WRITI

The McIlw

EVA-MARIE KRÖLLER

Writing the Empire

The McIlwraiths, 1853–1948

UNIVERSITY OF TORONTO PRESS
Toronto Buffalo London

© University of Toronto Press 2021
Toronto Buffalo London
utorontopress.com
Printed in the U.S.A.

ISBN 978-1-4875-0757-2 (cloth)
ISBN 978-1-4875-3652-7 (EPUB)
ISBN 978-1-4875-3651-0 (PDF)

Library and Archives Canada Cataloguing in Publication

Title: Writing the empire : the McIlwraiths, 1853–1948 / Eva-Marie Kröller.
Names: Kröller, Eva-Marie, author.
Description: Includes bibliographical references and index.
Identifiers: Canadiana (print) 20210099380 | Canadiana (ebook) 20210099666 | ISBN 9781487507572 (cloth) | ISBN 9781487536527 (EPUB) | ISBN 9781487536510 (PDF)
Subjects: LCSH: McIlwraith family. | LCSH: Ayrshire (Scotland) – Genealogy. | LCSH: Great Britain – Genealogy. | LCSH: Great Britain – Colonies – History – 19th century. | LCSH: Great Britain – Colonies – History – 20th century. | LCSH: Imperialism – History – 19th century. | LCSH: Imperialism – History – 20th century. | LCGFT: Family histories.
Classification: LCC CS39.M382 2021 | DDC 929.2 – dc23

Publication was made possible by a grant from the Scholarly Publication Fund, under the auspices of the Vice-President, Research & Innovation, and the Provost and Vice-President, Academic, University of British Columbia.

University of Toronto Press acknowledges the financial assistance to its publishing program of the Canada Council for the Arts and the Ontario Arts Council, an agency of the Government of Ontario.

Canada Council
for the Arts

Conseil des Arts
du Canada

ONTARIO ARTS COUNCIL
CONSEIL DES ARTS DE L'ONTARIO
an Ontario government agency
un organisme du gouvernement de l'Ontario

Funded by the
Government
of Canada

Financé par le
gouvernement
du Canada

Canadä

Contents

Illustrations

Acknowledgments

This book would not have been possible without the steadfast interest, assistance, and hospitality of the McIlwraith family. In particular, I thank Professor Thomas F. McIlwraith for knowledgeable discussions and shrewd feedback over many years, Duane McIlwraith for sharing her expertise as genealogist extraordinaire, and their son Professor Thomas (Tad) F. McIlwraith for suggestions pertaining to his grandfather's place in Canadian anthropology. My research began in the home of the late Mary and Michael Brian in Montreal, and their daughters Imogen and Jessica Brian, and especially Connie Brian, have generously continued their parents' support for this project. As well, I acknowledge the interest of Margaret (Peggy) Matheson, the late Murray Matheson, and their son, Hugh Matheson.

Numerous North American and international archives and libraries have hosted research visits or responded to inquiries. In Canada, I wish to single out Harold Averill, the formidable archivist of the University of Toronto Archives and Records Management Services (UTARMS), along with UTARMS's Special Media Archivist Marnee Gamble and Digital Records Archivist Emily Sommers. Equally impressive was the late Margaret Houghton, archivist of the Hamilton Public Library, where I also received assistance from Tracey Krause, Jennifer Dell, Charity Blaine, and Naso Sipsis. At the University of British Columbia, I was alerted by Chelsea Shriver at Rare Books and Special Collections to important papers in the McLennan Family Fonds, and I consulted the University of British Columbia Press Fonds in the University of British Columbia Archives (Erwin Wodarczak), as well as documents in the Audrey and Harry Hawthorn Library at the Museum of Anthropology (Alissa Cherry, Katie Ferrante). UBC's Interlibrary Loan service efficiently processed my many requests. I consulted the Archives and Records Management Department at Simon Fraser University (Alexandra Wieland, Paul Hebbard) and SFU's Canada's Early Women Writers database (Carole Gerson, Karyn Huenemann); the Archives of the Royal BC Museum (Ryan Cameron); Archives and Special Collections, University of

Manitoba Library (Tyyne Petrowski); the William Ready Division of Archives and Research Collections and Mills Services Desk, Mills Memorial Library, McMaster University (Bev Bayzat, Denise Johnson); the Thomas Fisher Rare Book Library, University of Toronto (Jennifer Toews); the Ontario Ministry of Government and Consumer Services, Toronto (Serge Paquet); the Art Gallery of Ontario (Marilyn Nazar); the George Metcalf Archival Collection of the Canadian War Museum, Ottawa (Carol Reid, Nancy Lauzière, Alain Simard); the Canadian Museum of Nature, Ottawa (Chantal Dussault); Library and Archives Canada, Ottawa (Sophie Tellier, Jessie Moolman, Valerie Casbourn); the Canadian Museum of History, Gatineau (Benoît Thériault, Erin Wilson, Vincent Lafond); Archival and Special Collections, University of Guelph (Jan Brett); the University of Waterloo Library (Martha Lauzon); the Queen's University Archives (Deirdre Bryden); the Leacock Museum National Historic Site, Orillia (Fred Addis); the Weston Corporate Archives (Derrick Clements); the Gravenhurst Archives (Judy Humphries); Rare Books and Special Collections, McLennan Library, McGill University (Mary Ellen Houde, Elis Ing); the Bibliothèque et archives nationales du Québec, Quebec City (Nancy Bélanger); the Musées de la civilisation, Quebec City (Peter Gagné); and Archives Nova Scotia (John MacLeod, Anne Catherine Williams). In the United States, I thank the Walter Houghton Library, Harvard University; the Ernst Mayr Library, Museum of Comparative Zoology, Harvard University (Dana Fisher); the Smithsonian Institution Archives, Washington, DC (Mary Markey); the Firestone Library, Princeton University; the Library of Congress, Washington, DC; the Harry Ransom Centre for the Humanities, University of Texas at Austin (Elizabeth L. Garver); the Bancroft Library, University of California at Berkeley (Lorna K. Kirwan, Jennie Hinchcliff, Michael M. Lange); the Raymond H. Fogler Library, University of Maine at Orono (Desirée Butterfield-Nagy); the Louis Round Wilson Special Collections Library, University of North Carolina at Chapel Hill (Elizabeth Shulman, Matthew Turi); the Beinecke Rare Book and Manuscript Library, Yale University (June Can); the Lincoln Library, Lake Erie College, Painesville, Ohio (Chris Bennett); the Laurel School, Shaker Heights, Cleveland, Ohio (Pamela Dean); the New Castle Public Library, New Castle, Pennsylvania (Chris Fabian); the Indiana Room, Anderson Public Library, Anderson, Indiana (Elaine Mathews); the Kelso House Collection, Special Collections and Archives, Kent State University, Ohio (Elizabeth Campion); the Linda Lear Centre for Archives and Special Collections, Connecticut College (Rebecca Parmer); the Saranac Laboratory Museum, Historic Saranac Lake (Amy Catania, Marc Wanner) and the Saranac Lake Free Library, New York (Michelle Tucker); the Adams County Library, Gettysburg, Pennsylvania (Susan Walton); and the Dauphin County Library System, Harrisburg, Pennsylvania (Ann Marie Megoulas). In the United Kingdom, I consulted the Cambridge University Library (Frank Bowles); the Cambridge Union Society (Louise Gamon); Special

Collections, St. John's College, Cambridge (Kathryn McKee); the St. John's College Library, Cambridge (Fiona Colbert); the Institutional Archives, St. John's College, Cambridge (Tracy Deacon); the Christ's College Library, Cambridge (D.J. Wagstaff); the Museum of Archaeology and Anthropology, Cambridge (Melanie Norton Huglow, Anita Herle); Balliol College, Oxford (Anna Sander); Magdalen College, Oxford (Robin Darwall-Smith); Eton College, Windsor (Penny Hatfield); the British Library (Annette Jackson); the Imperial War Museum, London (Katherine Phillips); the National Archives, Kew (Gillian Kirby, Bruno Pappalardo); Special Collections, Royal Anthropological Institute, London (Sarah Walpole); the Liverpool Record Office, Liverpool Libraries (Helena Smart); the Centre for Research Collections, University of Edinburgh (Rona Morrison); the University of Glasgow Archives (Gaby Laing, Claire Daniel, Catriona Perry); the Cadbury Research Library, Special Collections, University of Birmingham (Helen Fisher); and the Public Records Office of Northern Ireland (Paul Rea, Rachel Sayers). In Australia, I acknowledge the John Oxley Library, State Library of Queensland, Brisbane (Simon Farley, Katy Roberts); the Noel Butlin Archives Centre, Australian National University, Canberra (Sarah Lethbridge, Rachel Armstrong); the State Library of Victoria, Melbourne; the National Archives of Australia (Karan Oberoi); the National Library of Australia (Sue Chan, Isobel Johnstone); the Fryer Library, University of Queensland (Flic French); and the Australian War Memorial (Jane Robertson). In New Zealand, I obtained help from the National Library of New Zealand (Jenni Chrisstoffels) and the Auckland War Memorial Museum (Madison Pine). Jo Burger at the Johannesburg Art Gallery in South Africa assisted in piecing together the South African life of Hilda Phillips, as did the Johannesburg Public Library (Essie Chaphi); the Johannesburg Heritage Foundation (Sarah Welham); ARTEFACTS, South Africa (Dr. Roger Fisher, Frank Gaylard); Barlow Rand Archives South Africa (Julia Woolcott); and Historical Papers Research Archive, University of the Witwatersrand (Gabriele Mohale). In Germany, I obtained information from the Stadtarchiv Stralsund (Regina Nehmzow); the Stadtarchiv Dresden (K. Wagler); the Verkehrsmuseum Dresden (Ulrike Krautz); the Stadtarchiv Krefeld (Joachim Lilla); the Stadtarchiv Solingen (Karoline Riener); the Bundesarchiv Berlin (Ulrike Just); the Universitätsarchiv Leipzig (Katharina Holzbecher); and the Universitätsarchiv, Johann-Wolfgang-von-Goethe Universität, Frankfurt (Carsten Trautmann, Matthias Lorenz). Special thanks go to the librarians and archivists at the University of British Columbia, St. John's College in Cambridge, the Canadian Museum of History, and the National Library of Scotland who responded to queries despite COVID-19 lockdown.

Many individuals have contributed to this project by listening to my ideas, passing on information, and providing practical assistance. Coral Ann Howells, Ruth Blair, and Denver Beanland ensured that my visit to Australia was a well-organized success in helpful and knowledgeable company. Stephen Foster,

Australian National University, and Melanie Oppenheimer, Flinders University, responded to inquiries. In South Africa, Jillian Carman and Maryna Fraser helped to track down descendants of Sir Lionel Phillips, as did Eliza Banks and Patricia Reed in the United Kingdom. Clive Hunt provided photographs of his grandmother Hilda Phillips. Chris Meade and Clare Meade responded to inquiries about the descendants of A.C. and Marion Seward, and, along with John Sampson, gave me access to Marion Seward's travel diary. In composing the story of the von Gruber-Kromayer family, I benefited from genealogical information and family documents provided by Dipl.-Ing. Klaus Kromayer in Munich, and by Peter Kromayer and Edvige Kromayer Barrie in the United States. I acknowledge the great pleasure of talking to the late Maggie Tushingham and the late Martha Kidd about this research. At the University of British Columbia, John Barker shared scans of elusive field letters by T.F. McIlwraith. Colleagues and friends offered suggestions and advice. Allan Smith was helpful from the very beginning of the research, and I learnt from exchanges with Jean Barman, Susanna Egan, Linda Morra, William H. New, Ann Pearson, David Staines, and Carol van Rijn. The booksellers at Hager Books in Kerrisdale offered consistently excellent stock in history, imperial and otherwise, and kept me in all kinds of other reading. Office staff in the Department of English at the University of British Columbia were unfailingly helpful, especially Dominique Yupangco and Angela Kaija, as was Leonora Crema, scholarly communications and copyright librarian at the University of British Columbia and chair of the Scholarly Publishing Subvention Fund Committee. I acknowledge the wisdom and professionalism of Mark Thompson, acquisitions editor at the University of Toronto Press, the careful attention to all aspects of production by managing editor Lisa Jemison, and the superlative work of copy editor Ryan Perks. As well, I thank the anonymous readers of the manuscript for thoughtful suggestions.

The research was funded by a Standard Research Grant of the Social Sciences and Humanities Research Council of Canada. Application for the SSHRC grant was made with Dr. Christoph Irmscher (Indiana University Bloomington) as co-investigator, but other obligations prevented him from following through with the collaboration, and this is a single-authored work. Funding also came from a Hampton Fund Research Grant and several research grants from the Faculty of Arts at the University of British Columbia.

This book is dedicated to the memory of my mentors, E.D. Blodgett, Sandra Gwyn, and Pierre Savard.

Permissions

Quotations from the A.C. Haddon Papers are by permission of the Syndics of Cambridge University Library; from the T.R. Glover diaries by permission of the master and fellows of St. John's College, Cambridge; from Herbert Warren's "President's Notebooks" and the Tutorial Board minutes by permission of the Magdalen College Archives, Oxford; from the diaries of Edward Stanley, 15th Earl of Derby, courtesy of Liverpool Record Office, Liverpool Libraries, as the custodian of the Earls of Derby Collection; and from the Stanmore Papers by permission of the British Library Board. Quotations from the entrance records and transcripts of the Macdonald Institute and from the Bureau of Records, Graduates, Ontario Agricultural College, are by permission of Archival and Special Collections, University of Guelph Library; reference to the Douglas Cole Fonds by permission of the Archives and Records Management Department, Simon Fraser University; quotations from K.C. McIlwraith, "What I Know About Birds," courtesy of the Thomas Fisher Rare Book Library, University of Toronto. Quotations from the A.P. Watt Records by permission of Rare Book Literary and Historical Papers, the Wilson Library, University of North Carolina at Chapel Hill; from the Hardy-Eckstorm Collection by permission of Special Collections, Raymond H. Fogler Library, University of Maine. Quotations from Sir Lionel Philipp's personal papers by permission of Barloworld, South Africa.

Abbreviations

AU NBAC	Noel Butlin Archives Centre, Australian National University
BAAS	British Association for the Advancement of Science
BCI	T.F. McIlwraith, *The Bella Coola Indians*
Birds	Thomas McIlwraith, *The Birds of Ontario* (1886, 2nd ed. 1894)
CB	Thomas McIlwraith, "Catalogue of Birds Mounted Under Glass"
CMH	Canadian Museum of History
COTC	Canadian Officers Training Corps
CUL	Cambridge University Library
CWM	Canadian War Museum
DCF	Douglas Cole Fonds
ESS	Elizabeth Smith Shortt Fonds
FA	Family Album, JNMP
FHEP	Fannie (also spelled Fanny) Hardy Eckstorm Papers
"Genealogy"	T.F. McIlwraith's memoir, typescript, 1964, TFMP
HBCI	*At Home with the Bella Coola Indians: T.F. McIlwraith's Field Letters, 1922–4*, ed. John Barker and Douglas Cole
HCUL	Alfred Cort Haddon Collection, CUL
HH	Helen H. Holt diary, TFMP
HLHU	Houghton Library, Harvard University
HPL	Hamilton Public Library
JNMP	Jean N. McIlwraith Papers, Mary Brian (McIlwraith) estate
JOL	John Oxley Library, Brisbane, Queensland
KOSB	King's Own Scottish Borderers
LAC	Library and Archives Canada
LPP	Sir Lionel Phillips, private papers, Barlow Rand Archives
MAA	Museum of Archaeology and Anthropology, Cambridge
McLFF	McLennan Family Fonds, RBSC, UBC

MM	*More of a Man: Diaries of a Scottish Craftsman in Mid-Nineteenth-Century North America*, ed. Andrew C. Holman, Robert B. Kristofferson
MOA	Museum of Anthropology, University of British Columbia
PRONI	Public Record Office for Northern Ireland, Belfast
RAI	Royal Anthropological Institute of Great Britain and Ireland
RCI	Royal Colonial Institute
RBSC	UBC Rare Books Special Collections, University of British Columbia
ROM	Royal Ontario Museum
SD	Marion Seward Diary
TFMF	Thomas F. McIlwraith (1899–1964) Fonds, UTA
TFMP	Thomas F. McIlwraith (1899–1964) Papers, private collection, Professor T.F. McIlwraith (b. 1941)
TFRBL	Thomas Fisher Rare Book Library, University of Toronto
TMF	Thomas McIlwraith (1824–1903) Fonds, HPL
TRG	Terrot Reavely Glover Fonds
UBCA	University of British Columbia Archives
UCB	University of California Berkeley
UGA	University of Glasgow Archives
UGL ASC	Archival and Special Collections, University of Guelph Library
UTA	University of Toronto Archives
UWL	University of Waterloo Library
WD	Wartime diary, T.F. McIlwraith, TFMP
WIK	Kennedy C. McIlwraith, "What I Know About Birds and How I Came to Know It" (1882–90), TFRBL

WRITING THE EMPIRE

Introduction

In his volume on Scotland's Ayrshire for the Cambridge County Geographies, John Foster describes the county as "a maritime country, the broad estuary of the Clyde washing its western shore. Far out lies the busy ocean highway for vessels from and to the bustling commercial centres in the upper reaches" (John Foster 3). This busy highway also transported ships across the ocean, and with the sea on their doorstep, the Ayrshire McIlwraiths spread through the British Empire during the nineteenth century. The family name can be found in New Zealand and South Africa, but because of the large number of personal and official papers they have left behind, this study focuses on the Australian and Canadian branches, and those who migrated to the neighbouring empire of the United States. In addition to published and unpublished literary and scholarly works, the McIlwraiths' archive contains personal letters, diaries, logbooks, memoirs, estate papers, as well as business and scientific correspondence. Some of this material has been edited and published, but much of it remains scattered across family and public archives in North America, Great Britain, Australia, and South Africa.

The McIlwraiths include, among others, the flamboyant Sir Thomas McIlwraith (1835–1900), three-time premier of Queensland; Thomas McIlwraith (1824–1903), a cabinetmaker, gas works manager, and coal dealer turned ornithologist who settled in Hamilton, Ontario; his brother Andrew (1830–91), a draftsman and patternmaker who also emigrated to Ontario but temporarily crossed the border to the United States when work became scarce in Canada; Thomas's daughter, Jean Newton McIlwraith (1858–1938), author and editor with Doubleday Publishers in New York; Thomas's grandson, Thomas Forsyth (T.F.) McIlwraith (1899–1964), first head of the University of Toronto's Department of Anthropology; and T.F.'s sister, Dorothy Stevens McIlwraith (1891–1976), editor of *Weird Tales* and other pulp magazines. The public role of several members of the family has previously been acknowledged. Thus, Sir Thomas McIlwraith's biography appears in the *Oxford*

Dictionary of National Biography, and the *Australian Dictionary of Biography* includes articles on him as well as his brothers John and Andrew. The *Canadian Dictionary of Biography* features the ornithologist, and entries on Jean, T.F., and Dorothy McIlwraith are scheduled for the future. Several McIlwraiths have attracted the attention of historians, anthropologists, ecological critics, and literary scholars. For example, Denver Beanland's biography of Sir Thomas McIlwraith draws on its subject's private and public papers to reconstruct his political persona; Christoph Irmscher looks at the ornithologist's *The Birds of Ontario* as nature writing; Andrew C. Holman and Robert B. Kristofferson analyse Andrew McIlwraith's diary as a document of labour history; and John Barker and Douglas Cole discuss the anthropological field letters that describe the genesis of T.F. McIlwraith's magnum opus, *The Bella Coola Indians*. Patricia Twaddel and Duncan Waterson have brought some of the Canadian and Australian McIlwraiths together, but although Twaddel's genealogy provides information about the family that is not available anywhere else, it is not a scholarly work, and Waterson's research on the Canadian McIlwraiths is not always reliable (see Waterson, *An Ayrshire Family*).

The present study differs from previous specialized publications in its biographical, temporal, and geographical range. The texts on which it draws include the letters and diaries of young children, notes from individuals nearing the end of their lives, and writing from every age in between. By moving from generation to generation but also from one stage of a person's life to the next, the discussion investigates some of the ways in which various McIlwraiths, both men and women, articulated their identity as imperial subjects over time. Writing, including life writing, is an essential instrument in that articulation: these individuals not only exchanged information with others, tracked their own activities, and justified their actions, but also continually recapitulated and updated their lived experience as members of the British Empire. That experience was "construed ... through texts," Lambert and Lester point out, and "those lives themselves were lived out in large part through the textual representations that moved within and between different colonies and Britain: appeals, memoranda, despatches, and, of course, biographical writing were the forms through which individual agency was expressed, communicated across distance, and effected" (Lambert and Lester 28–9). Here Lambert and Lester highlight official communication and "biographical writing," but the distinctions between the official and the private, the imperial family and the personal family, were often blurred. Sir Thomas's various disputes with the Colonial Office, for example, repeatedly enacted colonial resistance as a vigorous young man's protest against Britain as "a ... grandmotherly old wreck" (Dilke, 2: 204). As numerous critics have pointed out (for example, Birk and Neumann), imperial metaphors were emotionally loaded and to view the mother country as an "old wreck" and a premier as "A Bad Colonial Boy"[1] was both a sacrilege and a declaration of independence.

As used by Sir Thomas and his supporters, the family metaphor draws a distinction between vigorous sons and feeble, though tyrannical, mothers (or grandmothers), with the daughters nowhere in sight. The other colonies were known to refer to Queensland as "our wayward and backward sister colony,"[2] but these adjectives designate the colony as delinquent and uncouth rather than spunky like her male counterpart. However, there is a pronounced feminine theme in the McIlwraiths' narrative as well, and it is not formulated to view the colonies as obedient daughters of the metropole. In her collaboration with William McLennan on the historical novel *The Span o' Life*, Jean McIlwraith resisted the disappearance of women into masculine allegories of nationhood. The subject of their book was the Battle of the Plains of Abraham and the Jacobites' role in it, but while the co-authors were happy enough with each other as they researched the historical background, Jean provoked her partner into a dispute about the meaning of eighteenth-century femininity and of its Victorian counterpart. In the process, she raised important questions about the ideological freight of historical romance in Canada, where it was often placed at the service of reconciling its British and French heritage.[3] In particular, she objected to the expectation that female characters were to submit to conciliatory marriages rather than choose defiant celibacy. Her letters were articulate and fierce, and her views about the obsolescence of romance were extreme enough to require McLennan's brother to act as umpire.

The difficulty encountered by educated women with bright minds and unusual talents in asserting their independence is a recurrent theme in the McIlwraiths' story and that of their associates. In the years just before and after the First World War, female scholars and aristocrats alike are seen to struggle for a rewarding life. Eileen Plunket's efforts to get away from the limitations of her upper-class upbringing that too often had her "sit[ting] alone doing nothing in [her] bed room" (TFMP, Eileen Plunket to Beulah Knox, n.d. [December 1913?]) were mostly futile in the long run, but she briefly found her calling when she joined the all-female Hackett-Lowther ambulance unit in First World War–France and when she acted on the stage. Much of post-war Cambridge, bursting at the seams with ex-servicemen, was violently opposed to granting

---

1 See the cartoon, reproduced in chapter 1, "Sir Thomas McIlwraith and his altercation with the Bank of England, as seen by the Boomerang," *Boomerang*, 17 October 1891, 1.

2 *Speeches on Australian Federation, by the Premiers of Victoria, South Australia, Queensland, Tasmania and Western Australia*, George Robertson & Co., 1899, 11, qtd. in McConnel, *The People's Stories*, 168.

3 On the historical romance as "national tale," see Trumpener; also see Cabajsky and Grubisic, Introduction, vii–xxiv.

women equal rights at the university, and for the duration of his studies there T.F. McIlwraith absorbed the hostile attitudes of some of his teachers and fellow students, although he revised them soon enough when he returned to Canada. Working-class women do appear in the McIlwraiths' writing, as servants, maids, washerwomen, and seamstresses, as harried Irish, Italian, and German mothers in Hamilton, New York, and Dresden, sailors' and soldiers' wives in the Tipperary Club, and bedmakers suspected of pilfering T.F.'s jam in Cambridge. Most of them remain anonymous, however, and we learn little about their views even if Jean McIlwraith considered the situation of servants in her essay "Household Budgets Abroad: Canada" for *Cornhill Magazine* in 1904, placed a housemaid at the centre of her story "The Assimilation of Christina," and described the working-class milieu of New York's Greenwich Village in her unpublished novel "Dominick Street."

Although the tone is more controlled than Jean's in her debates with McLennan, a similar passion is apparent on the repeated occasions when a McIlwraith, male or female, used the ledger-sheet approach to take stock of his or her life, probably influenced by the family's Presbyterian background. In none of their writing, however, is there the brutal determination to balance the books to which Ernest Thompson Seton's father subjected his son: when the former came of age, Joseph Logan Thompson demanded to be paid back, with interest, for all expenses incurred in Ernest's upbringing, including his delivery at birth (Seton 152). Characteristically, the McIlwraiths applied the ledger-sheet approach in the public format of a magazine article or a letter addressed to a collective of recipients rather than in an introspective document, despite some exceptions to the rule. In "How to Be Happy Though Single," published in *Harper's Bazaar*, Jean McIlwraith sorted herself out after her mother's death temporarily left her without a purpose in life and without a home. In making important decisions about a field of study and profession that would allow him to make a contribution to "this empire of ours" (TFMP, T.F. McIlwraith to family, 3 August 1919) after the Great War, T.F. also consistently used the ledger-sheet method to organize his letters to his family. Personal conversation did not replace writing about his intentions, as becomes strikingly clear when – perhaps in anticipation of domestic arguments that required him to be firm about his plans ahead of time – one of these letters was written just before he returned to Canada after demobilization. Any regrets or conflict involved in laying out his intentions to himself do not make it into the letter, but they are displayed in the jottings of his diary. The wartime letters are the only ones in the McIlwraith archive that come with a concurrent journal. His diary and correspondence do not necessarily record the same events, and when they do, the interpretation may be quite different. On the grounds of this complexity alone, T.F. McIlwraith's observant wartime writing qualifies as a noteworthy, if not exactly unique, contribution to the archive of Canadians in the First World War.

Given the linguistic skill with which some of these individuals take themselves through critical moments of their lives and the care with which they select the genres in which to do it, it is all the more distressing to read their writings when language no longer obeyed its user. By the time Jean left her position as an editor towards the end of the First World War, she had become increasingly forgetful, and by the early 1930s, her letters were incomprehensible. She continued to update her testament, but soon lost track of its different versions. The tight organization of the ledger sheet and the mentality that stands behind it shows up not only an individual's mental decline, but also exposes those family members who were unable to keep up with their successful spouses and siblings. These include Sir Thomas's first wife Maggie, who became an alcoholic, and his brother Hamilton, also a drunk, who wandered aimlessly through Britain, Australia, New Zealand, Canada, and the United States, unable to settle down to an occupation despite help from his parents and brothers.

Keeping these and other McIlwraiths apart can be a challenge for the researcher, and there is a certain irony in the anthropologist T.F. McIlwraith's struggle with Nuxalk genealogies when he first arrived in Bella Coola in 1922. In particular, the name Thomas occurs in both the Australian and the Canadian branches of the family, and the recurrence of this name for the eldest son in each generation of the Ontario McIlwraiths has sometimes caused confusion. In his review of the republication of T.F. McIlwraith's *The Bella Coola Indians* (1992), Ramsay Cook deplores the absence of a more detailed background discussion of the family, especially of "McIlwraith's father, Ontario's pre-eminent early ornithologist," but he muddles father and grandfather (Cook 89). In 2012, the anthropologist's son, the geographer T.F. McIlwraith (b. 1941), and his grandson, yet another anthropologist named T.F. McIlwraith (b. 1969), joined forces to write a book blog entry in which they pretended that T.F. McIlwraith (b. 1899) was a "Methuselah" who determinedly published books over the course of a whole century before they revealed that the works were produced by three generations of authors all of whom bore the same name ("Who is Methuselah?"). The names Andrew, John, William, and Jean McIlwraith, not to mention various middle names, have also had their moments, as has intermarriage between different branches of the family. In his study *Australian Imperialism in the Pacific*, Roger C. Thompson identifies the newspaper editor William McIlwraith, married to Margaret Baird McIlwraith, as Sir Thomas's brother, but William was his brother-in-law. Margaret was the sister of Sir Thomas and William the brother of the Ontario ornithologist. The errors in Duncan Waterson's account, in *An Ayrshire Family*, of the Canadian McIlwraiths are too numerous to mention. A descendant of Andrew McIlwraith of the McIlwraith, McEacharn Company shipping business scolded me politely via email for getting Andrew's biographical particulars wrong, but although they were – broadly speaking – contemporaries, they were different Andrews, one in Ontario (brother of the ornithologist) and the other in Australia (brother of Sir Thomas).[4] In literary criticism, the ornithologist's daughter, the writer Jean Newton McIlwraith, has been transformed into Jean Norman McIlwraith and even John Newton McIlwraith (Coleman; Kuttainen).

If, therefore, the information used to identify individuals in this volume may at times appear overdetermined with birthdate, occupation, place of residence, the name by which their family called them, or titles like "Sir" or "Bailie" ahead of their owners receiving them, there are practical reasons for proceeding this way. To assist the reader further, genealogies of the Australian and Ontario branches of the McIlwraiths are provided in the appendix, along with family trees for two of the women who married into the family and feature prominently in its story – namely, Mary Stevens, mother of the anthropologist, and Beulah Gillet Knox, who became his wife. These genealogies do not address the difficulties represented by the name itself. In 1878, a business correspondent with catastrophic spelling changed it into "Mackelray" (TMF, 56, Charles Wagner, 30 November 1878),[5] and when Jean McIlwraith opened an account at a New York bank frequented by German immigrants she found she had undergone a metamorphosis to "John Newton Micklehardt" (JNMP, "New York Impressions"). During the Great War, when he mingled with a great many Scots in the King's Own Scottish Borderers (KOSB) and became so immersed in a variety of dialects that he briefly began to speak Glaswegian himself, it was a surprise to T.F. McIlwraith to learn that his last name was pronounced with the stress on the "il" or on the "wraith" rather than the "Mc," as was his family's habit. Whatever the correct version, it remained a difficult name. One army superior calling the roll "came to [his] name and stopped for a few seconds, then deliberately refused to try the pronounciation [sic]" (CWM, T.F. McIlwraith to family, 3 February 1918).

In the company of his KOSB mates, T.F. began to acknowledge a strong division between the English and the Scots. Perhaps this sentiment was provoked by the high number of Scottish war dead and a tendency, among Scots, to compare the recent losses with those sustained during historical battles such as Culloden and Glen Coe. At Cambridge, T.F. repeatedly visited Scotland, and he was struck by the parallels between the war memorials that were being erected everywhere and "the simple gray stones" that commemorated the fallen Jacobites at Culloden. Both he and Dorothy were irritated by the "gabble of some wretched English tourists" as they travelled towards Glen Coe (TFMF, T.F. McIlwraith to family, 17 August 1920), and elsewhere Dorothy confirmed

---

4   Allison Harper, email to Eva-Marie Kröller, 19 August 2007.

5   I consulted these postcards when they were in private hands, but they have since been deposited in the TMF, HPL. An inventory of the postcards, produced by Professor T.F. McIlwraith (1941–), assigns a reference number to each, along with other annotations.

that "[a]s a family we have always been very proud of our Scottish descent [and] held it as sacred" ("CONCERNING"). The perception that the English and Scots did not belong to the same branch of the imperial family was a new development in T.F.'s thinking. At McGill, shortly before enlisting, he had hotly opposed anyone who argued that Canada was not obliged to fight Britain's battles, and he got into a "rabid dispute with ... a third year man and a blooming nationalist" (TFMP, T.F. McIlwraith to his mother, 13 November 1916). Likewise, his comments on Wilfrid Laurier and the Conscription Crisis became increasingly hostile as he and his fellow recruits were, as a special privilege, permitted to vote on board the train taking them to embarkation for Europe. On arrival at Hare Camp in Essex, he was lavish in his praise for receiving generous assistance from his officers "simply because we are colonials and in a strange land," and they "seem[ed] to appreciate that we had come over as volunteers" (CWM, T.F. McIlwraith to family, 17 January 1918).

The McIlwraiths' understanding of their civic identity was shaped by a second juxtaposition that affected their understanding of "home": Canada and the United States. T.F. and Dorothy were persistently critical of the States and its delayed decision to join the war. In the title of her essay "CONCERNING US CANADIANS: By One of Minor Importance," Dorothy – who had followed Jean into an editorial position at Doubleday – puns on her confusing status as a "US Canadian" but announces with a belligerence worthy of her aunt that "a change of his allegiance and citizenship is to a Briton not a matter of form to be undertaken lightly." When she speaks of citizenship, she sees herself as a "cosmopolite who loves [her] native country best," and for whom the meaning of "Britain" and "Canada" is identical ("CONCERNING"). Yet the McIlwraiths had strong connections to the States. The ornithologist's brother Andrew tramped across the border when an economic depression drove him away from Ontario in 1859–60. While in New York, he submitted a letter to the *Ayrshire Times* comparing working conditions in America and Britain for the information of prospective emigrants. Three of Jean's siblings moved to areas of the States where members of their mother's family had also settled. Dorothy's parents spent many weeks visiting with their daughter in New York, and when it came to consulting with medical specialists, the family routinely headed south.

While T.F. began to see Scotland as separate from England during the war, a Scottish element in an American's background appears to have consistently cancelled out most objections a McIlwraith might have raised against him or her as a desirable partner: T.F.'s wife Beulah was from Painesville, Ohio, and her mother's family came from New England, but her father came from Glasgow. In reversal of the usual migration, her uncle Will Addison Child moved north and became a leader in Hamilton's steel industry. His son Philip, T.F.'s childhood friend and future Governor General's Award–winning novelist, was as eager to fight in the British imperial forces as T.F. was. In adaptation of Linda Colley's insistence that identities do not resemble hats, of which only one can be worn at a time (Colley 6), one may conclude that the McIlwraiths, too, were normally comfortable with multiple identities. A crisis occurred only when it was suggested that they choose one over the other, and Dorothy wrote her essay when she had apparently been asked one too many times why she was not yet a US citizen. In contrast to Dorothy's insistence that despite the multiple allegiances in her life, Britain remained her emotional centre of gravity, one suspects that Sir Thomas was being opportunistic whenever he praised Britain as "home." He extolled the virtues of the Canadian Pacific Railway as a place where the passenger was "at home among his own people" ("Sir T. M'Ilwraith") but – as has been previously noted – under his leadership Queensland repeatedly strained away from British tutelage. McIlwraith's attitude was, however, not necessarily typical of the average Australian. Marion Seward, who travelled to Australia in 1914 and befriended T.F. in Cambridge, tells the story of "a Doctor from Katoomba" who married a young Australian woman because he did not want a British wife pining for home. The plan did not work, for when the couple returned from a visit with his folks in Britain, she longed to return "home" forever after (Seward, "Sketchbook").

As a type of prosopography, the study of large families over several generations has become an increasingly established way of "connecting the microhistories of individuals and families to the larger scenes of which they were a part: to important or 'macrohistorical' inquiries" (Rothschild 7), and there is a growing body of research associated with this endeavour.[6] At times, it may be less a question of "connecting" the two types of histories than one surging across the other. This happens when any sense of Sir Thomas McIlwraith's personal life is submerged by political crises that, admittedly, he has usually provoked himself, and when, with the advent of the First World War, the young T.F. McIlwraith turns into a rabid jingo whom his parents probably had difficulty recognizing as their son. In telling the story of empire through the stories of families, prosopographies often focus either on the elite or the working class, as demonstrated by Barbara Caine on the Stracheys (2005), Adele Perry on the Douglas-Connolly family (2015), Charles Drazin on an Irish family of surveyors (2016), Deborah Baker on a group of surveyors and geologists from the Auden and Spender families (2018), Melanie Nolan on a New Zealand working-class family (2005), Elizabeth Jane Errington on working-class emigrants to nineteenth-century Upper Canada (2007), Angela Woollacott on settler networks (2015), Nick Brodie's investigation of Australian history through the life stories of his own family (2015), and Janet Doust's various studies of settler families (e.g., 2008). Brian Young's study of two patrician families (2014), the McCords and the Taschereaus, is focused on "the making of Quebec," but nevertheless has much to say about the global implications of their story.

---

6 See, for example, Cleall et al.

In *To the Ends of the Earth: Scotland's Global Diaspora, 1750–2010* (2012), the historian T.M. Devine talks about the importance of trusted networks of family and friends to Scottish emigrants, points out that the study of these networks is "still at an early stage" for Scotland, and calls for research that matches the "extensive and impressive scholarly literature" already produced on the Irish equivalent (147). Two major works anticipate Devine's request – namely, Foster on the Macphersons (2010) and Rothschild on the Johnstones (2011), both of whom are concerned with "the inner life of empires" or the "private empire" of their subjects. These two volumes describe families of colonial administrators, merchants, planters, slave-owners, officers, judges, politicians, and scholars. Rothschild writes about the Johnstones that they were "not a celebrated family, even at the moments of their great successes" and "no more than minor figures in the public events of the times" (1, 4). Like the Macphersons, they were, however, a great deal more privileged in birth, connection, and education than the McIlwraiths. Practising the virtues of Prudence, Enterprise, Mechanical Science, and Learning that flank Caledonia in the portico of Edinburgh's Commercial Bank of Scotland, the McIlwraiths left the occupations of weavers and plumbers in the previous generations behind and, with differences in speed and success, established themselves as businessmen and entrepreneurs in the colonies. Of the generation who emigrated to Australia and Canada, only one – Sir Thomas – attended university, but he did not complete a degree, and his own lack of academic education sometimes made the ornithologist Thomas McIlwraith insecure in his many dealings with trained scientists. However, both his children and those of Sir Thomas were well educated, especially the girls. Sir Thomas's daughters attended expensive schools in Edinburgh and Brussels, and all three of the ornithologist's daughters excelled at the Wesleyan Ladies' College in Hamilton. His youngest son Kennedy attended the University of Toronto and became a medical doctor, while his three older sons were apprenticed as clerks by their mid-teens and, in varying degrees, became successful businessmen.

Important and wide-ranging connections were made at educational institutions such as the Wesleyan Ladies' College and Highfield School in Hamilton, the Ontario Agricultural College at Guelph, the Misses von Gruber's *Pensionat* in Dresden, not to mention Cambridge University. Several marriages resulted between partners who otherwise would have had limited opportunity to meet. Mary Stevens, who came from the Eastern Townships southeast of Montreal, was introduced to her future husband Thomas McIlwraith by his sister Helen, her fellow student at the Wesleyan Ladies' College. In researching the students from the college, I soon learned to look up each and every name because chances were that the students had either become career women like Jean McIlwraith or came from prominent families across North America and later married into equally well-established ones. One of them was Laura Miller Surles from Lafayetteville, North Carolina, who became the wife of James Dunsmuir, future lieutenant governor of British Columbia. While at the college, she delighted the ornithologist and his family with her singing during one of the many soirées at Cairnbrae, the McIlwraiths' home. Specialized institutions like the Ontario Agricultural Institute facilitated encounters between individuals from opposite ends of the empire. Dorothy's friend Hilda Wildman Hills met her husband, son of the South African financier Sir Lionel Phillips, at Guelph when Harold was studying at the Ontario Agricultural College and she was a student of home economics at the Macdonald Institute. In Dresden on the eve of the First World War, Beulah Knox forged friendships with young women from the British and European aristocracy and moneyed classes that lasted through several years of correspondence complicated by the war. In Cambridge, T.F. McIlwraith became a member of an academic family presided over by his teachers and mentors, A.C. Haddon, W.H.R. Rivers, William Ridgeway, and A.C. Seward, all of whom were devoted to his intellectual and personal welfare, sometimes well into his professional career. He made friends with fellow students who recommended themselves to him by their military achievements, their intellect, and their networking skills, including the Englishman Michael Sampson, the Australians E.W.P. Chinnery and L.W.G. Malcolm, and the American John D. Newsom.

As a result, the concept of networking could have been invented by the McIlwraiths. As part of their success, they carefully nurtured connections within their own expanding family and with their associates as they "careered" through Canada, Australia, Britain, and continental Europe.[7] The present discussion avoids the elegant conceptualizations of Niall Ferguson's *The Square and the Tower: Networks and Power, From Freemasons to Facebook* (2018) and similar studies of networking. Instead, it subscribes to the conviction that "Empire is in the Details" (Lutz). In this understanding, intimate relationships and the collective concerns radiating beyond them are equally important and sometimes closely intertwined. As Françoise Noël relates through a poignant set of personal documents, public and private crises became inseparable when *patriote* Amédée Papineau's family was left nearly destitute after his escape into American exile following the 1837 Rebellion. To adapt the historian Arlette Farge's concern about "the tacit consensus" that is sometimes practised about ambitious theoretical frameworks – "maybe it is time to return to the question of how this all worked" (*Allure* 44)[8] – and in so doing "identify ... the many fissures, contradictions, historical particularities, and shifts in imperial processes" (Lutz 593). What types of networks were activated in each case? What were the

---

7 In addition to Lambert and Lester, see Ballantyne; Ballantyne and Burton, *Empire* and *Moving Subjects*; Deacon et al.; Magee and Thompson; Woollacott, *Settler Society*.

8 The original phrasing is more specific. Talking about "la notion de 'cultures partagées,'" Farge adds that "peu de monde se demande à l'heure actuelle comment se sont effectivement opérés les partages." The translation renders the latter succinctly as "how this all worked." See Farge, *Le Goût de l'archive*, 58.

mechanisms of setting them in motion? Did they achieve the goals that were set for them? How did different types of networks compete with each other?

"How this all worked" is demonstrated in each of the following chapters, but particularly vivid examples of layered and competing networks occur in the Family Album, a communal diary kept by the ornithologist's children between 1867 and 1875, as well as their youngest brother Kennedy's bird diary and their father's book *The Birds of Ontario*. In these texts, the scene is "tremendously local to Hamilton, Ont" (McLFF, J.N. McIlwraith to William McLennan, 29 December 1897), as Jean McIlwraith put it in reference to some of her own fiction, and especially the ornithologists in the family seem to map out and go over every square inch of their immediate environment in search of rare species. Not bothered with provincial or national borders, the birds were in their turn part of a system of natural communication that preceded the man-made nexus but was all too often destroyed by it. The situation of Hamilton at the head of Lake Ontario and the location of the family home on the wharf, along with the McIlwraiths' frequent travels through the Great Lakes and down the St. Lawrence River, tied family events into an expansive circulation of commerce that extended across and beyond the North American continent. In this way, the Great Lakes area may be seen as a subsystem of nineteenth-century British and American imperialism, a "phenomenon that was economic at its base and global in its reach" (Northrup 14).

Rothschild characterizes the Johnstone family's story as "a history, in part, of the consequences at home in Scotland of distant events" (6). The city of Hamilton, as described in the Family Album, practically vibrates with events taking place across North America and Great Britain and elsewhere, news of which was delivered by newspaper, magazine, cable, letter, or word of mouth by the Great Lakes captains and other well-informed visitors during marathons of "at-home" visiting. At times, printed texts entered an explosive alliance with personal confidences. This happened repeatedly to Jean McIlwraith, who, notoriously indiscreet, wrote an unflattering portrait of her voice teacher, the improbably named William Shakespeare, in her story "A Singing-Student in London," and who used local gossip, passed on by a cousin's wife, for her first novel *The Making of Mary*. The story about Mr. Shakespeare, published in a magazine with high circulation, drew his ire and that of his admirers while the fracas surrounding *The Making of Mary* created a chill lasting several decades between Jean and members of her family. As indicated earlier, few of the texts in the McIlwraith archive track the "elusive, fluctuating conditions" of "the inner life" (Rothschild 8), though, given the difficulties that Jean McIlwraith created for herself, it would perhaps have been good if she had paid more attention to these "conditions" in herself and others. However, the archive contributes indirectly to the investigation of intimacy that sometimes accompanies the study of collective biography (see Ballantyne and Burton, *Moving Subjects* 1–28).

Judging from their written testimony, the McIlwraiths were not encouraged to display their feelings and avoided discussing them with family, but they do talk about their emotions in the rare instances that survive of correspondence with others. In her letters to Fannie Hardy Eckstorm, for instance, Jean talks about her grief over her mother's death but filters her sorrow into a practical discussion of future plans, and the anthropologist T.F. McIlwraith, careful to avoid the subject of Mary Stevens's death in letters to his father, did openly write about her suffering and that of her family to his teacher A.C Haddon and his wife Fanny in Cambridge. He kept the most intimate details for the memoir he composed for his children just before his own death in 1964 ("Genealogy"). Like Jean, he both displaces and evokes the horror of his mother's decline by dwelling on the practical difficulties of keeping an estranged sister away from his father, closing his parents' house, and having to rent a room in which to work on his book.

All of the McIlwraiths did pay a great deal of attention to the elements that affected the representation of the *outer* life, and any broader understanding of intimacy must be extrapolated from the surface details they provide. The Family Album in particular is a dynamic document that Jean continued to re-read and sometimes revise when the original report seemed to require adjustment to current circumstances. The anthropologist's memoir similarly combines the reading of family papers with personal stock-taking, and in the annotated typescript accompanying his father's wartime letters, T.F.'s son takes his parent to task for not finding the Fitzwilliam Museum in Cambridge "specially interesting": "[t]here was no need to TFM to be bored, and museums came to be central to TFM's later career" (CWM, T.F. McIlwraith to Dorothy McIlwraith, 2 March 1918). Stephen Foster, in commenting on the Macphersons, writes that "they did not just keep family records – they read them, sometimes commenting on them, sometimes censoring them, and sometimes alluding to the similarity of events past and present" (Foster 14). He might be talking about the McIlwraiths as well. In some prosopographies the author is a descendant of the family, and the research doubles as an investigation into his or her composite self. This complication can make for a difficult relationship to the scholarship, resulting at one extreme in a special case of "historians who love too much," to use Jill Lepore's phrase from her "reflections on microhistory and biography," and at the other in disillusionment with ancestors who, for a variety of reasons, fail to live up to their descendants' expectations. In keeping with their hesitation to display the "inner life," their own and that of others, the McIlwraiths' dialogue with family members both past and present has never been immersive enough to create this problem.

Official documents and life writing were important discourses that knit the empire's networks together but they were not the only ones. Magee and Thompson suggest that "migrant networks ... were powerful vehicles for disseminating

British styles of architecture, fashion, fiction, food, and music" (28). To illustrate the role of "food" from this list, Jean McIlwraith studied at London's National Training School for Cookery, one of several institutions with the ambition to teach food production and distribution within the empire. The Ontario Agricultural College and the Macdonald Institute at Guelph, where Harold Phillips and Hilda Wildman Hills fell in love, pursued similar goals. Jean's essay on "Household Budgets Abroad: Canada" systematically investigates the foodstuffs available for Canadians with different incomes, including the produce grown in the Niagara Peninsula, while in 1918 her niece Dorothy reported on wartime efforts of preserving fruit and "Sending Tommy his Marmalade." As teenagers, both T.F. McIlwraith and his future wife Beulah Knox were ravenous for sweets, and supplies of sugar and sugar-based products briefly became important bartering items for them. A year before the outbreak of war, Beulah and her fellow students at the Töchter-Pensionat von Gruber used chocolate to allow girls into their cosmopolitan circles or exclude them, and the directors of the school deployed food generally to keep their underoccupied students from becoming too restive. Before he and his mates discovered whisky, T.F., too, shared the contents of his many food packages from home and so strengthened his friendships in the army: a recurrent scene in his letters involves a group of cadets steadfastly eating their way through the supplies they had received. Sugar remained such a preoccupation that, after the war, he committed the faux pas of commenting on the saccharine on his professor's tea table despite the increase in sugar rations. Of course, maintaining the circulation of food within the empire often came at high cost to Indigenous people. Sir Thomas's attempts to annex New Guinea in order to obtain Native labour expose the exploitation sustaining Queensland's sugar trade, as did a seven-part report, published also as a book, in *Harper's Monthly* (1905–6) on the "modern slavery" that enabled cocoa production in Angola. The author was the journalist Henry W. Nevinson, whose name will appear repeatedly in the following.

Food for thought circulated in books, magazines, and pictures through the extended family and beyond. At a YMCA hut in France shortly before the Armistice, T.F. McIlwraith was astounded to see a print on the wall that had also hung in his childhood room in Hamilton showing Arthur John Elsley's painting *Late for School* (CWM, T.F. McIlwraith to family, 22 October 1918). The image, completed in 1898, was widely distributed by the *Illustrated London News* and *Pears Annual*, and perhaps the print at Cairnbrae had been clipped from one of these magazines.[9] The Ontario McIlwraiths read extensively and methodically; Jean, her father, and her nephew were writers, and Jean and Dorothy

---

9   See Arthur John Elsley, "Late for School," *Dallas Museum of Art Uncrated* (blog), https://blog.dma.org/tag/arthur-john-elsley/ (accessed 15 September 2019).

worked as editors. There was not enough money to succumb to the kind of book madness that, as will be described, gripped the Cambridge classicist T.R. Glover throughout his lifetime and over the years had him deposit a sizeable library in the house of his Canadian friends in Kingston, but books were always treated with respect in the McIlwraiths' homes. Although galley proofs of T.F. McIlwraith's *The Bella Coola Indians* served his household as scratch paper for years, books as such were not for recycling. Family members would have been aghast to learn that few complete sets of the British Parliamentary Papers exist because of "the convenient size of the blue book page, which the shopkeeper regards as the very model of an envelope for butter, cheese and sausages" (Charles Manby Smith qtd. in O'Neill 23). The children's Scottish grandmother presented them with inscribed copies of *The Legendary Ballads of England and Scotland* and *The Poetical Works of Walter Scott*, and their Uncle Andrew read Robert Burns with his beloved Mary. The Family Album records many instances of older children reading to the younger ones, of penny readings, and recitations, often featuring popular Scottish works. As a child, T.F. listed and ranked the books on imperial travel and adventure he checked out from the library, and as a young KOSB recruit he recited Kipling in letters to his sister, at concerts, and in private get-togethers with his mates. As was typical for a McIlwraith, he was uncomfortable when the author's verse seemed to become self-absorbed. He also loved light comedy, especially when it came from a Scotsman like J. M. Barrie or Ian Hay. Even before he got to Europe, he benefited from the visits in Montreal and Toronto of entertainers like Harry Lauder, who had braved the dangerous crossing of the Atlantic to drum up support for the military. Touring entertainers became an important element in knitting the English-speaking world together, even if the discerning audience did not always approve of the presentations.[10] In 1870, T.F.'s grandfather took his children to what they expected to be educational "readings" but found to be "just a theatre" by a British entertainer who was making a stopover in Hamilton (FA, 22 March 1870). It was not only the Canadians who were apt to take offence. In Dresden, Beulah Knox was scandalized when a travelling American dance troupe let the side down by performing a risqué tango.

The very materiality of the paper, packing material, and writing implements became part of the circulation of insider culture. Appropriately, two of the ornithologist's sons went into the box-making business, and one became wealthy doing so and registering patents for special-usage packages. Along with the visiting cards that the McIlwraith children carried from an early age, letterhead was an important professional and social marker, and in their correspondence, the McIlwraiths were careful to use stationery with appropriate details of their

---

10 Deacon et al. includes several chapters on entertainers who circulated throughout the English-speaking world.

standing. It was an indication of growing indifference to questions of social status when one of them, the ornithologist, no longer paid punctilious attention to these formalities in his later years. In general, however, this frugal family habitually recycled paper, even more so during the paper shortages brought about by the war. T.F. McIlwraith wrote letters from the Great War that were so long that they attracted the wrath of the military censor, but he took care to return the wrapping paper from some forty parcels his family sent him by using it for his own packages to Canada. When he suffered from "paper famine" (CWM, T.F. McIlwraith to family, 23 March 1918), his father helped out by mailing a stack of blank insurance forms from his office. The itineraries of some McIlwraiths can be reconstructed by following the trail of headed notepaper for which both the anthropologist and his grandfather had a passion, whether it came from hotels, Atlantic steamers, the Cambridge Union, the Victoria Memorial Museum, or even the Canadian Senate. The latter may have had its origin in a supply of "old 'senate' paper from the small trunk in the attic" that probably arrived at Cairnbrae with Mary Stevens, whose father was a Canadian senator, and over some thirty years was used up by various family members (TFMF, T.F. McIlwraith to family, 17 August 1920). T.F.'s letters are studded with stories about his writing materials. When he picked up a German soldier's notebook on his trek through Belgium in late 1918, he continued to use it. A typewriter borrowed from a fellow student in Cambridge was well-travelled loot indeed because the latter had brought it back from military service in the German Cameroons. Pounding away on this machine gave T.F. the satisfaction of seemingly conquering the enemy one more time.

Through the generations, the McIlwraiths had a talent for associating with individuals who came from backgrounds different from their own and who were themselves accomplished networkers. Magee and Thompson describe such individuals as " 'leaders,' 'architects' or 'agents' " who "could appear in any type of network" and "ensure[d] that information circulate[d] as freely and widely as possible" (Magee and Thompson 55, 54). Sir Thomas, who worked as a railway engineer in his early years in Australia, insisted on the development of communication by "railway, telegraphs, postal subsidies" as a basis of Australian federation ("Our Most Enterprising Colony," part 2, 21), and he joined Canada's Sir Sandford Fleming in the promotion of the Pacific Cable ("Sir T. M'Ilwraith"). Fleming visited Australia in 1893 in the company of Mackenzie Bowell, Dominion minister of trade and commerce and subsequently prime minister of Canada, aiming to encourage trade between Australia and Canada and "confer[ring] on the subject of a telegraph connecting Canada with Australia" (Begg 452). On his turn, McIlwraith met with officials in Ottawa the following year for further discussion of the Cable.

While Sir Thomas stands out, many of the McIlwraiths and their partners excelled in the role of networking "agents." As a result, this book features walk-on parts from unexpected adjuncts to their middle-class world. They include Eileen Plunket and Doris Blackwood, granddaughters of the Marquess of Dufferin and Ava, former governor general of Canada. Eileen was the daughter of William, 5th Baron Plunket, governor of New Zealand between 1904 and 1910 and his wife, Victoria, while Doris was trapped in Australia for the duration of the First World War when she was invited to accompany her uncle Ronald Munro Ferguson, 1st Viscount Novar and his wife upon his appointment as governor general in 1914. There are also Lionel Phillips, South African randlord, and his family; the scholar T.R. Glover, classicist at Cambridge and, for five noteworthy years, professor at Queen's University in Kingston; A.C. Seward, professor of botany at Cambridge and his wife Marion, painter and philanthropist, who kept in touch with a host of former students throughout the empire; W.H.R. Rivers, A.C. Haddon, and William Ridgeway, T.F.'s teachers at Cambridge, and their large circle of influential colleagues and high-ranking administrators from the Colonial Office. Although few present-day readers will understand it that way, Haddon intended it as a joke when he advised his student that the empire was so all-encompassing that "you can leave England on a British vessel, land only at British ports, and be killed, cooked, and eaten by British subjects" ("Genealogy").

Such networks and networking agents, however, also operated on rival fronts. By the 1880s, competition in the Pacific pitted the British against the French, Italians, Russians, and Germans. Sir Thomas was provoked into the annexation of Papua New Guinea[11] by an incendiary article composed by the German geographer Emil Deckert, while opponents to McIlwraith's plans for imported labour included the Aborigines' Protection Society and the Russian scientist and humanitarian campaigner Nikolai Miklouho-Maclay. Sir Thomas never met Deckert, and he may not have known Miklouho-Maclay personally either. But he heard a great deal from and about them through "[a] plethora of papers" that ensured "the flow of information and press communication ... within an imperial framework" (Magee and Thompson 28). Because of his expansive scientific and political activities, Miklouho-Maclay was also interesting to Russia and Germany while Deckert's widely circulated article in the *Augsburger Allgemeine Zeitung* recommending that Germany annex New Guinea was published in the ascending empire of Wilhelmine Germany. Deckert's own intellectual horizons reached well beyond Germany (and Australia, which he never seemed to have visited) when he married the daughter of the inventor Charles Goodyear and conducted years of fieldwork in North America, becoming one of the leading experts on its geography. Another combination of empires, each crumbling with the onset of the Great War, came into play when

---

11 Because the contemporary documents all refer to "New Guinea," I will be using this term to avoid confusion.

Beulah Knox enrolled at a *Pensionat* in Dresden for a few months in 1913. Without her knowledge, she was taught by teachers whose family of pedagogues, scholars, and scientists circulated through the Hapsburg and Ottoman Empires, as well as Northern Germany, the Rhineland, and Alsace-Lorraine. This mobility came to an abrupt stop with the Great War. When, in the 1930s, members of the family were caught up in the Nazis' racial laws, emigration to North and South America became the only way for them to save themselves.

More than once the McIlwraiths experienced global rivalry and conflict, culminating in the Great War and its aftermath, and the purview of their activities broadened and narrowed accordingly. The Pacific shows up repeatedly in this context, and together with the Atlantic, the Great Lakes, and important waterways like the St. Lawrence, it provides an oceanic element so strongly present that it can be seen to engulf the narrative as a whole. In 1898, fifteen years after Sir Thomas's attempted annexation, the Cambridge Torres Strait Expedition, including A.C. Haddon and W.H.R. Rivers as participants, completed its anthropological inventory of populations in Mer and Mabuiag. Another sixteen years later, in 1914, T.F.'s future mentors at Cambridge, the botanist A.C. Seward and his wife Marion, were overtaken by the war as they travelled to Australia for the British Association for the Advancement of Science (BAAS) conference. By the time they made their anxious return voyage to Europe, colleagues who had been friends on the voyage out had been interned as enemies alien and the first casualties among colleagues and students were being posted. Following the war, between 1919 and 1921, T.F. McIlwraith was enrolled at Cambridge and taught by members of the Torres Strait Expedition. He was keen to obtain a Colonial Service or research appointment in Melanesia, among other prospects, but instead the Anthropological Division of the Geological Survey of Canada employed him to study the Nuxalk in the Canadian Pacific Northwest between 1922 and 1924. The experience profoundly transformed his understanding of empire and his place in it. When it was finally published some twenty years after completion, the Nuxalk welcomed all that was useful to them in *The Bella Coola Indians* and ignored anything that was not. This latter process, too, has a global element that links it to the Pacific at large: it runs parallel to the use of Haddon's research data "as a reference guide" and source of inspiration for contemporary Pacific Island families and artists in the Torres Strait (see Patrick; Herle and Philp).

While T.F. McIlwraith worked among and was being educated by the Nuxalk, the premier of Queensland never deviated from the grasping mentality that informed his coup d'état. Sir Thomas's views of Aboriginals, Pacific Islanders, Chinese, and Indian labourers were proclaimed across the imperial press and printed in the British Parliamentary Papers. The principle was to exploit migrant labour for little money under adverse conditions for the workers, and to make certain that the latter were excluded from any power that came with membership in the empire. In commenting on Pacific labour, Sir Thomas deploys the tropes of dying and multiplying races to justify his government's policies: like Aboriginals, the "Polynesians" were "dying out in our island," he averred, and would soon no longer be a problem to those who objected to their presence. To offset any anticipated labour shortage, there was "[t]he Papuan [who] breeds and multiplies." As long as none of the groups of labourers was permitted to "swarm ... over like the Chinese," the situation was well under control ("Our Most Enterprising Colony," part 2, 21). The mass of documents about the Pacific labour trade fails to convey Islanders' own experience adequately. The few records that do exist are being restored from Parliamentary Papers and legal documents, in order to acknowledge Islanders as agents in their own narrative and "individuals with shared experiences and responses" (Banivanua-Mar, *Violence and Colonial Dialogue* 48) rather than as figures "shadowing" the imperial networks set up to exploit them.[12]

The stakes were not as extreme as those in Sir Thomas's Queensland, but the Canadian McIlwraiths, too, were clear about individuals and groups whose company they did not seek out. Thomas McIlwraith befriended ornithologists in Quebec, and in researching her fiction, Jean McIlwraith consulted with French Canadian historians, but the family in Hamilton generally kept its distance from French Canadians, Irish immigrants, Roman Catholics, and former Black slaves who had arrived in the border towns of Ontario via the Underground Railroad. When Jean McIlwraith wrote her essay on "Household Budgets Abroad: Canada," she included comments on the Chinese domestic, "that tireless, methodical machine" (812). She would have approved of the advertisement in the *Queen's University Journal* that had Hong Lee's laundry on Kingston's Princess Street announce to Queen's University students that he "like your trade goot, and he now give 1000 cent for this. Leave your address and John will call for washee."[13] She deplored the Chinese head tax not because it was discriminatory but because it drove up the wages for available workers. Although they appear as a source of knowledge about North American birds in *The Birds of Ontario*, Indigenous people are rarely mentioned in the McIlwraith archive during the nineteenth century. Jean's brother-in-law, John Henderson Holt, of the Holt-Renfrew store, employed clerks who were instructed to tell their American customers about "that primitive people, who have become almost extinct in Eastern America" (*Ten Days in Quebec*). In the Great War, T.F. McIlwraith was surprised to find he was comfortable mixing with fellow

---

12 As Banivanua-Mar has shown, however, it was possible to assert Native agency in "shadowing" as well, as Indigenous people "sought to resist, manage, or exploit emerging colonial settlements and trades" ("Shadowing Imperial Networks" 340).

13 Advertisement, *Queen's University Journal*, clipping, St. John's College Library, TRG, GB 275 Glover/F: Biographical Material.

soldiers who, in civilian life, were bankers, lawyers, and theologians. He concluded that in times of peace "we would never have met, or if we had would certainly never have been friends ... [but] when it comes down to brass tacks most fellows show up all right" (CWM, T.F. McIlwraith to family, 13 May 1918). It was a different story when he encountered Jewish recruits from East London, students from India at Cambridge, where he completed his officer training, as well as Native troops from around the empire and members of the Chinese and West Indian Labour Corps in France. With the exception of the Māori troops, whom he admired, he was wary of all of them, at the time.

In political, religious, and educational views, the McIlwraiths shared the ideologies of their class, and the networks to which they belonged mostly failed "to provide a counter-weight to the ethnic divisions, discrimination and dispossession associated with settler colonialism" (Magee and Thompson 57). The following narrative attends to the McIlwraiths' limitations, but it also pays tribute to the discernment and determination with which some of them stepped outside the boundaries that the idea of empire initially imposed on them. Using a psychoanalytical perspective on "the unconscious work of history," Michael Roper has insisted that "the intellectual and moral positions we adopt, and the adversaries we choose, cannot be wholly explained by historiographical trends, or by social class, gender, national or ethnic background." He concludes that "unconscious conflicts and desires" ("The Unconscious Work of History" 186) must also be considered. T.F. McIlwraith's readiness to be educated by the Nuxalk suggests that perhaps he, too, was motivated by such "conflicts and desires." More specifically, the angry clarity with which he came to recognize injustice when he saw it speaks to the intelligence and humanity that propelled him to change his views.

A word of explanation about the title and its dates. "Writing the empire" refers to a large range of written communications. It alludes to the written taxonomies with which administrations have traditionally regulated imperial possessions, including people, wildlife, and land. "Writing" refers to Parliamentary Papers, commission reports, interviews, and press coverage. It encompasses literary work and correspondence between authors, and it describes scholarship and the reader's reports, book reviews, and letters of recommendation that accompany it, along with the gatekeeping that prevented publication of Jean McIlwraith's novel about New York's Settlement House milieu and delayed T.F. McIlwraith's *The Bella Coola Indians* by twenty years. "Writing" refers to the daily business of exchanging personal letters, invitations, thank-you notes, and letters of introduction. It means business correspondence and keeping accounts. Even business letters that – like Jean's at Doubleday Publishers – ostensibly served to keep a rival empire going were always bracketed by her identity as a "Britisher." Indeed, Jean's situation is a reminder that the "empire" in this title can on occasion cover more than one empire, including the United States and Wilhelmine Germany, as competitors of Britain.

Finally, "writing" includes the inscriptions on plaques, memorials, and tomb-stones that time and again reminded the McIlwraiths of the lives that held the empire together, but they were not always aware of the silences that ruled collective memory. In one particularly elaborate example, T.F. perused the plaques commemorating the Wale family in the parish church of Little Shelford, Cambridgeshire, with generations in military service from the Great Siege of Gibraltar and the Siege of Lucknow to the Great War. The most recent were the eight grandsons and great-grandsons of Sir Charles Wale, last governor of British Martinique, who lost their lives in the First World War (TFMF, T.F. McIlwraith to family, 22 February 1920). One of them, the splendidly named Vernon Harcourt De Butts Powell, was employed as housemaster at Appleby School (now College) in Oakville, not far from Hamilton, before he joined the Canadian field artillery and received the Military Cross. His plaque does not mention that he was unable to overcome the trauma of his physical and psychological wounds and shot himself ("Vernon Harcourt De Butts Powell").

The opening date of 1853 chosen for this book emphasizes the significance of emigration by indicating the arrival of John McIlwraith, Sir Thomas's older brother, in Australia, with Thomas McIlwraith, the first of the Canadian branch, coming to Ontario the same year. The closing date of 1948 underscores T.F.'s education by the Nuxalk, which took place during fieldwork from 1922 to 1924 but whose significance became fully manifest only after his research was finally published. The manuscript was completed by early 1927, but government censorship and other problems delayed publication until 1948. I have chosen this date rather than 1992, when *The Bella Coola Indians* was republished with an introduction by John Barker, or 2003, when the field letters were published in an edition by John Barker and Douglas Cole, because the Nuxalk immediately acknowledged on first publication that the research was significant to them. The reviews following the publications in 1992 and 2003, including reviews by Indigenous authors, were an increasingly articulate elaboration of this initial response, and they are an important part of the following discussion. Together, the opening chapter of this book describing Sir Thomas's attempted annexation of New Guinea and the conclusion detailing T.F.'s fieldwork in Bella Coola provide a frame in which the ideologies of empire are confirmed and challenged. There is evidence of resistance throughout, however, ranging from the Indian Rebellion of 1857 to Sinn Fein, and the story of "writing the empire," as Priyamvada Gopal has impressively documented, is revealed not so much as one in which "the empire writes back" than as a narrative in which, despite appalling odds, the colonized never stopped composing their own script.

The archival situation is complex. As indicated earlier, some of the McIlwraiths' papers are available in public archives while others remain in private hands. Some documents will soon make their way into public archives, or they have already arrived there but have not yet been catalogued. As much as possible, I have indicated the up-to-date locations of papers and information on their identification in the "Manuscripts and Manuscript Collections" section included at the beginning of the bibliography. The fact that I consulted some of these papers before they were deposited in public archives may affect these details.

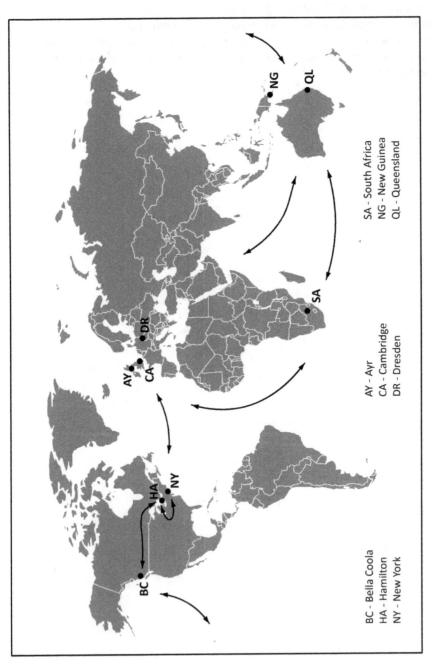

Movements and locations of the McIlwraiths and their associates as they circulated through the British Empire. (Created by Byron Moldofsky, GIS and Cartographic Consulting).

Chapter One

The Australian McIlwraiths

Scottish and Australian Family Relations

On 13 August 1886, Sir Thomas McIlwraith fired off a letter to his brother Andrew in response to the news that their mother had died in Scotland. One by one, the missive reproachfully ticks off recent communications from Andrew and John, their oldest brother, including "[o]n the 22 June ... a cable from [Andrew] that mother was seriously ill," and "on the 23 ... a telegram from John to say that my mother was dead." As the last straw, a letter from Andrew arrived on 13 August, dated "1st + 2nd July full of details of business connected with her property not a word about herself." Although he excused Andrew as having had to deal with "many cares and duties" in connection with the death, Sir Thomas was furious that "none of the dear old woman's relations daughters and grandchildren thought her illness or death worth [writing?]" to him about, and he vowed unspecified retaliation: "[t]he slight is not to me but to my mother but I wont forget it."[1] Ten days later he had to admit that he had been hasty, and that Andrew's note written on the day of their mother's death arrived some four days after the dispatch of his own angry letter. In the meantime, a further letter dated 7 July as well as a newspaper containing the obituary had also been received. Thomas acknowledged that "yours of the 23 was properly posted but I have no means of knowing what delayed it." Once again, he reassured his brother that he was not blaming him but "the others neglect nettled me."[2]

All of the correspondents in this book are preoccupied with the efficiency of the mails, but even during the First World War, when transatlantic communication was especially difficult, none of them spent as much time worrying about

---

1 McIlwraith/Palmer Papers, JOL, Box 8437, OM 69-19/55, Sir T. McIlwraith to Andrew McIlwraith, 13 August 1886, McIlwraith Letterbooks 1886–1887.
2 Sir T. McIlwraith to Andrew McIlwraith, 23 August 1886, McIlwraith/Palmer Papers, JOL, Box 8437, OM 69-19/55, McIlwraith Letterbooks, 1886–1887.

dependable shipping routes, punctual delivery, and the fastest cable services as the nineteenth-century Australians with whom this narrative begins. To cite Geoffrey Blainey's classic discussion of Australia's remote location, they had to contend with "the tyranny of distance" between their continent and virtually everywhere else, but especially Britain as their most important point of reference. Add stormy personalities to the many problems attending communication across long distances, the imprudence of mixing business with personal affairs, and the festering resentments all too common within a large family, and it becomes apparent why the mails for Sir Thomas, his siblings, and their father were a constant source of anxiety. His own family's interest in connecting swiftly with each other provides one reason why the politician among them, Sir Thomas McIlwraith, made efficient postal and telegraphic communication a chief mandate when he was in office. Among others, he initiated the Torres Strait Mail Service to enable Queensland to obtain faster mail service to Britain,[3] an effort that ran under the ambitious flag of an uninterrupted route to the mother country. One of the last projects of McIlwraith's political career was to join forces with Canada's Sir Sandford Fleming in promoting the Pacific Cable that, along with "the Canadian route" across North America, would provide a connection by which a citizen of the empire could "feel ... at home among his own people" from wherever he sent his message ("Sir T. M'Ilwraith"). At the same time, McIlwraith pursued a nationalist agenda, geared towards making Queensland competitive with New South Wales and Victoria, and his reasons for supporting Australian federation were topped by a list of "well-defined, common purposes, such as the construction of Trans-Continental lines of railway, telegraphs, postal subsidies, and the like" ("Our Most Enterprising Colony," part 2, 21).

Despite the problems it created for immigrants, the ocean also served as "a medium of connection" (Steel 356) that produced opportunities for entrepreneurs like the McIlwraith brothers to invest in transport and commerce. Sons of John McIlwraith, a plumber and town councillor, and his wife Janet Howat, Sir Thomas and his brothers John Jr. and Andrew came from a family of twelve in Ayr, Scotland. All three availed themselves of the empire's overseas opportunities. John, the oldest, emigrated to Australia in 1853, followed by Thomas a year later. John first tried the goldfields but, with supplies shipped by his father, soon founded a successful plumbing business in Melbourne. He became so well respected that he was elected mayor of the city and served as one of the royal commissioners of Victoria at the Centennial Exhibition in Philadelphia. For his collection of sheet lead, lead pipes, gas pipes, and "Block-tin Tubes, hydraulic pressed," the latter being "the first manufactured in the colony," he won a "Special award by Commissioners – Silver Medal for collection" at the Intercolonial Exhibition preceding Philadelphia, and samples of his merchandise were shown at

---

3 For the larger implications of the Torres Strait Mail Service, see Munro 282–3.

the Centennial Exhibition itself (*Philadelphia Centennial Exhibition* 148). John's ventures included shipping, but it was Andrew who made a name for himself in this business and, in dispatching the *Strathleven* from Australia to Britain in 1880 with a cargo of refrigerated beef and butter, he became a pioneer in the overseas transport of frozen food. He was a partner in the "Scottish line" of McIlwraith, McEacharn & Co., helped to finance the Australasian United Steam Navigation Co., and reorganized the Tokyo tramways (Waterson, "McIlwraith, Andrew"). As a result, he became "a key figure establishing a significant Scottish network ... forging valuable relationships between his Scottish connections and the investment needs of his adopted country" (Devine and Mackenzie 244). Andrew frequently travelled back and forth to oversee both ends of the shipping business and other enterprise in which he was involved.

Better educated than his brothers, Thomas excelled in mathematics at the University of Glasgow, winning numerous prizes (see Beanland 14), but changed his mind about a possible academic career and did not graduate before following John to Australia. Thomas's academic success appears to have convinced him that he did not need the services of "a bookkeeper or accountant to record and monitor his personal business undertakings" (Beanland 298), but with the collapse of the Queensland National Bank in 1896, it became apparent that in this area at least McIlwraith's practical skills fell short of his intellect. After the goldfields, he began a career as engineer and subcontractor on the railways with the company of Cornish and Bruce, receiving a government appointment as civil engineer in 1859 (Beanland 18). By the mid-1860s, he was established as a pastoralist in the Maranoa region west of Brisbane in partnership with the Irishman Joseph Capel Smyth. At approximately the same time, he entered political life, eventually serving three terms as premier of Queensland (1879–83, 1888, and 1893), as well as assuming the post of colonial treasurer and other ministerial appointments. Thomas received an LLD from the University of Glasgow in 1880, was knighted in 1882, and both he and John received the Freedom of Ayr in 1884. Thomas and Andrew were members of the Royal Colonial Institute, and at the RCI's meeting in London in 1893, Thomas was toasted for "showing so well ... that the ancient traditions and talents which thrive in the Old Country may flourish in a new soil" (*Proceedings RCI* 246). The toast was offered by James Bryce, Regius Professor of Civil Law at Oxford, future British ambassador to the United States, and author of *The American Commonwealth* (1888). The book, influential for its advocacy of keeping America white, became "a 'Bible' [to] white nation-builders in Australia and South Africa" (Lake and Reynolds 7).

Through marriage, the McIlwraith brothers consolidated their wealth and the connections that helped maintain it.[4] Thomas's first wife, Margaret

---

4 On family networks among Scottish immigrant pastoralists, see Wilkie.

Whannell, was a sister of John's wife Mary. Margaret, the brothers' sister, married another McIlwraith, the newspaper editor William McIlwraith.[5] William, who emigrated to Queensland in 1880 with his family of six, was the youngest brother of the Ontario McIlwraiths, who will be introduced in the next chapter. As owner of the *Morning Bulletin* in Rockhampton, William became an important ally in Thomas's political career who could be relied upon to give him positive press. He praised the annexation of New Guinea as "a bold and clever proceeding," characterized an opponent's writing as "watery," and laughed at the opposition's "sorry attempts ... at condemning your conduct."[6] For his part, Andrew married a cousin of the Whannells, Mabel Andrina Campbell, daughter of the engineer James Campbell, who assisted him in organizing the transport of frozen food on the *Strathleven*. Thomas may have married his first wife in preference to Isabella Simpson, the mother of his first daughter, Isabella, as a result of pressure from John to strengthen existing family connections (Beanland 24).[7]

Not all of these liaisons worked out as planned: Andrew divorced both his first and second wife, and Thomas's first marriage was also a failure. Shortly after his first wife's death, however, Thomas strengthened his political network by marrying Harriet Mosman, sister-in-law of one of his chief allies, Sir Arthur Palmer. His close connections with his brothers and with Palmer did also create problems for Thomas. In the so-called Steel Rails Case instigated in 1880 by his political opponent, Sir Samuel Griffith, the premier was accused of corruption for apparently favouring the McIlwraith, McEacharn Company in the purchase and transport of steel rails from Britain. Both Thomas and Palmer owned shares in one of the company's vessels. The charge was investigated by a royal commission and eventually dismissed,[8] but in hindsight even the premier's most ardent admirers felt that he, his family, and his associates should have been more circumspect. Thus, the journalist R. Spencer Browne gallantly concluded that it was "impossible ... for great English and Scottish firms to be parties to flagrant and small corruption," but he warned that "[a] politician's dealing with relatives on behalf of the country which he serves may be ever so free of evil, but it should be conspicuously in the open" (320).

---

5 Beyond this marriage, the exact family relationship between Sir Thomas and William McIlwraith has not been established. Beanland identifies him as "[a] distant cousin" (155).

6 William McIlwraith to Sir Thomas McIlwraith, 1 May 1883, McIlwraith/Palmer Papers, JOL,
   Box 8434, OM 64-19/590, Sir Thomas McIlwraith.

7 Information about Isabella's mother is sparse and inconsistent. Baigent gives her name as Victoria Findley and the daughter's birth as 1865, not 1863 as Beanland does.

8 For details of the case, see *The Law Reports* 120–34.

Father, Son, and Business

Despite their close ties, relations among the McIlwraiths were – as Thomas's letter to Andrew on their mother's death indicates – not always amicable. Between 1865 and the early 1870s, John conducted a rancorous correspondence with his father, who had helped him set up his business in Melbourne by sending merchandise that included everything from slates, zinc, and lead pipes to tiles and closet doors. Judging from his numerous errors in spelling and grammar, Bailie John was not well educated, and he appears to have been unable to keep up with the younger man's ambitious overseas ventures beyond the first ten years. As may be inferred from his son's responses, however, John demanded filial respect and was taken aback when his shortcomings as a business partner were pointed out to him:

> I dont [sic] clearly understand what you mean by saying you will not be responsible for merchants or manufacturers blunders. In ordering goods from you I have no one else to look to if any mistake or blunder is made and you surely dont mean to say that you will not see it rectified if a mistake is committed. (AU NBAC, John McIlwraith to Bailie John McIlwraith, 28 January 1866, item 2–3)[9]

John regularly sent large amounts of money, such as two drafts for £1,000 each in a letter dated 25 March 1865, preceded by a draft for the same amount the previous month, and was increasingly angered when his parent failed to acknowledge receipt by return of post or to keep copies of their correspondence. More than one shipment was delayed in customs because invoices had not been filled out properly: "I trust that you will for the future pay a little more attention to my orders, send me full particulars in invoices and advise me more fully of slates not forgetting to state on the invoice the Quarry from which the Slates come or rather the Port or both if you like" (AU NBAC, John McIlwraith to Bailie John McIlwraith, 28 January 1866, item 3–5). Shipments were ruined because inferior supplies had been purchased or items had not been safely packed. As a result of previous experience, John hotly refused to consider a cargo of Porthmadog slates, "& if the Best ... are not to be had I will do without them" (AU NBAC, John McIlwraith to Bailie John McIlwraith, 27 November 1866, item 3–5). He complained to Thomas that he had lost £1,000 over a delivery of slates that "beat anything I ever saw ... Had any other person sent them I should at once have had a Survey held on them & paid accordingly" (AU NBAC, John McIlwraith to Thomas McIlwraith, 27 November 1866, item 3–5). John expressed regret to his father "that our business relations should cause you any uneasiness & sorrow, and the more

---

9   In order to distinguish John senior and John junior, the former will be identified as "Bailie John McIlwraith" throughout, although he did not become Bailie until late 1865.

so than you seem to take it all personally" (AU NBAC, John McIlwraith to Bailie John McIlwraith, 28 June 1866, item 3–5). He could not comprehend, however, why his father should be offended at being taken to task: "Upon my word you are the most extraordinary business man ... instead of taking means to rectify the error which you ought at once to have done you indulge in personal remarks" (AU NBAC, John McIlwraith to Bailie John McIlwraith, 9 November 1868, item 6–8). In 1866, his father was so insulted that he did not inform his son that he had been named Bailie, and John had to learn of it through a third party (AU NBAC, John McIlwraith to Bailie John McIlwraith, 28 January 1866, item 3–5). At times, relations became so tense that their correspondence came to a virtual standstill, and they communicated through Andrew or Thomas (AU NBAC, John McIlwraith to Andrew McIlwraith, 24 April 1869, item 6–8). The ultimate insult came when John switched to different suppliers: "I can buy [slates] in London of the sizes & quality I want & land them in Melbourne cheaper" (AU NBAC, John McIlwraith to Thomas McIlwraith, 27 November 1866, item 3–5).

Difficulties in postal delivery were sometimes used as a pretext to cover up interpersonal problems, and given the distances between Scotland and Australia, it was not easy to dismiss this explanation. "I must accept your excuse for not writing in December," John wrote in March of 1865, "but how in the name of business the post office people could have the power of delaying the Australian mail I cannot conceive" (AU NBAC, John McIlwraith to Bailie John McIlwraith, 25 March 1865, item 3–5). Like Thomas, John fumed when there was no post. How was it that "such a large family" could not produce "a scrap" between them? (AU NBAC, John McIlwraith to Thomas McIlwraith, 27 August 1866, item 3–5). He was particularly anxious for the mails to arrive when business was dull, as happened in 1865. He obsessively reviewed the technicalities of impending delivery and the little time he expected to have for composing a response before the ship turned around: "The mail due on the 10th inst has not arrived yet. She was telegraphed from Adelaide last night and may be expected in the Bay through the course of tomorrow [sic] Sunday. The outgoing mail closes finally at the post office at 10 o'clock on Monday morning & unless the Gov-t keep the steamer back for a day I will not be able to reply to your letters" (AU NBAC, John McIlwraith to Bailie John McIlwraith, 24 June 1865, item 3–5). Most of John's mail to Scotland was dispatched via Marseilles (or "Marseillais," as his father had it), but he was on the lookout for alternative routes. After the launch of the Panama, New Zealand and Australian Royal Mail Company in June 1866, he was curious if mail delivery via Panama would be faster than the route through Suez (AU NBAC, John McIlwraith to Bailie John McIlwraith, 12 July 1866, item 3–5).[10] In 1870, another route connected

---

10   For details on this route, see "Mails for England via Panama"; also see Otis. The route had been promoted for some time; see "The Panama Steam Route."

to the sugar trade was opened up by the Oceanic Steamship Company across the Pacific "via Honolulu + San Francisco from Sydney," and John sent his father "a few lines with the view of seeing what time this mail takes compared with the P. & O. Co[mpan]y. It is given out the new Coy. will do it in 40 days, of this I am doubtful but we will see" (AU NBAC, John McIlwraith to Bailie John McIlwraith, 21 March 1870, item 6–8; see also Adler). John was alert to possible obstructions created by the Austro-Prussian War in 1866, but he says nothing to his father about similar problems caused by the Franco-Prussian War of 1870–1. In the end, neither war appears to have disrupted business communications between Ayr and Melbourne. Three months before the outbreak of the Franco-Prussian War, and in a rare show of harmony, father and son were even planning a trip for Bailie John to Australia. He was to come either on his own ship, the *Girvan*, via Suez or by commercial steamer via Panama, connecting first to the Pacific Railway across the United States and then to the Panama, New Zealand and Australia Royal Mail Company bound for Sydney. If he did cross the American continent by train, John warned, "take it in stages ... eight days & nights in a Railway Carriage is no Joke" (AU NBAC, John McIlwraith to Bailie John McIlwraith, 21 March 1870, item 6–8).

With these alternatives in place, the mails could be rerouted if necessary, but there was nothing to be done when a mail steamer was lost. In early December 1871, John wrote to his father regarding "the total loss of the mail steamer *Rangoon* with the Australian mails when she struck a rock in Galle Harbour." In panic, he took this as another opportunity to remind his father of "the necessity of sending me a duplicate of your correspondence" (AU NBAC, John McIlwraith to Bailie John, 4 December 1871, item 9). The papers gave plenty of details concerning the loss of mail: "All the European and Indian mails were lost, and the Ceylon mails were slightly damaged ... The Australian press despatches are all lost ... Duplicates of mails have been telegraphed for" ("Particulars of the Loss of the Rangoon"). Generally, these press despatches were expected to take six weeks to reach their destination, but with direct cable connection between Britain and Australia imminent, Reuter had signed an agreement with the Melbourne *Argus* and the Sydney *Morning Herald* earlier that year according to which the news agency was to "despatch daily by telegraph by retransmission from India, Jawa [sic] or Singapore ... the same telegraphic intelligence as shall be despatched by the Company to the Indian Press" (qtd. in Rantanen 38). The *Argus* and the *Herald*, which formed the Australian Associated Press following the agreement, were the exclusive recipients of the "intelligence."

The press coverage of the sinking of the *Rangoon* addresses a variety of the problems that afflicted maritime communications despite advances in steam travel and cable communication. One paper blamed a failure in coordinating three different mail steamers for causing the calamity, including the early arrival of a steamer from Suez with the English mail and of the *Rangoon* with the much delayed "appearance of the S.S. Travancore, from China," with "[p]assengers ... grumbling over the loss of three days at least in the dispatch of the Home mails to the colonies" ("Loss of the Rangoon," *Grey River Argus*).[11] Observers surmised that this lack in coordination was to blame for the difficulties encountered by the *Rangoon*, whose distress signals were initially misread (and therefore ignored) as an indication that the *Travancore* had finally arrived and that the two steamers were establishing contact. Additional problems arose from racial friction as technological progress did not imply improvement in race relations or diminish the fear that Native personnel were taking jobs away from white workers who, by nature, were assumed to be better qualified: "The Malay crew of the Rangoon behaved very badly," one letter to the editor complained, "not rendering any assistance in saving passengers or baggage ... It would be a great deal better to employ European sailors entirely, on the Australian line especially, than a lot of fellows not to be depended on in an emergency" ("Loss of the Mail Steamer"). This request anticipated the legislation of the Post and Telegraph Act in 1901, according to which – with the exception of "the coaling and loading of ships at places beyond the limits of the Commonwealth" – there was to be "only white labour" employed in the transport of Australian mails ("Post and Telegraph Act"). Other press coverage pointed out that "[n]o lives of passengers or crew were lost, but three native wreckers supposed to be drowned" ("Particulars of the Loss of the Rangoon"). The Otago *Daily Times* elaborated that the "three native fishermen, supposed to be plundering wreck" ("Loss of the Rangoon") had it coming to them because they belonged to a group that encircled the steamer on canoes from where "at the risk of their lives [they] snatched any articles swept off the decks." The fishermen then also boarded the sinking *Rangoon*, and some went down with her. Although lives were lost in this instance, the episode illustrates the existence of oceanic networks that knew to avail themselves of the "resources, technologies, energy, [and] transport options" developed by the imperial powers (Banivanua-Mar and Rhook).

Portrait of a Marriage

Thomas and Margaret ("Maggie") Whannell married in 1863, and they had four children together: Thomas in 1863 (Thomas Jr. died in early 1864), Jessie in 1864, Mary in 1866, and Blanche in 1872. The family was in Scotland between 1866 and 1868, and Margaret and the children stayed on until January 1869 while Thomas returned to Australia in early 1868. The social life she had enjoyed in Ayr and, one assumes, on visits to the Whannells in Northern Ireland

---

11   Spelling of "despatch" and "dispatch" is inconsistent in the originals.

must have made the rural isolation at the Merivale sheep station in Queensland difficult to tolerate,[12] but this is where the family moved on their return. Maggie capitulated only a few months later and left for Melbourne with the children. Her father-in-law was shocked, and intended "to tell her [his] mind" in a separate letter as he wrote to his son: "what is the use of all you have if you are to live in this miseryble [sic] way – why you may be taken away without any of your little ones or your wife being beside you to give any help – this is not as it should be."[13] The couple was back together by 1871, living at Eurella, a sheep station that Thomas had purchased the year before. Her husband's forceful personality, which impressed his political associates and opponents, probably crushed his wife, and his political ambitions and business interests distracted him from his family. As well, she may have had reason to suspect him of infidelity, and the concluding paragraph of his entry in the *Oxford Dictionary of National Biography* offers the disapproving summary that he "was a burly 6 foot womanizer with the instincts of a gambler" (Baigent). The reference to his overpowering physique suggests an inclination to dominate weaker individuals, including women, perhaps even intimidate them, while the phrasing of "the instincts of a gambler" implies the risk-taking of an innately unreliable individual.

It was not easy for his father to obtain news of Thomas's marriage or anything else because he was not a diligent letter-writer. Bailie John's letters are full of complaints, asking "how it is that you are not writing us" and counting as many as four mails "gone past and not one word from you." Maggie, who was then in Melbourne, appears to have complained about not hearing from her husband either, and even if their marriage was not the most harmonious, Bailie John McIlwraith admonished his son "to let your wife know where you are and what you are dooing [sic]" (OM 64-19/67, Bailie John McIlwraith to Thomas McIlwraith, 24 March 1870). The reminders had no effect, and four years later the complaints persist. Even political business did not count as an excuse: "I got yours dated Melbourne 28th Decr – all right where you say that with the election you did not write last Mail but you will see from my former letters that you have not wrote [sic] these three mails past" (OM 64-19/67, Bailie John McIlwraith to Thomas McIlwraith, [18?] July 1874). It was only when Thomas became premier that his father was ready to content himself with "a few lines now + again I can not expect them often but a few lines will do" (OM 64-19/81, Bailie John McIlwraith to Sir Thomas McIlwraith, 24 August 1882). By then, an ailing Bailie John had in any case lost his pugnacious personality, and his "period of activity was past" (qtd. in Dignan, "Sir Thomas McIlwraith: His Public Career" 3).

---

12 For discussion of the monotony of life in the outback, see Auerbach 141–4; L. Frost.
13 Bailie John McIlwraith to Thomas McIlwraith, 8 September 1869, McIlwraith/Palmer Papers, JOL, Box 8438, OM 64-19/67 Sir Thomas McIlwraith. Further references, all to Box 8438, in text.

Thomas was equally slow to respond to business correspondence. While the Franco-Prussian War was in progress, John wrote to his sheep-farming son that "[t]hare [sic] has been a great demand for woollen goods for both Germany and France," and he hoped that "trade generaly [sic]" would be stimulated by the hostilities (OM 64-19/67, Bailie John McIlwraith to Thomas McIlwraith, 26 January 1871). Under separate cover he mailed a copy of the Glasgow *Herald* with an article outlining these business opportunities. To his annoyance, the war further complicated postal delivery because mail to Australia had to travel via Brindisi instead of Marseilles (OM 64-19/67, Bailie John McIlwraith to Thomas McIlwraith, 29 December 1870). He had little sympathy with the French, whom he considered an "unsettled lot – I am much afraid the Germans will need to go in amongst them yet and humble them a little more" (OM 64-19/67, Bailie John to Thomas McIlwraith, 18 May 1871). While the relationship between John in Melbourne and his father in Scotland was affected by the latter's failure to keep up a prompt exchange of business correspondence, it was now Thomas who took his time to produce an explanation for "a draft being presented by a Mr. Robertson for £ 850 ... which I have paid although as yet you have not said one word to me about it" (OM 64-19/67, Bailie John McIlwraith to Thomas McIlwraith, [18?] July 1874).

But there were more serious problems than postal delay. By 1874, Maggie was drinking heavily, and her husband decided to send her and the children to Scotland to be supervised by his parents. Thomas himself drank too much, and he once was the object of a prohibitionist's "very sackcloth and ashes oration" in Parliament, in which he and two other members were singled out, in a rather strained metaphor considering McIlwraith's girth, as "shadows of their former selves" caused by excessive drink. One of these parliamentarians, Jacob Low, even insisted that his doctors had recommended "two or three dozen [sic] glasses of whisky daily ... for his material benefit" ("Political Froth"). (Low died a year later.) However, while social drinking was part of the culture of pastoralist and political mateship (see K. Inglis), alcoholism was unacceptable in women of the "affluent middle-class that valued sobriety and modest behaviour as a means of preserving bourgeois standing and attaining class mobility" (Piper 88). Performance of their duties as wives and mothers hinged on impeccable conduct, and any cracks in the social façade had to be concealed. Some husbands addressed the problem by withholding money from their wives that allowed them to buy liquor (Piper 89–90), but this may have been difficult to implement during the long periods that Maggie and the children spent away from Thomas. Bailie John instantly consented to taking charge of Thomas's wife and their children, and proving the efficiency of overseas family gossip transmitted through intersecting sets of correspondence (see McCarthy, "Ethnic Networks"), he told his son that he "had heard of this some time ago but never spoke of it to you because I never believed it" (OM 64-19/67, Bailie John

McIlwraith to Thomas McIlwraith, 30 September 1874). The family already had unhappy experience with an alcoholic, and Bailie John's letters document years of futile efforts to get his son Hamilton away from liquor and settled in a profession as an engineer in Scotland, Australia, New Zealand, Canada, or the United States. All attempts failed, and Hamilton eventually died by drowning in Chesapeake Bay (Twaddel 356–7). He may have been overwhelmed by his parents' expectations and the example of his successful brothers, and fear of his family is evident in "the stupid fellow" taking three months before he plucked up the courage to tell his father that he had married. His new wife was "first rate ... a very respectable one although not a rich one in money" (OM 64-19/67, Bailie John McIlwraith to Thomas McIlwraith, 2 November 1871, 30 November 1871). However, she, too, was unable to save Hamilton from himself.

John McIlwraith agreed that Maggie should be separated from her children once they arrived in Scotland, and emphasized that, for the sake of the family's reputation, her "conduct should be kept as quite [sic] as possible" (OM 64-19/67, Bailie John McIlwraith to Thomas McIlwraith, 30 September 1874). In November 1874, Thomas's parents travelled to Liverpool to meet their daughter-in-law, and John took care to "board ... the ship without any of the cabin passangers [sic] seeing me" (OM 64-19/67, Bailie John McIlwraith to Thomas McIlwraith, 25 November 1874). Perhaps it was a relief to Maggie to be away from Australia and her husband, especially as she had her children nearby, because reports from Ayr remained encouraging for several months. In January, Maggie had a "very bad cold, ... however thare [sic] is nothing wrong so far as drink is concerned," despite "every opportunity of taking it" over the holidays (OM 64-19/67, Bailie John McIlwraith to Thomas McIlwraith, 28 January 1875). In May, she was confirmed to be still "quite sober" (OM 64-19/67, Bailie John McIlwraith to Thomas McIlwraith, 15 May 1875). Thomas continued to insist that she be separated from their children, but his father declined because "she is doing all that we could wish her" (OM 64-19/67, Bailie John McIlwraith to Thomas McIlwraith, 10 June 1875). Two years later, however, Maggie had succumbed to drink again, and her in-laws removed the two older children, who were spending their school holidays with their mother in Dumfries: "I am very sorry to have to tell you so I thought for a time we would manage her, but I am sorry it has been out of our power to do so" (OM 64-19/81, Bailie John McIlwraith to Thomas McIlwraith, 11 October 1877). She died three days after he had sent this letter, and John in Melbourne passed the cabled message on to his brother. Their father followed up with a long, unhappy letter in which he mixes up an account of Maggie's death with worries about Hamilton. Maggie's steep decline convinced him that "she could not live long at the rate she was Drinking," that she "no dout [sic] was to be the ruine [sic] of your family," and that it was better for everyone that she was dead. Hamilton once again seemed to be settling down, "but I don't like his letters" (OM 64-19/81, Bailie John

McIlwraith to Thomas McIlwraith, 31 January 1877). His daughter-in-law's death appears to have caused the old man to anticipate his own because he began to think about his will, especially the provisions he intended to make for Hamilton. Thomas protested vehemently against the suggestion that his younger brother be made one of the trustees, and his father agreed that "however painfull [sic] it was for me to read it Still I am glad you spoke your Mind about Hamilton," because "he can scarceley [sic] mend" (OM 64-19/81, Bailie John McIlwraith to Thomas McIlwraith, 10 October 1878). As with Maggie, a major concern was the constant fear that he would embarrass the family and "only annoy and disgrace every one connected with him" (OM 64-19/81, Bailie John McIlwraith to Thomas McIlwraith, 12 September 1878).

Thomas's indifference to his deceased wife was further brought home when he failed to respond to several requests from his father to provide instructions for Maggie's headstone. McIlwraith's attitude towards her has caused him such dislike among historians that the evidence has been misread to make him look even worse. Thus, in an entry in the *Australian Dictionary of Biography*, Don Dignan claims that "McIlwraith tried to separate his wife from her children, but his father rejected the proposal because, despite her bitterness, Margaret's behaviour had been exemplary" ("Sir Thomas McIlwraith"). The correspondence gives a more complicated picture: his father initially agreed that "the children [should at once be taken] from her" (OM 64-19/67, Bailie John McIlwraith to Thomas McIlwraith, 30 September 1874), then resisted when his son urged him to follow through because his daughter-in-law seemed well "and quite happy with the children" (OM 64-19/67, Bailie John McIlwraith to Thomas McIlwraith, 13 May 1875), but finally gave in to his son's request when she once again succumbed to drink. Similarly, Waterson suggests that McIlwraith "arbitrarily sent her back to his parents at Ayr, rather cruelly and cynically alleging that she had become an alcoholic." Apparently drawing on interviews with family members, Waterson concludes that "she suffered from an acute urological complaint and tippled to alleviate her various pains," and that her death "was both a physiological and psychological consequence of disease and conjugal neglect" (*An Ayrshire Family* 132).

In Scotland, the two older daughters, Jessie and Mary, attended schools in Edinburgh that their grandfather had carefully selected for them (and for which he sent his son annual accounts), and he provided other luxuries such as "a nice little poney [sic] for Jessie and ... a new saddle and other mounting for it," along with a boy to supervise her riding (OM 64-19/67, Bailie John McIlwraith to Thomas McIlwraith, 13 May 1875). The darling of her grandparents was the youngest child, Blanche, who was only two when they first met her at the dock in Liverpool, and whom her grandfather described as "romping about dancing and singing all day" (OM 64-19/67, Bailie John McIlwraith to Thomas McIlwraith, 28 January 1875). When Thomas asked for his children to be sent back to Australia in 1879, his father wondered "how we are to part with Blanch [sic] I don't know but I suspect it must be so" (OM 64-19/81, Bailie John McIlwraith to Thomas McIlwraith, 23 April 1879). There appears to have been discussion of returning the children separately, Mary ("Dolly") first because she was susceptible to colds and expected to benefit from Queensland's hot climate, with Blanche to follow later, but her grandfather feared "she would have broken her little heart [because] she is so fond of Dolly" (OM 64-19/81, Bailie John McIlwraith to Thomas McIlwraith, 23 April 1879). Because the parting could not be helped, the grandparents did everything to make the children comfortable on the voyage back. A dependable "Nursery Governess" was hired to accompany them, with the suggestion that "should you require a governess for them in Brisbane I am sure would be pleased with her." As the daughter of a captain, Miss Baird would have found it relatively easy to make her way back to Scotland if her services were not required in Australia after all. A harmonium was ordered to "help pass the time" (OM 64-19/81, Bailie John McIlwraith to Thomas McIlwraith, 8 May 1879). The old man obtained a character reference to reassure himself that the captain was "a first rate seaman," and in Liverpool he spoke to the ship steward "to do all he could to make them right." He tipped him handsomely and suggested his son do the same at the other end. There is great sadness in the sentence that "thay [sic] started out of dock about 3 oclock [sic] [illegible] on Tuesday the 27th May with a fine wind – and I am sure must be well out to sea" (OM 64-19/81, Bailie John McIlwraith to Thomas McIlwraith, 5 June 1879).

The same year, Thomas remarried. His new wife, Harriet Mosman, was "robust, cheery, a delightful hostess, and very fond of the brighter side of life" (Browne 80) and so better equipped than Maggie to manage her husband. Before he had even received the announcement from his son, Bailie John had obtained reports from his other sources: "Andrew and his wife thay [sic] had meet [sic] her in Brisbane – and gives [sic] us good account of her." Their grandmother was worried about the children getting a stepmother "but I hope Miss Mossman [sic] will make a good mother to them" (OM 64-19/81, Bailie John McIlwraith to Thomas McIlwraith, 19 June 1879). Was it a comment on lack of attention from both her father and her stepmother when, five years later, McIlwraith's eighteen-year-old daughter Mary became secretly engaged and was on the brink of eloping with her admirer while she attended a boarding school in Brussels? (OM 64-19/26, W. Drury to Sir Thomas McIlwraith, 7 May 1884). In the style of a cheap novel, a shifty governess had served as go-between for the lovers. Thomas's father continued to be impressed with Harriet, however, and not the least of her attractions was an improvement in postal communications between father and son because she took it upon herself to keep her father-in-law in Australian newspapers. He was especially happy with "the Sydeny [sic] Mail and other of Melbourne papers" that gave his son "great praise for what [he had] done in Queensland for the Country" when he received his knighthood (OM 64-19/81, Bailie John McIlwraith to Thomas McIlwraith, 25 January 1883).

Sir Thomas McIlwraith: Admirers and Satirists

Sir Thomas McIlwraith was a politician, and his sparse collection of personal letters does not adequately capture that aspect of his personality. Journalism, satire, and political cartoons must also be consulted, as well as Parliamentary Papers documenting his political actions from 1868 onwards when he won the seat for Maranoa in the Legislative Assembly of Queensland. Contemporaries and historians alike describe him as a force of nature or even a manifestation of the supernatural rather than a mortal. The historian Duncan Waterson compared him to "a Cooktown cyclone" ("A Colonial Entrepreneur" 126) while Denver Beanland has him "thunder" across the Queensland stage (1). Although he thought of himself as "the prophet of colonial socialism" (Waterson, *Personality, Profit and Politics* 20-1), the poet Francis Adams was infatuated with McIlwraith and considered him "an Indian idol cut in bronze – strong, stolid, heavy, and puissant," and he thought there was "something of the element of the miraculous in him" (F. Adams, 75, 78).[14] No wonder that tourists like the novelist Gilbert Parker considered him one of the sights in the Queensland Parliament, as a man who "carries with him a dignity that could make an impression on any Chamber" (235-6). Descriptions of McIlwraith's characteristics, as evoked in newspaper coverage, political cartoons, and contemporaries' impressions, draw on a repertoire of imagery circulating throughout the colonial press. Some of the graphics were adapted from traditional British parliamentary satire but, when the conventional comparisons failed to do him justice, his Australian environment supplied even better analogies.

Friend and foe are in remarkable agreement over the outsized intellectual and physical presence of Sir Thomas (see McConnel, "Our Wayward and Backward Sister Colony" 113–17). Supporters and adversaries alike credited him with exceptional intelligence and "a mental equipment given to few" (Bernays 56).[15] The word "big" and its synonyms recur insistently: "he is a giant among midgets," thought the trade unionist Gilbert Casey (Casey);[16] "he grasps all he touches with big and powerful fingers," Francis Adams wrote admiringly (F. Adams 76), while the journalist Spencer Browne considered him "[a] great big man, big-brained, big-hearted, generous, dominating, and brave" (Browne

---

14   On Adams, see Murray-Smith.
15   On Bernays, see Lack.
16   On Casey, see Sullivan.

80). Browne was echoed by the politician William Corfield, who was "greatly struck with his personality. He was a man, big and broad, both physically and mentally" (Corfield 89). Both Browne and Corfield were admirers, but Gilbert Casey was not, and yet he found McIlwraith

> [s]trong, able and determined. He inspires confidence. He is neither weak, vacillating, nor irresolute. He goes the complete pig or none. He has grit, force of character, and will power. He is a born leader of men, and the pity of it is that he prefers to lead the Boodle party [i.e., the Tories].
>
> He is blunt, outspoken and brutal almost in his supreme disregard for the opinions of others. He is courageous, bold and defiant. He doesn't cringe or crawl to his enemies. Not he. He kills them with kindness. (Casey)

Similarly, Lord Derby, the colonial secretary – who was at the time flustered from Queensland's attempted annexation of New Guinea – mixed antipathy with grudging appreciation when he described him as "a heavy, rather clownish Scotchman of 50: shrewd & plainspoken, with a strong Scotch accent" (Stanley 638–9). McIlwraith promptly made it clear in a subsequent interview that he did not care for Derby and his associates either: " 'Yes!' said Sir Thomas McIlwraith, somewhat bitterly, 'I am going back to the colony with the deep conviction that so far as ... such leaders of the Liberals as Mr. Gladstone, Lord Derby, Lord Kimberley, and others – are concerned, they would not stretch forth a finger to save the colonies to the empire' " ("Our Most Enterprising Colony," part 2, 21). In contrast to his cumbersome size, McIlwraith had exceptional mental agility. Thus, in the recurring analogy with a circus *artiste* he is seen not only as a "clown" but also as an "entrepreneurial acrobat," one who entertained astonished crowds with "his pyrotechnics" (Waterson, "A Colonial Entrepreneur" 126). To his opponents, that quality translated into recklessness towards those entrusted to him. In a *Worker* cartoon from 1893, McIlwraith – "expected to lead the coalesced parties to general election" – becomes an enormous marshal who casually steps over the edge of a yawning abyss as he waves a flag of "Queensland for the Syndicates." Behind him follows a parade in "two-by-two" formation featuring, besides the Tories, the Patriotic League, the New Reform Party, and the Naval Tribute,[17] also Kanaka workers, "coolies" from India, and Chinese labourers.[18]

Depending on who was writing, McIlwraith's physical size either confirmed his intellect or his grasping nature. Casey introduces his character sketch of

---

17 "Naval Tribute" refers to the situation that developed from the McIlwraith government's dismissal of Captain Wright of the *Gayundah*, a gunboat of the Queensland Maritime Defense Force. See "The Queensland Government and Captain Wright."

18 *The Worker*, 17 February 1893, 1, reproduced in Beanland 288.

McIlwraith with an extended word play on his "*awful* epigastrium." One series of portraits, published in the Queensland *Punch*, shows the premier steadily expanding in size over the years like a balloon.[19] The press was so preoccupied with his bulk that an interviewer in London instantly "cabled the news out to Australia that [McIlwraith] was about to undergo a medical treatment prescribed in [a] book [on obesity]" that McIlwraith had requested from his secretary within the interviewer's hearing ("Sir T. M'Ilwraith"). Because he was a politician of idiosyncratic appearance and one who courted controversy, he was a boon to caricaturists, and the caricatures focusing on his physique underscore the role of satire as a bluntly manipulative form of life writing (Meskimmon 916). His entrepreneurial activities and recurrent entanglement in financial crises caused the Labour publication *The Worker* (Brisbane), which published full-page caricatures on its front page, to depict him as a variation of Mr. Fat Man, embodiment of the global capitalist (Dyrenfurth, "Truth and Time" 123). In one caricature, dated 21 March 1896, he appears as "Boodlewraith," an uncouth giant brandishing a club marked "Class Legislation" and defending the manacled Maid Queensland, whose rags proclaim her to be bound as a "White Slave" to the "Sweat System." Boodlewraith stares down the "Labour Party," a slender knight holding a sword announcing "Justice" and a shield inscribed "Truth and Time Against the World's Wrongs" (Dyrenfurth, "Truth and Time" 116). An earlier caricature has McIlwraith pose as Falstaff, holding the shield "Banks," the sword "Brisbane Property Vote," and wearing a hat named "Grab."[20] A poster on a tree trunk nearby lists his many offences: "Broken Pledge/Meat Works/Poor Job Q.N. Bank/Naval Tribute/The People's Money for Everything But Honest Government." He cowers before an advancing group of Labour knights, all of them slim and fit, flourishing the banner "Advance with Queensland, Justice for the People." In this juxtaposition between capitalist and worker, thinness means virtue and, in the Labour knights' confrontation with Boodlewraith, it points to the biblical courage of David before Goliath. This interpretation of physical size is, however, not always so obvious in comparisons between Samuel Griffith and McIlwraith, in which the former is seen as "the thin – I had almost said gaunt – pale, suspicious Welsh lawyer" and the latter as "the burly, thick-set, shrewd, Scotch business man" (Stirling 722). Here, each man's appearance echoes Julius Caesar's plea, in Shakespeare's eponymous play, for companions "that are fat" rather than those with "a lean and hungry look." Like Gilbert Parker, this particular writer, who is surveying McIlwraith and Griffith from the visitors' gallery of the Queensland Parliament, is a tourist who has come to take a look at the two opponents as if they were among the

19   Queensland *Punch*, 8 August 1893, reproduced in Beanland 38.
20   Montagu Scott, "Falstaff Up to Date," *The Worker*, 8 May 1893, 1, reproduced in Dyrenfurth 125.

colony's natural attractions. The qualities of one man are enhanced by those of the other. Indeed, the *Worker's* caricatures thrived on the interpretative possibilities of such pairs. Thus, in a variation on Lewis Carroll's Tweedledum and Tweedledee, who look and act alike, the fat "Reidle-dum" (George Reid) and the thin "Deakin-dee" (Alfred Deakin) look different but are both wearing capitalist-style top hats (Dyrenfurth, "Truth and Time" 132).

To some, McIlwraith seemed like a powerful animal, noble or grotesque depending on the writer's political convictions though here, too, the thinking behind the analogy is not always consistent. To the ever-admiring Francis Adams, McIlwraith's nose jutted "like the beak of the bird of prey," and his eyes were "hawk like ... glancing and penetrative" (F. Adams 75, 76). Some commentators were unable to locate the appropriate animal and instead fled once more into references to his size: "Regarded as an animal there ain't many points about M'Ilwraith. He is rather rotund" (Casey). Others compiled a whole series of comparisons in their effort to convey his overwhelming presence. The most frequently cited list occurs in a letter from Dr. William MacGregor, appointed administrator of British New Guinea in 1888, to Arthur Gordon, then governor of Ceylon. Among others, MacGregor seizes on a Pacific sea cow to depict McIlwraith as "an able bully, with a face like a dugong & a temper like a buffalo."[21] In his commentary on Queensland politics, Charles Arrowsmith Bernays sees him as "a big, portly frame, with a bulldog head and neck – something you would look twice at and thank God he was your friend and not your enemy" (Bernays 56). The references to "bully," "bulldog," and even to "buffalo" may point in the direction of "John Bull," suggesting to his supporters that he embodied Britain's qualities as a headstrong nation – so headstrong, in fact, that he was prepared to disagree with the head office.

A man this "bold, prompt and masterful" (Satgé 247) had no patience with anyone who obstructed his ambitious plans, or time for "littlenesses" (Browne 67), either in the sense of small projects or of personal pettiness, and "[h]is estimates of his bitterest enemies [were] tolerant and generous, not merely before the footlights, but in the friendliest privacy" (F. Adams 76). He offered help spontaneously. Observers were amazed at his willingness to set aside "old grudges" (Beanland 248) and enter a coalition with Samuel Griffith in 1890, the so-called Griffilwraith, with Griffith as premier and McIlwraith as colonial treasurer. Despite surprising eruptions of Presbyterianism that had him reprimand a fellow parliamentarian for reading the newspaper on a Sunday (Dignan, "Sir Thomas McIlwraith"), he did not take himself too seriously, as was apparent in his readiness to play the "bourgeois larrikin" (Waterson,

---

21 British Library Board, Stanmore papers, vol. 5, Additional MS.49203, London, letter 25 December 1888, p. 177; on MacGregor, see R.B. Joyce; on Gordon, see Mark Francis.

"A Colonial Entrepreneur" 130). Few biographers can resist the story of the "Maranoa Infant" that had him dress up for a fancy dress ball as a baby "of startling proportions and exceptional powers of speech and locomotion, being upwards of 6 feet high, of stalwart build, and an industrious dancer." The infant was "clad in long white garments, duly furnished with coral rattle, &c., and with a neat cap on his head" ("Fancy Dress Ball at Government House").

Gilbert Casey – who seems to have been both powerfully attracted and repelled by the man – saw the root of McIlwraith's charisma in his ability to seduce supporters into his way of thinking and "kill" his opponents "with kindness" but remain profoundly indifferent to anyone's opinions: "They yearn for his smile as a lover does for his mistress's favour, and his nod of approval fills and thrills them with the most exquisite delight." Casey appears to have seen McIlwraith as a totalitarian, characterized by his "matchless assurance, his wide, deep and lofty egotism, his towering assumption" that "abash and terrify most ordinary mortals" (Casey). Casey's elaborate character sketch appeared in the *Worker* in the fall of 1893, a few days before McIlwraith resigned as premier because of poor health. Earlier the same year, the paper had published a cartoon of McIlwraith as yet another mythical "animal" – this time a blood-sucking vampire sprouting wings marked "Q.N. Bank" that, by diverting an unfair share of profits for its directors, feasts on blood flowing from the bare breasts of Queensland.[22] Here, McIlwraith's ability to seduce his political followers and sometimes even his opponents becomes intertwined with the masculinist and sexualized imagery running through Australian frontier culture (see Lake). Such language was frequently heightened by perceived racial threat, a fear shared by Liberal and Labour adherents alike. Racial threat dominates the *Worker* cartoon discussed earlier of McIlwraith leading a circus parade, and both sexism and xenophobia underpin the caricature of Boodlewraith, with grotesque-looking Kanaka, Chinese, and Indian workers standing by as Maid Queensland is held captive by her giant. The Mackay *Mercury* even worked up a mini-drama to illustrate the situation. In four scenes that variously take place in a store, on a plantation, in a land court, and on a wharf, citizens under McIlwraith's premiership are seen to suffer economic duress because he has allowed coolies, "niggers," and the Chinese into the colony, and his personal business benefits from their presence ("Four Scenes"). The *Mercury* was obviously not impressed by McIlwraith's assurance, made five years earlier to the *Pall Mall Budget*, that it made good business sense to employ "coolies" instead of white men, who were believed to be constitutionally unable to perform heavy physical labour in the tropics: "We can get any number [of coolies] at £10 per head passage money. They can be shipped under Government supervision. They will

---

22 *The Worker*, 23 January 1893, 1, reproduced in Beanland 287. On this cartoon, see Waterson, *Personality, Profit and Politics* 22.

all go back, and there is no fear of them swarming over like the Chinese" ("Our Most Enterprising Colony," part 2, 21).

Surprisingly, McIlwraith's physical and intellectual presence did not translate into a gift for speech. As even Adams had to admit, he was "one of the worst average debaters in any Assembly," who "hesitates, and even stutters, coughing and *er*-ing in his pursuit of the exact 'business word' he wants" (F. Adams 76). His thoughts seemed to run ahead of his speech, such that one wonders whether he was suffering from some kind of neurological disorder: "If he is speaking of a building he will unconsciously call it a road; or if he speaks of a term of forty years he is just as likely to say four till someone corrects him, which breaks in upon his habit of abstraction and brings him back for a minute or two to the present."[23] It was only "in the hours of passionate debate or turbulent public gathering" that he became fluent in a "torrent of ... fiery words" (F. Adams 78). As the section on the annexation of New Guinea will illustrate, he also shone when it came to composing forceful government documents, but became awkward and tedious in more casual communication. For example, in an interview about his Canadian train journey from Vancouver to Ottawa in 1893, he laboriously relates various engineering details, especially the heating arrangements on board, where "the car conductor's thermometer showed an extreme of 43 deg., while Sir Thomas McIlwraith's own thermometer, standing in the sun at 2 p. m., registered some degrees below zero." He then performed a similar experiment at the hotel in Ottawa, "where all means of ventilation were carefully avoided" and "no less a number than 600 human beings were ... constantly rebreathing the poisoned air" ("Sir T. M'Ilwraith"). It was left to Lady McIlwraith to produce vivid travel impressions in a letter sent from Montreal describing the luxuries of "a private car, with our own cook & plenty of provisions" and the delights of joining the Earl of Aberdeen's "Gvt House party in four in hand sleighs" for a tour of the winter carnival (OM 64-19/42, Sir Thomas McIlwraith, Lady Harriet McIlwraith to "Cess," 1 February 1894).

Annexation of New Guinea, Part One: Imperial Webs of Communication

The networks connecting the McIlwraiths and their business partners were intricate but circumscribed, and when it came to keeping embarrassing secrets like a family member's alcoholism private, the family sealed their circle against outsiders as much as possible. Although analogies to a large and temperamental family impose themselves repeatedly, with Sir Thomas and other colonial leaders playing disobedient offspring to the Colonial Office's outraged parents, much more complicated webs of communication were spun during crises with

---

23 Carl Feilberg, journalist for *The Queenslander*, qtd. in Dignan, "Sir Thomas McIlwraith" 68. Dignan does not indicate the original source for this quotation, and it has not been located.

Sir Thomas McIlwraith, 1883. State Library of Queensland.

potentially serious consequences for Britain's imperial politics and its competitors in the Pacific, including Germany, Russia, France, the Netherlands, and
Italy. Sir Thomas's attempted annexation of New Guinea was one such crisis,[24]
but in contrast to his reluctant and cold letters to family, this was a type of communication on which he thrived. The official documentation of the episode, collected across several volumes of the British Parliamentary Papers, the Journals
and Printed Papers of the Federal Council of Australasia, and the *Weissbücher*
of the German Reichstag, vividly illustrates how colonial administrators produced avalanches of paperwork in order to legitimize the empire's actions, and
how they drew on an ever-expanding support system of journalists, scientists,
traders, sea captains, military personnel, philanthropists, entrepreneurs, engineers, and others for information that suited their purpose.[25] A researcher's

24 Commenting on the conflicts surrounding the annexation of New Guinea, Dülffer et al.
    (317–33) suggest that they brought Britain to the brink of war.
25 On the characteristics of colonial correspondence, see Goody; Laidlaw; Stoler.

head soon begins to spin when trying to keep track of it all, and she is likely to sympathize with the novelist J.G. Farrell's satire of this mountain of office files. In *The Siege of Krishnapur*, an administrator builds himself a nest with reports, correspondence, and statistics, the latter "rising to a mound beneath his knees and cushioning the rest of his body" (187). Greatly condensed, the following account of events surrounding the annexation is not about giving a detailed narrative of the episode. Instead, it is meant to provide an understanding of Sir Thomas as producer of shrewdly managed paper "mounds" of his own. Although he sometimes seems to disappear beneath the dossiers and behind their authors, this strategist is present throughout. He and his counterparts played the poker of imperial communication with gusto, but their skill disguises neither the callousness nor the eventual futility of the exercise.

On 4 April 1883 and at the premier's request, the magistrate of Thursday Island, Henry Majoribanks Chester, hoisted the Union Jack at Port Moresby on New Guinea in order to prevent Germany from laying claim to the area. In London, the colonial secretary was aghast at McIlwraith's chutzpah when he received a "[s]tartling telegram from Reuter, stating that the Queensland government has annexed New Guinea, which is impossible, being beyond the rights of any colony to do, but I telegraphed out to enquire" (Stanley 531–2). Normally, Derby was kept thoroughly informed through "the well-oiled perfection of the messenger service which circulated boxes to wherever a minister might be with relentless efficiency every day of the year, including Christmas and Easter" (Vincent, Introduction, Stanley xxiii). However, even he was unable to obtain an immediate explanation from Thomas Archer, agent general for Queensland in London, and had to content himself that "[w]e shall know all about the matter when the mail comes in" (Stanley 531–3).[26]

McIlwraith's actions were sparked by an article in the influential *Augsburger Allgemeine Zeitung* (*AAZ*) recommending that the Germans annex New Guinea to safeguard their commercial interests in the Pacific. In early December 1882, a vigilant Frederick Young, secretary to the RCI in London, had forwarded this article to the Foreign Office, which, in turn, alerted the Colonial Office. The RCI reminded the Foreign Office that in 1875 occupation had been recommended, but not pursued, to pre-empt annexation by a power other than Britain and that the recommendation was now being reiterated. The Colonial Office responded by the end of December that it was "not prepared at present to re-open" the question and in January wrote again, dismissing fears that the Germans had "any scheme of colonization" (Great Britain, C3617, 119, 120). On 28 February, Archer forwarded a telegram to the Colonial Office he had received from McIlwraith (to whom the *AAZ* article had also been sent) in which the premier

---

26 For a discussion of Derby's diaries, see Powell.

supported annexation by Britain to protect Queensland's and Britain's interests in the Torres Strait: "Urge Imperial Government annex New Guinea to Queensland; reasons, large increase in steamer traffic through Torres Straits. Population settled there require Government. Imperial coaling depôt established; danger to colonies if other powers take possession. Queensland will bear expense of Government and take formal possession on receipt of Imperial authority by cable; letters by mail" (Great Britain, C3617, 121). Before conveying the outcome of their conversation to the Queen's representative in Queensland, Governor Sir A.E. Kennedy, Derby requested personal assurance from Archer that annexation would receive the support of "public opinion" in the colonies.

In mid-February, representatives of the other Australian colonies – whom the RCI had also supplied with the article from the *AAZ* – appeared on the scene. Western Australia sounded generally supportive if somewhat irritated by Queensland's unilateral initiative, suggesting that the situation could be considered only "as a question of Imperial policy," not an exceptional case (Great Britain, C3617, 122). New South Wales weighed in through its governor, Augustus Loftus, who – as further proof that a problem was brewing – sent Derby a memorandum he had received from Dr. James R. Robertson.[27] The memorandum was one of many enclosures that typically accompanied such correspondence to amplify an argument with press clippings, expert reports, logbooks, maps, glossaries, and interviews. Robertson, who had been inspecting mines in northern Queensland, was alarmed at the prospect of powers other than Britain laying a claim to New Guinea, which was located just across the Torres Strait. The memorandum is a grandiose evocation of Britain's mission: "I have yet to learn, that these black races could fall into the hands of a wiser or more benign governing power, or one that over the whole Pacific is more respected and trusted by savage men, or one whose strong arm could better direct them and fit them too for fulfilling the behests of civilization" (Great Britain, C3617, 128). Leaving expressions of fervour to Robertson, Loftus himself crisply listed practical observations: there was evidence that not only the Germans but also the French, Dutch, Russians, and Italians were interested in the strategic location of New Guinea for naval and coaling stations. The *bêche-de-mer* and pearling fisheries in the Torres Strait provided lucrative incomes for Australia and required protection. A transcontinental railway connecting Brisbane with Point Parker on the Gulf of Carpentaria – "which line will eventually become the shortest route for communication with England" (Great Britain, C3617, 124) – was being considered, providing faster access to the Strait. International powers had been alerted to Australia's growing wealth following successful display of its riches at the Exhibitions in Sydney (1879) and Melbourne (1880), and as a result there

---

27   On Robertson, see Schmitz.

was competition for the opportunities enjoyed by Australians within the Pacific. In case of war, Loftus underscored, the consequences of having a foreign government established on Australia's doorstep, let alone several of them, would be alarming. Loftus's letter is dated February 1883. By March, other European colonial powers were becoming interested in the situation, and the Foreign Office brought another newspaper article into the discussion, this one published in Antwerp's *Précurseur*. The paper indicated the Netherlands' determination to protect their already existing interests in New Guinea against the Germans.

Repeatedly, the Foreign Office telegraphed requests for explanation to the governor of Queensland, who passed them on to the premier's office. For example, when Derby wanted the reasons for the sudden urgency behind McIlwraith's actions, Sir Arthur Palmer, Queensland's colonial secretary, cabled in the premier's name on 4 June: "General rumours of Germany and Italy; special rumour, German corvette 'Carola' was leaving Sydney for South-Seas without object of annexation. She left on 18th March" (Great Britain, C3691, 13).[28] The normal mail explaining the situation took a great deal longer to arrive. The Colonial Office did not officially file Chester's letter in which he described taking "formal possession" of New Guinea until two months after the event, on 19 June 1883 (Great Britain, C3691, 14). The letter was part of a large package of correspondence and documents Archer presented to Derby, containing "copies of correspondence received to-day from the Colony relative to the pearl shell and bêche de mer Fisheries in Torres Strait, and of the number and tonnage of vessels passing through the Straits to and from the Colony during 1882, and also a printed copy of Mr. Chester's report of his visit to Port Moresby, and of the ceremony of taking possession of New Guinea in the name of Her Majesty" (Great Britain, C3691, 14). Also on 19 June, Derby received Governor Kennedy's endorsement, with explicit support of McIlwraith's actions: "I have only to express my entire satisfaction with the action of my government, especially Sir Thomas McIlwraith, in the matter," and "Sir Thomas has laid his views before you, and we have the satisfaction of knowing that they are heartily adopted by all the Australian Colonies, which we trust may be our excuse for any irregularity we have committed" (Great Britain, C3691, 19). One of Kennedy's previous appointments had been as governor of Vancouver Island for three agitated years between 1863 and 1866, and he probably found the two frontier societies equally daunting.

Ten days after the annexation, Archer had produced a similar envelope of enclosures that underlined "the very great importance ... of preventing the acquisition of New Guinea by one of the great military powers of Europe which would exercise a baneful influence on the future prospects of the Colonies

---

28 The puzzling "without" in the cable is annotated with "Query 'with,' but sic in original" (C3691, 13).

by commanding the only channel of communication between them and Europe, India, and the islands of the Indian ocean by the northern route" (Great Britain, C3617, 131–2). All of the documents in this package predate the annexation by at least two months, including the *AZZ* article in translation as published in the Sydney *Morning Herald*. New South Wales, Victoria, and South Australia rallied round Queensland at the premier's request and sent telegrams between 19 and 21 April supporting the annexation, instantly followed by a cable from McIlwraith: "All Colonies heartily endorse our action, and are urging approval, consider annexation by Foreign Power calamitous. Assure Lord Derby no expense Imperial exchequer. Press early ratification" (Great Britain, C3617, 139).

"Telegrams have come in from all the Australian colonies, except Tasmania, approving annexation of N. Guinea in general terms," Derby noted on 21 April 1883 (Stanley 535). A deputation led by the Duke of Manchester appeared as the group that had urged annexation in the mid-seventies. Its members "were … afraid that the question might be settled without their having figured in the settlement" (Stanley 550). At the end of June, when he had finally received the detailed reports of McIlwraith's actions, the Australian agents general flocked into Derby's office, presenting "a gigantic scheme of annexation, including … all the South Pacific within about 1,000 to 1,500 miles from the Australian coast." Derby, who tried "a little mild sarcasm" with them without success, was "surprised, & puzzled at the wildness of their plans, and the quiet conviction which they expressed that we should do all they wanted" (Stanley 561). He was convinced that Britain intended to annex New Guinea in the near future, but would do so on its own initiative and in its own time. In response to the proposals of the Australian colonies at the Intercolonial Convention in Sydney in late 1883, he waxed sarcastic again. These proposals extended Queensland's demands to such an extent that Derby suspected "a piece of swagger" and made a point of "ridiculing their extent & vagueness" to Prime Minister Gladstone, but once again he hinted that "we must be prepared for a protectorate of New Guinea" (Stanley 611).[29] When Derby proposed a protectorate in cabinet in July 1884, however, Gladstone opposed it, wanting Derby "to ask the Australian agents what precedents they could find for the annexation of a country not occupied by the people claiming it?" Were Derby and his supporters being ironical or merely offering information when they "cited Australia itself & N. Zealand"? In any case, the colonial secretary decided to "reserve … the whole question,

---

29 At the Intercolonial Convention, the Australians were nervous about the French in the Pacific rather than the Germans, especially convicts escaped from the penal colony in New Caledonia. See, for example, Bergantz.

and at present I do not see how the Cabinet is to decide the matter, our differences being so wide" (Stanley 685).

The Annexation of New Guinea, Part Two: *The Way We Civilise*

McIlwraith's plans were, however, routed by a powerful philanthropic lobby. The Aborigines' Protection Society wrote to Derby on 14 May 1883 to express opposition to the annexation of New Guinea by "a Colony which relies for the means of prosecuting its tropical industries upon labour drawn from many of the Islands of the Western Pacific" (Great Britain, C3617, 140). Instead, the Society proposed that – in parallel with the status of the Fiji Islands – New Guinea be made into a Crown colony in order to ensure close supervision of its governance.[30] To underscore its case, the Society added an enclosure of its own – namely, a pamphlet entitled with deliberate irony *The Way We Civilise*. It was, as the subtitle indicated, compiled from "articles and letters" published in the *Queenslander* newspaper at the initiative of editor-owner Gresley Lukin and Carl Feilberg, a journalist and humanitarian activist from Denmark who had arrived in Australia in the hope of healing his tuberculosis and became deeply involved in local affairs. In the pamphlet, readers aired and challenged racist prejudice against Aborigines with equal force. In particular, the Society raised concerns about "the operations of the native police" in their dealings with Aboriginals in Queensland (Great Britain, C3617, 140) as described in the pamphlet where instances of police brutality were vividly documented.[31] An influential document in the discussion of Australia's Aboriginal policies,[32] *The Way We Civilise* has since been cited in *Bringing Them Home, the Report of the National Inquiry Into the Separation of Aboriginal and Torres Strait Islander Children from their Families* (1997) and other contemporary investigations, but it is marked as "not printed" in the British Parliamentary Papers of 1883. Its length may have something to do with it, along with the graphic descriptions of torture, murder, and rape. Whatever the reasons, the omission illustrates that important supportive documents were sometimes left out from the Parliamentary Papers, with the result that this one practically disappeared from view for many years.[33]

---

30 On the Aborigines Protection Society, see Swaisland.
31 On the native police in Queensland, see Bottoms.
32 See Reynolds 108–37. In the first edition of Reynolds's book, Feilberg was not identified as the author of the editorials in *The Way We Civilise*. This was corrected in the 2018 edition, in response to research by the Danish historian Robert Ørsted-Jensen. See also Daley.
33 In "Done and Dusted," Evans indicates that "[n]o copy of this important pamphlet [was] available in Queensland research collections. I finally tracked it down in the specialist library of the Royal Commonwealth Society in 1984."

McIlwraith denied in his response to Derby that, in annexing New Guinea, Queensland was primarily interested in obtaining Native labour,[34] and in 1884, during his meeting with the colonial secretary in London, he avoided the question altogether. Instead, he "was very earnest about the prevention of French convicts landing in Australia," and "did not seem to care much for the annexation for its own sake" (Stanley 638–9). This is quite a change of gears from McIlwraith's bullish protest, the year before, against Queensland being taken to task for exercising "powers which [it does] not possess": "That we had no right," he wrote then, "without the sanction of Her Majesty's Government, to annex territory in which there exists no settled Government, is contrary to the whole history of colonial acquisition."[35] Whatever McIlwraith's primary motivation, concerns about the methods used in the recruitment of Native workers and their treatment did become the turning point in Queensland's attempted annexation of New Guinea.

The dismissive comments with which administrators at the Colonial Office sometimes annotated correspondence from the colonies are not included in the Parliamentary Papers.[36] Nor are behind-the-scenes discussions such as those between Derby, Gladstone, Lord Selborne, the Lord Chancellor, and Gladstone's friend Sir Arthur Gordon, who had begun his diplomatic career as lieutenant governor of New Brunswick, followed by appointments as high commissioner for the Western Pacific, governor of Fiji, governor of New Zealand, and governor of Ceylon. All were agreed, as Gordon put it, on the "grave impropriety of allowing a colonial government to force the hand of the imperial government with regard to a matter of imperial policy" (qtd. in Knaplund 103), but more specifically, Gordon insisted that, based on its previous record in the treatment of Aboriginals, Queensland could not be trusted with the Native population of New Guinea. A few days earlier, Gordon had given Derby a hard time over dinner when, "with the odd mixture in him of brusque disagreeable manners with knowledge and intellectual ability," he "declaimed violently ... against the proposed annexation of New Guinea" because "he (& I suppose his is the view of a large party in colonial matters) looks entirely to the interest of native populations" (Stanley 533).

In July, Derby conveyed the British Parliament's decision to annul the annexation, citing as reasons that Queensland had overstepped its prerogatives as a colony; that the fear of German annexation was "altogether indefinite

---

34 There has been some disagreement over this question. Trainor writes that the "annexation ... was, it is now recognized, largely a product of the desire for further labor for the sugar industry" (41). In support, Trainor cites R. Thompson 56. For a dissenting view, see Mullins.

35 McIlwraith's response is listed in the table of contents of the relevant British Parliamentary Papers but is not reproduced in the digitized version. I am therefore quoting this response from *Journals and Printed Papers of the Federal Council of Australasia, January 25 to February 6, 1886*, 41. All quotations from this letter are taken from this page.

36 See, for example, Lake and Reynolds 199–200 on the Colonial Office's response to Alfred Deakin's invitation to the US fleet.

and unfounded" (Great Britain, C3691, 22); that annexing even part of New Guinea would require more of Britain's resources than it was currently willing to commit in order to subdue "a large coloured population, which would certainly resist subjugation and has apparently nothing to gain by it" (Great Britain, C3691, 23); that Queensland was already too large; and that any colonial expansion had to be coordinated by the British government "on broad and clearly defined principles" (Great Britain, C3691, 23). A somewhat conciliatory gesture that promised a "strengthening [of] the naval force on the Australian station" concluded the letter (Great Britain, C3691, 23). Although McIlwraith's supporters insisted that his initiative "delighted the Queenslanders and astonished the political coteries of Europe" (Traill 692), the matter was for the time being closed for the Colonial Office. Derby was pleased that, "[j]udging by the newspapers ... our decision not to annex New Guinea ... has satisfied the public," and that "the Australians ... have no right to claim that we shall seize on strange & unknown countries for their benefit" (Stanley 568). If any worry over the strange affair remained, it was dispelled soon after when "[t]he papers on New Guinea, including my despatch, [were] published, & well received" (Stanley 573). In February 1884, Derby heaved a sigh of relief that "just now" his "colonial ... difficulties [were] ... few." He checked off the colonies one by one, and emphasized that "in Canada there is no trouble of any kind" while "Australia is maturing the plan of confederation, & until that takes some definite shape the question of New Guinea need not be seriously dealt with" (Stanley 634). He felt a little vindictive against those who had sided with McIlwraith's efforts to push the annexation through. When Loftus requested "an extension of his term," Derby noted in his diary that he would be refused: "He is not only foolish, which might not matter, but pompous & inclined to swagger." The indictment extended to Loftus's sons, who "take after him, & are even less appreciated" (Stanley 718).

If McIlwraith delayed an official letter, it was – in contrast to his communications with family – part of a calculated diplomatic plan and not failure to keep up with his correspondence. In conducting the business of empire, administrators had to coordinate overland, maritime, and telegraphic postal services to ensure that individuals and offices separated by long distances were kept informed of deliberations on either side, and that the British government was sufficiently aware of the actions, authorized or not, of its colonies to address them where necessary. In order to achieve his ambitious goals for Queensland, McIlwraith played the card of diplomatic communication with as much skill as his superiors in London, whether it was a fait accompli announcement contained in a cable, the timing of an explanatory despatch that he knew would take up to two months to reach Britain, or the effect of massed telegrams from the sister colonies in Australia lobbying on Queensland's behalf. These tactics of "diplomacy, delay and duplicity" (Lake and Reynolds 124) were exercised by politicians throughout the empire[37] and illustrate that, despite the tight control exercised by the head office in London, nationalists like McIlwraith were ready to rebel in any way available to them once they were convinced that "the British Cabinet and the Colonial Office [were] a pack of old women, and the mother-country 'a composite grandmotherly old wreck ... tottering with a handbag and a cotton umbrella towards an open grave.' "[38] Throughout his political career, McIlwraith revelled in such provocation, including his anger at the Bank of England, unheard of because it was so public, for apparently not abiding by the details of a financial agreement when he was treasurer of Queensland (see Magee and Thompson 203), and a showdown with Sir Anthony Musgrave, governor of Queensland, over the "unfettered exercise of the prerogative of mercy" (Gibbney) that brought hundreds of Queenslanders out into the street in support of McIlwraith's government.

Deliberate as the delay of messages from the colonies to London could be, the tactic was applied in the knowledge that the Foreign Office had excellent resources for manipulations of its own. However voluminous the published Parliamentary Papers, or Blue-Books, they were edited before publication to suit the interests of the parties currently in charge, each of which tapped into its own ideological network.[39] A warning repeated in most descriptions of these documents alerts historical researchers that "[m]uch was always omitted and texts were frequently curtailed," and "total reliance on them on any period would be a cardinal error" (Temperley and Penson x). Partly because of the unique combination of historical and fictional elements in these papers, both the British and the German records with their blow-by-blow accounts of McIlwraith's attempted annexation of New Guinea make for reading worthy of a somewhat challenging thriller even 135 years later. At the same time, the abundance of different, often multilingual voices incorporated into the records

---

37 On Sir Henry Bartle Frere's delay tactics in the Anglo-Zulu War of 1879, see Bowman 122. See also Alfred Deakin's flouting of imperial authority in preparing the US fleet's visit to Australia in 1907, in Lake and Reynolds 196–7, 199.

38 Dilke attributes this quotation to the Sydney *Bulletin*, "which possesses ... a forcible style of its own" (vol. 2, 204). The citation in the *Bulletin* has not been located, but it is quoted, without precise attribution, in numerous contemporary newspaper reports. One that precedes Dilke's book appears, with slight variations, in "A 'Disloyal' Chief Justice."

39 "Blue-Book" (also White Papers or Command Papers) refers to the colour of the binding for the British Parliamentary Papers, but – independent of the actual colour of the bindings – the term has also been used generically for diplomatic collections of papers issued by the governments of other nations. However, the latter have also been named after the actual colour of the bindings. For example, the German equivalent is the "Weissbuch," the French "livre jaune," the Italian "libro verde," the Belgian "livre gris," and so on. See Strupp and Schlochauer, vol. 1, 507.

The *Boomerang*'s cartoon of Sir Thomas McIlwraith's provocation of the Bank of England. *Boomerang*, 17 Oct. 1891, p. 1. Fryer Library, University of Queensland.

creates a "jungly and labyrinthine" narrative[40] chafing against the rigid system of bureaucratic record keeping that barely contains them. The correspondent for *The Times* in Berlin alluded to the complicated cast, plotline, and high drama when he quoted *Macbeth* and *As You Like It* in a review of the "strange eventful history" of the annexation of New Guinea, as narrated in the German White-Book of 1885 ("Latest Intelligence"), and the *Pall Mall Gazette* evoked Charles Dickens's *Little Dorrit* when it referred to the imperial administration as the "Dawdle and Circumlocution Offices" in its handling of the New Guinea episode ("The Dawdle"). The literary analogy has persisted: Laura Ann Stoler repeatedly invokes poetic genres to characterize the grandiose ambitions and tenuous concept of reality that emerge from Dutch colonial archives.

The Annexation of New Guinea, Part Three: Nikolai Miklouho-Maclay and Emil Deckert

Although some historical commentary has tried, it is as impossible to introduce all of the players that were involved in McIlwraith's attempted annexation of New Guinea as it is to detail all of its different stages. Two individuals, one a Russian scientist and philanthropist, the other a German geographer and author of the provocative *AZZ* article, will give an idea of the multitude of participants who affected Sir Thomas's actions and of his response to them.

Nikolai Miklouho-Maclay

The concerns expressed by the Aborigines' Protection Society were reinforced in a letter, forwarded by Arthur Gordon to Derby on 16 June 1883 (Great Britain, C3691, 19), that had been submitted by Nikolai Miklouho-Maclay. He had trained with the Darwinian zoologist Ernst Haeckel in Jena before conducting research in marine biology, anthropology, and anatomy in the Pacific Islands, including New Guinea, from the 1870s onwards. Miklouho-Maclay established the first Australian marine research station in Sydney, and his ability to acquire influential friends was confirmed in 1884 with marriage to Margaret Emma Clark, the widowed daughter of Sir John Robertson, premier of New South Wales. Miklouho-Maclay, whose thought was influenced by the utopianism of Nikolay Chernyshevsky and whose humanitarian ideas impressed Leo Tolstoy, made it his business to look out for the welfare of Native populations in the Pacific region, especially the inhabitants of the north-east coast of New Guinea, which came to be known as the "Maclay Coast." Several scholars have drawn

---

40   See Temple commenting on "The Manipur Blue-Book."

attention to Miklouho-Maclay's ambivalent position between mythic protector of the Papua and "self-empowering" figure with "Kurtzian resonances."[41] Certainly, the scene in which he dissects the head of his just-deceased Polynesian servant in order "to obtain a dark man's larynx, with tongue and related muscles," is not easily forgotten (Webster 69). Assessing Miklouho-Maclay's role is further complicated by multilingual scholarship on his career, and – as his role in the annexation of New Guinea illustrates – the exploitation of his fame by political opponents. Even decades after the period under discussion, for example, the Soviets and their satellites continued to circulate redacted versions of his life story as proof that, in contrast to its Western opponents, Russia's motivations were anti-imperialist, non-racist, and humanitarian (see Fitzpatrick; Turmarkin).

Well before the Aborigines' Protection Society forwarded *The Way We Civilise* to Derby, Miklouho-Maclay had alerted Gordon to the pamphlet and, at Gordon's request, provided letters from Feilberg and the police magistrate R.B. Sheridan confirming its authenticity (Reynolds 128). Likewise, Miklouho-Maclay submitted a report addressing the question of "Kidnapping and Slavery in the Western Pacific" to the Commodore John Wilson, who had been tasked in 1882 with an investigation into the traffic in Native labour and related abuses (Great Britain, C3641, 82–5). In correspondence with the Colonial Office, Miklouho-Maclay kept up the pressure by joining forces with the missionary James Chalmers,[42] and he sent additional communications to coincide with the Intercolonial Convention in Sydney in 1883 (see Great Britain, C3863). Some of Miklouho-Maclay's most influential writing was done in these letters and cables of protest. Not surprisingly given the mass of correspondence he conducted, he was unable to complete a scholarly monograph aside from travelogues and diaries about his fieldwork, and any notes that may have existed towards one were destroyed when, at his request, his wife burnt most of his papers after his death (see Stagl).

In his report, included in the Parliamentary Papers on "Natives of Western Pacific and Labour Traffic" (1883), Commodore Wilson identified Miklouho-Maclay as "a well-known Russian traveller in these seas, and a gentleman of great scientific knowledge and research" whose testimony would "convince the most skeptical" that the labour traffic was "fraught with evils not even second to the slave trade which England expended so much money and labour to put an end to" (Great Britain, C3641, 80). By contrast, Loftus did his best to discredit the Russian scientist by first describing him as a type of vagabond, "a naturalist who has been wandering about the South Sea Islands for the past 12 years, and at times is a resident in Sydney" (Great

---

41 See George W. Stocking Jr., "Maclay, Kubary, Malinowski," 25. Also see O.H.K. Spate's foreword to Webster, which suggests that "[t]he elements were ... greatly mixed in Maclay" (viii).

42 On Chalmers, see Prendergast.

Britain, C3617, 124), and then insisting that Miklouho-Maclay was an agent for Russian interests in the Pacific.[43] McIlwraith was more aggressive in his criticism, taking particular care to disparage Miklouho-Maclay as an individual whose "eccentricities on the subject of anthropology" had made him "a most unreliable authority on the subject of the Island labour trade." Aiming at statements that were tangential to the matter at hand but which discredited his opponent as ill-informed, McIlwraith concluded that "Baron Miklouho-Maclay, no matter what his scientific attainments may be, is not worthy of being quoted as an authority on the labour question of Queensland." In this case, the disputed document is the Pacific Island Labourers' Act of 1880, which is said to use a new definition of "transfer of labour" that will make abuses more difficult in future: "It is a transfer of labour that has received the sanction of Her Majesty for many years, under which no abuses take place, and to which nobody could possibly apply the title of selling, except a man as thoroughly prejudiced as Baron Miklouho-Maclay" (Great Britain, C3641, 130). The force of his response suggests, however, that McIlwraith was aware of Miklouho-Maclay's wide-ranging influence and did consider him a formidable opponent. As has been documented from the archives of Imperial Germany's Department of the Exterior, the Baron – as the Australian press persistently referred to him – managed to rattle Bismarck too (see Germer 1: 153–70, 2: plates 51–4).

From the start, Germany – whose merchants and planters did have substantial interests in the Pacific – closely followed the discussion surrounding the annexation, and Lord Derby's explanation to McIlwraith that fears of Wilhelmine ambitions in the Pacific were "altogether indefinite and unfounded" did not hold up for long. "[W]ith contemptuous effrontery" (Traill 693), Germany moved to establish a protectorate in New Guinea in late 1884. The British and Australian public was shocked and, together, Derby and the Foreign Office bore the blame for running "the Dawdle and Circumlocution Offices" ("The Dawdle"). While, in 1883, he had sent a cable to Derby indicating that "Maclay coast natives claim political autonomy under European protection," Miklouho-Maclay now switched his attention from Great Britain to Germany, informing Bismarck, also via telegram, that "Maclay coast natives reject german annexation" (Germer 2: plates 52, 53). In "A Russian View of the Germans in New Guinea," published in the Sydney Morning Herald, he accused German traders of transgressions similar to the ones he had condemned in traders operating for Queensland ("A Russian View"). Like

---

43 Stocking refers to Miklouho-Maclay's transfer, on his return to Australia after a visit to Russia and Europe, "to a Russian naval ship which he was to accompany on a survey of suitable sites for [a] proposed naval station" as the trigger for the annexation of New Guinea ("Maclay, Kubary, Malinowski" 23). Stocking does not mention the AZZ article.

McIlwraith, Bismarck's Department of the Exterior went out of its way to neutralize Miklouho-Maclay's influence. His actions were dismissed as motivated by personal interest, and a campaign in the German press challenged his claims to the Maclay Coast, questioned his scholarly credentials and insisted that he was British rather than Russian because of his marriage.[44] His aggressive opposition to Germany's interest in New Guinea was seen as evidence that he had imbibed a typically Australian and therefore British mentality (Germer 1: 163).

Emil Deckert

McIlwraith never seems to have tackled Emil Deckert ad hominem the way he challenged Miklouho-Maclay, but as the author of the article that triggered the annexation, Deckert, too, deserves attention. It is a mystery why his *AZZ* essay was given such instant and widespread credence, well respected as the paper was. Nor does anyone appear to have been much interested in investigating the author, though it has been suggested that he was the cover for "higher origins than [the article] showed " (Webster 271) because the German press was closely controlled by Bismarck. And yet, Deckert's name was in the Australian papers in a related context only a year after his influential article first appeared. A report from the Berlin correspondent of the *Daily News* published in several Australian newspapers, including William McIlwraith's *Morning Bulletin*, described his lecture about "the British Colonial Empire" to the German Society for Commercial Geography. In it the speaker asserted that "England will never cease to be the ruler of the seas and of the world's trade," even if other nations with imperial ambitions were now appearing on the horizon ("A German View"). In short, the Australian papers concluded, "Germans generally regard our Colonial Empire with envy," though Deckert was said to "touch ... with manifest satisfaction on the dangers that threaten it" ("A German on Our Colonies").

One of several widely travelled academics who will appear in this book, Deckert was a rising but not yet well established scholar in the early 1880s. He was appointed to the chair of geography at the newly founded University of Frankfurt in 1906, but in 1882 he was only thirty-four, teaching geography at the rank of *Hauptlehrer* (senior teacher) at a business school in Dresden and pursuing his doctorate at the University of Leipzig.[45] In his dissertation (1883), he focused on the geographical attributes of major trade routes in

---

44 See Germer. Published in the GDR, Germer's article, confirming Fitzpatrick's observations, is painstakingly documented and pursues its own political agenda in discrediting Wilhelmine Germany's diplomacy but vindicating Russia's methods.

45 For biographical details, see Maull.

Europe, India, China, and North America, sorting them into a hierarchical system according to their usefulness to the world powers,[46] an approach he also pursued in the *Lehrbuch der Handels- und Verkehrsgeographie*, a textbook of the geography of commerce and communication published two years earlier. As a young man, Deckert travelled widely in Europe, learned languages, and spent extended periods in Hamburg, Copenhagen, and London. Like Miklouho-Maclay, he chose a wife from an influential family when he married Fanny Goodyear, daughter of Charles Goodyear, the inventor of vulcanized rubber (see Goodyear Kirkman 129). The Deckerts took up residence in the United States for several years, and he pursued an extensive program of field research in North and Central America in the 1880s and '90s that made him a leading expert on the subject. Deckert selected the family's various places of residence to ensure they were in geographically interesting locations, with libraries and archives nearby. Between 1892 and 1896, three of his five children were born in Waynesville, North Carolina, Charlottesville, Virginia, and Washington, DC, respectively, and the Deckerts also lived in New York. His wife seems to have accepted their nomadic existence in pursuit of his research as a matter of course, and for all we know his family also accompanied him to Canada, Arizona, Cuba, and the Caribbean.

There are no details about his employment when the family lived in America. Perhaps Deckert's income derived from the honoraria for the numerous geographical essays he published in magazines and the daily papers. He was a well-informed writer with forceful convictions that appealed to the general reader interested in travel and geography. Like his teacher Oskar Peschel, he was influenced by Alexander von Humboldt's ideas (see Banholzer 23), and as a result his work had an impressive sweep. Even now, some of his judgment – such as his observations about Australian federation or the prospect of Canada joining the United States – are prescient and perceptive. His authoritative but accessible writing may have been one reason why the *AZZ* article had such impressive distribution in Britain and Australia, in addition to Germany. Deckert's career demonstrates the absence of a sharply defined border between specialized and amateur science that persisted into the late nineteenth and even early twentieth centuries – a fluidity we will encounter again in the

---

46 Published as *Über die geographischen Grundvoraussetzungen der Hauptbahnen des Welt-verkehrs*, Frohberg, 1883. In keeping with contemporary guidelines for dissertations that assigned as much weight to the *disputatio* as to the thesis itself, this work is only thirty-six pages long. Both Adam (273) and Brogiato erroneously claim (probably in confusion over the meaning of "Bahn") that Deckert wrote his dissertation "on the creation of railway networks in Germany." My thanks to Katharina Holzbecher, Universitätsarchiv Leipzig, and Matthias Lorenz, Universitätsarchiv Frankfurt, for clarifying this in emails, 28 August 2018 and 4 September 2018, respectively.

career of Thomas McIlwraith the ornithologist – and his popular writing did not stand in his way when he was appointed to his academic post in Frankfurt without having previously held a university appointment. Between 1888 and 1890 he was editor of *Globus*, an illustrated magazine of geography, ethnography, and travel, a mandate to which Deckert added world trade. Just how prolific and wide-ranging a writer he was is illustrated in the volume of *Globus* for 1888, the year he began his editorship: he contributed essays, two long enough to be published in sequels, on Fiji, the Hoangho, the caves of North America, and railways in Asia. In contrast to Deckert's fieldwork approach to American geography, none of these essays appears to have been produced from personal observation, with the possible exception of the discussion of the North American caves.

Kirsten Belgum has pointed out that one of the magazine's methods was to splice together translations of previously published work, and in writing about Asia and the Pacific, Deckert, too, must have relied on statistics, maps, and travelogues prepared by earlier authors (Gräbel 89). Another hypothesis for the popularity of Deckert's article on New Guinea might therefore suggest that, because it expertly manipulated European views about the international rise of colonialism that were already in the public eye, it served as a pretext for the ensuing controversy rather than actually causing it. The essay on New Guinea was one of several studies of colonial geography Deckert published between 1882 and 1885, and together they created enough of a stir to have them collected in a volume, *Die Kolonialreiche und Kolonisationsobjekte der Gegenwart: Kolonialpolitische und kolonialgeographische Skizzen.*[47] The first edition appeared in 1884, two years after the éclat in Queensland, and the second followed only four years later. The "White Book of the Reichstag," so Deckert claimed in 1899 with no fear of hyperbole, recorded Bismarck's response to the essay as "giving the impulse for the annexation of that island by Germany, and consequently to the whole colonial movement in Germany" (Goodyear Kirkman 123).[48] This claim was later repeated in biographical essays about Deckert and in his obituaries (see Roemer 549; Maull 58; Banholzer 24). He did produce enough of a stir for Ferdinand von Richthofen, traveller, geographer, and uncle of the First World War flying ace, to thank Deckert for the book and his share in bringing about Germany's annexation of north-eastern New Guinea in 1884.

Deckert's volume on colonialism includes a largely admiring opening discussion of the British Empire apparently based on the lecture that attracted

---

47 Contemporary Colonial Empires and Objects of Colonization: Sketches of Colonial Politics and Colonial Geography (my translation).

48 Bismarck's own reference to the *AZZ* feature remains elusive, but a memorandum prepared by the Foreign Office in Berlin for the German ambassador in London does refer to Deckert's article. See Deutscher Reichstag, 141.

attention in the Australian press in 1884. There are special chapters on
Heligoland and Hong Kong, as well as essays on Borneo (the Sabah Territory), the French and British in Canada, and sections on French, Dutch,
Portuguese, and Spanish colonialism. The discussion of New Guinea has
been revised from its original version in the *AZZ* to refer to the "well-
known protests in Queensland" (*Kolonialreiche* 225; my trans.), and it rec-
ommends pursuing German annexation of the island despite Australian
opposition. He is affronted by Queensland's parvenu impertinence in evoking the Monroe Doctrine as if the colony were one of the "old European
world powers" (*Kolonialreiche* 74; my trans.). Perhaps McIlwraith was in
his turn sniping at the presumption of German colonization when he told
the *Pall Mall Budget*:

> We have had free passages and assisted and nominated emigrants. The last named
> class are those nominated by citizens of Queensland, each of whom on pay-
> ing £ 2 has the right to have brought out free of further expense any relative or
> friend whom he wishes to transplant from the Old World to the Antipodes. The
> Germans avail themselves greatly of this. The nomination is not transferable, but
> to Germans it makes no matter. If the original nominee cannot come it is passed
> on to his neighbor. We have many Germans. They are very clannish, and remain
> Germans long after the French colonists assimilate. ("Our Most Enterprising
> Colony," part 2, 21)

Once the First World War was underway, Deckert's advocacy of German
imperialism became shrill as he developed aggressive visions of *Panlatinis-*
mus, Panslawismus, und Panteutonismus (1914), and he took Great Britain
to task in *Das Britische Weltreich: ein politisch- und wirtschaftlichgeographis-*
ches Charakterbild (1916). His earlier, slightly jaundiced admiration is now
replaced by criticism of what he perceives as innate arrogance, envy, and deception. Once again, Queensland's annexation of New Guinea as provoked
by the *AZZ* article is cited, and he now claims not only that Bismarck's colonial politics were initiated by it, but also that it was Bismarck's intervention
that caused Britain to annul Queensland's annexation of New Guinea (*Das*
Britische Weltreich 3). He perceives Britain's declaration of a protectorate in
New Guinea in November 1884 as an act of aggression against Germany,
which had claimed parts of the island earlier that month. Deckert published
no more, however, because he died suddenly in 1916, in the middle of the
Great War.

Historians of German colonialism have pointed out that his work has failed
to influence subsequent discussions of the subject (Gräbel 90). While his pop-
ulist approach ensured the widespread success of his essay on New Guinea, his
method was no longer acceptable to a discipline increasingly defined by the

academy, and the chauvinism of his wartime writing disqualified him further from lasting recognition.

"The Black Fellows"

A year after Queensland's attempted annexation of New Guinea, McIlwraith was interviewed by the *Pall Mall Budget*. Primed by the protests initiated by Gordon, Miklouho-Maclay, the Aborigines' Protection Society, and others, the reporter asked probing questions about "the black fellows," "the Kanaka and slave labour," "the Polynesian labour trade," and "coolie labour," but the publication makes its approval of McIlwraith's actions known in the headline, "Our Most Enterprising Colony: An Interview with the Ex-Prime Minister [sic] of Queensland" ("Our Most Enterprising Colony," part 2, 21). For each of the controversies addressed by his interviewer, McIlwraith insisted that he had toured his colony and personally investigated the situation. The "black fellows" were "[d]ying out, sir; dying out," he asserted, referring to Aboriginal people as "[t]he offscouring of the human race," "the miserable remnants of these tribes," "the last dregs of a doomed race," and "decrepit apologies for manhood." Efforts to civilize them with dress, food, and education when famine had driven them "to eating some of the settlers" had failed because "[t]heir savagery is ineradicable." He denied as "a mistake" any reports that settlers shot Aboriginal people on sight, but he made some concession for miners "in the extreme north" who "have less confidence in themselves than the squatters" because they had to deal with an environment where "natives are wilder." He equally denied as "nonsense" reports that white men raped Black women, and instead blamed Aboriginal men who "would place [their] women at the disposal of any man" for a "sixpence or shilling" because they did not have "the most elementary ideas of chastity." In confirmation of McIlwraith's contempt for Aboriginal people and the support he enjoyed for it, the historian Raymond Evans cites a scene in which McIlwraith entertained a party of prominent Queenslanders with stories of how "he would undertake to disperse an army of [natives] with a stockwhip (laughter)."[49]

In the *Pall Mall Budget*, McIlwraith likewise dismissed as "nonsense" rumours about the ill-treatment of Kanaka labourers on Queensland's sugar plantations, let alone suggestions of "slavery." With his usual politician's method he attacked by name those individuals who had suggested that there were problems in the first place, dismissing these people as harmless eccentrics at best and impostors at worst. Thus, he singled out John Wisker, a chess champion and, according to McIlwraith, a "misanthrope soured by

---

49 Queenslanders at Dinner, June 1890–June 1895 (cuttings), Brandon Papers, JOL, 52–85, qtd. in Evans, "The Country Has Another Past" 19.

misfortune" ("Our Most Enterprising Colony," part 2, 21), who had attracted Australian and overseas attention with long articles on "Troubles in the Pacific" and "The Victim of Civilisation." In forming his judgment, Wisker was impressed with "one Sheridan." This was not an unknown tramp, as McIlwraith appears to suggest with this formulation, but Richard Bingham Sheridan, minister without portfolio in Griffith's government when McIlwraith talked to the *Pall Mall Budget*, and a man known for his support of Kanaka labourers (Sheridan, it will be remembered, joined Feilberg in the endorsement of *The Way We Civilise*). Commodore Wilson, too, was inclined to accept Sheridan's testimony on the native labour trade. Although McIlwraith conceded that he was an "excellent officer and charming man" ("Our Most Enterprising Colony," part 2, 21), Wilson now had two strikes against him: he believed Miklouho-Maclay, and he believed Sheridan. Two years earlier McIlwraith had addressed a long response to Wilson's report about the Pacific labour traffic to Queensland governor A.E. Kennedy, doing his best to discredit Wilson's approving references to Miklouho-Maclay's ideas. Kennedy in turn forwarded the missive to the Earl of Kimberley, secretary of state for foreign affairs (Great Britain, C3641, 126–30). Although this particular chain of communication worked in his favour, McIlwraith still found himself enmeshed in a tightening web of opponents. To strengthen his case, he pounced on a judgment of error Sheridan had committed eight years earlier when, as "inspector of Polynesians," he "had allowed his opposition to the abuses to Polynesian labour to overrule his discretion [in an official report]" and had been "forced to resign" (see Jones). To McIlwraith's obvious irritation, however, Sheridan's moral authority appeared to be unshaken, and a change of tactics seemed in order: as with Aboriginal people, McIlwraith predicted that any problems involving Kanaka workers would go away by themselves because they were "dying out in our island." In the meantime, they were useful because they – unlike white people – were able to stand the conditions "on the sugar brake" and did not go on strike at harvest time. Once the Kanaka had "died out," there were the Papuans to fill in for them: "The Papuan is of another breed. He increases and multiplies" ("Our Most Enterprising Colony," part 2, 21). It must be added that, "as a speculator and entrepreneur," McIlwraith "owned substantial sugar lands," and so had a vested interest in generating a supply of labour (see Megarrity 2–3).

Also typical of McIlwraith's argumentation is his attempts to increase his credibility by admitting to an occasional shortcoming. Thus, the interviewer, who likely expected another dismissive "nonsense" or "mistake" in response to his question about the "Polynesian labour trade," may have been taken aback to get the following instead: "No. There I admit there have been abuses. I investigated every case reported during my term of office and only discovered three.

But those three were bad." This admission is modified by the insistence that his government had addressed the problem and that it was now for Griffith to pursue further solutions:

> What Queensland can do to suppress abuses in this recruiting business she has done. She can do no more. What remains to be done is for the Home Government to decide. It has only two alternatives. Either it must decide to suppress the whole business, as the slave trade was suppressed, or it must take the whole task of supplying labour into its own hands. That is to say, instead of trusting to incompetent labour agents, who are not paid enough to secure good men, let the Home Government establish a regular service of labour vessels, recruiting in a regular way among the islands. There is no third course ("Our Most Enterprising Colony," part 2, 21).

If reliable information on some of the players involved in the dispute around the annexation of New Guinea can be hard to come by, it is infinitely more difficult when it comes to the Aborigines and Pacific Islanders who were McIlwraith's targets. Among the documents cited above, neither the ones that speak on their behalf nor those that advocate their exploitation cite much testimony from the "black fellows" themselves. In her investigation of "violence and colonial dialogue," Banivanua-Mar insists that "the colonial world, with all its reams of papers and wells of ink, when it mattered was incapable of recording or hearing [a Polynesian worker's] story and was not equipped with the language and words to do so" (*Violence and Colonial Dialogue* 4; see also Harkin).[50] As one of the few contemporary resources in which "Islanders, who were so thoroughly homogenized in colonial discourses, appeared as individuals with shared experiences and responses" (48), she singles out the *Report of the Royal Commission to Enquire into Kidnapping of Labourers in New Guinea and Adjacent Islands*. Tabled in 1885, the report became available a year after McIlwraith's interview with the *Pall Mall Budget*. To gather evidence, the commissioners held meetings during which close to five hundred labourers were examined. Oral testimony and information from logbooks describing the methods used by eight recruiting vessels were collected. The authors of the report offer detailed comments on the difficulties of communication, some of them created deliberately by the recruiters. Both language and body language are scrutinized, along with details about the culturally determined understanding of time and space ("The Labour Trade"). By contrast, there is little Native testimony in *Correspondence Respecting the Natives of the Western Pacific and the Labour Traffic* (Great Britain, C3641), the volume of

---

50 The literature on the Pacific labour trade is extensive, including numerous publications by Patricia Mercer, Clive Moore, Kay Saunders, and Ralph Shlomowitz.

Parliamentary Papers cited most frequently in this chapter. The few available examples nevertheless illustrate the difficulties of accessing an authentic voice that is not overwhelmed by the "discursive filter" of colonial administrative language (Banivanua-Mar, *Violence and Colonial Dialogue* 17). All of the items included in C3641 bristle with signifiers of bureaucratic accuracy and so render the lack of detail about the Native individuals at their centre even more conspicuous.

One of the documents, for example, concerns the "Leslie Massacre" on Russell Island, which took place on 19 February 1881. Labelled "Sub-enclosure No. 2," this item contains the "Examination of a Native Boy 'Tu Tolly [aged about 15 years],' who was an eye witness to the Murder of Captain Schwartz" (Great Britain, C3641, 59, 60). Tu Tolly's interviewer was Commodore Wilson, cited earlier, and the young man's responses are rendered in correct English, with Wilson providing annotations about the meaning of words, gestures, people's relationships or local rank, and ownership. Tu Tolly's detailed testimony of what he witnessed on the ground after he had rowed ashore with the captain is complemented by a much more condensed report, dated three days after the incident, from A. Robertson, "late Mate of the Schooner 'Leslie,' " who viewed the aftermath of the scene from the vessel. In each case, speakers of English, including interpreters acting for Native individuals of high rank, are mentioned specially, but outside of their function as translators and assistants, no other details about their person are given. Thus Robertson comments in his letter that "two of the native boys" from the "Leslie" "[spoke] very good English" (Great Britain, C3641, 60), and Wilson's interview of Tu Tolly refers to " 'Harry,' a Native of the place (and the Chief Cookey's right-hand man of business)" who "speaks English" (C3641, 59). By contrast, the statement of Tomwito (Charlie) about the kidnapping of his wife, dated 3 July 1882, is rendered in Pidgin, but signed by "Cyprian A.G. Bridge, Captain," who presumably also provided the annotations in brackets:

Boat come ashore at Saviri; my wife go in boat. Vessel go over to Nyunga; me go after her; me go see captain. Me say, "Captain, me want my woman go home." Captain says, "No, I no want give you her to go home." When I see my wife on board ship, she cry and want to come with me. Longfellow man (*i. e.* Government Agent) sent her below.

When that boat go ashore again all man say, "That boat steal woman belong to Charlie (Tomwito's name amongst the whites); very good; you and me shoot him." Me say, "No, no you no shoot him, me go see Mr. Michelsen." Then I go see Mr. Michelsen. He write along ship. Longfellow man (*i.e.* Government Agent) he go ashore see Mr. Michelsen. Longfellow man he gammons, he say he give me the woman. Mr. Michelsen talk me. I say to longfellow [sic] man, "What for

you gammon, I want my ... woman home." Then he go along ship, ship go away.
(C3641, 136)

As in the case of Tu Tolly, the report is corroborated by that of a white observer writing in correct English, in this case Captain Bridge's report to Commodore Erskine about the same event (C3641, 135). The use of Pidgin lends
authenticity to this report, but also signals "a lack of complexity, structure, and
dynamism" (Banivanua-Mar, *Violence and Colonial Dialogue* 5) in speech and
thought. To address these shortcomings, the recovery of Indigenous labourers'
experience through archival papers, government publications, and oral history,
as conducted by Banivanua-Mar and other scholars, is all the more necessary.
Although these particular records exist only because their employer took them
to court, it is a relief to read about labourers' verbal and physical resistance to
exploitation. One worker on a Queensland plantation informed his employer,
a sugar farmer, that he was a "bloody shit," "spat in [his] face," and "hit [him]."
Another refused to go to work, announcing, "No bloody fear – too bloody cold"
(qtd. in Saunders 171, 173).

With the next few chapters, the narrative moves on to the McIlwraiths
who emigrated to Ontario, and it switches from the high stakes of imperial
politics to empire as lived in the intimacy of close-knit family and local geographies. Documentation of the links between the Australian and Canadian branches is slight, but it does exist. The most important tie connects Sir
Thomas's brother-in-law William in Rockhampton, Queensland to William's
brother Thomas in Hamilton, Ontario. A trained printer turned journalist
who emigrated to Australia in 1880, a year after McIlwraith became premier,
William became an important local figure who promoted "literature, science
and natural history" (McDonald 473) through the *Morning Bulletin* and other
involvement in civic activity. Like his brother Thomas, he was a keen naturalist and served as "chairman of the Fishing Club and the Dog and Poultry
Club" (McDonald 474), but he also appears to have corresponded with his
brother about Canadian ornithology and applied his ideas to his Australian
environment. When Thomas died in 1903, an obituary appeared in *Emu*, the
Australian journal of ornithology, offering condolences to William, who may
have been the one to inform the journal of his brother's death. The idea, cited
in the obituary, of implementing "the system of observing stations which the
Aust. O. U. [Royal Australasian Ornithologists' Union] has endeavoured to
establish throughout Australia" ("Thomas McIlwraith [Obituary]") was inspired, it seems, by Thomas's work on the Migration Committee of the American Ornithologists' Union. Fourteen years earlier, in 1889, the brothers had
seen each other for the first time after an interval of over thirty years when
William and his daughter passed through Canada on their way from Scotland
to Australia.

The connection between the families remained strong enough for Australia to be one the possible destinations considered by Thomas's daughter Jean when she was looking for a new home and occupation after her mother's death in early 1901, and she offered to pass on the addresses of their Australian cousins to T.F. McIlwraith when he met Anzacs in Britain during the First World War. Perhaps through William's introduction, Sir Thomas also seems to have met the Ontario McIlwraiths. In a photo taken in late 1879, he, his second wife, and what may be the ornithologist's oldest son pose in front of Niagara Falls. The occasion was probably Sir Thomas's second honeymoon. Unfortunately, no details about this visit have emerged, and we know nothing about the impressions the nineteenth-century Australian and Canadian branches of the family may have formed of each other.

Chapter Two

The Ontario McIlwraiths

From Ayrshire to Ontario

On 8 May 1857, Andrew McIlwraith wrote in his diary: "Commenced to drawing of Sarnia Depot Grounds. Day most beautiful and clear. Bro. Thos arrived with the 'Clifton' by moonlight between eight and nine at night, bringing with him a live specimen of a small owl. Had a most happy meeting with him. Called on R. Mackenzie and talked late." A day later, he followed up: "Day very sultry and lowering with gusts of wind from the south. Got the day to myself and Tom and I with guns a-piece, went a-shooting. Went out the London Road beyond the Perch Bridge. Shot Jays, Woodpeckers, etc. and came home very tired but having some nice specimens and enjoying ourselves well. Had R. Mackenzie down in the evening and spent it pleasantly" (*MM*, 8 and 9 May 1857, 82).

Brief as they are, these journal entries bring together most of the main themes that describe the Ontario McIlwraiths, specifically the immigrant brothers Andrew and Thomas McIlwraith, their lives in Ontario, and their close relationship with each other and their extended family. Unlike the Australian McIlwraiths, their Canadian counterparts were affectionate and wrote and visited often. Their ambitions never became as towering as those of Sir Thomas and his brothers: in 1857, Andrew was a patternmaker and draughtsman employed in Sarnia and Thomas the manager of the Hamilton Gas Light Company, and both eventually became moderately successful businessmen. They nevertheless cultivated a large circle of friends, many of them also immigrants from Scotland, with numerous prominent people among them. In the diary entries quoted above, "R. Mackenzie" is Robert Mackenzie, one of seven brothers from Perthshire who settled in Sarnia and "became one of Canada's most politically prominent families and leading Liberal Party lights." The Mackenzies produced Canada's second prime minister, Alexander Mackenzie (*MM*, dramatis personae, xvi). As the entries also illustrate, Andrew and Thomas shared a love of the outdoors, and Thomas became an acclaimed ornithologist. He contributed to "writing the empire" by producing bird taxonomies discussed in postcard exchanges with other researchers and published in the two editions of *The Birds of Ontario* (1886, 1894). While for the Australians the "empire" always means the British Empire, the reference is less straightforward for the Canadians: Thomas's eloquent narratives of bird lore are shaped by his younger years in Scotland, but more often his point of reference is the United States. American scientists offered important help in his studies, but they also expected Canadian ornithologists to hand over their results so that they could be conceptualized by scientists who, it was assumed, had superior qualifications. Partly because of these and other unavoidable entanglements with their self-assured neighbour to the south, the Canadian McIlwraiths' understanding of "nationalism" differs from that of Sir Thomas and his supporters because challenging the authority of the British Empire and possibly forfeiting its protection would have been too dangerous a gamble.

Thomas (b. 1824) and Andrew (b. 1831) were two of ten children born to Thomas McIlwraith, a weaver, and his wife Jean Adair Forsyth in Ayr, Scotland (*MM*, appendix 1, 403). Thomas Jr. trained as a cabinetmaker, a skill that later served him well when he crafted display cases for his collection of stuffed birds and skins. For undocumented reasons he changed his occupation in 1851 by becoming manager of the Newton Gas Works, a post that prepared him for his appointment as manager of the Gas Light Company in Hamilton, Ontario in 1853. Of his siblings, four others also left for overseas. Andrew followed Thomas to Canada a few years later, and as mentioned in the previous chapter, their youngest brother William emigrated to Queensland, Australia in 1880. Because widowhood put them in an economically uncertain situation, two sisters joined their brothers in North America. By 1857, Margaret ("Mrs. Logan," b. 1814) was living in Brooklyn as housekeeper to a fellow Scotsman, the merchant Robert Renfrew. When Andrew returned to Ontario in 1860 after a shortage of work had temporarily driven him across the border to New York the year before, she came with him and opened a boarding house in Galt. Another sister, Helen ("Mrs. Hunter," b. 1810), joined Andrew's household by 1881.

Dated 1857 to 1862, Andrew's diaries about looking for work in Canada and New York before settling in Ontario for good, along with the archive related to Thomas's careers as a businessman and ornithologist from the 1850s until his death in 1903, illustrate how punctilious communication, both in writing and in person, sustained the immigrant community, enriched business, and facilitated scientific exchange. Thomas's collection of papers allows us to observe him more closely and over a longer period than Andrew. Despite his obsessions and eccentricities, Thomas enjoyed his family's affection and the respect of his acquaintances. In turn, he tolerated in others a similar unwillingness to conform – as long as their unconventional manner did not seriously disrupt his own comfort or the accepted beliefs within his circle. But other aspects of his personality also emerge that show him not to be so firmly grounded. Thus, in his letters to some of the scientists he met through the American Ornithologists' Union (AOU) and to John Macoun of the Geological Survey of Canada, he appeals to their counsel as a pupil would to a mentor, and his typically jovial, laissez-faire attitude is sometimes replaced by melancholy about "the mass of the people" to whom "the beauties of birdlife are a sealed book" (*Birds*, 1894, 291). He is troubled by competition with other ornithologists and by anxiety about his own stature as a scientist and author. In short, his life writing shows this charming man to be more complex and contradictory than he first appears.

Family, Friendships, and Work

Shortly before leaving for Canada, Thomas married Mary Park. They had four daughters (one of whom died in infancy) and four sons. Several of these children play a role in this section focusing on their father and uncle, but the childhood of Thomas, Mary, Helen, Jean, Jack, Hugh, and Kennedy was adventurous enough to deserve a separate chapter, as does Jean's career as a well-respected writer.

In addition to some of the siblings of Thomas and Andrew, members of Mary Park's family also emigrated to North America, and circulating packets of letters, newspapers, and occasional photographs, not to mention many personal visits, helped to connect the North American and the Scottish branches of both families. Marriage, friendship, and business affiliations within and beyond the immediate family steadily expanded and tightened the network, creating "[a] host of ... friends, relations, and former co-workers" who provided "extra eyes and ears" in the search for employment or who offered shelter, financial assistance, and companionship away from home (*MM*, Introduction, 17). Quite often, emotional and practical ties became one and the same. Thus Andrew found a friendly refuge in Thomas's home at all times but especially when he was out of work, as repeatedly happened to him in his early years in North America. At his brother's home, he could rely on the sympathetic counsel of "Mrs. Mc." and on her husband's advocacy, not to mention the entertainment provided by a steadily growing flock of children, the youngest of whom might enliven afternoon tea by "accomplishing the feat of rising to her feet and standing alone for a moment" or even walking "nearly half across the dining room" a few days later (*MM*, 15 February 1858, 21 February 1858, 143, 144). When Andrew left his parental home in Scotland, Thomas's guidance in person and by letter became essential to his success. Judging by the epistolary models provided in contemporary letter manuals, we find that older brothers played an increasingly important role in their siblings' lives from the mid-eighteenth century onwards, by assisting "a man's movement towards independence and freedom from his family of origin" (Bannet 159).[1] Although he was only in his early thirties himself when Andrew arrived in Canada, Thomas took his role seriously.[2]

As with the Australian McIlwraiths, a potent mixture of family and business was at work when Andrew was hired in 1860 as bookkeeper by his future father-in-law, John Goldie from Kirkoswald in Ayrshire, and when, likewise with Goldie's support, he partnered with a business associate in setting up a foundry twelve years later. Andrew's marriage, though motivated by love for Mary Goldie strong enough to make him feel "crippity crappity" (he crossed out this vivid expression on second thoughts) for delaying his proposal of marriage (*MM*, 3 May 1958, 156), coincided with "his entry into the growing entrepreneurial network that was the Goldie family" (*MM*, epilogue, 388) and that eventually comprised two mills and two foundries in Ontario, located, respectively, in Galt, Ayr, Guelph, and Listowel. It helped that – like Thomas – Andrew was an adaptable worker who was forever striving to increase his education and skills. In his younger years at least, these self-improvements allowed him to adjust, apparently without much difficulty, to fluctuating conditions in the labour market and to the demands of his growing family.

To maintain this web of connections required diligence, especially in times of economic uncertainty. As Eric Richards has pointed out, "[n]etworks generate documentation because migrants used their correspondence to oil the wheels of settlement, adapation, and colonial advancement" (153). According to Andrew's notes during a period when work was scarce and banks failing,[3] much of his leisure was spent keeping up with his personal and professional correspondence, and lists of letters – as in, "Had letters from Hamilton, from John Stewart and Thos. with enclosures of letters of Mrs. Mc to Thos. and one for me from T. Anderson, Dumbarton" (*MM*, 17 September 1858, 178) – appear almost daily during the months when he kept conscientious records of his post. Delays, especially delays in overseas mail, were monitored anxiously. There was relief all around when "[p]ackets of letters arrived from home some of which should have come with last mail," with "home" always referring to Scotland (*MM*, 21 August 1858, 174), or when Thomas finally heard from his wife, who was on the other side of the Atlantic for a visit with her folks.

---

1 To illustrate this shift, Bannet cites *The Complete Letter-Writer, or Polite English Secretary*, 2nd ed. (1756), and H.W. Dilworth, *The Complete Letter-Writer, or Young Secretary's Instructor* (1775).

2 See also Vibert 67–88, which highlights the strength of the relationship between the brothers Donald and Murdoch Stewart, with the older Donald acting as substitute parent.

3 On 11 November 1857, during a visit to Scotland, Andrew reports "[g]reat money panic and run upon the banks at Ayr and elsewhere" when the Western Bank of Scotland and the Borough Bank of Liverpool failed. His letter to the *Ayrshire Times*, 29 August 1860, also refers to "the great money panic of '57" (*MM* 120, 52).

Although the Ontario McIlwraiths were not as quick as their hot-tempered Australian cousins to suspect negligence in the sender when letters were slow to arrive, they, too, instantly followed up with a letter-writer who had inexplicably lapsed in his side of the correspondence: "Had a short note from Thos. to know what was up with my not writing" (*MM*, 3 November 1859, 241). The extent of these communications becomes apparent when, for a few months in 1857, Andrew kept track of his correspondence in a systematic list: between January and August, he received as many as 432 letters and dispatched 530, not counting the enclosures of letters initially directed to other correspondents and then circulated among an extended group of secondary recipients. Expenditures for postage, stationery, and ink are listed each month in his cash accounts between 1857 and 1861 (*MM*, cash accounts, 418–29).

Given the number of letters recorded in McIlwraith's diary, it is disappointing that the only letter that appears to have survived is one entitled "Is the Working Man Better Off in America Than in Britain?" and published in the *Ayrshire Times* 29 August 1860 (*MM* 51–8). In it, using an important genre among "sources of information ... that enabled judgements about emigration to be considered" (Devine, *The Scottish Nation* 101), he compared working conditions in Scotland and America. Such letters anticipated the "impartial advice and information on land grants, wages, living costs, and passage rates" (96) that in later years became readily available from the Emigrants' Information Office in Westminster, opened in 1886 and operating under the supervision of the Colonial Office. Andrew McIlwraith's letter and others like it provided the more spontaneous alternative of "informal settlerism" to the occasional sugar-coating practised by governments keen to increase the number of immigrants from specific countries of origin and ethnic backgrounds (see Belich 153–65). Aggressive agents, some of them able to converse in Gaelic if required or skilled in the presentation of magic lantern shows, pressed a colony's cause at "markets, hiring fairs, agricultural shows and village halls" (Devine, *The Scottish Nation* 96).

As a document carefully composed by a well-read writer, McIlwraith's letter commands respect, and his diaries confirm him to be versed in rhetorical practice. He spent weeks drafting an essay for presentation to his "Mechanic's debating club" on Alexander Wilson, ornithologist and weaver (*MM*, 8 June; 18, 21 September; 7, 21, 22 October 1858, 178, 179, 181, 183); participated in an "animated discussion" about an essay "on the Morality of Burns" at the YMCA in Hamilton (*MM*, 14 March 1859, 204); read "Burns' Centenary Speeches" to his sweetheart Mary Goldie (*MM*, 25 February 1859, 201); and was critical of sermons that failed to keep him interested in church: "Thought Dr Candlish a dry sort of a customer and felt very drowsy under him," he complained about one such preacher (*MM*, 11 October 1857, 113). In keeping with the principle that, in order for instruction to take effect, a presentation had to follow a familiar design even as it intrigued its audience, he used the double-entry format in his letter to the *Ayrshire Times* that, as mentioned earlier, shows up repeatedly in the McIlwraith archive. The principle is also evident in individuals' conduct. Andrew himself "balanced" the assistance he received from his family and friends by conscientiously looking for work that would keep him financially independent. Both in Ontario and in New York, he walked for miles in search of jobs in foundries or architectural ironworks and did not stop until he had found one.

In the *Ayrshire Times*, Andrew McIlwraith aims for a tone both authoritative and conversational. He begins by stating his credentials: "eighteen months' experience in knocking out life as a mechanic here" (*MM* 52) and then presents the question to be discussed, namely: "Is the working man better off in America than in Britain?" (52). Troubling developments, such as a recent economic depression, are duly acknowledged, but so is America's ability to "rall[y] bravely from the dire tribulation" (52). A discussion of the practical aspects of obtaining work follows: how employers advertise vacancies, what wages may be expected by foundry workers, machinists, and those in the building trade, and for what contingencies to prepare oneself. A discussion of the characteristics of the American labour market includes the division of work into increasingly specialized branches, such as "Sash, Blind, and Door Factory," "Scroll Sawing," and "Kindling Wood Factory." A special section is devoted to "the manufacture of iron-work for buildings" (54), an area in which he became an expert soon after his arrival, and to the success in exporting such work across the States, to South America and, "can you believe it" (55), to British North America. The expression of surprise refers to the view, presumably shared by his readers, that to rely on such imports is a blemish on Canada's record of self-sufficiency that reflects poorly on its status within the imperial family. Also based on shared assumptions is the prejudice against Irish and German immigrants he expresses, and feels no need to explain, in a review of ethnic groups competing in the labour market. Remarks about lodging, board, and hygiene round off the letter.

For each point introduced, he notes possible disadvantages that the emigrant must consider – namely, the scarcity of permanent work and the resulting reduction in annual income, the lack of "organized protection among the workmen" (53), and some employers' tendency towards speculation and dishonesty, leaving them sometimes unable to pay their workers' wages. He maintains this balanced perspective on the good and the bad until the conclusion, where he suggests an exploratory advance visit. A trip is easy enough to arrange "[i]n these days of cheap locomotion" (57) before hesitant emigrants make up their minds for good. The editor of the *Ayrshire Times* clearly expected the letter to be distributed widely among readers because he informed them that "[b]y folding [this] letter like a newspaper, open at the ends, and writing 'Press Copy' on the wrapper, the postage will be cheaper than if forwarded the usual way"

(58). At a moment in postal history when correspondents used cunning ruses to avail themselves of the cheaper postage of newspapers, this was important information.[4] The editor also expressed the hope that Andrew would contribute a monthly column on the subject of immigration, but this scheme does not appear to have materialized.[5]

The list of library books McIlwraith borrowed from the Mechanics' Institute Library in Newton-on-Ayr before his emigration does not include a letter manual,[6] but the polish of this one surviving letter indicates that he had mastered the requisite epistolary conventions. As early as the 1700s, popular letter manuals emphasized the importance of a traveller "assur[ing] those at home" of his welfare and of their returning the favour by "cheerfully support[ing] the adventurer's endeavors" and getting on with their own duties. To convey this attitude unequivocally in a letter, the manuals implied, was the "*sine qua non* for empire and for extension of Britain's trade into the New World" (Bannet 123).[7] McIlwraith's letter to the *Ayrshire Times* illustrates that he understood his responsibilities within the epistolary network to extend beyond his immediate family.

Like letter-writing, visiting whenever possible was considered a communal duty that could be turned to personal advantage, and as the next chapter will illustrate, the McIlwraith children were educated from an early age to carry calling cards on their frequent travels through the Great Lakes and to participate cheerfully in the taxing rituals of "at-homes." When Andrew broke his promise to drop in on his sister Margaret on New Year's Day in New York, he made up for it by "spend[ing] all day with her" at the next possible opportunity as well as escorting her downtown to do her shopping (*MM*, 3 January 1860, 253). In contrast to their Australian cousins, irritations among the Ontario McIlwraiths were, in general, swiftly addressed and closely monitored if their causes seemed more elusive, especially if the individual in question was crucial to one's own well-being: "Thos. aguish ... and I fancied rather snappish to me," Andrew writes about his brother, normally a genial man, but the problem resolved itself soon enough because no more is said of this friction in subsequent entries (*MM*, 11 October 1858, 182).

Even if they involved lengthy travel on foot or complicated conveyance by relay, most of these visits were to relatively nearby places. However, in an effort

---

4 Postal reformer Rowland Hill relates a particularly elaborate scheme in volume 1 of his *Post Office Reform: Its Importance and Practicability* (1837), 92–3.

5 On the importance of newspapers and the privileges they enjoyed in postal exchange, see Amyot and Willis, 128–9; Henkin, 42–3; Golden, 123–4.

6 "Andrew McIlwraith's Mechanics' Institute Library Loans, Newton-on-Ayr, Scotland, 1846–1852,"*MM*, 404–12.

7 Bannet cites John Hill, *The Young Secretary's Guide or Speedy Help to Learning*, first published in London in 1696, with numerous reprints until 1737.

to enjoy the advantages of both permanent and temporary migration, trans-atlantic crossings, too, were undertaken to keep up with family and friends in Scotland. It would be going too far to call the Atlantic "a minor impediment" for the McIlwraiths, as has been suggested for the numerous crossings under-taken by the Brodie family (Gibson 137), but between 1857 and 1859, Andrew's diaries record one trip each to Ayr for himself, for Thomas's wife Mary, along with her two oldest children, and for Thomas on his own, a high tally com-pared to other immigrants' practices (see Gerber 163). Although Andrew had to excuse himself from tea "and peuk [sic] three times" as the *Indian* sailed into the Atlantic on his return trip to Scotland (*MM*, 18 August 1857, 101), none of the McIlwraiths seems to have been much bothered by crossing the ocean, certainly not enough to stay away from Scotland. In this, too, they differed from others who longed to see their families but had to admit that they did not "like the see [sic]" (Joseph Hartley qtd. in Gerber 164) and so were better off stay-ing on firm land once they had reached North America. Later diaries from the McIlwraith archive, the children's Family Album and the logbook kept by Thomas's youngest son, Kennedy, indicate that at least some family members continued these visits into the next few decades, even if business kept Thomas mostly at home: Mrs. McIlwraith visited Scotland in 1874 and again in 1883, and there may have been other trips for which there are no records. Once the children were grown, several of them continued the tradition and advanced their education by spending extended periods with family in Scotland or on their own in London or Dublin, not to mention tours of the Continent.

In addition to the McIlwraiths' easy mobility between North America and Britain for the purpose of maintaining the family bond, Andrew's departure for New York in search of work – along with his letter to the *Ayrshire Times* – may be seen as part of a labour-oriented circulation that not only encompassed North America but also seasonal migration across the Atlantic. Increasing from the 1880s onwards, these migrations temporarily took granite workers, coal miners, masons, and building tradesmen to North America (Devine, *The Scottish Nation* 95–6), including the three hundred Scottish stonemasons brought to Ottawa between 1905 and 1911 to build the Victoria Memorial Museum, which was to play an important role in the career of Andrew's great-nephew T.F. Because both his brother and Mary Goldie lived there, Andrew's chief point of reference within North America was south-western Ontario, but his decision to "tramp" across the American border was facilitated because he had an alternative sup-port system in New York, thanks to his sister Margaret and her employer Robert Renfrew. Conversely, Margaret resolved, apparently on the spur of the moment, to accompany her brother back to Ontario and settle in the vicinity of several members of her family. From Andrew's descriptions of his trip to Ayr, it is clear that he relied on an equally strong nexus on the other side of the Atlantic, where he kept up a busy program of visits to people's homes and workplaces.

At times, these contacts expanded into an articulate awareness of the ideo-logical ties binding the British Empire and of the communication technologies that brought its subjects ever closer. The event might be a collective abstention from food "on account of [the] Indian Revolt" (*MM*, 7 October 1857, 112), or news, "telegraphed from New York," of the death of Sir Henry Havelock, one of the generals of the Siege of Lucknow (*MM*, 25 January 1858, 139). The occasion could also be the "Railway Celebration at Goderich" to mark the completion of the Buffalo and Lake Huron Railway (*MM*, 8 July 1858, 166–167) or Robert Burns's hundredth birthday, "celebrated ... in Dundas and all over the world" (*MM*, 25 January 1859, 196). A public holiday with fireworks marked the laying of the Atlantic Telegraph Cable (*MM*, 18 August 1858, 174), a momentous new stage in global communication, even if this particular cable failed soon after (see Müller 26).

Business Postcards

In 1871, a year before Andrew, too, became an entrepreneur by setting up a foundry with partner Adam Austin, Thomas McIlwraith left his post at the Gas Light Company in Hamilton. Ship owner John Proctor had bought the wharf at the foot of Hamilton's MacNab Street in 1869, originally leased by Routh and Munro.[8] In his turn, Proctor sold the property "with horses waggons and so on" (FA, 1 December 1872) to McIlwraith three years later.[9] The two entered a business relationship, with Proctor acting as uptown agent for the Western Express Line, and McIlwraith becoming "wharfinger and coal merchant" (FA, 1 December 1872). In addition to selling coal, McIlwraith became a forwarder of a wide range of industrial products, including foundry facings as well as "crates and boxes, pig iron, scrap iron, cut nails, soda, soap, castor oil, bleaching pow-der, cement and vinegar" (Middleton and Walker 11). As his twelve-year-old daughter Jean wrote admiringly, he also made "stock bricks by steam, the only ones of the kind to be had in the city" (FA, 18 June 1872). Finally, he sold ice for use in cold storage, and borrowing his son Kennedy's bird logbook, he describes two frantic days before the end of the winter season with all available workers cutting ice in Burlington Bay and loading it (WIK, 2, 8, 12 March 1890).

Also in 1871, Canada became the first country outside of Europe to intro-duce the postcard (Steinhart 5), and to communicate with his suppliers and customers, McIlwraith availed himself of this low-cost and efficient means of

---

8 John Proctor (1831–1908), born in Scotland, owned a large fleet of boats for transport be-tween Hamilton and Montreal before becoming a dealer in heavy hardware and railway sup-plies. See Obituary, Hamilton *Spectator*, 18 August 1908.

9 McIlwraith's great-grandson has tracked these developments through Hamilton's city directo-ries. See Thomas and Duane McIlwraith, "508, 389, 179, et al.," 2–3.

transmitting "brief, casual messages" (Henkin 174). When the United States followed in 1873, sending postcards across the border was an inexpensive two cents
while postage within Canada was one cent. An archive of over 570 of these cards
documenting McIlwraith's trade throughout the Great Lakes area has survived,
ranging from printed price lists and offers from competing dealers and shippers,
to orders, invoices, and reminders. Sketchy and even cryptic as these messages
are at times when writers lacked practice in producing them, the postcards not
only represent a detailed business record but, in offering glimpses into both the
coal dealer's and his correspondents' lives, they also sketch a broader range of
educational and social backgrounds than is otherwise typical of the McIlwraiths'
middle-class literacy. Andrew, as we have learned, knew how to handle the language of business with confidence when required: the fragmented brevity of
his entries in his diary was in keeping with the conventions of journal-keeping,
but his letter to the *Ayrshire Times* displays epistolary polish. The postcard, by
contrast, "helped democratize the act of correspondence by bringing it within
reach of all but the very poorest" and of the least literate (Distad). In this way,
the postcards documenting McIlwraith's coal dealership also track aspects of
the "mutual assistance and reciprocity" that enabled frontier communities to
function, as well as illustrating how the existing formalities for letters had to be
adjusted to the new medium. Such adjustments were especially necessary as this
process took "family life ... beyond the front door" and into communities with
whom the McIlwraiths did not readily mingle otherwise (Noël 246, 192).

No matter how basic their requirements, the postcards still had to meet
certain standards of effective communication, and the sender was not always
equipped to provide them. Many of Thomas McIlwraith's correspondents
struggled with penmanship, spelling, punctuation, and grammar, let alone the
formalities of address, salutation, acknowledgment, and tone, and some cards
are soiled by ink blots or coal dust to the point of illegibility. Practice taught
Thomas McIlwraith to decipher such messages, just as he automatically knew
to fill in various requirements such as providing transport when the customer's
own horse was "away" (TMF, 593, E.C. Fearnside [?], 23 February 1885), or
when – as in the following note from a man in the small community of Bin-
brook – there were no "teems" of horses to begin with:

> Please to let me know by return of mail what you will [send?] me out 2 or 3 tons of
> coal for on my contract from last year [illegible] I have not teems [sic] of my own
> Mr. [illegible] got 3 tons brought to hear [sic] for [illegible] will you do the same
> with me. Please to let me know at once and oblige yours. (TMF, 382, S.G. Harris,
> 15 November 1882).

Variously addressed to "Commercial Coal Yard, Hamilton," "Coal Merchant,
Main Street," "Mr. McIlwraith, Coal Driver, City," "Any Wholesale Coal Dealer,

Hamilton," and "Mr. Mackelray, Hamilton Ontario, on the foot of Megnab St north," the cards still reached the correct recipient. The apparent ease with which they were delivered reflected on McIlwraith's status, evocative of the suggestion in some eighteenth-century letter manuals that excessive precision in the address implied "the person was too obscure to be easily found" (Bannet 68). For daily life to proceed, it was essential for citizens to establish themselves in their community well enough so that their names could serve as guarantee that their credit was good. Likewise, the ability to receive an order for coal and fill it from minimal information was important for business success in an environment where standards of education or income were far from uniform and where there was competition from other dealers.

The long, harsh Canadian winters made planning for sufficient fuel in homes and offices a crucial task, and the types of coal available, cost, delivery, and storage made enough of an impression on Thomas's daughter Jean to give the topic pride of place in her essay "Household Budgets Abroad: Canada." Customers found that additional provisions were often required to get them to the beginning of warmer weather: "The three tons of coal did not reach the winter through. Please send another half ton of Nut Coal and charge the same to Me," one of them writes towards the end of March (TMF, 427, D. Hausser, 21 March 1883). Another is "down to the dust" as early as November (TMF, 103, George Collis, 21 November 1879). Several customers ask for delivery of coal for which they will pay after receiving their wages, and the phrasing suggests that because they are personally known to McIlwraith, they expect him to oblige. In order to obtain daily supplies of coal or other necessities, some customers were able to vouch for each other. If the connections became tenuous or the recipient was completely unknown, the business risk became too great: "All coal sent to the country is payable in advance," McIlwraith responded curtly to an enquiry from Hamish Hamilton at Ryckman's Corners (TMF, 100, 18 November 1879), possibly recalling a lesson he had been taught early in his career as coal dealer. When Routh and Munro went under and before McIlwraith and Proctor entered their business arrangement, McIlwraith's oldest son was concerned because his father "had some coal on the wharf of which [Routh and Munro] sold a considerable quantity and kept the money" (FA, 31 March 1868). The cost was not recovered.[10]

Business was not charity, and McIlwraith had a firm notion of what could and could not be expected of people from "the humbler walks of life," even as he allowed himself to be pleasantly surprised when, despite "little education,"

---

10 Thomas Jr.'s comments suggest that his father was dealing in coal as early as the late 1860s, when he was still working for the Hamilton Gas Light Company. It is also possible that the coal was for Thomas Sr.'s household.

a member of "this class" proved to be circumspect and perceptive (*Birds*, 1894, 335). He reluctantly gave permission, judging by the character modelled on Thomas McIlwraith who appears in his daughter's autobiographical novel "Smiling Water," for Jean to set up a night school for young labourers in the basement of her parents' house in the late 1870s. These students were "sturdy, rough-looking lads" from the Irish families who lived near the McIlwraiths' home by the wharf. They, too, she decided, were her "neighbours,"[11] and she may have learned how to write about them from the "slum stories" in H.W. Nevinson's collection *Neighbours of Ours* (1895) or Arthur Morrison's *Tales of Mean Streets* (1894). Her father, however, remained sceptical and was relieved when the venture fizzled after four years. Some correspondents anticipated the difficulty of not fitting into the category of trusted customers, and they appealed to the dealer's compassion. "L.G." from 10 Magill Street in Hamilton entreated:

> Will you please to favour me a stranger to you by sending me a ton of stove coal
> but I have not the money until pay day that is Friday the 9 and I will give it to you
> then I thought my coal would hold out but the weather being so cold I burn more
> (TMF, 402, 6 February 1883).

We do not know how McIlwraith responded to this particular plea, but as subsequent chapters will illustrate, the family drew distinctions between the individuals that it did or did not want to admit to its circle.

It was not only customers who sometimes had to be on the defensive, but also the dealer. When demand was high, McIlwraith found it difficult to keep up with orders and had to be reminded that a customer had "ordered 6 tons + have up to date received 2 ½" (TMF, 227, J. O'Derry [?], 1 December 1880). Discussions of the postcard as a medium of communication have suggested that its "tendency ... was toward the reduction of correspondence to formal gestures" (Henkin 174) and to an attendant decrease in intimacy. Such is certainly the case in the unequivocally stern reminder Mr. McIlwraith received from W. & F.P. Currie and Co. in Montreal: "Have you got completion of pig iron Langloan. We wired you for rate on pig iron to Pittsburg [sic] and Alleghany [sic] and are surprised you paid no attention to it" (TMF, 130, 30 January 1880). Another correspondent threatened "there will be trouble" if merchandise was not delivered to his warehouse as agreed (TMF, 44, B.E. Charlton, 27 September 1878). Inexperienced correspondents might complicate their message by switching inadvertently between different levels of formality and so exposing more about their situation than they intended. In insisting that the balance of his order be

---

11 "Smiling Water" is the first of a trilogy of autobiographical novels that also includes "Casual Kate's Letters" and "Springs Eternal" (JNMP). These appear to have been written during McIlwraith's time in New York, probably sometime after 1905, but were not published.

delivered as soon as possible, one writer alternates wildly between elaborate civility in the opening ("I should feel glad if you could make it convenient") and in the salutation ("I am yours J. O'Derry [?])" on the one hand and imperious briskness in the body of the message on the other – namely, the request to "Send number 4 coal as ordered. Tell men to bring basket with them" (TMF, 227, J. O'Derry [?], 1 December 1880). This unevenness in language could spring from annoyance directed at an unreliable dealer but, given the unpredictable level of diction in many of these cards, lack of epistolary experience was an equally likely reason. Letter manuals routinely taught appropriate expression in business correspondence, and postcards drew on well-established formulas for salutation, acknowledgment of receipt, and so on (see Bannet, 58, 78, 113). It quickly became apparent, however, that for harmonious business relations to continue, the brevity and lack of privacy characteristic of the postcard required an adjusted etiquette. After all, any reminders of "delinquencies" such as late delivery or tardy payment spelled out on it could be "read by a message boy, clerk, &c." before the recipient got to the message himself (C.A. Fleming, 67).

Occasionally, McIlwraith failed to respond in good time because he was for once unable to read the correspondent's name. On the other hand, he would have found it difficult to plead postal delays. Hamilton may not have had up to twelve mail deliveries a day, as was customary in Victorian London, but several postcards received in McIlwraith's wharf office indicate that writers expected their order to reach its destination within hours and coal to be delivered "this afternoon" or even "today by noon" (TMF, 617, Mrs. Wallace, 22 September 1885; 118, James Hinchcliffe, day and month missing, 1879). No wonder the postcard was known as "the poor man's telephone" (Gendreau 29). Despite a supplier's best intentions, however, muddy roads or frozen rivers could annihilate the best-planned delivery schedule. It must have required steady nerves to deal with frantic individuals like H. Moore in Dundas, who was waiting to receive a shipment of nails and launched a steady stream of inquiries, demanding to be kept up to date by postcards twice a day as well as by telegraph:

> Is there no word of the nails and Other Goods. I am out of Stock for 6 days and waited daily. Send card when Vessil [sic] enters the Bay now 12 days on the way and I fear disaster. Say name of Propeler [sic] and when she left Montreal. Answer by return as we watch the street for your teams daily. How many Vessils in your line is that the delay short of Vessils & that the Boat did not start 28th or 9th May. Give all the information you can by return post and send Imediat [sic] your telegraph. Send that day. Do hurrie all you can and reply & oblige and card twice a day until goods come. (TMF, 19, Hugh Moore, 10 June 1878)

Such problems notwithstanding, Thomas McIlwraith's services were essential to the community. He was a respected businessman, and his trade connections

in the Great Lakes area were impressive.[12] Membership on educational, financial, and civic boards confirmed his standing, including the Hamilton City
Council (if only for one year in 1878) and the Central Presbyterian Church of
Hamilton, and he was a long-time president of the Mechanics Institute. Andrew speaks of his brother attending to "parliamentary business" in Quebec,
though he does not specify its nature (*MM*, 25 April 1860, 270). His family
was immensely proud of Thomas's prominence in the local community. His
son Jack, for example, linked his own success as a businessman in Indiana to
his father's example and, implying that his own standing gained from his parent's stature, reported that "the flag on the Government building was hung at
half-mast"[13] when Thomas McIlwraith died in 1903 (Forkner 778).

Thomas McIlwraith, the Ornithologist

It is doubtful, however, whether the flag would have been flown at half mast for
Thomas McIlwraith's business and civic accomplishments alone. Jean captured
the reason for his fame more accurately when, writing in 1895 for a British
readership, she underlined that her father was "well-known as the leading ornithologist of Canada" and "his name and book [were] familiar to 'bird men'
all over the continent." She had several literary achievements to her name by
the time she wrote this, but concluded that editing the second edition of her
father's book *The Birds of Ontario* (1894) had been her "most important service
to the public."[14] Jack's biographer – probably acting on confused information
from Jack himself, who brimmed with family pride but knew nothing about
birds – does acknowledge the scientific work but commits several errors at once
when he claims that Thomas McIlwraith became "president of the American
Ornithological Society" (Forkner 777). More correctly, he was one of only three
Canadian founding members of the AOU.

Hamilton's unique position at the head of Lake Ontario was not only advantageous for McIlwraith's coal-dealing business, but it also had an exceptional
wealth of birdlife. When McIlwraith arrived, the birds were no longer as plentiful as in the days "when Hamilton was but a village" and "the flocks of water-
fowl, which frequented Burlington Bay, were so great as frequently to darken
the light of the sun by day" (McIlwraith, "Notices" 9), but a large number of

---

12 For biographical information, see his great-grandson's *DCB* entry on him: Thomas F. McIl-
    wraith, "McIlwraith, Thomas." Holman and Kristofferson provide a wealth of genealogical
    information on the family, including Thomas.
13 Jack does not specify the "Government building" to which he is referring.
14 Clipping from *Good Reading: A Monthly Advice*, n.d. [1895?], Notebook of Newspaper Cut-
    tings and Advertisements for the Correspondence Classes," DC 233/2/8/3/23/5, Queen Mar-
    garet College, Correspondence Courses, UGA.

Cairnbrae, ca. 1898, with Thomas McIlwraith in the garden and his wife,
Mary Park, on the porch. TFMP.

species continued to visit the area nevertheless. Andrew has "Bro. Thomas
speaking about beginning birdstuffing operations" in early 1857 (*MM*, 1
February 1857, 65), but Thomas himself dated his interest in the birds of Ontario a year earlier when he "indulg[ed] in a series of morning rambles along
the edge of the mountain, west of the city." He challenged himself to identify
each species he encountered, despite the absence of "not even the beginning of
a museum in the city" or of helpful reference works in the library ("Notices"
11). In his determination to collect his own information if none was available,
he avoided the fate of the Abbé Léon Provancher in Quebec who was reprimanded by the entomologist George Henry Horn of the Academy of Natural Sciences in Philadelphia that he was wrong to have tackled entomology in
the absence of the necessary reference sources: "You say you have no library
and no large collections, therefore why enter a field where both of these are
absolutely necessary?" (qtd. in Duchesne 112). In the pursuit of ornithological data, McIlwraith became "a familiar figure walking along the bayshore, to
Coote's Paradise, and along the Niagara Escarpment" (Henley 108). The garden

of Cairnbrae had birdhouses aplenty, variously installed "[o]n a peak of the stable," "about the out-houses," and "in an apple tree" to encourage seasonal visitors to hatch their young (*Birds*, 1894, 306, 307). In *The Birds of Ontario*, he describes the drama of nesting swallows and house wrens being displaced from their boxes by aggressive house sparrows that, when McIlwraith came to the aid of the original occupants, promptly made a home for themselves "under the veranda around the house, which brought frequent complaints from the sanitary department," namely, his wife (307). Over Mary Park's protests, McIlwraith tolerated the sparrows because they decimated the insects around the stables and near the water, but when they attempted to destroy his grapevines, his patience ran out, and he shot as many sparrows near the house as he could reach (308).

Swallows, house wrens, and at times even the sparrows were accepted as neighbours at Cairnbrae, and the garden was a carefully tended wilderness to attract as many birds as possible. In "Smiling Water," written after she had left Cairnbrae, Jean McIlwraith remembers the place as a small Eden, and she has the main character

> enter ... her home garden by a gate in the high board fence that bounded its southern end. Before her stretched a straight, long path, bordered on either side by a broad belt of flowering shrubs and perennials. Roses were in full bloom, also columbines in every shade of pink, yellow and purple. Behind these borders extended a trellis of grape vines, screening raspberry and currant bushes, the asparagus bed and several big old snow-apple trees among which a hammock was suspended. Overhead, at the junction of cross paths were arches of clematis, purple or white, and more grape vines, while nearer the house was a high rockery, with a tiny spray of water coming out at the top, as well as a natural wall of the same rough stones in which grew ferns and wild flowers. But [her] gaze leaped at once to the end of the path, framed by green-draped verandah pillars, through which she saw her own blue Smiling Water. (11).

This garden was "a natural resting-place of many warblers and other small migrants, and it was there that many rare birds were taken" (Saunders, "In Memoriam" 2). One day in May 1882, McIlwraith and his son Kennedy obtained more than a dozen different species without setting foot outside their own grounds: "I will give all the different kinds we got," Kennedy writes. "They were: the Blackburnian Warbler, the Black-throated Green Warbler, the Black and Yellow Warbler, the Yellow Rump Warbler, the Cerulean Warbler (female), the Nashville Warbler, a Red Start (female), the Yellow Warbler (male + female), a small Flycatcher, the Great Crested Flycatcher, an Oriole (Baltimore), a Rose-breasted Grosbeak (female), besides seeing a small hawk and a redstart" (WIK, 9 May 1882).

This wealth of species notwithstanding, McIlwraith offers abundant evidence of the threats to birdlife in the Hamilton area. The birds' migration paths intersected with the communication technology produced by the spread of settlement and the growth of North American industries.[15] On the one hand, telegraph, railway, and lock stations, as well as post offices and older structures such as fur-trading posts – including the Hudson's Bay Company's York Factory and Norway House – and military buildings no longer in use such as Fort George, became the ideal "laboratory outposts" (Müller 169)[16] from which to study birdlife. McIlwraith cites numerous observations collected by occupants of these outposts, several of whom evoke places of work that enabled rare concentration on the natural world. Edward C. Nelson, appointed by the Smithsonian to the United States Army Corps Signal Service because of his expertise as naturalist, listened to the whistling swans near the mouth of the Yukon River, admiring "the organ-like swell and fall in their notes, as they were wafted on in rich, full harmony" (qtd. in *Birds*, 1894, 103). McIlwraith produced evidence that birds and other creatures did successfully adapt to cohabitation with humans; this was the case, for example, with the pomarine jaeger, which was "especially common along the border of the ice-pack and about the whaling fleet, where they fare abundantly" (Nelson qtd. in *Birds*, 1894, 40), the eels that attached themselves to the wheels of a wagon for a ride to another location, or "a pair of Mourning Warblers" observed while "waiting for the train at a way station on the Kincardine branch of the Grand Trunk Railway" (*Birds*, 1894, 57). The warblers were made anxious by his presence but apparently not by the trains, and from the window of his carriage a few days later he saw one of the birds again, this time sitting on a tree by the track (378). Similarly, the White-rumped shrike's favourite perch was "on a fence-post or on the telegraph wire by the railroad track" (347).

On the other hand, the technologies represented by these "outposts," some more remote than others, also significantly interfered with the birds' natural "highways" or "runs" (*Birds*, 1894, 104, 108). The "haunts" of the Canada goose had "been invaded by trolley cars, electric lights, telegraph wires and other innovations, which cause them to fly high and pass on with fewer stoppages" (98). Ducks became entangled and died in gill nets (95), the cutting of timber drove the pileated woodpecker away, "one of the grand old aborigines who retire before the advance of civilization" (249), and large numbers of birds migrating at night were destroyed by flying against lighthouses (13). The "snorting of the locomotive" may have been responsible for the disappearance of the long-billed

---

15 For a discussion of environmental issues related to Hamilton's vicinity to the waterfront, see Bouchier and Cruikshank.

16 Müller applies the term "laboratory outposts" to telegraph cable stations and the research they facilitated in ocean and land surveys, astronomy, and thermodynamics, but the term can be seen to have broader application. See also Binnema on the role of HBC factories for naturalist observation.

curlew from Ontario (158), and a "Red-billed Rail ... probably ... killed by the telegraph wires" was found lying in the street and brought to Mr. McIlwraith (WIK, 10 September 1883). Environmental pollution and climate change may have had something to do with the sudden, though temporary, disappearance of birds in early 1886, when Kennedy noted: "During the passed [sic] two months, although we made several excursions, we did not succeed in capturing a single specimen of any sort, except now and then a bad cold from going out in wet weather" (27 February 1886).

McIlwraith rails against the wholesale destruction of certain species, and he reports on ecological damage in various areas of North America. Thus, he cites *The Auk* on "a most barbarous practice called 'fire-lighting,' " by which birds like the knot were killed by the barrel-full for food. The ones that survived their journey on a "Cape Cod packet for Boston" without spoiling sold for "ten cents per dozen," while the ones that had rotted were "thrown overboard" on arrival (*Birds*, 1894, 136, 137).[17] Writing about the passenger pigeon, an important food source for Indigenous people and settlers alike, he reports on the massive hunts on the bird, with at one time "[a]t least five hundred men ... engaged in netting pigeons [in Petosky, Michigan] and sending them to market." It was believed that each netter "captured 20,000 birds during the season," with as many as "two carloads ... shipped south on the railroad each day." There seemed to be no end to the abundance of this bird, but it is now extinct (184).[18] While McIlwraith generally accepted the need to kill birds for food and included information on tasty or unpalatable meat in his book, he disapproved of hunting for sport, claiming that the activities of collectors were "more refined and elevating" than those of the "ordinary sportsman." The latter cared only about "the number he brings home at night" whereas the "collector [must] exercise his skill" in ensuring that the beauty of the bird is not destroyed when it is killed so that he has "feathered gems" to bring home "to enrich his cabinet" (354–5).

Despite McIlwraith's objections to the killing of birds for sport, collectors' activities also affected the survival of certain species. Historians of ornithology have explained that in the nineteenth and early twentieth centuries, "the gun ruled supreme as the natural tool for studying birds" because neither binoculars nor cameras were sufficiently advanced to replace the weapon (D. Lewis 5),

---

17 McIlwraith cites Mackay, "Observations on the Knot (*Tringa Canutus*)." The latter explains the procedure of "fire-lighting," which was for "two men to start out after dark at half tide, one of them to carry a lighted lantern, the other to reach and seize the birds, bite their necks, and put them in a bag slung over the shoulder" (29). Mackay also wrote a detailed description of the practice: see Mackay, "Fire-lighting."

18 McIlwraith draws on William Brewster's "The Present Status of the Wild Pigeon (*Ectopistes Migratorius*)."

but a modern reader of McIlwraith's book and those of his contemporaries will find it difficult to accept their authors' "shotgun ornithology" (Quinn) and the conclusion that, in order for the beauty of a bird to be enjoyed, it must be killed. "Once when driving north in the township of Beverley," McIlwraith writes in a particularly striking scene, "a cream-colored specimen [of the flicker] kept ahead of me for half a mile. How beautiful he looked in the rich autumnal sunlight, as with long swoops he passed from tree to tree by the roadside! I could not but admire him, and that was all I could do, for I was unarmed" (*Birds*, 1894, 253). The American naturalist John Burroughs, in introducing Neltje Blanchan's *Bird Neighbors* (1897), insisted that "the bird in the bush is worth much more than the bird in the hand" (Burroughs xi), and Ernest Thompson Seton made his plea for "camera-hunting" in 1900.[19] By the turn of the century, however, McIlwraith's work in ornithology was over, and it is doubtful in any case that he would have forsaken the habits of a lifetime.

The moment of observing the flicker, although it has him longing for his gun, is remarkable for its gentleness, but birds were trophies, and a rare specimen produced a "tingling sensation" (*Birds*, 1894, 360) and was given pride of place in the bird cases. His treasures included an evening grosbeak, "the first of the species which came into [Thomas McIlwraith's] possession" in 1863, and a "Summer Red-bird," "shot ... in the bush above the reservoir" and "the only one of the species I have ever heard of being found in Ontario" (CB). A bald eagle, one of the most spectacular items in McIlwraith's collection, occupied most of a case by itself, paired only with a "weasel-stoat-ermine." Innkeeper John Dynes on the Beach – a distinctive geographical feature of Hamilton – baited the bird with strychnine when it proved impossible for anyone to get close enough to shoot it, and in admiration of its beauty, McIlwraith "kept [the bird] living for a week at the end of which time his life was taken to save the plumage" (CB). As is typical of trophy hunters, fierce resistance increased the attraction of a bird. Thus, a male great horned owl, to which McIlwraith refers as "he," was kept "in a wire enclosure for several days" and got "so enraged" when a "farmer – a bird man" was taken to see him that he "shook his enclosure asunder" and flew off. McIlwraith and visitor pursued the owl by buggy until they found him "sitting on a lower branch [of a tree], and shot him" (CB). It is ironical that McIlwraith's writerly talent in evoking the power of birds before he and other hunters got to them has in the long run given them greater permanence than his carefully prepared skins and stuffed specimens (see Irmscher).

Thomas was one of several naturalists in the extended family that included Andrew's father-in-law John Goldie, a trained horticulturalist who – before

---

19 See Greer and Cameron, 38. Most of the shift to birdwatching they discuss postdates the period relevant to McIlwraith's activities.

emigrating to Canada in 1844 – was employed by the Botanical Gardens in Glasgow, studied under William Hooker of Kew Gardens, became acquainted with the botanist Frederick Pursh during two tours of North America, and assisted in the creation of the Botanical Gardens in St. Petersburg, Russia ("John Goldie"). Andrew, who often accompanied his brother on his shooting expeditions in the 1850s, tried his hand at taxidermy but decided that skinning a loon was "a very tough and dirty job" (*MM*, 24 April 1857, 80). Instead, Andrew – characterized as "thoughtful, retiring and quiet in demeanour" by his pastor – preferred catching and mounting butterflies and collecting wildflowers (Dickson 306–8). By contrast, Thomas's achievements in ornithology began to attract public attention soon after he came to Hamilton until, by the time of his death, he was "recognized everywhere as the highest authority" on the birds of his province ("Old Resident"). The ornithologist J.H. Fleming, who purchased McIlwraith's collection after his death, covetously referred to it in an unfortunate figure of speech as "the fleshpots of Egypt."[20] As early as 1860, McIlwraith won the first of numerous Canadian prizes for his work. This was for "his cases containing 180 mounted birds ... at the 15th Provincial Exhibition of the Agricultural Association of Upper Canada" ("Flashlights"),[21] and was followed in 1864 by first prize for "Canadian Birds, stuffed, named, and classified" ("Nineteenth Annual Exhibition" 332) in a competition adjudicated by William Hincks, the University of Toronto's first professor of natural history. In 1860 and 1861, respectively, McIlwraith published a "List of Birds observed in the vicinity of Hamilton, C.W., arranged after the system of Audubon," as well as "Notices of Birds observed near Hamilton, C.W." Both items appeared in the *Canadian Journal*, a publication of the Canadian Institute edited by Hincks.

These publications immediately extended McIlwraith's scientific connections beyond Ontario. In 1860, he visited James Macpherson LeMoine, lawyer, polymath, and author of *L'Ornithologie du Canada* (1860–1), at Spencer Grange in Sainte-Foy, where the two walked "in a musing mood" along "[o]ne of the umbrageous, winding avenues" near LeMoine's property (Lemoine, "Thomas McIlwraith" 91). The romantic vocabulary is LeMoine's as is his extravagant reference to McIlwraith as "the Laird of Cairnbrae" (91), but despite their differences in personal style, the two got along well, and reminisced about Audubon who, on his way to Labrador twenty-odd years earlier, had stopped off at Spencer Grange as guest of its previous owner, Henry Atkinson. A merchant, collector of antiques, and horticulturalist, Atkinson

---

20 J.H. Fleming, undated letter (probably 25 or 26 January 1904), James Henry Fleming Fonds, ROM, SC29 Box 6.

21 According to T.F. McIlwraith's *DCB* entry on Thomas McIlwraith, "Flashlights" appears to have been jointly written by James Little Baillie, Percy Parker Ghent, and Thomas Forsyth McIlwraith, the ornithologist's grandson.

was no doubt delighted to be shown "a portfolio containing the engravings to be embodied in [Audubon's] projected work, 'The Quadrupeds of America'" (J. Cooper 512). In one of his *Maple Leaves*, a series of "budgets of legendary, historical, critical, and sporting intelligence" that bear witness to their author's eclectic interests, LeMoine included a letter from McIlwraith dated May 1861 regarding "the recent appearance of a flock of pelicans" in Burlington Bay, and he reprinted most of the *Canadian Journal's* "Notices of Birds Observed Near Hamilton, C.W." (LeMoine, *Maple Leaves* 189–90, 191–206). The friendship continued by mail for decades, and thirty years later, LeMoine enthusiastically welcomed the second edition of *The Birds of Ontario*. He also acknowledged McIlwraith's son Kennedy, a medical doctor by 1894 as well as a bird enthusiast who published his observations in *The Auk*,[22] as a worthy successor to "the name of his respected father" (LeMoine, "Thomas McIlwraith" 91). Most of LeMoine's tribute went to quoting at length from his own ornithological work, perhaps in the nervous realization that his old friend had long overtaken him in the study of birds and that some compensatory self-promotion was in order. The connection between the two was strong enough, however, to have the Reverend Duncan Anderson dedicate his poem "The Arctic Owl or, A Naturalist's Dream" in his collection *Lays of Canada* (1890) to both of them.

McIlwraith's stature was impressively recognized in 1883 when, as mentioned earlier, he became one of only three Canadian founding members of the AOU, along with Montague Chamberlain and W.E. Saunders, a businessman and pharmacologist, respectively, for whom ornithology was – as it was for McIlwraith – a parallel occupation. The publication of *The Birds of Ontario* three years later later strengthened McIlwraith's reputation. The first edition appeared in 1886, published by the Hamilton Association for the Advancement of Literature, Science, and Art, followed by a second, extensively revised and illustrated edition in 1894, jointly published by T. Fisher Unwin in London and William Briggs in Toronto and dedicated to the governor general's wife, the Marchioness of Aberdeen. McIlwraith's reputation was such that John Macoun of the Geological Survey of Canada approached him in the late 1880s about undertaking a joint survey of the birds of Canada. As will be discussed later in this chapter, McIlwraith was enthusiastic but the prospect was undermined by the Survey's internal politics, and to his intense regret the collaboration was not approved (see Waiser 93–4, 103). Instead, Macoun co-authored a *Catalogue of Canadian Birds* (1900–4) with his son James Melville Macoun.

---

22 See K.C. McIlwraith, "Prothonotary Warbler."

Family Obligations

Alongside his activities in ornithology, there were McIlwraith's obligations to his large family, financial and otherwise. It is true that Hamiltonians occasionally turned to him when they required a particularly fine bird to give away as a gift, and they presumably paid for the favour. Thus, the sewing-machine manufacturer R.M. Wanzer requested a box of birds to take along to the Old Country, where he intended to have them stuffed before presenting them as a Canadian memento (WIK, 29 May 1884). For McIlwraith's hobby to generate money seems to have been the exception, however, and more typically a good portion of the family's budget went to the purchase of guns and ammunition, taxidermist equipment, books, magazines, and rare birds, and to postage to send packages with bird skins across North America. Kennedy, the only one of McIlwraith's children to share his enthusiasm, reports on his father's willingness to pay top price for red grosbeaks when he found himself competing with someone else for specimens: "someone, we could not find who, had engaged a darkey boy to shoot Red Grosbeaks @ 50 cents per doz. Father told him to bring in any Red ones he got to the office, and he would give him 10 cents a piece for them" (19 January 1884). (The "darkey boy" and other Black citizens mentioned in the McIlwraith archive are taken up in the next chapter). Likewise, in the absence of an appropriate collection of books in the public library, Andrew's journal repeatedly describes shopping expeditions with his brother to purchase expensive volumes for his reference library such as Audubon's *A Synopsis of the Birds of North America* (1839) and John Cassin's *Illustrations of the Birds of California, Texas, Oregon, British and Russian America* (1856) (*MM*, 20 February 1858, 144). The painstaking documentation of ornithological literature in *The Birds of Ontario* suggests easy access to such works on Thomas's own shelves, along with the latest issues of *The Auk, Forest and Stream, Canadian Sportsman and Naturalist, Canadian Horticulture and Home Magazine*, the *Canadian Journal*, and other specialist magazines. When he sought scientific advice about his book from Joel Asaph Allen, then at Harvard's Museum of Comparative Zoology, he confirmed that in addition to Audubon's *Synopsis* he had "beside [him]" Jacob P. Giraud's *The Birds of Long Island* (1844), Elliott Coues's *Birds of the Northwest* (1874), Winfrid A. Stears's *New England Bird Life* (1883), Coues's *Key to North American Birds*, in both the "new and old" editions (1872, 1884), as well as the "9th vol.: R.R. Reports."[23] At times, McIlwraith became as

---

23 Thomas McIlwraith, letter to Joel Asaph Allen, 1 June 1885. Thomas McIlwraith Fonds, R7460-0-6-E, LAC. Photocopies obtained by Thomas F. McIlwraith (Mississauga) in 1985. No reproduction copy number noted. The "R.R. Reports" presumably refer to the reports produced by the Pacific Railroad Surveys; see J. Moore.

enchanted with the beauty of a book about birds as by the birds described in it. A.K. Fisher's *Report on the Hawks and Owls of the United States in their Relation to Agriculture* (1893) was one such work, and McIlwraith lovingly consulted the volume as he finished work on the second edition of *The Birds of Ontario*: it was "neatly bound [with] twenty-six beautiful, colored illustrations" and "nothing seem[ed] wanting which should be there" (*Birds*, 1894, 189).[24]

As his children's tributes underline, Thomas McIlwraith's love of birds did not isolate him from his family. He appears to have been a good provider who handled money with responsibility and, given the family's apparent prosperity, also with some aplomb. Andrew entrusted him regularly with the investment of his savings. As a result, Thomas's wife and children took his relative indifference to any occupation that did not have to do with birds in stride. There were apparently no complaints about either the expense or the clutter caused by an accumulation of stuffed birds around the house. Instead, we hear Mary Park's indulgent defence of her husband in eleven-year-old Jean's explanation that "he doesnt smoke or do anything else that's nasty" (FA, 21 March 1870), and Mrs. McIlwraith occasionally brought birds home from the market that she thought would interest him. An "unfortunate day" for the bird cases meant entertainment for the young McIlwraiths, especially as their father accompanied the repairs with muttered expressions of self-reproach:

> Early this afternoon Papa thought he would be awful smart in moving the cases when just when he was thinking how nice he was doing it down [came] one of the smaller cases; but the worse [sic] of it was that he did it himself; if it had been anybody else, he could have had somebody to blame, which would have been some consolation. (FA, 23 March 1870)

For McIlwraith, family duty, civic obligations, and ornithology were at best one and the same, for then none distracted him from the others. Family and ornithology were splendidly combined in his collaboration with his son Kennedy, but ornithology could also be turned to civic advantage. "Of Birds and Bird Matters," the introduction to the 1886 edition of *The Birds of Ontario*, first delivered as a lecture before the Hamilton Association for the Advancement of Literature, Science, and Art, may have been one such opportunity. He gladly presented a paper to the Fruit Growers' Association of Ontario about the English sparrow and the damage caused by it (see "The English Sparrow"), was available to judge displays of taxidermy locally or at the Toronto Industrial Exhibition, or to "read a paper on birds before the Teachers' Association in the school room of Wesley

---

24 According to the First World War letters of T.F. McIlwraith (1899–1964), a third edition was being considered, but nothing came of these plans.

[United] Church" when the school inspector requested it. "[N]obody hurt," he drily concluded about the latter engagement (WIK, 20 February 1890). He also advised a reader of the Fruit Growers' Association's *Canadian Horticulture and Home Magazine* – who had his own information from a newspaper forwarded from Bath, England – on whether or not it was a good idea to import starlings to Canada as "useful insect destroyers" ("The Starling"). He did, however, extricate himself from casting his vote when Isaac Buchanan challenged Allan Napier MacNab as member of Parliament in 1854. Instead, McIlwraith took "[his] skiff down the Bay," where he came on "three cormorants preening their plumage in the sun" (CB). He shot one of them and put it in a glass case.

McIlwraith's impatience to get on with his true interest rather than attend to his business did occasionally clash with other people's ideas of everyday decorum. The incident is not as gruesome as Ernest Thompson Seton's efforts to dispose of a decomposing dog in the Paris sewers that he had dissected in his room (Seton 292), but McIlwraith still provoked excitement when during a business trip to Quebec City he purchased a hawk owl in the market and "skinned [the bird] with his pen-knife in his hotel room." He dropped the remains in the waste-paper basket, causing the maid to report that "a body had been found in room 24" ("Flashlights"). Eventually, his preoccupation with birds became so all-consuming that on a rainy February morning, a month away from the robin's first appearance in March (an event important enough to be announced in the local paper), he could be found sitting in his office at the wharf, observing that "[e]verything [was] miserable blue being the prevailing colour" (WIK, 14 February 1890).

In later years, Jean appears to have become more critical of her father, possibly because she recognized in him her own inclination to become completely absorbed by her various enthusiasms, although these, unlike her father's, tended to be relatively short-lived. In her novel "Smiling Water," written after his death, she transforms McIlwraith into an amateur botanist who, immersed in the study of rare plants and expensive books, takes a casual approach to his business, allows for a "happy-go-lucky style" in his house, and overburdens his exhausted wife with responsibilities: "He contented himself with going through the world as easily as the world would let him" (12). Perhaps, in addition to numerous personal reasons, there was some underlying resentment against her father in Jean's decision to move to New York after her mother's death in January 1901. She nursed Mrs. McIlwraith after a stroke but then left it to her older brother and his wife to look after their father until he died two years to the day after his wife. In his final years, McIlwraith's mental and physical health broke down severely. As described by Jean and his grandson (FHEP, J.N. McIlwraith to F.H. Eckstorm, 14 July 1902; "Genealogy"), his symptoms, such as depression and kidney failure, may have been the normal result of old age but it is also possible that he, like other ornithologists, suffered from the long-term effects of arsenic poisoning (see D. Lewis 97).

When the first and second editions of *The Birds of Ontario* were first published, however, both this radical decline and Jean's criticism of her father
were as yet well in the future, and the family's tolerant response to Thomas
McIlwraith's passion for birds influenced their style of social communication generally. This was vividly illustrated when John Henderson Holt of the
Holt-Renfrew store fell "violently in love" with McIlwraith's daughter Nellie at
the International Exhibition of Science, Art and Industry in Glasgow in 1888.
Holt complained that she took her time to register his growing devotion: had
"she ... not notice[d] that he was neglecting his business for her?" he finally
prodded, only to be told that to a McIlwraith this was not necessarily cause
for concern because "her family was always prepared to neglect its business"
("Genealogy"). Indeed, any man who came courting at Cairnbrae did well to
show appropriate enthusiasm for birds in addition to proving that he could
support a wife. Even a few years before their encounter in Glasgow, Holt had
commended himself to Nellie's father by sending ptarmigan skins from Quebec, while daughter Mary's husband, the Reverend Robert Service from Detroit, was treated to a bird-shooting expedition when he came visiting later that
year (WIK, 25 February, 25 August 1885).

This interplay between convention and resistance to it also affects McIlwraith's writing about ornithology. Throughout *The Birds of Ontario*, McIlwraith projects his society's expectations for the ideal citizen onto birds, and he
classifies their actions as intelligent, ambitious, and sociable when he approves
and as stupid or overbearing when he does not. His standards for the ideal
avian family are high, and at times his expectations for their conduct seem to
exceed the ones he has for humans, including himself. Although his tone is
often humorous, he is critical of birds that neglect their spousal or parental
duties, or avoid their obligations towards their young altogether, as does the
cuckoo, or that ignore the traditional division between male and female roles.
In speculating about the reasons for bird migration, he observes that " 'love
of the nesting ground' and 'strong home affection' ... are usually strongest in
the female sex," and he scolds male ducks for "getting together in flocks ... in
the open water" once mating is complete and "ignor[ing] all further family responsibilities" (*Birds*, 1894, 14). Showy mating rituals like those of the ruff, in
which the males "charge each other with a great deal of fuss and flutter" (154),
are cited with fascination but also a certain degree of disapproval. Sometimes
there is so much commentary of this kind in the first edition that the second
trims some of it, perhaps because the original would have provoked probing
questions from the children who were specifically included in the anticipated
readership of the 1894 version. For the Wilson's phalarope, for instance, McIlwraith notes in the 1886 edition that the "female is the largest and most gaily
attired" and that "from choice or necessity the eggs are incubated by the male."
He cryptically adds that "in some other respects their 'domestic relations' are

not in accordance with the recognized rules of propriety," but that he prefers to "leave that part of the history without further comment" (*Birds*, 1886, 89). This latter addition, which probably would have increased the young reader's curiosity rather than deflected it, is left out in the 1894 edition.

The practice of anthropomorphism in the Victorian study of ornithology has been characterized as a tool to reinforce the "passive and dutiful roles" expected of Victorian women (Greer and Guelke 333). In McIlwraith's case, however, these projections double as an oblique form of life writing with more complicated results: he does endorse society's conventions of propriety but practical experience has taught him that some of these rules may be difficult to enforce, both in the life histories of birds and in the human lives around him. His earthy sense of humour has him describe the American bittern as producing "love notes" that make him sound "as if he had recently taken a violent emetic" (*Birds*, 1894, 106). This is one instance from a rich repertoire of parallels between birds and humans that draws on life in a house crowded with seven children. McIlwraith disapproves of "whining" and "ferocity" as much in the birds as in his young family, and his own brood has taught him to recognize the "dignified look of injured innocence" displayed by the American rough-legged hawk when suspected of marauding among the chickens because "the evidence now goes to show that he never touched a hen in his life" (207). Birds mimic humans, and animals mimic each other: the English sparrow is a "pugnacious tramp," the great horned owl "a perfect flying tiger," and the canvas-back dives into the water "with a curve," much like Hamilton Beach boys doing "a header" into the lake (413, 235, 79). But he readily admits defeat when the birds' behaviour cannot be captured by human categories, and when the usual categories do not apply to the humans of his acquaintance either. He repeatedly cites his fellow ornithologists' efforts to render the songs of birds in human language, but he is not convinced that it can be persuasively done. Thus, the black-throated green warbler "announces its arrival ... by its characteristic notes, which are readily recognized when heard in the woods, but difficult to translate into our language" (371). He questions the necessity of subspecies for birds like the hairy woodpecker because, as the father of a tall daughter, he concludes that "we see among the members of the human family individuals who differ in size far more than the woodpeckers do, and yet we do not make subspecies of them" (244).

Sons and Daughters

This reluctance to assign overly rigid categories to either humans or birds is also apparent in McIlwraith's outlook on gender in the practise of ornithology. Many of his views echo conventions of his time, including the notion that the outdoor exercise associated with bird hunting would help to turn a boy into a man, especially when this activity included not only the effective handling of gun and knife but also "killing, skinning, dissecting, and stuffing birds" (Greer and Guelke 326). A lengthy review in the *Canadian Baptist* insistently refers to "boys" as the appropriate readers of *The Birds of Ontario*; in this way they would be taught both manliness and patriotism by practising ornithology:

> Those who have boys who are old enough to look around them and ask questions should prepare themselves to be the companions of their children by reading such books as that which Mr. McIlwraith has written, or such as Mr. Ernest Seton Thompson has given us in "Wild Animals I have Known." And those whose boys are not quite old enough to ask many questions had better be getting ready. For it helps to give a boy a love for his home and country, and to give him a capacity for innocent pleasure, if he learns to know the birds that God has given to teach and to help and to entertain us.[25]

Dr. George Alexander MacCallum, a bird enthusiast frequently cited in McIlwraith's book, agreed that *The Birds of Ontario* was "really a book which should be in the hands of every boy or student of [ornithology]." The naturalist Robert Elliott praised the work as a suitable gift to "the eager boy," although in this case a rather emotional one "who peers with wondering eyes into the deftly-woven nest of some beautiful, unknown feathered tenant of his father's underwoods and sighs and is silent."[26] Speaking for the boys themselves, decoy maker Peter Pringle called McIlwraith's book the "Bible" of his childhood (qtd. in Reeve 60). Not a single informant cited in *The Birds of Ontario* is female, and the world of ornithology as described there and in McIlwraith's other writing about birds is entirely male: a domestic servant who forgets to note down the donor's name when a bird is delivered is the only woman he mentions (CB).

Nevertheless, he does not address himself as emphatically to "boys" in *The Birds of Ontario* as his reviewers suggest he does. In acknowledging that "[a]ll our Canadian boys and girls are familiar with the Snowbird" (*Birds*, 1894, 311), he still follows convention because he implies that watching birds rather than shooting them is an appropriate activity for girls (see Greer and Guelke). His introduction, however, insistently uses a pedagogical "we" or the passive voice, refers to the "writer" of the recommended logbook, and addresses his "younger readers," "youthful readers," and "juvenile readers." He maintains this inclusive approach throughout (*Birds*, 1894, 11, 15, 311). Perhaps his hesitation

---

25 TFMP, J.L.G., "Browsings among Books: *The Birds of Ontario*," *The Canadian Baptist*, n.d. [but after publication of the 2nd edition in 1894], 586, clipping.

26 Advertisement for *Birds*, 1894, Thomas McIlwraith, letter to Joseph Grinnell, 30 April 1895, Joseph Grinnell papers, BANC MSS C-B 995 box 13, Bancroft Library, UCB. On Robert Elliott, see Moffat 281.

to separate boys and girls into sharply separate categories had something to do with observing his daughter Jean, who submitted to conventional expectations of femininity only when they appealed to her, which was not often. Neither parent appears to have been bothered by her tomboyish ways, and if Kennedy had not shared his father's enthusiasm and Jean had been inclined towards ornithology, she, too, might have become her father's companion. There were precedents for this practice because several daughters among Thomas McIlwraith's acquaintances mastered outdoor skills. Most notable among them was Jean's friend Fannie Hardy Eckstorm, daughter of Manly Hardy, a fur trader and ornithologist from Maine and one of Thomas McIlwraith's correspondents (see Krohn). In a fitting introduction to her close collaboration with her father in his naturalist work, Eckstorm "played school with fox skins stuffed with hay as [her] pupils" in her childhood, later "remember[ing] how their black legs used to hang down and their pointed noses would stick up as if they were ranged in line" (MacDougall 9). Neither of Eckstorm's brothers shared their father's enthusiasm to the same extent, nor did her sisters. Although the social dictates of their time restricted their ambitions, other female naturalists like Florence Merriam, Eckstorm's fellow student at Smith College, were supported in their scientific interests by their fathers, brothers, and husbands.

Given his extensive reading in naturalist literature, McIlwraith must have been aware of contemporary discussions that not only limited women to certain approaches to ornithology, but also declared different types of nature study off-limits for men. His correspondent Robert Ridgway at the Smithsonian, for example, was concerned that "the Love of Trees and Flowers" might be "a Sign of Effeminacy,"[27] while forty years earlier the physician J.F.A. Adams considered it necessary, in an essay frequently quoted in research on the role of women in nineteenth-century science (for example, in Slack 77), to defend botany as "a suitable study for young men." By unfortunate implication, he diminished the women involved in the field as dilettantes (J.F.A. Adams). Although botany did not become as much of an obsession with him as the study of birds, McIlwraith loved his geraniums and was delighted when the white lilac burst into bloom, and as young children Jean and her younger brother Hugh helped to dig up wildflowers and ferns for the rockery at Cairnbrae. While they were gathering flowers in the early morning under his direction, they learned to identify birdsong (FA, 4 May 1870), but neither Jean nor Hugh appears to have had any strong desire to shoot and skin birds, and Tom and Jack were only mildly interested. When the collector J.H. Fleming[28] purchased Thomas McIlwraith's

---

27 Robert Ridgway, "Is the Love of Trees and Flowers a Sign of Effeminacy?" *Olney Times* (IL), 28 March 1925, 5, qtd. in D. Lewis 201. Wetmore gives 1926 for this publication. The original article has not been located.

28 On Fleming, see Quinn.

bird skins, he met Hugh to whom, oddly and to Kennedy's irritation, their father's bird skins had been left – this in spite of the fact that he "did not know a skin from a dead bird and frankly said so."[29] By contrast, Kennedy was keenly interested in ornithology while the only "botany" to which Kennedy's logbook admits is collecting moss, presumably to protect the bird skins he and his father sent to collectors in Canada and the United States, and also to create small dioramas for the display of stuffed birds. For her part, Jean McIlwraith became a keen gardener whose alter ego in "Smiling Water" locates rare plants for her father, among them "aesclepias" and "some blue fringed gentians" (213).

Father and Son

For a few years while he was a teenager, Kennedy and Thomas McIlwraith became a father-and-son team of the kind that appears to have been quite common among naturalists. Thus, the Smithsonian's Robert Ridgway "spent a great deal of time [with his father]" in his childhood, "sometimes going out at 3:00 am to hunt wild turkeys" (D. Lewis 5). Other ornithological pairings included J. Parker Norris Sr. and Jr. from Philadelphia, the Australians Neville Henry Cayley and Neville William Cayley, and, in Canada, William Edwin Brooks and Allan Brooks, as well as the Macouns. McIlwraith was particularly inspired by the partnership of John and James Macoun when he decided – rather abruptly, it appears – to train Kennedy in ornithology.[30] Begun as an experiment, these joint excursions became the joy of McIlwraith's later years, so much so that he became reluctant to go out alone on bird expeditions when Kennedy was not available.

The record of this collaboration is Kennedy's logbook "What I Know About Birds and How I Came to Know It," begun in January 1882 and kept until 1890, when all the pages had been used up. Although Kennedy started out as his father's apprentice, he came to be repeatedly cited as "K.C. McIlwraith," an experienced ornithologist. The format he adopted for his logbook was later recommended to young students of birds in the 1894 edition of *The Birds of Ontario*, and in general the teamwork of father and son doubled as a trial run for some of the revisions to and the pedagogic program behind this book:

---

29 J.H. Fleming, undated letter (probably 25 or 26 January 1904), James Henry Fleming Fonds, ROM, SC29 Box 6.

30 See Thomas McIlwraith to John Macoun, [?] March 1884, Rudolph Martin Anderson and Mae Bell Allstrand Fonds, MG 30, Series B 40, vol. 15, file 8, Ornithology – Department of Interior Files (1884–1890), LAC. It has not been possible to check Macoun's letterbooks. Waiser cites these as located in the National Museums of Canada Library. The holdings of this library have since been dispersed to other archives, but despite a thorough search the current location of Macoun's letterbooks has not been confirmed.

For a beginner I would recommend a plain page on which to enter notes of the
birds seen at such a place on such a date, with any facts relating to their numbers,
occupation or manners which may have been observed.

When this book has been kept for two or three seasons, even the writer of it will
be astonished at the amount and variety of the information accumulated, and the
reading of it in after years will recall many of the pleasant experiences of the time
when the entries were made. (*Birds*, 1894, 11)

The diary paused for three years beginning September 1886, presumably because Kennedy became increasingly busy with studies and travel, including a
visit to the Natural History Museum in South Kensington in 1888. His father
wrote fondly to John Macoun about the hours his "boy Kenny" spent "gazing
in delight at the collection of native birds" and the details he passed on about
displays that gave "the life history of [a] species in one group," with male, female, and "the nest being placed as nearly in the natural position as possible."[31]
In January 1889, Thomas McIlwraith suddenly decided to resume the journal
himself and make his own regular entries, including reports on Kennedy's ornithological successes. Because he found that the book was initially started at
the wrong end, he first swivelled it to the correct position. Nor is it only the
layout that takes a different direction. While Kennedy kept a log, strictly and –
though probably so instructed – rather numbingly focused on the subject of
birds with none of his father's eloquence, Mr. McIlwraith wrote a more conversational journal, covering also his business and travels, deaths in the family,
including the death of a horse, work in his garden, dealing with the furnace
and the roof of the coal shed, and seeing his brother for the first time after
thirty-three years when William passed through Canada on his return from
Scotland to Australia.

At the beginning of the log, Kennedy notes as a reason for their joint excursions that his father had always been "very fond of collecting birds and also
of his children," but there was a specific and urgent reason to take Kennedy
on these outings. McIlwraith meant to expose his youngest to lots of fresh air
and physical activity, in the hope that they would strengthen him because, as
his father confided to Macoun, he "was rather delicate."[32] Kennedy (no matter
what his age, he was "Kenny" or "K." to his father except when he is cited as the
ornithologist "K.C. McIlwraith") worried his family with poor health. These

---

31 Thomas McIlwraith to John Macoun, 18 February 1889, Rudolph Martin Anderson and Mae
    Bell Allstrand Fonds, MG 30, Series B 40, vol. 15, file 9, Ornithology – Department of Inte-
    rior Files (1884–1890), LAC.
32 Thomas McIlwraith to John Macoun, [7?] March 1884, Rudolph Martin Anderson and Mae
    Bell Allstrand Fonds, MG 30, Series B 40, vol. 15, file 8, Ornithology – Department of Inte-
    rior Files (1884–1890), LAC.

concerns obviously predate the beginning of their bird expeditions in 1882, but they also continued for several years after. In August 1889, Kennedy came down with respiratory illness serious enough to leave him for weeks unable even to sit up in bed. He briefly resumed his journal in April 1890, with short addenda by his father, and the sketchy back-and forth makes for a touching dialogue tenuously replacing their earlier outdoors companionship. A year after completion of the log, Kennedy's condition worsened, and on a visit from Michigan his brother Jack resolved that it was time to take him to New York for consultation with the lung specialist Dr. Alfred Lebbeus Loomis. The diagnosis was pleurisy, which was serious enough but still better news than the dreaded tuberculosis, and immediate steps were taken to have Kennedy interrupt his studies and to get him to the warmer climate of North Carolina, perhaps at one of the state's many sanitaria such as the Mountain Sanitarium for Pulmonary Diseases in Asheville.[33] "What I Know" closes four years before Kennedy's graduation from medicine at the University of Toronto, preceded by "a year abroad studying obstetrics at the Rotunda Hospital in Dublin and at Queen Charlotte's Hospital in London" (Shorter 526). Coincidentally, Thomas McIlwraith published the second edition of *The Birds of Ontario* the same year his son completed his medical training. Kennedy's name joined his father's in *The Naturalists' Directory of the United States and Canada* in 1895.

A year before McIlwraith's departure for New York to attend the inaugural meeting of the AOU (WIK, 25 September 1883) and four years before the publication of the first edition of *The Birds of Ontario*, father and son began a routine that, as soon as the days were getting longer, had them rise at 4:30 or 5:00 a.m. and drive by democrat buggy to farms, woods, swamps, and shores in and around Hamilton or row across the bay to places where birds were known to gather. If an early morning expedition could not be arranged, then McIlwraith waited for his son outside his school at 4:00 p.m. and both were disappointed when, for one reason or another, they missed each other. McIlwraith appears to have given instructions on what was to be noted in Kennedy's logbook, and at the beginning there are occasional annotations in a different hand to suggest that the entries were being monitored. Kennedy recorded the tally of birds shot on any given expedition, noting the species, the number obtained, and sometimes their sex. When a bird could not be immediately identified, it was described provisionally ("a plain-looking warbler which we haven't got the name of yet") and, after consultation of reference books and other specimens at home, it was given a name: "female black-throated blue" (WIK, [?] May 1882). They were excited when they got a bird that Mr. McIlwraith "had never shot before,"

---

33 McIlwraith, Jean N. Letter from Jean N. McIlwraith to Elizabeth Smith Shortt. 31 January 1891. UWL, WA-10, File 280, ESS.

such as a "Blue-gray Gnatcatcher" (15 May 1882). On a fine day in spring, the catch could be enormous, and Kennedy never fails to produce the full list:

This morning Papa went out to Flock Bush above Calder's, and in the afternoon I went to the bush west of McNab's; the result of the expeditions was as follows: (4) Blackburnian Warbler, (2) Black-throated Green Warbler, (10) Black-throated Blue Warbler, (1) Red-headed Woodpecker, (1) Whippoorwill, (1) Blue Yellow-back Warbler, (1) Chestnut-sided Warbler, (3) Black-and-yellow Warblers, (1) Rose-breasted Grosbeak, (1) Solitary Vireo, (1) Little Flycatcher, (1) Redstart male, (1) Indigo Bird, (1) Yellow-Red Poll Warbler, (1) Water Thrush, and a Vireo the kind of which we have not yet decided [a footnote clarifies: brotherly love vireo]: in all 21 birds. We saw besides these: the Great-crested Flycatcher, White-crowned Sparrow, Scarlet Tanager and heard lots of Winter-wrens singing. (WIK, 11 May 1883)

To locate flocks of birds, Kennedy was trained to identify birdsong such as the "Winter-wrens singing" in the preceding scene. He records, "we heard some kind of a warbler singing in the bush, which we thought was the Maryland Yellow-throat" (WIK, 9 June 1882), and "we heard Nuthatch but as we went farther into the bush we did not see a bird" (1 April 1882). He studied behaviour such as a bird's efforts to deflect attention from its eggs or fledglings: a sandpiper "ran away from us pretending to be lame so as to draw us away from his nest. I fired at him but missed him" (24 May 1882). Sometimes he shot a bird that was in the process of killing or eating another, including a hawk with "a kingbird in its claws" (17 May 1884) and a shrike: "I shot two 'Big Shrikes' to-day. One of them I saw killing a sparrow. He had the head of it in his throat when I shot him" (19 December 1882).

When father and son returned home from their first outing, Kennedy was introduced to the business of skinning and stuffing birds, and Jack equipped his brother with the necessary tools by producing "a nice little knife" for the first few skinning operations (WIK, 7 January 1882). Kennedy practised his taxidermist skills with "a nice little owl" to add to his collection: "It was a male. I got a female did the same with it" (7 January 1882). These lessons in taxidermy may have contributed to the section in *The Birds of Ontario* that introduces bird enthusiasts to the skills involved in "Collecting and Preparing Specimens." The scene is gruesome to the modern reader, but it is sketched as a domestic idyll, showing "the collector divest[ing] himself of his muddy boots" and "get[ting] a pair of slippers and a change of coat" (*Birds*, 1894, 18) before he attends to the birds he has brought home wrapped in paper cones and laid out in a fishing basket. Likewise, his father attentively watched Kennedy's skills with the gun and applauded when, as his "first [flying] bird," he shot "a Herring Gull in immature plumage" (WIK, 18 November 1882), or when he managed to shoot "twelve (12) [snowbirds] with one shot and three (3) with another" (21 March

1883). Mr. McIlwraith was unhappy when birds were wasted because they had been hit too hard "to be of any use" (29 April 1882), and he groaned at his son's reluctance to let go of bad habits even with several years' worth of bird expeditions behind him:

> A consultation was held on an Eider Duck ... as to whether he could be shot and could be got. Both queries being decided in the affirmative K. blazed away and as usual got him in the head which sent him dancing. We two + Smith then got on the ferry scow ... the duck was drifting and it drifted within our reach and was then retrieved in good style. (WIK, 4 February 1889)

Tracking the Weather, Mapping the Region

Because they affected the birds' behaviour, the time of day and weather were punctiliously observed, and to keep track of patterns in bird migration, Kennedy noted the dates: on 25 March 1882, for instance, towards the beginning of his lessons in ornithology, he and his father "saw a black-shouldered blackbird which Papa said was very early for them," and in early November 1883, the observant Captain Thomas Campbell, keeper of the Burlington Canal Main Lighthouse, informed them that snowbirds had been around for a couple of weeks whereas the previous year they "did not make their appearance in large quantities at least as far as we know until March 20th" (WIK, 2 November 1883). The longed-for spring generally took its time to arrive even after the Robin had sung for the first time in the season, and Kennedy's diary is full of anticipatory drama, talking about "ice 18 in. thick all over the Bay" (4 March 1883) and "no signs of ice breaking up" (11 April 1885). Even when there was "a great thaw" that caused "a perfect torrent of water coming down [the mountain]" (10 March 1884), it could take over a month for the ice to be gone completely and for warm weather to begin. As long as it was safe to do so, father and son took the cutter or sleigh out on the frozen bay to watch snowbirds and compare their winter plumage to the previous year's, but spring weather was treacherous and sometimes violent. Three days after the "ice [was] blown out of this end of the bay by a strong west-wind" (3 April 1886), Kennedy writes of

> a storm such as has seldom if ever visited this locality before. The gale was from the North-east and was accompanied, in the afternoon, by a heavy snowfall. So great was the force of the wind that the waters from the lake were forced across the beach in many places, washing out the railroad track and doing great damage to other property. (WIK, 6 April 1886)

There was no bird-shooting on Sundays, at least not when Mr. McIlwraith was around, a principle that earned him (and the Scots generally) praise in the

Canadian Baptist "for observing that respect to the Christian Sabbath which
has been such a strong factor in the national character of the stock from which
he has sprung" (J.L.G., "Browsings"). Kennedy notes: "3 Red Grosbeaks were
feeding on the berries of a mountain ash in front of our house: we did not like
to shoot them on a Sunday, but they came back on Monday and we shot two of
them" (WIK, 3 February 1884). Once he began to go out shooting on his own,
Kennedy did not observe the Sabbath quite so strictly because on Sunday, 8
February 1885, he shot a bird but records no compunction.

Along with precise times of day and meteorological conditions, Kennedy's
bird diary carefully notes the pair's itineraries that, together, create a map of
the McIlwraiths' expeditions between the Niagara Escarpment and the bay and
of the neighbourly friendships that allowed them to frequent the places where
birds were plentiful. Several locations, like "McNab's farm," were visited so often that on their return, the pair was "pretty well known by this time" (WIK,
24 May 1882). The owners of "McNab's farm" and other properties welcomed
father and son as they criss-crossed the area: "up the mountain to Mr. Calder's
house where the water reservoir is" (1 April 1882); "over the mountain on the
Ancaster Road" (7 April 1882); to the Rock Chapel (9 June 1882); "a mile past
Millgrove and ... back by the Brock Road" (23 September 1882); "12 miles
straight east on Barton St." (14 October 1882); to "out to Ancaster over the
Mountain ... and home by the Dundas Road" (31 March 1883); to " 'Inglewood'
at the head of James St." (21 April 1882); to "Bamberger's" (8 May 1883), Ainslie
Wood (15 April 1882), the Albion Mills (1 April 1882), Stoney Creek (17 April
1883), and "on the Bayshore near the Hamilton Northwestern R.R. elevator"
(14 October 1882). When he was out on his own or in the company of visiting
bird enthusiasts, Kennedy sometimes chose to walk along the railroad or wa-
terworks pipe tracks. Many times, father and son decided to go to the Beach,
where they were regular visitors in the garden of Dynes's tavern. Repeatedly,
they "got" rare birds in the " 'willow hedge' at the Beach," such as a prothonotary warbler in 1888, "the only appearance of the species in Canada so far as
known," as well as a "Hooded Warbler," likewise a "species [not met] except on
that occasion" (CB).

The brief and serviceable notations about their itineraries cited above are
Kennedy's, but when his father took over the diary the notes became elaborate,
and Thomas appeared to find it an enjoyable mnemonic exercise at the end of
the day to run over his perambulations once more. Thus, in addition to "West
Flamboro" (WIK, 29 January 1889), "Flock's Bush" (16 March 1889), "Edmonds
Bush" (22 March 1889), and "Smith's Ranch" (4 February 1889), there is the
recapitulation that "K. + I went up James S. this aft took the [first?] line west
after passing the Asylum thence south 2 or 3 miles then east to the stone road
and home down John S." (20 March 1889), as well as this particularly detailed
itinerary:

A fine bright cold day K + I went across the bay after dinner – on the bank below Oakland we got two cherry birds red tips I had 8. Thence up to Kerry's Tavern – then 1 mile east then north to near Capt. Spence's, turned at the toll gate on the mountain slope + came south via Kerry's tavern + on the ice near Brown's wharf got a purple finch in the woods (+ 1 d[itt?]o) near the shore the racers were trying the track as we came back (WIK, 25 February 1889).

These complex movements, along with switches from close-up to long shot and back again, create a panorama of McIlwraith's immediate neighbourhood, but he also employs such detailed mapping in *The Birds of Ontario* to draw out the failure of man-made borders to impede a bird's flight. The lavish three-page entry on the bald eagle creates a varied regional backdrop including Pelee Island, Niagara Falls, and Hamilton, as well as adding references to Alaska and the Aleutian Chain. Hunters are shown as they lurk near "Niagara River below the Falls," where they shoot eagles sitting "on the dead trees by the river bank and watching for any dead or dying animals that came down the stream." Juxtaposed with this lugubrious scene there is the drama of an iceboat race across the frozen Burlington Bay to pick off an eagle inexorably driven into the boat's way by the wind until he is brought down on the ice with "a flash, a crack." The sketch concentrates on the strength and intelligence of the bird but avoids anthropomorphism, and the scientific documentation is scrupulous. Always ready to acknowledge the skills of daring boys, McIlwraith concludes with a suspenseful story around the exploits of Willie Smith, one of Hamilton's "Beach boys," who demonstrates his talents as an athlete and huntsman as he races after an eagle across the ice (*Birds*, 1894, 209–11).

Ornithological Networks

Daily, McIlwraith scanned the paper for bird-related notices such as the one announcing "Pine Grosbeaks being got near Georgetown" (WIK, 9 February 1883), and a small army of people was kept busy in and near Hamilton reporting sightings and delivering birds to the wharf office and to Cairnbrae. The messengers' names were always conscientiously noted, and it was annoying when the maid took delivery of a goshawk but forgot to record "the donor's name" (CB). On the same day that the paper reported the sighting of pine grosbeaks in Georgetown, "Reid the gardener's son ... shot one or two" (WIK, 9 February 1883). The next month, "Mr. Pring from Dundurn" brought "two Cherry-birds" to the wharf office (9 March 1883). Reports of a barn owl, "the second one of that kind that has been got around here this season although they were never found in Canada before" (9 February 1883), had Thomas and his son drive to Dundas a couple of weeks later to meet the fellow who shot it. Alick Brown promised that "if he got another he would bring it to Papa" (24 February 1883).

A "young man named Kerr whose home was on the mountain near the reservoir" appeared "with a sack over his shoulder from which he shook [a golden eagle]" (CB, [?] October 1867). Although they were able to identify the species that McIlwraith wanted to obtain from them, few of these individuals appear to have been passionate bird collectors, but Cairnbrae was also a port of call for those who were, and Kennedy was helpful in handling the many visitors who sought McIlwraith's advice.

Father and son preferred to go out together, but soon after he had been instructed in the principles of bird observation and shooting, Kennedy began to venture out on solo expeditions when his father was not available. He also partnered with other male companions intermittently interested in ornithology such as his brother Tom or the Park cousins from Detroit. Kennedy willingly escorted visitors who wanted to view Mr. McIlwraith's collection of bird skins and look over his favourite birding locations. His son's readiness to pair off with others was particularly welcome to his father when he did not like the individual in question but considered it impolitic to send him away. William E. Saunders, who visited often, as did his son Percy (Kennedy's contemporary at the University of Toronto), was not a favourite. Thomas McIlwraith appears to have thought of Saunders père as "a young man possessed of a large am't of self conceit"[34] even before his antipathy was justified by Saunders's pedantic review of the first edition of The Birds of Ontario. To extricate himself from Saunders's company, McIlwraith claimed the privileges of old age by showing himself, as Saunders later reported, "disinclined to brave the dews of early morn and the other necessary vicissitudes of weather which must be encountered in field work" when the two first met "in 1883 or 1884," around the time when both became founding members of the AOU (Saunders, "In Memoriam" 1). Kennedy's bird book demonstrates that throughout the eighties there was nothing wrong with his father's health or his willingness to get up before sunrise. Indeed, Mr. McIlwraith complained in 1890 about Kennedy's new habit of getting up late, possibly an outcome of his illness.

McIlwraith was held in such respect that these visitors sometimes arrived bearing a letter of introduction, as did William Keays.[35] Naturalist and conservationist H.P Attwater called in person and corresponded by postcard,[36] and

---

34 Thomas McIlwraith, letter to William Brewster, 9 September 1887, from the Archives of the Museum of Comparative Zoology, Ernst Mayr Library, Harvard University.

35 William Keays, about whom Kennedy does not give further details, may be identical with William Jeremiah Keays, owner of the Huron Signal, railroad investor and agent in Goderich, Sarnia, and Buffalo, as well as lieutenant in the United States Union Army (whose platoon chased down and shot the assassin of Abraham Lincoln), and captain of the McPherson on Conesus Lake. See C. Baker.

36 See "Henry Philemon Attwater."

Allan Brooks, who was to become "Canada's main bird and mammal illustrator in the first half of the 20th century" (Winearls 133), learned the art of preparing bird skins from McIlwraith in 1885 when he was sixteen years old (Brooks). Between 1885 and 1890, a frequent visitor was "Ernie Thompson" – that is, Ernest Thompson Seton – then working as an illustrator in New York, preparing his book *The Birds of Manitoba* (1891), and occasionally checking in with his parents in Toronto. McIlwraith sent him bird skins on request, presumably to assist him with his illustrations, and together they served as "the natural history judges at the [Toronto Industrial Exhibition]" in 1888 (TMF, 665, 3 November 1887; 676, 11 August 1888). In spring 1890, Seton appeared at Cairnbrae on his way to study art in Paris and requested to see the collection of stuffed birds in Mr. McIlwraith's absence. Four years later, when – according to the editor of the *Oologist*, Seton's "reputation as a painter of birds [was] not surpassed ... by that of any other living artist" – he provided some of the illustrations for the second edition of *The Birds of Ontario*. Identified in the publisher's advertisement as "Naturalist to the Manitoba Government," Seton was happy to support a work that frequently cited his own observations, claiming in his praise for McIlwraith that "since the days of Gosse I believe there has been no Canadian naturalist who more happily combined accurate knowledge with a felicitous manner of expressing it."[37] Surprisingly, neither Thomas nor Kennedy is acknowledged in Seton's autobiography.

These were exchanges with individuals close enough to home for frequent personal contact if necessary. After his appointment as superintendent for the district of Ontario on the AOU's Migration Committee, however, McIlwraith began an extended correspondence with volunteers throughout Ontario and beyond who assisted him with his work. Some of these individuals did not know much, if anything, about ornithology, and he claimed that *The Birds of Ontario* sought to address the "appalling ... ignorance" in those who were unable to distinguish one bird from another.[38] To improve the situation he wanted a list that was "cheap and popular and yet correct."[39] His correspondence with these largely inexperienced volunteers tapped into an "open network" of "weak ties" that provided him with sporadically helpful information but also with the impetus to shape *The Birds of Ontario* towards a specific pedagogic goal. Conversely, there was a circle of knowledgeable individuals who represented the "closed circles" in which "strong ties" bound a specialized research community

---

37 Qtd. in advertisement for *The Birds of Ontario*, 2nd ed. *The Oologist* vol. 11, 1894, 271; on Gosse, see Wertheimer.

38 Thomas McIlwraith, letter to Joel Asaph Allen, 12 June 1885, Thomas McIlwraith Fonds, R7460-0-6-E, LAC. Photocopies obtained by Thomas F. McIlwraith (Mississauga) in 1985. No reproduction copy number noted.

39 McIlwraith to Allen, 1 June 1885.

of professionals and experienced amateurs together.[40] In the second edition of *The Birds of Ontario*, the acknowledgments have been increased to three pages from the original one, and the impression is of an expert confidently moving among his peers, ready to instruct those who want to know more. In the documentation for each species, the entries lay out where, when, and by whom each species or information about it was obtained, and in order to offer a complete picture, McIlwraith draws on "the notes of those who have visited the remote homes of the birds, at points often far apart and not easy of access" *(Birds, 1894, vii–viii)*.

Because it permitted quick and inexpensive communication, the preferred means of communication to obtain information for the Migration Committee and for his book was once again the postcard, and approximately 150 cards related to McIlwraith's work in ornithology have survived. Most of the members of the "closed circle" wrote formal letters, but some of them also found the postcard useful: W.E. Saunders, for example, switched to postcards when they turned out to be a less complicated medium: "As I'm so slow at letter-writing, let's try cards" (TMF, 657, W.E. Saunders, 6 November 1886). Almost daily, bird-related post was received at McIlwraith's home and parcels of bird skins were dispatched or received from collectors in Canada or the United States. In Ontario, correspondents wrote from Toronto, Ottawa, London, Dunnville, Chatham, Chippawa, Colchester, Cornwall, Amherstburg, Lynn Valley, Lucknow, Hyde Park, St. Thomas, Sarnia, Bowmanville, Pembroke, Ingersoll, Plover Mills, Gravenhurst, Strathroy, and Hoodstown, and there was "a man with an unspellable Dutch name, who lives at Mildmay," by whom Kennedy probably meant W.A. Schoenau (WIK, 4 April 1883). Postcards came from British Columbia and Quebec, and from a large number of American bird collectors, variously located in Warsaw (IL), Perth (MI), Saint Cloud (MN), Brookville and Rockyriver (IN), Britt (IA), New Lisbon and Boscobel (WI), Taunton (MA), Bangor and Brewer (ME), Pawtucket (RI), Danielsonville (CT), Boston, New York, Rochester, Washington, Charleston, New Orleans, Camp Verde (AZ), San Antonio and Giddings (TX), Perin Creek (NM), and San Diego and Lakeport (CA).

The resulting correspondence may not have amounted to the 3,000 to 5,500 letters produced by the Smithsonian's Spencer F. Baird, who sought "to build a national network of correspondents to aid the institution's work in the earth and life sciences" in the United States (Goldstein 576), let alone the extensive postal exchanges of prominent nineteenth-century scientists like Charles Darwin and Alexander von Humboldt, but McIlwraith's contacts nevertheless

---

40 On the role of "weak ties" and "strong ties" in the formation of scientific knowledge, see Lux
    and Cook, drawing on terminology developed by Granovetter.

illustrate that he actively participated in building the "sociable knowledge" of North American natural history and that it was customary to draw on experts and laypersons alike to collect scientific evidence (Yale). The result was "the web of co-operative and mutually supportive cross-class practices of Victorian science" (Pettit 4). The phrase "sociable knowledge" is taken from a study of early modern natural history, where it refers to the custom of circulating valuable manuscripts and books among fellow scientists, as well as to the augmentation of scientific works with textual and pictorial annotations by author or reader. Although it is of a different era, the continual revision of knowledge undertaken by McIlwraith and his associates in their correspondence serves a similar purpose. Indeed, McIlwraith impresses on readers of *The Birds of Ontario* that, though these adjustments are annoying, it is impossible to avoid the periodic "changes ... in the nomenclature, and in the arrangement of the different groups" that come with refinement of knowledge (*Birds*, 1886, 6). In other words, he encourages readers to look upon his work and similar undertakings as provisional no matter how thorough the documentation is at any given moment.

The range of McIlwraith's contacts is all more impressive as he was an autodidact and did not have the support of a governmental department like John Macoun or A.R.C. Selwyn at the Geological Survey of Canada or of an educational institution like Louis-Ovide Brunet and J.-C.-K. Laflamme at the Université Laval. Even a parish priest like Léon Provancher enjoyed helpful connections through the church, including collegial relations with Brunet, towards his research in Quebec and on his travels in North America and Europe. A tabulation of the most frequent correspondents in the collections of Brunet, Laflamme, and Provancher shows these men to have communicated extensively with scientists in Canada (of whom the majority were English-speaking), the United States, and Europe (see Duchesne).

His business and family obligations prevented McIlwraith from transatlantic travel that would have allowed him to establish personal contact with European naturalists, and he had to be content with enjoying such overseas riches by proxy through Kennedy.[41] By contrast, his contacts to ornithologists across North America were extensive, and the connections were greatly facilitated by personal acquaintance with some of them at the first meeting of the AOU in New York in 1883. Invitations reflected on McIlwraith's growing stature south of the border following this conference, such as one to give a lecture to the Ridgway Ornithological Club in Chicago (TMF, 589, H.K. Coale, 5 February 1885). As was his family's practice, he immediately followed up in writing when

---

41 Thomas McIlwraith to John Macoun, 18 February 1889, Rudolph Martin Anderson and Mae Bell Allstrand Fonds, MG 30, Series B 40, vol. 15, file 9, Ornithology – Department of Interior Files (1884–1890), LAC.

important contacts had been made. Thus he acknowledged the pleasure of meeting William Brewster of the Museum of Comparative Zoology at Harvard University shortly after the AOU meeting.[42] McIlwraith corresponded with the Smithsonian's Robert Ridgway; A.K. Fisher and Clinton Hart Merriam, both of the United States Department of Agriculture's Division of Economic Ornithology and Mammology; Joel Asaph Allen, first of the Museum of Comparative Zoology at Harvard and then of the American Museum of Natural History in New York; Joseph Grinnell, the future director of the Museum of Vertebrate Zoology at Berkeley; and Jared Potter Kirtland at the Western Reserve College in Cleveland. Several of these men were to give supportive advice when McIlwraith found it difficult to deal with competition and criticism. Aware that the appearance of a letter "could signal all one needed to know *a priori* about the rank and importance of the addressee and the education and 'good-breeding' of its writer" (Bannet 67), McIlwraith was generally careful to use professional stationery such as his personal letterhead or that of the AOU's Migration Committee. He seems to have slipped in his later years when, in his correspondence with Macoun, he also used stationery from his coal dealership although he had by then largely retired from the business. On one occasion he got his hands on letterhead from the Canadian Senate, probably from his supply of writing paper in "the small trunk in the attic" mentioned earlier. McIlwraith may have tried to impress Macoun, with whom he was eager to co-author a book on Canadian birds, or he was simply recycling whatever paper came to hand.

Volunteers and Fellow Scientists

McIlwraith's helpers throughout Ontario for his work on the AOU's Migration Committee were located using his own wide-ranging connections and through recommendation. Assistants included lighthouse keepers, captains, postmasters, farmers, fruit growers, horse breeders, fishermen, taxidermists, illustrators, and a mayor – namely, Woodstock's ambitious Thomas Cottle, who was known to receive royal visitors at his Altadore estate. D.A. Maxwell, a school inspector in Amherstburg, suggested suitable individuals in his own town, on Pelee Island, and in Cottam (TMF, 554, D.A. Maxwell, 8 April 1884). Respondents were gratified to be asked to help and flattered to be contacted by an ornithologist as well known as McIlwraith. E. Odlum from the Ottawa Field Naturalists' Club expressed satisfaction "to see such definite movement in this direction [of collecting systematic information about bird migration]" (550, E. Odlum, 27 March 1884). Others were eager to see McIlwraith's collection of bird skins and to show off their own, however modest, and to request help in

---

42   Thomas McIlwraith, letter to William Brewster, 27 October 1883, from the Archives of the Museum of Comparative Zoology, Ernst Mayr Library, Harvard University.

identifying birds. A few hinted at scientific interests in Hamilton's environment that went beyond ornithology by asking him to send small rock samples from the Niagara Escarpment.

A letter cited in *The Birds of Ontario* illustrates just how complex the relay between administrators, scientists, military people, bird catchers, and kinsmen could become and how "thickly layered" the resulting information (Yale 197). "Since writing the above," McIlwraith notes in his entry about the passenger pigeon, then swiftly nearing extinction in Ontario, "I have received a letter from Vernon Bailey, of the Department of Agriculture, Washington, dated October 14th, 1893, in which the following passage occurs: 'I stopped at Elk River, Min., and while there asked my brothers and several others about Wild Pigeons. My brother had seen two or three flocks of about four to six birds during the past summer, and had killed two pigeons, but had seen no nests, neither had he heard of any of the birds breeding there' " (*Birds*, 1894, 185). This letter serves as a postscript to other richly cross-referenced eyewitness sources documenting the bird, including William Brewster at Harvard, Charles Emil Bendire (major of the United States Army and ornithologist), Jonathan Dwight (physician and ornithologist), and Mr. Stevens, a "veteran pigeon-netter" (184).

Despite their eagerness, helpers sometimes found that keeping up with bird observation as well as their daily work was too much. Some lost their forms or forgot to sign them, and had to be prodded with reminders. Like McIlwraith himself, several of his correspondents were often "very busy. Rushed" (TMF, 688, C.K. Worthen, 22 March 1889). Others gave up altogether. One suffered too badly from rheumatism to go out bird watching, and George Pearse wrote from Colchester, Ontario that "[t]he blank forms for reports on Bird Migration have been handed me by Capt. L.B. Hackett, with a request for me to fill them out and return to the dept., as neither himself nor his lightkeeper felt capable of doing it" (TMF, 568, George Pearse, 28 July 1884).

Ornithology attracted some colourful personalities who, at best, were knowledgeable eccentrics, but at worst could become troublesome. In the former category was Robert Elliott (1858–1902) from Plover Mills, a hamlet near London that had received its name from Elliott in consultation with the local postmaster. Elliott wanted to become a schoolteacher but poor health kept him on his parents' homestead, where he wrote poetry and studied the plants and animals of western Ontario. A painfully shy individual, he nevertheless attracted "a host of friends" (Garrett) including W.E. Saunders, educator John Dearness, writer Cy Warman, and lawyer Frank Lawson. After his early death, a minor cult sprang up around Elliott: his room was preserved and shown to visitors, and his poems were collected by Dearness and Lawson. As soon as Elliot was recommended to McIlwraith, he bombarded the older man with queries about the AOU's migration survey, along with questions about the forthcoming *Birds of Ontario*: "Do you wish to have a report on the Fall migration of kinds from this station this year? ... Does the AOU propose to receive further reports? Have they issued a list yet? How is your book progressing? Please [illegible] my name for a copy, and let me know where and when I can get it" (TMF, 630, Robert Elliott, 7 December 1885). Despite his eagerness, Elliott was an unusually soft-hearted bird enthusiast who – in contrast to virtually all of McIlwraith's other correspondents and to McIlwraith himself – plaintively reported that he "had a chance of killing a pair of pileated [woodpeckers] the other day but had not the heart to do it" (7 December 1885). Elliott was sufficiently well known in Ontario to have Briggs's publishers ask him to endorse the second edition of *The Birds of Ontario*, alongside celebrities like Ernest Thompson Seton, D.C. Scott, and James LeMoine. In his typically fulsome style, Elliott delivered a panegyric predicting that the "date of its appearance will be written in red letters in the calendars of all who watch for the coming and going of the birds in their seasons."[43]

Several country doctors reported to McIlwraith, including Dr. John Hutchison Garnier in Lucknow, a widely travelled and multilingual physician trained in Dublin and Paris whose personal life and reasons for settling in rural Ontario have remained a mystery. An "awesome figure" who seemed to have stepped out of a Scottish legend, Garnier was known as "an idiosyncratic and eccentric man with a reputation for violent language" (Roland). He was nevertheless greatly respected by his patients for his medical skills, especially in obstetrics and ophthalmology. His gun accompanied him everywhere and his house was filled with birds and reptiles he had shot and preserved. McIlwraith noted that Garnier's views about birds were "not entirely in harmony with the modern school of ornithologists" and that he resisted – probably in choice language – what he considered "unnecessary subdivision" of the Barrow's goldeneye from the American goldeneye (*Birds*, 1894, 83). F.B. McCormick, another physician, though one who repeatedly got into trouble for practising without a licence,[44] reported from Breeze Point on Pelee Island,

---

43 Advertisement for *The Birds of Ontario*, 1894, Thomas McIlwraith, letter to Joseph Grinnell, 30 April 1895, Joseph Grinnell papers, BANC MSS C-B 995 box 13, Bancroft Library, UCB.

44 See *Grip*, vol. 31, no. 795, 1 September 1888, 3:

A paragraph like the following, which we clip from the Chatham *Planet*, is well calculated to make a Canadian blush:

Dr. F.B. McCormick, Pelee Island, has been prosecuted again for practicing without a licence. The case was tried Tuesday at Kingsville, and was appealed to the County Judge. It is one of peculiar hardship. The doctor is owner of the greater part of the island, and customhouse officer there. There is not practice enough on the island to support a regular licentiate, the advent of whom the doctor would gladly welcome, and resign his practice to him. Meanwhile he does not feel like leaving the people of the island to die, fifteen miles in Lake Erie, for the want of medical advice, and his work has been very successful from a medical standpoint.

most of which was owned by his family[45] and where he was also the customs collector. Dr. George Alexander MacCallum, who served as president of the Ontario Fish and Game Commission and superintendent of the London Asylum for the Insane, wrote from Dunnville on the north shore of Lake Erie. Like the houses of McIlwraith and Garnier, the MacCallums' home was "filled with stuffed wildcats, foxes, snakes, birds and other animals; with birds' eggs," and like McIlwraith, MacCallum had a particularly close bond with one of his sons. When the latter, William George MacCallum, became professor of pathology at Columbia University, his seventy-year-old father was appointed "pathologist of the Bronx Zoo and the Aquarium," where he began "a study of worm parasites in captive animals" (Rich 570). An infinitely more troubling individual than these country doctors was Dr. Robert W. Shufeldt in New York, known for his racism, headhunting, and a marital scandal so lurid that a posthumous diagnosis of neurosyphilis has been proposed (D. Cook).

There is no record of McIlwraith and Shufeldt locking horns in their correspondence, but like the postcards related to business, the postal exchanges involving birds did not always go smoothly. Cross-border communication came with various difficulties. One correspondent, from St. Cloud, in Minnesota, fretted over the address: "[c]ould not make out your name but copied the letters as neatly as I could, I hope it will reach you" (TMF, 587, H.P. Bennett, 5 March 1885). He need not have worried: McIlwraith was so well known that two postcards from Brewer, Maine addressed to him at "Hamilton, Ontario, Canada West" correctly arrived at Cairnbrae (TMF, 659; 7 January 1888; 670, 4 February 1888). Preparing the boxes and documents for the post was time-consuming, even more so with an ever-critical correspondent like Amos W. Butler from Brookville, Indiana, who persistently complained about McIlwraith's packing and paper work. Butler berated him for using "a paste-board box" that left "10 of the birds torn to pieces" (TMF, 547, 26 February 1884) and was irritated by the delay when customs returned a package to sender because the box was too large (WIK, 16 February 1884). Customs is repeatedly a concern: when McIlwraith sent a copy of *The Birds of Ontario*, Butler advised him to address packages to him as "Secretary, Natural History Society" to obtain an inexpensive rate and, if they contained birds, to mark them as "not dutiable" (TMF, 661, 23 April 1887). Butler is so perpetually inclined to complain that even the compliment that a shipment is "in the best condition of any birds I ever received from you" (TMF, 584, 10 January 1885) sounds like a reprimand.

Overall, the barter system of exchanging one shipment of bird skins for another seems to have worked well, but some correspondents found McIlwraith's estimates of a bird's value too high, and there were disagreements, some

---

45 On Pelee Island and the McCormicks, see Pryke.

potentially costly, over what had been ordered and what had been sent. Arthur
T. Wayne from Charleston thought that McIlwraith "must value [his] Goshawk
very highly as you want so many skins for it." The "Southwick + Jencks price
list" set it at only $3.50 whereas his own Swainson's warbler was "a very rare
bird," and Wayne estimated his own whole shipment at "$13.00 cash" or "$20.00
in exchange" (TMF, 605, Arthur T. Wayne, 13 April 1885).[46] Even more irate,
and not hesitant to vent their annoyance in an open postcard, were two other
correspondents. C.K. Worthen sarcastically apologized for sending "what you
did not want I sent them because you ordered them!" (TMF, 708, 27 February
1893). Meanwhile, John A. Morden from Hyde Park, with whom McIlwraith
usually had friendly relations, exploded when he was apparently accused of
"pull[ing] leg wires out of [stuffed birds] and palm[ing] them off as skins ...
I wish I had never seen a stuffed bird" (TMF, 654, 7 October, 1886). If Morden
was familiar with the business etiquette that advised against airing disagreements in an open postcard, he was too angry to observe it. For one quarrel with
Morden, Robert Ridgway acted as umpire when McIlwraith suspected that
Morden had been cheated with a couple of golden rails.[47]

Marketing Ornithology and "Indian Artefacts"

As the Southwick and Jencks price list wielded by one of McIlwraith's correspondents illustrates, ornithology spawned numerous specialized businesses.
When they published work related to ornithology, magazines sent advertisements, such as a notice of W.E.D. Scott's essay included in an 1897 issue of
Scribner's on arranging stuffed birds into effective poses. Among McIlwraith's
correspondents were taxidermists, collectors, dealers, and illustrators, and the
commercial section in a sports magazine like Forest and Stream listed page after page of advertisements for guns, gunpowder, taxidermical equipment, and
other supplies.[48] As a potential customer, McIlwraith was contacted by establishments practising aggressive marketing in his area of interest. For this purpose
too, the postcard was an effective medium. Messages arrived from gun dealers,
one of whom advertised himself as a "Dealer in Breech and Muzzle-loading Rifles, Double and Single Shot Guns, Pistols, Cartridges, Powder, Shot Lead, And
a General Assortment of Sportsmen's and Hunters' Goods" (TMF, 595, H.P.
Bennett, 5 March 1855). Another individual in Detroit insistently followed up

---

46 James M. Southwick and Fred T. Jencks ran a "Natural History Store" in Providence, Rhode
    Island, and also published a short-lived magazine, Random Notes on Natural History. See the
    section on Southwick and Jencks in Barrow 516–18.
47 Thomas McIlwraith, letter to Robert Ridgway, 19 February 1889, Smithsonian Institution,
    Record Unit 105, box 22. United States National Museum, Division of Birds, 1854–1959.
48 See, for example, Forest and Stream, vol. 7, 1876, 205–8.

on an enquiry made ten days earlier: "What about the gun? Wrote full particulars 10 days ago and have had no word. Please let me hear about it if you want us to supply the gun" (443, Jack [McIlwraith?], 24 April 1883).[49] Although it is not clear what they have to do with soap, the supplier A.L. Ellis, in Pawtucket, Rhode Island, offered artificial eyes for the use of "Taxidermists, Jewelers, Soap Mfrs, and Fancy Work": "Browns, Hazel, Red, Straw, Yellow, White, Blue, Flint, Elongated Pupils, 20 per cent extra. Elongated Pupils, Veined ... extra" (202, A.L. Ellis & Co, 7 November 1880).[50] Some taxidermists combined their work with a variety of other activities, such as one outfit that – alarmingly – was also a "Dealer in all kinds of Fruit and Confectionery" (591, E.S. Bowler, 6 February 1885).

Noteworthy is the number of dealers who, besides selling stuffed birds, catered to tourists' interest in Indian artefacts (M. Hamilton 63), a combination likewise practised at agricultural exhibitions where taxidermy appeared alongside "Indian Work" in the display cases (see, for example, "Halifax County" lxi). Some ornithologists became amateur archeologists with a special interest in Indigenous "relics." Among them were the doctors McCormick and Mac-Callum, and the inventory of MacCallum's "Catalogue of Indian and Other Relics" (1887) lists well over two hundred items.[51] The persistent proximity of taxidermy and Indian artefacts underscores a parallel between the exploitation of the natural world and the commodification of Aboriginal culture. In *The Birds of Ontario*, the popular name for the long-tailed duck is listed as "Old Squaw." Used "in reference to [its] talkative behaviour,"[52] the name speaks of prejudice against Indigenous people generally and Native women in particular, as does the "translation" of "*Wis-Ka-Tjan*" as "Whiskey Jack" for the Canada jay (*Birds*, 1894, 275). However, *The Birds of Ontario*, whether intentionally or not, also offers ample evidence of the close connection between Indigenous people and birdlife, although references to them in the Hamilton region are rare except for "some Indians from the Grand River" who delivered "to the

---

49 The phrasing of "if you want us to supply the gun" seems to speak against it, but "Jack" could be McIlwraith's son John Goldie, who was seventeen in 1883 and, by the following year, is documented as working in a hardware store in Detroit.

50 With his business partner Frank Blake Webster, A.L. Ellis operated a "Naturalists' Supply Depot" in Pawtucket, Rhode Island. See the section on Webster and Ellis in Barrow, 510–15.

51 Queen's University Archives records describe the catalogue as "an accessions register listing native artifacts, possibly collected by G.W. McCallum [sic], mainly from Ontario locations, but also including aboriginal artifacts from Australia and New Zealand." Some of the artefacts are located in the Agnes Etherington Art Centre, Queen's University. The artefacts from New Zealand and Australia listed in the catalogue are, however, not part of MacCallum's collection (archivist Deirdre Bryden, email to Eva-Marie Kröller, 17 May 2017).

52 "Long-tailed Duck (*Clangula hyemalis*)," *Audubon Field-Guide*, http://www.audubon.org/field-guide/bird/long-tailed-duck (accessed 17 May 2017).

Hamilton market specimens of a race [of the ruffed grouse] decidedly red, their tails being fox-colored, but these were seen during one fall only" (175). Many of the discussions in *The Birds of Ontario* of the links between Indigenous people and birds come from Edward W. Nelson's *Report on the Natural History Collections Made in Alaska Between the Years 1877–1881*, and McIlwraith borrows extensively from Nelson's commentary on the uses of the black-throated loon for clothing, the ptarmigan for food, the grey-cheeked thrush for the training of young hunters, and the whistling swan for its role in young men's competitive exercise (*Birds*, 1894, 33, 176, 408, 102). Likewise, McIlwraith draws on Nelson's discussion of Native beliefs, highlighting the "family" connections among animals and between humans and animals. The former connection has "the natives call [the Oven Bird] the Grandfather of the Ruby-crowned Kinglet" (374), while the latter saddles the American pipit with a bad reputation because "the Eskimos regard this bird as an enemy, and accuse it of telling the reindeer when a man is in pursuit" (386). Meanwhile, the goshawk is disliked for "its habit of stealing birds from their snares, as well as for hunting the Ptarmigan, upon which, at certain seasons, the Eskimos depend largely for a food supply" (199). In this way, although none of the informants is given a name or tribal affiliation, Indigenous peoples' knowledge is shown to circulate among North American ornithologists and to shape their understanding of the natural world (see Binnema 272–4; Greer).

The Birds of Ontario and the National Project

Most of McIlwraith's correspondents in the 1880s knew that his book *The Birds of Ontario* was in the works, and they anxiously enquired about its progress. The first edition sold out quickly, but several years after publication, booksellers John Henderson in Kingston and John Durie in Ottawa were still requesting copies from the author. Bird enthusiasts were just as anxious to know about plans for the second edition as Robert Elliott had been about the first. They were satisfied that, compared to the first edition, which was "very unpretentiously gotten up" and with little effort expended "to push its sale," Briggs and Unwin were more aggressive about presentation and marketing, and that "Illustrations by Ernest E. Thompson and Others" were an attractive addition.[53] It was all the more important to give the work appropriate prominence because, as *The Canadian Baptist* had it, knowledge of the natural world instilled "a love for ... home and country." The display of native birds at international exhibitions took this patriotic idea to a proudly competitive level, and McIlwraith appears

---

53   J.E. Bryant, endorsement for *The Birds of Ontario*, 2nd ed., and announcement of forthcoming publication, Joseph Grinnell papers, BANC MSS C-B 995 box 13, Bancroft Library, UCB.

to have supplied some of the exhibits included in the Canadian display at the Paris Exhibition in 1867. Oddly, the Ontario Department of Public Works confirmed as late as 1886 that a cheque for these exhibits had been sent to him in 1867 (TMF, 653, William E. Thomas, 11 September 1886). Ambitious plans for these displays sometimes exceeded the supply, and a curlew sandpiper listed in the catalogue prepared by Professor Hincks was impossible to find in good time, though there were a trumpeter swan, a pair of black-throated loons, and an Arctic tern among the birds sent to Paris (*Birds*, 1894, 146, 104, 32, 56).[54]

No Canada goose was included in the collection sent to the Paris Exhibition, but McIlwraith was alert to the national symbolism of this bird, "whose well-known call is welcomed by the Canadian people as the harbinger of spring." Given Hamilton's proximity to Queenston Heights, site of a major battle in the War of 1812, there may be a Canadian wariness of Americans in the annotation that "farther south ... [the geese] are subjected to continual persecution," so that for vigilance "sentinels are placed on the outskirts of the flock" (*Birds*, 1894, 98, 99). McIlwraith was not alone in the notion that the sober habits of the Canada goose made it a suitable national symbol, more so than the white-throated sparrow, which could be said to whistle either a song to "sweet Canada" or a tune addressed to the Peabodys, one of New England's foremost families (Greer and Cameron 42). The latter is the version cited in McIlwraith's book, where he has a white-throated sparrow, "his whole attitude indicating languor and weariness, drawl ... out the plaintive, familiar 'Old Tom Peabody, Peabody' " (*Birds*, 1894, 320). By contrast, Canadian nationalism is plainly expressed in an anecdote about a bald eagle that dates back to McIlwraith's early days as a Canadian bird enthusiast, and perhaps the witty but blunt anti-Americanism of the story had him decide not to include it in his book. A specimen captured in the 1850s by a Hamiltonian "whose chickens had been disappearing with undue rapidity along the shore of Burlington Bay" was temporarily incarcerated in the new jailhouse because no other space could be found for it. The situation caused "much jovial comment about the ... prisoner ... being the symbol of American freedom" ("Flashlights"). Another bird, the ptarmigan, provided the title for a comic opera with a patriotic theme co-authored by Jean McIlwraith and the British-born Hamilton musician J.E.P. Aldous. "Ptarmigan, or, a Canadian Carnival" (1895) satirizes the dilemmas of Canadian nationalism through characters whose names suggest trees (Maple Leaf) and flowers (Hepatica, Blue Belle, Trillium) associated with national symbolism, as well as a flock of birds: P. Tarmigan, Wis-Ka-Tjan (the Canada jay), Robin, and Bob O'Link. To represent the French Canadians, there are Al Louette and Corbeau. In this opera, the migration of birds suggests the back-and-forth travel of some Canadians across

---

54 On the bird collection for the Paris Exhibition and McIlwraith's involvement in it, see "The Birds of Western Canada."

the border between Canada and the United States, and the difficulties that arise from these displacements for maintaining a clearly defined Canadian identity. The concluding chorus suggests that "Our ladies take in / The fact that the sin / Of loving th'American vulture, / Is worse beyond doubt than being without / A fraction of what they call culture" (223).

Despite these self-ironical expressions of defiance, Canadians were the junior partners in North American ornithology. In order to underscore the timeliness of his own publication, Montague Chamberlain used the preface to his book *A Catalogue of Canadian Birds*, published a year after McIlwraith's *Birds* in 1887, to compile leading American scientists' damning assessments of the state of Canadian ornithology. Allen, Ridgway, Merriam, Coues, and Brewster are all cited, with a particularly blistering comment from Brewster: "What has Canada done for ornithology? In general terms, simply nothing except the little that has resulted from purely private investigations, or from work instigated, and in some cases paid for, on this side of the line. The results of this work are trifling compared to the as yet untried possibilities."[55] American expertise and money allowed US naturalists to mentor their Canadian colleagues but they expected favours in return and dealt with collectors such as John Macoun as if they were employed by "Washington, not Ottawa." In a similar vein, Canadian scientists' alleged shortcomings justified the assumption that instead of original research they would provide "the field data upon which [American naturalists] based their theoretical work" (Waiser 110, 111).[56] Elliott Coues drew "attention to the great amount of work that needs to be done before your country can stand side by side with the United States in [ornithology]" (qtd. in Chamberlain iii). He distinctly exempted McIlwraith from his criticism, however, and, reviewing *The Birds of Ontario* in *The Auk* in 1887, accorded its author the rank of "first place in his own field" (Coues 246). There may of course have been an implied suggestion that the author's "own field" was modest to begin with.

McIlwraith's book served Canadian nationalism in more creative ways as well. *The Birds of Ontario* appealed not only to bird collectors and institutions such as the Bureau of Industries at the Ontario Department of Agriculture, which requested to be put on the mailing list (TMF, 712, C.C. James, 18 October 1893), but also to authors for whom nature was a source of literary inspiration. E.S. Caswell at William Briggs passed on the compliments of Catharine Parr Traill, "a warm admirer of your work" (718, E.S. Caswell, 8 January 1896),[57] and D.C. Scott's praise for the book in the *Globe*'s At the Mermaid Inn column of

---

55 Undated letter qtd. in Chamberlain, *A Catalogue of Canadian Birds* iv.
56 Duchesne describes similar scenarios but questions the notion that these exchanges were symptomatic of "colonialism," describing them instead as normal procedure in scientific networks.
57 On E.S. Caswell, see Peterman and Friskney.

10 June 1893 was cited in Briggs's publicity blurbs. Towards the end of *The Birds of Ontario*, in the entry on the wood thrush, McIlwraith asks, "When will some divinely gifted Canadian appear to sing the praises of our native birds, as men of other lands have done for theirs?" He goes on to offer models by which poets might orient themselves: "Hogg and Shelley have eulogized the Sky Lark in strains so musical that they rival those of the birds they have sought to honor" (*Birds*, 1894, 406). At times, the narrative offers lengthy quotations from poetry, from well-known sources such as Longfellow's *Evangeline* (387), assumed to be so recognizable to his readers that the poet's name can be omitted, and from more obscure ones such as verse about the nighthawk issued by an unnamed poet "from the unromantic plains of Chatham" (256).

It is possible that, in researching these literary allusions, McIlwraith had assistance from Jean, even if he resisted her services for the first edition in 1886 when he brushed off her complaint that one of his sentences lacked a verb with "Whsst, Jeannie, what's a verb" ("Genealogy"). A manuscript copy of the second edition of *The Birds of Ontario* bears annotations in her handwriting,[58] and although her contributions cannot be clearly established from these notes, she did edit her father's book while she was a correspondence student of literature at Queen Margaret College in the early 1890s. The influence went both ways: in her own *A Book About Shakespeare Written for Young People* (1898), she made a point of drawing out references to the "sparrows, eagles, kites, choughs, and the vulture" populating *Macbeth* (*A Book About Shakespeare* 134), not to mention her libretto for *Ptarmigan* cited earlier.

The references to literature, music, and history that enrich the entries about individual birds made McIlwraith's work doubly attractive to literary authors, especially as the book – despite its title – does not restrict itself to Ontario or Canada or even North America. *The Birds of Ontario* includes references to the United Kingdom, especially Scotland, and so acknowledges McIlwraith's country of origin and that of many of his readers. McIlwraith's passion for ornithology began in boyhood, and although he may have acquired these after his arrival in Canada rather than bringing them with him, a case of British birds is included in his "Catalogue of Birds Mounted under Glass." McIlwraith's rich documentation of natural life in Ontario implies a Canadian nationalism that encompasses the writer's Scottish birthplace. Thus McIlwraith cites Archdeacon Donald Munro's sixteenth-century *Description of the Western Isles of Scotland*, reissued in 1805 and 1818, as well as William Macgillivray's *A Manual of British Ornithology* (1840–2) and *A History of British Birds, Indigenous and Migratory* (1837–52), and Robert Gray's *The Birds of the West of Scotland, including the Outer Hebrides* (1871). The section on the American bittern quotes Robert Burns's "Elegy on Captain Matthew Henderson," and Burns – along

---

58 Thomas McIlwraith, *The Birds of Ontario*, 2nd ed., manuscript, TMF, HPL.

with Robert Tannahill and William Shakespeare – appears in the item on the barn owl. There are also references to Scottish folklore, such as superstitions associated with the magpie and the catbird.

As a result, some of the entries on individual birds resemble densely textured essays in which autobiography and cultural cross-reference join scientific information. The 1886 edition gives a laconic description of the common puffin as a bird for which there was only one sighting in Ontario documented for 1881 by the Ottawa Field Naturalists' Club, explaining that it was a specimen that "had probably been blown inland by a severe storm" (*Birds*, 1886, 32), but in the second edition McIlwraith adds a recollection of his school days in Scotland when he "frequently visited ... Ailsa Craig on the west coast" (*Birds*, 1894, 35), a rock crowded with seafowl. Along with a story about the birds' habitat, their behaviour, and the local custom surrounding them, he tells anecdotes of human interaction with them, including employment of a Scotch terrier to retrieve birds that came back with "several ... hanging on to his hair." Birds covered the rocks in such "incredible" numbers that the lighthouse keeper, in wanting to "mak[e] up a lot to send to the market," merely had "to club down as many birds as he needed while they flew past" (36). This is one of several references to plenitude that has the hunter almost too bored to bother with the embarrassment of riches. Elsewhere, in recording the birds' local names of "Paties" or "Coulternebs," McIlwraith links them to the land when he explains that their name is derived from the resemblance of their bills to "the cutting part of a plough" (36). He concludes the section with an image of the lugubrious cormorants that often roost alongside the puffins, auks, and guillemots on the shore of Mochrum, citing a local "wut" who named them the "Mochrum Elders" (37).

The library at Cairnbrae contained two copies, each inscribed by "Grandmother McIlwraith" and one each given to her grandchildren Thomas and Jean, of *The Legendary Ballads of England and Scotland*, edited by John S. Roberts (1868?), but by the time her father published the second edition of *The Birds of Ontario*, Jean had also taken singing lessons with a member of the Royal Academy of Music in London, and her repertoire of traditional Scottish song was extensive. She may therefore have had something to do with the references to folk music in McIlwraith's book. When Thomas McIlwraith describes the willow ptarmigan, he turns to the traditional Scottish song "The Braes Aboon Bonaw" to draw a vivid analogy between the bird and a lass, both as shy as a doe and both as worthy of capture. The entry on the barn owl, in addition to Shakespeare's *Julius Caesar*, cites Robert Burns's "Tam o Shanter" and Robert Tannahill's "Are Ye Sleepin' Maggie?" A sense of irony generally keeps McIlwraith from bombast: his long dissertation on the barn owl also mocks his countrymen's superstitions about the bird by claiming that though "many a stalwart Scot may have quailed at the cry of the 'hoolet,' " clansmen "have performed deeds of personal valor" because they were inspired by an even more horrifying sound – namely, the screeching of "the national instrument," the bagpipe (*Birds*, 1894, 224). Nowhere is the symbiosis between bird and human underscored quite so charmingly as in a quotation from Macgillivray wherein a guide, contemplating a flock of gannets, explains his fascination with them: "I was only thinking how like they are to *oursel's*" (qtd. in *Birds*, 1894, 60).

Yet, the references to Old World beliefs are not always bathed in fond nostalgia, and in one of several indictments of superstition and its tendency to travel from the Old World to the New, an introductory section in the second edition describes the reputation of birds of prey "[i]n Scotland ... as the thieves and robbers of the bird creation," ready to carry off grouse, ducks, poultry, lambs, and even young children. Keepers, McIlwraith remembers, were held "to kill ... whenever opportunity offered" and to display their trophies by "nail[ing them] upon the outside of their houses" (*Birds*, 1894, 187). The recollection impels him to offer a more appreciative view of "our beautiful and interesting Birds of Prey" (187, 189). Citing the ornithologists working for the Department of Agriculture in Washington, he does remain pragmatic in his distinctions between "beneficial" or "harmless" birds on the one hand and "harmful" ones on the other (190).

By drawing on Old World culture, *The Birds of Ontario* supported ancestral memory at the same time as its descriptive catalogue of North American birds helped to shape "a self-governing nation, more confident in its attempts to control its water, minerals, forests, and wildlife" (Greer and Cameron 40). To McIlwraith, the resulting world view was both pragmatic and poetic, and he would have agreed with John Burroughs that "the birds link themselves to your memory of seasons and places so that a song, a call, a gleam of color, set going a sequence of delightful reminiscences in your mind" (Burroughs viii). These poetic qualities, however, did not sit well with at least one admirer of McIlwraith's work, John Macoun at the Geological Survey of Canada. When Macoun approached him with his plan to produce a joint catalogue of Canadian birds, he apparently asked his intended co-author to refrain from literary allusions, either because an unadorned style was his own preference or because he was concerned that the politicians who controlled the Survey's activities would consider such features frivolous adornment rather than useful information. Because McIlwraith was eager to undertake the collaboration, he immediately concurred: "As you do not seem to care for the literary part of the work, it might be called a Manual of the Birds of the Dominion of Canada."[59] Given how important the "literary part" was to the distinctive character of McIlwraith's

---

59 Thomas McIlwraith to John Macoun, 4 March 1889, Rudolph Martin Anderson and Mae Bell Allstrand Fonds, MG 30, Series B 40, vol. 15, file 8, Ornithology – Department of Interior Files (1884–1890), LAC.

writing, one does wonder just how successful the result of this co-authorship would have been if it had taken place.

Mentors and Students

The bird enthusiasts who flocked to McIlwraith's home to consult with him looked to him as a mentor, but he needed advice and reassurance himself, and he was generously tutored by several prominent naturalists, especially the Americans. It is therefore difficult to fathom the self-image he appears to have periodically created for himself as someone labouring in isolation. He wrote to Ridgway in 1887, one year after the publication of *The Birds of Ontario*, when his work was widely acclaimed, as if he were mostly done with ornithology.[60] Two years later, when it came to persuading John Macoun that he would be an appropriate co-author on a proposed inventory of Canadian birds, McIlwraith contradicts himself, assuring Macoun that he "[kept] up [his] connection with the A.O.U." and that he had replaced Montague Chamberlain on its council.[61] Marianne Gosztonyi Ainley, one of the first scholars to discuss McIlwraith's place in the history of Canadian avian science, seems unsure whether to take him at his word that he worked in isolation or to base her conclusions on ample evidence to the contrary (Ainley, Foreword, x).[62]

A particularly generous mentor was Joel Asaph Allen. When McIlwraith was preparing the first edition of his book, Allen guided him through the preliminaries of publication, advising on the conventions of citing the work of others, offering to read the proofs, and providing updated taxonomical information. Likewise, when William Saunders – a frequent guest at Cairnbrae – produced a review of McIlwraith's book that made its author feel as "one wounded in the house of his friend"[63] and that, according to McIlwraith, his friends thought "ill-natured and spiteful,"[64] both Brewster and Coues were ready to advise him on a reply. Saunders claimed to have written the review in response to a request from "a few of the prominent members of the A.O.U." (Saunders, "Review" 246),

---

60 Thomas McIlwraith, letter to Robert Ridgway, 13 December 1887, Smithsonian Institution Archives, Record Unit 105, box 22. United States National Museum, Division of Birds, 1854–1959.

61 Thomas McIlwraith to John Macoun, 18 February 1889. Rudolph Martin Anderson and Mae Bell Allstrand Fonds, MG 30, Series B 40, vol. 15, file 9, Ornithology – Department of Interior Files (1884–1890), LAC.

62 See also also Ainley's doctoral dissertation, "From Natural History to Avian Biology."

63 The correct quotation, from King James 2000 Version, Zechariah 13:6, is: "What are these wounds in your hands? Then he shall answer, Those with which I was wounded in the house of my friends."

64 From the Archives of the Museum of Comparative Zoology, Ernst Mayr Library, Harvard University, Thomas McIlwraith to William Brewster, 13 July 1887, 9 September 1887.

and McIlwraith suspected C.H. Merriam, but was not sure about the others.[65] In the end, McIlwraith did not submit his response, but Saunders's criticism continued to rankle, and two years later, McIlwraith reiterated his complaint to another correspondent, this time Macoun, that Saunders was "a young man full of self-conceit" who had produced a "trivial, hypercritical, and incorrect" review of his book. As he indicated once more, others "looked upon [the criticism] as spiteful and ill-natured."[66]

Just as he finds it politic in his dealings with Macoun not to emphasize his mostly imagined isolation from other ornithologists, so, too, does he cite Saunders's review this time perhaps not so much because he felt betrayed but because he wanted to clear any competition out of the way for his projected book with Macoun. Other potential rivals are identified as owing him favours but also deficient in various professional areas, including Montague Chamberlain, who obtained a letter of introduction to the journalist and politician Thomas White from McIlwraith but who "was not quite enough of a field man for my taste" even if he was ready to admit that "Mr. C. has a great deal of energy and writes very nicely."[67] Likewise, McIlwraith declined to assist Chamberlain and Ernest Thompson Seton ("a Mr. Seton") in their plans for a book on the birds of Canada because neither of these men had the thorough knowledge of a specific area that McIlwraith had of Ontario, and because he meant "to give the result to the public at what they think the best time," and not to his rival naturalists.[68] At one point in their correspondence, several of McIlwraith's letters to Macoun appear to have gone missing in the far reaches of the Geological Survey of Canada, and both were nervous that their exchange had "fallen into the hands of someone else in the department." Macoun had to be reassured that "there was nothing in them offensive to any one," that all McIlwraith had done was "to collect information and specimens." He had "said nothing about [their plans] any where." The episode disturbed him enough, however, to have him urge Macoun to make their plans public before Macoun's departure for another expedition across Canada in the spring.[69]

---

65 Thomas McIlwraith to William Brewster, 14 July 1887, from the Archives of the Museum of Comparative Zoology, Ernst Mayr Library, Harvard University.

66 Thomas McIlwraith to John Macoun, 19 October 1887, 418, Correspondence McDunnough-McInnes, RG 132 vol. 29, file 8, Botany Division, Geological Survey, LAC.

67 Thomas McIlwraith to John Macoun, 13 June 1888, Rudolph Martin Anderson and Mae Bell Allstrand Fonds, MG 30, Series B 40, vol. 15, file 8, Ornithology – Department of Interior Files (1884–1890), LAC.

68 Thomas McIlwraith to John Macoun, 4 May 1885, Rudolph Martin Anderson and Mae Bell Allstrand Fonds, MG 30, Series B 40, vol. 15, file 8, Ornithology – Department of Interior Files (1884–1890), LAC.

69 Thomas McIlwraith to John Macoun, 18 February 1889, Rudolph Martin Anderson and Mae Bell Allstrand Fonds, MG 30, Series B 40, vol. 15, file 9, Ornithology – Department of Interior Files (1884–1890), LAC.

These fears of being outflanked by other authors with similar interests were, of course, characteristic of scholarly enterprise long before McIlwraith studied the birds of Ontario. Elizabeth Yale, for example, describes John Aubrey's complicated efforts to protect his work and his readiness "to attack when he felt his own work was threatened" (150). Even if the scholarship advertises itself as no more than "collect[ing] information and specimens," this is one of several areas where the correspondence and reviews generated by scientific work become life writing as well. The extent of McIlwraith's indiscretions in his long letters to Macoun indicates how anxious he was for the co-authored book on the birds of Canada to come to fruition before the competition got wind of the project. He may have been eager to attach himself to an undertaking sponsored by the Geological Survey because to do so would give his work and legacy official cachet. He even held out briefly for having his name go first as author, but, possibly afraid of his own courage, swiftly indicated that he was also amenable to the formulation "by Professor Macoun edited by Thomas McIlwraith member [of the AOU]."[70] Although he includes brief personal news in his letters to them, McIlwraith's correspondence with Allen, Brewster, Ridgway, and Grinnell is characterized by its focus on the subject of birds and by its even tone. By contrast, his correspondence with Macoun shows a man in crisis, one who looks forward to institutional recognition but is then disappointed in his hope. No letter appears to have survived that articulates his response to the change of plans at the Geological Survey, but the failure of their project did not destroy the McIlwraiths' friendship with the Macouns. Thirty years later, McIlwraith's grandson noted with sadness the death of Macoun's son James, and when T.F. passed through Ottawa on his way to fieldwork in British Columbia, "the Macoun-Scotts ... asked [him] to supper."[71]

With the next chapter, the narrative returns to an earlier period in the McIlwraiths' lives, picking up the thread five years after the end of Andrew McIlwraith's diaries and in the year before Kennedy's birth. The focus is on Thomas's children and their communal diary, but Thomas and Andrew remain on the scene. Here, Thomas McIlwraith is the genial hero of his young family, and as far as they are concerned, he knows nothing about anxiety and doubt.

---

70 Thomas McIlwraith to John Macoun, 4 March 1889, Rudolph Martin Anderson and Mae Bell Allstrand Fonds, MG 30, Series B 40, vol. 15, file 8, Ornithology – Department of Interior Files (1884–1890), LAC.

71 TFMF, T.F. McIlwraith (1899–1964) to family, 29 March 1920, 28 February 1922. James Melville Macoun had married Helen Douglas, sister of Duncan Campbell Scott.

Chapter Three

The "Family Album"

The McIlwraith Children

In October 1867, a few months after Canadian Confederation, twelve-year-old Thomas McIlwraith – no longer the youngster who caused his uncle Andrew "a sad dilemma" by "bawling all the way" home from church because his mamma had gone ahead without him (*MM*, 13 March 1859, 203) – began a "Family Album" at his father's request, designed to chronicle his activities and those of his siblings. The result is a remarkable document of the day-to-day activities of a sociable family in Hamilton with strong ties to their Scottish origins. Devoted believers in the ideals of the Scottish Enlightenment, the McIlwraiths championed reading and writing as vehicles of knowledge from an early age, and they urged their children to keep a daily record of their activities. Like Kennedy's bird book, the Family Album is an exercise in literacy initiated by Mr. McIlwraith, but its purpose is broader. In narrating the emotional and practical rewards of maintaining an ever-expanding circle of family and associates, it emphasizes the role that writing plays in it. Thus, several of the children wrote for publication in children's and college magazines, and they corresponded with pen pals in the United States. Intended to be written communally, the album tempers Mr. McIlwraith's lofty educational project with a perspective that is often endearingly spontaneous, but that also illustrates prejudice – specifically against Irish immigrants and against Black citizens in the cities near the border between Canada and the United States – that the children absorbed from the adults around them.

The names, ages, and birthdays of the young McIlwraiths are listed at the beginning of the album: in addition to Thomas, there were Mary Duncan ("Pollie," ten years); Jane Newton ("Jean," "Jeannie," or "Jennie," eight and a half); Helen Adair ("Nellie" or "Nell," seven); Hugh Park ("Hughie," five); and John Goldie ("Johnny" or "Jack," one); with their youngest brother Kennedy

("Kenny" or "Ken") to follow in 1868.[1] Another sister, Marion Reid, was born between Hugh and John but died in infancy. In ten pages or so, many of which have since faded to illegibility, Tom did his best for a few years with the task he had been given, writing about bird hunting and chestnut gathering with his father, collecting books from the library and reading a story in *Harper's Magazine*, going to the lime kiln or down to the dock "to see about some coal that was to be sent up" (FA, 18 March 1868), building a rabbit hutch and henhouse, and relating the shocking news of the assassination of Thomas D'Arcy McGee and the hunt for his murderer. He was not a fluent writer, however, and as he seems, according to the *Dictionary of Hamilton Biography*, to have been as "retiring in nature" in his youth as in adulthood ("McIlwraith, Thomas Forsyth"), he may have lacked material and motivation. Moreover, by 1870 Tom was a post office clerk with the wholesale grocers' firm of Kerr, Brown and McKenzie in Hamilton – or a "P.O.C." as his disrespectful brothers and sisters called him "because he thinks that he's somebody" (FA, 18 March 1870) – and the job of coordinating the journal fell to twelve-year-old Jean. She was Tom's opposite in temperament and, despite her young age, a more talented writer than any of her siblings, including the academically gifted Pollie.

As the first point of order, Jean introduced the most recent addition to the family, Kennedy Crawford ("Kenny" or "Ken"), who "toddles about all day after Mamma sometimes crying for a 'Goodie' + sometimes to be 'Up' " (FA, 18 March 1870). She also presented the two servant girls, Big Jeanie, so-called to avoid confusion with herself, and Annie. Despite interruptions of weeks or even months when she was too busy "to have very much time to write in this book" (10 July 1871), Jean faithfully kept the journal until July 1875, when all of the remaining 156 pages of the volume sturdily bound between black covers had been filled. The plan was for Jack to take over from her with a new album but if he did, the result has not come down to us. Jean herself intended to write a private journal and was already filling the pages of a "diary book" she had been given for Christmas a few months earlier. Neither this journal nor an autograph book, adorned with images she cut out from old valentines, appears to have survived either. Nor is there any trace of the scrapbooks kept by both the children's father and their uncle Andrew although care and money was spent on these, such as the purchase of "some plates in Gentry and Brown's" in downtown Hamilton (*MM*, 25 and 26 January 1858, 144). The only additional journal that appears to have survived is Kennedy's bird book, begun seven years after the end of the Family Album and discussed in the previous chapter.

---

1   The dates of the children's birth were: Thomas, 22 May 1855; Mary, 20 February 1857; Jean, 29 December 1858; Helen, 18 April 1860; Hugh, 29 November 1861; John, 31 December 1865; Kennedy, 3 September 1868.

The Album as Commonplace Book

The distinction between these different genres suggests an awareness in Jean's family of the various traditions behind keeping a journal. The Family Album was intended as a "record of family events," with Jean as "chief editor" (FA, 18 March 1870) inviting contributions from those of her brothers and sisters who were old enough to write. Practically speaking, this approach avoided placing all of the responsibility on one person and therefore once more risking failure of the project, but the public, collaborative, and eclectic nature of the album also ties it into other traditions of record keeping. These include the family register in which births, marriages, deaths, and – depending on local custom – additional events like migrations may be recorded, as well as the almanac, the logbook, the ledger, the guestbook, and the commonplace book. *Miller's Canadian Farmer's Almanac for 1870*, for example, provided calendars for each month, with extensively annotated predictions of weather and recommendations towards propitious dates for planting and harvesting. As well, there were charts and tables by which to track festivals, bank holidays in Ontario and holidays of public offices in Quebec, equinoxes and solstices, and movements of the planets. Details about the royal family, the new Canadian Parliament, postage rates, banks, and legal courts rounded off the information. A blank facing page prompted users to enter memoranda regarding their personal lives and those of their associates (see Smyth, *Autobiography* 15–56). These annotations did not discriminate between the mundane and the momentous, and records of bank account numbers or payments might sit side by side with annotations over several pages about a neighbour's death by drowning, finding his body, and burying him.[2]

Without referring to a printed template, the McIlwraiths' album oriented itself along similar guidelines of tracking the year and using each entry to structure what might otherwise appear to be random reports about domestic experience. Thus, dated entries about the family's activities are complemented by accounts of recurrent religious and civic ritual. Christmas was generally the time to assess progress in school, apprenticeship, or profession, to list everyone's presents (and thereby reflect on age, talent, level of achievement, and future aspirations), and to recite the menu for a communal feast so abundant with oyster soup, turkey, and cranberry sauce, as well as mince pies, plum pudding, canned peaches, and jelly cakes, that the "mashed potatoes and turnips" could be declared superfluous "trash" to be consumed only if the guests were against all expectations capable of eating even more (FA, 25 December 1872). Births, deaths, and marriages were recorded throughout the year, as were calamities

---

2 See *Miller's Farmer's Almanac for the Year of the Lord 1870*, 7, 11 for such entries. The owner of this particular almanac is not identified.

involving injury and loss of life. On the Queen's Birthday and Dominion Day, the latter introduced only recently to celebrate Confederation, family and friends enjoyed picnics, fireworks, and parades, and the children eagerly participated in the traditional pranks permitted on Valentine's Day, April Fool's Day, and Halloween. Thanks to Ontario's harsh winters and their impact on the region's commerce, the seasons punctuate the narrative as sharply as they do Andrew McIlwraith's craftsman's diaries, Thomas McIlwraith's business correspondence, and Kennedy's bird book, and problems caused by inclement weather are as punctiliously listed as they would be in a meteorological log. Business transactions, closely linked to climate in the Great Lakes area, were also recorded, even if their implications were not always fully comprehended by these youthful authors.

Before the advent of gaslight and the railway, the moon and the stars were important means of orientation on unlit country roads, and many of Geoffrey Blainey's observations on the influence of "moon, sun and stars" on daily life and travel in the Australian outback apply to nineteenth-century Canada as well (*Black Kettle and Full Moon* 3–44). Likewise, safe traffic on the Great Lakes depended on a thorough knowledge of both sky and water, in addition to the powerful beams of the lighthouses, such as the one on Turtle Island guarding the entry to the Maumee River since 1831 (and closed in 1904) that Jean and her siblings saw on one of their excursions through the Lakes. By the time Jean edited the Family Album, moon and stars were often eclipsed by the glitter of city lights near a busy port, but as they travelled through the waterways, the children still observed the constellations in a clear sky, and they noted shooting stars and knew about comets. Well before he began his regular bird expeditions with Kennedy, their father often had the older children up at sunrise for excursions on Hamilton Mountain, with everybody else's blinds still down. Observation of the skies was one of several useful skills they learned during these outings, and Jean later used her knowledge to create the character of Major Robert Mathews, Quebec governor Frederick de Haldimand's military secretary in her novel *A Diana of Quebec* (1912). Mathews is an amateur astronomer who watches "[t]he earth ... spinning round on its axis towards another day" (219). From this perspective, "it does not seem to matter much what flag flies over a small globe in one of the lesser solar systems" (29).[3]

Unpredictable weather and other incalculable influences were apt to disturb at any moment the organizational scheme stipulated by the almanac, but the format of the commonplace book responds easily to the sometimes chaotic realities of human lives. Unlike the typical commonplace book, the McIlwraiths' album is not a scrapbook of letters, pictures, quotations, clippings, and recipes.

---

3 On the historical Robert Mathews, see Sutherland.

All of the inclusions characteristically featured in such a book are nevertheless sooner or later mentioned in the Family Album, and the flow of daily routines is furthermore disrupted by the insertion of several lengthy travelogues with their own rhythms of organizing the day. Adam Smyth has written about the early modern *album amicorum* that it promoted an understanding of "[t]he compiler's self" as "the cumulative product of the world in which he moved: each new signature another mooring" ("Social Networking" 10).[4] With some modification, Smyth's comment can also be applied to the McIlwraiths' Family Album. Jean and her team of writers did not collect signatures, but they did produce a kind of compendium of "the world in which [they] moved." Despite the inclusion of female writers in his discussion, Smyth uses the masculine pronoun to describe the typical compiler of the album during the early modern period, while Kathryn D. Carter has pointed to the female communities apparent in nineteenth- and twentieth-century women's diaries[5] and their possible roots in the commonplace book. Jean's unmistakable presence notwithstanding, hers is a *Family* Album, both in the sense of a text designed to be written jointly and of one that is always concerned with a multitude of related characters, both female and male. More than once in writing about the McIlwraiths, I have sympathized with Barbara Caine, who explains in the preface to her book on the Stracheys that she "[i]nitially ... was concerned primarily to explore the lives and activities of the Strachey women" but found "that it was impossible to separate the lives of the Strachey women from their father, brothers, and husbands" (vii).

Keeping a Family Journal

In getting his daughter started on the project, Jean's father appears to have given some supervision. Her sometimes adventurous spelling of difficult words ("Kalathumpians" for "Calithumpians," "trussel" for "trestle," "smiflicate" for "spiflicate") is left uncorrected, possibly because her tutor found it amusing or did not want to crush her motivation with too much criticism, but the early entries do have small stylistic emendations added in a different hand that may be her father's. Or, a more mature Jean made these revisions herself as she re-read the album in preparation of drawing from it for her publications such as the autobiographical sketch "A Bright Girlhood" and her novel "Smiling Water." Her father may also have attempted to tame Jean's delight in slang and earthy detail, vividly displayed in her first entry and temporarily replaced by greater formality the next day. Her racy language can, however, never be repressed for

---

4   On the autobiographical aspects of the commonplace book, see Smyth, *Autobiography* 123–58.

5   See Carter, 1997, and her introduction to *The Small Details of Life*, esp. 12.

long and she frequently peppers her writing with expressions of youthful enthusiasm, including "first-rate," "high" (as in "it is so high to ride everywhere";
FA, 19 September 1874), and "hunkey" (as in "hunkey fun"; 4 May 1875), an
expression apparently made popular during the American Civil War.[6] As her
section of the album opens, she goes from "We have 5 hens and a rooster, a dog
called Dash and an innumerable number of rats" in her first entry (18 March
1870) to "In the afternoon, Clara Gray came over to play with me, and together
we proceeded to make a snow-cave, which was finished by a grand explosion in
the shape of Clara falling through the roof of it" in the next (19 March 1870),
but she relapses into colloquial idiom soon enough when she becomes a kind
of ventriloquist for Mr. McIlwraith's exasperation at a calamity involving his
bird cases.

As this was an affectionate family always ready to poke good-natured fun at
each other and their acquaintants, any parental censorship of Jean's writing
that may have taken place was probably light. The parents, especially Thomas
McIlwraith, set an example with their readiness to entertain others: Jean's father
complained that his wife would not "let him sleep in church in peace" (FA, 13
November 1874) and, in response to Miss Morton changing her mind half a
dozen times about whether she or her daughter – or indeed either of them –
ought to accompany Mrs. McIlwraith to Scotland, he commented drily that "in
the morning it would be *Mr.* Morton that would be going" (18 May 1870; emphasis added). As the episode involving the collapse of the bird cases illustrates,
Thomas McIlwraith was happy to make fun even of his own all-consuming
passion for ornithology. This playful tone and their father's indulgent readiness
to spoil the children when he felt they needed it (for example, after their mother's departure for Scotland for two months) did not preclude a robust understanding of responsibility. Jean, for example, had to replace out of her pocket
money the cost of a girl's ring she had lost and that could not be found although
the plumbers came to look for it in the water closet. She was expected to help
out with household chores such as harvesting huckleberries, red currants, or
"rasps" to make jam, or picking peas and catching bass for the family supper,
even if this comfortably situated family would hardly have gone hungry if she
had not collected her quota of berries or caught enough fish. Above all, once
school was over for the day or year, it generally fell to her to look after her
younger brothers. This, as will become apparent, was fortunately a job she thoroughly enjoyed, and her fondness for children persevered into her later years.
Decades into the future, when Jean was in her fifties, her favourite sister Nellie
affectionately observed her with some young passengers on board a ship that

---

6   See the Civil War song "Whack row de dow, Hunkey boy is Yankee Doodle" (1861), http://
     www.loc.gov/resource/amss.cw106500.0 (accessed 24 September 2014).

was taking them both to Europe: "full of life as usual playing with the children" (HH, 11 March 1912).

This joy in the company of children not only carried over into several teaching jobs later in her life but also shaped a number of characters in her books, all notably unsentimental individuals. Among them are Captain Mathews, the gruff narrator of *A Diana of Quebec*, who is devoted to the entertainment and welfare of the Baron and Baroness von Riedesel's young daughters, and Rory the maverick in *The Curious Career of Roderick Campbell* who persuades himself that the "two wee lassies" Elsie and Mysie Buchanan are better off playing to their heart's content under his supervision in an Iroquois camp than being immediately returned to their anxious mother and her lessons in feminine etiquette (242). Teaching as an activity that benefits both instructor and student is often an element in these relationships, as is illustrated in the character of Margaret Nairn in *The Span o' Life* (1899), who spends a few weeks on the Isle aux Coudres, an island downstream from Quebec City in the St. Lawrence, where she schools "the infant population of the parish." Margaret finds their company "the greatest boon which could have been granted [her]" because it "kept [her] sane and healthy" (175, 172).

Because writers use both the first and third person to refer to themselves, it is not always easy to confirm which parts of this communal journal were composed by whom unless the author is specifically identified or Jean indicates that she has designated a space for someone else to fill. The large number of identical first names in the extended family, including that of Jean, sometimes tempt the reader to assume – erroneously, as it usually turns out – that contributors beyond the McIlwraith children were involved. As well, Jean's handwriting varied quite considerably throughout the five years (and throughout her life), ranging from the careful penmanship of the first few pages to the hurried notes towards the end. There are so many different types of handwriting in between that it sometimes seems as if she were trying out different personalities to go with them, an impression enhanced by the several variations that circulate of her first name. This is not even to mention the different noms de plume she was to adopt during her career as a writer, beginning with the period covered by the Family Album. At times, her handwriting was altered by the circumstances of specific situations. For example, she was writing on a moving boat or train or on a "blowy verandah,"[7] could not get the ink to write properly, or spoiled the page with ink blots. The resulting impression is one of "gradual construction, refinement, and rehearsal of a textual identity" (Smyth, *Autobiography* 136), and Smyth's comment that the "reiterated signature" in commonplace books

---

7 The expression "blowy verandah" is borrowed from a later context. See McLFF, J.N. McIlwraith to W. McLennan, 13 July 1897.

points towards "an identity in the process of being made, reformed, practiced, tried out" (136) applies here as well.

The Family Album is all the more remarkable because it records the adolescence of a young woman who did not fit the standard feminine mould of her time. She enjoyed unhurried freedom within her family in finding a place for her talents, even if some of them – such as her easy way with children – were undoubtedly useful to those around her. Despite contributions by two of her siblings – namely, her sisters Pollie and Nellie – the great majority of the album seems to be Jean's work. This, however, did not prevent her from becoming the mouthpiece for a chorus of McIlwraith voices.

Stories concerning the family and their circle of acquaintances always remain the focus, but the narrative gradually changes character from the jointly written chronicle her father had intended to an exercise with which to hone her own storytelling skills. This transformation may have been partly in response to Tom's and her sisters' reluctance to contribute entries, even as she sometimes corralled writers by ostentatiously leaving part of a page blank and requesting it to be filled. She encountered this difficulty also with her autograph book and became something of a menace by bringing it along to parties and pressing it on guests and, in doing so, subjecting them to a milder version of the "albumean persecution" endured by literary celebrities like Charles Lamb and Felicia Hemans (K. Harris 79, 76). On one occasion she requisitioned a friend's fishing-pole cover that she had stitched up for him "until he had written something in my [autograph book]," but he thwarted her plan by snatching the cover away while she was distracted "playing shinney or baseball" (FA, 28 May 1874). However, if early on she used other assignments, such as completion of a geographical puzzle, to excuse the brevity of some her entries in the album, she realized a couple of years into keeping it that writing in it allowed her to accomplish two jobs at once, especially after she successfully submitted several essays to children's magazines and was handsomely paid for them.

The Album and the Young Girl's Journal

Her talent and her father's clever educational scheme for the Family Album, along with the whirl of activities within her family and the city of Hamilton, gave Jean plenty to write about, ensuring that this became a better-written, livelier, and less solitary-sounding document than the childhood journals kept by Sir Allan Napier MacNab's daughter Sophia and by the medical pioneer Elizabeth Smith (later Shortt, after her marriage to the historian Adam Shortt). Jean McIlwraith became friends with Smith when the latter attended the Hamilton Collegiate Institute, taught in Hamilton, and after completion of medical school at Queen's opened a medical practice on MacNab Street only a few blocks from Cairnbrae (see McLaren). These journals are the opposite of communal documents. Fourteen-year-old Sophia's journal, most of which was written at Dundurn Castle in 1846 during her mother's final illness, is governed by the strict rules that determined all of her and her sister Minnie's conduct, and they were trained to feel guilty when these rules were not obeyed. The family's religiosity and Sophia's anxiety at disappointing her parents' expectations place her diary in the Roman Catholic tradition of young nineteenth-century girls whose punishment for failing to write regularly in their diaries might result in not being "allowed to take Holy Communion the following Sunday" (Lejeune 141). In addition to the diary serving as a regulatory and punitive instrument, MacNab writes about a life characterized by such monotony that she proposes "to write one day and copy all the rest down from it, there is so little variety" (MacNab 43). Part of this uniformity comes from the rigid schedule imposed by the duty of looking after her ailing mother, but much of it also derives from the social ambitions of the MacNab household and the prescriptive rules for feminine conduct that went with them. Unlike MacNab, Smith grew up on a farm in Winona, east of Hamilton, but according to the childhood journal she kept between 1872 and 1875 she did not fare much better than Sophia. There was a governess, but at thirteen Elizabeth was expected to interrupt her formal schooling, forego the daily company of her friends, and instead provide full-time help around the house and babysit her newborn sister Violet, a duty she did not enjoy. The brief entries that make her childhood diary "more a note book than a diary" are full of dismay at the tedium of "the same thing over & over same day & every day" and express her envy that "the other girls go to school." Much too often, considering her young age, Elizabeth's feels "sleepy" and "tired" as a result of these dull days (E. Smith 4–6).

Despite some similarities with Sophia MacNab and Elizabeth Smith, Jean's world was very different. Her family also had social ambitions, observed the strict rules of their Presbyterian faith, and expected the older children, especially Jean, to look after the younger ones. She was allowed brief sulks when it was Pollie and not she who was chosen to accompany their mother to Scotland or when she was not invited insistently enough to join an excursion to the Niagara Falls, but she did not generally dwell on her feelings, not only because that was not the purpose of the Family Album but also because life around her was too interesting for her to succumb for long to melancholy or boredom. To capture all her impressions and experiences, she variously adopted the persona of a civic reporter, an amateur naturalist, and a travel writer and, to use one of her own expressions, she did it with "sass." Years later, she acknowledged the positive effect of the album on her observational skills and credited it with "[making] us open our eyes the wider" ("Bright Girlhood"). Unlike the homes described by MacNab and Smith, Jean's environment was neither geographically nor socially narrow. The McIlwraith girls' freedom of movement was no more restricted than that of their brothers: they mingled freely with both boys and girls of their own age, and when Jean went to Scotland in the early eighties to stay with her Aunt Sarah she found that she was "kept ... in more closely than [she had] ever been kept at home" (FHEP, J.N. McIlwraith to F.H. Eckstorm, 12 June [1902?]). Sophia had to promise her mother "that we should never waltz" (MacNab 38), but there is no suggestion that the young McIlwraiths' dancing lessons were censured in this way even if their mother decided that Jean was too young to dance at a ball given in honour of Prince Arthur, the governor general, in 1870.

By choice – and in Nellie's case also by necessity because she had a weak ankle and her health was generally delicate ("Genealogy")[8] – the conduct of Jean's sisters and cousins was more conventionally feminine than her own, even when they were young children. On the day following a three-hour Christmas banquet with cousin Hugh Park and his wife Lizzie in Saginaw, Jean tried her best to get Pollie and Lizzie "out of the house," but had to set out on an energetic walk "all over the town" by herself, on which she crossed "the river on the ice." She finally returned "in a cutter with two gentlemen" (FA, 26 December 1872), but had difficulty locating the Parks' home because to her all the houses in its neighbourhood looked alike. The episode projects an astonishing atmosphere of trust that is confirmed as not unusual when on the return journey from Saginaw she walked all over Detroit and watched the sleighs on Lafayette Avenue and Fort Street race fast enough to run down a pedestrian. The driving was sufficiently reckless for young children to be kept indoors and have them watch from the safety of a window, but Jean was in the middle of the action. On that occasion at least, Pollie was persuaded to come out with her sister on a second sortie into Detroit's streets. It was, incidentally, rare for Jean to take the lead when she was with Pollie, who, although she was only two years older, acted very much the older sister throughout their lives. After their mother's death when she was staying with Mary (now "Mrs. Service") in her home on Woodward Avenue in Detroit, Jean confided to Fannie Hardy Eckstorm that "[Mary] rather seems more like a mother to me than any one I have left now" (FHEP, J.N. McIlwraith to F.H. Eckstorm, 12 January 1902), though Pollie's brand of motherliness was bossier than Mrs. McIlwraith's gentle guidance. Likewise, the intimacy that Jean and Nellie established in their shared room at the top of Cairnbrae and "in [their] favourite place under the big apple tree in the garden, Nell – darning stockings and I writing letters" (FA, 7 July 1874) carried over into adulthood, and they remained "great ... chums" into Nellie's marriage to John Henderson Holt (FHEP, J.N. McIlwraith to F.H. Eckstorm, 12 January 1902). Because of her slight handicap, Nellie did not participate in the family's boisterous activities, and Jean watched over her sister's welfare like a lioness.

---

8   Her obituary points out that she was "[p]hysically never strong" (see "Mrs. Helen Holt").

Jean's vigorous physical activities give the lie to the assumption that middle-class young women of her generation automatically succumbed "to a mawkish celebration of domesticity" (Katz 55).[9] It is true that she could be found embroidering a footstool to present to her mamma on her return from Scotland, participating in a quilting bee, learning to bake "scons" [sic] and apple fritters, and taking part in genteel croquet parties or a dance on the propeller "Dromedary." She was, however, much more often busy playing hide-and-go-seek, swinging, rowing, swimming, and wading in the creek, playing baseball, sliding, snowshoeing, sleighing, skating, and performing "the Dutch roll down a flight of four steps" (FA, 21 December 1874). Her athleticism was such that she was later able to spin it into stories and articles, and she often enriched her enjoyment of physical activity with her knowledge of literature. She cited Robert Burns to her co-author William McLennan when she assured him that "a good skate" made her "feel 'o 'er a' the ills o'life victorious" (McLFF, J.N. McIlwraith to W. McLennan, 31 December 1896), and she may have thought of the skating episode in Wordsworth's *The Prelude* or Mary Mapes Dodge's popular children's book *Hans Brinker, or The Silver Skates* (1865), which introduced North Americans to speed skating, when she described the pastime as "the king of winter sports, the most individually independent, the most graceful and the most universally possible" for "the Canadian girl flying before the wind ... [w]ith her jacket outspread in lieu of a sail" ("Winter Sports" 180). The latter quotation appears in an essay with the resounding title "Winter Sports Old and New: The Joyous Possibilities of Sleighing, Snow-Shoeing, Skeeing [sic], Curling, Bobbing, Tobogganing – What Canada Can Teach Us in Open-Air Holiday-Making," published in *Country Life in America* (1905–6) and full of precise information on sports equipment and technique. Indeed, the article was considered informative enough for two excerpts, on snowshoeing and tobogganing, to make it into J.C. Dier's edited collection *A Book of Winter Sports: An Attempt to Catch the Keen Joys of the Winter Season* (1912). For McIlwraith, physical fitness was one of several ways in which a woman was able to match her worth against a man's, and her story "On Georgian Bay" (1900) introduces a "woman, or girl, broad, sturdy ... with flowing black hair and wildly waving arms" (181) who eventually outsmarts a young man from Boston with her canoeing skills. When McIlwraith moved to New York at age forty-three, she was not in the least intimidated by the prospect of cycling to work to save on tram fare: after all, her "muscle [was] A1" (FHEP, J.N. McIlwraith to F.H. Eckstorm, 29 August 1902).

In her pursuit of outdoor exercise, Jean was well ahead of the advice on how to be a "healthy girl" dispensed by girls' magazines a few years later (Moruzi

---

9 For other young women who defied the stereotypical image "of languid Victorian maidens," see Fanny Marion Chadwick and her friends as described in Hoffman and Taylor 205.

83). In a rare moment when no friend or equipment was handy, Jean had a good time "poling around on an old door on the swamp" by herself (FA, 7 June 1875), but generally her exercise took place in the cheerful company of others. Christmas presents for the children often included sports gear of one kind or another, and for 1874 Hugh and Kenny each received half of a new sleigh. At times one of the children became too enterprising, and Johnny was just in time pulled out of a barrel filled with water that he intended to explore headfirst. Several of the young McIlwraiths had whooping cough when they were very young (MM, 21 June 1862, 372), and as we know, Kennedy fought respiratory illness for much of his youth, but plenty of fresh air and outdoor activity were perhaps one reason why the health of the children was, apart from the occasional cold or infection, remarkably sturdy during the period recorded in the Family Album. There was no guarantee in the absence of vaccination, but the way the children spent their days, along with excellent meals, probably helped most of them to build up resistance to infectious diseases while other children of their acquaintance died of typhoid fever (FA, 14 June 1874) or succumbed to smallpox, a disease raging at various times in the country around Hamilton. On their way to visit with Andrew and Mary McIlwraith in Listowel, Mrs. McIlwraith and Jean saw a "board nailed at a door of a house near the station [of Elora]" that warned anyone about to enter that there was a patient suffering from smallpox within: "[a] woman behind us in the car said that there were a great many cases in the village" (14 May 1874).

Sports and Family Bonds

Their outdoor games definitely strengthened the siblings' bond with each other. Tom or Hugh often obtained "the loan of a schooners [sic] yawl" (FA, 20 May 1875) to row their sisters and their friends around the lake, including Tom's future wife, Mary Stevens, but Jean was an expert sailor herself who was not flustered when she had to do "more hammering than rowing [because] one of the lockers had burst from the fastening" (14 June 1875). Babysitting the younger boys was an excellent excuse to teach them the games she enjoyed herself, and she was gratified when Jack, "a remarkably good skater for a little fellow ... beat ... [Hugh and her] all hollow" (19 February 1874). She was happy to laugh at her own comparative awkwardness on the ice. Because it seemed to her that they lived this kind of freedom all the time, she liked "country girls first rate," and though she found them "very homely," two such girls she met on vacation were "just as funny and nice as they can be" (9 June 1875). By contrast, we can almost see Jean rolling her eyes as "Nellie and Peggie Big Anger as we call her practice dressmaking. They sit in a little place under the kitchen window and make dolls dresses etc. all day long" (28 July 1871). In her novel *The Curious Career of Roderick Campbell* she is practically cheering with her male narrator when Elsie and Mysie Buchanan escape the feminine drill of "sit[ting] for hours at [their] tiresome samplers" (240), and instead play "beaver ... build[ing] dams and houses and ... flop[ping] in and out of the water in a fashion the animal himself might have envied" (242). While Nellie and Peggie made doll's dresses, Jean herself was getting lessons in baking scones and learning the difficult art of getting the fire to burn just right for them. Meekness was not her method even in the kitchen, as she proved when "she made the young ones eat [the scones] all up at breakfast" so that she could bake some more at an hour when she did not have to compete for space on the stove with the maid who was doing the family wash (FA, 31 July 1871). She did enjoy baking, cooking, and entertaining and, as will be discussed in the next chapter, even obtained a diploma from the National Training School in Cookery in London to improve her skills.

Transport and Mobility

The many vehicles that move through Jean's diary entries are like extensions of her own energy: in addition to the cargo travelling on schooners, steamers, and propellers on Lake Ontario, and powerful tugs taking on six of these vessels at a time, everyone seems to be in constant motion on skiffs, yawls, trains, tram-cars, stagecoaches, buggies, democrats, sleighs, cutters, and one-hoss-shays. Road and bridge work was carefully noted and alternative routes mapped out to avoid delays and, like her father, Jean delighted in retracing the day's route as precisely as possible. One drive was particularly circuitous because there was construction on the Desjardins Canal, the site of a disaster in 1857 when a Great Western Railway passenger train plunged through the bridge over the canal, killing fifty-nine people:

> At a little before six Papa and I in the front seat and Maggie and Pollie in the back started for Rock Chapel in the buggy. At the Desjardins Canal we had to take the low bridge as they have pulled down the high one to rebuild it newly. We went quite a long way on the Waterdown road when we came to another bridge that was being pulled down so we had to back up and turn round. A man on the roadside directed us to the road that went up the hill beside the long trussel [sic] work bridge on the Toronto branch. (FA, 16 July 1874)

Also like her father, Jean always paid attention to the working animals' response to their changing environment, and when they "had the pleasure of seeing a long train cross [the bridge]," she noted approvingly that unlike other horses that had been known to panic at the approach of a train, "Barney pricked up his ears but stood quite still" (16 July 1874). Jean liked her vehicles stylish and fast, and when given a chance she steered them with panache. Her boldness was such that it fired up her Uncle Bill to encourage daredevil driving: "We went down on the ice and saw the races and then drove all over town," she wrote. "I nearly tipped the cutter over going round a corner too sharply but except that we got on hunkly" (28 January 1875). When she was sixteen, one of the Great Lakes captains even allowed her to take the wheel of his steamer "quite a distance" on Lake Erie (6 August 1874). No wonder she was not impressed with the stagecoach taking her from Listowel to catch the train in Palmerston, "a rather rickety old vehical [sic]," but she consoled herself by observing "a swell in glasses" who got in the front seat, as well as spying "a great brown beast with a huge tail, waddling into the bush." The passengers agreed that this was most likely "a porcupine" (22 May 1874).

The extent of Jean's outdoor exercise, which later included diving, cycling, golf, and motoring (and was replaced by workouts in the gymnasium during bad weather), impressed her acquaintances well into her sixties until heart disease put a stop to vigorous exercise. The American-born Anne Elizabeth Wilson, who became the first editor of the women's magazine *Chatelaine* but was working in the editorial department of Stodder and Houghton when Jean won the publisher's award for her juvenile novel *The Little Admiral* (1923), wrote in her obituary about her "beloved friend" that "the photograph of [Jean] I then most admired was one wearing a flyer's helmet, for she had taken several flights, even in those early days of air-travel!" (Wilson).[10] Given the helmet, it is not clear whether Jean was only a passenger or was in fact taking flying lessons.

The McIlwraith Wharf and Great Lakes Commerce

In addition to her naturally active constitution, Jean's curiosity in the world around her was stimulated by her father's business, which from the 1870s onwards tied the family's fortunes closely to the shipping and railroad routes that linked the city's prosperity to the Great Lakes economy. In one of her earliest published sketches, written under her first pseudonym, "Jeannie Newton," Jean succinctly describes the scene and her family's home and business within it:

My home in Hamilton is on the heights above Burlington Bay. As I sit now at my window, looking to the east, I can see the blue waters of Ontario stretching away toward the horizon. To the west, the southern shore of the bay is lined with wharves, and the workshops and elevators of the Great Western Railway. Steam and sailing vessels are constantly passing to and fro, and there is any amount of boating. (Newton, "Burned to the Water's Edge" 755)

---

10 Unfortunately, the photograph has not come to light. For biographical information on Wilson, a remarkable woman in her own right, see "Anne Elizabeth Wilson."

Once their father had become a wharfinger, the children were awakened by "[t]he 'Go he-ead' ... and the never ceasing tramp of horse's feet going up the [coal] dump which has been greatly raised," requiring "Papa ... to make another one" (FA, 6 May 1874).

Thomas McIlwraith bought the wharf at a time when commerce on the Great Lakes was at an all-time high, with as many as 5,600 vessels in operation and "bumper-to-bumper traffic" (M. Thompson 22) through the locks, as Jean frequently confirms in her travel notes when she can write barely fast enough to note down the name of each vessel. Shipping was closely tied into an expanding railroad system and, because it was less dependent on the climate, increasingly displaced by it. In her descriptions of Hamilton and her travels south, Jean deftly cites the initials of Canadian and American railway companies, such as the Great Western, the Detroit and Mackinac Railway, and the Michigan Central Railroad, along with the names of executives such as Hugh Allan, Thomas Swinyard, and W.K. Muir, but it was the ships that captured her and her family's attention most. On an outing to Egerton Ryerson's Normal School in Toronto, her young brothers were especially fascinated by "the models of every kind of craft from a yacht to a line-of-battle ship" on display there (FA, 20 August 1874). Observing the weather was an essential condition of successful shipping, and at times her entries build up to elaborate meteorological drama that goes well beyond Kennedy's sketches of wild weather. This is especially true of the spring thaw, when "the life blood of commerce" was, to cite Thomas Keefer's plea for the building of railways, no longer "curdled and stagnant" (3) but burst forth powerfully. Jean writes on Monday, 23 March 1874, "Intensely cold and very windy. The water looks very cold and muddy. The steamers are sagging against the docks and there is a heavy swell, ice round the surface of the boats."

That chilly day was bracketed by one earlier in March when the sound of "a blow" preceded the "ice [coming] steadily down from the Desjardins Canal" (FA, 19 March 1874), and the beginning of the shipping season three weeks later when "the first steamer of the season" left for St. Catharines, although "[t]he boat cannot get down to Montreal yet" (9 April 1874). By mid-April, "the first steamer arrive[d] ... hauling three barges to load with lumber" (12 April 1874). There was a setback a week later: "Monday 20th [April 1874]. Cold, and raining heavily. The 'Acadia' at our front dock pitching six feet[;] she had to come round to the high dock."

Jean talks about arriving and departing ships as if they were so many friends, and she carefully lists the name of each: "There are five schooners at our dock now," she writes three weeks later, when shipping is in full swing. "The 'Melrose' just going out; the 'Azov' being unloaded; and the 'Kate Kelly,' 'Austrailia' [sic], and 'Twilight' waiting" (6 May 1874). Just as she was taken aback by her brothers' suddenly unfamiliar, sun-tanned and long-legged appearance when she had been away for a few weeks, she critically assessed the appearance of the schooners when they had been repainted during the winter. When John Proctor's *Africa* exchanged her elegant green paint, set off by a white funnel with red top, for a black-and-white colour scheme, Jean curtly judged that "[s]he doesn't look the same" (8 June 1874). As with horse-drawn carriages and sleighs, she liked her ships to be handsome. One afternoon on deck of the *Africa* in the port of Montreal, minding the boys and "watching the operations going on around," she found "our backed up lake propellers" badly wanting compared to the "fresh and clean" look of the *Caspian* and the *Prussian* (15 August 1874). As on other occasions, her ambition to list every vessel she saw was – despite a hastily scribbled list in the back of the Family Album – foiled by the sheer number of them.

Quite often, one of the ships became a temporary home for one or several of the children. As soon as the Lakes were navigable, the captains, in return for the warm hospitality at the McIlwraith home when they were anchored at the dock, frequently invited the youngsters to come along on a run. Thirteen-year-old Hugh, for example, travelled to Ashtabula on Lake Erie that way. His family was on the lookout ten days later for the return of the *Picton* as she came "slowly up from the canal against a head wind," revealing a very sun-tanned Hugh in a straw hat. He, too, had been allowed to steer in the canal, had "seen such lots of propellers and schooners," and was loaded with gifts: a drum for Kenny, a "Yankee hoop" for Jack, and "an abundant supply of hickory nuts for us all" (FA, 25 June 1874). A few months later, Jean, Nellie, Pollie, and Kenny were up at three o'clock in the morning to board the *Africa* for a trip to Montreal that first took them through the Welland Canal into Lake Erie and on to Toledo and then back into Lake Ontario before heading into the St. Lawrence and its canals. At the last minute, they were joined by Jack and "his bundle of clothes" because "[h]e had cried so much at the thought of Kenny going without him that Mamma let him come" (3 August 1874).

In describing these travels, Jean's diary complements the rare narratives by women who came to know the water not only as a venue for tourism but also as a place of work, either the crew's or their own. In the 1860s, Amelia July worked as a cook on the *Mayflower*, "plying the Great Lakes (Ontario and Erie), the Welland Canal and the Detroit River" with her husband Peter, the captain (Hoffman and Taylor 4). Closer to Jean's age but from New Brunswick and crossing the ocean rather than travelling through the Great Lakes was eleven-year-old Amelia Holder who, in the late 1860s wrote about travelling with her mother and younger sister Aggie on her father's ship, the *Hannah H.*, "from Ireland to Spain, then back across the Atlantic to South America before returning to New Brunswick" (Carter, *Small Details of Life* 97). This was one of six sea voyages Amelia undertook and recorded. She, too, was allowed to steer the ship under the captain's supervision, though, in writing about her adventures, she lacked Jean's lively style. Amelia Holder's story reminds us that captains and crew were separated from their families for long periods of time. For them, the

McIlwraith children sometimes played the role of temporary substitutes, and Kenny especially charmed everyone. During one of their trips on the *Africa*, he was declared "a great favourite on board" (FA, 5 August 1874). The children were attentive listeners when crew members wanted to talk about their families, as did Captain Anderson from Milan, Ohio, and "a regular Yankee," who showed them "tin types of his five children that he carries about in his pocket book." Jean adds: "The eldest girl is just a little older than I" (26 June 1874). Members of the crew's family sometimes boarded to keep them company for part of the way, and "George, the second mate, brought his little girl on board. She is a pretty little thing and he is awful proud of her" (12 August 1874). Such visits were not always without danger, and another child was drowned as she came to visit her father on the Welland Canal.

While the McIlwraiths do not appear to have suffered the economic disasters experienced by other Hamiltonians (see Katz 176–208), the business that made these childhood adventures possible was not created without some stress to the family. Perhaps Mr. McIlwraith felt that, in the prosperity that Hamilton was experiencing after the depression of the fifties, his family's fortunes would be better served if he set up a coal dealership, and that he was sufficiently well off to take the risk. The gas works did not bear him a grudge for leaving, and he soon obtained the contract to transport coal for them. His son's situation also changed when his employer, Kerr, Brown and McKenzie, split into three separate firms, and Tom became chief bookkeeper at John Brown and Co. before finally joining his father's business. There was then some instability in the family's situation at the time when the album was in progress despite everyone's apparent cheerfulness, increased by the fact that the McIlwraiths moved house several times during the seventies. Jean records three of these removals within the first three years of keeping the Family Album, including a new spacious home with "stable, woodshed, and henhouse" on the corner of Hamilton's Charles and Hunter Streets. This house was completed in August 1871 and is the most concrete evidence we have of the family's affluence at the time. Although the McIlwraiths were reluctant to leave their new house again so soon, the wharf came with a large brick building, and Jean reported belatedly in 1873 that they had moved there. This is presumably the dwelling that remained the family home until 1912 and that they named "Cairnbrae." Although the family appears to have settled quickly into their new situation, it was a worry that the mare in the "splendid span of working horses" that Mr. McIlwraith had purchased for the dock "was found to be rather weak in the joints" and had to be sold (FA, 18 June 1872).

Anxieties and Separations

Gaps in the Family Album can, as suggested earlier, have a variety of reasons, but they do appear to signal some anxiety during this period in the family's lives when they were upset by one worry or new adjustment after the other. Entries for 1872 are extremely sparse, with none between 1 January and 18 June 1872, and another six-month gap between that day and December. The whole of the summer is summed up in the sentence "I spent two weeks of this summer at Greenfield with Jack" (FA, 1 December 1872). A long description of a two-week trip to Saginaw during the Christmas holiday season barely compensates for these interruptions. Writing for 1873 is more sustained and proceeds in fits and starts for most months, but neither year has the almost complete day-by-day record that is provided for 1874 and 1875. There were a number of disruptions in the family's life that accompany these gaps in the record. In late 1871, Mrs. McIlwraith's mother died in Scotland, and Mary Park herself suffered from crippling rheumatism throughout the winter – clearly a worry for Jean, who adored her "Mamma" and "nearly choked her" with affection on her return from Scotland two years earlier, as Pollie observed in one of her rare entries (3 September 1870). For unspecified reasons, fourteen-year-old Pollie did not attend school for part or all of 1872, though she must have returned soon enough because she graduated with honours in 1873 (an achievement on which the Family Album is oddly silent), and there are oblique references that she did not enjoy herself at the Wesleyan Ladies' College[11] as thoroughly as Jean appears to have done throughout her time there. In 1874, it was Nellie's turn to take a break from school; once again no reasons are given.

Opened in 1861 with Mary Adams as founding principal and occupying the former Anglo-American hotel in downtown Hamilton, the college pursued a non-sectarian policy despite its Methodist orientation, and it set high academic standards, "offering preparatory studies as well as collegiate courses in mathematics, logic, rhetoric, classical languages, philosophy, modern languages, natural sciences, music, and fine arts" (Selles 82).[12] Because the school attracted students from all over Canada and the United States, often from well-connected families, the McIlwraith girls not only received an excellent education there but also formed lasting friendships with young women from all over North America. One of these friendships was the catalyst for marriage when Nellie introduced her brother Tom to her fellow student Mary Stevens from Quebec's Eastern Townships. Given the intellectual and social advantages that the college provided for the girls, it is fortunate that all three did stay there until graduation, whatever it was that kept Pollie and Nellie at home for a while. In fact, thanks to the Wesleyan Ladies' College, the McIlwraith girls had a better academic education than their brothers, with the exception of Kennedy, who went on to study medicine.

---

11 The college has been referred to as both the Wesleyan Female College and the Wesleyan Ladies' College. To avoid confusion, I will use the latter throughout.

12 See also John G. Reid, "Adams, Mary Electa."

If 1872 was a difficult year for the McIlwraiths, then there were problems large and small to report throughout the five years in which Jean kept the Family Album. While travels on lakes, canals, railways, and country roads made for a lively childhood, they also frequently took friends and acquaintances away from the family. Jean was very sorry to lose her best friend Clara Gray when her father was appointed principal in Galt, and she offered Clara a "pretty plated locket" as a farewell gift (FA, 23 and 28 May 1870). Galt was close enough to allow them to maintain their bond by letter and by visit but this was more difficult when people moved "away out west to live," as did the family of Ida Sawyer, who had to board at the college in order to finish her education (20 June 1872). Because students generally left town when their studies were over, there were frequent farewells. Sometimes, to Pollie's delight, former classmates returned as teachers a few years later. At other times, looking up their friends' homes had to suffice. While visiting in Montreal, the girls tramped up and down Belmont Street to locate the home of Thomas Macfarlane Bryson,[13] merchant and father of an apparently inexhaustible supply of daughters who studied at the college, although some of these Brysons may have come from the families of Thomas's brothers George and John, lumber merchants and politicians.

Teachers and preachers also moved away. In 1874, the girls lost their teacher Emma Douse when she married the Methodist missionary Thomas Crosby and moved with him to northern British Columbia.[14] Another attraction was New York, and several of Hamilton's most popular preachers departed for a more prominent posting there. William Ormiston, first president of Hamilton's Association for the Advancement of Literature, Science and Arts, close friend of Egerton Ryerson, and a frequent presence in Andrew McIlwraith's diaries, left the city's Central Presbyterian Church for the Dutch Reformed Church in New York in 1870 ("Ormiston"). A year later, David Inglis, the first minister of the MacNab Street Church that Ormiston had helped to create, resigned to take up "the chair of systematic theology at Knox College in Toronto," from where he visited to give the occasional sermon before moving on to the Dutch Reformed Church in Brooklyn in 1872 ("Inglis"). The departure of these preachers was often a loss twice over because their wives, too, were active in the parish. Ormiston's wife Clarissa, for example, was Jean's Sunday school teacher, and Mrs. Ormiston's pupils presented her "with a magnificent fancy clock, and two beautiful large vases" when all were invited to tea at her house to say goodbye (FA, 19 August 1870).

In order to maintain contact with friends who had moved away, the mails were essential. Jean kept conscientiously in touch with school friends who had left town, such as Clara Gray and Jean's "great school friend" Lilly Thompson,

---

13 See Starke's *Pocket Almanac*, xi. For George Bryson, see Gillis.
14 See Hare and Barman; see also the Thomas and Emma Crosby Fonds, RBSC, UBC.

and a cooling of friendship was measured by fewer letters or a complete stop in correspondence: "I have got cool with ... L. Thompson," Jean writes before adding philosophically: "Last year it was Fan Bryson" (FA, 19 February 1874). There was more at stake than school-girl quarrels in the letters that, in order to hold the widely scattered McIlwraith clan together, flew back and forth between Hamilton and Scotland, and between Hamilton and places in the more immediate Canadian and American neighbourhood: "[a]s ... a carrier of letters, the railway ... pulled the old country closer to Hamilton" (Weaver 74), as well as pulling the whole of North America closer to Hamilton. There were news of the birth "of a son and heir" to the Parks in Saginaw, and black-edged envelopes announcing the deaths of "Uncle John's little girl" and of Grandma McIlwraith (FA, 17 February 1874; 15 April 1874; 1 December 1871). John Stevenson in Liverpool, Mrs. McIlwraith's second cousin, wanted to emigrate to Canada with his family and wrote expressing his hope for support in getting settled.

Their parents' matter-of-fact assistance to emigrants before they left the Old Country and after they arrived was the model for Pollie and Jean when, on a train to the United States, they did their best to make a weary emigrant family comfortable who had been travelling since dawn: "Pollie sat by the fire talking to one of the grown up girls while I went around [and] pulled down all the shutters" (FA, 23 December 1872). No matter with how much freedom the McIlwraith children moved about, they kept in close touch with their parents and frequently wrote to their mother, and she wrote back just as often when they were on vacation with relatives or hitching a ride on one of the boats that loaded at their father's dock. To ensure his offspring was safe, Thomas McIlwraith sent letters of introduction ahead to his business associates asking them to pick up his children for dinner or a carriage ride when they arrived in Montreal. In turn, business friends like G.E. Jacques, a forwarder on Common Street, produced the letter as a kind of identity card: "Mr. Jacques and Edith came with a letter from Papa and took Pollie away with them. She did not come home till we were all in bed" (29 August 1873). Only intimate friends like Thomas W. Raphael, a produce and commission merchant in Montreal, were able to take the children away without such identification.[15]

Mail, Telegraph, and the Imperial Archive

When Mrs. McIlwraith travelled to the Old Country, she was able to rely on an efficient and speedy postal service, complemented by telegraph transmission to the Hamilton *Spectator* that her ship had been sighted off the coast of Ireland, to reassure her family of her safety. Mr. McIlwraith read his wife's letters to the

---

15 On Jacques and Raphael, see *Lovell's Montreal Directory for 1881–82*, 441, 590.

children, and he shared her reports with extended family. When Jean published her book on Canada for young readers in 1899, she underlined the role of the imperial penny postage stamp, introduced in 1898, "making it cost no more to send a letter from Canada to London, England, than to London, Ontario" (*Canada* 246). By the time she wrote this, she had spent a decade pursuing her literary education via mail, by taking correspondence courses in English literature with Queen Margaret College in Glasgow, and she had co-authored a novel with William McLennan, *The Span o' Life*, which would have been impossible without the efficient express service that allowed them to exchange almost daily letters and packages between Hamilton and Montreal. Logically, letter-writing is an important motif in her historical novels, for example in *A Diana of Quebec*, in which Frederick Haldimand's military secretary spends weary hours "quill-driving" (34) as he decodes espionage mail and duplicates correspondence to ensure that it reaches its recipient even if the original is intercepted or destroyed. By dwelling on the mass of written political communication handled by Major Mathews, Jean McIlwraith shows how imperial administrations weave connections between "the state, the bureau, and the file" in order to document and so formalize their claims to governance (Goody 87, 113).

By letter-writing and other means, her own family contributed to the practical assistance and emotional support that sustained the ambitions of the empire, although survival of the Family Album is the result of accident, not bureaucratic planning, and Jean and her siblings were encouraged, rather than required, to write daily entries. Unlike reports, statistics, and coded official correspondence, the album lacks a rigorous system and tracks fluctuations in human behaviour even if it does not dwell on its writer's moods. While the house was in turmoil preparing for her mother's departure for Scotland, for example, Jean stopped writing in the album for a month because she was too preoccupied with the "fuss in the house" (FA, 4 May 1870) and too disappointed that she was not allowed to come along, and she did not consider it to be much of a consolation that her father promised she would accompany him on *his* next trip. By contrast, she wrote almost daily while her mother was away, presumably so that Mrs. McIlwraith would have a record of her children's activities in her absence, including the defiant "We have just been having splendid fun in the yard playing 'Pussy wants a corner,' 'Hide-+-go-seek,' + tag, not very like children whose mother had just gone away" (19 May 1870). As soon as her mother returned eight weeks later, Jean took a ten-month break from journal-keeping, and the last important activity noted before the interval was opening the trunks that contained, one assumes, many presents for the children who had stayed behind in Hamilton.

Jean often mentions keeping up with the Family Album and writing letters to her mother and Pollie in the same breath, and it seems that the diary entries also served as an aide-mémoire. These detailed reminders to herself – some of which were elaborate enough that they could be copied verbatim into letters – were no longer needed when Mrs. McIlwraith returned, but there were other times when Jean used the album as a notebook for her correspondence, either to collect material to write about or to document an exchange of letters that was especially important to her. She conducted an efficient correspondence with several editors of children's magazines, one of whom sent her a geographical puzzle with which to compete for a prize. She and Nellie acquired pen pals through advertisements in *Our Young Folks*, one of these magazines. Nellie wrote to "a Presbyterian minister's daughter" by the name of Emma Wheeler while Jean corresponded with Lulu Dunn, "quite a flirt I believe," in La Grange, Missouri (FA, 5 April 1873). As with her school friends, the connection faded after the first enthusiasm. Jean and Lulu seem to have exchanged letters with long gaps in between because a year after first contact Lulu pleaded to "recommence [their] correspondence," perhaps as a way to comfort herself because "[h]er little sister Josie is dead" and Lulu herself had been sick with typhoid fever: "I wrote her a long letter immediately," Jean announced (6 June 1874). To enliven their long-distance acquaintance and give it additional stability, Jean and Lulu exchanged photographs, although this does not seem to have made much difference because Lulu is not mentioned again. The McIlwraith siblings enjoyed visiting the studio of Mr. Robert Milne, the Hamilton daguerrotypist, especially on landmark birthdays such as their "sweet sixteen." In putting their trust in photographs as effective mementoes, the older McIlwraith children followed the example of their parents' generation. Their uncle Andrew, for example, regularly had his likeness taken to send home to Scotland.

Hamilton Reporter

A mother's two-month absence and the permanent departure of friends and family upset the McIlwraith children's sense of security, but there were more serious events in their neighbourhood. Hamilton's picturesque location between bay and mountain could be treacherous, and the city's infrastructural opportunities came at the price of calamities, especially on the water, both on the lake and in the waterways connected to it. The rail disaster of 1857, when dozens of passengers lost their lives as a derailed train plunged from a swing bridge into the frozen Desjardins Canal below predates the Family Album, although Andrew reports on it in his diary (*MM*, 14, 15 March 1857, 72). There were, however, plenty of accidents on the lake between 1870 and 1875. In an incident close to Cairnbrae, old Mr. Muir[16] was fortunate after he had slipped stepping from his boat on to the wharf. He was hauled out of the water by Tom and other workers,

---

16 Probably the father of railway executive M.K. Muir.

brought to Cairnbrae to be "doctored" by Mrs. McIlwraith, and finally driven home in a cab by her husband (FA, 25 November 1874). By contrast there was terrible heartbreak when Amy, Constance, and Irene, the young daughters of Thomas Swinyard, general manager of the Great Western Railway, perished in a yachting accident one summer evening in 1870 (28 June 1870). They were eulogized by the Reverend John Hebden at the Church of the Ascension (see Hebden). Equally tragic was the news in the summer of 1874 that the yacht *Foam* had capsized near Niagara-on-the-Lake, taking seven young men from some of Toronto's most prominent families with it.[17] Charles Beckett, the organist of Christ's Church, lost heart because a scheme to seek his fortunes out west had not been successful, and he took his own life. The Hamilton *Spectator* was blunt about the gruesome details of his suicide, committed by tying his knees together, slitting his throat with a razor and managing to slide into the water before he died. Two boys demonstrated remarkable sangfroid when they attempted to fish the body out of the lake by "[fastening] a rope around the neck and ... [towing] the corpse to the shore."[18] The McIlwraith children discovered nothing quite so shocking on their many trips around the lake, even if they had "a nice sail out to a dead dog in the Bay" one July afternoon (FA, 28 July 1874). In general, they were free to roam in the extended neighbourhood, including the water, but sometimes even their normally relaxed parents greeted their offspring "with angry relief " when they did not return from an expedition up Waterdown Creek until late at night ("Bright Girlhood"). As mentioned earlier, Jean paid conscientious attention to the working animals, and on a visit to Woodland Cemetery in Cleveland she related the nervous response of a team of horses to a noisy funeral band, or she reported on accidents involving the many horses employed on the wharves and along the canals. "Strawberry," one of her father's workhorses, slipped into the bay as he was brought on deck of the *Twilight* to hoist coal and "swam around for about an hour before he was rescued" (FA, 9 May 1874). In a more serious accident observed alongside the Welland Canal, "two of the towing horses ran away, dragging another one after them, causing it to hit its head against the lamppost and then roll over and over in the dust." Happily, the horse survived and was soon seen "towing again" (10 August 1874).

Maintaining Connections

Still, the ever-present danger of accidents and the departures of friends, teachers, and pastors did not spoil Jean's love of her hometown. Opportunities to

---

17 See *The Daily News* (Kingston, ON), 22 July 1874. http://images.maritimehistoryofthegreat-lakes.ca/20730/data (accessed 1 September 2019).

18 Hamilton *Spectator*, 27 April 1870, n.p.

reconnect with acquaintances who had left town were eagerly pursued, such as a trip to the market where, just before Christmas, "we saw a great many boys and girls who had come home for the holidays" (FA, 20 December 1873). It is unusual that she does not list the names of each and every one of these "boys and girls," because the names of almost all of Hamilton's well-known families, from Ambrose, Browne, Crerar, Dynes, Fairgrieve, Ferrie, and Gourlay to Proctor, Rae, Wanzer, and Zealand show up sooner or later in the Family Album, either as Mr. McIlwraith's business associates or as school friends of one of the children, especially the girls. The children were brought up to be sociable and their parents' generation demonstrated to them how useful, even essential, "gregarious outreach toward respectability" could be in helping to weather crises and the threat of "[i]solation and transiency" that came with them (Weaver 24).

The preparations for Mrs. McIlwraith's trip to Scotland demonstrate that this outreach was reciprocal: soon after she decided to travel to the Old Country, she visited the extended family in Galt to say goodbye and to collect letters and parcels from them to take along with her to Ayr. In addition, a stream of visitors appeared as her departure came closer to wish her safe travels and to drop off more mail and packages. A recurrent scene in the McIlwraith archive involves the last-minute arrival of a relative or acquaintance as one of the Canadian McIlwraiths prepares to return home from Scotland. Andrew McIlwraith's diaries contain such a scene involving a distant cousin, a plumber, who rushed to Liverpool and "knocked us up at 7, he coming from Ayr by the night train" when Andrew was getting ready to return to Canada (MM, 18 November 1857, 122). Jean's nephew T.F. McIlwraith, then a student of anthropology at Cambridge, described a similar scene when he accompanied her to Greenock in 1921 to see her off after a tour of Europe.

On their travels, Jean and her brothers and sisters easily chatted with other passengers and accepted calling cards from them. They did, however, have a clear sense of "tribe." A good example is Pollie's report of a Dominion Day excursion by train to Niagara Falls. The account is all names: "There were Nellie Sawyer and her Mother three Miss Fairgrieves, Maggie Amos and her sister [,] three of the Angiers and five or six others whom I did not know besides Tom Ormiston who is here on a visit from New York and Bobbie Mitchell the friend with whom he is staying." At Sawyersville, the train took on another group, "the Sawyers, Penningtons, Coburns, Aineses, and Mr. Scrimger." All of them defended the territory of their "Special Party" against an irate gentleman "who insisted on sitting in our car ... and said he would write to Mr. Muir," general superintendent of the Great Western Railway, about the outrage of being asked to move to another compartment (FA, 1 July 1871). Naturally, any Fairgrieves who happened to be in Britain in 1921 when Jean was visiting her nephew were paid a visit, and news of events in Hamilton that had occurred while she was travelling on the Continent was obtained from them at the same time (TFMF, T.F. McIlwraith to family, 15 September 1921).

Always including lists of names, Jean kept careful track of the many hospitable gatherings in her parents' home for which, if they were especially fancy, supper was ordered from Ecclestone the confectioner. At these times, the Family Album doubles as a guestbook and social program. Besides animated conversation, there were usually music and games such as croquet in summer, and carpet croquet, bagatelle, euchre, charades, and tableaux vivants in winter. In addition to teas organized to keep business relations friendly, including visits from Mr. McIlwraith's clerk and his wife or the various captains of the ships that transported cargo for him, most of the gatherings were organized by age into parties for the "old folks" of the parents' generation or for the children's school friends. The former might include "Mr. + Mrs. Morton, Old Mr. + Mrs. George Thompson, Annie Osborne, and Mr. + Mrs. Taylor," and were popular even with the young McIlwraiths because "[i]t was a good treat to hear Mama and Mrs. Taylor go over the old Ayr worthies" (FA, 8 February 1875). Conversely, the parents were on hand to welcome the younger visitors: "[s]ix of the College girls spent this evening with us," Jean writes on one such occasion: "3 Brysons, L. Surles, M. Webster + J. Wilkins. Laura sang a Dutch song that delighted Papa" (24 December 1873).[19] Along with other middle-class families, the McIlwraiths diligently practised the social rituals of visiting and leaving calling cards.[20] In her cousin Lizzie's home in Saginaw, Jean endured an afternoon of nine callers. During a visit in Listowel, Uncle Andrew's wife Mary accompanied Mrs. McIlwraith and Jean on "calls" through town that were both social and charitable, taking them from Andrew's foundry to "poor little Charlie who has hurt his spine jumping" (20 May 1874). As was her custom, Jean improves with deft character sketches what may otherwise have been a tedious afternoon for her. Thus, she singles out the wife of Dr. Nichol, "who is something of an authoress" but "appeared in house cleaning rig at the door" (20 May 1874). The transition from the easy commerce of childhood to greater adult formality was not always negotiated smoothly, as three young gentlemen found out when they appeared at Cairnbrae to invite the girls to a dance: the invitation was gladly accepted, but Picton C. Brown, Frank R. Waddell, and R.M. Wilson, "as their cards indicated," were pelted with pebbles as they departed (1 January 1875).

The adult Jean continued her parents' practice of hosting convivial parties at Cairnbrae. Writing in the Hamilton *Spectator* about social life in the city during the 1890s, Charles R. McCullough, founder of the Canadian Club, called

---

19 As mentioned in the introduction, L. Surles was Laura Miller Surles from North Carolina, who married James Dunsmuir, entrepreneur, politician, and lieutenant governor of British Columbia. In Nanaimo, she often entertained "the local élite ... with songs at concerts" (Karr).

20 See the chapter on "Visiting," Hoffman and Taylor 135–50.

her a "brilliant hostess" whose gatherings of writers, critics, artists, and other public figures included the poet Pauline Johnson, the violinist Nora Clench, the critic Hector Charlesworth, the politician W. Sanford Evans, as well as local relatives of the American William Dean Howells, of whom Pauline Johnson, through her mother Emily Susanna Howells, was one.[21] As for using letters of introduction and calling cards to expand her social and professional network, Jean was – as we shall see when she moved to New York – her father's well-prepared daughter.

The family's circle was therefore large, and charity was extended to those less fortunate, including the homeless "Miss Jones [who is] subject to fits" and who was taken in by Mrs. Goldie, Uncle Andrew's sister-in-law, in return for "mak[ing] herself generally useful" (FA, 29 May 1874). But Miss Jones was Mrs. Goldie's "old school friend" and therefore still belonged to the middle-class individuals, most of them Scots or maintaining close connections to Scotland, with whom the McIlwraiths typically socialized. Hamilton "was part of a[n] ... extended trade empire managed by Scots" (Weaver 15), and individuals from families who had distinguished themselves in its service were sure to be pointed out to the children. In Uncle Andrew's neighbourhood in Listowel, for example, there was John Livingstone, brother of the missionary and explorer Dr. David Livingstone, while Hamilton's citizens included Richard and Thomas Rae, siblings of the Arctic explorer John Rae. John Rae himself was one of Hamilton's celebrities when he briefly took up residence there between 1857 and 1860.

The Black Community and French Canadians

While the world of Jean's childhood was much less constrained than that of Sophia McNab and Elizabeth Smith, it still had its restrictions. We learn little from her about Hamilton's Black community, which, like the ones in other Canadian cities close to the border such as Windsor and St. Catharines, had its origin in the fugitive slaves who had arrived via the Underground Railroad. They were relatively safe in Canada but not protected against segregation and ridicule, especially during times of economic depression when work was scarce (see Winks 178–232). Jean reports on a scene of "babtizing [sic] the negroes in the bay," which was "great fun to Johnnie" (FA, 4 May 1870), and "a lecture given by a darkie in the school house" that she considered "funny" and "not the most refined imaginable" (10 June 1875). Elsewhere she talks about buying apples from a "polite darkie" in St. Catharines (3 August 1874). Her dismissive

---

21 Charles R. McCullough, "The Old Verandas," *Famous People, Landmarks and Events*, 75–6. Presented in a series of reviews published in the Hamilton *Spectator* 8 March 1941–20 February 1943, Special Collections HPL, qtd. in Huyck 38.

expressions echo similar ones in Andrew's diaries, Kennedy's bird book, and Thomas McIlwraith's *The Birds of Ontario*. In Ontario, Andrew observed "old Pumphrey, a nigger wanting an arm and blind of an eye dancing on the sidewalk" (*MM*, 15 June 1858, 163), and in New York he hoped "to find a Nigger church open" to observe Watch Night services (31 December 1859, 251). Twenty-five years later, Kennedy talks of "a darkey boy" who was engaged "to Shoot Red Grosbeaks" by another collector but was offered more money to do the same for Mr. McIlwraith (WIK, 19 and 25 January 1884). His father argued with "an ancient negro" about the white-rumped shrike but had to admit reluctantly that "Sambo was probably right" in assuming that the bird meant harm to chickens (*Birds*, 1894, 347). As Robin Winks has documented (294), Canadian attitudes towards Black citizens were often condescending, and Jean's and Kennedy's comments reflect what they heard at home and at school. An article she wrote for the Saturday edition of the New York *Post* on "a negro camp meeting" (Pringle, "Jean McIlwraith") has not yet come to light, but judging from her novel "Dominick Street," about New York's Lower East Side, and from other sources, her views did not change over time. Walter Hines Page, her employer at Doubleday, Page, was concerned with the situation of African Americans after the Civil War, and the racial divide was debated in his home by journalists like Ray Stannard Baker from the *American Magazine*. Jean's comment, in her "Jottings" about Page, that she was not interested in the subject suggests that, at best, she replaced her prejudice with indifference (JNMP, "Jottings"). On her visit to Cambridge in 1921, she was curious about coloured students from India, either because she found them exotic or because she was surprised that they should be entitled to study at one of Britain's foremost universities, or both.

These attitudes are consistent with those of other Canadian women writers of her time who, although otherwise progressive, hesitated to extend to others the freedom and respect they claimed for themselves. She also shared this inconsistency with the suffragists at Greenwich House in New York, where she volunteered sometime between 1902 and 1905: despite her inclusive politics, the reformer Mary Kingsbury Simkhovich practised segregation so as not to alienate her wealthy sponsors.[22] At the same time, McIlwraith may have thought about the topic more than she was able or willing to articulate, as her effort to compare the situation of servants, Blacks, and Aboriginal people in her story "The Assimilation of Christina" illustrates. Here, McIlwraith tackles a love story, in a resort in Georgian Bay, between an Ojibway and a Scottish housemaid. In response to Christina's "Black men dinna count," her employer cautions her that "[t]hese Ojibways are not the descendants of slaves from Africa. They used

---

22 For an overview of the Canadian situation, see Fiamengo; for Greenwich House, see Adickes 85; McFarland 63.

to own all this part of the country. We are the land thieves," and Christina concedes that as a domestic she is "no better than a black slavey [herself]" (610, 611). In creating Christina, she may have been influenced by H.W. Nevinson's unusual story "Sissero's Return" from *Neighbours of Ours* (1895), which relates the cross-racial romance between a young woman from London's East End and a Black deckhand who is fascinated by her red hair.

To the young Jean, the French Canadians in Montreal were even stranger than the "darkies" of St. Catharines, including "little boys paddling their feet in the water, ... jabbering in French and <u>chewing tobacco</u>" (FA, 28 August 1873) and bargemen who "danced a clog perfectly splendidly to the music of a fiddle played on another barge across the canal" (16 August 1874). In contrast to her persistent indifference to Blacks, the change in language from the first to the second quotation does indicate some growing appreciation of French Canadian culture that quickly came to fruition in her mature writing, made her a connoisseur of French Canadian history and geography, and had her enjoy the friendship of the Abbé Henri-Raymond Casgrain. "In the Earthquake Region" (1890), the first story she published as an adult and under the pseudonym of "Jean Forsyth," displays her knowledge of the Baie-St-Paul region and its history of earthquakes. As in "The Assimilation of Christina," the rapprochement between individuals of ethnic backgrounds traditionally hostile to each other is handled through a love story. "In the Earthquake Region" features a clumsy romance between Philippe, a student of the University of Laval, and "Miss Pettit," whose "thick fringe of copper-colored hair" suggests Scottish origin. Philippe handles a dangerous situation with ingenuity and courage, thus proving Miss Pettit's friends wrong about him and his folks. McIlwraith's lifelong fondness of the Charlevoix area displays the ambiguity typical of much nineteenth- and early twentieth-century women's travel writing about "exotic" or "picturesque" locales and their inhabitants: on the one hand, these places give the visitor a freedom that would be difficult for her to enjoy at home, while on the other she participates in their commodification.[23]

Canadian Nationalism and the Americans

Jean's loyalty to Hamilton's citizens, selective as her awareness of them may have been, was matched by her intense pride in the city itself, and she hotly argued with a boy from Toronto about that city's merits compared with Hamilton's, the discussion made all the more enjoyable because he was "pretty smart ... nearly as old as I" (FA, 5 August 1874). Probably inspired by daily reading of the Hamilton *Times* at home and family discussions about the news, she adopted

---

23   On the commodification of the Charlevoix region, see Hamel; Neatby.

the voice of a roaming local journalist, reporting on civic festivities and spectacles such as the Queen's Birthday, Dominion Day, St. Patrick's Day, and an
excursion from Toronto of the Freemason order of which her brother Tom later
became a member, with the Ancient Order of Foresters decked out in "white
breeches, green or white velvet blouses, large gray felt hats with scarlet feathers,
bows and quivers" (1 July 1875). She wrote about illuminations to celebrate
the governor general's visit that "did great credit to the Gas Works" where her
father was still manager at the time (17 March 1870), and she reported on the
Caledonian Games at the Crystal Palace, erected in 1860 to make the city a
competitive site for holding fairs and thus improve its economic opportunities
(Weaver 68). Here, Mr. McIlwraith was "judge of broad sctotch [sic] poems
and ... of bag pipe playing" (FA, 11 September 1874), a duty he also performed
at the Provincial Fair in Toronto. She wrote about a barn destroyed by fire on
Hess Street, the damage caused by a thunder and hail storm, the excitement of
Election Day, and brawls between Fenians and Orangemen. She also reports on
a labour dispute among the workers on the McIlwraith dock and channels her
father's anger at the disruption to his business.

Such disturbances, however, did not significantly interfere with her conviction that her city was practically paradise on earth. "Rounding the curve ap-
proaching Hamilton I think I never saw as beautiful a sight in all my travels,"
she exclaimed as she returned from a visit to Guelph, and the other travellers on
the train agreed because they "got up to look out the windows; and it was worth
looking. The bay was dotted with row boats and there was a yacht race going
on. Several schooners were making their way towards the canal and we could
see the mail boat lying at Browne's wharf" (FA, 30 May 1874).[24] She was not
alone in her enthusiasm: a poem from 1895 compared the location to Naples,[25]
and Henry Rushton Fairclough, who became a renowned classicist at Stanford,
thought that in his childhood Hamilton "was one of the most attractive of the
small cities of Ontario ..., beautifully situated on land-locked Burlington Bay"
(Fairclough 7). Years later, when Jean worked in New York, Walter Hines Page
was curious to know if there were any other cities worth knowing in Canada
besides "Ham. Can.," the heading by which Hamilton "figured in the card catalogue of our circulation department" (JNMP, "Jottings"). At Doubleday, Page,
Jean emphasized the achievements of the city's citizens rather than its physical
beauty. However, she certainly did not miss any opportunities for "tooting the
fame of said city – the birthplace of Julia Arthur – the spot where so many
runners were trained to run the Marathon events and of a race horse who [sic]

---

24 Michael Wilson Browne (ca. 1816–1879), born in Ireland, a businessman and politician,
    maintained a wharfing business with Daniel C. Gunn, in addition to working as agent and
    manager of a number of railway lines. See "Browne, Michael Wilson" 28.
25 William Murray, "Hamilton," qtd. in Rosenfeld 79–80.

won the [illegible] etc. etc." To support her claim, she also cited the success of the golfer Florence Harvey, who won the Canadian Ladies' Championships in 1903 and 1904 – an achievement particularly worth mentioning because Jean, too, enjoyed golf.[26]

Jean insisted that Hamilton was superior not only to other Canadian cities like Toronto and Montreal, but also to the American cities she visited. The Great Lakes shipping routes ensured that major events within their range registered in her hometown. The Great Chicago Fire of 1871, for example, seriously affected shipping and it saw Hamilton organize relief efforts for "Shercargo," as one of Jean's little brothers pronounced it (FA, 11 October 1871). Even as a young child, Kenny knew his share of world events as far as they affected his own safety. Briefly left alone on Hamilton Beach (9 July 1875), he refused to accept a buggy ride from a young man because he had been told of young Charley Ross's kidnapping in Philadelphia in 1874 (see Hagen). This precaution does not appear to have occurred to anyone when Jean set out two years earlier, in 1872, to explore the city of Saginaw by herself and did not return till nightfall. But, normally, supervised relays were organized to convey even the older children from one place to the next when their parents did not accompany them on frequent visits to family dispersed across rural Ontario. In June 1862, for example, Thomas's entire family descended on Andrew and Mary McIlwraith in Listowel though the children were suffering from whooping cough and "Janey in particular [was] very dowie." A few months later during another visit from "[o]ur Hamilton friends" (MM, 21 June 1862, 372; 8 August 1862, 375), two-year-old Nellie was left behind to spend a few days with Mrs. Logan, sister of Thomas and Andrew, but became so sick during the night that she was swiftly returned to her parents. Everyone became skilled at packing hastily when transport became available at short notice, and sometimes the children had to accept disappointment when safety trumped enjoyment. Thus, cousin Maggie in Galt was left to cry her eyes out when her uncle decided that, in the absence of permission from her mother, she had to stay behind, and Jean duly reports on the drama:

> We had a visit of Aunt + Uncle Ferguson today, and they carried off Nellie and Maggie for a visit to them out in the country. But several hours after when I had done all my baking I went out, and there sitting in their little house was poor Mag her eyes all swollen with crying. They had gone down to bid the Uncle "Goodbye"

---

26 Julia Arthur (1869–1950), Hamilton-born stage and film actor; Jean probably refers to the Marathon runners Billy Sherring (1877–1964) and Robert Kerr (1882–1963). The horse could be either William Hendrie's "Martimas" or "Butter Scotch." The former won the Futurity in 1892 and the latter the 1899 Queen's Plate. On Arthur, see E. James et al., vol. 2, 60; on Sherring and Kerr, see their entries in the Canada's Sports Hall of Fame; on William Hendrie, the Canadian Horse Racing Hall of Fame; on Florence Harvey, the Canadian Golf Hall of Fame.

and he had sent her back saying that she could not go in her Mamma's absence. Auntie was expected home tonight but she has not come and has likely gone on to Hamilton. (FA, 1 August 1871)

Their interest in news from the United States and the frequency with which the McIlwraiths crossed the border did not prevent Jean from making critical comments. She was thrilled when a couple of "Yankees" on the train whom she overheard criticizing Canada as a "wretched country" were left behind at the station because they took too long over dinner (FA, 6 January 1873). She concluded a report on a fortnight of "dissapation" [sic] with family in Saginaw with the reluctant admission "that there are other cities besides Hamilton and that though Canada is certainly the nicest country in the world it is not the only one," but demolished this concession with the hilariously irrelevant jab that "the Yankees do fix their hair horrid" (7 January 1873).

There was only one occasion when Jean's determination to criticize the "Yankees" failed her and no tart comparisons with Hamilton came to mind, and that was when her mother took her to visit the Hannas in Cleveland. In 1874, Marcus Alonzo Hanna, generally known as Mark Hanna, was a wealthy merchant trading in coal and iron as well as the owner of a railway,[27] and he and Thomas McIlwraith were probably connected through Great Lakes business.[28] A Republican, Hanna coordinated William McKinley's presidential nomination twenty years later and shortly after became an influential US senator. Much of his money and social standing initially came from the family of his wife, Charlotte Augusta Rhodes. Her brother James won the Pulitzer Prize in 1918 for his *History of the Civil War*, but in September 1874 he and his new wife had just moved into a "splendid large house – everything about it new and elegant," where they served Mr. and Mrs. Hanna and their Canadian guests "a capital dinner" (FA, 19 September 1874). Because Mrs. Hanna was deeply religious, she probably felt an affinity with Mary McIlwraith. Whatever the reasons for their acquaintance and for the invitation, the Hannas rolled out the red carpet for their visitors. Mrs. McIlwraith and her daughter hastily sorted themselves out from a bout of travel sickness when Mr. Hanna arrived at the wharf to pick them up in his carriage for the drive home to his sumptuous Italianate villa on Franklin Avenue. In the next few days, their program included a tour of the

---

27 See M. Thompson 25; see also "Hanna, Marcus Alonzo," *Encyclopedia of Cleveland History*, http://ech.case.edu/cgi/article.pl?id=HMA (accessed 20 August 2014). The article incorrectly states two rather than three children.

28 There may also be a connection through David Blythe Hanna, a Canadian railway executive, although no relationship with Mark Hanna or with Thomas McIlwraith has so far been established. See Regehr.

city, with Euclid Avenue – "said to be the finest street in America" – and its
Nicholson pavement as one of the highlights. They visited Woodland Cemetery and made a scenic detour through the countryside to the Ohio State Fair,
where Mrs. McIlwraith "got quite excited" watching the races (18 September
1874). More sedate were several lengthy church services, a church supper, as
well as shopping at Baldwin's Dry Goods and Ingham's Bookstore for a hostess
gift and "curious toy for Kenny" (21 September 1874). Not least, there were
excellent meals topped off by large saucers of ice cream and peaches, chocolate cake, and Concord grapes. Jean loved all of it: "You'd better believe it was
high – spanking along over the soft roads past vineyards just overflowing with
heavy clusters of grapes – the gold jiggers on the horses' harness shaking and
everything just as bright as could be" (18 September 1874). She gamely accompanied "the old folks" to church and politely admired the screaming youngest
child, "Miss Mabel Hanna ... three years old, just as cute as a spoiled child can
be, but cannot talk plain" (16 September 1874), but as usual she enjoyed herself most with a boy of her young brothers' age. She played ball with Danny,
the Hannas' eight-year-old son, stood on a trunk with him through a performance of *Aladdin*, with the coachman as chaperon, and played "Casino" with
Danny and Mr. Masters, presumably his tutor. Daniel Rhodes Hanna, the "fair
haired dark eyed rather nice looking youngster" (16 September 1874), became
a prominent publisher and businessman with four marriages and a fifth pend-
ing, eight children, and a fortune of $10 million to his name when he suddenly
died in 1921 ("Hanna, Daniel Rhodes").[29] In shock, his widowed mother passed
away only a few days after him. Senator Hanna's protégé, President McKinley,
was murdered at the Pan American Exhibition in September 1901. A couple
of months later, Nellie and her husband John Holt took Jean, still grieving her
mother's death earlier that year, with them to see the sights in Buffalo, including
the "Pan Am." McKinley's assassination by the anarchist Leon Czolgosz goes
unmentioned (FHEP, J.N. McIlwraith to F.H. Eckstorm, 3 November [1901?]),
but it does appear a few years later in Jean's "Dominick Street," which features a
cast of Italian and Bohemian anarchists. Overall, her views of the United States
remained as conflicted as those of her father and other Hamiltonians. In her
case, these mixed sentiments are even more striking because they persisted
through some twenty years she spent working in New York.

Learning About the Natural World

These excursions taught Jean about people in the world at large and how they
mattered to her family, but she also learned a great deal about the natural world

---

29 See obituary, "Dan R. Hanna," 1921, for details of Hanna's colourful personal life.

on her travels and in her city. Because of their father's interest in birds specifically and the outdoors generally, all of the McIlwraith children, not just his favourite Kennedy, were taught from an early age to observe the animal and plant life around them. Jean, too, demonstrates knowledge in this area, and the Family Album at times becomes a nature lover's logbook. As she wrote in "A Bright Girlhood," she was able to identify an "indigo bird, brown thrasher, wood thrush, rose-breasted grosbeak, scarlet tanager, flicker and redheaded woodpecker." In later life, she thanked her father for teaching his offspring about "the true inwardness of everything connected with skinning and mounting of specimens," although she seems to shudder slightly while writing it, and for inviting his children's suggestions on how to arrange the backgrounds for small dioramas, "such as green stuff for marsh ducks, and grey sandy floor and rocks for those of the seashore to perch upon" ("Bright Girlhood").

She much preferred living animals, however, and just as she had something to say about the working horses at the wharf or on the towpath, she was as apt to exchange friendly "bows" with a dog encountered on her travels as she was to have a conversation with interesting humans. Sophia and Minnie MacNab were thrilled to be given small "Poodle dogs" (*Diary* 47) for company, but at Cairnbrae there was a succession of family dogs variously named Dash, Lassie, and Ponto, and horses named Dan, Gyp, Barney, and Strawberry, and a photo of the entire family after the children were grown up includes Larry the dog front and centre, firmly clutched in place by Kennedy. Jean's love of dogs was surely one of the qualities that made her the "beloved friend" of Anne Elizabeth Wilson, author of *That Dog of Yours* (1941) and founder of a pet cemetery in Aurora, Ontario (see A. Wilson). The arrival of puppies or a new calf caused excitement all around, even as any surplus of young animals was swiftly "smiflicated [sic]" (FA, 15 July 1871). A new harness that made "Gyp" look "firstrate [sic]" was as much of an event as the delivery of a new carriage from Pronguey's Coach Factory (13 November 1874). In later life Jean collected the showy face pieces of workhorses, noting the local differences in southern England, Scotland, and Quebec, and making a special bequest of these "amulets" to one of her nephews in her will.[30] Though failing memory made her increasingly shy of new acquaintances by 1921, knowledge of horse brasses steered her through an animated conversation with her nephew's professor at Cambridge.[31]

On vacation in Listowel with Aunt Mary and Uncle Andrew, a much younger Jean and a friend entertained themselves by naming the cows Nancy Reid, Black

---

30 See her essay, "Robbing the Clydesdales"; "Disposal of Effects of Jean N. McIlwraith, June 14, 1932," TFMP.

31 TFMF, T.F. McIlwraith, letter to family, 28 July 1921.

Bess, and Lily, and their calves Bob and Jessie. They found "two such dear little kittens" (FA, 19 July 1870) and christened them Star and Comet in allusion to Biela's comet that was making its appearance in the skies in the 1870s, an event closely followed in the Hamilton *Times*. Comet was trampled by a horse but was licked back into shape by its mother, "and it is all better now I guess" (19 July 1870).

The contemporary reader may wonder about the discrepancy between shooting birds en masse for Mr. McIlwraith's collection and providing a haven for animals, but the McIlwraith household could be relied on to take in creatures that others had tormented, such as a kitten that "a boy had thrown up in the air" (FA, 2 August 1871), and it was unusual for the children to poke a stick at "two black bears in cages near a bazar," among "everything ... Niagra-ish [sic]" on an outing to the Falls (27 June 1874). The family's doghouse, rabbit hutch, and back verandah at times housed a fox, a pet skunk, and a horned owl that "glared at us out of a roomy cage on our back verandah" ("Bright Girlhood"). Chipmunks, squirrels, and bats were caught to entertain the smaller boys but were usually allowed to escape. In *The Curious Career of Roderick Campbell*, Jean revives some of these childhood scenes as Rory produces a pet raccoon and a bear cub as playmates for Elsie and Mysie Buchanan, and they enjoy the company of a tame grey jay. By 1901, when this novel was published, a new generation of McIlwraith children was being introduced to animals and plants, and given Jean's tendency to draw the life around her into her fiction, the two young sisters may be modelled on her nieces Marjorie and Dorothy, who were then growing up in Cairnbrae.

On occasion, however, the animals were too big and frightening even for the McIlwraith children. In her story "What We Did at the Beach," "Jeannie Newton" writes about a lively encounter between a young bull and Jack that had the "calf, with tail flourishing aloft, in full pursuit; and Jack making for the house yelling as if a hyena were after him" (497). Even more traumatic was the experience of being set upon by the bald eagle kept by Mr. Dynes near his popular inn on the Beach (FA, 4 June 1870), and Jean's father may for once have gone too far in pulling his daughter's leg. She remembered the incident all of her life but edited Mr. Dynes and her father out of it, replacing the latter with "a naughty boy":

> I remember once going with father and the boys to see a live bald-headed eagle that a fisherman at the Beach had caught and kept in an empty barn. I gazed awe-struck at the majestic bird, perched upon the rafters, but one of my brothers heard the owner say that it always flew in the same direction, rested on the ground for an instant at the same spot, and made a half-circle in flying back to his perch. So the naughty boy directed me to stand directly where the eagle alighted, and then

Marjorie and Dorothy McIlwraith, ca. 1901, costumed for performance in Jean McIlwraith's "The Days of the Year, or The Masque of the Months." TFMP.

he stirred him off – to come flopping down almost on top of me, while I ran in the very course he always took to return, shrieking like mad, for I was sure the eagle was bent on having a little girl for his supper. ("Bright Girlhood")

Mr. McIlwraith was less mischievous when he took his daughter and Hugh on an early morning excursion to the mountain to collect wildflowers for his garden, and this time the scene that she remembered as part of her "bright girlhood" is pastoral even in her twelve-year-old voice. They spent the whole day "crawl[ing] over fences and up and down hills ... until at last [we] came upon a whole patch ... in the shade of the fence," where they collected hepatica and dogstooth violets into an increasingly heavy basket, enjoyed a picnic of apples and biscuits, and lay "flat down by the streams to suck up the water." Thomas McIlwraith shared with other Hamilton gardeners the Victorian enthusiasm for ferns, and Jean watched him dig some up for his rockery. Another friend, Mrs. Osborne, showed her how to compose a fern basket, first lining the wire construction "with moss," allowing "several of the ferns to peep out at the sides." This was followed by "some fine black mould and more ferns the maidenhair standing up in the centre." Moss on top finished off the arrangement (FA, 20 July 1870). McIlwraith learned from such instruction, and interviewers who visited the author at Cairnbrae and, after retirement, in her bungalow in Burlington, were enchanted by the skilful layout of the gardens and their "sunny grounds" (Fenton).

Academic Education

The education Jean and her siblings derived from travel and observation of nature was underpinned by solid formal instruction. The fluency of Jean's writing owes much to her talent to be sure, but the whole scheme of the Family Album is an expression of the high regard in which the McIlwraiths held education generally. The year young Tom began the album, his father was listed as president on the act of incorporation of the Hamilton & Gore Mechanics' Institute and its catalogue of library (Hamilton & Gore Mechanics' Institute). The parents encouraged diligent study habits, regular attendance, and excellent performance at school, and renowned educational institutions such as Egerton Ryerson's Normal School were as much part of the sightseeing program as the new Union Station when the family visited Toronto. Although Jean writes little about her daily lessons, teachers are invariably named and their pedagogic skills acknowledged. Every year, usually at Christmas, Jean reported on everyone's scholastic or professional progress. In 1870, Pollie "goes to the College where she learns to put on airs, to talk French and a lot of other things." Jean and Nellie attended the Central, and while Nellie's teacher was "awful cross," Jean's was "so kind and tells us such nice stories about our lessons." Hughie "goes to the primary school," and Johnnie attended a type of dame school: "too young to go to school [he] goes up to Mrs. Tailors [sic] where he gets lessons in baking" (FA, 11 March 1870).

At the end of the Family Album, Tom was twenty and "still in the wharf office," Pollie at eighteen was "getting thin" and had been at home for the past two years, Jean was sixteen and had another year at the Wesleyan Ladies' College, fifteen-year-old Nell had two more years at the college, thirteen-year-old Hugh was beginning to ease into his professional life by keeping "the [?] office sometimes," nine-year-old Jack was "in 7th division," and six-year-old Kenny was not yet at school (FA, 21 July 1875). There was no mercy for a reluctant Jack on *his* first day at school when the blissful days of baking lessons with Mrs. Tailor (who may be Mrs. Taylor, Mrs. McIlwraith's Ayrshire friend mentioned elsewhere in the album) were over: "Polly had a great deal of trouble to get him inside of the door of the little Central and even when she did manage it he behaved so badly that Miss Fairgrieve had to give him a slight salute with the strap" (12 September 1871), Jean writes, but adds not too long after that her brother has become so fond of his teacher that he wants to save his pudding and take it to her in "a bit of paper."[32]

Formal education even shaped the siblings' teasing of each other, as Jack realized when he was suffering from nightmares and crawled night after night into bed with a greatly annoyed Tom. Not only did Kenny, then "a knowing little chap of five," make fun of Jack, but Jean produced an acrostic poem describing the nightly interruption of "[k]ind young Tommie's/manly snoring" and spelling out "Jack McIlwraith" consecutively in the first letters of the lines (FA, 31 December 1873). Surprisingly their father sometimes permitted a child or even several of them to stay home as a special favour or when it was "cold, windy, and rainy" (11 June 1874), a practice that does not seem to have been uncommon because bad weather or the after-effects of an opulent Sunday school picnic had teachers occasionally confront a half-empty classroom.[33] Still, the McIlwraith children often carried away prizes, such as a volume by James Grahame, *The Sabbath: Sabbath Walks and Other Poems* (1857), presented to Thomas "for general proficiency" at Hamilton Central School when he was eight. Or, they were found to have done such excellent written work that oral examinations were waived. Along with their diligence came a remarkable sense of self-confidence. Thus, eight-year-old Hugh "march[ed] right out of the [school] yard" requesting to switch to another school because he felt he had been insulted by a schoolmate. He was eventually persuaded to change his mind by the boy and their teacher, both of whom showed up at Cairnbrae to explain the situation (FA, 25 March 1870).

---

32 The Family Album dates this entry 10 September 1871, but this must be an error as Jack's first day in school is 12 September.

33 For a study of school attendance in Hamilton, see Davey.

Writing for Children's Magazines

For Christmas or birthdays the children received the annuals of British and American children's magazines such as *Chatterbox*, *Children's Friend*, and *Our Young Folks*. These widely distributed magazines targeted a family of children reared in the pursuit of intellectual curiosity, industry, and competitive achievement. To describe the process, one editor aptly combined the new technology of the telegraph with traditional techniques of composition when she announced that the "paragraphic wires [had been] laid" (Dodge 46; see also M. Phillips). Because there were male and female children of different ages to entertain at Cairnbrae, the magazines were selected both for character-building and breadth of interest. In addition to stories that appealed to both genders, such as the Jack Hazard series by John Townsend Trowbridge, the magazine *Our Young Folks* included features on camping, meteorology, window gardening, constructing a fernery, building a boat, and a variety of academic subjects ranging from literature to algebra intended to entertain active boys and girls alike. The editors maintained a lively correspondence with their young readers, and diligently – and apparently with a straight face – answered questions such as, "Of what use is Algebra?" ("Our Letter Box" 318). In addition to receiving the Christmas annuals, the children pleaded for a monthly subscription to *Our Young Folks* because it had a "Young Contributors" section to which they were eager to submit their compositions. Both Jean and Pollie sent in stories and had them accepted for publication, though we do not hear any more about Pollie's writing beyond an essay inspired by her travels in Scotland (see Duncan). Jean's first publication in *Our Young Folks* was a brief sketch, "What We Did at the Beach," composed at the age of fourteen and drawing on entries from the Family Album. She received $3.00 for it. A second successful submission by "Jeannie Newton" described the burning of the propeller *City of Chatham* and how it was tugged out into the lake "to save the elevator" ("Burned to the Water's Edge" 755). The story conveys the drama of a night-time fire, but it also alludes to economic hardship. The Family Album elaborates on 15 October 1874 that a "propeller built on the keel of the 'City of Chatham' was launched" without much fanfare. The new ship was named *Zealand* after its owner, but would have "no flags till spring as 'times are hard.'" It was probably the combination of geographical, social, and economic interest that earned the story acceptance in *Our Young Folks*. This was an achievement, as "Our Letter Box" makes clear: while *Our Young Folks* diplomatically did not list rejected essays, Jean's "What We Did at the Beach" was one of only three successful submissions, compared to eighteen "honourable mentions." The editors sometimes cited praiseworthy excerpts from rejected work, but their criticism was generally blunt, and unsuccessful contributors were encouraged to do better and try again. The editors, who did not allow their judgment to be clouded by sentiment, did not relent when one young contributor sent in work by a disabled sister. They regretted that they could not "make use of at least one of the pieces" and cited instead "from the accompanying letter [a] touching description of the invalid." Maude H., Effie S., and Edith C. were all told that their "compositions are pretty well written, but the subjects treated are not particularly interesting" ("Our Letter Box" 320).

When *Our Young Folks* merged with *St. Nicholas* in 1873, the "Young Contributors" section was dropped to Jean's keen regret. Instead, she sent her work to *Kind Words for Boys and Girls* in London, a Sunday School Union publication that later became a boys' magazine with the ringing title *Young England: An Illustrated Magazine for Boys Throughout the English-Speaking World* (see Kirkpatrick 285–7). The magazine accepted her story "Under the Sea" for the "Our Young Authors" page, based on a school assignment written when she was thirteen years old. She was apprehensive about this submission because it was longer than the usual contributions to *Kind Words* and "not like anything that has ever been in before" (FA, 10 November 1873), and so success was all the sweeter. "Under the Sea" is indeed unlike the reportage characterizing her first published essays or the Family Album entries. It is the story of a mermaid with a remarkable resemblance to Walt Disney's spunky Ariel. While Ariel finds a fork and is told by Scuttle the Seagull that it is a "dinglehopper" with which to curl her hair, Jean's mermaid finds a boot and quizzes all her acquaintances, including a hermit crab, pike, cod, and mackerel, about the purpose of the object. Assuming Scottish, Irish, and New England accents, they variously inform her that "'Tis what men wear on their heads," that a "boot" must not be confused with a "boat," and that man tries to catch fish because he "has no intillict." The story has a wry moral about the pitfalls of research and the challenges of creating a plausible story from it, both of which were concerns to this young writer as well. The idea of the mermaid's story may have come to Jean because – in yet another instance of the pervasive presence of the era's new communication technologies – news coverage of the laying of the transatlantic cable frequently used "the mermaids' song" as a trope for intercontinental communication (see Müller 87–8).

Together with acceptance of her story, Jean received an invitation from the magazine's editor, Benjamin Clarke, to "write 'a paper of Canadian life and adventure with plenty of incident' " (FA, 15 April 1974), a challenge she was happy to accept. She sent in "Autumn in Canada," but Mr. Clarke does not appear to have been impressed this time.[34] Perhaps she failed to sensationalize "Canadian life" sufficiently, though she certainly understood elsewhere that this was

---

34 Her entry in Morgan, "McIlwraith, Miss Jane" 470, indicates that she also wrote for *All the Year Round* (AYR) and *The Youth's Companion*, but these stories have so far not been identified. Possibilities are "Down at the Salt Water," AYR, vol. 12, no. 291, 28 July 1894, 79–84, and "Bewitched," AYR, vol. 12, no. 297, 8 September 1894, 228–33, 236–40. Both are unsigned.

expected of her. In the Family Album, there are casual references to "Indian remains" on Lake Medad (30 May 1875) or to an "Indian encampment" near Prescott (18 August 1874), but in "What We Did at the Beach," she offers information "about the red men" said to have been obtained from her father and a farmer and she adds that the children "almost expected to see a screaming Indian start up and scalp us." In later years, Jean's growing appreciation of French Canadian culture was paralleled by extensive reading about Indigenous history and customs. She incorporated the results in *The Curious Career of Roderick Campbell* after failing to have quite as much of this research featured as she wanted in *The Span o' Life*, her novel with William McLennan.

The adult Jean continued to submit work to children's magazines, but she found that some of these publications were controlled by men or else by women who thought these magazines should be controlled by men. When she arrived in New York in 1902 in search of an editorial job, she was eager to work for *St. Nicholas Magazine* but was neither able to obtain a position nor publish a serial for young boys she had submitted to them. She was advised by Associate Editor Tudor Storrs Jenks, a Yale-educated lawyer, journalist, author, and artist by profession and "a funny little man with a bald head" by appearance, that the magazine operated with a skeleton staff and that the market was glutted with stories for boys: "[H]e said that women liked boys and were always writing for them while they were positively stuck for decent girl stories." Her serial had cleared the first hurdle and gone up to Editor William Fayal Clarke, she was told, and this was an important success "as most [manuscripts] were sent right back." However, her submission, which has not been preserved, appears to have been turned down in the end (JNMP, "New York Impressions").

Storytelling, Music, Church, and Public Lectures

For the whimsical "Under the Sea," Jean was probably inspired by the copious reading of newspapers and books encouraged at the McIlwraith home. Hamilton was by then well equipped with libraries, and Kerr, Brown and Mackenzie, the firm to which Tom was apprenticed, featured a book room for its employees (see C.M. Johnston 218). Jean read a wide range of British and American children's classics, along with the occasional translation, such as *Alexander Mezikoff, or, the Perils of Greatness* (1853) by the German children's author Gustav Nieritz. Her selections include Charles Reade's *Put Yourself in His Place* (1870), novels by Walter Scott, Louisa May Alcott, Charles Dickens, and A.G. Riddle's *Bart Ridgeley – A Story of Northern Ohio* (1873). To her younger brothers, she read a novel from the Jack Hazard series, published from 1871 onwards and written by J.T. Trowbridge, an editor of *Our Young Folks*. Hugh, Jack, and Kennie particularly enjoyed Longfellow's *Hiawatha*, with everybody acting out different characters inspired by the poem: "They like it firstrate," Jean reports, using her favourite adjective of the moment (FA, 18 April 1875). Perhaps the memory of this session inspired her when she wrote *A Book About Longfellow* twenty-five years later, although she came to dislike Longfellow in the process of research. The enjoyment of reading to her brothers certainly carries over into her books for young readers, and she dedicated *The Little Admiral* (1923), with its boy heroes, to her four nephews. Recitation from popular books, especially poetry, was part of convivial evenings such as the strawberry festival at the Presbyterian church, with "ice cream [and] a soda water table," where "the choir sang once" and – perhaps as part of a penny reading – Mr. Crerar "read such a funny piece from Mansie Waugh" – that is, D.M. Moir's humorous *The Life of Mansie Waugh, Tailor in Dalkeith* (1828) (FA, 30 June 1874). This book was a particular favourite in the family's larger circle, and Andrew had read it fifteen years earlier to Mary Goldie when they were courting (*MM*, 5 March 1859, 202).

There was also storytelling that did not have its origins in a book but nevertheless strengthened geographical, genealogical, and linguistic bonds. As mentioned earlier, the captains were often invited to the McIlwraiths' house, and the girls contributed to their entertainment by playing the piano, though Hugh and Jack were probably prevented from beating the drum, their favourite instrument. To expand their repertoire for companionable evenings, both Jean and Pollie received sheet music for Christmas 1874, "The Queen's Lancers" and the "Violetta Mazurka," respectively. In return for the musical entertainment, the captains told stories about their seafaring adventures: "Captain Spence came up here after tea to play bagatelle and listen to our music. He ... has been all round the world" (FA, 23 September 1874). Mr. McIlwraith brought anecdotes back from his travels throughout Ontario, told stories of "the Munchhausen variety," and sang "old Scotch and Irish songs with a story in them" ("Bright Girlhood"). Ghost stories were a favourite, and a pleasant shiver accompanies Jean's tale of "a certain woman who is said to be dressed all in black and to go about the streets at night but never to touch anybody" (FA, 10 May 1870). Tom, though not as flamboyant as his father, continued the tradition of singing and storytelling, and Tom's own son – famously unable to carry a tune himself – reported that "[h]e had a range of very popular songs and stories; he had a powerful voice" ("Genealogy").

Likewise, as we have seen, the children enjoyed listening to their mother's conversations with friends from Scotland (FA, 8 February 1872). In later years, interviewers commented on Jean's broad Scots accent, despite her upbringing in Canada. She had learned it mostly from her mother who, hard of hearing early on, never lost the language of her native Ayr. This did not stop Jean from observing that a young emigrant who had arrived from there "to be apprenticed to the barque 'Undaunted' " did "seem like a nice kind of boy though he does talk very Scotch" (19 July 1874). As her skilful imitation of her father's self-mocking speech about his display cases illustrates, she had a keen appreciation of different voice registers. She enjoyed listening to chatty old gentlemen on the train even when they were a little tedious, and several of her books experiment with a variety of narrative voices. She was especially partial to male narrators, usually a middle-aged Scot, such as the bemused newspaper editor in *The Making of Mary* (1895), or Rory, the jack-of-all-trades in *The Curious Career of Roderick Campbell*, and the prickly Captain Mathews in *A Diana of Quebec* (1912). But with William McLennan she also ventured into the dual male and female perspectives of "Maxwell's Story" and "Margaret's Story" in *The Span o' Life* (1899). Above all, she loved singing and used every opportunity to insert lyrics and scores of Scottish and French Canadian songs into her novels, making some of her characters into gifted performers, such as Mary Simpson in *A Diana in Quebec* and Hugh Maxwell of Kirkconnel in *A Span o' Life*. The songs were a useful plot device, she reminded McLennan, when their character Hugh "[hadn't] warbled any for awhile": after all, his "lovely voice" was helpful in "get[ting] him out of various scrapes."[35] The Family Album features many enthusiastic singing sessions, especially on Sundays, when the family sat on the verandah late into the night singing hymns. On their travels, too, the young McIlwraiths sang "to their hearts [sic] content" to the accompaniment of a flute played by a "little French fellow who cant [sic] say 'too thin' "(FA, 8 August 1874), but they encountered serious competition from a fine choir led by the canal missionary who boarded the *Africa* at Port Colborne at the south end of the Welland Canal: "The crew ... knew lots of hymns so that treble was almost drowned in the bass" (9 August 1874). Singing in choirs remained a favourite activity in Jean's adult life, and within weeks of arriving in New York in the fall of 1902 she resolved to join the choir of St. George's Church on Stuyvesant Square, in time for the Christmas service.[36]

While they were travelling, the family improvised attendance at Sabbath services in whatever way available, but at home, Sundays were devoted to serious churchgoing throughout the day, and this was often complemented by prayer meetings during the week:

> Sunday March 20th [1870] Hugh, Nellie + I went to Sunday School in the morning and Papa, Mamma, Tom, Polly and Nelly went to church. In the afternoon Hugh + I went to the Baptist Sunday School, and at night Mr. Muir having come over to take tea with us Tom + Polly went with him to church.

Not surprisingly, books of a devotional nature show up repeatedly, both as a hostess gift to Mrs. Hanna, who received Elizabeth Prentiss's *Stepping*

---

35 McIlwraith, Jean N., Letter from Jean McIlwraith to William McLennan, 26 November [1896?]. Box 4, File 3. McLFF.

36 On the role of music in nineteenth- and early twentieth-century Ontario, see Morrison.

Heavenward: One Woman's Journey to Godliness from her Canadian visitors, or as the subject of a lecture series by the Reverend John McColl on *Pilgrim's Progress*. Likewise, churchgoing offered various types of instruction and even surprisingly light-hearted entertainment. Presbyterian allegiances did not prevent family members from attending other Protestant services if a Presbyterian one was not available or if, like other Ontario folks, they were curious about unfamiliar church rituals even if they "seemed strange to our Presbyterian ears" (FA, 25 December 1872).[37] They did not mind being conspicuous when they were not familiar with the conventions of other churches; such was the case with Mr. McIlwraith, who committed a gaffe by sitting with his wife in the women's section of a Methodist church – either because he did not know any better or, as would have been typical of him, because he enjoyed creating a mild stir (see Newton, "What We did at the Beach"). Nor, as we already know from Andrew, did anyone hesitate to criticize the sermons. Dry sermons, Jean found, made hard seats even more objectionable. As a sharp observer of differences in social choreography and speech, Jean gives this snappy account of a service at St. Andrews in Montreal: "They have an organ, sing very fast, sit at prayers, stand at singing, and chanted the Te Deum at the close" (FA, 15 August 1874).

There were limits to the willingness to experiment: both Jean and her nephew T.F. attended Church of England services when pressed but vowed that they would not do so again if it could be helped. As Jean informed McLennan, her mother drew the line at Roman Catholics and, despite his fame, would not welcome the Abbé Casgrain into her home when McIlwraith and McLennan obtained historical and other advice from the Abbé for *The Span o' Life* in 1898.[38] Her friendship with Casgrain notwithstanding, Jean did find Roman Catholics unusual enough to mention their religion specifically when she met one. On arrival in New York in 1902, she briefly roomed with a "Miss Flanigan," identified as a "milliner ... who comes here twice a year to buy goods" and is "an R.C." (JNMP, "New York Impressions"). Still, when she was eager to join its choir in 1902, she did not find it off-putting that St. George's Church on Stuyvesant Square was Episcopalian, and her relaxed approach to dogma was probably a reason for an awkward confusion created by Walter Hines Page when "the wife of the Dean of the [Cathedral of the Incarnation]" came calling to ask him "if there was anyone of the feminine gender among the employees who might be considered eligible to receive some attention from herself + her select circle. Mr. Page mentioned me – a stout Presbyterian in every sense of the word" (JNMP, "Jottings"). It is obvious from Jean's acquaintances, however, that even

---

37 See also Hoffman and Taylor, 21.
38 Jean N. McIlwraith to Henri-Raymond Casgrain, 20 April 1899, Musée de la civilisation, fonds d'archives du Séminaire de Québec, 0470.

Presbyterians had their colourful moments. Thus, the eccentric Reverend Robert E. Knowles, preacher of rousing sermons in Stewarton and Galt, as well as a successful novelist and interviewer of celebrities for the Toronto *Daily Star*, gifted presentation copies of his novels *St. Cuthbert's* (1905) and *The Attic Guest* (1909) to her.

The McIlwraith children enjoyed the circus, the magic lantern, Pepper's Ghost, and a ventriloquist, but as Jean grew into a teenager,[39] public readings and lectures were often on the program, and just like the preachers, the lecturers were carefully evaluated for their performances. She was very impressed by Huldah McMullen, "sister of the celebrated politician [Harvard C.] McMullen," who at a meeting of the Literary Society of the Wesleyan Ladies' College delivered "a splendid parody on Mark Antony's oration; all about John A. + George Brown" (FA, 1 June 1874; see also Kiefer). Jean enjoyed a lecture on "Life and its Possibilities," though the speaker "stammered a good deal" (14 April 1875), and she also appreciated being informed about "Peculiar People," an evangelical group, but she was merciless on "Travelling," a speech by one of her fellow students, thus practising the sharp tongue that later made her a formidable manuscript reader at Doubleday, Page: "the lecture showed haste and was a rather rambling discourse that might have been on any subject as well as 'Travelling' " (21 May 1875). She, too, was required to make a presentation and worked all week on her speech about "Geography" to the Literary Society, finding when she had given it that it was not such an "awful drag" after all (5 May 1875). As well, Jean and her sisters contributed to *The Portfolio*, a publication of the students at the Wesleyan Ladies' College, but because the contributions are not signed, it is not possible to determine which ones were written by the McIlwraith girls. Occasionally, the family landed at a performance that they had not bargained for. Thus, Thomas McIlwraith took a couple of the older children to what he thought were "readings," only to find – as Jean paraphrases his somewhat disapproving response – "that it was just a theatre" (March 22, 1870). In fact, they had stumbled into a performance by Grace Egerton (1835–81), a touring British *artiste* who formed an internationally acclaimed duo with her concertina-playing husband George Case. Her specialty was impersonation of a dozen characters or more per evening involving rapid changes of costume ("Mr. and Mrs. George Case").

Jean's increasingly close attention to music specifically and sound generally resulted in experiments, towards the end of the Family Album, in impressionist writing using a real-time approach. She had already practised some

---

39 Wagner and Plant 9, describe nineteenth-century stages as "built with trapdoors and machinery for [spectacular] effects so that Pepper's Ghost, the Vampire Trap and the Corsican Trap which allowed actors to appear or disappear as if from nowhere are but three illusions easily manufactured in front of the audience." An illustration of "[t]he 'Pepper's Ghost' illusion as produced at the Grand Opera House in Hamilton, 1863" is added, without indication of the source.

Thomas and Mary Park McIlwraith and their children, ca. 1890. Front: Kennedy with Larry the dog; middle, left to right: Mary Duncan, Thomas Sr., and Mary; back, left to right: Jean, John, Thomas, Hugh, and Helen. TFMP.

of this technique in her meteorological reports describing the wild weather preceding spring thaw. During the children's trip from Hamilton to Toledo and Montreal, she maintained a log by noting the time of day at the end of each entry, commenting on weather conditions, and describing the stars. Whenever possible, her entries were not composed in retrospect but in immediate response to the noise and movements of a working ship. The idea possibly came to her because she was kept awake by the commotion when it was too dark to see, and the tactile and auditory senses had to do the work of gathering her impressions:

> Wednesday August 5th 1874 I did not sleep very well last night there being such a number of sounds and shocks to keep one awake. We were in the part of the canal where the locks are very close together, and every few minutes the boat would brush up against the sides of one of them and we would hear the shouts of the men on shore and boat mingled with the noise of the capstans turning and the roar of the water over the lock. Then there was the quiet thud, thud, of the screw the drawing of the rudder chains and often the ding dings or the short sharp whistle.

She concluded the album in similar immediacy: "I am sitting at the open bedroom window[.] The lamp on the sill has attracted innumerable insects that are buzzing around. It is about 10 p.m. Now I'll close this book. Amen." (21 July 1875).

Epilogue

Information about their later lives rounds off the Family Album's account of the McIlwraith siblings, and also gives some background to the sometimes controversial use Jean was to make of her family's biographies in her fiction. By the late 1870s, most of her brothers and sisters were entering an age described by Michael Katz as a semi-independent phase for young professionals between childhood and adulthood that was often characterized by boarding out before founding a household of one's own (see Katz 209–308). Thus the Goldies in Galt not only sheltered a homeless and invalid schoolfriend of Mrs. Goldie but also hosted a young lawyer who was in the process of establishing his practice (FA, 22 May 1874). In keeping with this principle of semi-independence, the path immediately after school was relatively straightforward for most of the McIlwraith boys. They began an apprenticeship, usually in one of the many companies in the Great Lakes region with which their family was associated. Tom, as we learned, started his professional life in 1870, beginning as a clerk in local companies until he became his father's second in command at the dock. From 1872 he was listed as a boarder at the McIlwraiths' home until he set up his own household following his marriage in 1886. In 1893 Tom replaced his father as head of the firm. Family lore has it that he was eager to go south, either before his marriage or with his young family, but that loyalty to his father's business and perhaps also a lack of ambition kept him in Hamilton ("Genealogy").

By the late 1870s, Hugh also had his own entry in Hamilton's city directory as boarder at Cairnbrae, but both he and Jack – neither held back by the responsibilities of an eldest son – soon headed to the United States. Both brothers had a career in box making, and a 1914 business profile of Jack that includes a proud biographical sketch of his father along with brief notes about the achievements of his brothers and sisters, has Hugh "engaged in the manufacture of boxes in New Castle, Pennsylvania." Hugh, who according to his obituary remained unmarried, though there are rumours within the family of a wife named Mary, suddenly died of pneumonia in 1916. He was lauded as a "Well Known Business Man" and an individual "of quiet and unassuming nature[,] of broad education and of great generosity," a description that makes him appear closest in temperament to his brother Tom. His body was taken by the Pittsburgh and Lake Erie train to Hamilton, where he was buried with his parents.[40]

---

40   See "H.P. McIlwraith Called By Death"; "H.P. M'Ilwraith Dies Suddenly."

In contrast to Hugh's quiet manner, Jack gave notice even as a child that he was adventurous and ambitious, and while Hugh did quite well for himself, Jack became a wealthy businessman in Great Lakes transport. His business profile lists the different steps of his career in order to illustrate that "among the most successful are men who have been content to start at the bottom of the ladder and to force their way steadily upward to their rightful place among their fellow-citizens." Thus, in 1884, nineteen-year-old Jack took up a position as "a clerk in a ... wholesale hardware store" in Detroit. A few months later "he became freight clerk for the Detroit & Cleveland Steam Navigation Company," before moving the next year to the lumber-processing Munroe Manufacturing Company in Muskegon, Michigan, where his cousin Hugh Park was treasurer. In 1891, Jack founded the Indiana Box Company "with two Muskegon lumbermen" at Anderson, Indiana, purchasing in 1899 the Elwood Box Company and doing so well that soon after he was able to add the same Munroe Manufacturing Company at which he had begun his career. Subsequently, he built further box factories in East Chicago, Indiana; in New Castle and Vandergrift, Pennsylvania; and in Martin's Ferry, Ohio. In 1897, he made an advantageous marriage to Martha Chittenden, a native of Anderson and daughter of a local doctor and Civil War veteran, Dr. G.F. Chittenden, and had three children with her (Forkner 777–8). In 1923, Jack died in Florida, where he had gone to recuperate after serious illness and surgery at the Mayo Clinic in Rochester, and he was returned to Indiana for burial ("John G M'Ilwraith").

Like Jean's career, Kennedy's was not typical for his generation of the family. He studied medicine, graduated from the University of Toronto in 1894 following a year at Rotunda Hospital in Dublin and Charlotte Hospital in London, and became an obstetrician in Toronto, first at St. Michael's and then at the General Hospital, as well as being appointed head of obstetrics at the University of Toronto (see Shorter 526). Kennedy married May Fison Saunders from Bristol, England. Their son Archibald, educated at Upper Canada College, the University of Toronto, and Oxford, became a Shakespeare scholar in Liverpool.

Jack went to Detroit in 1884, the same year his sister Pollie moved there following her marriage to the Reverend Robert J. Service, and perhaps she helped to pave her brother's early days in that city. Although she was "one of the four scholars who attained the highest rank in the [college],"[41] was class valedictorian, and "took part in a debate arguing in the affirmative on the question 'Should Universities be Opened to Women?" (Huyck, "Adapting Through Compromise" 27), Pollie did not choose an academic career. There are early indications in the Family Album that she was being prepared for a suitable marriage. In 1874, when she turned sixteen, her presents were elaborate: "a real thread

---

41 "Ladies' College," Hamilton *Spectator*, 25 June 1873, qtd. in Huyck 27.

lace collar and pale blue ribbon" from Mrs. Caven and "a gold locket" from her mother (FA, 20 February 1874). Christmas presents a couple of months earlier included "a black silk dress" and a "purse" (24 December 1873), both of which were useful accessories when she attended carefully selected social gatherings in Hamilton and Toronto, where the Cavens, members of the extended Goldie family, were her hosts. She had three children with the Reverend Service, but shouldered her share of nursing her mother after Mary McIlwraith was paralyzed by a stroke in 1897. During a summer on Hamilton Beach, she relieved Jean from the gruelling duties of nursing and housekeeping (McLFF, J.N. McIlwraith to William McLennan, 13 July 1897). The first of the adult McIlwraith children to die, Pollie passed away in 1907, only a few years after her parents' deaths and when her youngest child, Willis, was only eleven. In subsequent years Jean often chaperoned Pollie's daughters, such as when she accompanied Marion on a trip to Europe in 1912. Jean's novel *A Diana of Quebec* is dedicated to Mary's memory and contains a historical character named Mary Simpson, also known as "Polly" to her friends.

In 1891, Nellie, too, married, making a socially impressive match with the merchant John Henderson Holt of the Holt-Renfrew store in Quebec City. By the mid-eighties, the shop had become the official purveyor of furs for the royal family and was acclaimed for creating a "dreamland of almost barbaric splendor" when it opened its Montreal branch in 1910, following stores in Toronto and Winnipeg.[42] Born in Quebec, and educated at the Ottawa Commercial Academy, Holt acquired his affiliation with the store through his mother Isabella Henderson's Irish family of hatmakers. A "big + good + reliable" man, as Jean described him, he was just the person to take care of her delicate sister. Ever protective of Nellie, Jean was "sorry ... to lose [her] but could not wish her to be in better hands."[43] The Holts had been introduced by Jean, who was "great friends" with John's sisters Emily and Matilda and regretted only that the family was not Scots. To make up for this shortcoming, Nellie – who like Jean and Kennedy repeatedly visited with relatives in Scotland and received part of her education there ("Mrs. Helen Holt") – met her future husband "over there," namely, in Glasgow in 1888 at the International Exhibition of Science, Art and Industry, where his company was showing furs.

The childless Holts were an affectionate couple who kept a hospitable house on Quebec's Grande Allée embellished with stained-glass windows created by local artists. Premier Louis-Alexandre Taschereau was a neighbour. Both Holts were strongly involved in the affairs of Quebec City: during his lifetime, John Holt's name was attached to virtually every activity promoting municipal

---

42   See "New Fur House Opens"; also see Benoît, "Renfrew, George Richard."

43   McIlwraith, Jean N. Letter from Jean McIlwraith to Elizabeth Smith Shortt, UWL, 31 January 1891, WA-10, File 280, ESS.

welfare and prosperity, including the Jeffery Hale Hospital, the Quebec Tercentenary, and the Stanley Cup, while Nellie poured her energies into the Ladies' Protestant Home that cared for immigrant women and their children. During the First World War, she worked for the Quebec branch of the Red Cross ("Mrs. Helen Holt"). The couple frequently travelled overseas, combining Holt-Renfrew business with tourism. Between 1906 and 1912, for example, they went on at least three extended trips, one taking them from San Francisco to Hawaii and Japan, through Russia on the Trans-Siberian Railway, and on to France and Britain. Unlike their leisurely sightseeing in such places as Italy and Switzerland, entertainment in Paris and London was usually accompanied by business. Thus, Holt consulted with Revillon frères furriers in Paris, and Nellie's dresses and suits were custom-made at such Parisian couturiers as Boeklage and Margaine-Lacroix, not only because she was an elegant woman but also because her fashionable appearance enhanced Holt-Renfrew's cachet and buying European fashion for herself was a good way to try out potential international suppliers for the store. Nellie was clearly used to talking shop with her husband, and they "had it hot" with American passengers on the express train to Paris discussing Prime Minister Wilfrid Laurier and President Taft's recent plans for a reciprocity agreement that, as the couple had learned from the papers, would have resulted in "mak[ing] Canada 'just an adjunct of the U.S.'" (HH, 22 April 1912).Nellie fully participated in the wide-ranging social contacts necessary to support her husband's business, including dinners and visits to the theatre, sports events, and clubs with the leaders of London's garment industry, many of them nervous in 1912 because of recent strikes by East End workers. The networking extended to wealthy clients, and an afternoon call took the Holts to tea with Mrs. Thomson at Caen Wood Towers (now known as Athlone House), the opulent mansion occupied by Thomas Frame Thomson of the Otis Steel Company in Highgate, London.

When John Holt died in 1915, Nellie settled into a long widowhood looked after by two maids and a chauffeur, going for drives at noon, resting in the afternoon, and playing bridge with selected family and friends such as the University of Toronto's registrar, A.B. Fennell, and architect J.C.B. Horwood ("Genealogy"). Ironically, considering her frailty, Nellie outlived her husband by thirty-five years as well as surviving all of her brothers and sisters. She took to spending the winter months at the Empress Hotel in Victoria, British Columbia, but her obituary praised her for the active interest she had taken for many decades in the affairs of Quebec. Most of her husband's fortune was left to charity.

We have to wait until Jean's impressions of her arrival in New York in 1902 to obtain writing as detailed and immediate as that of the Family Album from her again, but unfortunately the later journal consists of only a few pages and the archive documenting her personal life becomes generally scattered. For the years following the conclusion of the album, the details of her life have to be assembled from a variety of sources, including letters, reminiscences, interviews, and biographical handbooks, and intensely populated archival islands are separated by extensive waters of biographical silence. Still, because she was a well-respected writer, Jean's life story is better documented than that of any of her siblings. The portrait that emerges of her later years is – as is to be expected of a woman this unconventional – not fully predictable either.

Chapter Four

Jean McIlwraith's Story

Teaching in Hamilton

In a letter written in 1925 to Margaret Cowie, a teacher who was collecting books by Canadian authors, along with their photos and biographies, for a school library in Vancouver, Jean claimed that she had never been a teacher herself, except – as she corrected herself in an afterthought – as "a substitute."[1] Perhaps she meant that she had never trained as a teacher for, immediately after she graduated from the Wesleyan Ladies' College, she turned the experience of looking after her young brothers into an educational occupation. In the basement of her parents' home, she "organized free evening classes for working boys, and for 4 yrs. taught them ... 4 nights in the week and on Sunday afternoons" (Morgan, "McIlwraith, Miss Jane" 740).[2] Jean inherited her father's fondness for pedagogical schemes but used them to reach beyond the McIlwraiths' usual circle and towards their working-class neighbours, and she was similarly motivated when she briefly worked at a Settlement House in New York following her mother's death.

McIlwraith's reputation as a published author in Canada, the States, and Britain was mostly established with historical fiction, biography, and travel journalism, but she also wrestled with literary modes that captured contemporary life. Her night school made its way into fiction – autobiographical in varying degrees – that she continued to revise under different titles between the late 1890s and early 1920s but failed to publish. Followed by "Dominick Street" (1905), "Smiling Water" (after 1905), and "Casual Camilla" (after the First World War), the first of these was "The Altrurian Maid," submitted to T. Fisher Unwin around

---

1 McIlwraith, Jean N., Letter from Jean McIlwraith to Margaret Cowie, 5 April 1925, Box 1, File 13, Margaret Cowie Fonds, UBC Library, RBSC.
2 Note that "Jean" was occasionally referred to as "Jane." Morgan's title follows that usage.

1897, but apparently too "tremendously local to Hamilton, Ont." in setting and topic to be attractive to the overseas market she was hoping for (McLFF, J.N. McIlwraith to William McLennan, 29 December 1897). Little information is available about this manuscript, but the allusion to W.D. Howells's utopian romance *A Traveller from Altruria* (1892–3) suggests that McIlwraith was motivated by high-minded Christian socialism in setting up her basement school, an ambition recognized by her friend Elizabeth Smith, who noted that the endeavour was "truly a great missionary work."[3] In her title, McIlwraith may be paying homage to the suffragist Sarah B. Cooper, who "had gone into the dark and dreadful places of the city and gathered the little ones into [the] fold [of her kindergarten]" (De Aguirre 929), and whose work earned her praise as "A Woman from Altruria" when she died under tragic circumstances in 1897. Like McIlwraith, who was "passionately fond of children – all children" (J.N. McIlwraith, "How To Be Happy" 454), Cooper loved children and even "earned the distinction of being tried for heresy [by the Presbyterian Church] because she refused to believe in infant damnation and everlasting punishment" (De Aguirre 930). Together with her scrutiny of the marriage plot in national romance when she collaborated with William McLennan, McIlwraith's experiments in "radical romance" (see, for example, Cella) show her immersed in contemporary social debate, particularly as it related to the education of working-class immigrant children, and its literary depiction in ways that have not been acknowledged in existing accounts of her work, largely because it did not see print. Despite a few impressive coups that had her publish in two or even three English-speaking countries simultaneously, acceptance of her work by American publishers was impeded by, among other things, her outspoken allegiance to all things British even if she did not hesitate to criticize them when necessary, and her equally outspoken objection to American republicanism. As a result, her repeated failures to gain recognition for her work in the States become increasingly painful to behold.

McIlwraith drew inspiration from children throughout her life. They have a special place in her narratives as characters whose energy and imagination must be protected from the limiting dictates of society, and she won an award for her children's novel *The Little Admiral* (1924) a year before she wrote to Miss Cowie. Like the Family Album, the descriptions of the "working boys" in her night school show her to be caring in her dealings with children even if she could be tactless with adults. The Irish teenagers whom her alter ego Jonquil (or "Jonk") Ames in "Smiling Water" gathers in her father's house in "Macassa" present their teacher with "barrenness of the land with respect to the Three R's." Undaunted, Jonquil spots a future bookkeeper and engineer among them, and she has high hopes for one whose "ready tongue was all that was needed

---

3 Shortt, Elizabeth Smith. "Diary." 14 March 1881 UWL, WA-10, File 1763, p. 31, ESS.

to make a lawyer out of him, who would eventually get into Parliament." She triumphs when she believes to have detected a precocious poet, only to realize that – with the best of intentions – he has copied his poem out of a book. All of the students reluctantly agree to sign a temperance pledge for a year, and she impresses upon them that "[i]n this grand big country of ours nobody needs to be hopelessly poor who is willing to work and can leave the liquor alone." Her ambitious plans for the school include "a lending library, coffee taverns, free lectures" ("Smiling Water" 31, 101, 17). The real-life Jean was able to "get enough books to go round and sent [the boys] off rejoicing."[4] She obtained donations of books and money from the Literary Society of the Wesleyan Ladies' College and from her brothers, now grown-up, as well as small financial contributions from the students themselves. Despite these auspicious beginnings, both the fictional and the actual library soon ran into difficulties because few of the boys read fluently enough to benefit from it, and many of the books they borrowed were not returned ("Smiling Water" 127).

An important sponsor of Jean's educational experiment was Elizabeth Smith, with whom McIlwraith corresponded into Smith's marriage to Adam Shortt. In 1881, Smith was teaching in Hamilton (Strong-Boag, Introduction, Smith xxv) and admired Jean's devotion to her students. She helped to organize an "entertainment" in support of Jean's proposed library and even taught the occasional class for her. The two women wondered about the effectiveness of prizes in motivating students, but Jean's experience taught her to be wary of the practice: "Those who were unsuccessful were so greatly disappointed that I feared none of them would ever come again."[5] For similar reasons, Jonquil learns that it is not a good idea to present her students with report cards or, worse, take the assessments to their mothers: "Many of these documents were torn to bits before her eyes ere she saw it was unwise to express anything but the heartiest approval of her scholars' performances" ("Smiling Water" 127).

Despite Jonquil's efforts, "Smiling Water" ends on a discouraged note, one that has her feel "like a wreck, a failure." She accuses herself of "lack[ing] religion" and therefore being unable to make an "impression on the souls of my boys" (204). Things go downhill badly when she must serve as a character witness for one of her students who has become involved in crime though there is no evidence that this episode is based on actual experience. As became characteristic of Jean's modus operandi through much of her life, she abruptly switched direction when the school seemed no longer rewarding. In this case, she left for Europe in 1881. She did organize volunteers, including

---

4 McIlwraith, Jean N., Letter to Elizabeth Smith, 4 June 1881, UWL, WA-10, File 280, ESS.

5 McIlwraith, Jean N., Letters from Jean McIlwraith to Elizabeth Smith, 19 March 1881 and 4 June, 1881, UWL, WA-10, File 280, ESS. On the nineteenth-century discussion of prize-giving at Ontario schools, see Houston and Prentice.

Nellie, to continue with the classes in her absence before setting sail for Scotland for a stay of over two years with her Aunt Sarah in Ayr. She does not mention teaching these boys again in her letters to Smith or to others, and it is doubtful that the school survived much beyond her departure because Nellie, too, began to travel abroad. Given Jean's interest in helping disadvantaged children, it seems fitting that her father's house was eventually sold to the Children's Aid Society and used as a children's shelter from 1913 until the society purchased another building in 1956, and Cairnbrae was torn down. The welfare of destitute children remains a theme in her family's story in other ways as well. Thus, the family of Jean's brother Tom was friends with the superintendent of the Stephenson's Children's Home in Hamilton, Frank Hills, whose daughter Hilda will feature in the chapter about T.F. McIlwraith's wartime letters.

Despite disappointments, organizing the school in Cairnbrae's basement was a forceful indication that Jean was not prepared to live through the "awkward period ... when there might be little ... to do" (Hoffman and Taylor 205) for many young women of her background other than wait for a suitor. As a city with well-established philanthropic traditions (see Nielson), Hamilton offered plenty of other outlets for her talents even when she was finished with her basement school, and she found ways to include children in these activities as well. She immersed herself in theatrical and musical performances,[6] including a benefit concert organized by the Garrick Club "for the old folks in the House of Refuge" that forced her to delay a visit to Kingston with Elizabeth Smith. Not long after her return from this trip she reported on the performance of a play called "The Elevator" that was so successful that "we had to give the play twice the same night so that all might see it."[7] The play was repeated "up at the Asylum," complemented with a musical program in which Jean sang duets.[8] Hamilton's musical talent was brought together for the comic opera "Ptarmigan, or, A Canadian Carnival" she co-authored with J.E.P. Aldous in 1895, and repeat performances filled the coffers of the Ladies' Benevolent Society. This local success paled before the popularity of "The Temple of Fame: A Spectacular Play," which appealed to audiences of all backgrounds and ages. The pageant was registered for interim copyright under McIlwraith's name in 1892 ("Interim Copyrights") and circulated in typewritten copies throughout Ontario. The idea came from "a rough, hand-written copy" of a similar American spectacle that Pollie had sent her sister after it had been performed at the "Sunday School [of her husband's Detroit parish] with great success," along with a note suggesting that

---

6 See the long list of such organizations in Hamilton in H. Murray 217–21.
7 No information on this play has been found.
8 McIlwraith, Jean N. Letters from Jean McIlwraith to Elizabeth Smith Shortt, 13 December 1890, 31 January 1891, UWL, WA-10, File 280, ESS.

Jean "write it up to suit a Canadian audience" (JNMP, Editorial Correspondence, J.N. McIlwraith to Henry Lanier, 30 May 1907).

In a feminine response to Alexander Pope's representation of fame, McIlwraith's version features the Goddess of Fame, to whom a large and eclectic cast
of historical, fictional, and allegorical women apply for admission to the Temple. Among them are Hypatia, Xanthippe, Helen of Troy, Joan of Arc, Shakespeare's Portia, Mary Queen of Scots, Flora MacDonald, Jenny Geddes, Mrs.
Grundy, the Empress Josephine, Mother Goose, Jane Austen, George Eliot,
Christina Rossetti, Pocahontas, Laura Secord, Marie de l'Incarnation, Made-
leine de Verchères, "Canada" (who appears arm in arm with Queen Victoria),
"Mother," Emma Albani, and many others. In her stage directions, McIlwraith
suggests alternating idealized figures with comic ones to keep the audience interested. The reviews proved her right: though lip service is regularly paid to
the prominence of "Canada," it was Xanthippe, Socrates's "vixenish wife [who]
was one of the stars of the evening" at the pavilion of the Horticultural Gardens
in Toronto, and the actress playing "Mother Goose" received the dubious compliment that she "looked and acted her part to perfection" ("Chit Chat"). The
grand prize of admission to the Temple of Fame eventually went to the character selected separately by each performing company, and favourites appear to
have been "Mother" and "Queen Victoria." Anywhere between forty and sixty
participants were involved in staging the play in Hamilton as well as "in almost every town and village of Ontario,"[9] among them Port Hope, Welland,
Brantford, Carleton Place, London, Bowmanville, Woodstock, Galt, Stratford,
and Toronto.[10] The performance was usually under the auspices of a church or
a charitable organization like the YMCA or the Ladies' Hospital Aid Society,
and proceeds went to a worthy cause. This did not stop the participating ladies,
especially the ones in Toronto, from competing in their acting, singing, dancing, and costumes, and the *Globe*'s "Chit-Chat" column assessed the situation
correctly by dwelling on what everyone was wearing and hastily printing a correction when a participant had inadvertently been left out.

Success for "The Temple of Fame" came in two waves, first in 1892 when
the play premiered and then at the turn of the century, especially in the
turn-of-the-century year of 1900 and in the midst of the Boer War, but the pageant was also staged in the mid-nineties. The "news of the Relief of Ladysmith"
arrived while some performances were in progress ("South African War"). In
addition to "The Temple of Fame" permitting large groups of women to display
their talents and finery, its genius was flexibility. Available local talent could be

---

9 "The Temple of Fame," *The Globe*, 5 October 1901.
10 The Toronto *Globe* covered many of these performances. For particularly detailed comments on a performance in Woodstock, see "The Temple of Fame: A Brilliant Dramatic
Entertainment."

added impromptu, such as performers of Scotch or Irish dialect or Florence Glover Woodland's performance of an aria from Gounod's *Faust*.[11] The prominence of "Canada" notwithstanding, organizers were not dogmatic about nationalism, and a polite invitation was issued to a visiting American teenager to play Laura Secord. (Only one reporter thought this particular casting was a little odd.[12]) Some theatrical societies found it politic to include at least a few well-known men, and in Welland "Col. Wm. Buchner and Major Clarke Raymond" acted as heralds.[13] As well, the play's flexible set-up allowed it to respond instantly to current historical developments. The performances in 1900, for example, featured painter Elizabeth Thompson (Lady Butler), temperance campaigner Carrie Nation, the philanthropist Baroness Burdett-Coutts, and, in acknowledgment of the turn of the century, a "Twentieth-Century Girl." The update for 1901 included Queen Wilhelmina of the Netherlands and Gezina Kruger, Paul Kruger's wife. As mother of sixteen children, she seemed to be owed greater respect by a Canadian audience than her husband. In this latter version, the "Red Cross Nurse" – who, as McIlwraith proposed, could be specified as Clara Barton, founder of the American Red Cross – was accompanied by "Guards in Khaki" and guided to a seat close to royalty, Queen Victoria and the Empress Eugénie.

McIlwraith produced a similar spectacle at the request of the Ladies' Aid in Hamilton, "The Days of the Year, or the Masque of the Months," which may be seen as a theatrical version of the seasonal chronologies shaping the Family Album. The play probably had its premiere in Hamilton, and McIlwraith's notes on the script also refer to performances in Halifax and Galt in 1893 and in Detroit in 1895. In Halifax, the pageant – here entitled "Pageant of the Seasons" – was "given in Aid of the Sailors' Home," under the patronage of the lieutenant general's wife, with Captain Duffus as stage manager and the lieutenant governor, the mayor, and high-ranking military in the audience.[14] Furthermore, the spectacle was performed in March 1901 at the opening night of the Gravenhurst Opera House in Muskoka with a "thundering well-dressed crowd" in attendance (Hind). McIlwraith appears to have had another look at the play during the First World War because her notes suggest recital of Kipling's "For All We Have And Are" (1914) to accompany Empire Day, but the details of this renewed interest are not known. In addition to celebrating

---

11 "Chit Chat," *The Globe*, 24 February 1900.

12 "The Temple of Fame," *The Globe*, 26 October 1892.

13 "The Temple of Fame," *The Globe*, 13 February 1897.

14 For the performance of the play in Halifax, see Scrapbook Collection, Nova Scotia Archives, MG 9, vol. 10. The Scrapbook belonged to Mrs. J.F. Kenny, wife of the mayor of Halifax. With thanks to John MacLeod and Anne Williams, Nova Scotia Archives, for background information.

"The Days of the Year, or the Masque of the Months," opening at the Gravenhurst
Opera House, 1901. Gravenhurst Archives.

the seasons, interspersed with the birthdays of various composers and poets,
the pageant relied on ethnic humour. The latter was linked to the days devoted
to St. David, St. Patrick, St. George, St. Jean Baptiste, and so on, and complemented with political, educational, and other landmark days such as Dominion Day, Emancipation Day, and Commencement Day. As with "The Temple
of Fame," the strength of the entertainment was its flexibility, which allowed
for all or portions of the pageant to be performed as required (Halifax, for
example, concentrated on winter because the spectacle was staged in December), for the inclusion of actors of all talents and ages, as well as adjustments
to local context, and the addition of music, dance, tableaux, and pantomimes
as required. Child performers were often highlighted, and even a baby in a
crib could be featured if desired. Photographs survive of the young actors at
Gravenhurst, some looking glum (see photo above), and of Jean's nieces in
costume: Marjorie as a bewitching "Day and Night Equal" and Dorothy as a
flower-bedecked attendant of the May Queen (see photo in chapter 3). For all

its ethnic stereotyping, McIlwraith's script is remarkable for the critical voice it gives to various groups and entities seeking to assert themselves, including the Dominion of Canada. Thus, "Canada" takes John Bull to task for "many ... transactions .... that I haven't approved of at all," and for once a voice is given to Black citizens when an "old negro" speaks about "[d]e grand people ob de Norf, dey made us free we can vote, an' w'en its de 'lection time dey tinks a lot ob de kullad population, but dey won't sit at de table with us, nor hab us in de kyars wid them – 'cept as porters or barbers." He claims "'Taint so bad in Canada."

After her arrival in New York, McIlwraith offered "The Temple of Fame" and "The Days of the Year" as proof of her success in writing for children when she proposed an anthology of "Games That Every Child Should Know" to Doubleday, Page. As was her habit, she cited an impressive supporter of her project, in this case Professor F.H. Sykes from Columbia University, "the leading American authority on vocational studies" ("Selects Dr. F.H. Sykes"), who was originally from Toronto. And as Sykes was the editor of the Scribner's English Classics series,[15] she impressed on Henry Lanier that if Doubleday, Page did not want the book, then Scribner's was sure to be interested. Nevertheless, neither publisher picked up the idea.

Glasgow and London

The 1880s and '90s were a time for McIlwraith to learn as much as possible and immediately put it to use. On one level, her travels were the equivalent of the costlier finishing year enjoyed by young women from the social elite, but in another and more important way she was not so much "finishing" as she was searching for a way to turn her interests into a fulfilling and well-paid occupation. Her brother Jack's biography in a *History of Madison County, Indiana*, composed when he was an established business man, proceeds briskly through family background, stages of career, marriage, and children, and religious and political affiliation. By comparison, Jean's first biography in Morgan's *The Canadian Men and Women of the Time* (1898) is scattered and, unlike its more tightly composed revision in the 1912 edition, does not appear to have been much edited from notes submitted to the publisher. Yet, precisely because of its lack of organization outside of a somewhat breathless chronology, this entry gives a good sense of the various directions she pursued

---

15 JNMP, Editorial Correspondence, Jean N. McIlwraith to Henry Lanier, 30 May 1907. See "Sykes, Frederick Henry," typewritten biographical entry for the *National Cyclopedia of American Biography*, Frederick Sykes Biographical Information, Box 1, Presidents Historical Collection. Linda Lear Center for Special Collections and Archives, Connecticut College.

between 1881 and 1898, including details about this period in her life that appear nowhere else:

> For the next 2 and a half yrs. [following 1881] Miss McI. was in the Old Country, most of the time engaged in the study of singing, varied by pedestrian trips in Scot. and a session at the National Training Sch. of Cookery in South Kensington. Five months of 1892 she also spent in European travel, followed by more singing lessons in London. By far the greater part of her literary work consists of critical essays written for the correspondence class in modern literature in connection with Queen Margaret Coll. Glasgow, of which she had been a mem. off and on since 1886. (Morgan, "McIlwraith, Miss Jane" 740)

The original purpose of her singing lessons in London was to set herself up as a voice teacher after her return home. Perhaps she was looking for a life that allowed her to earn enough as a music teacher and so free her to write at leisure and entertain her wide circle of friends in some style. Characteristically, she was not content to be a dilettante and obtained formal training in all three areas. It speaks to her mercurial temperament, her limited economic resources, and the few career opportunities available to women generally that she nevertheless found it difficult to organize these skills into a life that made her financially independent.

Both Queen Margaret College and the National Training School for Cookery were pioneering institutions in women's education. From the late 1870s onwards, the Glasgow Association for the Higher Education of Women, convened under the leadership of Jessie Campbell[16] by women from wealthy families and patronized by nobility such as the Duchess of Argyll, offered a range of academic subjects with the goal of withdrawing "the charge of flimsiness ... from the education of girls" ("Queen Margaret College: Correspondence Classes" 556). Instruction took place through lectures and both on-site and correspondence courses. The latter, carefully planned to ensure effective independent learning, attracted students from all over the United Kingdom and, eventually, close to five hundred women "in 19 different countries." Many of them came from within the British Empire (Myers 363). By 1891, Jean was well launched in her distance study of modern literature and excitedly reported to Elizabeth Smith that she had "joined the correspondence class again in time to take up Browning's 'Ring and the Book.' "[17] To the college, it was "[g]ratifying testimony to the value of these Classes ... that the students [were] drawn from almost all classes of society and quarters of the globe," including participants from Africa

---

16 See "Jessie Campbell of Cullichewan."
17 McIlwraith, Jean N. "Letter from Jean McIlwraith to Elizabeth Shortt," 31 January 1891. UWL, WA-10, File 280, ESS.

and Canada.[18] Although there is no evidence in the college's records that she enrolled in on-site courses while she was staying with her Aunt Sarah, Jean may have attended public lectures on subjects as diverse as "Development of the Constitution of England," "English Literature," "Music," and "History." All of these were offered during the early 1880s, and all of these subjects play a role in her subsequent writing (Myers 358, 360, 363, 369–70). In a letter to T. Fisher Unwin, reproduced in a monthly pamphlet giving advice on "Good Reading" and drawing attention to her novel *The Making of Mary*, she describes how important the correspondence courses were to her, and her testimonial was saved in the college scrapbook as that of a particularly successful student.[19] For all we know, the college's 1889–90 report was referring to Jean McIlwraith when it pointed out that "some of the ablest papers received have come across the Atlantic, from Canada."[20] As one of the highlights in some ten years of taking these courses, she did win an award for best essay on the subject of "How far is the history of the nineteenth century reflected in its literature?" (Morgan, "McIlwraith, Miss Jane" 740).

She repeatedly told William McLennan that "[t]he writing [she had] enjoyed most was the work [she] did for her Correspondence Class of Queen Margaret College – stacks of literary criticism" (McLFF, J.N. McIlwraith to William McLennan, 15 December [1897?]), and she was convinced that this was the area in which she was most talented. In the course of her career as a writer, she confided to at least three different interviewers that her real desire was to concentrate on literary criticism, showing "an armful of closely written manuscript" (Fenton) as proof of the work she had already done. This plan "would be a mistake," Marjory MacMurchy from the *Canadian Magazine* cautioned, given the acclaim with which *The Curious Career of Roderick Campbell* had just then been received (MacMurchy, "Canadian Celebrities" 134). McIlwraith did, however, find opportunities to demonstrate her knowledge of English literature. Shortly after her arrival in New York in 1902, she was commissioned to write encyclopaedia entries on Thomas Hardy and George Meredith for the *New International Encyclopedia* published by Dodd, Mead, as well as introductions to Doubleday, Page's editions of *Wuthering Heights* and Charles Reade's *Love Me Little, Love Me Long* (both 1907). Several of her compositions for the Queen Margaret College courses made it into print, such as her essay on "Emerson's Choice of Representative Men," published in the

---

18 Report, 1889–1890, DC 233/2/8/3/23/4, College, Queen Margaret College, UGA.
19 Clipping from *Good Reading: A Monthly Advice*, n.d., Notebook of Newspaper Cuttings and Advertisements for the Correspondence Classes," DC 233/2/8/3/23/5, Queen Margaret College, Correspondence Courses, UGA.
20 Report, 1889–1890, DC 233/2/8/3/23/4, Queen Margaret College, Correspondence Courses, UGA.

Canadian Magazine, and, in a brief excerpt, "George Meredith on Women," which appeared in the *Globe*. Yet, her love of literary criticism apparently did not extend to the desire to become an academic, and – considering that several women of similar background in her acquaintance, such as Elizabeth Smith and the mathematician Louise Cummings, did obtain advanced degrees and pursued academic careers despite the chronic difficulties facing women who do so – the reason seems to have been lack of inclination towards the scholar's life rather than lack of money.

Jean does not appear to have enrolled in the course in domestic economy offered at Queen Margaret College, but she did build on her youthful enthusiasm for baking by studying cookery in another innovative educational environment, this time on-site in London. The South Kensington Training School of Cookery was first established as part of the 1873 International Exhibition and was thought to be "designed for ladies ... and not for the training of servants," with the goal of making a woman the "accomplished ruler of her own house" (Dickens 90). The clientele became rather more diverse than this entry in the contemporary *Dictionary of London* would have it. On the one hand, acquiring a diploma at the school became the thing to do for young women from privileged backgrounds, including American girls touring Europe. An irritated writer signing herself "Belgravia" in the New York *Times* scoffed at the concept; she proposed instead that they would be better off training in the kitchens of their parents' homes, or better yet in those of orphanages and prisons ("The National Training School"; see also Stone). On the other hand, the respectable matrons and spoiled teenagers at the school were joined by participants of "the most extraordinary mental and social diversity. There were cultivated ladies, the daughters of country gentlemen, old housekeepers, servants, cooks, and colored girls from South Africa, together with a large proportion of intelligent young women who were preparing to become teachers" (Youmans, Preface, R. Cole vi). This is Eliza A. Youmans writing, a botanist from a family of scientists and editor of the American version (1878), published only a year after the original, of *The Official Hand-book of the National Training School for Cookery* (1877). In both the British and the American editions, the textbook was quickly adopted throughout the English-speaking world, and the popular *Mrs. Clarke's Cookery Book*, published in Toronto in 1883, includes many of the recipes in simplified format (see Driver 348–9). The connections claimed by the author of the British edition, Rose Owen Cole, were every bit as impressive as Eliza Youmans's: Cole was the daughter of Sir Henry Cole, whose many achievements as civil servant, educator, and industrial-design pioneer included the planning of several international exhibitions in London, one of them being the 1851 Great Exhibition.

In other words, McIlwraith learned cookery in a school that taught the subject as part of the imperial project, in a setting devoted to a woman's scientific, creative, and managerial training. The school exposed McIlwraith to a larger cross-section of the female population of the British Empire than she would have experienced at a teacher's college or in a secretarial course, even if McIlwraith was an early enthusiast of the typewriter and bought hers with the proceeds of her book on Longfellow. The school brought her in contact with women with whom she would otherwise have had little opportunity to mingle, such as "colored girls from South Africa" although it is another question whether she appreciated them. As a writer, McIlwraith may have enjoyed the analogy the *Handbook* drew between cooking and writing, offering "rather a grammar than a dictionary" (R. Cole 3) and leaving plenty of room for creativity.

"Household Budgets Abroad: Canada"

Her experience at the National Training School was part of a larger interest in imperial economics, as becomes clear from McIlwraith's "Household Budgets Abroad: Canada," published in *Cornhill Magazine* in 1904. The article trains a lens on her understanding of the choices available to young men and women depending on their backgrounds, as well as revealing first-hand knowledge of much of Canada, the United States, and Great Britain. The essay was part of a series begun in the magazine in 1900 to illustrate turn-of-the-century financial management in low-, medium-, and high-income British families and selected "households abroad," and its contributors included well-known writers like Arthur Morrison, author of *Tales of Mean Streets* (1894), writing on "A Workman's Budget" (A. Morrison, "Family Budgets"). The question of financial management also shapes the *Handbook of the National Cookery School* when it seeks to "illustrat[e] many degrees of cost," according to which "the rich may have a dish of curried rabbit at 3s. 8d., and the poor a dish of curried tripe at 10¾d." (R. Cole 3). (The *Handbook* avoids answering the question of how the poor might also go about having curried rabbit on their tables.) Four years after the inaugural feature, the *Cornhill Magazine* published similar profiles for households in the United States, France, Germany, Italy, Australia, and Canada. The format of these essays resembles Settlement House publications like the famous *Hull-House Maps and Papers* (1895) or Louise Bolard More's *Wage Earners' Budgets: A Study of Standards and Costs of Living in New York City* (1907). But while these seek to furnish the necessary evidence towards reform of social inequity, McIlwraith outlines Canada's national economic profile as it exists rather than as it should be, and she filters any sense of social injustice into occasional grim humour. Given the criticism that she has Anna Trnka, an anarchist in her novel "Dominick Street," voice about the invasive investigation of the poor that produced the data for such publications, it would be interesting to know how McIlwraith collected her information.

"Household Budgets Abroad: Canada" draws comparisons between the Canadian situation on the one hand and that of Britain and the United States on the other before taking a systematic tour of each province beginning with British Columbia. McIlwraith specifies salaries by working her way through the hierarchies of politics, banking, education, the clergy, and commerce. Young households are established, she explains, by "board[ing] until [the couple] can afford to keep house" or by "liv[ing] out of town" in a rural area where the rent is cheaper and where the "weary brain-workers" can "escape the telephone, the typewriter, the trolley car, the automobile" ("Household Budgets" 807). She comments on the social function of dress, does not believe that fashion is a reliable marker of class in North America, and underlines the significance within the community of "a good dressmaker [who] will have her winter's work laid out for weeks ahead." Horses and carriages are relatively cheap, but "labour ... is dear," and "Canadian men and women" are used to doing "many odd jobs in and about the house – carpentering, gardening, plumbing, and so on – and they are none the worse for the doing." Canadians proved their resourcefulness in the recent Boer War, she reminds her readers, where the "Dominion Tommies" became known as the "Thousand Thieves" for their skill in foraging.[21] This is not the only swipe she takes at what she assumes to be British arrogance, and she commends Canadian "colonials" for their unconventionality that has them "drive themselves, wash their own buggies, or even venture forth with them unwashed, which would be considered a crime in England" (808). Nevertheless, the Boer War fired up Jean's imperialist fervour: a notice in the *Globe* of 5 October 1901 has her "arrange ... an entirely new set of characters" for "The Temple of Fame," "bringing the programme up to date" in honour of the "Dominion Tommies."[22] One of these "Tommies," a Canadian doctor and fiancé of Jonquil Ames, appears in McIlwraith's novel "Casual Kate's Letters." Although he is a saintly figure who refuses to kill even "a dirty Boer," he echoes Jean's insistence that "[i]t is always our business to fight when the Empire is at war."[23]

Outsiders are valuable only insofar as they contribute to the Anglo economy, and a family's fortune is signalled by its ability to hire one or more servants. In commenting on the cost of domestic work, she is critical of the Chinese head tax, not because she finds it discriminatory, but because it has become more expensive to hire Chinese domestics "to perform the duties of cook, house maid, [and] waitress" ("Household Budgets" 809), do the weekly laundry, and complete the laborious annual canning of fruit and vegetables, all for 16 shillings a

---

21 She is referring to officer Edward Thomas Henry Hutton, who described the Canadian troops "as the worst thieves in the British army, on one occasion they had stolen his horse." See Miller.

22 "The Temple of Fame," *The Globe*, 5 October 1901.

23 "Casual Kate's Letters," 37, 34.

month serving a family of three. She talks about the ethnic composition of each province, such as the "Germans, Irish, Icelanders, Galicians, [and] Norwegians" (812) in Manitoba, the "coloured servants" (817) in Nova Scotia, and the mix of nationalities in ports like Halifax. Her sample budget for a merchant's family in Vancouver with three children on a £400 annual income allows for rent, labour tax, one servant's wages, light and fires, clothing, education, and extras. The next level is occupied by a clerk and his family of two, with an annual income of £200 pounds. To make ends meet, he has to make do without a servant, live at "some distance from his work" (810), and allow for carfare in addition to rent, light, fuel, clothing, insurance, groceries, and savings. He has the choice between paying his medical bills or having money to spend on amusements. Workmen, the final group, are paid by the day, hoping to earn a total of £144 a year. In Jean's budget, they are not given a family as their income is insufficient to provide for one. A workman's expenditures are stripped to the essentials of rent, food, and light and heating, with clothing and savings ranking at the same level of low urgency as incidentals. A servant is obviously out of the question. As a coal dealer's daughter, Jean discourses knowledgeably on the cost of coal, adding her "congratulation that wood can be bought for 16s a cord, and bark to burn in grates for £1" (810) in British Columbia, but she has much more to say about the subject of fuel when she gets to provinces with a severe climate like Manitoba. An analysis of the financial situation of Prairie farmers is included in the section on that province.

From her visits with Nellie, she knew something about the complications and cost of snow removal in Quebec, which "gives employment to a great number of men" ("Household Budgets" 816) and compelled large stores like Holt-Renfrew on Rue Buade to take out accident insurance in the event that ice or snow falling from the roof injured a customer. Although he traded in the finest fox and mink, John Holt was also able to tell her about the furs typically worn by low-income Quebeckers, including "'coon, rabbit, or other cheap skin," and about their preferred types of "woollen overstockings" and "felt overshoes" (817). Likewise, he may have encouraged her to acquaint herself with his store's wide range of snowshoes for her essay on Canadian winter sports ("Winter Sports").[24]

McIlwraith is equally knowledgeable about local foods when she gets to Ontario, listing the "apples, pears, plums, peaches, grapes," as well as the "strawberries, cherries, rasps, brambles, and blueberries" that could be had from "the western end of Lake Ontario" ("Household Budgets" 812), not to mention the fish from the Great Lakes: salmon, salmon trout, white fish, and herring. She elaborates on methods of food preservation practised in specific areas, such

---

24 See also the Smithsonian's Otis Tufton Mason, *Primitive Travel and Transportation*, which features snowshoes manufactured by Renfrew & Co.

as the freezing of meat in Quebec. In one of several expressions of ethnic stereotype, she deems the citizens of the province "a cheerful, contented, thrifty class" (815) whose charming but antiquated ways make them "a brake upon the Dominion wheel not always appreciated by the party of progress" (815–16). In Quebec, "held in great esteem by ... the seekers for the quaintly picturesque" (816), fowl, mutton, and partridges are "preserved out of doors, in a box, packed in snow, and ... thawed out as required" (815). Beef cannot be frozen because it "spoils the flavour," she claims, although her Australian relatives who had made the long-distance transport of frozen meat their business would have protested. The virtue of resourceful thinking remains a persistent theme, and she lists the tutoring of "backward scholars," early morning paper routes, "attend[ing] the house furnaces in a given block or two," "teach[ing] in a country school" (813), and farm labour during the vacation as so many ways for young persons to finance their education. As a sportswoman and frequent tourist, she does not omit opportunities for outdoor leisure. "The annual influx of American tourists" is to blame for driving up the cost of "hotel charges, the house-rents, board, lodging, driving, domestic service and food in every summer resort they frequent," especially in "Murray Bay, Cacouna, and Tadousac [sic]." As a result, these locations are beyond the means of ordinary Canadians (813), but renting a room in a modest cottage still ensures a good holiday.

Successful Author

By the time this article appeared, McIlwraith had been publishing steadily for more than a decade, and her success was notable enough to earn her inclusion in Morgan's *Canadian Men and Women of the Time*, as cited earlier. Following her first published story as an adult, "The Earthquake Region" in *Harper's Bazaar* (1890), she wrote several books for the juvenile market that allowed her to draw on her teaching experience, the expertise in literary criticism she acquired in her courses at Queen Margaret College, and her increasingly impressive research skills. These publications included *A Book About Shakespeare Written for Young People* (1898), *Canada* for the Children's Study series (1899), and *A Book About Longfellow* (1900). The first and third of these books were published by T. Nelson in Edinburgh and the second appeared with T. Fisher Unwin in London. W. Briggs issued a Canadian edition of *Canada*. The Nelson publishing firm had Canadian connections through its managing trustee, George Mackenzie Brown, the Canadian-born son of the Toronto newspaper man George Brown and a cousin of the Nelsons. McIlwraith may have benefited from her dual Canadian and Scottish connections in gaining an introduction to the publishers.

She drew on her singing lessons in London in "A Singing-Student in London" for *Harper's Magazine* (1894). Her novel *The Making of Mary*, her first book published by T. Fisher Unwin, also appeared in 1894. Collaboration with the

Montreal notary and author William McLennan on the historical novel *The Span o' Life* followed. It was serialized in *Harper's* throughout 1898 and 1899 and published as a book in 1899, also by Harper, along with a Canadian edition by Copp, Clark. Shortly after another historical novel, *The Curious Career of Roderick Campbell* (1901), appeared. The publisher this time was Houghton, Mifflin in Boston, with a British edition by Archibald Constable. A study of Sir Frederick Haldimand (1904) for the Makers of Canada series, edited by Duncan Campbell Scott and Pelham Edgar for George M. Morang in Toronto, was next. During the same fifteen-odd years in which these books appeared, McIlwraith wrote a steady stream of essays and stories for British, American, and Canadian magazines such as *Cornhill Magazine*, *Harper's Magazine*, *Harper's Bazaar*, the *Atlantic Monthly*, *World's Work*, and the *Canadian Magazine*, as well as articles for the New York *Post*.[25] Although she continued to publish books after she moved to New York in 1902 and after her return to Canada at the end of her career with Doubleday, Page,[26] it was not at the same prolific rate because she found it increasingly difficult to place her work with publishers. Publication of her final books is spaced well apart. *A Diana of Quebec* (1912) drew on her research on Frederick Haldimand. It was followed by the children's book *The Little Admiral* (1924), which took her back to the Seven Year's War, the historical background for *A Span o' Life*. Her final novel, *Kinsmen at War*, about the War of 1812, appeared in 1927.

Especially at the beginning of her editorial career in New York she produced articles on Canadian scenery and sports for "life-style" magazines, such as her "Salt Water Vacation in Canada" for *Travel* (1907),[27] "Bracing Outings on the Great Lakes" for Doubleday, Page's *Country Life in America* (1905), and the previously cited "Winter Sports Old and New," also for *Country Life*. In this way, she ironically contributed to encouraging the American tourism that, as she wrote in "Household Budgets Abroad," was making it difficult for Canadians

---

25 In her interview with Pringle in 1926, McIlwraith suggests that her decision to move to New York was motivated by acceptance, by the New York *Post*, of a sketch "of a humorous nature, touching on the adventures of camping out," and the encouragement to submit "further articles from her pen," which "they featured in their Saturday Edition" (Pringle, "Jean McIlwraith" 21). These articles have so far not come to light. McIlwraith's correspondence with Fannie Hardy Eckstorm does not confirm that the connection to the *NYP* was the reason for moving to New York.

26 It is somewhat difficult to determine when she left New York. She repeatedly speaks of a fourteen-year career in editing but does not clarify whether she includes the year or so before she was permanently hired by Doubleday, Page and whether she briefly stayed on in New York after she left the firm. T.F. McIlwraith's letters to his sister in New York towards the end of the First World War continue to include greetings to "Aunt Jean."

27 The Hathitrust database lists Jean N. McIlwraith, "Salt Water Vacation in Canada: The Northern Shore of the St. Lawrence Below Quebec," *Travel*, August 1907, 470ff., but the essay has not been located, and the page range is not available.

to have an affordable holiday in their own country. Given the popularity of French Canada, specifically Quebec City, as a substitute Europe, her article for *World's Work* on the Quebec Tercentenary (1908) fits into the category of her travel essays,[28] but she also wrote about her travels in Europe, such as "A City of Fountains" (1910), about the fountains of Rome, published in *The World Today*. In her letters to Fannie Hardy Eckstorm about the types of jobs she could see herself doing in New York, McIlwraith cites the writing of advertising copy as a possibility (FHEP, Jean N. McIlwraith to F.H. Eckstorm, 30 June 1902), and these travel sketches do indicate an aptitude for such work. Unlike "In the Earthquake Region," her later essays and stories about French Canada are openly commercial. Because of her many visits with the Holts, she may have been influenced by Holt-Renfrew's strategy of linking its merchandise to tourism along the St. Lawrence. The firm distributed promotional publications such as *Ten Days in Quebec* and kept them up to date. In these, as part of a trip to the historic city of Quebec and its picturesque surroundings, the store is packaged "as one of the sights." Its merchandise doubled as an educational experience to visitors from Boston or New York that they could not easily obtain in their own country because "[t]he firm buys its pelts direct from the Indians, and the employees can tell many stories of the customs of that primitive people, who have become almost extinct in Eastern America" (*Ten Days in Quebec*). The reasoning expressed in the booklet was clearly effective because a version of these views, bolstered with reference to the firm's million-dollar capital, appears in Ella G. Farrell's *Among the Blue Laurentians* (1912). One of many American travel books about Quebec, it notes Holt-Renfrew's own zoo near Montmorency Falls, where fur-bearing Canadian animals were displayed (E. Farrell 32; see also Little).

The reviews of McIlwraith's books were favourable, many highlighting her sense of humour, scrupulous research, and grasp of her readers' expectations. Both her non-fiction and her fiction were a success. The keeper of the Legislative Library of Ontario was sufficiently impressed to acquire a copy of her book about Canada for young students.[29] She made the study of Shakespeare "simple" (*School Journal*) for students because "things [were] put ... clearly and attractively" (*Education*), and her volume on Longfellow was "[a] pleasant, chatty book about the poet, his friends and surroundings" that the Church Library Association gladly recommended to its members.[30] Overall, the wholesomeness of her writing made her publications a favourite for school curricula, in

---

28 "Re-enacting 300 Years of Quebec's History." In her interview with Pringle, she mentions writing on the Tercentenary for the New York *Post* as well, but this work has so far not been found.

29 *Catalogue of Books in the Legislative Library of the Province of Ontario* 108.

30 *A Catalogue of Books Recommended by the Church Library Association* 96.

public libraries, and even in penitentiaries,[31] and when she became a reader for Doubleday, Page, she shared with Walter Page a dislike of risqué books.[32] Despite her enjoyment of bohemian company, she was straight-laced and, in her entry on the writer for the *New International Encyclopedia*, disapproved of Thomas Hardy's frank depiction of sexuality ("Hardy, Thomas" 85–6). Perhaps her primness was another reason why she found it difficult to locate a place for herself that satisfied both her talents and her temperament.

However, her writing had more to offer than stout morality. For one, she consistently impressed scholars in particular and readers in general with the thoroughness of her investigations. Her book on Frederick Haldimand was widely cited, for example in R.W. MacLachlan's *Fleury Mesplet, the First Printer at Montreal* (1906) and Jean Charlemagne Bracq's *The Evolution of French Canada* (1924). *Haldimand* was recommended for college libraries along with the other Makers of Canada volumes,[33] and praised by the *Handbook of Canadian Literature* as "a notable biography" that would make its subject better known (A. MacMurchy 178). Her historical fiction was well received for similar reasons. The accuracy of its facts, "based upon an actual historical occurrence" (Hamilton *Spectator*), distinguished *The Little Admiral*, which was recognized in 1923 with first place in the Canadian Contest for Juvenile Fiction by the Hodder and Stoughton and Musson Book Company. *Kinsmen at War* proved her to be "a skilful and experienced romancist [sic]" and a writer who remained commendably "faithful to recorded fact."[34] The journalist M.O. Hammond sent his review of *A Diana of Quebec* in the *Globe* to her, which included the reservation that "Miss McIlwraith has, perhaps, suffered from ... limitations of exact history, and exhibits some puzzlement as to where to leave facts and begin romance" (Hammond). In her response, she sets him straight on these concerns, and lists her sources as a "tombstone in the Royal College at Chelsea" that she checked for dates of birth and death, letters at the Literary and Historical Society of Quebec, diaries, and conversations with "[l]ocal lights" about Nelson's "Quebec charmer [who] used to sit at her window near the present Post Office and watch for him coming up Mountain Hill." To dispel Hammond's doubts about the authenticity of other details, she cites "Elbert Hubbard in his 'Famous Lover' Series" for corroboration.[35] She is equally clear

31 See Trotter 61, 66, 68, 73, 156, citing *Sir Frederick Haldimand* under five different rubrics; *A Classified Catalogue of 3500 Volumes Suitable for A Public Library* 20, 44, which includes both *A Span o' Life* and *Canada*; and *Catalogue of the Library of the Illinois State Penitentiary Joliet, Illinois* 91, which lists *The Curious Career of Roderick Campbell*.

32 For her dislike of risqué books, see "Jottings."

33 See *A List of Books for Junior College Libraries* 199.

34 Review, TFMP, identified on the clipping (but not confirmed) as having appeared in *The Globe*, 21 April 1928.

35 See Elbert Hubbard, *Little Journeys to the Homes of Great Lovers: Lord Nelson and Lady Hamilton*, The Roycrofters, 1906.

about the reasons for making the few changes that she did introduce. For example, it was probably one of the "local lights," most likely the Abbé Casgrain, who alerted her to the complications of local genealogy that would make it wise to select a different name for one of her characters because he was "the great-uncle of the wife of the present Lieut-Gov of Quebec." The original Laterrière was "a strange fellow and a pathological liar" jailed for espionage (Dufour and Hamelin), and in *Diana* he becomes Vallière instead of Laterrière because his present-day relatives would not appreciate being reminded of their shady ancestor. Given her three-page defence of the novel, it comes as a surprise that she claims that she is "not very caring" about the success of *Diana*, and merely wanted to get the book out of her system.[36] As we will see, however, she used this kind of smokescreening repeatedly, perhaps in an effort to protect herself against criticism and disappointment.

The most acclaimed of her novels was *The Curious Career of Roderick Campbell*, with its "lively invention and a ready pen," and *Vogue* printed a lengthy excerpt along with this positive assessment to whet readers' appetites ("What They Read"). To the non-Scottish reader, some of the dialogue could be a challenge, and *The Academy* was not altogether complimentary when its reviewer thought that *Roderick Campbell* was "[v]ery Scotch," offering an excerpt he considered virtually impenetrable.[37] By contrast, Scottish reviewers were happy with McIlwraith's characterizations of their countrymen, whom, as *The Scotsman* wrote about *Roderick Campbell*, she made "appear courageous, humorous without descending to the fanciful travesties that find favour in some quarters."[38] Together with *Haldimand*, *Roderick Campbell* is one of McIlwraith's most enduring books, and it is a study of the Scottish literary tradition in Canadian literature that is most appreciative of it. In it, Roderick is described as "a turncoat before Culloden, ... an engaging Falstaffian figure, an opportunist, who stirs memories in his readers of a long roll of literary prototypes from Scott to Stevenson."[39] McIlwraith wrote *Roderick Campbell* when the market was glutted with imitations of Robert Louis Stevenson. It was no small feat to produce a fresh formula for the historical novel, but by using a system of different points of view for which she may have drawn on her study of Robert Browning, she came close. When it came to *Haldimand*, writing the book practically turned into a love affair with this "patient, calm, reserved + very fine gentleman" (FHEP, J.N. McIlwraith to F.H. Eckstorm, 12 January 1902). The excitement of working on historical manuscripts comes with an attractive sense of self-mockery that has

36 J.N. McIlwraith, letter to M.O. Hammond, 9 October 1912, M.O. Hammond Fonds, F 1075–10, Archives of Ontario.

37 *The Academy*, no. 1,511, 20 April 1901, 346.

38 Qtd. in publishers' advertisement, Maurice Hewlett, *New Canterbury Tales*, Archibald Constable, 1901.

39 Waterston 220. It may be going a little far to call McIlwraith "a graduate of Glasgow" as Waterston does.

her lament the failure of a historical figure to tell her all she wants to know: "Why did he not name these periodicals and thus gratify a present-day public, curious to know what were the well-thumbed pages sent from post to post to beguile the tedium of a lonely winter?" (*Sir Frederick Haldimand* 24).

Her contemporaries agreed that McIlwraith had established herself in the transatlantic literary world, with publication of *Roderick Campbell* by Houghton, Mifflin as an especially impressive coup, and she was included in *Women of Canada*, the volume prepared by the National Council of Women of Canada for the Paris International Exhibition in 1900 and the Pan-American Exposition in Buffalo in 1901. She was one of the few women featured in the *Canadian Magazine*'s series "Canadian Celebrities" (M. MacMurchy). For interviews with Jean McIlwraith, magazines and newspapers dispatched some of their best-known female writers, or the editor came herself. Faith Fenton, editor of the *Canadian Home Journal*, visited Cairnbrae in 1895,[40] and Marjory MacMurchy arrived in 1901 on behalf of the *Canadian Magazine*. In 1926, *Saturday Night* sent its frequent contributor Gertrude Pringle, niece of Ernest Thompson Seton and soon to publish *Etiquette in Canada: The Blue Book of Canadian Usage* (1932), to Jean's retirement bungalow in Burlington. Fenton romanticizes McIlwraith as "a bonnie Scotch-Canadienne" with "a ripple of natural curl," "eyes, whose color varies from blue to grey, from grey to black, as the light or shadow fills them." Although she declined to sing for her interviewer, Fenton confirmed that McIlwraith had "a soft, full-sounding voice." All of these features lightened the strength of her "broad forehead and heavy eyebrows," and the well-tended gardens at Cairnbrae were "harmoniously fitting for the fine and wholesome nature of the daughter of the house" (Fenton). McIlwraith appears to have been at pains to project a dignified image in these conversations, but perhaps she did manage to have some fun at the expense of Gertrude Pringle, who concludes her otherwise glowing essay with a reference to McIlwraith's "racy and graphic conversation." In Pringle's books that was not a compliment, and in *Etiquette in Canada* she included a list of slang to be avoided in polite conversation, such as "Gosh," "Darn," and "Gee" (Pringle, *Etiquette* 106). McIlwraith's language tended to be rather more colourful than this.

Collaboration with William McLennan

The success of her early novel *The Making of Mary* may have been the trigger for the collaboration between McIlwraith and William McLennan on *The Span o' Life*. *The Making of Mary* was published in T. Fisher Unwin's Half-Crown series in the company of such bestselling authors as Olive Schreiner, Ouida, John Buchan, and William Clark Russell, and it enjoyed an American edition by Cassell

---

40 On Fenton, see Downie.

in New York and a Canadian one by William Briggs in Toronto. Reviewers found "a fund of originality" ("Leads the Reader") in the story and thought it a delectable confection, "amusing and brightly written" ("The Making of Mary"), "sparkling and vivacious" ("New Novels"), and "one of the ... best constructed and most entirely interesting bits of fiction ... that the literary world has seen in many a long day" (*Colonies and India*).[41] Perhaps it was reviews like these that persuaded McLennan, a historical novelist and translator of French Canadian folktales, that a jointly written novel with Jean would be advantageous to both of their careers. Such collaborations had become a popular novelty, especially in the highly commercialized genre of magazine serials (see Ashton). The variations on well-established themes produced by two or more authors in dialogue with one another helped to rejuvenate genres, characters, and plots, sometimes sensationally so. The *ne plus ultra* of such collaborations was *The Whole Family, a Novel by Twelve Authors*, brainchild of W.D. Howells and serialized in *Harper's Bazar* (which had not yet added a third *a* to its name) throughout 1907 and 1908 under the direction of its editor, Elizabeth Jordan, with Henry James as the most famous participant and Mary E. Wilkins Freeman the boldest. We do not know whether previous collaborations by Canadian authors, such as G. Mercer Adam and Agnes Ethelwyn Wetherald's *An Algonquin Maiden: A Romance of the Early Days of Upper Canada* (1887) or Agnes Maule Machar and T.G. Marquis's *Stories of New France* (1890), inspired McIlwraith and McLennan or why and when, exactly, their partnership came about, but the two were able to draw on an impressive web of professional and personal acquaintants. Jean knew McLennan's wife Marion ("Minnie") Paterson, apparently a former student at the Wesleyan Ladies' College: Jack McIlwraith, as Jean reports, immediately recognized her in a photo when he came visiting with his "Indiana bride" (McLFF, J.N. McIlwraith to W. McLennan, 13 July 1897). Minnie came from Quebec and knew the Misses Holt, sisters-in-law of Jean's sister Nellie and close friends of Jean. As well, McLennan's father Hugh and brother John Stewart were grain and coal merchants and as such probably business contacts of Mr. McIlwraith's.[42] Finally, both McIlwraith and McLennan were featured in volume 88 of *Harper's Magazine* (1893–4), in the impressive company of W.D. Howells, Owen Wister, Sara Orne Jewett, George du Maurier, and a fellow Canadian, Ch.G.D. Roberts. For McIlwraith, "A Singing-Student in London" in *Harper's* was one of her first publications as an adult writer while McLennan, here represented with "As Told to His Grace: Tales of the French Revolution," was well established as a frequent contributor to the magazine. The frequency with which Harper publications appear in Jean McIlwraith's career

---

41 *Colonies and India*, qtd. in McIlwraith's entry in Henry James Morgan, "McIlwraith, Miss Jane" 741.

42 See *DCB* entries on members of the McLennan family: A.J.B. Johnston on John Stewart McLennan, Leslie Monkman on William McLennan, Allan Levine on Hugh McLennan.

and elsewhere in this book confirms the publisher's role as "a powerful, extended cultural apparatus" for the period (Howard 58).

McIlwraith was the junior partner in the arrangement and, as she jokingly put it herself, travelling on the "coat-tails" of her co-author (McLFF, J.N. McIlwraith to W. McLennan, 18 September 1897) to whom she willingly – and as it turned out to her financial advantage – surrendered negotiations for their contract with *Harper's Magazine* (McLFF, J.N. McIlwraith to W. McLennan, 25 September 1897). A notice in *The Academy* after their book had appeared barely acknowledges her ("Notes on Novels"), and a very positive notice in *The Bookman* noted that "[c]ollaboration has not hampered Mr. McLennan" ("Review of *The Span o' Life*"), although the effect was somewhat spoiled in the latter by confusing his novel *Spanish John* with Neil Munro's *John Splendid*. For marketing reasons, it was quite common in such collaborations for the better-known partner to receive all or most of the credit (see Ashton 3). Throughout their correspondence, Jean acknowledged McLennan's greater experience and sought his advice on questions of publishing. Thus, he counselled her on an effective title for her book on Shakespeare and about the advantages and disadvantages of continuing with her pseudonym "Jean Forsyth" at this stage of her career. They were almost contemporaries but her salutation "Dear Father William" speaks to an important aspect of their working relationship. Her name for him alludes to his title "Mon Compère Melchior," a collection of seven stories first published in *Harper's Magazine* (1891) that established McLennan's literary reputation. By using this salutation she acknowledged his guidance, although she dropped this form of address soon enough in favour of the occasional "My Dear Partner" or, most frequently, "Dear William," as one of many signals that she wanted her contribution to be taken seriously even if she occasionally adopted a pose of docility – a rare and startling thing for her to do. Despite their unequal stature and their sometimes heated disagreements over *The Span o' Life*, they were an amicable pair who exchanged gifts of a pretty pin for McIlwraith and a box of home-made shortbread for McLennan, and he steadfastly supported her with letters of introduction when she looked for a job in New York a few years later. He eagerly anticipated reports of her progress there as he and his family travelled through Italy to improve his health.

As their joint project got underway, McLennan's novel *Spanish John* was being serialized in *Harper's Magazine*, followed by book publication. *The Academy's* criticism of the book as lacking "the breeze and swing of good narrative" ("Review of *Spanish John*") was all the more reason to work with a writer who had only recently been praised for her "sparkling and vivacious" style, especially as they shared a preoccupation with historical accuracy. The details of their collaboration are well documented in McIlwraith's letters to McLennan. Although his side of the correspondence is missing, its gist can be gleaned from her responses, and the collection is a fascinating record of late nineteenth-century collaborative writing in progress: the authors' sometimes substantially different ideas – specifically their disagreements over the characteristics of a "female" perspective as opposed to a "male" outlook – their negotiations toward a consensus, and for both of them the interference of serious personal problems with their work. Writing in the *Canadian Magazine*, one critic found the result almost too "gracefully written and carefully polished" ("Books and Authors"), an ironical conclusion considering that there was nothing smooth about the discussions that preceded it. With few exceptions, historical fiction dates fast, and a modern reader will be inclined to dismiss *The Span o' Life* as "a rather stiff and slow-moving book" (Dean). By contrast, the reviewer writing in *The Bookman* (London) in 1899 thought that the book was vigorous, handled "historical romance in a responsible fashion," and presented "real human beings, not mere puppets." The heroine's decision to follow the male lead to North America was deemed mildly and appealingly risqué, and the authors had "broken fresh ground [in] a particularly interesting country of romance" ("Review of *The Span o' Life*"). The *Saturday Review* also liked the book for its "very attractive love story" ("Novels"), a satisfying outcome considering that both authors thought love stories were not their forte. Whatever one may now think of the book, the conversation between McLennan and McIlwraith shows two well-informed and articulate writers seeking – within the limitations imposed by their mentality and times – to address the difficult relationship between Canada's English- and French-speaking citizens. It was important to them that the narrative express their respect for the French tradition. At least twice in her letters to McLennan, McIlwraith cites the report allegedly received by the dying General Wolfe on the defeat of the French Canadians – " 'They run – they run!' ... 'Who – who run?' ... 'The enemy, Sir ... they give way everywhere' " (R. Wright 586). This episode impelled her to tell the "enemy's" story with as much fairness as possible, and McLennan fully agreed with her. McIlwraith cited the scene yet again almost twenty-five years later when she published *The Little Admiral*, and when she felt that the recent world war had put a stop to her generation's belief that "the French [were] a running race" ("Hamilton Woman"). As her nephew's wartime letters illustrate, these stereotypes were unfortunately far from extinct while the war was in progress.

McLennan and McIlwraith chose a subject that occupied them individually as well – namely, the aftermath of the '45 Rebellion, its colourful cast of Roman Catholic, French-, Gaelic-, and English-speaking Scottish Jacobites, the parallels between this traumatic event and the victory of Britain over France on the Plains of Abraham fourteen years later, and the difficulties of drawing clear battle lines between enemies who shared numerous loyalties and values. Walter Scott in *Waverley* (1814) and Robert Louis Stevenson in *Kidnapped* (1886) had written acclaimed novels about the subject but the same review in *The Academy* that found McLennan's treatment of the Jacobite theme in *Spanish John* wanting also pointed out that "[t]he novel of the 'Forty-five remains to be written, for Scott and Stevenson have only played with the fringes of the thing ... But the man who would write it must have an eye for the subtle and strange in character, and the nerve to achieve the dramatic" ("Review of *Spanish John*"). Work on *The Span o' Life* was completed by the time this review appeared but for all we know it stung the pair into the ambitious hope that theirs would be that novel. Their main character, Hugh Maxwell of Kirkconnel, was modelled on the Chevalier de Johnstone, who fled to North America following Culloden, became aide-de-camp first to Lévis, then to Montcalm, and saw action during the campaigns of 1759 in Quebec and 1760 in Montreal.[43] The Chevalier's life story and fluid identity – which, among other peculiarities, had him write in imperfect English as if he had "forgotten or ... never thoroughly known the language" (LeMoine, Introduction, de Johnstone) – had been interesting to historians of Quebec for some time. It received renewed attention with the publication in 1868, under the auspices of the Literary and Historical Society of Quebec, of the Chevalier's *Memoirs* and "A Dialogue in Hades" between the ghosts of Generals Montcalm and Wolfe about the military errors committed by both the French and the British. The introduction was written by James LeMoine, friend of Jean's father. A few years later, McIlwraith borrowed the conceit of a "dialogue in Hades" between Omar Khayyám and Walt Whitman. The dialogue was published in the *Atlantic Monthly* and features the deliciously 1960s-style phrase "That's poetry, man" in response to the complaint "Thou speakst in riddles" ("A Dialogue in Hades," 808). Perhaps also inspired by Walter Savage Landor's *Imaginary Conversations* (1824–9), McIlwraith tried the genre again for a conversation between Frederick Haldimand and Ethan Allen and was advised to send the result to the *New England Magazine*, but without success.

To situate their book in the market, both authors familiarized themselves with their literary competition and studied their likely audience. Thus, they agreed that it would be best not to dwell yet again on the Intendant Bigot and Madame Péan, both "done to death" (McLFF, J.N. McIlwraith to William McLennan, 29 January 1897) in Gilbert Parker's very successful *The Seats of the Mighty* (1896), and instead they decided to emphasize the role of Montcalm. They had no need to specify that both Bigot and Péan had also been "done to death" twenty years earlier in William Kirby's popular *The Golden Dog* (1877), a traditional measuring stick by which to evaluate Canadian historical fiction: when McIlwraith published *A Diana of Quebec* in 1912, it was praised for being "in its own way ... almost as useful to read for the history of Quebec City as the famous 'Golden Dog' " (MacMurchy, "Retrospect" 7). McLennan's brother, John Stewart – connoisseur of the history of Louisbourg – had urged *The Seats on the Mighty* on

---

43 See T.A. Crowley, "Johnstone, James." Also see Kröller, "Jacobites in Canadian Literature."

the collaborators before they got too far into their project because he suspected overlap even after William had carefully laid out the differences to him. Certainly there were differences, John Stewart conceded, but would the average reader not take *The Span o' Life* as duplication of what had already been done, much as a reader of a novel about Paris during the Revolution, as narrated by a witness, would be dismayed to find he was merely given another version of *A Tale of Two Cities*? (McLFF, John Stewart McLennan to William McLennan, 15 January 1897). Either as part of the collaborators' arrangements from the beginning, or as the result of conflicts they found difficult to resolve by themselves as they began their work, John Stewart played the role of umpire. His family loyalties must have been strong indeed to read lengthy chapters and the authors' commentary on each other's work at short notice, as well as to compose multi-page responses to his brother at the end of a busy day at the Dominion Coal Company in Boston.

Joseph-Edmond Roy and the Abbé Casgrain, important figures in the historiography of Quebec, are both warmly acknowledged in the published book. McIlwraith sent an inscribed copy to Casgrain, expressing the authors' thanks and their hope that he would like the result better than *The Seats of the Mighty*. To assist her, Casgrain had visited historical sites with McIlwraith, "besides giving [her] so many points about Rivière Ouelle and the spirit of the times."[44] The authors sought to clarify everything from the correct salutation for James Murray (was he entitled to "Your Excellency"?), the colour of the Young Pretender's eyes, the precise view of the battle scene to be had from the windows of Quebec's General Hospital, and the date when potatoes were first introduced to Lower Canada. Members of the McLennan and McIlwraith families became informal consultants. Jean's parents repeatedly advised on correct Scottish idiom, and Minnie McLennan and Kennedy McIlwraith offered their views as "average" readers. For the scene in which Margaret, disguised in her brother's uniform, prepares to cross enemy lines, Minnie advised kilts rather than trousers and Jean agreed that "anything in the shape of petticoats is less repugnant than trousers to the feminine taste, even if they are a trifle short" (McLFF, J.N. McIlwraith to W. McLennan, 29 January 1897). Facetiously, she proposed to make up the deficit by having Margaret don the woollen stockings that the local nuns had knitted for the Scots, either out of compassion or scandal at the display of their bare legs. Jean longed for more opportunities to discuss the book in person with Nellie, but mostly had to be satisfied with letters such as one reporting a chance encounter between John Holt and Casgrain in the streets of Quebec. On a visit from the University of Toronto, Kennedy was drafted into reading the manuscript to gauge his response to the contentious character of Margaret, and he was family-minded enough to support his sister's views.

---

44 Jean N. McIlwraith to Henri-Raymond Casgrain, Musée de la civilisation, fonds d'archives du Séminaire de Québec, 0470.

All the while, Jean was reading through the latest publications and plumbing them for insights on invention, drafting, and marketing. On her list were books as diverse as Stevenson's *Vailima Letters* (1896), J.M. Barrie's memoir of his mother, *Margaret Ogilvy* (1896), and Maurice Hewlett's bestselling medieval romance *The Forest Lovers* (1898) – the *Game of Thrones* of its time – which, she reported from her reading of the Glasgow *Herald*, "had made the reputation of its author" (McLFF, J.N. McIlwraith to W. McLennan, 21 January [1898?]). She did not like the book (FHEP, J.N. McIlwraith to F.H. Eckstorm, 3 November 1901), probably because she found its female character, Ysoult la Desirous, too self-effacing. She strongly resisted the notion that Margaret Nairn, their own main female character, should be similarly ready to annihilate herself. *The Span o' Life* combines first-person narratives by both Hugh and Margaret, and rather than assigning composition of the female voice to McIlwraith and the male to McLennan, both authors seem to have drafted sections across both narratives and criticized each other's work so thoroughly that collaboration did in fact shape the entire book. The story has the amorous convolutions typical of the historical romance, involving both comic and tragic misunderstandings, along with ingenious disguises and hideaways. Having rejected her lover, the Vicomte Trincardel, and her brother for lacking commitment to the Jacobite cause, Margaret impulsively follows Hugh to Quebec, not knowing that he is secretly married (a situation he is not at liberty to reveal) and feeling encouraged in her affections by his friendly attitude.

The authors' disagreement, pursued over several letters, was over Margaret's response to the revelation that, until his wife's death, Hugh had not been free to court another woman but gave every indication of being so. In McLennan's version, Margaret forgave Hugh quickly enough for his deception, providing readers of *Harper's* with the happy ending that the genre had taught them to expect. Jean railed against what she perceived to be an egregious misunderstanding of the female psyche and her tone went from the humorous to the aggrieved. She was used to expressing forceful opinions, including in an essay on George Meredith's *Diana of the Crossways* for Queen Margaret's College in 1895, which in many ways reads like a trial run of her dispute with McLennan and which, curiously, one of her tutors annotated as "violent[,] dare I say woman-like?" (JNMP). In the argument with McLennan, she was increasingly beside herself. She threatened to "roll you in the snow or drop you in the ice for a cold bath" as well as "perch myself on your breast-bone and pick your eyes out – one by one!" (McLFF, J.N. McIlwraith to W. McLennan, 29 January [1897?]) should the mature Margaret not be allowed to vent her outrage at having been deceived when she was a gullible young woman. Better yet, in Hugh and Margaret's first meeting in Quebec, McIlwraith thought that Margaret should be "the self-possessed woman of the world who can hardly ... remember where she has seen his face before," and that it was best to put the emphasis not on Margaret's infatuation with Hugh but on her ability to win "the friendship of men like Montcalm." McIlwraith adds that this was "much more complimentary to her than their love" (McLFF, J.N. McIlwraith to W. McLennan, n.d., January 1897). The logical conclusion to the humiliation that Hugh had inflicted on Margaret, McIlwraith insisted, was to have them go their separate ways. Since her other suitor, Trincardel, had become a priest out of disappointed love and was no longer available, Margaret must enter a convent – not necessarily out of disillusionment but because there at least a single woman would find something worthwhile to do (McLFF, J.N. McIlwraith to W. McLennan, 31 December 1896).

This suggestion was immediately vetoed by McLennan's brother. He read Margaret as "a very affectionate soft creature jumping at the call of her emotions without looking," whose impulsiveness has her repeat her youthful mistakes later in life (McLFF, John Stewart McLennan to W. McLennan, 11 January 1897). At times, the reader cannot but suspect that in addition to her advocacy for women's independence, McIlwraith projects personal experience onto Margaret Nairn – for example, when she writes, "I could not marry a man I'd knocked down, but then I'm not 18th century!" or when she cynically concedes that "a book that ends happily is more certain to please the majority who still labour under the delusion that marriage means 'happiness ever after.' " She expressed similarly critical views of marriage in *The Making of Mary* and in her essay on *Diana of the Crossways* (1885). As for *The Span o' Life*, she proposed that "the real climax can now be the arrival of the ships" – namely, the British fleet that confirms the conquest of the French (McLFF, J.N. McIlwraith to W. McLennan, 31 December 1896).

In battling McLennan over the plot of their novel, McIlwraith put her finger on a fundamental problem that came with grafting an ideological program onto romance. In their effort to describe both sides with equal respect, the authors denied themselves the drama derived from pitching ideological opposites against each other. To keep the suspense going, conflict was shunted into tangled and, as McIlwraith thought, trite intrigue that no more than delayed the inevitable reconciliation between Margaret and Maxwell that McLennan intended for them. The couple's final union was meant to mirror the friendship that, in both authors' view, the English and the French would find sooner or later within a common nation. For the traditional conflict between opposing armies, McIlwraith sought to substitute a conflict between the main characters over a woman's freedom of expression and, with it, her freedom of movement. As she admitted, her reading made Margaret into a "bold miss of the 19th [century]" (McLFF, J.N. McIlwraith to W. McLennan, 29 January 1897). This was an anachronism, considering that the story played out more than a century earlier, but also a necessary revision considering the misinterpretations of female psychology that, in her view, had already taken place in any number of literary texts: "If she were a 'new woman' she would prefer the devotion of a

strong-minded spinster like me, to any amount of delicate attention from you"
(McLFF, J.N. McIlwraith to W. McLennan, 5 January 1897). As a replacement
for the conciliatory marriage between former enemies, McIlwraith proposes
independence. She does not say how life in a convent would allow Margaret to
achieve it, nor does she clarify whether both men and women are allowed independence and, if so, how their relationship outside of marriage is going to work.
Finally, she does not analyse, let alone straighten out, the confusing political allegory of English and French cohabitation that would result from her proposal.

For his part, McLennan's ideas were so different that he was not ready to talk
her through her concerns, which amounted to a comprehensive attack on the
gender politics embodied in romance. McIlwraith did not fully articulate her
ideas, first because her partner was clearly not sympathetic and second because
sudden time-consuming family obligations impelled her to compromise –
probably causing McLennan to heave a sigh of relief. His and McIlwraith's disagreements anticipate the rows that bedevilled the composition of *The Whole
Family*, well documented in Elizabeth Jordan's autobiography *Three Rousing
Cheers* (see also Howard, 106–57; Ashton, 127–66). Mary E. Wilkins Freeman,
one of the collaborators, was more successful than McIlwraith in asserting
herself. Asked to contribute a chapter on an old-maid aunt, Freeman did not
produce the faded character expected of her but – despite protest from Howells –
created "Aunt Elizabeth," a sexually alluring single woman in her thirties. Her
belligerent defence of Margaret Nairn's perspective notwithstanding, McIlwraith evaded the problem in subsequent historical novels *The Curious Career
of Roderick Campbell* and *A Diana of Quebec*. The narrators in these books are
not spinsters but middle-aged men who, although Robert Mathews surrenders
to love for Mary Simpson in the end, prefer to live alone but have strong parental instincts. Despite her own independence and the company of successful
women around her, McIlwraith may have concluded that independent men had
the freedom to be more unconventional than even the most unconventional
woman, that the lives of such men made for better stories, and that they – rather
than women – were therefore her own ideal fictional counterpart. It speaks to
her own doubts, and those of her publishers, about the permissible extent of
women's independence that the fiction featuring contemporary female characters she attempted between 1905 and 1920 did not see the light of day.

Family Problems

For both McIlwraith and McLennan, the dialogue over their joint novel occurred against the backdrop of serious family problems. The McLennans endured numerous illnesses while the collaboration on *The Span o' Life* was in
progress and moved to Europe shortly after the publication of the book in
the hope that the Mediterranean climate would improve William McLennan's

respiratory ailments, but he died in Fiesole in 1904. While on a European tour three years later, Jean visited his grave. In her home, too, catastrophe struck when Mrs. McIlwraith suffered a debilitating stroke in early April 1897, and Jean's letters express her anxiety, exhaustion, and depression at the prospect of never having her restored to full health. The worry had Jean lash out at McLennan and her comments on "the thing" and "the stuff," normally unemotional terms they used between themselves to refer to the manuscript, assumed a sharpness that evidently had as much, or more, to do with her current anxiety as with their work. Kennedy, who had rushed to his mother's bedside from Toronto, was asked to read and comment on the draft, and Jean cites his views to bolster her own objections and perhaps also to have an excuse for language she might otherwise have hesitated to use in addressing McLennan: "One gets tired to death of this dodging about + spying from corners," Kennedy reportedly said about the relationship between Maxwell and Margaret. Towards the end of the letter, Jean relents enough to explain herself and offer an apology: "I am incapable of thought these days + haven't a literary aspiration left in me ... Forgive me if I seem unsympathetic about the [manuscript] – I can't help it" (McLFF, J.N. McIlwraith to W. McLennan, 8 April 1898). McLennan wisely appears to have taken her outburst for what it was, and a couple of weeks later she has calmed down enough to adopt a friendlier tone. She praises his efforts to respect her views and expresses her gratitude for a partner with the necessary "buoyancy" when she is incapable of generating it herself while under pressure to look after the patient and "driv[e] away at the house cleaning ... to get it done before the nurse leaves" (McLFF, J.N. McIlwraith to W. McLennan, 19 April 1897).

Cairnbrae, a lookout onto scenes of endless interest during Jean's childhood, now at times seemed like a freezing outpost: "Our house is so exposed on every side that we catch it from 'a' the airts the win' can blaw,' " she writes, quoting Robert Burns, "and it has 'blawn' steadily + bitterly for two days now. I had to make mother stay in bed today to keep her warm." Mrs. McIlwraith, who seemed so self-effacing compared to her gregarious husband when the children were young, now required "a lot of looking after," not only because she was not well but also because "her little ways" had moved centre stage (McLFF, J.N. McIlwraith to W. McLennan, 25 January [1898?]). Jean found some solace in her reading when her mother's personal habits reminded her of the charming eccentricities of Margaret Ogilvy, whose memoir her son J.M. Barrie had just published. In her exhaustion, McIlwraith may well have identified with Barrie's sister who was "dying on her feet" as she looked after her mother, with the important difference that Jane Ann Barrie did in fact die three days before her mother (Barrie 188). Mr. McIlwraith, whose mental faculties were failing, had become a rather shadowy presence and after his wife's death merely "seems interested" (FHEP, J.N. McIlwraith to F.H. Eckstorm, 14 July [1902?]) when his daughter told him about her correspondence with Fannie Hardy Eckstorm, daughter of one of his ornithological contacts in Maine.[45]

These were the most serious areas where the two authors' personal worries overshadowed professional ones, but there were others. One attraction for McIlwraith of writing historical fiction may have been that it promised to avoid the problems she had encountered with *The Making of Mary* and "A Singing-Student in London," both of which had embroiled her in criticism from individuals whose stories or characters she had too closely reproduced. The source of the story about the manipulative young woman in *The Making of Mary* was Jean's cousin Elizabeth (Lizzie) Park, an "awfully funny + witty [woman]" devoted to spiritualism, an interest changed to theosophy in the novel, possibly because it sounded more respectable. Now living in Muskegon rather than Saginaw, Lizzie had given Jean "permission to do exactly as [she] pleased with [the material]" – or so McIlwraith had understood her – and as a result Lizzie became the model for the character of Belle Gemmell,[46] a journalist's wife who takes in the orphaned Mary and humours her capricious behaviour. When both Lizzie and the townspeople of Muskegon objected to their portrayal, the author was flabbergasted – "I never dreamt of the blamed thing reaching Muskegon, or indeed of getting a publisher at all" – and she accused herself of losing "a gold mine, in the way of material, when [she] fell out with Lizzie Park" (McLFF, J.N. McIlwraith to W. McLennan, 25 September 1897). The Parks did not forgive her for forty years, but not many family members seem to have read the book to find out for themselves what exactly the problem was. As a result, a distorted version of the reasons for the disagreement continued to circulate even after Jean's death ("Genealogy").

"A Singing-Student in London" likewise brought a storm of protest down on her head when readers, and worst of all the instructor himself, recognized the voice teacher she described in it, giving her "much notoriety, of an undesirable kind, all over the States."[47] The professor's name was William Shakespeare, and Jean changed it to the equally improbable "Francis Bacon." Shakespeare, a tenor trained in Leipzig and Milan, member of London's Royal Academy of Music, and author of several books on vocal technique, was popular with "'smart' young ladies," especially American ones, "who [were] driven to and from his door in the smartest of carriages" (Forsyth, "A Singing-Student" 388).

---

45 On Eckstorm, see MacDougall; also see "Eckstorm, Fannie Pearson Hardy (Mrs. Jacob A. Eckstorm)." This entry cites her as "an honorary member of the National Bird Museum of Canada." Existence of this museum has not been confirmed.

46 McIlwraith may have adapted the name from Alexander Bell Gemell, proprietor of the Ayrshire *Advertiser*.

47 Clipping from *Good Reading: A Monthly Advice*, n.d., Notebook of Newspaper Cuttings and Advertisements for the Correspondence Classes," DC 233/2/8/3/23/5, Queen Margaret College, Correspondence Courses, UGA.

One admirer estimated that, by 1896, as many as six hundred singers and voice teachers had been trained by him, many of them Americans who advertised themselves as pupils of Mr. Shakespeare (Tubbs 301). In other words, criticism like Jean's – especially if published in a popular magazine like *Harper's* – could have interfered with a well-oiled business on both sides of the Atlantic. The narrator of the story, a young woman named "Jean," cannot claim to be "smart." She is supported by her far-from-wealthy brother "Reuben," probably based on Hugh, and has to go without meals to pay the guinea charged for each lesson at Shakespeare's "charming and compact little house" near the Langham Hotel ("An Interview with Mr. William Shakespeare" 67). Her main complaint is that she and others in her position were not given their money's worth in Shakespeare's lessons. The response from the instructor's supporters was forceful, and *Werner's Magazine*, dedicated to the teaching of elocution and voice, concluded that because she had "lived all her life in a backwoods town," she could not be expected to appreciate "the best known vocal teacher since Lamperti," the most illustrious of Shakespeare's own teachers. McIlwraith's criticism, in short, was suspected to be motivated not by expertise but by a display of "personal pique," and it was "bad form" to display ingratitude towards "the man who gave you the foundation" (Wilbor 104, 105; Tubbs 303). Shakespeare himself was angry enough to form a troublesome association between his own name and McIlwraith's pseudonym of "Jean Forsyth." When she made the rounds among the publishers' offices on her arrival in New York a full eight years later, Henry Mills Alden at Harper remembered that "Mr. S. was quite exercised over that article and had required considerable smoothing down, implying that [Alden] himself had had to do the job." To herself, Jean added grimly: "I wonder if the publication of [Shakespeare's] picture in Harper's Weekly when [Shakespeare] was out in this country had anything to do with the smoothing process" (JNMP, "New York Impressions"). The fact that not only Alden but also numerous contemporary "reviews of reviews" refer to "A Singing-Student" as an "article" rather than as a "story" suggests that, probably with the editors' encouragement, "A Singing-Student" deliberately sat between reportage and fiction.[48] Although Shakespeare's anger was more than Harper had bargained for, the magazine may have found notoriety like this quite useful for its sales, and therefore did not prematurely draw McIlwraith's attention to the possible consequences of her naivety.

In 1897, near the beginning of her writing career, Jean was upset enough by these events to consider dropping her pseudonym, "having a perfect 'scunner' at

---

48   In another illustration of this ambiguity, Elspeth Cameron has used "A Singing-Student" to reconstruct the voice lessons of Jean Forsyth (1851–1933), Canadian soprano, with Shakespeare. Cameron speculates that Jean McIlwraith's pseudonym was inspired by her namesake, but "Jean (Adair) Forsyth" was the name of McIlwraith's paternal grandmother.

everything I've done under [the pseudonym of Jean Forsyth]." The coincidence that she had studied singing with a teacher named William Shakespeare and also written a book on his famous namesake had her anticipate "a paragraph headed 'Jean Forsyth after Shakespeare again' " from "a musical critic or two" (McLFF, J.N. McIlwraith to W. McLennan, 25 January 1897). She proposed to publish from now on under her own name in order to dissociate herself from this controversy as well as the quarrel over *The Making of Mary*, and she consulted with McLennan about the advisability of doing so, especially since she also had the marketing of their collaborative novel in mind. She thought that whatever name she used for her juvenile book on Shakespeare, going through final proofs at the time and promising to be a success, should also appear on *The Span o' Life*. This would help their joint book "so much" despite the "terribly clumsy conjunction" of "[t]he two Macs" on the cover (McLFF, J.N. McIlwraith to W. McLennan, 25 January [1897?]).

Like other female authors, such as McIlwraith's interviewer Alice Freeman, whose pseudonym "Faith Fenton" allowed her to combine careers as a school-teacher and journalist, Jean did appreciate the "irresponsibility" of a nom de plume, especially as she could always create new names for herself and find new venues, but if she were to run into controversy under her own name, "whaur'll I flee to next?" She was probably right to assume that her publishers, having spent promotional money on "Jean Forsyth," would be reluctant to agree to additional pseudonyms but might grudgingly consent to her own name because she could be expected to stay with it (McLFF, J.N. McIlwraith to W. McLennan, 25 January [1898?]). McLennan appears to have counselled her to keep the pseudonym, but *The Span o' Life* – and with few exceptions her other publications from then on – were published under her own name. She did consider returning to a pseudonym when she wrote a thinly disguised account of her work as a publisher's reader in New York, but the resulting manuscript remained unpublished. For her books on Shakespeare and Longfellow, Nelson found a solution by adding "Jean Forsyth" in smaller print and in brackets below her own name. However, indiscretion of the kind that provoked this whole debate in the first place seems to have been a recurrent problem. Her lamentations to McLennan over *The Making of Mary* and "A Singing-Student in London" notwithstanding, she had a brief contretemps with him over confiding in an "injudicious friend" that she was collaborating with McLennan on a novel, thus provoking an awkward "press notice" (McLFF, J.N. McIlwraith to W. McLennan, 21 October [1897?]). She may also have been a little disingenuous when she claimed surprise at having upset the Parks and Mr. Shakespeare: considering her own interest in effective marketing, she surely knew that a book and article as well placed as *The Making of Mary* and "A Singing-Student in London" would sooner or later come to the notice of those concerned.

Escape into historical fiction was, however, no guarantee against controversy. Ironically, given the author's punctilious scholarship, the scholarly integrity of

McLennan's *Spanish John* was questioned the year *The Span o' Life* began to appear in *Harper's*. T.G. Marquis, a notary like McLennan and a competitor in the field of historical fiction whose novel *Marguerite de Roberval* was reviewed together with *The Span o' Life* in the *Canadian Magazine* ("Books and Authors"), accused McLennan in *The Bookman* (New York) of having plagiarized his historical source, the memoirs of Colonel John M'Donnell (Marquis). The speed with which this accusation was traded through the contemporary magazines says something about efficient communications within the periodical press, and by implication, the episode also reflects on the rapid thoroughness with which Mr. Shakespeare's supporters were able to disparage McIlwraith's "A Singing-Student." The *Publishers' Weekly* headed its coverage with "Plagiarism Extraordinary" the same month Marquis made his allegation, while *The Dial* commented on "a clear case of pilfering" ("Recent Historical Fiction") three months later. In between, in April, the *Canadian Magazine* investigated the question, "Was 'Spanish John' Stolen?" but came down on McLennan's side.

McLennan's own response to Marquis in *The Bookman* reveals a great deal about his archival expertise but perhaps even more about the way in which his writing had become determined by the popular-appeal dictates of serial publication. In compliance with *Harper's* editorial guidelines, he clarified, an explanatory preface included in the original manuscript had been sacrificed to meet the thirty-five-thousand-word limit imposed by the magazine, where such preliminaries were "not required." Proof of originality, he continued, was established by the greater proportion of the overall word count compared to the historical source. The alleged literary quality of M'Donnell's memoir (a quality appropriated, as Marquis suggests, by McLennan and offered as his own) became questionable when "those portions suggested by the editor for omission in serial form ... contain more than half the *literal extracts* used in the whole story" (McLennan, "Response" 138). Marquis's accusations did not exactly give a boost to McLennan's career but the *Canadian Magazine*, which had already made its support of McLennan known, ostentatiously ignored the affair in the author's "Canadian Celebrities" profile a year later. Instead, it underlined the "immense value" of his legal profession in helping him to assess "the nature of old documents" (E.Q.V. 252). The *Dial's* reviewer, too, though conceding that an accusation of plagiarism was "naturally bad for Mr. McLennan's reputation," thought that it did "not make his book any the less readable and remarkable" ("Recent Historical Fiction").

Marketing *The Span o' Life*

McLennan was influenced by editorial guidelines seeking to please "the large mass of readers to whom study of any description is irksome, unless relieved by pleasing incident and sustained interest" (E.Q.V. 252). In addition to their

different views about Margaret and Hugh, the co-authors' disagreements often stemmed from McLennan's fear of the editor's blue pencil. Thus, he had
McIlwraith reduce or delete passages describing Canadian scenery and "Indian lore" with which she had "crammed" herself (McLFF, J.N. McIlwraith to
W. McLennan, 29 January 1897). McIlwraith urged him to consider that these
details would distinguish the book from *Seats of the Mighty*, "with which undoubtedly this will be compared *ad nauseum* [sic]" (McLFF, J.N. McIlwraith to
W. McLennan, 29 January 1897), but because of his experience with serializa-
tion, McLennan claimed better knowledge of what was required to make their
manuscript marketable.

By the time McLennan's "Celebrities" profile appeared in the *Canadian
Magazine*, one of the poems from *The Span o' Life* had been "set to music by
Mr. Frederick F. Bullard," a well-known American composer. It was perhaps
overly ambitious to predict that "the world will sway to the rhythm of the song"
(E.Q.V. 252), but the song did tie the novel cleverly to another medium. As with
the financial arrangements, McIlwraith gave the lie to her claim that she could
"not [be] bothering her head about style or publishers, nor any such vexatious
things" (McLFF, J.N. McIlwraith to W. McLennan, 15 December [1897?]) when
she involved herself in the production of the book. She agreed that the music
threaded through the narrative could be turned to profit, and was particularly
insistent on finding a better title than the original *The Losing Side*, wanting a
"*talking* title, something that will make the book sell" (McLFF, J.N. McIlwraith
to W. McLennan 25 September 1897).[49] After they had tossed a number of possibilities back and forth, she proposed a refrain that would keep readers connected to the serialized narrative as they were waiting for the next issue of the
magazine. She suggested hitching the title to a recurring song, and McLennan
agreed to change the title to *The Span o' Life* (McLFF, J.N. McIlwraith to W.
McLennan, 25 September 1897). Illustrations by a well-known artist were an
additional selling point, and the Austrian Felician de Myrbach, renowned illustrator of Jules Verne, Alphonse Daudet, and Victor Hugo, as well as founding
member of the Vienna Secession, was commissioned to sketch the images for
The Span o' Life. She worried that, as a European, he would not be able to do
justice to the Indian scenes and urged McLennan to visit Rivière Ouelle with
his Kodak so that the illustrator had the authentic scene to work from. At first
she did not care for Myrbach's images, finding that "the illustrations don't add
anything to the story," and complaining about a squint in Hugh and a wooden
expression on Margaret's face (McLFF, J.N. McIlwraith to W. McLennan, 23
September [1898?]). By the time part 3 appeared in *Harper's Magazine*, she had
changed her mind, thinking "Margaret [was] perfectly stunning in the kilts,"

---

49 McLennan's detailed proposal for the novel, using *The Losing Side* as its title, is held in the
    William McLennan Fonds, Rare Books and Special Collections, McGill University.

and confessed that she had "wept on every single page" as she was reading their story (McLFF, J.N. McIlwraith to W. McLennan, 21 January [1898?]).

Making money from her books was clearly important to McIlwraith. She was happy with the $850 honorarium that McLennan negotiated for her share in *The Span o'Life*, and retroactively, she asked her publisher to pay royalties for *A Book About Shakespeare for Young People*, a work that she hoped would become a school textbook and so guarantee solid sales. Her optimism stemmed from T. Nelson thinking so highly of the Shakespeare volume that on completion it was immediately followed by a commission to write a similar study on Longfellow within the tight deadline of six months (McLFF, J.N. McIlwraith to W. McLennan, 29 December 1897). She was disappointed in the hope that these assignments would generate royalties, and both T. Nelson and T. Fisher Unwin "paid ... very shabbily for the young folks books I did for them" (FHEP, J.N. McIlwraith to F.H. Eckstorm, 14 July 1902). Her book on Haldimand, she resigned herself, was "a labor of love ... no money in it that I can see + ten per cent royalty in Canada, 5 elsewhere and not 1000 copies sold anywhere" (FHEP, J.N. McIlwraith to F.H. Eckstorm, 12 January 1902), but against her expectations this volume was republished in 1904, 1906, 1909 (Canadian Club edition), and 1910 (Parkman edition). There was a British edition by T.C. and E.C. Jack in 1905, and an anniversary edition of the Makers of Canada series by Oxford University Press in 1926. Meanwhile, she drew *Cornhill Magazine* to McLennan's attention for paying "a guinea a page" for a "small [page], with such a wide margin" (McLFF, J.N. McIlwraith to W. McLennan, 21 January [1898?]).

As we have seen, Mrs. McIlwraith in her old age reminded her daughter of J.M. Barrie's mother, but in her thrift, Jean herself resembled Margaret Ogilvy. Before reading a new article by her son, Margaret "first counted the lines to discover what we should get for it," wondering "whether that sub-title meant another sixpence," and she kept the empty envelopes in which his first cheques arrived tied with a special ribbon (Barrie 65). Account keeping was part and parcel of the McIlwraiths' Presbyterian background, as described in the chapter on Andrew and Thomas McIlwraith, and several of Jean McIlwraith's stories and non-fiction are constructed to reflect the waxing and waning of disposable income. Thus, "A Singing-Student in London" persistently matches hard-earned money spent by the student against unsatisfactory services rendered by the voice teacher, and the narrator concludes that the resulting deficit logically requires that the student abandon the venture and return home (as well as expose the professor as a fraud). Most poignantly, McIlwraith applies the method of double-entry bookkeeping with which Robinson Crusoe famously "mak[es] the best of his circumstances" when she imagines how worthless her life might appear to others after her mother's death. Published in *Harper's Bazaar* alongside articles on "Trials of a Young Housewife," fashions for brides and old ladies, playhouses for children, and suggestions for a "rational diet," McIlwraith's

"How to Be Happy Though Single" at first cheerfully tackles one by one the cli-chés that see a spinster's life as lonely and wasted before she concludes with the brutal "I am first with nobody; it will be a crowning grief to nobody when my death occurs" on the debit side, followed by "Then it will not be hard to die" as the balancing credit ("How to Be Happy," 454, 455). The subject occupied other writers seeking to define the characteristics of the "New Woman": McIlwraith's brief feature anticipates articles on unmarried women by Lilian Bell and Anne O'Hagan, both also published in *Harper's Bazaar* (in 1902–3 and 1907, respec-tively), and it is more direct and daring than either of these.

McIlwraith was not only careful in looking after her well-earned money, but also enjoyed managing it, and the investment portfolio that was part of her estate after her death speaks to shrewd handling of funds. In "Robbing the Clydesdales" (1924), she admits to the thrill of bartering for the face pieces of horses, but when it came to money, she pretended with both McLennan and Gertrude Pringle that she was an ingénue who "hate[d] business details – hate[d] having anything to do with money at all" (McLFF, J.N. McIlwraith to W. McLennan, 25 September 1897). She even claimed that "the commercial side of authorship she has not cultivated. While other well-known writers succeeded in making their own terms with publishers, Jean McIlwraith left financial ar-rangements entirely in their hands, taking what they agreed to give her" (Prin-gle, "Jean McIlwraith"). This from a woman who managed to place one story, now best known under its Canadian title "The Assimilation of Christina," un-der three different titles with reputable magazines in the States, Great Britain, and Canada.[50] She appears to have convinced even members of her family, such as her sister Pollie, that she knew nothing about money or indeed anything that required precision (FHEP, J.N. McIlwraith to F.H. Eckstorm, 29 August 1902). Perhaps this pose of cluelessness, like her pseudonym, was a form of protection against envy or outside interference with her affairs. Judging from Hamilton matron Mary Baker McQuesten's comment to her son, McIlwraith may have had a point: "Mrs. Mullin heard that Jean McIlwraith was making $50 a week in New York and I am going to find out how she does it" (McQuesten, 30 October 1902, 101).

Leaving for New York

In her interviews with Marjory MacMurchy and with Gertrude Pringle twenty-five years later, Jean did not let on just how difficult her mother's decline had been for her, emphasizing instead "[t]he bond ... of unusual fidelity and understanding" with her parent, and her determination not to allow anything

---

50 See bibliography for details.

"to tempt [her] away from her ... side ... for more than a few hours at a time" (M. MacMurchy, "Canadian Celebrities" 132). Irritation at having to leave her desk in order to attend to her mother's needs, she explained, was followed by the realization, enforced by her mother's teachings, that the patient "deserve[d] attention and [got] attention" (Pringle, "Jean McIlwraith"). One biographical sketch of Jean McIlwraith published in *World Biographies* in 1901 says that she "took a training course as nurse" ("Jean N. McIlwraith" 76). Details of her training have not emerged, but the experience seems to have motivated her to include a Red Cross nurse in the Boer War version of "The Temple of Fame" and a nurse representing Hospital Sunday in "The Days of the Year." She featured nurses in her fiction, notably the lead character in *The Making of Mary*, who mends her thoughtless ways while looking after patients during a chicken-pox epidemic until she almost dies herself and, a few years after Mrs. McIlwraith's death, the community nurse Miss Harry in "Dominick Street." For the duration of Mrs. McIlwraith's illness, her daughter's nursing skills were put to use at home, and her mother's invalidism kept Jean virtually captive at Cairnbrae with the exception of brief skating expeditions on the lake or "an old-fashioned 'twirl' " with friends in Toronto (McLFF, J.N. McIlwraith to W. McLennan, 31 December 1896). Her mother's death in February 1901 was such a blow that she needed to make a decisive change to her life so as not to be consumed by grief and "do nothing but miss her + mourn for her" (FHEP, J.N. McIlwraith to F.H. Eckstorm, 14 July [1902?]).

In addition to the sorrow, there were practical considerations to be thought through, and she was fortunate to have a compassionate and well-informed listener in a woman she called her "Godmother," Fannie Hardy Eckstorm, who had recently lost both her husband and young daughter. A priority was for Jean to find a place of her own and an occupation to pay for it. To look after the ailing Mr. McIlwraith, her brother Tom and his young family moved into Cairnbrae with the understanding that the house would be theirs on his death, and the scheme seemed to work once a servant, "an A1 specimen ... from Scotland," had been hired and, unlike previous domestic help, persuaded to stay on (FHEP, J.N. McIlwraith to F.H. Eckstorm, 12 June 1902). (This paragon was possibly the model for Christina, the "prize in the domestic lottery" drawn by Miss Maitland in McIlwraith's story "The Assimilation of Christina.") While this arrangement relieved McIlwraith of the responsibility of looking after her father, it also meant that "this old home ... is no longer my home," though she "dread[ed] the thought of leaving [it] for good" (FHEP, J.N. McIlwraith to F.H. Eckstorm, 30 June 1902). She happily babysat the three children of Tom and Mary when the couple went off to visit Pollie in Detroit, but – enjoyable as looking after her own brothers had been – Jean obviously did not want to become a full-time nanny to her nieces and nephew, nor would their parents, who doted on their children, have wanted her to ("Genealogy"). She spent extended

periods with Nellie in Quebec and Pollie in Detroit, enjoying the warm friendship of the former and, when staying with the latter, the freedom to write in "a
comfortable study" with a "typewriter rented, student lamp bought, no household + social demands" (FHEP, J.N. McIlwraith to F.H. Eckstorm, 12 January
1902). The attraction of "no household + social demands" was one reason why
the idea of moving permanently or even temporarily to Scotland to look after
her Aunt Sarah did not appeal to her but she was prepared for the possibility
that if "my Aunt in Scotland positively needs me," her niece would have "to go
to Ayr Scotland, for the winter" even if she did not intend to settle there (FHEP,
J.N. McIlwraith to F.H. Eckstorm, 30 June 1902).

The prospect of becoming dependent on her siblings – or rather her
brothers-in-law, because both were at the time better off than her brothers –
was intolerable to her (FHEP, J.N. McIlwraith to F.H. Eckstorm, 12 June
[1902?]), and in another show of not caring about money she assured William
McLennan that she "should positively refuse to take a cent for what I've done
in [*The Span o' Life*], were it not that I have an eagle eye to the future when I
don't want to be left dependent on my brothers and sisters" (McLFF, J.N. McIlwraith to W. McLennan, 25 September 1897). She had $180 dependable income
a year, she told Eckstorm, and would have twice that amount when her father
died, but as his condition was stable, at least while she was writing her first few
letters to Eckstorm, there was no telling when that would be. In other words,
if she wanted her freedom, she had to find herself an occupation with a regular salary rather than the limited royalties she was typically receiving for her
publications. She did obtain advice on how to increase her revenue from fellow
author Agnes Laut, "a thorough business woman" whom she visited in Ottawa
while researching her book on Haldimand in the Dominion archives and who,
"though younger," made her "feel like a babe." By contrast, Duncan Campbell
Scott, also located in Ottawa and editor of the Makers of Canada series to which
she contributed her volume on Haldimand, seemed "a melancholy chap with
not half the breezy go about him Miss Laut has" (FHEP, J.N. McIlwraith to F.H.
Eckstorm, 3 November [1901?]).

Where was she to go? Mrs. McQuesten's prying note confirms McIlwraith's
growing suspicion during the late 1890s that, for professional purposes, Hamilton was not quite the Garden of Eden that it had seemed during her childhood: although she dreaded leaving Cairnbrae and its memories, she was now
apt to find both the city and most members of her own family philistine and,
with the exception of Nellie and John Holt, not prepared to express enthusiasm
for anything she had done. Like her father, she was prone to occasional black
moods that had her feel isolated and unappreciated. "Nobody here cares anything about [*The Span o' Life*]," she wrote to McLennan, "though my mother
did her best to read it, but had to stop – found it too much for her 'poor head' "
(McLFF, J.N. McIlwraith to W. McLennan, 23 September [1898?]), and earlier

she conceded: "I'm afraid we are not a gushing lot" (McLFF, J.N. McIlwraith to W. McLennan, 18 September 1897). Jack certainly did not gush about her success as a writer when, in his business profile, he curtly introduced her as "a book reviewer" in New York but did not say a word about her own books (Forkner 778). Likewise, the reason why Jean was left in peace in her study in Detroit was, she felt, that Pollie was not interested in her writing (FHEP, J.N. McIlwraith to F.H. Eckstorm, 12 January 1902). This vagueness about Jean's career became something of a family tradition, and her nephew, the anthropologist T.F. McIlwraith, was less than clear about the nature and extent of her publications when he compiled notes on family members for his memoir. He noted that the historian George Brown, "his colleague at the University of Toronto, once looked over her bibliography and was impressed, to his surprise" ("Genealogy").

Although she would soon be disillusioned, one unexpected satisfaction of making the rounds among publishers when she did get to New York was to realize that not only was "her work ... known and appreciated more than in Canada," but that she was "liked all the better just because I have not made [a big scoop]," whereas Hamilton "considered [her] a failure in the literary world" precisely because none of her books so far had been a bestseller (JNMP, "New York Impressions"). In running through her options for where to settle after her mother's death, she ruled out "the intellectual atmosphere of Hamilton [as] extremely enervating" (FHEP, J.N. McIlwraith to F.H. Eckstorm, 12 June 1902). Perhaps she feared being absorbed into a narrow circle of people closely watching each other, and she was certainly not above gossip herself. Passing on the regards of "Mrs. Brownlon [who] was feeling more reconciled to Hamilton than she was a while ago," she informs the McLennans that "[t]he principal factor in her reconciliation is her clergyman ... 'a very scholarly man' she says – who goes to see her frequently. His wife is a great invalid + in England at present" (McLFF, J.N. McIlwraith to W. McLennan, 15 March [1897?]).

At one point, she even concluded that it was best to put the greatest possible distance between herself and Hamilton: "I believe I should go to Australia," she announces out of the blue (FHEP, J.N. McIlwraith to F.H. Eckstorm, 30 June 1902), but does not pursue this plan. Eckstorm, who had worked as a manuscript reader for D.C. Heath in Boston, suggested she consider that city, but Jean – who had spent several weeks there when she was researching her book on Longfellow and liked the place as little as the author – dismissed it as "a sort of intellectual snob-centre," one "travelling on its past reputation," that was not likely to impress anyone who had lived in London as she had. The chief reason for her dislike, one suspects, was "all the revolutionary relics" on display that irritated the patriotic "Britisher" in her (FHEP, J.N. McIlwraith to F.H. Eckstorm, 30 June 1902). Given the critical undertone of *A Book on Longfellow*, it is no wonder that there was no American edition of it. In any case, she was looking for a "more [b]ohemian" place because "that is the sort of life [she was] out for at present," and for this, New York was the better fit (FHEP, J.N. McIlwraith to F.H. Eckstorm, 30 June 1902). As documented by W.H. New (1987) and Nick Mount, a large group of Canadian writers relocated to the city, but she was motivated by a variety of practical reasons rather than the wish to move to a place that would be better for her writing. Her fierce loyalty to the British Empire generally and to "Ham. Can." specifically attest that she certainly did not "expatriate" to the United States (Mount 138), and her move south had as much to do with family traditions, such as Andrew McIlwraith's tramp to New York, as with the example of other writers.

In her interview with Gertrude Pringle, she leaves out the difficulties that needed to be overcome to get to New York. In consulting with Eckstorm (rather than turning to McLennan, who was "a wealthy man [with] great ideas about what it is beneath one's dignity to do" and whom she did not want to bother because he was already unwell enough to require the attendance of a nurse), she ran through her qualifications. She assured her friend that she would do "anything within [her] powers" to secure her independence, and requested advice on the kind of introductions that would help her get a foot in the door as manuscript reader for "a big firm of publishers" (FHEP, J.N. McIlwraith to F.H. Eckstorm, 12 June 1902). Jean agreed with Eckstorm that their exploitative practices made it best to steer clear of authors' agencies, and she did not think she had it in her to become a full-time journalist. The ambition to work for a well-known publisher suggests that no matter how flexible she intended to be, she did set high standards for herself. Besides warning her against employers with a bad reputation in the business, such as McClure, Eckstorm encouraged her to aim high by suggesting that she introduce herself to publishers as someone seeking experience in writing "copy," not someone who was obliged to earn her living. Jean confided that, after working with Houghton, Mifflin on *Roderick Campbell*, she was reluctant to associate herself with lesser publishers (such as the W.A. Wilde Company in Boston that wanted her to do a book for the juvenile market), let alone do hack work that would have required her "to write a love story of Canadian farm life advertising agricultural implements." She would not have minded the machines, she quipped, but it was the love story that didn't appeal to her (FHEP, J.N. McIlwraith to F.H. Eckstorm, 12 June [1902?]).

Her family weighed in with advice too: as "trusting Canadians" and her cheering section, the Holts believed that she was able to do anything she set her mind to, but Pollie gave her an earful. Her lecture is worth reproducing at some length because it gives a sense of the limited range of occupations thought available to a spinster; of the parental role that Mary adopted with her only slightly younger sister; of her failure to sympathize with Jean's vivacious temperament; and perhaps also of a tone she had adopted from her husband, "a stiff-necked parson" disliked by the McIlwraiths as "narrow, [with] an unpleasant accent, and violently anti-British" ("Genealogy"). The dressing-down takes on additional zest if it is considered alongside Jean's wisecrack, when Pollie had graduated from the Wesleyan Ladies' College, that her older sister was now "loafer in general" about the house (FA, 31 December 1873):

> [Pollie] says I've always been my own mistress + have worked or laid off as I pleased and she believes, strong + all as I am, that steady occupation under a driver would finish me, that all I have hitherto done has been by spurts. She is also encouraging (?) in her doubts as to my capabilities for any kind of situation or work for which there is a demand + says if I could be secretary or companion to an elderly lady – that is where I might fit in – not as housekeeper nor as governess – nor indeed in any position where business training or exact information upon any subject is required.

In Pollie's mind, her sister's range of interests was a problem rather than an advantage, and producing books, articles, and stories to tight deadlines did not count as proof that her sister had the mental equipment to manage a "steady occupation."

Although she was not keen to adopt one of Pollie's suggestions by becoming a companion to her Aunt Sarah, Jean adds dryly that "Well, I wouldn't mind wheeling an old lady in Central Park, not a bit. My muscle is A.1 + I'd love to be out of doors, instead of being penned up in an office" (FHEP, J.N. McIlwraith to F.H. Eckstorm, 29 August [1902?]). She was not deterred by Pollie's wrist-slapping either, but busily activated her circle of friends. One of the people advising her on New York boarding houses was the painter Arthur Heming, "a Hamilton boy [and] a chum of mine," who knew of places "where art students board" (FHEP, J.N. McIlwraith to F.H. Eckstorm, 30 June 1902).[51] Particularly helpful in sorting out her living arrangements were her old friends Alice and Louise Cummings. They came from a remarkable family: their father James Cummings was a businessman, briefly mayor of Hamilton, and a tax collector ("Cummings, James" 5), and his wife Anne, the first female principal of Hamilton's Central School. Of their five children, two sons became physicians, and Alice and Louise, too, had impressive talents: when Jean was getting ready to move to New York, Alice taught music at St. Margaret's College in Toronto, and Louise joined the mathematics department at Vassar in the fall of 1902.[52]

---

51 On Heming, see Getty, Cassandra.

52 On Louise Cummings, see Green and LaDuke 165. This book cites the 1881 Canadian census as listing five children, while *Dictionary of Hamilton Biography* mentions only three. At the Central Collegiate Institute, Alice Cummings was also friends with Elizabeth Smith, and letters from her are included in Smith's archive: UWL, WA-10, Files 113–114, ESS.

The Stanford classicist Henry Rushton Fairclough, who grew up in Ontario and attended the Central Collegiate Institute in Hamilton with Alice, remembered her academic and musical talents as awe-inspiring (Fairclough 17), and he also followed Louise's academic success with interest.

Because Louise and Alice were coming through New York on their way back from Europe only a few days after Jean's arrival in the city and John Holt's sisters visited for six weeks soon after, Jean was immediately surrounded by friends with whom to go shopping at Wanamakers, see plays starring Mrs. Leslie Carter and Eleonora Duse, conduct "prowls in foreign quarters" (FHEP, J.N. McIlwraith to F.H. Eckstorm, 12 November 1902; 24 November 1902), and generally enjoy the freedom to have company whenever she pleased. An explosion of energy replaced the sadness and uncertainty after her mother's death. Louise Cummings, whose bicycle Jean had brought along from Hamilton, enlarged the group by introducing an instructor in German at Vassar, Charlotte Reinecke, "a graduate of the Royal Seminary for Teachers in Berlin [who had] done graduate work at Radcliffe College."[53] She was the daughter of Carl Reinecke, a Leipzig musician who had trained Jean's voice instructor in London, Mr. Shakespeare. For additional company, should McIlwraith need it, there was Eckstorm's brother, Walter Hardy, an illustrator working in New York.

The boarding house recommended by the Cummings sisters was 44 Irving Place. Located in a previously fashionable neighbourhood, it was so popular that McIlwraith, while being able to take her meals there, had to stay in over-flow rooms of dubious cleanliness next door. No wonder that Louise and Alice were delighted with this place: "[m]eals at 44 Irving Place were enjoyed in the company of [the landlady's] artistic and literary tenants, including industrial designers, artists, actors and actresses, [and] schoolteachers" (Eidelberg et al. 135). After dinner, "[t]here were charades, performances of plays, cards, and reading aloud – including Plato's *Apology of Socrates* and Jane Austen's *Emma*. In 1904, a co-ed group of boarding house friends undertook to enact George Bernard Shaw's newly published comedy *Man and Superman*, an interesting selection given the play's overt theme of sexual attraction" (136). The entire neighbourhood of Irving Place "exuded a [b]ohemian atmosphere that must have felt welcoming to a well-educated, single woman in the arts" or, in Louise Cummings's case, in mathematics (138). We know as much as we do about Mary Owens's boarding house because her long-time tenants included Clara Driscoll, one of Louis Tiffany's team of women designers, whose contribution to the firm's achievements has finally been acknowledged. Driscoll met her husband Edward Booth at Mrs. Owens's, and McIlwraith, too, made friends with Booth, who managed the American branch of a well-known British export

---

53 *Vassar Miscellany*, vol. 29, no. 1, 1 October 1899, 64.

firm, John G. Rollins, on New York's Whitehall Street (*Exporters' Encyclopedia* 46). A few years into her stay in New York, McIlwraith's friendship with Edward was to worry his brother William, an editor at Houghton, Mifflin, when it came to rejecting one of her manuscripts. Perhaps Jean, Clara, and Edward became friends on bicycle outings together, an exercise enjoyed by all three.

Because McIlwraith had to count her pennies, it was nevertheless a relief to find an apartment at 206 East 17th Street, where she intended to split the rent with Miss Taylor from Oakville, Ontario, an "accountant in a big publishing house down town which gets out works on engineering etc." (JNMP, "New York Impressions"). Eckstorm suggested that, instead of setting up house with Miss Taylor, Jean share rooms with Imogen Harding, a music student from Oregon where Eckstorm had spent most of her marriage. The piano and the singing practice would "drive her wild," Jean objected with typical directness, but with equally typical generosity she helped "Imo" get settled, welcomed her visits, and introduced her to her friends. Both women resolved to join the choir at St. George's Church, just around the corner from Jean's apartment, and while busy at her desk, McIlwraith enjoyed music from the organ and choir practice drifting over from the church. Agnes Laut, who had so impressed Jean on her visit to Ottawa, had moved to nearby Wassaic, a "lovely spot," where she occupied the "old place" of Laurence Oliphant, British author and diplomat, and McIlwraith hurried to pay a visit to this energetic woman (FHEP, J.N. McIlwraith to F.H. Eckstorm, 12 November 1902).

Most of the old and new friends who rallied around Jean were in the literary or musical milieu, but on arrival at Grand Central Station she was welcomed by Margaret ("Peg") Somerville from Dundas, daughter of newspaperman and politician James Somerville and recently graduated nurse at the New York Hospital. After an exhausting week of getting settled, Jean was glad to be spirited off to Brooklyn to stay for the weekend. There she met Oluf Tyberg, the Danish-born husband of Peg's sister Marjorie, whose judgment McIlwraith later trusted enough to ask her to assess a novel based on Jean's experience as an editorial reader. Tyberg was a typewriter inventor with several patents to his name, but more importantly, he and Marjorie were prominent members of the Theosophy community at Point Loma in California. His name had recently appeared in the papers in connection with a group of Cuban orphans destined to become "lotus buds" at Point Loma. In a vivid example of the dramas that often played out at the Immigrant Inspection Station, the children were held up at Ellis Island at the instigation of the New York Society for the Prevention of Cruelty to Children but later released in an elaborate operation that had them "Taken from Ellis Island in a Tug to Prevent Interference" and guarded by "twelve private detectives" ("Lotus Buds," 3).[54] The Tybergs were

---

54 See also "Children from Cuba Held on Ellis Island," 7. For a detailed description of the episode, see Greenwall 57–66.

hosting a "young German musician" recently arrived from Leipzig, "an odd little chap – a genius, I think[,] with dimples in his thin little cheeks," who played for them and extemporized "an operatic aria on the words Omega Oil" (JNMP, "New York Impressions"). Perhaps emboldened by her success in introducing the Holts to each other, Jean declared this gentleman an excellent match for Imogen, certainly a better one than "that man in Oregon who ... I'm sure is not good enough for her" (FHEP, J.N. McIlwraith to F.H. Eckstorm, 30 December 1902). Her young friend does not appear to have listened because in due course Imogen married the Oregon politician Edward Everett Brodie. Some of this frantic socializing on McIlwraith's arrival in New York took place in quarters that were a little too Bohemian even for her. When Imogen came to visit her at the boarding house, Jean had to explain the smell of gasoline that the exterminators had left behind in her room in destroying the "bugs ... not many, but quite enough to give one a scunner" (FHEP, J.N. McIlwraith to F.H. Eckstorm, 17 September 1902). But however modest her living arrangements, her expenses were greater than she had anticipated, and she needed to find work fast to pay for her upkeep and the social life she was enjoying with old and new friends.

Looking for Work in New York

Before leaving Hamilton, McIlwraith had collected a pile of letters of introduction, and, with Peg Somerville to accompany her, she began to make the rounds among New York's publishers. From William McLennan she had introductions to Henry Mills Alden at Harper Publishers and to Henry W. Lanier, junior partner at Doubleday, Page. William Belmont Parker at Houghton, Mifflin provided letters for James MacArthur at Harper, Robert Underwood Johnson at Century and Company, Lincoln J. Steffens at McClure, and Walter H. Page at Doubleday, Page. She had letters from Hamilton friends, including the minister of her church, for the New York *Daily News* (whose editor was "a Canadian lad") and *Texas Siftings*. Eckstorm's father wrote introductions for Scribner's and for "bird people" (presumably publishers of ornithological works). Jean was reluctant to ask for a letter from Ernest Thompson Seton, an old acquaintance of her father and Kennedy but one whom she did not like (FHEP, J.N. McIlwraith to F.H. Eckstorm, 29 August [1902?]). As becomes apparent in her recollections of Walter H. Page, she cared even less for Seton's wife, who inflicted "a very nasty [manuscript]" on the publisher (JNMP, "Jottings"). In addition to the letters of introduction, she typed up a list of her own publications, and was repeatedly told that this – and the fact that her name was well known among American publishers – was a more important document than the letters. The list helped interviewers to determine whether her skills fit their business and whether she was sufficiently attuned to the requirements of different readerships. Some of the people she talked to – such as Tudor Jenks at *St. Nicholas* and Mr. Chapin at Pearson – readily offered advice on places where to submit work or they updated her on the progress of work she had already submitted. Still, the letters of introduction did not hurt her cause, and the note from McLennan ensured a warm reception from Mr. Alden at Harper Publishers who, while he could not employ her, invited her to his place in the country. Unfortunately, she was also confronted with racism when Jenks, trying to encourage her in the midst of her wearying search, "told of a young man who was a Jew, a foreigner, he was not even clean and yet he got a good position." Elsewhere, on a job-hunting expedition to an office at 21 Washington Square, she noted that "there are Jew sweaters apparently at work on the lower flats" (JNMP, "New York Impressions").

Jean recorded her interviews with publishers in her "New York Impressions," a typewritten excerpt apparently taken from a regular journal that is not included in toto among her papers. The document often resembles a chatty letter, and as she did occasionally in the Family Album, she may have used her diary entries as an aide-mémoire for correspondence with which to keep family and friends informed of her activities. Some of the formulations in the "New York Impressions" and in her letters to Fanny Eckstorm are identical. On the other hand, the style of the "Impressions" is polished enough to suggest that she meant to use the story of her search for work in a future article, story, or novel. On one day alone, she presented herself at Scribner, Pearson, McClure, Harper, and Doubleday, Page, followed by Collier, *The Outlook*, *St. Nicholas*, and Houghton, Mifflin on subsequent days. The very first interview at Scribner netted an introduction (and another trek across town) to Professor Colby, one of the editors of the *New International Encyclopedia* at Dodd, Mead, who warmed to her when she enquired whether he was a relation to Professor Colby at McGill. "[H]e said 'Cousin,' " and gave her "some minor bibliographical work to do" (JNMP, "New York Impressions"). Involving hours of research at the Astor Library, this task had her "hunt up James De Mille," and she recommended reinstating him, though his entry was already marked "kill," because she "found out he was the man who had written 'A Castle in Spain' that ran in Harper's as a serial in 1882–3." She was familiar with the serial but because it was published anonymously, some sleuthing at Harper Publishers had to take place to confirm her hypothesis. The encyclopedia staff were impressed enough with her initiative to commission entries on Thomas Hardy and George Meredith. The meeting with Hamilton Mabie at Dodd, Mead produced a promise for some book reviewing, while the interview with Henry Lanier at Doubleday, Page resulted in the freelance job of "cut[ting] a novel of 180,000 down to 120,000, correct the grammar + constructions throughout, make suggestions as to plot, change of title + anything else that occurred to me." She agreed to be paid $25 because, in her usual pretence of not knowing anything about appropriate payment, this "was what [she] was short in what I might have made in the same time on the Ency[clopedia]" (FHEP, J.N. McIlwraith to F.H. Eckstorm, 12 November 1902).

By mid-November, she was so busy that she fell behind in her correspondence, and Pollie must have been sufficiently curious about her sister's activities to accept an invitation to New York for the Christmas season but had to cancel the trip. Perhaps the prospect of a Christmas on her own and away from Cairnbrae briefly depressed Jean because she immediately tried, but failed, to persuade Mrs. Eckstorm to come instead. More encouragingly, there was enough money coming in to require a savings account.

While McIlwraith was surrounded by impressive women in her personal life, and she was aware of female leaders in the magazine business such as Ida M. Tarbell at McClure (FHEP, J.N. McIlwraith to F.H. Eckstorm, 30 June 1902), all of the people with editorial positions to whom she introduced herself were men. The only woman she mentions, Mary Mapes Dodge, the children's author and editor at *St. Nicholas*, had become a mere "figure head" following her son's death (JNMP, "New York Impressions") and was not keen on employing other women. Told that Tudor Storrs Jenks was about to retire from his post as associate editor, Jean offered to "step into his shoes," but was informed "that Mrs. Dodge had lifted her hand unto heaven and had sworn that she would never have another woman on the staff of St. Nicholas." Mr. Jenks did not elaborate on Mrs. Dodge's reasons. McIlwraith described Jenks as a "funny little man with a bald head," and she created similar sketches of each of her interviewers, gauging enthusiasm and helpfulness, and she amused herself by grouping them into either white-haired and fatherly gentlemen or brunette and brown-eyed young fellows. She sized up Doubleday, Page's junior partner Henry Lanier, the twenty-eight-year-old son of the poet Sidney Lanier, as "a bit of a masher" (JNMP, "New York Impressions"), and suspected that the "lovely young men" in the publishers' offices would have created "havoc ... in [her] affections" had she come to New York "in [her] susceptible youth" (FHEP, J.N. McIlwraith to F.H. Eckstorm, 17 September 1902). She was quick to discern if any of "these lovely young men" were full of themselves and "saunter[ed]" about the office with "a consequential air." A guarantee to get into her bad books was any kind of condescension in response to her age. One individual at McClure's insisted that "all their working staff [were] young girls," and suggested that it would have been "wiser for her to stay [in the eighteenth century]." She concedes that he was referring to "good field for romance etc." and that he said it "in a most gentlemanly way" (JNMP, "New York Impressions"), but she was not as reassured by this encounter as with others where she was treated politely, like a "maiden aunt from the country" (FHEP, J.N. McIlwraith to F.H. Eckstorm, 17 September 1902).

This was a role in which her nephews and nieces had given her plenty of practice, so much so that she often adopted the guise of "auntie," even with correspondents such as McLennan and Eckstorm, though she preferred to describe herself to the former as a spinster who was "hard-pushed," "independent," and "strong-minded" (McLFF, J.N. McIlwraith to W. McLennan, 29 December 1897; 18 September 1897; 5 January 1897). Her photo in an article on "The Modern School of Canadian Writers" is captioned "J.N. McIlwraith, 'Auntie Jane,' " without any further explanation (Wendell 515). The choir at St. George's Church immediately appealed to her because of the presence of "women in it, in surplices [who] do not march in procession but slide quietly out of the side." Even better, some of them "look as old as I am" (JNMP, "New York Impressions"). At times, McIlwraith seems like a forerunner of Agatha Christie's Jane Marple, with whom she not only shares a habit of camouflaging her spunk behind an innocuous façade but also one of categorizing new acquaintances in relation to familiar faces in her hometown: a man in Scribner's subscription department looked like "young Pottinger" and "a dark young chap" at Collier's resembled "the Glasscos" (JNMP, "New York Impressions"). Her banter with editorial staff shows her ready wit with anyone who cared to spar with her. One man with "a well-developed funny bone" was Lanier, who enjoyed her assurance that, though she "looked large," she "could be compressed into a very small hole, like an eider down quilt." Nor did an arrogant young man get the better of her when he bragged "that he arrived in New York at seven-thirty and by 11.30 the same day ... had a situation." She "had arrived at 7.50 and it was now 12.20 and I had not got one yet, so [she] was behind him," she mock-lamented in return (JNMP, "New York Impressions").

She was as curious about the look of the workplaces she visited as she was about the people inhabiting them, finding the lack of privacy in most offices off-putting and noting that a higher position did not guarantee a separate workspace let alone a pleasant one. McClure reminded her of "a dress-making establishment," with the "editorial rooms ... caged off at one side of the big long room where the stenographers sit" as if they were "at sewing machines," and areas "divided off by half mast partitions" as the "fitting rooms ... where the mss are made to fit the magazine." Even worse was Harper on Franklin Square, which reminded her of "a railway station with a news stand, waiting room etc," with the noise of the printing machines clattering "at the back" and the trains of the elevated rail roaring past the windows. This was the first time that McIlwraith was exposed to the business of publishing in all of its stages, and while she found much of it ugly, she was not put off by it, concluding that "from the chrysalis comes the butterfly." The city itself was not attractive. In 1902, the whole of Manhattan was one enormous construction site, with the building of the underground and several bridges underway to ease the flow of workers into and out of the city. McIlwraith, who had travelled on Hamilton's first tramcar twenty-five years earlier, now plotted her trips to the Astor Library to avoid

The McIlwraiths, ca. 1907, with Jean McIlwraith and T.F., future anthropologist on her lap. At the rear, left to right: his father, T.F. McIlwraith; his sister Dorothy; Martha Chittenden, wife of Jack; Mary Duncan McIlwraith Service, T.F.'s aunt; John Goldie ("Jack") McIlwraith, his uncle; and Mary Stevens, T.F.'s mother. Middle, left to right: Marion Reid Service, cousin; Helen McIlwraith, cousin; Mary Park McIlwraith, cousin; to the right of Jean and T.F. McIlwraith, Archie McIlwraith, cousin; May Saunders, wife of Kennedy; and Marjorie, sister. Front, left to right: Willis James Service, cousin; John Worden McIlwraith, cousin; and Helen Service, cousin. TFMP.

some of the worst congestions, but observed that the city "reminds me of a man who has had some of his fingers cut off by machinery" (JNMP, "New York Impressions"). Her startling analogy anticipates Saul Bellow's comment that "[a] Chicagoan as he wanders about the city feels like a man who has lost many teeth" (Bellow 374). The sight of New York suggested dystopia to her, specifically H.G. Wells's novel *The Time Machine*, with construction workers toiling below to serve "the people on top riding or driving at the fashionable hour of the day" (JNMP, "New York Impressions").

Reader at Doubleday, Page

Occasional assignments for Doubleday, Page, which included "reading manuscripts for a month during the summer while the regular member was off on vacation" (JNMP, "Jottings"), became a permanent manuscript reader's post in November 1903, just over a year after Jean's arrival in New York. She occupied this position until her retirement and return to Canada towards the end of the First World War. During these years, she observed American book publishing from within a new and flourishing firm that prided itself on publishing some of the great names in late nineteenth- and early twentieth-century literature in English, among them Mark Twain, Joseph Conrad, Rudyard Kipling, John Galsworthy, Christopher Morley, and Charles, Frank, and Kathleen Norris (see Doubleday). While junior partner Henry Lanier had been her initial contact, and she continued to report to him, McIlwraith came to work closely with Walter Hines Page, who as recently as 1900 had entered a partnership with F.N. Doubleday. Born in North Carolina and educated at Trinity College (later Duke University) and at Randolph Macon College before becoming one of the first fellows of the new Johns Hopkins University, Page left an academic career for publishing. His excellent contacts, along with his diplomatic skills, shaped the success of Doubleday, Page from the start. As a close friend of Rudyard Kipling, he acquired "exclusive American book rights for [his] work," persuaded Ellen Glasgow to transfer to his firm from Harper, and arranged "to publish Booker T. Washington's autobiography before the Black leader had written the book" – and, for that matter, before Doubleday, Page had even begun operations (J.M. Cooper 162, 163). He was known for exceptional tact in dealing with difficult authors and became a "diplomat who can write an unpleasant truth without offense," as he phrased it in the anonymously published *A Publisher's Confession* (91). One of his most popular authors, the short-story writer O. Henry, claimed that "Page could reject a story with a letter that was so complimentary ... that you could take it to a bank and borrow money on it" (Hendrick 2: n.p.).

Page's social skills extended to keeping his staff happy. McIlwraith typically prepared as many as twenty reader's reports per week, and she had the satisfaction that only two years after she had settled into her job, Sara Jeannette Duncan – apparently an old friend and by then married to Everard Cotes – believed her to have enough clout to expedite the manuscript of *The Viceroy* (published as *Set in Authority*). Duncan even temporarily bypassed her agent, A.P. Watt, before she thought better of it and retraced her steps. It is clear from Henry Lanier's response to Duncan's manuscript that McIlwraith's advice was being heard.[55]

---

55 See Letter from Sara Jeannette Duncan (Mrs. Everard Cotes) to A.P. Watt, 13 March [1905], folder 91.04, and Letter from Henry Lanier to Sara Jeanette Duncan (Mrs. Everard Cotes), 4 April 1905, folder 85.08 – both in A.P. Watt Records, 1888–1982, # 11036, Rare Book Literary and Historical Papers, Wilson Library, University of North Carolina at Chapel Hill.

A reader's daily routine was anything but glamorous, however, and in the "Jottings" she prepared about Page after his death, McIlwraith affectionately credited his affable presence with making this monotonous task interesting and enjoyable. As well, because he had previously occupied the positions of literary adviser to Houghton, Mifflin and editor of the *Atlantic Monthly*, Page's very presence reminded her of her proudest accomplishments as a writer to date. It was also helpful that his magazine *World's Work* had published a brief but positive review of *Roderick Campbell* well before she was introduced to Page ("A Short Guide" 891). As she was to confirm repeatedly, Page's influence on McIlwraith's life in New York was significant.

His air of leisure as he ambled out of his office "perhaps swinging his glasses but more likely ... looking over the top of them at his extremely busy staff" (JNMP, "Jottings") created a collegial environment despite the chronic frenzy of imminent deadlines. While on closer acquaintance she found Lanier, the "most charming of all the charmers" when she first met him (FHEP, J.N. McIlwraith to F.H. Eckstorm, 12 November 1902), remote in his dealings with staff, Page cultivated friendly routines such as passing on complimentary tickets for authors' readings (she remembers one featuring Richard Le Gallienne), allowing himself to be teased with favourable reviews of books that McIlwraith had recommended but that he had rejected, and asking her advice on handling manuscripts submitted by his many friends. To McIlwraith, Page was above all the anglophile southerner who made her exile in Yankeeland pleasant, and his son Arthur grouped him and Jean together as people of one mind. Thus, "a long poem in blank verse" with the proposed title of "Britain tu anathema" was, as Arthur Page thought, "a fine line of goods to find favor in a nest of British + Southerners!" ("Jottings"). She quite liked having her feathers ruffled by the "fascinating youths running [*World's Work*]," Page's public-opinion magazine, and she humoured their efforts to "stir ... the British lion in the corner" ("Jottings"). These "youths" were often recent graduates from Harvard who were gaining experience in journalism towards their eventual careers in law or politics, but they seem like older and upmarket versions of her young brothers and the boys in her night school. If she found the lack of privacy in Harper's and McClure's offices disagreeable and did not acquire an office of her own until the company moved to Garden City in 1910, she did not mind having her "desk ... shoved around to suit bumptious young editors" ("Jottings"), and she was generous with assistance when they came running for help. One of these young men was Isaac Frederick Marcosson, who started as editor with *World's Work* the same year McIlwraith took up her post, before he moved on to *Saturday Evening Post* and *Munsey's Magazine*. Some people, Marcosson among them, suspected Page of using his charm to get his staff to work for less than they would have received elsewhere, but such rumours did nothing to diminish McIlwraith's respect for him.

Partly because Mrs. Page came from a Scottish family, she and her husband took a particular shine to Jean and often invited her to their home in one of the "Apostles" buildings, part of A.T. Stewart's planned community in Garden City. McIlwraith participated in after-dinner discussions about the literary merits of Mark Twain and Longfellow, and in the Pages' home and at work she met Christopher Morley, Frank, Charles and Kathleen Norris, and Vachel Lindsay, as well as public figures such as the journalist Ray Stannard Baker from the *American Magazine*. At some of these encounters, she might have realized that Page in fact had little use for the cliché of the southern gentleman and considered "the 'epidemic vocabulary' of the ex-Confederate states ... a false screen behind which a new generation was shirking its responsibilities." Like Baker, he concerned himself intensely with the "fearful problem of the Negro," more correctly, the fearful problem of America's racial division (Sedgwick 377, 376). But if she acknowledged this aspect of Page's thinking and allowed it to influence her own ideas, she did not elaborate on it in her recollections of him.

Editorial Correspondence

Although her employers probably would have been shocked if they had known about it, McIlwraith saved copies of correspondence with some of Doubleday's more eccentric authors (JNMP, "Editorial Correspondence"). One particularly acrimonious exchange was with an individual who submitted a manuscript entitled "Race Corrupters," a novel dealing with "Ohio, the Negro and sentimental fools." The news that the manuscript had been rejected was not well received, and by calling the publisher "a little one horse house ... afraid of offending the 'niggers,' and their sympathizers," the aggrieved author hoped that the publisher's "business [would] soon go to 'the wall.' " Walter Page attempted to smooth the waves by conceding that "it is somewhat rash to put any limit to the possibilities of earnest effort and determination," and he promised "to read anything you may care to submit to us," only to provoke almost immediate submission of a revised manuscript that, the author thought, would not "offend ... the negro race." Both Page and McIlwraith were flooded with apologetic letters wheedling for sympathy with the writer who had stencilled the words "courage," "determination," "persistency," "nerve," and "starve" on the "dirty walls of [his] dingy room." To no avail: the manuscript was rejected again. This correspondence persistently and contemptuously refers to McIlwraith as a "Busy Member" of the Doubleday, Page staff.

She appears to have been able to preserve anonymity in this case but was not so lucky with W.B. Trites and his wife Estelle, who "assumed full charge of the necessary correspondence [and] relieved [her husband] of the petty details that were always as thorns in his flesh." Mrs. and Mr. Trites formed a rather frightening pair who declared to a New York *Times* reporter that "We can't mix work and play. We've almost forgotten how to play" (Stimson). The bone of contention between the couple and Doubleday, Page was Trites's novel *John Cave*, rejected although the author had "typed the manuscript on Japanese vellum and ... had it bound by Zaehnsdorf in [b]lue crushed levant" (Stimson). Mr. and Mrs. Trites appear to have arrived in person in McIlwraith's office because the ensuing correspondence over the rejection of the manuscript dwells on a "short-haired old lady" who issued the bad news. This description provoked an irate response from McIlwraith in which she congratulated Trites on his "unquestionably youthful virility" and assured him that she had "no recollection whatever either of the book, or of the writer's personality." Indeed, she had to look up the firm's records to find that the manuscript was "declined on account of the unpleasant nature of the plot, though commended for convincing realism." Half a year later, on 16 February 1913, this business made it into the New York *Times*. Jean appears as a "[c]ruel lady" who obstructed the success of *John Cave*. He was now being fêted by W.D. Howells as "a new literary light," not to mention favourable citations from Joseph Conrad and H.G. Wells (Stimson).

An article about the publishing world that had appeared in *The World's World* of 1901 twelve years earlier, shortly before she arrived in New York, might have prepared McIlwraith for the contempt in which some authors held the profession of manuscript reader. Publisher's readers were a "bizarre and nondescript lot [of] college tutors, decayed ex-editors, faded gentlemen wearing long hair for appearance and economy, truculent *Bludyers*, unsuccessful writers who have sunk to professional readers, or busy newspaper men who sample a manuscript as a grocer would a firkin of butter, by reading a few sentences in the middle[.] And typewriter girls!" ("The Unknown Writer" 1221).[56] McIlwraith defended herself and her qualifications by referring to her own publications and biography in *Who's Who*, but her job had already taught her to adopt the view that "if fiction is not entertaining enough to catch the general public it is not worth publication at anybody's expense" (JNMP, "Dialogue").

This particular pronouncement appears in a dialogue between a casual visitor to a publisher's office and her friend, a manuscript reader named Aurelia, in which McIlwraith summarizes her experience at the Doubleday, Page. Aurelia "has learnt the editorial trick of making the visitor front the window," thus revealing "the expression of the outsider ... while the insider has help in concealing the same." Aurelia explains the challenges of her craft, gives practical advice, surveys the features that characterize successful and unsuccessful manuscripts, and classifies the types of authors that make her life difficult. The dialogue, a format that she had successfully applied elsewhere, softens the sharpness of Aurelia's pronouncements because the evidence has her visitor arrive at some

---

56 The *Bludyers* are an allusion to "Mr. Bludyer, an English gentleman of the press; editor of the 'Weekly Bravo' " in William Makepeace Thackeray's *Reading a Poem*, Chiswick, 1891.

unpleasant conclusions by herself. She also gets to observe the kindness of "the rabid" Aurelia with "really charming unsuccessful folk." The editor has a sense of humour, displayed when she responds with "I am ... it bothers me sometimes" to the compliment that she must be "awfully clever" to do the job of a publisher's reader, and she gives a parodic summary of a novel about a society woman who falls in love with her chauffeur. However, a whiff of disillusionment with the trade of writers and publishers hangs over the whole exercise. She does not appear to have succeeded in publishing the dialogue, possibly because there were already too many similar advice books, including Page's own *A Publisher's Confession* (1905) and William Stone Booth's *A Practical Guide for Authors* (1907). One of the problems of assessing McIlwraith's experience at Doubleday, Page is that, with the exception of the "New York Impressions" of her early days in the city and a few letters to Eckstorm, most of her autobiographical writing covering the years until her return to Canada was composed in retrospect, when the initial euphoria of securing her freedom had worn off.

Walter Hines Page, Ambassador to the Court of St. James

In March 1913, Woodrow Wilson appointed Page to the post of United States ambassador to the Court of St. James, and McIlwraith claims to have been present when he received the telephone call from the president (JNMP, "Jottings"). At the time, Page did not anticipate the outbreak of war or his role as mediator before the United States entered it. Although the extent of Page's influence on Woodrow Wilson has since been questioned, there was no such doubt at the time. In addition to McIlwraith's own faith in the righteousness of Britain's cause, the First World War shaped the lives of Jean's nephew Tom and her niece Dorothy, both of whom will feature in subsequent chapters. Given the objections of all three McIlwraiths to the delay in the United States' entry into the war and Jean McIlwraith's pride in her association with him, it is appropriate to acknowledge Page's ambassadorial role and the fame he gained from it.

Following his early death in 1918, Page was acclaimed as the "Allied Standard-bearer" of Anglo-American friendship (J.M. Cooper 374). His work and death were commemorated with a plaque in Westminster Abbey, installed in 1923 and dedicated to "The friend of Britain in her sorest need" (Jenkyns 159). To date, he is one of only a small group of Americans including Longfellow, James Russell Lowell, Henry James, and T.S. Eliot to have been so honoured. Celebrated by Ellery Sedgwick, editor of the *Atlantic Monthly*, as "the incarnation of those qualities we love to call American" (Sedgwick 375), Page's achievement was enshrined in the two-volume *The Life and Letters of Walter H. Page* in 1922, followed by *The Training of an American: The Earlier Life and Letters of Walter H. Page* in 1928. These compilations were edited by Burton J. Hendrick, who, after Page's departure from Doubleday, Page, had become managing editor of

World's Work, which serialized *The Life and Letters* starting in September 1921. Both books won the Pulitzer Prize and became "a publishing sensation" with "156,000 copies [sold] in the United States over six years" (J.M. Cooper 398), producing revenue in excess of a million dollars for its publisher. At the dedication service of the tablet in Westminster Abbey, the dean referred to "those letters which at once have won an enduring place in the literature of the English-speaking world."[57] Jean McIlwraith was one of the people whom Hendrick asked to submit reminiscences and letters for his volumes. He notes that she agreed eagerly, and her "Unimportant Jottings" were a draft towards her contribution. Like the submissions of her fellow Canadians Sir Gilbert Parker and Ernest Thompson Seton, however, her offering was not considered worthy of inclusion.[58] If her blunt criticism of the editorship of *World's Work* after Page had left and Hendrick had taken over made it into the final draft, that could have been one reason for the rejection. She omits to clarify this outcome in her conversation with Gertrude Pringle, to whom she mentions Hendrick's invitation but not what became of her submission (Pringle, "Jean McIlwraith").

Settlement House

Eckstorm had warned her friend that the work of a publisher's reader would not necessarily be good for her own writing (FHEP, J.N. McIlwraith to F.H. Eckstorm, 22 June 1902), and while she did in fact write a great deal, McIlwraith found it difficult to get her work accepted well before Hendrick rejected her submission. Her claim, in conversation with Pringle, that virtually everything she ever wrote was also published is not based on fact. One major rejection was of her novel "Dominick Street," submitted in 1905 and written in response to Houghton, Mifflin's encouragement to try her hand at "a novel of modern life" (FHEP, J.N. McIlwraith to F.H. Eckstorm, 12 June [1902?]). Her narrative was set in a Lower-East-Side Settlement House and focused on its population of community workers, young university graduates among them, and the Italian, Irish, and Central European immigrants whom they assisted in finding their place in their new environment. Her cast of characters was complemented by the engineers overseeing the construction of New York's underground railway and the labourers building it.

The plot centres on a spoiled young woman, Barbara Ellwood, who leaves her home in Troy, Michigan after her mother dies and her father remarries in

---

57 "Programme, Memorial Service for Walter Hines Page at the Unveiling of the Tablet Erected to His Memory, Westminster Abbey, Tuesday, 3rd of July, 1923, at 5.30 p.m." Walter H. Page papers, MS Am1090.2, HLHU. There were also detractors who were not convinced of Page's reputation as "the greatest and noblest American since Lincoln"; see, for example, Grattan.

58 Burton Jesse Hendricks papers, MS Am1090.6, HLHU.

order to work in a Settlement House in New York, or as one of her critics puts it, to perform "philanthropic stunts" there ("Dominick Street" 141). Barbara is courted by two men, Jack Allister, an engineer on the subway and also her stepbrother, who wants to marry her, and Raffaele Tafuri, a handsome Italian anarchist, graduate of the University of Bologna, and "her soul's kin," whose principles forbid marriage (103). Allister wins her hand, and Tafuri dies after saving Allister's life in the 149th Street Tunnel. Allister in turn foils a dynamite attack that would have flooded the new tunnel and killed dozens of inaugural riders of the subway. In her previous work, McIlwraith repeatedly projected herself into her male characters, and as we know she fought with McLennan to keep their female characters as independent as possible. Now she attempted the complicated feat of distributing autobiographical features of her younger and older selves among the female figures, in addition to creating a conventional romance with a happy outcome. In order to drive the plot, Barbara displays the emotional flightiness typically associated with the young women in such fiction before they learn their lesson, but confusingly she is also a "red-haired Amazon," even a "giantess," and she has the looks and demeanour of "a manly boy" (6, 94, 39).[59] Barbara is befriended by the middle-aged Scottish Canadian Miss Harrison (whose own masculine characteristics are underlined by her nickname Miss Harry), a no-nonsense community nurse who, despite her feisty independence, also enjoys a romance with a German bookseller as the narrative concludes. Along with Barbara's religious beliefs, Miss Harry's interventions into the young woman's romantic entanglements act as a brake on social transgression, such as when she attempts to set up house with Tafuri. For much of "Dominick Street," there appears to be a conflict between two types of narrative: the novel about a woman unencumbered by marriage that the author wanted to write and the novel that would sell and therefore required heterosexual (and eventually legitimized) romance.

In this, the narrative resembles the "radical romance" of Settlement House fiction, a well-established genre by the time "Dominick Street" was being composed (see Szuberla; L. Fisher; Cella). Hervey White's *Differences* (1899), for example, draws on its author's work at Jane Addams's Hull House in Chicago to highlight the contradictions between the middle-class status of many Settlement House workers and their striving towards social equality with disadvantaged "neighbours." White's main character, Genevieve Radcliffe, rejects inheritance and a suitor from her own class and marries a widowed labourer, but it is clear that, although her work will contribute to their income, he will be her "prince" and she his "own little wife" (H. White 311). "Dominick Street" does not propose such sweeping redefinitions of class distinction but it does shift away from convention as Miss Harry comforts Barbara Ellwood, who is

---

59 See Mitchell, "To Be a Boy," 103–38.

distraught by Tafuri's and Allister's demands on her. In one scene, men become increasingly extraneous to their friendship when the older woman brushes Barbara's hair to calm her, calls her "honey," and agrees to have her sleep in her bed. Nevertheless, the men remain the main subject of conversation even then, and at the end Barbara cannot wait to leave New York with Allister once Tafuri is out of the way.

Most of the story is, however, not taken up by Barbara's love triangle with the two men or her respite from it with Miss Harry, but rather by descriptions of the immigrant milieu. In addition to chasing down overdue library books for the Settlement House, thereby gaining access to tenements and the families who live in them, Barbara teaches gymnastics to young girls, attends political rallies, and visits neighbourhood entertainments such as the Italian puppet theatre on Elizabeth Street. In scenes inspired by McIlwraith's school for young workers at Cairnbrae, she teaches Italian, Irish, and Jewish boys in the basement of the Settlement House, takes them on excursions around the city, and gets them to take a temperance pledge. Enhanced by greater ethnic variety, many scenes are lifted from "Smiling Water," but – in contrast to Jonquil, who fails to instil religion in her students – Barbara invites the boys to join her on Sundays in a pew she has taken for them in a local church.

McIlwraith undertook much of the research towards this novel by walking the streets of New York, visiting buildings, piers, and bridges, and looking at the construction sites for the subway. There was also a great deal of helpful information in magazines like *World's Work*, which published article after article about the "rebuilding" of New York.[60] Here she learned about the physical challenges of working underground, and she has one of her characters die of "caisson disease," or decompression sickness. She read up on anarchism, including J.H. Mackay's *The Anarchists: A Picture of Society at the Close of the Nineteenth Century* (1891). Studying the milieu of one of the more than thirty Settlement Houses operating in New York was a little more complicated. As a busy manuscript reader, she did not have the time to become a full-time Settlement worker. Instead, she collected the material for Barbara Ellwood's activities by helping out in the lending library of Greenwich House, which was founded in 1902 by Mary (Kingsbury) Simkhovitch, a social reformer and suffragist acclaimed as "one of the most articulate spokespersons for the movement" (Stebner 1065; see also Simkhovitch). Greenwich House offered instruction in infant care and hygiene, athletics, reading, languages, legal classes, drama, music, and arts and crafts, and over the years attracted prominent supporters in Gertrude Vanderbilt Whitney, Amelia Earhart, Eleanor Roosevelt, and others (Caves 406). Like other Settlement Houses, Greenwich House continues to this day as an important institution supporting immigrants in their new lives.[61]

---

60 See, for example, Cunniff and Goodrich; Cunniff; Wheatley.
61 See "Settlement Houses," Treasures of New York series, PBS, 2016.

Two of the three readers at Houghton, Mifflin were impressed with McIlwraith's novel, praised the manuscript for being "written from first-hand and accurate knowledge"[62] of the Settlement Houses, and enjoyed its humorous and unsentimental treatment of the subject. They also felt that the love triangle was well handled and the writing "eminently readable." By contrast, Barbara's character was a problem: "an impulsive egotist with a variety of crude humanitarian notions" whose dealings with her two suitors were not always believable. Both of these readers leaned towards recommending publication but were cautious about anticipated sales. One noted that *Roderick Campbell* had sold 2,150 copies to date, with "plates and advertising cost[ing] nearly $1500, and ... a debit balance of over $800," but that "without illustrations and not lavishly advertised," the new book "ought at least to pay for itself." In submitting her manuscript, McIlwraith – who apparently was not aware of these problems – had requested special advertising for "Dominick Street."

These largely positive views were, however, vetoed by the third reader, William Stone Booth (see "Booth, William Stone"), who was the one to identify that the Settlement House in the novel was based on Greenwich House. His response appears to have as much to do with his impatience with certain aspects of the Settlement movement generally as with McIlwraith's novel specifically. In particular, he railed against "the freaks and weak-kneed brothers and sisters," including the "Harvard and Yale graduates in sociology and religion," whose alleged charity amounted to little more than "laboratory studies in unwashed human nature." Booth was not convinced that McIlwraith knew enough about Settlement Houses to write about them. His hostile report trumped the two others, and the manuscript was rejected. Nine years later, Houghton, Mifflin had no such scruples when it published Elia Wilkinson Peattie's *Precipice* (1914; rpt. 1989), in which an increasingly lurid plot has the social worker Kate Barrington choose a suitor from three contenders. The winner, Karl Wander, is her equal in class but displays views about women as conventional as those of Genevieve Radcliffe's labourer husband until, speaking to each other across a "precipice" in the Colorado mountains, the couple agrees to a marriage that allows both to do their work but live apart. Neither Hervey White nor Peattie shows their unconventional couples' married lives in action.

Interestingly, Booth's outburst is prefaced by the caution that McIlwraith is nevertheless to "be handled with kid gloves" because she had not only published in the *Atlantic Monthly* (though, for no apparent reason, he then crosses out this reference) but was also "a friend of Professor W.A. Neilson and ... a friend of my brother." This was Booth's brother Edward, whom McIlwraith, as mentioned earlier, had met at 44 Irving Place. Neilson, on the other hand, was an older acquaintance and part of the McIlwraiths' Scottish network. Educated at

---

62 Reader's reports, Houghton, Mifflin archive, MS Am 2516 (A 1539), HLHU.

the University of Edinburgh, Neilson emigrated to Canada in 1891 and taught at Upper Canada College until 1895 before moving on to Harvard, where he obtained his doctorate in 1898. He taught at Bryn Mawr and Harvard until 1917, when he became president of Smith College, a post he occupied until his retirement in 1939. Neilson's brother Robert, who emigrated first, established himself in the milling business with the help of the Goldies, the in-laws of Jean's uncle Andrew (Thorp 57; Glazer 273). Booth's nervousness about McIlwraith's connections is the clearest indication we have that her network was so extensive as to be intimidating. Although it did her no good in this case, it did guarantee extra courtesy.

Years later, McIlwraith attempted to recycle "Dominick Street" as part of a trilogy she wrote for submission to a prize competition for the juvenile market. No details about the competition or precise dates are available. Openly autobiographical, each of the novels is closely tied to a period in McIlwraith's life: "Smiling Water," as discussed earlier, draws on her experience teaching working-class boys in her father's home; "Springs Eternal" describes her time with Aunt Sarah in Scotland; and "Casual Kate's Letters" divides the narrative of "Dominick Street" between the milieux of Settlement Houses and of publishing, enriched with expeditions to the opera, collecting antique furniture, and staging tableaux vivants. Once again, McIlwraith projects different aspects of her life onto separate characters. Kate Frost, a graduate of Vassar and resident of Grand Rapids, Michigan, arrives in New York in search of an editorial job that will prepare her for a career as an author, and reports on her adventures in letters to her mother. She becomes the flatmate of Jonquil Ames, now nicknamed "Johnny," which has Kate guess that her name is "Jean or ... Joan" ("Casual Kate's Letters" 33). Ames, a nurse from Canada, has lost her fiancé, a doctor, in the Boer War, and is devoted to her half-brother Hearty. Kate must choose between three men: Hearty, "a clear-skinned, healthy, curly-headed Canadian boy" (35); Martin Avery Carcross, a good-looking and flirtatious author; and Ben Thornton, a Jewish Settlement House worker. In the end, Hearty – who appears to be modelled on Kennedy – wins her hand, but not before Johnny has whisked him off to a healthy climate to cure his lung disease. The complications in the plot derive from Kate's "casual" character: she not only finds it difficult to settle on an occupation, but her irresponsibility also causes serious problems for herself and her friends.

The trilogy apparently did not go anywhere, but after retirement from her editorial position McIlwraith prepared a revised version of "Casual Kate's Letters." It was now entitled "Casual Camilla"[63] and featured the recent war. This

---

63 It is clear from the letters that revisions to "Casual Kate's Letters" have taken place, but no manuscript of "Casual Camilla" has been located to confirm what exactly they were. The choice of title may have been inspired by Margaret Cameron's novelette "Pragmatic Patricia," *Harper's Magazine*, vol. 132, 1915–16, pp. 703–16, 871–86.

time, there are no reader's reports from a publisher, but there are several letters from friends and family whom she canvassed for their views (JNMP, "Editorial Correspondence"): Lillian Comstock, long-time secretary to F.N. Doubleday and a good friend; Marjorie Tyberg (whose sister Peg Somerville had welcomed McIlwraith in New York when she first arrived); and Jean's niece Marion Service, a librarian. Comstock, who was McIlwraith's frequent travel companion and later became a close friend of Dorothy McIlwraith, protested that she "enjoyed the book immensely, of course" and buried her dislike of the heroine among a few innocuous comments on technical details that needed adjusting such as office mores and royalty agreements. By contrast, neither Tyberg nor Marion even tried to be diplomatic. McIlwraith's description of "mating season" at the office and her tone of "unbroken flippancy and familiarity" had Tyberg exhort her friend "not [to] give circulation under any circumstances" to "vile" suggestions of rampant sexuality and to remember that she herself had always been "absolutely free from mush." To make sure her correspondent got the message, Tyberg – who by then had been teaching for years at Point Loma – put on her professorial cap and underscored her warning that "[t]he written word has proven to suggest as well as to correct."

While it is easy to smile at Tyberg's straight-laced response, she also offers a brief glimpse into McIlwraith's uneasy life as a Canadian in New York during the war, an important period of her life but one about which there is virtually no information. Through Camilla, McIlwraith not only satirizes (or, as Tyberg puts it, "knocks") the working environment at a publisher's office but also revised the references to the Boer War in the original manuscript to comment critically on America's role in the First World War. Tyberg was having none of it: "During [the Great War] there was such widespread and sincere effort on the part of girls to do the work on hand and do it thoroughly that to turn the light on this casual type of girl is untimely." Tyberg approved of the sections in "Casual Camilla" that revived Jean's "early experience" with her "night-school," but she urged her to "eliminate the knock at the Americans. But oh Jean do not knock those publishers!"

Tyberg's second significant criticism was shared by all three readers, who agreed that McIlwraith's conception of young office girls' speech, conduct, and motivation was out of date, that her story had a " 'before the war' atmosphere" (Tyberg), described routines that are "not done at the present time" (Comstock), and created a heroine who did "not say the right kind of thing nor say it in the right kind of way" (Service). This criticism must have been hard to bear by a woman known for her "racy and graphic conversation" (Pringle). Marion suggested that, to get a better idea of how things were now done and expressed, her aunt look at contemporary novels about the office milieu, including Elizabeth Jordan's *The Wings of Youth* (1918), Lewis Sinclair's *The Job* (1917), or Sophie Kerr's *The Blue Envelope* (1917), but in their strong consensus McIlwraith was not, or was no longer, sufficiently au courant to write such a novel.[64] Marion attempted to soften her criticism with family chit-chat, such as the sensational news that Aunt Nellie had met the pugilist Georges Carpentier, but the message was more than clear. McIlwraith appears to have given up on "Casual Camilla," and the manuscript has disappeared.

Tenaciously, McIlwraith continued to approach Houghton, Mifflin with a variety of projects throughout her years in New York. She hoped to increase sales for *The Curious Career of Roderick Campbell* by having it "resuscitate[d]" in a Canadian edition by Macmillan Canada in 1906, following a none-too-amicable exchange about the business details between Macmillan's Frank Wise and Houghton, Mifflin representatives. She turned to Ralph Connor, asking him to "[w]rite a piece for the Winnipeg papers + sign it with your famous nom de plume" to help advertise the publication, but no evidence has come to light that Connor complied.[65] In 1908, three years after "Dominick Street" had been rejected, she tried to persuade Houghton, Mifflin to bring out an American edition of *Sir Frederick Haldimand* but Haldimand was deemed to be of insufficient historical interest to Americans.[66]

McIlwraith tried the publishers again in 1914 with a historical novel about the War of 1812 entitled "Of One Blood: A Romance of the War of 1812–14" and featuring "a Canadian hero and an American heroine," but there is only one brief reader's report, and the book was rejected as "curiously inadequate."[67] This manuscript appears to be a version of *Kinsmen at War*, published thirteen years later by Graphic Publishers, a short-lived but influential press devoted to the publication of Canadian books (see Kotin). Fortunately, this string of rejections was relieved in 1912 by the acceptance of *A Diana of Quebec* by Smith, Elder & Company in London, publisher of some of the great names of nineteenth-century British literature and of *Cornhill Magazine*. *Diana* appeared jointly with Bell & Cockburn, Stephen Leacock's publisher in Toronto. There was also the triumph of *The Little Admiral* (1924) winning the Stodder

---

64 Letters from Lillian Comstock (25 May 1920), Marjorie Tyberg (n.d.), Marion Reid (18 June, 30 June [1920]), "Editorial Correspondence," JNMP.

65 Letter from Jean N. McIlwraith to Charles William Gordon, 14 July 1906, University of Manitoba Archives and Special Collections, Charles William Gordon (Ralph Connor) Fonds, MSS 56 (A 34–42), box 3, folder 8, item 34.

66 Houghton, Mifflin archive, MS Am 4305, HLHU.

67 Houghton, Mifflin archive, MS Am 2516 (A9307), HLHU. This publication history may explain McIlwraith's insistence on reading the Canadian and American enemies as "brothers" and their conflict as "fratricide," as discussed in Coleman 48, 59. McIlwraith generally drew sharp distinctions between Canadians and Americans, but she also wrote with an eye to her market. Although there are parallels, the situation with *Kinsmen at Arms* is not quite the same as with *The Span o' Life*, where she and McLennan underlined the similarities between the enemies because the authors were keen to rehabilitate public opinion of the French side.

and Houghton Prize, and the continuing success of *Sir Frederick Haldimand* in Canada.

Throughout the war, Jean's nephew Thomas sent greetings to "A.J." in his letters to his sister Dorothy, who began her own connection with Doubleday as early as 1913. Jean McIlwraith appears to have left New York near the end of the war to stay with Nellie Holt, now widowed, in Quebec. She travelled with Helen Service to California in 1920 and to Europe in 1921, and the two attended T.F. McIlwraith's graduation from Cambridge as a festive conclusion to their journey.[68] Her nephew noticed, however, that Jean was no longer physically fit, repeated herself constantly, and was nervous about meeting his professors. By 1922, she had found a house in Burlington. After her sister-in-law's death in 1923, she shared her bungalow with her brother Thomas until his death in 1932, and the siblings avoided the cold months in Ontario by wintering in St. Augustine, Florida. She continued to write but published little. Now that she was no longer well known in the literary world, she sadly reported to Margaret Cowie, her name had been dropped from *Who's Who*. She did some editorial work, such as editing Charles Norris's novels until she began to object to the direction his work had taken, or so she said (Pringle, "Jean McIlwraith"; Wilson). When her nephew was completing his study of the Nuxalk in 1924, she offered to help, but he quickly concluded that it was "useless" because "she kept complaining about my insistence on facts" ("Genealogy"), an odd thing to say for a writer who had prided herself on the accuracy of her research. She looked after her garden and collected antique farmhouse furniture and old silver, a hobby she had taken up while she worked for Doubleday, Page,[69] but heart problems began to take their toll and her mental health declined rapidly.

By 1932, six years before Jean's death, letters written to her nephew Tom had become completely incoherent: she no longer remembered his name (though Kennedy's still came to her), was unable to reconstruct even simple events, and seemed to find language itself an unsolvable puzzle: "That's all right, I'll I'll pull out both shees + that must have been the time both sheets to Kennedy whose name I can always remember while while Toms I can't."[70] One wonders, too, if the many inconsistencies in her interview with Gertrude Pringle seven years earlier were not merely the result of her resolutely arranging her life story to suit herself but also of a failing memory. The only "editing" she did in her

---

68 See T.F. McIlwraith (1899–1964) to Jean McIlwraith, 2 March 1920, T.F. McIlwraith to family, 28 July 1921, TFMP.

69 In this, she was possibly inspired by Henry Lanier, whose collection of furniture, textiles, pottery, and firearms filled an entire catalogue when it came up for auction. See *The Collection of Mr. Henry Lanier*.

70 Jean N. McIlwraith to T.F. McIlwraith, 11 December [year?], Jean N. McIlwraith Estate, TFMP.

last few years concerned her estate, and she obsessively revisited the details of where her belongings should go, revising the list when recipients such as her old friend Alice Cummings died or when old family grudges surfaced and then were once again forgotten. When she died in 1938, T.F. – who closed the houses of several of his aunts and uncles – had the unhappy task of sorting out the different versions of her will.

In her book on Haldimand, McIlwraith used a set of daily entries from his diary to evoke his last few years. In the concluding chapter, entitled "His Relics" (which also include his last will and memorial plaques), McIlwraith combines excerpts from Haldimand's private journal with brief commentary in order to create the day-by-day drama of his decline as his formerly busy public life dwindles into a frail indifference to the world around him. At his death, Haldimand's journal is replaced by a letter from a friend in North America because, "before the letter crossed the Atlantic," the "diary jottings [had] come to an abrupt conclusion" (*Sir Frederick Haldimand* 340). In this book in particular, probably her best, McIlwraith was alert to different types of life writing and how each might contribute to a complex portrait of individuals and their circle. So, too, her own scattered archive offers glimpses of a rich and fragmented life.

With the next chapter, the narrative moves to the next generation, represented by Jean's nephew T.F., his sister Dorothy, and their associates. While there is almost no information on Jean McIlwraith during the First World War, there is ample correspondence from these younger family members about the war. Indeed, this phase in the McIlwraiths' story begins somewhat earlier, with letters by T.F.'s future wife Beulah Gillet Knox written from Europe written in 1913 and the first half of 1914.

Chapter Five

Beulah Gillet Knox in Dresden

The Child and Knox Families

A year before the beginning of the First World War, Beulah Gillet Knox, from Painesville, Ohio, was on tour through Europe with the Childs: her uncle William Addison ("Will") Child, his wife Elizabeth Helen ("Nellie" or "Nelly"), and their son Philip ("Phil"), all from Hamilton, Ontario. In the generation following Jean's, the Childs and McIlwraiths were close acquaintances, so well connected in fact that they eventually became family. The lifelong friendship between Philip and Jean's nephew Tom began at Highfield School and was strengthened when they both joined the British imperial forces and when, in 1921, they were both at Cambridge. Tom knew Philip's cousin Beulah from her frequent visits with the Childs before the couple became engaged in 1924. When Philip married Gertrude Potts in 1925, Beulah and Gertrude also became best friends.

Like previous chapters, this one, too, is about education, but this time it features the luxury of finishing schools and elite tourism made all the more surreal because it takes place on the eve of the war. Less than a year after the travellers' arrival in Dresden, the world enabling such privilege was in shambles. For Beulah, who did not come from an affluent family, this environment was the exception rather than the rule, but she took to it with aplomb. The ease with which she made friends in the fashionable set resulted in correspondence – variously written in English, French, and Spanish – with fellow students, instructors, and a Spanish "Comandante," one of her uncle's high-ranking European acquaintances. Notably, she participated in a relay of letters complicated by the war with young women from the British aristocracy and wealthy European families. This correspondence provides a glimpse into the entitlements, duties, and deprivations that distinguish imperial girlhood from the solid upbringing of an American middle-class teenager (see Oppenheimer, "The 'imperial girl' "). Privilege was of course no guarantee against illness and death: not long after Beulah's departure from Dresden, one of her former fellow students was diagnosed with tuberculosis and several of her closest friends lost a parent or even both parents. The war affected all of them, and the death toll in some of the military families among them was staggering.

Will Child moved across borders with ease, and while some of the McIlwraiths discussed so far travelled south to find work, he reversed the direction and came north to Canada. Born in Wisconsin and a graduate in history from Kenyon College in Ohio, Will Child became "one of the pioneers in the steel industry in Hamilton" ("Active Mind")[1] after he relocated to the city in 1883. In response to Prime Minister John A. Macdonald's National Policy tariff of 1879, which drove up prices for American-made machinery selling in Canada, "Hamilton industrialists [approached] the American steel companies with an offer to establish a branch plant in Hamilton" (Rosenfeld 48). As he remembered in a long retrospective published in the Hamilton *Spectator* ("Iron Trade"), Will Child was one of a group of American entrepreneurs who leased the shop of the Great Western Railway and founded the Ontario Rolling Mill Company. That company eventually merged with the Hamilton Steel and Iron Company, among others, to form the Steel Company of Canada. Members of the group came from Youngstown, Cleveland, and from Child's own hometown of Painesville, and they included Richard Brown, C.E. Doolittle, and H.H. Champ (see M. Campbell 140), as well as P.M. Hitchcock and Charles Seward Wilcox, who were related to the Childs by family. After Beulah Knox's marriage to Thomas F. McIlwraith, another business link strengthened by family ties emerged: the firm of Goldie & McCulloch, co-owned by Andrew McIlwraith's father-in-law John, had built "an enormous vertical single-cylinder engine" for the Great Western shop that lasted until 1925, when it was replaced by "an electric motor." Despite these local connections, the industry was oriented towards the United States and Europe. "Skilled labour" was imported from Ohio, while "common labour" was supplied by immigrants from Ireland, Germany, and the Baltic countries (Child, "Iron Trade").

As one of the city's most prominent and public-minded citizens, Will Child had many interests outside the steel plant. He immersed himself in the natural sciences and, like many Victorians, he was particularly interested in the study of ferns. He made a name for himself as a mostly self-taught but erudite and widely travelled anthropologist and photographer, and his work was respected enough to earn him election to the Royal Anthropological Institute of Great Britain and Ireland (RAI). In 1910, he told an audience that he had covered around seventy thousand miles in his travels, visiting every continent except Australia (Child, "Notes," 1911, 50). On their European tour, the Childs

---

1 For additional biographical information on the Childs, using the Philip Child Fonds, HPL, see Calhoun, Introduction.

and their niece benefited from friendships he had made on previous trips, and they were taken around Granada by one such acquaintance, the Comandante Agustín Mateo y Fernández, who "knows all the places and stories and everything worth seeing or doing about the whole city" and also introduced them to "some of the really high up natives" (TFMP, Beulah to Agnes Knox, 7 May 1914). Presumably because Will Child did not consider them interesting to either Beulah or his sister, full accounts of his wide-ranging scholarly connections throughout Europe are missing from his niece's and his own letters, but he does allude to such contacts in a talk to the Hamilton Association for the Advancement of Literature, Science, and Art, also referred to as the Scientific Association or the Scientifics, after his return from Europe (Child, "Notes," 1914, 15). While in Dresden, he may have called on the association's honorary member, Professor Ernst Haeckel at the University of Jena, who a few decades earlier had collaborated with Nikolai Miklouho-Maclay. The Scientific Association repeatedly called on Child to share his many interests by speaking about subjects ranging from German literature to ethnology, and in 1911 he gave a presentation about his travels in India to mark the beginning of his term as the association's president. Child's large house on Hamilton's Hess Street, described in his son's poem *The Victorian House* (1951), was renowned for its splendid gardens, and its owner was determined that, despite industrial developments, the whole city should look its best. In his obituary, he was remembered for insisting that trees be planted to cover "the barren spots on the mountain side" ("Active Mind"). In 1913, Will Child had recently retired, and the family was grieving the sudden loss of nineteen-year-old Helen Mary, who had suffered from epilepsy since early childhood. Beulah was invited to come along on their trip to Europe to take her cousin's place.

Beulah's father was the Glasgow-born architect William Knox ("Wilm" or "Tougal" to his family). He, too, crossed borders readily. On an 1886 visit to Chicago, he decided to stay there and took up work in the offices of Burnham & Root, subsequently forming a partnership with John Eliot, with whom he set up practice in 1888 in Toronto. They were joined a year later by architect Beaumont Jarvis. As the firm of Knox, Eliot and Jarvis, they won the competition for the Confederation Life Association of Canada head office, not only because of their professional excellence but also because the team's "acceptably Canadian" credentials gave them an advantage at a time when the American competition for public buildings was perceived as overpowering Canadian talent (Osbaldeston 98). Commissions for other important public buildings, such as the West Toronto Junction Presbyterian Church and the Victoria-Royce Presbyterian Church, followed, but Knox and Eliot returned to Chicago to work with Henry Ives Cobb on the Columbian Exhibition, and they resumed their partnership in the United States shortly after Knox moved to Cleveland. Just before before his return to Chicago, he married Agnes ("Aggie") Julia Child from Wisconsin.

Their son Carlos was born in 1892, followed by daughters Beulah in 1895 and Neilson in 1898. A watercolourist in his spare time, Knox filled his home with etchings from the works of famous artists, and Beulah used her knowledge of these reproductions as an aesthetic guide when she visited European galleries. Interested in the natural sciences like his brother-in-law, Knox was knowledgeable on the subject of mushrooms and owned "the finest collection of seaweed in the country" ("Knox, William").

Laurel School, Finishing Schools in Dresden, and the "Music-Loving Anglo-Saxon Tribe"

Beulah had so recently graduated from Laurel School at Shaker Heights in Ohio that she was keen to see the graduation photograph that appeared in the local paper even as she was crossing the Atlantic. The trip was intended as a crowning conclusion to her years at Laurel, well respected for its credentials in the education of women. Like the Wesleyan Ladies' College attended by Jean, Mary, and Helen McIlwraith, the Shaker Heights school had high scholastic standards and prepared students for "entrance examinations at Bryn Mawr and Radcliffe," as well as "giv[ing] certificates of entrance to Vassar, Smith, Wellesley, and the College for Women of Western Reserve University" (*Laurel School* 5). The school emphasized the building of character and insisted that, along with "culture, accuracy, and the power to work cheerfully and continuously, without nervous tension," this goal ranked higher than "exclusive attention to ... the text-book" (5). Physical health and vigorous exercise to maintain it were emphasized, as were frugality and self-discipline. Parents were advised that "girls ... should be provided with warm, plain and practical clothing," and that "dinner dresses" should be "simple" and "evening dress ... inexpensive." At US$175 per year for the "Academic Department," not counting extras, fees were substantial.

They were, however, not as steep as the £100 per annum or £12 per month, not counting extras, charged by the *Pensionat* in Dresden where Beulah studied German, French, and Spanish from September to December of 1913. Fees at a second school in Lausanne in the spring of 1914 did not include boarding but were probably not far behind. Like Laurel School, the *Pensionat* in Dresden insisted that it was located "in the best and healthiest part of the town" and underlined the importance of physical exercise, but unlike Laurel, its prospectus suggests an environment of opulence: the grounds included "a large garden with lawn-tennis-court" and "every comfort [was] provided" that would "give the pupils the feeling of a refined home." The school offered "a thorough education in all the branches of knowledge and art by first rate teachers" but did not provide a full academic curriculum or formal graduation certificate. Instead, courses emphasized subjects considered essential for social polish, such as languages, painting and drawing, singing, dancing, and needlework,

PENSIONAT VON GRUBER

DRESDEN-A., Eisenstuckstrasse 45

The Misses P. and R. von Gruber, North German ladies, receive only a limited number of pupils, who wish to finish their education. They enjoy all the comfort and care of home-life as well as a thorough education in all the branches of knowledge and art by first rate teachers. The parents are at liberty to choose which of the lessons their daughters are to attend.

Pupils also may enter who intend studying only one or the other special branch.

Particular advantages are offered for acquiring a thorough knowledge of German and French within the shortest possible time.

Prospectus, Töchter-Pensionat von Gruber, Dresden, 1913. TFMP.

with occasional lectures on special subjects such as religion.[2] There were visits to galleries and the opera, and physical exercise included "gymnastics," "long walks every day," and "skating in winter." Students recovered from these exertions with naps and scheduled periods of rest. Students' outings "in a crocodile" were strictly chaperoned but as "the oldest in school," Beulah was allowed "much more freedom than most I am allowed to go out any time I want to alone" (TFMP, Beulah to Agnes Knox, 14 November 1913, 23 October 1913). She normally used this privilege to visit her aunt and uncle at their pensione. The school's prospectus describes a sophisticated setting, with idiom slipping briefly when parents are assured that "the domestic arrangements are liberal," meaning that pupils had access to every imaginable convenience. Bedrooms were decorated in feminine pink, kept cozy by porcelain stoves, and lit by oil lamps. "[Beulah's] heart's desires were satisfied when she found a school that had the bedrooms papered in prints to match her kimono," Will Child quipped in a note to Carlos and Neilson (TFMP, 9 October 1913). Compared to the "warm, plain and practical" clothing recommended at Laurel, attire was as elegant as pocketbooks allowed, and a brief crisis ensued just before the Christmas holidays when the directors declared that no student was allowed to leave for her holidays until the seamstress had completed the necessary repairs to everyone's clothing.

Finding an appropriate set-up for Philip was more challenging. In general, the facilities for boys were wanting in elegance compared to their female counterparts. There were only a dozen boys' schools to choose from, and on inspection a dispirited Will Child found them "so mean & dirty & miserable." The overall impression was "simply dreadful," reason enough to modify the plan, settle Philip into language lessons with a private teacher, Harry Virgin on Reichenbachstrasse, and board him with fifteen German-speaking boys in a pensione (who then taught him to speak the language with a Saxon inflection). This establishment also offered tennis facilities – an amenity all-important to Philip's sense of well-being (TFMP, Will Child to Agnes Knox, 8 October 1913). Under the guidance of his uncle William Harvey in Hamilton, he had developed an interest in tennis, football, and other athletics that contrasted with the Childs' studious habits, and in his letters to T.F. McIlwraith after the war, he is preoccupied with joining the varsity team at the University of Toronto.

Despite the naps, the program at the *Pensionat* sounds busy enough but, compared to the rigorous schedule at Laurel School, "the general run of things [was] very casual" (TFMP, Beulah to Wilm Knox, 8 October 1913), such that Beulah briefly feared she would "mildew" waiting for the action to accelerate (TFMP, Beulah to Carlos Knox, 16 October 1913). She and her uncle concluded that,

---

2 TFMP, "Prospectus," Pensionat von Gruber, Dresden, Eisenstuckstrasse 45, n.p.

compared to the teaching she was used to, the academic expectations were "simply a joke" (TFMP, Will Child to Agnes Knox, 8 October 1913), but the travellers did not allow themselves to succumb to sloth. Learning languages was a serious project, and even before Beulah and Philip were set up, respectively, at the *Pensionat* and with Mr. Virgin, Will Child organized private instruction for himself, his son, and his niece almost immediately upon arrival. A language school in Lausanne followed from January to March 1914, described approvingly by Beulah as "a day school run by the government especially for foreigners," after Will Child had rejected another institution that – in allusion to Hathaway Brown College in Shaker Heights, Ohio – looked too "toney Hathawaybrownish" (TFMP, Beulah to Wilm Knox, 22 January 1914). English was off-limits for conversation when the Childs met with "the children" outside of their lessons, and as proof of her progress, Beulah addressed her folks at home as "Liebe Herrschaften von Cleveland" (TFMP, Beulah to family, 1 October 1913).

To ensure that Beulah did not feel overwhelmed or homesick, aunt and uncle showered her with attention, including a large bouquet of roses delivered on her first day at school in Dresden, regular presents of fine candy by the box-full, visits to the *Konditorei* where Uncle Will invariably left some of his cake on his plate for Beulah to finish in addition to her own, and lavish gifts for Christmas and birthday. There were a "perfectly ducky ... little silver box enameled in blue" from Aunt Nellie and opera glasses "with a handle in a pinky mother of pearl in a red velvet bag" from Uncle Will in her stocking (TFMP, Beulah to Agnes Knox, 25 and 26 December 1913), and she received a chiffon and lace dress, also in blue, for her birthday. Uncle and niece had races up the hotel stairs (as a result of which Beulah ran into a wall and acquired a colourful bump on her forehead), and they enjoyed leisurely conversations. One of these covered everything from her current reading, "the quantity of ribbon used on diplomas," and "the history of England and waterclocks," but "was chiefly on anthropology." Beulah happily concluded: "If Uncle Will enjoys talking with me as much as I with him he must have a most frightfully good time" (TFMP, Beulah to Agnes Knox, 14 November 1913).

While Philip and Beulah were pursuing their courses in languages, music, and art, the Childs stayed in a nearby elegant pensione on Lukasstrasse. All members of the party reunited on the weekends for excursions into Saxon Switzerland, visits to a coffee house, cinema, or other local diversions. Styled "Florence on the Elbe," Dresden – whose population had shot up from fifty thousand in 1805 to half a million a century later – was a favourite location for finishing schools because few cities in Europe matched its outstanding architecture, art collections, and music, the study of which was a significant part of the program. Although he was not easy to impress, Uncle Will agreed, calling it "one of the most splendid cities in the world" and admitting to Agnes that although he had "seen acres of Raphaels without caring for many of them," the Sistine Madonna

Beulah Gillet Knox in Dresden, 1913. TFMP.

was "beyond words" (TFMP, Will Child to Agnes Knox, 8 October 1913). In 1913, Dresden listed more than sixty girls' *Pensionate* and close to fifteen hundred students studying in them. This was almost double the number recorded only seven years earlier. Even some twenty years earlier, the census for Saxony noted the disproportionately high number of women among the large groups of visitors from the United Kingdom and the United States, nationalities that were eclipsed only by the Austrians and Russians. The census explained this phenomenon as linked to the popularity of the girls' finishing schools with "the music-loving Anglo-Saxon tribe" (Böhmert 223; my translation). Indeed, several schools were run by English-speaking staff in order to respond specifically to the needs of this clientele, and Philip Child's studies – though conducted in German – were directed by a teacher from Britain. The Childs' "very swell and dressy" pensione was frequented almost exclusively by Americans, and Will Child despaired that his own German was therefore not getting the workout for which he had hoped. Ever attentive to its well-paying clientele, the management laid on a sumptuous dinner dance for Thanksgiving: "out of about 40 half were from New York and the other half from California + Oregon," Beulah reported; "Uncle Will and I were the only middle state representatives there." In this gathering of "good old Americans," the Canadian-born Aunt Nellie and a French count were the only "foreigners." The table was decorated with "place cards with turkeys standing on them" and "with festoons of little flags and had baskets made of pumpkins hollowed out and filled with fruit + nuts at intervals down the long table," and the menu featured "grape fruit ...; turkey broth; sweet bread + mushroom paté; roast turkey with cranberry mashed potatoes and succotash; tomato salad (which I ate !!!!); ice cream; candies nuts + fruit" (TFMP, Beulah to Agnes Knox, 30 November 1913). An orchestra played American tunes, with tango dancing by the New Yorkers and Californians to follow.

Töchter-Pensionat von Gruber

In 1891, when the census cited above was taken, Charlotte von Gruber presented herself at Dresden's trade licensing office to have her school registered in compliance with the local health insurance act.[3] Her establishment had existed in Dresden since 1875, when Charlotte and her sister Hedwig were first listed as directors. Charlotte – who advertised herself as having lived in Britain and France for seven years – had previously run a similarly tony school in Wiesbaden-Biebrich on the Rhine.[4] The von Grubers operated their *Pensionat*

---

3 See "von Gruber, Charlotte," Aktenheft, Rath zu Dresden, Gewerbeamt A, 1891, Lit. G, No. 523, Rep. VII, Stadtarchiv Dresden.
4 Advertisement, *Schwäbischer Merkur*, 20 April 1872, 1547.

in Dresden at several subsequent locations before 1900, when they settled into a new building on Eisenstuckstrasse 45 for the next seventeen years.[5] The street, in Dresden's Südvorstadt, was part of a well-heeled neighbourhood of nineteenth-century mansions, a surprising number of which have survived the destructions of the Second World War. These were inhabited by company and museum presidents, architects, physicians, lawyers, high-ranking military officers, artists, and opera singers, along with a troupe of gardeners, window cleaners, carpenters, cobblers, caretakers, barbers, and milliners to look after their needs. Although they continued to teach some classes and take meals at the school, Charlotte and Hedwig ("Tante Hede") had by 1896 retired from their posts as directors, moved to private lodgings, and passed the reins to their younger sister Pauline (variously nicknamed "Tatie," "Tattie," or "Tantie" by the students) and their niece "Richie" (derived from "Mariechen," the diminutive of her first name, "Marie") (Klaus D. Kromayer, letter to Eva-Marie Kröller, 27 August 2013). The von Grubers' emphasis on "aesthetic education," including mandatory weekly visits to the opera, was clearly a success with their clients and attracted students from prominent families across Europe, Russia, and North America.

Beulah explains somewhat flippantly that the school "is run by 2 aunts + 2 sisters who are nieces of the aunts" (TFMP, Beulah to Agnes Knox, 12 October 1913), and the Irish students disrespectfully referred to them as "the Grubs," but the directors came from an impressive family of teachers, scholars, and scientists with generations of experience in the higher education of girls. The von Grubers originated in Hungary before settling in Stralsund, a Hanseatic city in Northern Germany, where Charlotte and Hedwig's father Johannes was a prominent pedagogue and democrat acknowledged by the University of Greifswald with an honorary doctorate (see Weiske).[6] His daughters were well educated and productive: Charlotte translated Lady Augusta Noel's children's book *Effie's Friends, or, Chronicles of the Woods and Shore* (1864) and other English children's authors, and she published juvenile stories of her own, while Hedwig produced a phrase book for students and tourists, *600 Idiomatic German and English Phrases*.[7] Another daughter, Franziska, collaborated as translator with the composer and pianist Marie Jaëll and the theologian Jules Breitenstein. Unfortunately, their father did not provide for his daughters, leaving them so

---

5   For demographic and other information about Dresden throughout this chapter, see *Historische Addressbücher Sachsen.*

6   This obituary is interesting not only for the biographical information on von Gruber, but also for its criticism of the City of Stralsund for failing to support his widow and children financially except for covering their removal costs. The obituary was held back from publication for a year.

7   Advertisement, *Collier's New Practical Guide to Dresden* 88.

destitute on his death in 1875 that they turned to Stralsund's city council for assistance. In the same year, Charlotte and Hedwig opened their school in Dresden, and making a success of their establishment was an economic necessity. When Beulah arrived on Eisenstuckstrasse, both generations of the von Gruber women were getting on in years but a third was in the ascendancy. Their niece Ulla acted as a mediator between the older ladies and their students because she was young, lively, and studied singing, an important qualification with these girls, many of whom were obsessed with opera. As a result, Beulah – despite some initial grumbling – confessed after she had moved on to the less congenial school in Lausanne that the Grubers' establishment in Dresden had been a wise choice and that she wished she were going back there.

Part of the success of the *Pensionat* was the management's skilful handling of discipline. Some of the problems were part of a vicious cycle caused by the lack of sufficient intellectual and physical challenge that was endemic to the education of upper-class women, but that the von Grubers were in no position to correct too drastically without disappointing their customers' expectations and so endangering their own livelihood. Some students were on principle mutinous about regulations, mild as they were, and suspected the staff of being harder on some girls, and some nationalities, than others. The directors allowed the girls one treat, but not two, and if they wanted to attend the opera, they could not also enjoy the carnival. For a different reason – namely, to avoid overtaxing the girls' nervous capacity – students had to choose between church and opera on Sundays. Because opera was, as Beulah observed, "a form of religion" in Germany, certainly in Dresden, it was invariably preferred over church (TFMP, Beulah to Agnes Knox, 12 October 1913). At times, the girls expressed their rebellion at little or nothing by childish means such as arriving late for breakfast "just to see what would happen" (TFMP, Beulah to Wilm Knox, 15 and 16 November 1913), taking more than the allotted number of rolls, sucking on rinds of pineapple in the street, or sliding "down stairs head first à la alligator fashion" (TFMP, Beulah to Agnes Knox, 23 November 1913 – her second letter that day.).

Sometimes the students let off steam by feuding among each other over trivia, such as when to put curling papers in their hair, whether to scrub off all of their theatre paint after a fancy-dress party or leave some of it on, or whether it was healthier to open the window at night than closing it. Quarrels easily became a matter of nationalities ganging up on each other. Beulah gleefully reported that "[a]ll the Germans hate us English speakers and we cordially reciprocate the feeling so our bunch consists of 4 Irish, 1 Austrian, 1 Swede, 1 Dane, 1 Norwegian and myself we all get along beautifully and all are fresh air fiends much more so than we would be ordinarily just to tease the Germans." In turn, she was informed, "[A]ll English people are fools," by her room-mates who had already endured a similar clash with a few Irish students, and there was sullen silence until the directors wisely moved Beulah to join "some Norwegians," where she expected to "be blown away by the air" (TFMP, Beulah to Carlos Knox, 16 October 1913). She was finally happy in a room where "almost all the important nations are represented French, German, Norwegian + American" (TFMP, Beulah to Wilm Knox, 22 October 1913), all of them fond of fresh air, including the sole German student (TFMP, Beulah to Carlos Knox, 16 October 1913). In this new room, the girls' multilingualism paid off and "we all get along very well because we all understand three languages" (TFMP, Beulah to Wilm Knox, 22 October 1913). They also shared a sentimental bond. As Christmas approached, some of them organized "a midnight carousel," consisting of "one lighted candle ... five girls laid around it so that each head lapped over on to the next one's hip two hampers of cakes and other deadly concoctions, several bunches of pine tree branches. They burnt the needles in the flame of the candle so that the room smelled simply lovely and guzzled sweets to the tune 'Oh Tannenbaum' 'Oh du heilige'[8] etc until late in the night" (TFMP, Beulah to Agnes Knox, 30 November 1913). Luckily, they did not burn the place down.

No matter how much they were at war with each other, the girls presented a united front against outsiders.'Any man unfortunate enough to enter the *Pensionat* barely made it out alive. One dismayed pianist was confronted with the question, allegedly taken from a popular piece of music, "Du liebst mich! Weisst du [das]?" ("You love me! Do you know?"; my translation)[9] (TFMP, Beulah to Wilm Knox, 18 or 19 November 1913). The eccentric appearance of a "polished and grand" instructor of religious studies had Beulah and an Irish friend "turn ... blue with suppressed laughter" as they sat "nudging each other the whole hour" (TFMP, Beulah to Carlos Knox, 16 October 1913), and the "fruit man" who came on Saturdays was "immediately fallen upon by an ambuscade and stripped of his [fruit, candies and cakes]" (TFMP, Beulah to Neilson Knox, 18 October 1913).

The hothouse ambiance of girls' boarding schools has intrigued novelists and playwrights for a variety of reasons. One nineteenth-century approach was to look at these establishments as social laboratories where wayward upper-class femininity was directed into socially acceptable channels of behaviour.[10] This is what happens in Emmy von Rhoden's juvenile novel *Der Trotzkopf* (1885), based on the experiences of von Rhoden's daughter Else at a school in Eisenach.[11] The book appeared in numerous translations, including *Taming a Tomboy* and *An Obstinate Maid*, both published in the United States in 1898

---

8   Beulah presumably refers to the carol "Oh du fröhliche, oh du selige, gnadenbringende Weihnachtszeit."

9   Perhaps Beulah confuses the verbs *kennen* and *wissen* and the piano player is being asked whether he knows a song entitled "Du liebst mich!"

10 For the role of *Pensionats* in female education, see Hardach-Pinke.

11 See Johann on German-language literary works using boarding schools as a setting.

(Brunken et al. 529), and it may have been doubly attractive to the von Gruber students because the author was a local celebrity: von Rhoden spent the last few years of her life in Dresden, died there the year her book was published, and was buried in Neuer Annenfriedhof, located not far from Eisenstuckstrasse. Despite its dated understanding of professional ambition in women, this story remains much loved by German readers, as well as acquiring a following in French and Spanish. Ironically, the book's chief attraction may lie in its main character being too headstrong to be completely subdued by a pedagogical regime, no matter how strict. As Dagny Dahll, a fellow student from Norway, reminded Beulah after they had both left the school, the girls all devoured the book and appear to have used its title as a nickname for each other because they were in sympathy with Ilse Macket, its rebellious heroine. The directors would certainly have been appalled to have their establishment referred to by the colloquial "Penne,"[12] as Dagny does. "[A]n awful little beast" who never wanted to "do a thing that anyone else wants to" (TFMP, Doris Blackwood to Beulah Knox, 23 December 1913), Dagny was relieved when she was back in Norway, where she read Jack London in the woods and went snowshoeing in the winter. Compared to this freedom the *Pensionat* in Dresden was a prison, and she was sure that as an American Beulah knew all about freedom too (TFMP, Dagny Dahll to Beulah, 12 February 1917). When two students cut their fingers to ribbons to avoid practising the piano, they may have been inspired by a troubling scene in *Der Trotzkopf*: in von Rhoden's novel, Ilse's best friend Nelly etches the name of a favourite teacher, later her husband, with a penknife into her arm. Even for this incident, the von Grubers' punishment was light: "they will have to say a poem and miss the next opera" (TFMP, Beulah to Agnes Knox, 18 October 1913).

Der Trotzkopf's cast of German, Austrian, English, French, and Russian characters vividly mirrors the Dresden school's international ambiance, with its impromptu coalitions and easy-to-flare hostilities. As such, the school was a microcosm of contemporary diplomacy, an analogy developed in Gwethalyn Graham's pre–Second World War novel *Swiss Sonata* (1938), where the Canadian Vicky Morrison acts as a neutral mediator among her feuding companions in a Swiss girls' boarding school. To keep the peace, the von Grubers used a method more elementary than mere talk: one of their chief weapons was good food. The girls' social privilege and the cost of their fees guaranteed that their meals did not become a form of chastisement, as they often did in institutions for less fortunate children. The girls themselves habitually used candy – especially chocolate – as a barter item for getting along or not. The factions warring over whether or not the windows should stay open underlined the seriousness of

---

12   Slang, derived from "Pennal" (high school).

their position by refusing to share chocolate with each other. One eternally hungry waif did not comprehend these complications and late at night came around to each room begging for chocolate to tide her over until breakfast, but because she did not observe the rules – whatever they were – she was sent away.

Beulah quickly acknowledged that "the eats" at von Gruber were "awfully good" (TFMP, Beulah to Carlos Knox, 16 October 1913). Always ready for a good meal, partly because she enjoyed it and partly because it may have allowed her to deal with various anxieties, she was suspicious of unfamiliar cuisine. The menu at the *Pensionat* thankfully did not include the outrage of "venison [that] tasted like a queer cow" (TFMP, Beulah to family, 21 September 1913), "a slab of raw ham on a bun" (TFMP, Beulah to family, 15 September 1913), or "raw herring for supper" (TFMP, Beulah to Carlos Knox, 30 December 1913) that she had encountered at various restaurants and hotels. But when meals like "sauerkraut + queer looking sausages" (TFMP, Beulah to Carlos Knox, 16 October 1913) appeared on the table, the cook was quick to accommodate Beulah with an egg dish especially prepared for her. When all else failed, one of the Fräuleins fed her cashew nuts and cocoa, or Beulah nibbled on a bar of chocolate. Normally, however, the school's caramel and walnut cakes, jam-filled doughnuts, and servings of up to fourteen different kinds of sandwiches displaced her earlier longing for her mother's crispy-skinned "leg of lamb and a dozen muffins" (TFMP, Beulah to family, 21 September 1913). A month into her stay in Europe, a "weighing machine" informed her that she had gained weight (TFMP, Beulah to Agnes Knox, 27 October 1913), and Uncle Will thought her face looked chubby. Food packages from the girls' families, including the Childs, were so plentiful that directors had to plead for a halt when an epidemic of stomach aches and general listlessness spread through the school. This episode did not stop Beulah from having a go a few days later at the "Chrystoline" (her idiosyncratic spelling of "Christstollen") that showed up among the breakfast offerings in a Berlin pensione on Christmas Day, and she and Philip treated themselves to slices of this rich seasonal fruitcake first thing in the morning (TFMP, Beulah to Agnes Knox, 25 and 26 December 1913).

Dance, Opera, Popular Entertainment, and Reading

To work off some of the students' surplus energy, the von Grubers organized dances and fancy-dress parties. One fellow student performed a solo in bare feet, wearing "nothing but a little voile dress that came to her knees" and doing "all kinds of little hops + runs + walks" (TFMP, Beulah to Agnes Knox, 18 October 1913). The student was "a pupil of Isadora Duncan," and her performance was a reminder that Dresden was an important centre of innovative dance, featuring such influential dancers and choreographers as Mary Wigman, Gret Palucca, and Heinrich Kröller (see Toepfer; *Sprache des Körpers*). Beulah watched with interest, but she preferred a different type of dance. For a Halloween party, organized by the English-speaking girls for their fellow students, she and her group dressed up as "Apaches" inspired by the demi-monde scenes in Bizet's *Carmen*, an opera they had just attended, and the girls got into its spirit as much as their resources and the *Pensionat*'s directors allowed. Beulah's own costume, as she breathlessly reported to her mother, "consisted of a skirt very tulle and ballet dancerish one of my slips with nightgown sleeves in it. They were both short but one I looped up so that my arm was absolutely bare to the shoulder around my waist I had my red sash ... and in the right side of my hair the bunch of red roses off my red dress ... I had a big brass ring fastened with invisible wire in each ear and my cheeks rouged nice and pink. I wore my red slippers + stockings of course." She regrets that the overall effect was "gypsyish" rather than "tough ... looking," but she assures Agnes Knox that "[t]he three who went as men were great they looked tough all right alright." Beulah and her "tough" companions practised kangaroo dips and other contortions:

> And the dances we danced were the weirdest I danced most of the time with Irene who was a "man" and is very tall one of our dances consisted of an exaggerated one step with her arm around my neck then she would pick me up and carry me a ways and we would go on. Another one was a sort of "horse trot" arm in arm – we first bent nearly double backwards for about six steps and then the same thing bent way forward My but that was great and the most rolicking thing I ever had any thing to do with. (TFMP, Beulah to Agnes Knox, 1 November 1913)

Beulah taught the group the Virginia Reel, but modified it for a more energetic performance: "we did not stand still in between times but kept hopping up and down in time to the music all the time and instead of walking up dignifiedly to curtsey etc we ran all the time" (TFMP, Beulah to Agnes Knox, 1 November 1913).

The prize for best costume – a box of chocolate tied with a blue ribbon – went to a young woman who sounds as if she did not quite fit into this wild company. She was dressed up as Queen Luise of Prussia as she strides down the stairs in Gustav Richter's popular painting of 1879. Beulah and her fellow students clearly knew the image, distributed in dozens of reproductions for the hundredth anniversary of Luise's death in 1911, and they may even have seen the motion picture about the Queen's life released in 1913. The nationalist worship that had sprung up around Luise probably went over the heads of students from outside Germany,[13] but it would have been difficult to overlook the Queen's idealized

---

13 The scholarship on the cult of Queen Luise is extensive. For its significance to girls' education, see Askey.

femininity that fed into this cult. Beulah and her group were impressed, but their preference was for the student who won the second prize and was at least as energetic as the English-speaking "bunch," as they liked to refer to themselves: dressed up as "a cow boy" and trained by "eight brothers," this girl sported "a real pipe and every few minutes she would turn a hand spring and walk across the room on her hands" (TFMP, Beulah to Agnes Knox, 1 November 1913).

A similar element of unruliness underlies the girls' passion for the opera. The quality of Dresden's opera was such that it engendered "a strong disinclination ever again to take the trouble of sitting out a performance in any English, French, or American opera house," as Jerome K. Jerome observed in *Three Men on the Bummel* (1900), adding that an extended visit was required in order to appreciate the city's attractions: Dresden's "beautiful and historically rich environment ... provide[s] pleasure for a winter but bewilder[s] for a week" (240). In Dresden and on other stopovers, Beulah and the Childs attended performances of *La Bohème, Eugen Onegin, Carmen, Mignon, Aïda, Hoffmann's Tales, Hänsel und Gretel, The Huguenots, The Mikado,* and the operetta *Orpheus in the Underworld.* Above all, 1913 was the centenary of the birth of Richard Wagner,[14] whose name was associated with Dresden, where he had been director of music until his involvement in the 1848 revolution sent him into exile. The Childs and their niece saw performances of most of Wagner's works, several more than once: all four operas of the *Ring,* as well as *Parsifal, Die Meistersinger,* and *The Flying Dutchman.* They attended the five hundredth performance of *Tannhäuser* in the presence of Saxony's royal family. Beulah was, however, bewildered by her friends' complete devotion to the *Hofoper's* stars. Even normally clearheaded students succumbed to the allure of tenor Fritz Vogelstrom, as Beulah observed: "Last night I said 'Isn't that march great' ... [Irene Lambert] said 'Uhm ... hasn't Fritz (one of the favourites) got perfectly ripping legs?' they talk of nothing else and the air is just saturated with operatic gossip" (TFMP, Beulah to Agnes Knox, 23 November 1913). Some students appear to have sent amorous notes to their preferred singers: one student mentions a "[B]riefchen" for Waldemar Staegemann, but he "did'nt [sic] rise to occasion offered him most clearly" (TFMP, Eileen Plunket to Beulah, from Paris, n.d. [December 1913?]). (With this particular young woman, it is never clear whether she was aware of her double entendres or if they were the result of careless writing.) In the same letter, she instructs Beulah to "HISS Adolf [Löltgen] ... and clap my adored ones!" Uncle Will was even more baffled by this madness than his niece, wondering how a tenor "with a face like a potato & short pudgy legs" and a soprano "with an arm like the side of beef" (TFMP, Will Child to Agnes Knox, 6 December 1913) could inspire such worship.

Nevertheless, opera became a shared medium for the girls, and at a performance of *The Flying Dutchman,* the last she attended as a student at the *Pensionat,*

---

14   On the social and political role of opera in Central Europe 1815–1914, see Ther.

Beulah kept on clapping with her special friend Doris Blackwood until "they raised the curtain just for us and [the opera singers] came out and bowed to us" (TFMP, Beulah to Wilm Knox, 21 December 1913). In preference to Eileen Plunket, Doris was repeatedly invited by the Childs to join them at the opera, probably because she had the better manners. A letter from Doris when Beulah had moved on to Lausanne recites a roll call of opera singers in yet another performance of *Die Hugenotten*, with Fritz Vogelstrom (the one with the "perfectly ripping legs"), Grete Merrem, Helena Forti, and Margarete Siems. Doris furthermore reports that Eva von der Osten died "ever so much better" in *Carmen* than Irma Tervani did: "She rushed to the curtain at the back shrieking Escamilio [Escamillo] at the top of her voice & [Fritz] Soot stabbed her in the back. Then she tottered slowly backwards till she was quite near the front & then fell just as Escam[illo] arrived." "Wasn't it a rag," she annotated the whole episode, not without informing Beulah that Mrs. Soot, who was sitting nearby applauding her husband, was "a funny looking freak" (TFMP, Doris Blackwood to Beulah, 17 January 1914).

Opera, oratorios, and carol services did not stop the travellers from enjoying popular entertainment, including a performance by the belle époque cabaret singer Yvette Guilbert, known for her "racy, sarcastic manner" and "drawling, monotonous voice" (Gammond, "Guilbert, Yvette" 246). Beulah, who asked Carlos to tune her mandolin so that she could try some of the music she was bringing back to Painesville, hummed along with the latest *Schlager*, "Puppchen, du bist mein Augenstern." She heard the organ grinder play it for dancing children in The Hague, and it was a favourite with salon orchestras in Berlin.[15] Everyone was reminded of home when the ragtime tune "Oh You Beautiful Doll" was played in the streets of Berlin.[16] The tango had recently arrived in Dresden via Paris and London,[17] and the group were taken aback by a troupe of louche dancers, all the more objectionable because they were Americans and therefore a personal embarrassment to Beulah and her uncle: "One girl had a skin tight grey satin slit to the knee and a thing more like a rose coloured corset than anything else over the skirt and a little scrap of lace for a waist – she was a beaut" (TFMP, Beulah to Wilm Knox, 10 December 1913).[18] The Childs and Beulah

---

15 "Puppchen" was composed by Max Winterfeld (who later changed his name to Jean Gilbert) in 1912. On Jean Gilbert, see Gammond, "Gilbert, Jean" 223–4; see also Zenck et al.

16 "Doll" was composed in 1911 by Nat D. Ayer, with lyrics by Seymour Brown. See Gammond, "Ayer, Nat D." 28.

17 See Gammond, "Tango" 564–5; also see, Lange, "Argentine Tango."

18 The number of touring Americans in Europe at the time is remarkable. One of them was the Lakota Sioux Edward Two Two, who was hired as a participant in the ethnographic show of Hagenbeck's Zoo in 1910. He returned to Germany in 1911 to work for Dresden's Sarasani Circus, followed by a second contract with Sarasani in 1914. He died in Dresden, and the announcement of his death appeared on the day the First World War was declared. At his own request, Edward Two Two was buried in Dresden. See Locke.

enthusiastically plunged into the latest crazes, such as auto shows, the cinema, tango teas, and an automat restaurant established on Dresden's Prager Strasse in 1910, two years before automats made their first appearance in New York (see Roberts). They were a welcome novelty to an ever-hungry Beulah and her fellow students: "We went to church but it was somewhat boring so just before the sermon we all solemnly filed out we then made for the 'Automat.' " There, Beulah selected ham sandwiches and cake from the slots although everybody had eaten a substantial breakfast only an hour earlier (TFMP, Beulah to Agnes Knox, 18 October 1913). Wherever they went, Beulah and Philip "[made] tracks for" the zoo "if there [was] one" (TFMP, Beulah to family, 10 September 1913). They liked the circus and, in Tangier, watched a magician who had toured North America for years with Barnum and Bailey's Circus.

A similar mixture of the highbrow and the popular characterizes the rich web of literary references that Beulah, like Jean McIlwraith, used to make her experiences as vivid as possible to her folks at home. Besides knowing her Robert Browning, Walter Scott, Arthur Conan Doyle, and Rider Haggard inside out – and she complained bitterly when one hotel failed to provide a generous selection of books or at least a few recent copies of the *Saturday Evening Post* and *Leslie's* – she was steeped in the German classics and history, even if her language skills were not always up to the task of reading them in the original. She endured Gotthold Ephraim Lessing's *Minna von Barnhelm* (a play her uncle had wanted to see ever since he had read it in college), but nodded off twice. She visited Weimar because of its association with Goethe and Schiller, climbed the Brocken mountain "where one of the scenes in Faust is laid" (TFMP, Beulah to family, 21 September 1913), and explored Barbarossa's cave and the Wartburg. As the Rhine steamer passed the Lorelei cliff – a disappointing sight to most North American tourists – she recited Heinrich Heine's Romantic poem "Die Lorelei." She repeated the performance at her school in Dresden, where it was pointed out to her that she had learned the words phonetically and that her recital did not make as much sense as she had hoped.

Elsewhere, she reached into familiar children's and magazine stories and into satire to anchor her impressions. When a fabulous production of *Rheingold* had the "Rheindaughters [swimming] under the Rhein" and "you could see the river flowing on above," she was reminded of a scene in *Peter Pan* that had Peter and the children fly around the stage suspended from similar contraptions (TFMP, Beulah to family, 3 October 1913). The fairy-tale atmosphere of the Thuringia woods recalled George MacDonald's children's book *The Princess and Curdie* (1883), while an elderly German teacher looked like Lapidowitz the Schnorrer, a character from Bruno Lessing's Jewish American stories.[19] Mark Twain's travel

---

19   The stories, first published in *Cosmopolitan* and other popular magazines, were collected in *With the Best Intention* (1914). Bruno Lessing was the pseudonym of Rudolph Edgar Block.

writing was a welcome relief when the imposing presence of European culture became crushing, and she viewed many of her travel impressions through the comical lens of *A Tramp Abroad* (1880) because it was "just chucked full of things we are noticing all along" (TFMP, Beulah to Agnes Knox, 6 October 1913). She cites Twain when, at a performance of *La Bohème*, the absence of a synopsis prevented her from appreciating "the true inwardness of it."[20] As well, Twain-inspired slang was her best friend when the sights became tedious and yet another castle "full of junk from the 16th century" (TFMP, Beulah to Agnes Knox, 12 October 1913) had to be visited, or when there was "simply enough [scenery] to burn" (TFMP, Beulah to Wilm Knox, 22 October 1913).

Sightseeing

Dresden exposed Beulah to the best in traditional and avant-garde culture, and her uncle spared no expense in making it available to her. The group's European tour began in the Netherlands in August 1913, and proceeded through Germany, Bohemia, Austria, Switzerland, France, Spain, and North Africa before ending in Gibraltar in late May of 1914, when they boarded the *Saxonia* for the passage home to New York. In rugged terrain, they rode horses, mules, and camels, but for the most part, the family travelled in comfort by train or by hired motor car (which Beulah often calls "the machine"), a mode of individualized tourism that had become increasingly popular by 1913 for those who could afford it.[21] Beulah regaled her family in Painesville with stories about the excellent view to be had while she was perched on a pile of luggage in the back seat, and the delights of driving open top in "a fine big brand new car ... painted pale yellow," but she also talked about the frequent bother of repairing punctured tires on rough country roads, especially if the driver was a fast-driving "scorcher" (TFMP, Beulah to Agnes Knox, 11 and 12 April 1914). Their program of sightseeing was so intense and her reports so detailed that Beulah's father found her letters sounded "like so many pages from Baedeker" (TFMP, Beulah to Wilm Knox, 22 October 1913), a comment that left her uncertain as to whether he was offering a compliment or a criticism.

As a seasoned tourist, Will Child steadied his companions by providing comparisons and contexts, along with strong opinions, for the more unusual places when Beulah's own familiarity with travels to Bermuda or other holiday locations in or near the United States was not enough to do so. The area around Avignon was "very like the land on the gulf of Corinth" (TFMP, Beulah to Neilson Knox, 8 April 1914), he suggested, while Burgos was "just like South America"

---

20 See Twain's comic description of a performance of Franz Kotzwara's "The Battle of Prague" (1788) in *A Tramp Abroad*.
21 On the rise of the motor car for tourist travel, see Mullen and Munson 200–3.

(TFMP, Beulah to Wilm Knox, 24 April 1914). Because he regularly perused the New York *Herald*, the London *Times*, the American weekly *Outlook*, and two Canadian newspapers to keep himself and his fellow travellers au courant, this particular comparison was possibly provoked by the Battle of Vera Cruz, of which he had just read in the paper. For her part, Aunt Nellie proposed that the Elbe Valley resembled the Grand Canyon and the Hudson Palisades, and Beulah ventured a comparison of the Dutch canals with Doan Brook in Ohio.

Because Will Child was keenly interested in botany and horticulture, Beulah observed the native flora on excursions into the countryside under his guidance even if she never did this with the vivid precision that characterizes the McIllwraiths' writing about nature. The travellers also encountered wild boars, and while in Bohemia she was convinced she saw wolves from the train, though Phil uncooperatively thought they were probably tree stumps. However, the Childs' trip placed an emphasis on culture rather than nature. Beulah and Philip dutifully visited cathedrals, palaces, monasteries, Roman ruins, art galleries, armouries, marine exhibitions, and collections of crown jewels. Despite Beulah's eager interest in novelty, she had strong opinions about anything too experimental. Her taste in art, whether traditional or contemporary, was – in keeping with what she had been taught at school and at home – conservative and rather prim.[22] She was encouraged in her views by Uncle Will, although he was happy to indulge, and supervise, her curiosity in anything new and even faintly scandalous. Through the expressionist group Die Brücke, Dresden was closely associated with important developments in modern art, but Beulah and the Childs were not impressed by these. With her uncle, she did visit an exhibition of the Italian Futurists that has become well known for its influence on Germany's avant-garde painters, but one suspects that she was chiefly interested because the *Pensionat* would not allow its pupils to go for fear that exposure to such work would spoil their taste. Alluding to her frequently cited dislike of Albrecht Dürer's unforgiving realism, she found the Futurist paintings "almost as bad as some of Dürer's!!" (TFMP, Beulah to Wilm Knox, 2 November 1913). In Madrid, both Beulah and Philip groaned at the thought of having to look at many paintings by Rubens who, she felt, "should be hung in a dark closet and shown only at midnight when the light is not working" (TFMP, Beulah to Agnes Knox, 27 April 1914). She and her folks much preferred the Romantic landscapes and historical paintings of Friedrich von Preller der Jüngere, and Aunt Nellie was so enthusiastic that she thought of having one of his paintings copied for her home in Hamilton.

From a particularly hectic stay in Berlin, she forwarded one of her characteristic running totals: "[N]o one can say we did not do our duty by Berlin in

---

22 She shared these conservative tastes with Jean McIlwraith's friend Elizabeth Smith, who toured Europe with her husband Adam Shortt two years earlier, in 1911. See Dembski.

18 days we went to: 10 museums or galleries; 5 theatres or operas; 2 concerts; 1 aquarium + 1 zoo; Potsdam; Charlottenburg; Christmas eve carol service; New Years parade; 1 grand shopping expedition and piles of little window gazing jaunts" (TFMP, Beulah to Wilm Knox, 3 and 7 January 1914). After visiting Roman ruins in the South of France, Beulah agreed that the tour was so educational that she "might read Caesar with pleasure now" (TFMP, Beulah to Agnes Knox, 11 and 12 April 1914), but their schedule was taxing enough that towards the end of their trip all four were "anxious to get home." Even Uncle Will, whose energetic sightseeing so exhausted everyone else at the beginning of their trip that he had to be restrained by his wife, now "frankly admits he is blasé." Sixteen-year-old Philip – in the habit of complaining about a great many things and worrying his father with his gloomy disposition – was "simply bored to death with life in general" (TFMP, Beulah to Carlos Knox, 10 May 1914). Some of his melancholia may have been the result of his sister's recent death, which is never discussed or even alluded to in any of these letters. Beulah became briefly exasperated enough by their gruelling program to find even Granada's nightingales annoying because they "keep me awake they are commoner than robins" (TFMP, Beulah to Wilm Knox, 12 May 1914). However, her zest never flagged for long.

On the last leg of their travels in North Africa, she listened to a storyteller recite the *Arabian Nights* in a bazaar and confessed that she would have loved to venture even further afield, to visit Fez and cross the desert by camel. A few years later at Lake Erie College, she turned this scene into a wild story of wartime espionage after she realized in retrospect just how close their party had come to being trapped in Europe by the outbreak of the First World War. In "An Arabian Night," she fancies that her fictional alter ego, a Western woman exploring a *souk* with a native guide, is "a strategic point" that allows the French to expose a German agent disguised as an Arab.[23] The latter's "tangled thatch of red-gold hair" gives pause, but the narrator remembers hearing about "red-haired Berbers, remnants of an old Neolithic race" – a learned detail probably passed on by Will Child. There is no doubt that the situation is a hostile cabal, however, when the allegedly blind minstrel in a hasheesh-perfumed Moroccan cafe throws back his hood "to show the helmet of a 'death's head hussar!'" She had seen members of the Leib-Husaren regiment with their distinctive death's head emblems in Berlin ("An Arabian Night" 9, 10).

Nationalities

Study of languages and cultural riches did not automatically do away with national stereotype. Germany stood for its classics in literature, music, and art,

---

23   *The Lake Erie Record*, May 1918, 8–11, Lincoln Library, Lake Erie College, Painesville, OH.

but it also stood for "fat + beery" people, and Beulah was disappointed that these did not immediately present themselves on arrival (TFMP, Beulah to family, 10 September 1913). Instead, she drew on Romantic and fairy-tale motifs to categorize her acquaintances. In Eisenach, they noticed a sign advertising the services of a teacher of German, and "immediately a head came out of a window and he raked us in like a spider gathering in flies" (TFMP, Beulah to family, 19 September 1913). The analogy comparing the language teacher with an insect continues as the elderly gentleman "hopped around like a flea on a hot griddle" while his pupils were squeezed behind "children's desks" and con-jugated "Ich bin, du bist, er ist" (TFMP, Beulah to family, 15 September 1913). Some of the German girls at the *Pensionat* also seemed to have emerged from a slightly sinister tale, resembling E.T.A. Hoffmann's mechanical doll Olimpia in *The Sandman*, when they "spieled off their [poems] like little machines." All the other nationalities, Beulah claimed, made a charming mess of theirs, though some of these performances sound suspiciously engineered. In full histrionic flight, one of the Irish students recited Thomas Campbell's "Lord Ullin's Daugh-ter," but "forgot more than half and skipped whole verses bodily she also took the book and read some of it the affect [sic] was anything but solemn" (TFMP, Beulah to Carlos, 16 October 1913).

In Lausanne, by contrast, Beulah slotted the French and French-speaking as wily and feminine when she described her teacher as "the cunningest kind of a little Mlle," nicknaming her "goo goo" because her name "is something like that and her eyes are decidedly [goo goo]." Unlike the spidery gentleman in Eisenach, this teacher stepped outside her alleged ethnic characteristics when she revealed herself as "great sport" and "a freshman at the university" and went shopping with Beulah (TFMP, Beulah to Carlos, 31 January and 1 February 1914). Mademoiselle's full name was Marguerite Guigou, and she and her for-mer student got on well enough to begin a brief correspondence in early 1915 in which Beulah responded in French to Guigou's English. A similar corre-spondence, this time in Spanish, ensued between Beulah and the Comandante Agustín Mateo y Fernández, one of Will Child's old European acquaintances. A model of Hispanic gallantry, the Comandante showered Beulah with com-pliments, assuring her that she was in "[his] thoughts as a honeydew" (TFMP, Agustín Mateo y Fernández to Beulah Knox, 17 February 1918). He asked for news from and a photo in uniform of "Felipe" once the latter had joined the army because Philip Child was himself slow to write (TFMP, Agustín Mateo y Fernández to Beulah Knox, 23 April 1917).

Throughout her travels, Beulah's store of ethnic stereotypes was alternately confirmed and challenged, but like most tourists she was also quick to create new ones when her encounters seemed to require them to reassure herself about her own identity. In an early letter from the *Pensionat*, she divided "American" and "foreign" girls into two distinct categories. Writing to her mother, she was apologetic about the classification, probably because she had been taught not to criticize others without cause, "but I am just chucked full of [impressions] and ... simply have to get them off my mind some way or I will burst." In any case, her categories broke down soon enough:

> Foreign girls are very different from Americans[;] here are a few of the points. A foreign girl is about four years younger than an American of the same age. They are not half so toplofty. They are the dowdiest dressed things you ever saw and the average 17 year old is not half as dignified as Neilson in her most abandoned moments. They also use more bad language (the English ones I mean now) than I heard in Laurel in my three years and they are absolutely without consideration + tact. That does not sound awfully complimentary and it is not but I like them all very much and have a splendid time. I think it is partly because I have so much nicer things than they and always feel well dressed whether I am playing tennis or going to the opera. (TFMP, Beulah to Agnes Knox, 9 November 1913)

Here, the English are subsumed under "foreign," even if the girl with "bad language" was probably Eileen Plunket, who was from Ireland. More frequently, however, the adjective "English" seems a type of linguistic joker that can be detached from nationality and reassigned as required, allowing Beulah on certain occasions to claim alliance with the Irish, English, Americans, Canadians, and – despite their "foreign" accent – even Australians, while still distancing herself from any one of these groups when necessary. Her judgment fluctuated with the conflicting standards of femininity she encountered and that, as far as it was socially acceptable, she cautiously tried out for herself. At times she found informality in a young woman scandalous and un-American, while on other occasions informality distinguished an emancipated American girl from her repressed English counterpart, although the latter was a view she was more likely to share with Neilson than with her mother. The length of her stay in Europe, the intensity of her interactions with some of the people she met, and the ability to observe nationalities in different contexts were important factors in this process. Thus, she observed disapprovingly that English girls smoked and crossed their legs while American ones did not (TFMP, Beulah to Agnes Knox, 6 October 1913). A few months later she concluded that English boys were "awfully formal in their speech and kind of prim" while American boys knew how to respond when a girl said "Hullo there" to them as she had done (TFMP, Beulah to Carlos, 31 March 1914). Oddly, Eileen Plunket, who defied as many rules of etiquette as possible, turned to Beulah with bewilderment when, during the war, an American soldier addressed her with "Honey, you're some dancing kid!" This, she thought, "seem[ed] rather an odd remark considering I'd never seen him before!!! Is it usual?" (TFMP, Eileen Plunket to Beulah, 11 July 1918).

As a way of maintaining her sense of identity in a sometimes confusing environment, Beulah turned to clothes and selected her outfits for each occasion with care. As fashionable dressers, Aunt Nellie and her niece paid frequent visits to the seamstress, and Beulah's letters are full of details about the latest designs and fabrics, such as the "duvetyne" from which her new suit was made. She knew her mother would be interested because in her youth Agnes had studied art in San Francisco, and Neilson was to follow in her footsteps by studying at the Cleveland School of Arts. Beulah's mother at times pressed her daughter to tell her more about her fellow students at the school, but her daughter usually complied for only a few lines before slipping back into an enthusiastic account of fashionable pleats and buttons. Beulah and her aunt did shy away from eccentric styles such as the belle époque "lampshade dress" first presented two years earlier by fashion designer Paul Poiret at his fancy-dress version of *A Thousand and One Nights*, and they recoiled from anything too risqué. High spirits in a woman were commendable, she thought, as long as her manners were impeccable. It was therefore more than a frivolous comparison when she underlined that English girls were "frouzy" while American girls were "dressy" (TFMP, Beulah to Agnes Knox, 7 and 8 February 1914), and it was obviously high praise for the Spanish queen and for American women in general when Beulah found Queen Ena "very pretty and stately" and concluded that she "looks American" (TFMP, Beulah to Agnes Knox, 27 April 1914). Appearance was, however, no guarantee for respect. Beulah was aghast when she realized that America and all it stood for did not have as firm a profile in other people's minds as in her own, and that it could even be confused with Canada or Mexico. One guest at the Hôtel Beau Séjour in Lausanne, where "America" tended to be equated with "South America," wanted to know if Americans spoke "Spanish, Portuguese or Indian," and if the country "was a British Colony." He may have been teasing her, but Beulah was furious, not at all convinced that she had corrected the error for good, and addressed the letter in which she describes this particular scene as going to the "United States of North America" (TFMP, Beulah to Carlos Knox, 9 February 1914). In an earlier outburst of patriotism, following a fancy-dress party at the von Grubers' school, she announced: "America certainly shone last night – if I do say it – I engineered the whole thing" (TFMP, Beulah to Agnes Knox, 1 October 1913).

Beulah obviously wanted nothing to do with misbehaving Americans like the sexy tango dancers in Dresden or the vulgar Cook's tourists the family encountered in Spain. Her sophisticated appearance, her growing linguistic skills, as well as her "southern" looks protected her from being mistaken for one of them. Sometimes this mimicry backfired when Beulah became "the observed" precisely because her appearance did not fit the stereotypical American. As mentioned above, she was informed by her roommates that "all English people are fools" (TFMP, Beulah to Carlos, 16 October 1913) and she was also told by a teacher that "like all Americans [she was] anxious to learn but very lazy" (TFMP, Beulah to Agnes Knox, 23 November 1913), but because of her naturally dark complexion, enhanced at the time by a sun tan, fellow travellers repeatedly took her to be Mediterranean or even Asian (TFMP, Beulah to Agnes Knox, 19 and 21 February 1914). Listening to the Childs and Beulah converse "in French, German, Spanish and Italian equally fluently besides English," one American tourist was overheard to say about them: "the man I should say was a Spaniard who ha[s] lived a great many years in England and that would account for the girl's looks but I don't see where the boy [i.e., the blonde Philip Child] comes in" (TFMP, Beulah to Agnes Knox, 27 April 1914).

Travel and Correspondence

Beulah's letters from her European tour built on the Laurel School's "[e]special attention ... to letter and note writing" as a useful element of education, pursued with similar intentions as Kennedy's bird book and the Family Album. Presumably to help students settle in, letter-writing at the Dresden *Pensionat* was permitted on two days of the week only, but this was a rule that Beulah for one flouted brazenly. Like Mr. McIlwraith, Agnes Knox monitored her daughter's expression, development of ideas, and handwriting, and she reprimanded her when Beulah claimed she had nothing to say (but wrote lots anyway) or when letters were barely legible because written in pencil on her knee or under the desk. Her mother did of course fret when Beulah injured her thumb, the one she used for writing, and so had a legitimate excuse for messy penmanship. Above all, letters were an ill-important way for this affectionate family to stay in touch, and the Childs' spoiled their niece not only to express their affection but also to make up for her parents' absence. When a serious crisis developed back home in Cleveland, Will Child's letters to his sister began to intertwine with his niece's correspondence.

Child immediately took charge of the situation when Wilm Knox's health – already frail on their departure from the United States – deteriorated, surgery became necessary, and Agnes Knox was torn in her anxiety between asking her brother to return with Beulah or allowing her daughter to enjoy her travels as planned. Child gently broke the news to his niece, and repeatedly sent large cheques of $200, $300, and $400 each to Agnes, underlining that "there [was] lots more where this came from" (TFMP, Will Child to Agnes Knox, 5 November 1913). He wrote encouraging messages to his brother-in-law, disentangled the logistics of sending overseas cables and telegrams for his sister, advised on resorts in Florida and Bermuda in which to recuperate, and all along also ensured that his wife and son were sufficiently settled in Europe for the eventuality that Child might have to return to the States with his niece. Despite ongoing worries, the group managed to complete the journey as planned. Not long after their return, however, in 1915, Wilm Knox died at fifty-seven. His wife followed a brief eight years later.[24]

Given his niece's copious letters, many of them ten and more pages long, Will Child worried at the beginning of their trip that any additional detail about sightseeing from him would be "superfluous or a bore," and he all but apologized to his sister for writing at all. Since wife and son were travelling with him, and he no longer had a daughter to send letters to, he felt lost because he had "no one to write to. I mean no one who especially wanted to hear all that I was doing & to write to me" (TFMP, Will Child to Agnes Knox, 20 October 1913). A few times, he penned a geography lesson about the Netherlands or Saxony for the benefit of Beulah's fifteen-year-old sister Neilson, and Beulah urged the "dearest infant" (TFMP, Beulah to Neilson Knox, 1 November 1913) to write to the Childs: "Say, it seems to me you haven't written to Aunt Nelly or Uncle Will for a long time – get busy" (TFMP, Beulah to Neilson Knox, 25 January 1914). Ironically, the crisis over Tougal's health resolved the dilemma of Will Child having nobody to write to because he now had plenty of reasons to do so, and he wrote frequently. His consoling and business-like letters to Agnes provide a steady bass note to Beulah's correspondence, normally cheerful and overflowing with news but frantic and incoherent when she was worried.

During the nine months of travel through Europe, the bulk of the letters come from Beulah. By replacing her earlier letters written collectively to "Dear People" with individual "postals" to family and friends, she contrived to get as many family members and friends as possible to write to her. After Dresden, new correspondents were added to the list, and by the time she reached Lausanne, she kept up a regular correspondence with at least ten different people and set aside special days on which to write to each member of her family.[25] All of her letters were probably shared among the Knoxes, but she still adapted her style to her relationship with the recipient. She was most confiding and emotional with her solicitous mother, who worried when cold weather was reported if Beulah should be cabled to wear her flannels (TFMP, Agnes Knox to Beulah, 9 September 1913). By contrast, the persistent tone with her father is cut-and-thrust banter, so much so that his own longing and fear that his illness

---

24 In the later lives of Beulah's other correspondents in the Knox family, Carlos studied engineering at Case Western Reserve University and Cornell, became an employee of Duquesne Light in Pittsburgh, and, between 1934 and 1951, worked as an electrical engineer in Shanghai and Korea. He was a veteran of the First World War and interned in Shanghai during the Second. Neilson studied at Wells College and the Cleveland Institute of Art. According to her obituary in the *Adirondack Daily Enterprise*, 2 April 1964, she was "a patient at Trudeau Sanatorium [at Saranac Lake] and later taught arts and crafts at the workshop there." At her death, she was sharing her brother's home in Gettysburg, PA.

25 For the connection between travel and letter-writing, see "Hearing from Home," in Mullen and Munson 292–303.

might prevent him from seeing her again were captured in Scottish verse to his "ane girlie" rather than the prose of a letter. She is a respectful younger sister to Carlos but a bossy older sibling to Neilson, who may have been slow to write because she did not enjoy having all of her spelling errors listed, being reminded not to wear Beulah's clothes in her absence, or given errands to run.

Although, to the Childs' delight – and in contrast to their own son – she was not one to complain or give in to melancholy, Beulah clearly missed her family and repeatedly hoped that they would join her in Europe in the spring of 1914. She made the strange more familiar by comparing new acquaintances to people at home, such as a roommate at the *Pensionat* who "is something [like] Eleanor Seymore's type very dainty + fastidious" (TFMP, Beulah to Agnes Knox, 23 October 1913). She sent stamps to friends she knew to be in want of them and even paid postage for those who – like Eileen Plunket – were "regular highway robber[s]" in never putting enough stamps on their envelopes (TFMP, Beulah to Carlos Knox, 30 December 1913, 1 January 1914). Neilson was drafted to put pressure on Beulah's friend Elizabeth[26] to write, and the success of the operation was celebrated with three exclamation marks (TFMP, Beulah to family, 28 September 1913). The same letter (which continued, journal-style, over several days) was decorated with a border of "WRITE WRITE WRITE" in different types of script as well as correct French but faulty German equivalents, followed shortly after by the lament that on three trips to the mailbox in one day she had found only the hotel bill. She announced that in future she would save herself the bother of spelling out "Write Often" and "just say W.O. and you will know what I mean" (TFMP, Beulah to family, 5 October, 1913; Beulah to Wilm Knox, 15 October 1913).

She complained vigorously when, despite her many letters, the responses were slow in coming. "WHY DON'T YOU WRITE you bad man," she asked her father, "here I am writing every night and wasting gallons of ink for which I get no reward why if you haven't time to write a regular one write it in short hand and I will imagine what is in it. It is eight days since I got a letter! Are you not ashamed of yourselves? You ought to be" (TFMP, Beulah to Wilm Knox, 8 October 1913). She enviously sat by a pile of four letters that had arrived from her mother for Will Child at his pensione, waiting for his return from an errand, and she made another trip from her school later in the day hoping for permission to read them. To ensure that no letters were lost but also to instigate a competition among her correspondents, she regularly presented her family

---

26 Elizabeth Buell (1896–1985) was a lifelong friend of the Knox family, and Beulah – who considered her "the right sort" (TFMP, Beulah to Agnes Knox, 30 November 1913) – hoped that Carlos would marry her (Thomas McIlwraith, email to Eva-Marie Kröller, 10 March 2015). For more on the Buell Wilder family, see Katherine Buell Wilder Family papers, YCAL MSS 18, Beinecke Rare Book and Manuscript Library, Yale University.

with tabs of mail received. A month after her arrival the tally was as follows: "I got a letter from Papa this afternoon I have had 4 letters from him 5 from Mama 1 from Neilson + Carlos each, 1 from Eleanor Merrell + 1 from Elizabeth [Eleanor, like Elizabeth, was a friend] Mama has the record so far you see Papa says he has written six so I suppose I have some coming to me" (TFMP, Beulah to family, 21–4 September 1913). She even wrote her father a letter in verse to provoke a detailed response as reward, and when he was feeling better he did reciprocate with his own six-page letter in verse to "My dear Girlie Boo" that concludes with "You have my love, I have no more, / And I have yours, so on that score, / We both are even. Papa" (TFMP, Wilm Knox to Beulah, 22 March 1914). Naturally, she became very anxious from the late fall of 1913 onwards when her father was not well, and a delay in letters could mean (and repeatedly did mean) bad news. When she felt he needed extra cheering up, she produced a collection of cheeky limericks (TFMP, Beulah to Wilm Knox, 10 November 1913).

Because their sightseeing had the Childs and their niece move frequently from place to place, Beulah often commented on the ease, or lack thereof, with which letters could be posted. At the hotel in Tangier, for example, she was impressed with the presence of "four post boxes French, German, Spanish and English and [you] use the stamps of those countries surcharged, then you just put your letter in the box that corresponds to your stamps" (TFMP, Beulah to Carlos Knox, 18 and 19 May 1914). The cosmopolitanism reflected in this practice is worth underlining, along with the ease with which Beulah's uncle was able to obtain British and American newspapers at most hotels, because the war soon put an abrupt stop to such ample and efficient means of communication. As Paul Fussell has pointed out in *Abroad* (1980), his study of literary travel between the wars, British tourists were shocked when they suddenly required passports in areas of the world where, thanks to their nationality, they had previously been able to move at their discretion. As well-to-do Americans, Beulah's family claimed the same privilege for themselves. Beulah experienced Europe in the last few months of apparently boundless freedom of movement before the outbreak of military hostilities abruptly ended it. Her correspondence with her school friends in the months after August 1914 gave her sharp impressions of a changed world, even as the girls did their ingenious best to manoeuvre around the various obstacles preventing them from writing freely to each other. Together with Beulah's light-hearted letters and Will Child's solicitous correspondence, these exchanges with former fellow students are the third collection of papers on which this chapter is based.

Preparations for War

By mid-April, reports of military conflict between the United States and Mexico began to appear in Uncle Will's newspapers, and the group's ability to blend in according to circumstances acquired a serious element, even if the military presence they witnessed in Gibraltar and North Africa had nothing to do with the conflict between the United States and Mexico. "There are French and British cruisers in the harbor," Beulah wrote from Tangier, obviously acting as a mouthpiece for Uncle Will's views. "So while we are here we are all British because you see if we got carried off by Beduoins [Woodrow] Wilson would only talk about the rights of man while England would hop right in and make things hot incidentally annexing the country probably. We are usually Americans because Uncle Wills passport is that" (TFMP, Beulah to Carlos Knox, 18 and 19 May 1914).[27] Here, Beulah was joking about British diplomatic mores as opposed to American ones, but to the reader privileged with the wisdom of hindsight, Beulah's comment on 1 January 1914 that "the year looks about the same as the last" is fraught with unbearable irony. Her observations of massed military presence in garrison towns also become ominous, as does the ceremonial changing of the guards at the royal palaces in Dresden, Berlin, and Madrid. A marine exhibit in Berlin featured "dreadnoughts ... about a yard long and fitted up perfectly with cannons and torpedo things and everything" and "a chart ... of all our naval boats" (TFMP, Beulah to Carlos, 30 December 1913), not to mention the "ships and torpedo boats etc." that crowded the harbour in Gibraltar (TFMP, Beulah to Agnes Knox, 17 May 1914). All of these sights she considered picturesque and exciting, and whenever possible the parading soldiers were fitted into her own fashion-and-etiquette universe: "The men marched splendidly just as Miss Flinn always tried to teach us to walk – putting the little toe down first," she wrote from Madrid, where "[t]here was a full military band in gorgeous uniforms" (TFMP, Beulah to Agnes Knox, 27 April 1914).

In Coblenz, a garrison of five thousand soldiers near the confluence of the Rhine and the Moselle, she observed that "you can't look out the window without seeing the landscape dotted with [military]." Their hotel looked out on the pontoon bridge connecting Coblenz with the Ehrenbreitstein Fortress, and one morning she saw a convoy of thirty Red Cross ambulances rumbling across, "with a troop of cavalry to head + to foot each man with a red cross on his arm[.] We haven't been able to decide what they were for" (TFMP, Beulah to family, 10 and 14 September 1913). Their hotel, the Bellevue, was completed in the year they arrived, but it was renamed Coblenzer Hof as early as 1913 to expunge its French name. In Berlin, the Siegesallee, with its recessed niches containing marble sculptures of Prussian royalty, was "particularly gorgeous" (TFMP, Beulah to Wilm Knox, 21 December 1913),[28] and the sight of a "Totenkopf Husar"

---

27 Presumably, Will Child held dual citizenship and also carried a British passport. See "History of Canadian Passports."

28 In 1913, the Siegessallee was relatively recent. Commissioned by Emperor William II in 1895, it was dedicated in 1901. Berliners were not impressed with it and referred to it as the "Puppenallee," or "Boulevard of Dolls" (my translation; see Sprengel 44).

The Zeppelin *Sachsen* passing over Dresden, 1907. Verkehrsmuseum, Dresden.

that later made its appearance in one of the stories she wrote about her European travels commanded all of the design detail that Beulah normally lavished only on her own new clothes: "you know that is the crack cavalry regiment of Germany he had a little black jacket lined + edged with white fur and strips of white braid across his chest and black cavalry trousers + boots and a black helmet with a skull + crossbones on in front in white" (TFMP, Beulah to Carlos Knox, 30 December 1913).

As Beulah began her German lessons in Eisenach, she saw her first "Zeppelin war air ship," and learned from her teacher that some days there were "as many as twenty." Initially uncertain how to spell the word, she thought it safer to compare it to "a huge white sausage or perhaps more like a gigantic silk worm" (TFMP, Beulah to family, 19 September 1913). Because there was regular passenger service between Dresden and Leipzig, "I think only $50 for a ticket and you take all the responsibility yourself" (TFMP, Beulah to Carlos Knox, 26 November 1913), airships passed so frequently overhead at Eisenstuckstrasse that soon they became little more than a welcome excuse to run to the window and interrupt a lesson. In their curious mixture of fantasy and menace, these scenes resemble Hayako Miyazaki's anime, where gingerbread architecture, decorative uniforms, and droves of insectoid flying machines create an environment that manages to be both picturesque and threatening.

Two sailings after the Childs and Beulah returned to the States on board the *Saxonia*, the ship was held up in Liverpool in August to replace the Hungarian and Austrian crew, now enemy aliens, with British sailors and stewards. The first September sailing from Liverpool to New York carried refugees and people stranded in Europe at the outbreak of war, most of them Americans not as fortunate as Will Child's party to leave in good time. By the next departure from North America, the ship had been requisitioned by the military. From then on, it was used to travel in convoy to transport Canadian troops – and, from 1917, American soldiers as well – to Europe. Moored in London, it served at times as accommodation for prisoners of war. War munitions were taken to Europe on it, and securities for J.P. Morgan and other banks were sent from Liverpool to the United States. If American tourists like Beulah had anxiously waited for delayed letters in peacetime, overseas mails were now subject to much greater hazards. The *Saxonia* seems to have escaped direct attack, but not sabotage: during a 1917 sailing, the mail room containing 1,350 mail sacks was broken into and numerous sacks slit open.[29] "Hoist with His Own Petard," one of the stories that Beulah wrote at Lake Erie College, describes another kind of interference. It relates how an American shipping magnate receives his deserved

---

29 See Norway Heritage, "Passenger Lists and Emigrant Ships," http://www.norwayheritage .com/p_ship.asp?sh=saxon (accessed 16 July 2017).

Eileen Plunket, ca. 1914. TFMP.

punishment for collusion with the Germans: he has helped them steal supplies from neutral ships only to have one of his own boats, powered by the very fuel he helped to confiscate, torpedoed by them.[30]

Eileen Plunket

Beulah and her fellow students had no idea that their language skills would soon do more than provide fond memories and a stream of chatty letters. A few

---

30 *Lake Erie Record*, November 1917, 10–12.

weeks into her stay at the school in Dresden, Will Child drew Beulah's attention to the fact that Doris Blackwood and Eileen Plunket shared an illustrious grandfather in the 1st Marquess of Dufferin and Ava, who – besides postings in St. Petersburg, Constantinople, Rome, and Paris – served as governor general of Canada (1874–9) before his diplomatic career reached its pinnacle with his appointment as viceroy of India (1884–8). The name Dufferin did not mean much to Beulah when she first heard it (and misspelled it as "Duffran"), but – probably exaggerating for Neilson's sake – she took Uncle Will's word that he was "the biggest person in England next to the King" (TFMP, Beulah to Neilson Knox, 18 October 1913). She refused to be intimidated by the many baronesses at von Gruber's, however, and claimed that to be "really exclusive" at this school, one had to be "Miss," a democratic view made easier by her friends' refusal to be "top lofty" (TFMP, Beulah to Agnes Knox, 19 and 20 November).

The first few missives Beulah received from the Dufferin granddaughters after her departure for Lausanne via Austria were bubbly reports adorned with many exclamation marks. Doris wrote about performances of *Carmen*, *Die Hugenotten*, *Tosca*, *Madama Butterfly*, and *Die Götterdämmerung*, about parties, and piano playing. Her passion for tenor Fritz Vogelstrom continued unabated, as did her many objections to the *Pensionat*'s house rules (TFMP, Doris Blackwood to Beulah, 25 February 1914). Both Doris and Eileen expected to settle into the social life prescribed by their class, following an education that was at best cursory compared to Beulah's own thorough academic preparation. Eileen's first few letters after her return to Britain were so like her cousin's that it takes the researcher a while to disentangle the two, especially as their handwriting is similarly careless, their spelling eccentric, and the dates usually missing. At the Plunkets' townhouse at Ormonde Gate in Chelsea and at Clandeboye, the Dufferin estate in County Down, Northern Ireland, Eileen flirted and danced with her "latest" or "bestest" suitor (TFMP, Eileen Plunket to Beulah, n.d. [probably before August 1914]). She was presented at court, attended any number of coming-out balls, participated in tenants' dances, was closely chaperoned on a visit to Paris, went to the French seaside with her family, and looked forward to a performance at Covent Garden of *Der Rosenkavalier* with Dresden stars Margarethe Siems and Eva von der Osten. The letters are light-hearted but also full of boredom, and more than once Eileen confesses that she has torn up a letter she meant to send because she had nothing to say. In a note written from Paris, she exclaims that she would "give worlds to be [back in Dresden] absolute worlds" and maps out her days as punctuated by "Sit alone doing nothing in my bed room." (TFMP, Eileen Plunket to Beulah, n.d. [December 1913?]). The schedule, annotated with "Thrilling isn't it?," consists of the following highlights:

8.30 Get up & have breaker alone in my room
9–9.45 Sit alone doing nothing in my bed room

10–10.45 French with Melle de Léonté

10.30–11.45 Walk [with Melle de Léonté]

11.45–12.30 Sit alone doing nothing in my bed room

12:30–1.10 Lunch

1.10–2.15 Sit alone doing nothing in my bed room

2.15–3 Walk with Melle de Léonté museum etc.

3–4.30 Sit alone doing nothing in my bed room

4.30–5 Tea

5.15–6.15 Lecture (this occasionally)

6.15–7.30 Sit alone doing nothing in my bedroom

7.30–8 Dinner

8–10 Melle P. plays patience. Melle de L. sews. E.H.P. does nothing.

However, the war brought fundamental changes to the lives of both Eileen and Doris. By full name, Eileen Plunket was Lady Eileen Hermione Hamilton-Temple-Blackwood-Plunket. Eileen's father was William, 5th Baron of Plunket, and her mother Lady Victoria Alexandrina Hamilton-Temple-Blackwood, daughter of the 1st Marquess of Dufferin and Ava and sister of Terence, Doris Blackwood's father. Victoria was born in Canada when her father was governor general there, and she and her siblings spent part of their childhood in Ottawa. Baron Plunket's term as governor of New Zealand (1904–10) had ended just three years before Beulah met the cousins in Dresden. Throughout her correspondence Eileen refers to her father's continued obligations to New Zealand, especially during the war, including his chairmanship of the New Zealand General Hospital at Mount Felix in Walton-on-Thames. These duties were also taken up by his family, and towards the end of the war Eileen dressed up as an allegory of "New Zealand in some priceless tableaux at the Alhambra" (TFMP, Eileen Plunket to Beulah Knox, 11 July 1918). Mother of eight children, Plunket's wife lent her name to a New Zealand organization devoted to the health care of mothers and infants, in parallel to her sister Helen's engagement in Australia's Red Cross during the First World War. Both sisters were influenced by the example of their mother, Hariot, who as vicereine of India worked towards improved health care for women. The Royal New Zealand Plunket Society, or "Plunket" for short, remains a New Zealand institution. On her father's side, Eileen's connections were no less distinguished. Her paternal grandmother was a daughter of Sir Benjamin Guinness, of brewery fame, and her paternal grandfather was archbishop of Dublin (1884–97). Like Beulah, both Eileen and Doris lost their fathers not long after the girls met in Dresden. Terence Hamilton-Temple-Blackwood died in 1919, and Baron Plunket in 1920.

With the declaration of war, the gossipy tone of Eileen's letters changed abruptly. Although she continually worried that she would have to marry "weak weed with a game leg + a glass eye, everyone else being smashed to bits by those – – – Germans!" (TFMP, Eileen Plunket to Beulah, 23 May 1915), she began to speak the "language of duty" (J. Lewis 224) and diligently looked for something useful to do. No matter how capricious they were, young women of Eileen's background were expected to acknowledge that their "roles within the imperial space were about charity, philanthropy and social reform" (Oppenheimer, "The 'imperial girl' " 514). The von Grubers rightly assumed that these would be typical duties in many of their students' future lives. Thus, the girls were required to tip the staff at Christmas though few of the students were able to tell the maids apart. The school also organized a "sewevening" during which the girls made clothes for dolls to give to a dozen poor children, as Beulah reported, using one of the compound nouns she began to create under the influence of learning the German language. The gift was complemented by "a thick dress a warm petticoat a pair of bedroom shoes and two toys" for each child, as well as "flour + sugar and bread + cake" for the mothers. The children, ranging "from two to thirteen years old ... [and] the tiniest things you ever saw," thanked their hosts by reciting "the most absolutely killing things" (TFMP, Beulah to Neilson Knox, 14 November 1913). Eileen, too, was drafted from early childhood into charitable work and official duties. A few months after arrival in New Zealand, for example, Lady Plunket sponsored a Nursing Guild Bazaar in aid of the St. John Ambulance Guild at which eight-year-old Eileen and her sisters Helen and Moira were in charge of "a fish pond" game that allowed children to angle for a prize ("Nursing Guild Bazaar"). They were also assigned fish-pond duty at a "Grand Garden Fete in aid of Veterans' Home" ("Advertisements"), while two years later, as a pupil of "Miss Estelle Beere's dancing classes," Eileen performed "a gay tarantella" following "a display of useful hygienic exercises [by all the pupils]" when Lady Plunket came visiting in her official role ("Rickards' Vaudeville Company").[31]

In 1914, Eileen immediately signed up for a household management course, trained in a baby crèche, took "blind soldiers out walking," helped out as "pantry-girl" in an officers' hospital installed in a hotel, and participated in shows staged for charity. Like everybody else, she took her knitting wherever she went, enjoyed the display of the "Allies colors," and found that as an empire, "we seem to be getting on well." Theatres and shops remained open and in the warm summer weather "everyone [is] rushing about with wide hats and full skirts," but "at night London is very dark" and "[s]o many people are walking about in black." Only "old ladies ... that one did'nt [sic] want to meet" showed up for three days' worth of "at-homes" at Ormonde Gate (TFMP, Eileen Plunket to Beulah, n.d. [but after 17 October 1914]; 23 May 1915; 11 July 1915). Eileen congratulated Beulah when Philip Child signed up; her own seventeen-year-old brother, she reciprocated,

---

31   For "hygienic exercises" for children, see Schreber 91–5.

had applied for admission to the military academy at Sandhurst and was waiting for notification. With relish, she described the complicated routine that kicked in at Ormonde Gate when Zeppelins – now much more threatening than in Dresden – were expected overhead. As "Inspector of special reserve of special constables," Baron Plunket's job (and that of his family) was to make "35 telephone calls in the middle of the night," some of which were received by "sleepy footmen," others by "hystericle [sic] wives." Then "the whole family fly up on to the roof in our dressing gowns, hoping to see the Zepps: we have never seen anything though" (TFMP, Eileen Plunket to Beulah, 11 July 1915).

Throughout her letters to Beulah, the prejudices that Eileen inherited from her class remained intact even as the military alliances with various nations traditionally held in contempt required some adjustment. Her uncles and cousins, back from the front, told her that "the Belgian soldiers are jolly brave ... but they are like a lot of raw recruits," the French are "awfully unde[pe]ndable" and forget to show up for battle, and "[t]he Zouaves are always on the run." The "Indians" were detailed to keep an eye on the French, she heard, but they, too, were defeated by the Frenchmen's lack of organization. Still, Eileen conceded, "[t]he French must be quite good because they have held their own so long in Alsace etc. etc." (TFMP, Eileen Plunket to Beulah, n.d [but after 17 October 1914]). She did find it difficult to shake her affection for her German fellow students ("Only wish it were Dresden + no war," she wrote on 14 September 1914), but the Germans were now generally beneath contempt, and she let fly some of the language that not only Beulah found shocking: "I wonder how our very dear friend Lisbeth Meyer & Carola von Garlick are getting on!!! And Erika Peters; dirty pigs!" (TFMP, Eileen Plunket to Beulah, 11 July 1915; "pigs" is underlined three times).[32]

Eileen's ambiguous attitude towards her former schoolmates was particularly apparent when she asked Beulah to act as a go-between between herself and Alice Schaefer. Alice was a silk merchant's daughter from Krefeld, a textile-manufacturing city on the Rhine. Because the civilian mails between Britain and Germany were disrupted and the United States had not yet entered the war, Eileen pressured her American friend to ask Alice for German wartime cartoons or "characertures" and to pretend they were for Beulah's own use. Their real purpose was to make a scrapbook for an uncle, also her godfather, "who is at the war and if I could get some German ones it would be doubly interesting." Even if direct communication between Germany and Britain had been possible, Eileen would – one hopes – have thought twice about making

---

32 Beulah's autograph collection identifies these students as Elisabeth Meyer, Carola von Garlik, and Erika Petersen. Bad language, generally blamed on the influence of their ancestor Richard Brinsley Sheridan, seems to have been something of a tradition among the women of Eileen's family. See Lady Cowper, qtd. in Gailey 315.

this request of Alice herself. As it was, she did have some doubts about the ethics of it all, and her tone with Beulah alternates between wheedling ("Do be a saint + try") and threat ("I hope the Germans are not so much in yr. favour that I shall get this letter returned with thanks as a snub!") (TFMP, Eileen Plunket to Beulah, n.d.; postmarked 14 September 1914). Beulah, for whatever reasons of her own, agreed and the proposed relay of letters succeeded. Pleased to have the cartoons, Eileen did have some pangs of conscience, and to alleviate them, she worked out a postal route through Thora Daverkosen, a Danish fellow student, that would allow her to write to Alice. Like Alice, Thora was the daughter of a textile merchant and the oldest of eight children born in rapid succession. She therefore had practice at being "very motherly," as Beulah characterized her, and so seemed a good intermediary to choose for the purpose (TFMP, Beulah to Neilson Knox, 14 December 1913). Eventually, Eileen and Alice managed to communicate because Eileen informed Beulah of Alice's work in a baby crèche, though she could not help the catty observation that compared to the adorable babies in her own care, Alice's – judging from the forwarded photographs – are "such big ones" (TFMP, Eileen Plunket to Beulah, 23 May 1915).

Known as the "pet" and the "baby" at von Gruber, according to the limericks Beulah wrote about each of her fellow students for Christmas (TFMP, Beulah to Neilson Knox, 14 December 1913), Alice was not quite as naive as Eileen and Beulah seemed to consider her, and she thought it strange that Thora, as she knew from a letter from Denmark, had received an identical request for cartoons from Eileen. But Alice, too, agreed to the relay. While we have to guess Beulah's motives (Was she flattered by Eileen's attention and allowed herself to be manipulated? Had she come to share her dislike of all Germans? Or was it all simply another prank in the spirit of the *Pensionat?*), we can be more positive about Alice's reasons. Written in uncertain English, the long letter to Beulah that accompanied the cartoons vividly projects a young woman determined to keep up her connections with both students and teachers: "I get letters of quite a lot of the Dresden girls; Thora, Lotte Loewig; Dulla v. Schw. Anie v. M. Elisabeth R. ... others" (TFMP, Alice Schaefer to Beulah, 17 October 1914).[33] Before the declaration of war, Eileen was one of her most faithful correspondents, writing every two or three weeks: "I am sure she hates me now, she didn't like the Germans before the war, we quarrelled very often about it." Like Eileen, Alice was patriotic, reported on her volunteer work in a military hospital and knitting "woolen things for millions of men," and she insisted that newspaper coverage of the German nation as close to defeat was "only lys [lies] out of the French

---

33 Beulah's autograph album lists most of these students: Thora Daverkosen, Dulla von Schwertzell, Anie von Mycielska, and Elizabeth Rudolph. Dulla (a favourite), Freda-Marie Gräfin Rittberg, and her sister Christa were Beulah's roommates.

and English papers." In fall 1914, Beulah was a few years away from knitting socks for American soldiers, but when she did, she and her American fellow students were duly pitied as "pobrecitas" by the Comandante in Granada, who thought there were better things for pretty girls to do – though he thought the same about girls who wrecked their looks by going to college (TFMP, Agustín Mateo y Fernández to Beulah, 17 February 1918). He was therefore asking for it when Beulah and Eileen snickered behind his back. Eileen wrote to Cleveland that she hoped Beulah's "behaviour is & always will be as perfect as mine but from yr. account of the Spanish colonel I doubt if it is so." She signed "Yrs. till Hell freezes" (TFMP, Eileen Plunket to Beulah, n.d.; postmarked 23 July 1914).

Alice probably agreed to send the cartoons in part because they allowed her to distribute her own national narrative among her circle of international friends. Her version of events was of course as much shaped by propaganda as Eileen's. One reason why Alice's letter, sent unsealed as regulation required it, may have escaped postal censorship by the German military was the fact that her stirring picture of the home front was welcome publicity. However, like Eileen, Alice, too, clearly longed for the friendships at the Pensionat to continue despite the war. If this meant spending hours writing letters, many of which were returned to her as undeliverable, she cheerfully did the job: "I am longing to see all again." The languages reluctantly crammed at the Pensionat assisted the girls in their endeavour. While at school, they wrote dutiful letters in French and German to their parents in order to illustrate their academic progress, but Alice's and Thora's ability to write in English or a Norwegian friend's spotty fluency in German in a letter to Beulah, who had an equally imperfect but serviceable understanding of it, facilitated communication that otherwise would not have been possible.[34]

Meanwhile, the school and the whole of Dresden were changing beyond recognition. Doris, Dagny, and Alice reported on new girls arriving early in the year, including students from Canada and Sweden, who kept the number of residents at a healthy twenty or so, but only two girls remained at the Pensionat when Alice wrote in October 1914. The language teachers and chaperones had abruptly returned to Sweden, France, and Great Britain. From one day to the next, the directors' livelihood was destroyed. The school hung on for a while, but by 1915 it was no longer listed, though the premises were later occupied by Pensionate under different names. The von Grubers' private addresses vanish from the directory too, and nothing has come to light about their subsequent lives. The opera was closed when Alice wrote her letter, and the singers had enlisted: "Eileen would be sad, if she could read that, her Waldemar Staegemann

---

34 For a comparison of responses to the First World War in German and Anglo-American writing for girls, see Redmann.

is in France too[;] poor man they were not obliged to do it, but no one likes to stay at home in this awful war" (TFMP, Alice Schaefer to Beulah, 17 October 1914).

By 1917 Eileen had learned to "motor" and was acting as chauffeur at a nurses' rest home established in Nancy Astor's seaside residence, Rest Harrow in Sandwich (TFMP, Eileen Plunket to Beulah, 1 March 1917). When she sent her last letter to Beulah, written 11 July 1918, she had just joined the Hackett-Lowther unit in France. Her deployment was high profile enough to be especially acknowledged among the accomplishments of his children in Lord Plunket's obituary in 1920 ("Death of Lord Plunket").[35] The Hackett-Lowther was originally planned as an all-English unit, but soon American drivers were also accepted. Founded by Norah Hackett and May "Toupie" Lowther and staffed by women from well-connected and usually wealthy backgrounds, the unit was a private ambulance and canteen service attached to the French army because neither the British nor the Americans would allow women this close to the front. As a member of the Earl of Lonsdale's family, Lowther was able to tap into her aristocratic network in order to obtain cars and drivers from Britain. The individuals attracted to the unit were often daredevils impatient with the passive role assigned to women in war; Eileen for one was satisfied that "it all sounds very thrilling & I believe we go up nearer than any other women we go to the casualty clearing stations." She had her hair cut short to get around the lack of much "in the toilet line out there," but worried enough about hygiene to ask Beulah to organize for a package of Odorono deodorant to be sent from the States because "all our chemists have run out." Considering that there is well over a year between Eileen's previous letter and this one, it is possible that the chief purpose of her message was to get "as many bottles" as possible for herself and others equally desperate for the product rather than resume correspondence with her American friend (TFMP, Eileen Plunket to Beulah, 11 July 1918). Perhaps this time Beulah's realization that she was being used outweighed any delight she may have felt in hearing from Eileen because the correspondence now definitely came to a standstill.

Unlike Le Bien-être du blessé, a women drivers' unit initiated by Grace Gallatin, Ernest Thompson Seton's wife, the Hackett-Lowther unit was efficiently run, and Maud Fitch from Utah, daughter of a wealthy mine owner, joined up when the disorganization of Gallatin's unit had her spend months idly waiting in French hotel rooms and volunteering in canteens to fill the time (see Murphy, "World War One Heroine" and "Utah Women in World War I"). Lowther responded with a brisk "Yes ... that is what we have been asking" to the question

---

35 On the Hackett-Lowther unit also see Hamer 51–2, 99.

whether they "wanted to be killed" ("Englishwomen"),[36] and she forcefully ensured discipline among the women under her command. The unit, some of whom already had extensive experience on the eastern front, worked as close as "350 yards from the German lines awaiting the wounded, under camouflage" ("Englishwomen"). *In the Soldier's Service* (1918), Mary Dexter, an American nurse and ambulance driver, describes her experiences nursing in Britain, Belgium, and France, including an assignment with the Hackett-Lowther unit. She evokes the abrupt transition to life at the front from upper-class London, where class distinctions were maintained even in air raids, with the servants huddling in a separate corner and the butler enquiring whether dinner should be served before or after the raid. Although the unit included several titled women, such social distinctions did not matter in the gruelling routine that had them transport the wounded along clogged roads, service defective cars, and live in unsanitary and freezing conditions. If there were any formalities to be observed, they had to do with details of military etiquette, such as the question of whether or not members of the unit were expected to salute senior officers.

To give a sense of members' reckless courage, Dexter repeatedly singles out "Miss P." as a particularly fearless member of the unit (with Dexter leaving the unit in May 1918 and Eileen Plunket arriving in July of that year, this unfortunately cannot be Eileen). In one episode, Miss P. is surprised by "a Boche aeroplane" immediately overhead during "a walk in a snowstorm" undertaken near the sign that says "Zone dangereuse." The pilot takes aim at her, but is driven away by anti-aircraft guns. Together with a French soldier, she seeks shelter in a ditch from flying shrapnel, only to have him exclaim the classic "Mais vous êtes femme!" ("But you are a woman!") as they climb back on to the road. Her "greatcoat and cap and boots" were clearly an effective camouflage (Dexter 166). Another incident has Miss P. rush two badly injured civilians to the hospital, find them rejected because they are not military, race back to headquarters to obtain the necessary permission, and then return to the hospital: "They were taken in, but it was just about too late," Dexter writes. "Their faces haunted me all that day" (188).

The valour of the Hackett-Lowther unit was such that it earned them the Croix de Guerre, but according to Lowther their "proudest moment came with the invitation to go to the German town of Wiesbaden with the 10th Army as part of the French army of occupation" ("Englishwomen"). The unit's liaison officer, Victor Châtenay, describes how they lived in splendour in the Hotel

---

36 Châtenay gives a somewhat different version according to which General Doumenc asked
    Lowther whether she and her unit wanted to be sent towards "une mort possible." Her response: "Bah, mon général! Quelques femmes de plus ou de moins dans ce monde, ça n'a pas
    d'importance" ("Ah well, general! A few women more or less in this world do not make any
    difference"). Unless otherwise noted, all translations are my own.

Victoria for two months, under the resentful eye of local citizens enduring curfews, evictions, and shortages of food. An elegant spa popular with the recently deposed emperor Wilhelm II, the city was suffering a fate similar to Dresden: during the war, business dropped off sharply and conditions under French occupation did nothing to revive it. A slightly sinister scene occurred when Eileen fell while skating and was helped up by a German. She told him: "Ce n'est pas en patinant qu'on aurait gagné la guerre" ("We would not have won the war if it had been a skating competition"). Though she smiled as she was saying it, he responded, possibly also with a smile: "Il y aura une revanche" ("There will be revenge").[37] In an ironical footnote, this exchange likely took place either in the French or German that she had learned in the *Pensionat* on Eisenstuckstrasse, some forty years after Charlotte von Gruber had founded her school in Biebrich, an elegant suburb of Wiesbaden. According to Châtenay, the Hackett-Lowther drivers became local celebrities and were visited by important personages, including a Chinese diplomat whose speech to them had them subside in giggles worthy of the *Pensionat*: "[m]es conductrices ont tellement mal à cacher leur hilarité qu'elles se mouchent sans cesse" ("my drivers have so much trouble hiding their hilarity that they incessantly blow their noses"). A politician and member of the French Resistance in later life, Châtenay married Barbara Stirling, a member of the Hackett-Lowther unit.

After the war, Lowther was interviewed by *The Times* in her home, with "the yellow regimental fanion of her corps with the cock of France on one corner and the lion of England on the other" hanging behind her on the walls, along with her own tin hat as a "companion trophy." However, as *The Times* underlined, Lowther had attracted attention well before the war, for reasons that are also germane to Eileen Plunket's life. Lowther was "a brilliant fencer and sportswoman" and composer, held "a Bachelor of Science of the Sorbonne," and was "one of the first women to ride a motor-cycle" ("Englishwomen"). Her work with the Hackett-Lowther unit served as a model for the wartime experiences of Radclyffe Hall's character Stephen Gordon in the Lesbian classic *The Well of Loneliness* (1928) and in Hall's story "Miss Ogilvy Finds Herself" (1926). Eileen herself appears to have had a relationship with Enid Elliott, also a driver with the unit. Elliott shows up repeatedly in Una Troubridge's diaries about her life with Radclyffe Hall. Hall and Troubridge attended a "dance at Toupies [sic] house," likewise attended by Eileen and Elliott, and Châtenay describes Elliott as especially devoted to Lowther. The guests furthermore included the Australian singer (and Lowther's lover) Nellie Rowe and the painter Romaine Brooks.[38]

---

37 It is worth noting here that "revanche" can have a double meaning of "revenge" and "return match."

38 Entries for 20 March, 15 April, 20 June, 1921, Una Troubridge diaries, Lovat Dickson collection, MG30 D237, vol. 1, LAC.

Perhaps Eileen was inspired, however briefly, in both her personal and her professional life by her aunt Hermione, whose work as a nurse at the front earned her the Médaille de la reconnaissance française and who shared her post-war life with a fellow nurse, Cathlin Cicely du Sautoy. From Dresden, Beulah reported that, with a German girl costumed as "Elsa," Eileen dressed up as Lohengrin for a party and that it was a natural character for her to choose "because she is always acting it." Because this description says more than it intends about Eileen and also about the characteristic distance Beulah was careful to maintain between herself and anything too much out of the ordinary, it is worth quoting at some length. Eileen's outfit, designed by Beulah, consisted of "two towels fastened so that one hung in front and on[e] in back and fastened on the shoulders this came about half way to her knee and had a wide white girdle around the waist, under this she had a yellow bloomer thing and white stockings and over her shoulders a pale blue opera cloak pinned on carelessly. She certainly looked great. Half of the girls dressed as boys and the other half as themselves I was myself and wore my white chiffon" (TFMP, Beulah to Wilm Knox, 19 November 1913). It was of course routine at all-girls schools for some of the students to dress up as men for plays and dances because, except for the occasional lecturer or handyman, the opposite sex was not allowed anywhere near them. At the same time, Eileen's costume is a reminder that, besides serving as microcosms of female socialization and of cordial relationships among different nationalities, as they do in *Der Trotzkopf* and *Swiss Sonata*, girls' boarding schools have featured as the literary settings of same-sex relationships. Among the best known are Christa Winsloe's novel and play *Gestern und heute* (1930), about a strict Prussian boarding school, more widely known under the title of its film adaptation, *Mädchen in Uniform* (1931), and Lilian Hellman's play *The Children's Hour* (1934), made into a film in 1936. In a parallel scene to *Der Trotzkopf*, a student in *Mädchen in Uniform* etches the name of a favourite female teacher into her arm. The costume parties may have allowed Eileen to live out her true self within a group of young women without risking social censure. Similarly, her work at the front with the Hackett-Lowther unit temporarily freed her from heterosexual convention. To avoid disapproval became more difficult when these liberating contexts were no longer available.

Immediately after demobilization, Eileen travelled to New Zealand with her sister Helen, who in 1916 had married Major Arthur Tahu Gravenor Rhodes, son of New Zealand pastoralists and newly appointed military secretary to the governor general, Lord Liverpool. We do not know the reason for Eileen's decision to return to New Zealand on this and subsequent occasions, other than that there was probably "nothing to do" for her at home, but there is a poignant snapshot of her in the diary of Lieutenant Colonel Charles Mackesy of the New Zealand Mounted Rifles in which he describes the troops' 1919 return voyage on the *Remuera*. She "works practically all day," he reported, joining the other women on board in "making drawings on canvas for the men to work."[39] The sisters participated in theatrical performances and fancy-dress shows, during which Eileen gave "a good 'Boy Scout'" and possibly had a hand in her brother-in-law's costume as an "Apache." Her language, as Beulah also had observed, was unpolished, and Mackesy witnessed how she told one of the passengers off with, "You dirty lousy old man." Indeed, he worried that she "will have a very bad effect on Wellington society. Her manners can be called nothing else but vulgar." Altogether, she made him uncomfortable as "Something of a Tom-boy," a peculiar label for a young woman who was by then twenty-three years old. "Glad I have no daughters," he concluded (Diary of Lieutenant-Colonel Charles Mackesy, 7, 11, 15, 16, 19, and 22 October 1919). Although her social life was soon disrupted by the news of Lord Plunket's death, Eileen was submerged into the smart set at events like the New Zealand Cup, where she sported a "navy blue satin charmeuse frock, relieved with white satin" (*Northern Advocate*, 18 November 1919, 1), and at the fancy-dress balls hosted by Tahu and Helen Rhodes at their home Te Koraha. At one of these, Eileen appeared "as a student from the Quartier Latin," wearing "pantaloons and a short smock" along with a "cap on her bobbed hair." If anyone was taken aback by her boyish appearance or, for that matter, by the Countess of Liverpool appearing in the "dress of a native woman of the Cook Islands, with weird headdress and fibre skirt,"[40] it did not make it into the society column reporting on the event ("Fancy Dress Ball At Te Koraha"). However, Eileen continued to make waves and was shortly after her arrival fined near Wellington for speeding. Driving ambulances, often converted from private luxury cars capable of high speeds even on roads ploughed up by troop movement, had turned her and other female drivers into "the progeny of war ... exceptionally strong, toughened, weather-beaten and mechanically savvy" (Doan 28). It was not only her language that had become masculinized well beyond the expressions that shocked her teachers and fellow students at the *Pensionat*, but also her physical presence.

In subsequent years, Eileen continued to search for something worthwhile to do that would give her an income even if it was difficult to match her adventures with the Hackett-Lowther. She trained at the Royal Academy of Dramatic Art for a career on the stage, encouraged by her brother Terence, the

---

39 A newspaper report clarified that the wounded on board took "[l]ittle interest ... in the educational classes," nor were they eager to participate in sports. Instead they preferred reading and "[m]any of the men who had learned to do fancy work in hospital in England took this up as a recreation" (Troops Return Home").

40 Dressing up as Native women appears to have been routine. On the *Remuera*, the prize went to "a most excellent 'Maori Woman'" (Diary of Lieutenant-Colonel Charles Mackesy, 11 October 1919).

new Lord Plunket, who was "very interested in his sister's ambition to 'make good' on her own account" ("Advertisements"). Brother and sister made "a notable pair" when they took to the dance floor together, and "[t]all and pretty," Eileen was considered "one of the most accomplished dancers in society" ("A Letter from London"). When the plan to become an actress failed, she partnered in a decorating business in Beauchamp Place in Knightsbridge, keeping as a memento of her days on the stage "a working model of the theatre" in her shop ("Interesting Engagement"). Together with the mystery writer Ngaio Marsh, her sister Helen Rhodes operated a similar establishment across the street (Harding 130), thus confirming the vogue among upper-middle-class and society women – of whom Syrie Maugham was the best known – of turning to interior decoration and antique shops for an occupation. As Deborah Cohen has illustrated in *Household Gods: The British and their Possessions*, these establishments could be expressions of the search for independence among women from privileged backgrounds, and Eileen's shop may have been yet another attempt to find a fulfilling occupation for herself (104). Considering that the Plunkets were not wealthy at the best of times, the resources that Eileen and Helen brought to their venture were connections rather than money, and their shops were meant to support them in an economically uncertain period ("A Letter from London").[41] Some social columnists claimed that Eileen's wish for a profession was "not a question of earning a living, for she is well-to-do. Girls nowadays want a profession. They are not content to do nothing gracefully," but another reporter was closer to the mark when she praised the sisters for their "charm, good looks, and a true Irish sense of humour, which remains unaffected by any financial crisis" ("Interesting Engagement"). Economy was also behind Eileen's reputation as "a very witty person" who asked her party guests to "bring a bottle of something else with them" if they did not like beer ("Rags or Tags").

In 1931, at thirty-five, Eileen married Captain Rowland Lionel Barnard of Cairo. He was former private secretary to Lord Edward Cecil and, at the time of his marriage with Eileen, "a prominent official of the Jockey Club there" ("Interesting Engagement"). She had met him during a lengthy stay in Egypt. The papers duly reported on their stylish wedding, followed by a motor trip to Trieste. The Barnards lived in Cairo and had a son and daughter; the children were evacuated to family and friends in Canterbury, New Zealand in 1941 ("For Women"). A correspondent writing from the New Zealand Forces Club in the Middle East in 1943 reported that "Mrs. Barnard [was] a marvelous war-worker" ("For Women: Current Notes"). After this notice, information about Eileen dries up.

---

41   For the Plunkets' financial situation, see also McLean 159.

Doris Blackwood with the viceregal party in Australia, 1914. Front row, left to right: Captain Anstruther, Lady Doris Blackwood, His Excellency the Governor General Sir Ronald Munro Ferguson, Lady Helen Munro Ferguson, Lady Blackwood, and her two children. National Archives of Australia.

Doris Blackwood

In Dresden, Doris Blackwood charmed everyone with her "fly-away" temperament that, on one of the *Pensionat*'s "cozy evenings," had her attempt to recite a poem in her characteristic lisp, but "skip ... the next 5 or 6 [stanzas]," and having come to the last stanza, she "[sat] down among roars of applause" (TFMP, Beulah to Carlos Knox, 16 October 1913). Doris's letter to Beulah of 25 February 1914, however, conveyed momentous news: "My uncle has been made Gov. Gen. in Australia + he has invited me to go crash with him + his wife and I've accepted. I'm only going for a year. We set sail April 10th I believe." Doris Blackwood's uncle was Sir Ronald Munro Craufurd Ferguson (1864–1920), later 1st Viscount of Novar, who was married to the Dufferins' second-oldest child, Lady Helen Hamilton-Temple-Blackwood (1865–1941). The couple did not have children of their own and, following the custom of other imperial officials, including Helen's parents (see Gailey 200), they enjoyed taking one of their nieces along to their new Australian posting. Doris's full name was Lady Doris Gwendoline Hamilton-Temple-Blackwood, and she was the daughter of Terence John Temple Hamilton-Temple-Blackwood, 2nd Marquess of Dufferin and Ava, and his American-born wife Florence (Flora) Davis, the daughter of a banker and one of many American heiresses who married into the British aristocracy. Because the amount of money Flora was bringing into the match was not clear until her father's death, the Dufferins' circle was sceptical whether the marriage was profitable (see Gailey 424n7). By contrast, the American press consistently spoke of Flora's "millionaire father," praised her pretty looks and pleasant voice (said to have been passed on to her daughters Doris, Ursula, and Patricia), and lauded her fashion sense. The American papers were, however, condescending about her husband's qualities. When Terence unexpectedly became the 2nd Marquess of Dufferin and Ava following the death of his older brother Archibald in the Boer War in 1900 and of his father in 1902, the San Francisco *Call* commented – on the front page no less – that "Lord Dufferin, unlike his distinguished father ... is not, exactly, clever but he is charming ... The Marquis is small, slight and clean-shaven. He has a hobby in his bicycle, and particularly enjoys riding about the most crowded streets of London. But books and things of that kind are not in his lordship's line. It is said that the late Queen, out of deference to Lord Dufferin, helped his boys into the army, else their bad examination marks would have kept them forever out" ("Elevation in Rank"). Because of her dual background, Doris felt a special connection to Beulah because she came from the States, and Doris wrote – two weeks into the war – that she "discovered from her Ma that her Mama came from Cleveland" and that Doris would like to "go out there sometime" and visit her "relations in New York" (TFMP, Doris Blackwood to Beulah, 28 August 1914).

By this time, Beulah knew enough about the family history of Eileen and Doris to realize that Munro Ferguson's posting in Australia was only the most recent in a procession of similar appointments. Although she did not mention her grandparents' viceregal posting to Ottawa in her letters, Doris was intrigued with Canada as well as the United States, and reported on the arrival of a new Canadian pupil, Annie Pemberton, at the *Pensionat* who is "quite nice, but awfully quiet" (TFMP, Doris Blackwood to Beulah, 25 February 1914).[42] Because Beulah often visited the Childs in Hamilton, she knew Canada well even before she eventually married a Canadian, and so she and Doris had another interest in common. "[I]t would have been great if it had only been Canada," Beulah wrote when she heard of the appointment to Australia. "I think I shall ask her

---

42 Possibly the granddaughter of Joseph Despart Pemberton, Hudson's Bay executive and first surveyor-general of Vancouver Island (1821–1893), but her identity has not been confirmed.

to have some of her family appointed G.G. of Canada. That family seems to run to governorgeneralships" (TFMP, Beulah to Neilson Knox, 28 February 1914). Like Eileen, Doris had grown up at Clandeboye. In his efforts to educate Beulah about European history through the people and objects she encountered on her travels, Uncle Will alerted her that the stamp on one of Eileen's letters from Clandeboye was "one of the new Irish covenant stamps saying 'we will not have home rule.' " This envelope, he thought, would "become very valuable so I am keeping it carefully" (TFMP, Beulah to Agnes Knox, 25–8 January 1914).[43]

With the outbreak of war, Doris was trapped in Australia because travel back to Britain was too dangerous; she did not return until 1919. Not that she minded very much. Writing from Government House in Melbourne, she described the declaration of war as if it were another opera performance ("Isn't it thrilling about the war"). She objected to having "civilians in as A.D.Cs" as if they were lesser understudies of the real thing, and bemoaned having to give up dances in order to "knitt [sic] socks for the soldiers" (TFMP, Doris Blackwood to Beulah, 28 August 1914). In short, she did her best to impersonate the "Fluff Girl" soon to be decried by the pilot and bestselling author Alan Bott (Bott 109), and she went seamlessly from gushing about "a perfectly angelic brown monkey which turns over & over when you wind it's [sic] arms round" she had purchased in Dresden (TFMP, Doris Blackwood to Beulah, 23 December 1913) to waving young men off to war. Doris's letter from Melbourne was the last from her that Beulah received, but she was told that "Doris never writes to anyone" when she complained to Eileen (TFMP, Eileen Plunket to Beulah, 23 May 1915).

The reason for her silence may well have been that Doris had too much to do because her imperious aunt immediately set her to work on arrival in Melbourne. Unlike Eileen, Doris had avoided official duty as a child, but she made up for this omission over the next five years when she accompanied the governor general's party on dozens of official occasions. She was there for the races and the launch of ships, but once the war had begun, there were countless visits to military hospitals, crèches, the Infants' Home, as well as a concert with Madame Melba in aid of the Italian Red Cross and a matinee of Wirths' Circus presented to the Friendly Union of Soldiers' Wives and Mothers. There were Anzac memorial services, a march of the Third Light Horse Brigade through the streets of Melbourne, an exhibition of battle pictures, and a call on the

---

43 This was a so-called "poster stamp," in use before the First World War: "Like full-sized posters, poster stamps were advertising or propaganda vehicles, used to publicize products, events, or (as is the case here) political issues. They frequently reached the public by being affixed to letters, invoices, and other documents and literature of the sponsoring agency." Anti-home-rule stamps bore the portrait of Sir Edward Carson. See Rare Books and Special Collections, Hesburgh Libraries, University of Notre Dame, http://www.rarebooks.nd.edu/digital/stamps/irish/set7L/set7L.html (accessed 13 July 2017).

concentration camp Enoggera[44] (that is, a camp in which, prior to shipping out, recruits were gathered and kept busy in order to prevent them from rioting). She participated in unveiling memorials, including the Dardanelles Memorial in Adelaide to commemorate the Anzacs' landing in Gallipoli and the Hobart's Soldiers' Avenue, where she planted the first tree.

It is true that this endless round of participation in viceregal duties came with leisure, such as having her go "tripping" to "the Hunter Petersons at the Delinquin sheep acres, after which she will go on to the MacArthur Onslows at Camden Park" (*Graphic of Australia*, 30 November 1917, 8). The society pages raved about "the dimpled Lady Doris" and her pleasant disposition, alternately considered her as "overflowing with vitality" and ready "to enjoy any amusement that comes along" (naturally so, it was believed, because she had an Irish father and an American mother) or as "a quiet, retiring" young woman who was "fond of tennis and hockey." The papers speculated on an impending engagement with a "Victorian man,"[45] a rumour confirmed by Eileen when she wrote to Beulah that "Doris is privately engaged !! to an Australian, absolutely no money, however" (TFMP, Eileen Plunket to Beulah, 11 July 1918). Perhaps it was the lack of money and subsequent intervention from her family that brought this particular relationship to an end. The Australian papers were disappointed when, shortly after Doris's return to Britain, her forthcoming marriage not to an Australian but to Lieutenant Colonel H. St. George Eagar was announced. This wedding, too, was cancelled.

However, Doris was not only immersed in duties of official representation, but also formally trained to play her part in the war effort. Even before her departure to Australia, Helen Munro Ferguson impressed a reporter of the Bathurst *Times*, in New South Wales, with her commitment to nursing and to female occupation generally. She was president of the Fife Red Cross Society, a member of the council of the Queen's Jubilee Institute of Nurses in Edinburgh, and a member of the Nurses' Committee for State Registration. She was involved in the Colonial Intelligence League, which "occupie[d] itself in finding openings for educated women in various parts of the Empire." Well before the declaration of war in 1914, Lady Helen organized "voluntary aid detachments for service in times of war." These were committed to training "women of every class to learn first aid, cookery, and nursing" and having them properly "certificated"("Lady Munro Ferguson"). With the outbreak of war, Doris trained as

---

44   "Brisbane Concentration Camps and the White City," Queensland State Archives, http://blogs.slq.qld.gov.au/ww1/2015/01/19/brisbane-concentration-camps-and-the-white-city/ (accessed 17 July 2017).

45   Compiled from *The Truth* (Brisbane), 20 December 1914, 4; *Graphic of Australia*, 30 November 1917, 8; *The Observer* (Adelaide), 13 September 1919, 40; *The Critic* (Adelaide), 10 September 1919, 32.

a VAD (Voluntary Aid Detachment) nurse. When she left Australia in 1919, it was not her dimples but her qualities as "a most energetic V.A.D." ("Melbourne News") that earned her praise, similar to the tribute Eileen Plunket received in her father's obituary for her work with the Hackett-Lowther unit.

Lady Helen converted the ballroom of Government House into the headquarters of the Australian Red Cross Society, of which she was president. Within weeks of the beginning of war, she oversaw the collection of £5,000 and arranged to have the money cabled to London for medical supplies and food. Along with Lady Stanley, the prime minister's wife, and a throng of society women, Doris sorted piles of "clothing, foods, comforts, books, tobacco, handkerchiefs, pyjamas, towels ... [r]olls of flannel and flannelette, butter-cloth and calico," as well as sheets, pillow cases, and felt slippers. Boxes of mosquito nets, tins of cocoa, bottles of cordial, and surgical sponges arrived, along with "woolen goods" knitted by women all over Australia, including Doris. An article describing the Government House headquarters and activities of other groups such as the Victoria League, the Salvation Army, and Victoria's Patriotic League powerfully evokes the promotion of "friendly understanding between British subjects all over the world." The bond was obviously all the more crucial in these times of crisis (Stenberg; see also Oppenheimer, "Lady Helen Munro Ferguson").

After her return to Britain in 1919, and instead of marrying Lieutenant Colonel Eagar, Doris and her sister Ursula briefly joined the British Committee of the French Red Cross in Reims. Shortly after, Doris married Captain Cecil Gunston of the Coldstream Guards, who had returned to his profession as stockbroker after the war. With him she had two daughters, both of whom made excellent matches: Hermione married Sir Walter Luttrell, and Sonia became the wife of the Thirteenth Lord Fairfax of Cameron. Doris's sister Patricia succeeded her in Australia as protégé of the next governor general, Henry Forster, and his wife Rachel. Like Eileen Plunket, Patricia took to the stage, but retired from acting when she married Henry Russell, former director of the Boston Opera Company, in 1926.

An enigmatic notice in an American newspaper in 1925 notes that "Lady Doris Gunston, whose mother is the daughter of John H. Davis of New York, has forsaken society to work as a clerk in a West End, London, shop" (Hutchinson Herald 19 November 1925, n.p.). Perhaps, like Eileen, she was looking for something to do and helped out in her sister Ursula's "fashionable dressmaking establishment in the West-End of London" ("An Engagement"), which would have hardly been akin to "forsaking society." One assumes that the shop came to an end when, a year later, Ursula married Arthur Swithin Newton Horne from the King's Own Royal Border Regiment and a former colonial administrator in Malaya. Doris's life became absorbed by the society rituals to which at least some of her five years in Australia had introduced her: royal receptions, weddings, funerals, dinners, and balls. She travelled to Scotland and St. Moritz as the seasons dictated, presided over charity events and horse shows, and was a keen golf player. Colonial newspapers were especially diligent in following up on the activities of former governor generals' families. In 1936, the Sydney *Morning Herald* praised Lady Gunston, "still the same friendly, warm-hearted person ... remembered in Sydney and Melbourne," for her skill in using old books "as main motif in house-furnishing scheme" to liven up "a room that threatened to be trivial" when she moved to a smaller house after her husband's early death ("Books as Main Motif"). Nothing is being said about her plans to read the books, but then the reading of books did not fall under the typical purview of the society pages.

The von Gruber and Kromayer Families

Beulah's trip to Europe saw her tap into yet another network. It is unlikely that she and her fellow students were aware of any these connections, but they add an important historical dimension to her months in Dresden. When she was interviewed for admission to the *Pensionat*, the director enquired urgently if her new pupil was "Church of England." The question was possibly motivated by Beulah's dark complexion, which, as we have seen, had other travellers wonder repeatedly if she had "southern or oriental blood" (TFMP, Beulah to Agnes Knox, 19 and 20 February 1914). Miss von Gruber added that although "she wasn't 'narrow-hearted' herself," the girls' families would not accept non-Christian fellow students, especially Jewish ones (TFMP, Beulah to family, 2 October 1913). The school's prospectus indicated that Protestantism was the preferred denomination, and that students were expected to "attend the English church."[46]

Dresden practised segregation by offering a special *Pensionat* for "israelitische Töchter,"[47] but the director's insistent question is remarkable for another reason: members of her own family were soon to be subjected to racial persecution. Franziska, sister of Charlotte and Hedwig, was married to Karl Kromayer, a teacher and school director who moved his family from Northern Germany to Alsace-Lorraine when it was annexed by Germany following the Franco-Prussian War. In her advertisement for her first school in Wiesbaden-Biebrich, Charlotte lists him as one of the personages willing to endorse the establishment. Guided by their wide-ranging academic and professional interests, the von Gruber-Kromayer families circulated freely through both the Austro-Hungarian Empire and the new Prussian Empire, and they repeatedly settled in politically volatile areas where education was deployed as a means of stabilization. The marriage of Franziska and Karl produced several accomplished children, including Johannes Kromayer (1859–1934), professor of

---

46 "Prospectus," Pensionat von Gruber, TFMP.
47 See the listings for girls' schools in the *Addressbuch für Dresden und Umgebung, 1913*, Verlag der Buchdruckerei der Dr. Güntzschen Stiftung, 1913 (*Historische Addressbücher*).

ancient history; the dermatologist Ernst Kromayer (1862–1933); and Hedwig Kromayer (1870–?), who achieved the rank of "Studienrätin" in the higher education of girls. Following a career at the University of Czernowitz in Bukovina (now Ukraine), an institution created to strengthen the north-eastern part of the Austro-Hungarian Empire, Johannes Kromayer accepted a chair at the University of Leipzig in 1913, which brought him near to his aunts' *Pensionat* when Beulah was their student. As a classicist, he often travelled in the lands of once-great empires surrounding the Mediterranean. This is where he met his wife, Henriette Topuz, daughter of a merchant in Smyrna (Izmir) whose family tree mingles Turkish, Dutch, and Italian names and backgrounds (see Volkmann).

Probably because he was forced to do so in order to continue in the medical profession, their son Ernst – a dermatologist like his famous uncle and namesake – applied in 1937 to the Reichsstelle für Sippenforschung, the Nazi office in charge of confirming German families' Aryan origins, to have his family tree cleared from the suspicion that his mother's origins implied Jewish ancestry. The Reichsstelle complied with his request, and the administrative language describing the procedure is as chilling as it is absurd. After scrutinizing his features both in person and in a photo and confirming that he saw little evidence of foreignness in Kromayer's looks, the examining physician concluded that the Topuz family's origins did not cause concern and that Ernst should therefore be certified as belonging to the Germanic race.[48] Four years earlier, Ernst's uncle Ernst Kromayer (1862–1933) had committed suicide. A brilliant dermatologist, he gave up a university career in Halle for a practice in Berlin, where he specialized in dermatological illness associated with warfare, including venereal disease, gunshot wounds, and bacterial skin disorders. Despite his wealth, Kromayer belonged to the circle of the Social Democrat Rudolf Breitscheid, eventually murdered in Buchenwald in 1941. When Kromayer killed himself in 1933, the papers reported that he suffered from an incurable illness, but the timing also suggests that Nazi ascendancy had something to do with his desperate decision ("Chronik vom Tage").[49] His wife also committed suicide in response to her husband's death, and both of their daughters emigrated to South America in 1937 (See "Kromayer, Ernst").

---

48 "Abstammung des Dr. Ernst Kromayer," Letter from the Reichs- und Preussische Minister des Inneren to Reichsstelle für Sippenforschung, 2 June 1937, Bundesarchiv Berlin R 1509/49.

49 Weyers suggests that Ernst Kromayer was Jewish and that this is why he committed suicide. Members of the Kromayer family dispute this, but confirm that a nephew of Johannes and Ernst escaped persecution in Nazi Germany by emigrating to the United States. Heinrich Kromayer, who held a doctorate in economics, was a social democrat and his wife Erika was part-Jewish, both reasons for harassment (email from Edvige Barrie to Eva-Marie Kröller, 30 July 2013; with special thanks to Peter Kromayer for providing a copy of the Kromayer family tree). Heinrich Kromayer's unpublished memoir "Mein Leben in Deutschland vor und nach dem 30. January 1933," is held at HLHU as part of the "My life in Germany contest" papers, MS Ger 91.

Will Addison Child, 1915. TFMP.

For his part, Will Child presented a lecture to Hamilton's "Scientifics" in the fall of 1914 that illustrated how his intellectual universe had been turned upside down by the war. During their European travels, Beulah repeatedly speaks of her uncle as having gone out "typing." By this she meant that he was out gathering visual evidence of different ethnic types and taking photographs of them. He did this sometimes on his own but also in the company of guides, who appear to have been either amateur scholars like himself or professors. Thus, he walked through

Dresden "with a German professor" observing the large number of Slavic-looking faces belonging to migrant workers and domestic staff, and commenting on the effect of these outsiders' presence on the original population. Based on a pre-war lecture, "Notes on Ethnology" rehearsed the theories then prevalent about the races of Europe, illustrated with dozens of photographs of representative "types" (*75th Anniversary Meeting,* 28). It was now impossible to display his love of German culture because, if he had done so, Child would have appeared to endorse the enemy's "superiority." It was certainly not a good idea to alert the association that it was their honorary member, Professor Haeckel, who coined the term "world war" (Haeckel) and, together with ninety-three scholars and artists, endorsed German military action against Great Britain by signing the manifesto "An die Kulturwelt." Instead, Will Child drew the attention of his audience to the "aggressive qualities" signalled by the shape of the head of "many German officers," particularly "the Aviation Corps." At the end, his twenty-page lecture subsides into a series of observations about the European way of life and art, "written some years ago." But the journal entries that, before the war, would have been a way to ease his way casually out of a serious talk now reflected a fragmented world in which previous categories no longer made any sense. After some critical comments about cleanliness in Italy and other places, he concluded: "So in North Germany, everything is neat, beautifully formed, square and exact" (Child, *Notes on Ethnology* 18, 19).

It was for a member of the next generation, Beulah Knox's husband T.F. McIlwraith, to denounce the racially defined thinking of anthropology when it was taken to its extreme by the Nazi regime.[50] McIlwraith's teacher A.C. Haddon and his co-author J.S. Huxley published their book *We Europeans: A Survey of "Racial" Problems* in 1935, and the topic of "Genetics and Race" was also on the agenda of the 1936 BAAS meeting. In his address, the geneticist H.J. Fleure concluded that "[a] pure race ... probably does not exist; indeed it is better not to use the term race at all in view of its purified misapplication in political discussions."[51] But as the next chapter will illustrate, T.F. McIlwraith was as yet a few years away from these realizations when he eagerly enlisted in the British imperial forces during the First World War.

---

50 See T.F. McIlwraith, "Race and Race Concepts"; See also "U.S. Negro 100 Per Cent Aryan Says Anthropology Professor," *Globe and Mail,* 2 September 1944, 5.

51 *Report of the British Association for the Advancement of Science* 459.

Chapter Six

The Wartime Letters of T.F. McIlwraith

"We're Winding Up the Watch on the Rhine"

Six years after Beulah Knox observed a convoy of ambulances rumbling across the pontoon bridge in Coblenz and in the same month that Eileen Plunket crossed the Rhine near Wiesbaden with the French army of occupation, nineteen-year-old Thomas F. McIlwraith reached the end of a gruelling march through Belgium when he walked across a pontoon bridge near Cologne with the British army of occupation. Special efforts were made to include men enlisted since 1914 and members of the Dominion troops among the first to cross the Rhine. As part of the official ceremony, McIlwraith's battalion was welcomed by the King's Own Scottish Borderers' regimental march "Blue Bonnets O'er the Border" on the east bank of the river. In a fifty-four-page letter to his family in Hamilton, he described the experience:

> The 13th [of December] was the big day and everybody was up early. Our luck was out, however, and the rain came down in torrents, a steady heavy drizzle. That meant water-proof sheets and trenchcoats, and no troops can look smart under those conditions. We marched off at 9:00 ... [and] halted for our ordinary 10 minute halt at 09:50 within a few 100 yards of the Rhine, our first view of it. It was very dark and cold-looking, but hardly as imposing as I had expected [from] the hills on either side.
>
> The bridge we crossed by is what is called "The Bridge of Boats." It is nothing more nor less than a pontoon bridge, though of pre-war construction and very solid workmanship. It was 10:10 when we marched out on it, past sentries with fixed bayonets. That was the way we crossed "Der Deutscher Rhin" [sic], and I think everybody was a bit keen on the thought. We marched at ease once we were past the sentry, but nobody tried to sing or anything of that kind. It was half smiles and things of that kind that showed the way the land lay. I wouldn't like to say how

many men wound their watches. I know I did, that the old song "When we wind up the watch on the Rhine" might pan out.[1]

We marched past more sentries at the other end of the bridge and a few yards further along Sir Charles Fergusson was waiting to take the salute.[2] It was quite an affair even in the rain ... He was standing on a platform and backed by our divisional commander, Maj-Gen [Henry Hugh] Tudor,[3] and our three brigadiers, not to mention various other red-capped worthies. All the bands had been sent ahead and were massed beside the platform and played the different battalions' regimental "march past" as they came along. It was quite a stunt, but sun would have made all the difference in the world ... It was worth the march to be in such a show – and on the other side of the Rhine. (CWM, T.F. McIlwraith to family, 27 January 1919)

Because it deals with the extreme circumstances of war, this chapter, more than any other in this book, is about asserting the ideology of the British Empire, and because of the volume of T.F.'s wartime correspondence, the discussion must be selective. To begin with, even before war was declared, imperialism moulded Tom McIlwraith's upbringing and everyday life, and his perceptions of wartime culture were filtered through the reading, theatre, and music preferred by his family and teachers. Second, loyalty to the beliefs that shaped his upbringing carried over into his overseas connections: T.F. cultivated friendships with fellow officers, entrepreneurs, and academic families who offered emotional support, provided hospitality during furlough, and advised him on his professional life after the war. Because he arrived at the front shortly before the Armistice, T.F.'s encounters with the enemy did not take place in the trenches but during the occupation of Germany. Thirdly, while this episode also drew on the understanding of empire in which T.F. had been inculcated, he began to differentiate between the military's English and Scottish components in the company of his KOSB mates. This distinction signalled that he was gaining a new understanding of plurality in the imperial troops, but McIlwraith was also confronted with the meaning of "world" in World War when, in addition to Australians, New Zealanders, and South Africans of European descent, he encountered Māori, Indians, and Africans, as well as the West Indian and Chinese Labour Corps. Fourth, his wartime impressions show the emergence of an

---

1 "When We've Wound Up the Watch on the Rhine," written by F.W. Mark (E.V. Lucas), composed by H.E. Darewski, for the musical revue *Business as Usual*, premiered in the London Hippodrome on 16 November 1914. Ironically, given the British patriotism of his work, Darewski was born in Minsk, then located in Russia, and trained in Vienna. On Darewski, see Gammond, "Darewski, H.E." 147–8.

2 On General Fergusson, who became military governor of Cologne and the third governor general of New Zealand, see Wheeler-Bennett.

3 On Tudor's wide-ranging imperial career, see Boyle.

independent spirit among the Dominion troops, especially the Australians, but there is as yet little indication that the presence of various Indigenous peoples had him question the segregations that school and cadet training taught him to take for granted. These questions and the change in his thinking that came with them had to wait until fieldwork in Bella Coola after he had completed his studies at Cambridge.

The troops' arrival at the Rhine was tactically, psychologically, and symbolically significant to both the Germans and the Allies. British newsreel and stereoscopic images recorded the moment when occupation struck "in one comprehensive sweep at the deepest and most fundamental source of German pride" ("On the Rhine"). Darewski's "When We've Wound Up the Watch on the Rhine," a satirical version of the German patriotic anthem "Die Wacht am Rhein,"[4] influenced McIlwraith's word play about the Allies "as chief watch-makers" (CWM, T.F. McIlwraith to family, 17 November 1918), and the pun may have been strengthened by advertisements asking, "Does your Watch suffer from Shell Shock?" and citing satisfied customers who had used the advertised Ingersoll "to time the firing of a gun."[5] Parodies like Darewski's song diluted the Rhine's mythic aura, as did the army of occupation's corps newspaper entitled *The Watch on the Rhine*, of which McIlwraith sent a copy home to his family. *The Times* predicted that the original anthem would now "become untuned, perhaps forever" ("On the Rhine"). The writer of this article conveys his disillusionment all the more vividly because he displays intimate knowledge, and probably a previous admiration, of German history and culture. The title selected by *The Times*, "On the Rhine: More than Geography," alludes to Victor von Scheffel's popular verse narrative *Der Trompeter von Säckingen* (1854), well known in English translation and in its adaptation to opera, but the article quotes the original German. To get a better sense of the river and the myths surrounding it, McIlwraith was keen to go on the boat trip from Bonn to Coblenz in summer 1919 that the army organized as one of many activities to keep restive troops busy as they were waiting for demobilization. The excursion aboard the steamer *Lohengrin* allowed him to view "the castled crag of Drachenfels" described in Byron's *Childe Harold's Pilgrimage* and the *Nibelungenlied*, but he did not think the river compared favourably to the Lower St. Lawrence, and he and his companions were bored soon enough. At least, the excursion allowed him to take photographs of the Germans' abandoned Zeppelin sheds and military equipment on the shore.

---

4 "Die Wacht am Rhein," lyrics by Max Schneckenburger, 1840, music by Carl Wilhelm, 1854. See Grove and Fuller-Maitland 342–3 for an overview of the song's contentious nationalism.
5 Advertisement for Ingersoll watches, *Red Triangle* (YMCA), 20 July 1917, 651, MAA, AA1/1/41, Box 328.

In December 1918, the population of Cologne nervously expected arrival of the foreign troops, and Konrad Adenauer, the city's lord mayor (and the first chancellor of the Federal Republic of Germany after the Second World War), urged citizens to remain calm. As the religious and political heart of the Rhineland, hub of the railways in the west of Germany, and home to important banks and industry, Cologne was a logical choice as the organizational centre for the British occupation (see Limburger 94). Because the city housed the administrative bureau for the army, McIlwraith reported to Cologne repeatedly over the next nine months in order to clear paperwork for his leave in London in early 1919 and, in August of that year, to prepare for demobilization. However, for most of his time in Germany, he was stationed in Wald (Solingen), in Germany's steel belt, with brief interludes in Mülheim, Leverkusen, and Niederhausen. Here he experienced a region "wrestling with the potentially explosive social, political and economic problems of post-war Germany" (D. Williamson, *The British in Germany* 32), including lack of work, food, and living space. Bolshevik sympathies were strong in the Ruhr industrial area that bordered the manufacturing town of Solingen. Five years later saw a campaign of bloody suppression by French and Belgian troops when German workers, encouraged by their political leaders, practised passive resistance against the harsh enforcement of reparation payments. Although the period of McIlwraith's stay was relatively uneventful, his letters do capture the incipient unrest.

He had left Canada for Britain in late 1917, spending Christmas at sea. On arrival, he was first assigned to the Artists' Rifles and began his training at Hare Hall in Romford, two years after the poets Wilfred Owen and Edward Thomas had completed their own officer course there. A few weeks later, he became an officer cadet in Cambridge and, in summer 1918, he "won his commission in the King's Own Scottish Borderers" as a second lieutenant.[6] He was keen to join the KOSB because its dress regulations were in keeping with his "wishes ... for a Scottish regiment wearing trousers" (CWM, T.F. McIlwraith to family, 13 May 1918). An epidemic outbreak of influenza stopped his cohort from going to the front immediately after their exams, which he had passed at the top of his group although he was convalescing when he wrote them. His battalion was quarantined in Cambridge until there was no further danger of spreading the disease. At Hyderabad Barracks in Colchester in mid-October 1918, he received his orders for France, not knowing that the Armistice would be declared only a few weeks later. The farewell letter that he, like all other recruits going to the front, was urged by his commanding officers to write told his family that he was "ready for anything, and if that anything should prove the next world, well I know my family will be brave until I meet them there"

---

6 "Won Commission: Son of T.F. McIlwraith, of This City," TFMP, unidentified clipping.

(CWM, T.F. McIlwraith to family, 19 October 1918). Although he saw plenty of war-torn Belgium and somewhat less of France, he was never in actual combat, and he had to be content with "working in a place where men have actually fought within the last few days, and where ... one can find relics of war, an empty cartridge case, a bit of a shell or something of that kind" (CWM, T.F. McIlwraith to family, 30 October 1918). After the Armistice, he served most of 1919 in occupied Germany as an assistant education officer under the "Khaki University" scheme (see T. Cook). He was reluctant to leave the army and considered deployment in Russia, for which he was turned down because he lacked the linguistic skills. Instead, he briefly returned home to Canada in August 1919 before beginning his studies in anthropology at Cambridge in the fall of 1919.

Childhood and Highfield School

Mclwraith's letters home from the First World War were written to his family, consisting of father, mother, and two older sisters, Dorothy and Marjorie. In 1886, Jean McIlwraith's oldest brother Thomas had married Mary Stevens. As mentioned earlier, the two were introduced by Thomas's sister Nellie, Mary's fellow student at the Wesleyan Ladies' College. Thomas's wife came from a well-situated family in Waterloo, in the Eastern Townships. Her father, Gardner Green Stevens, was a banker who repeatedly served as mayor and, between 1876 and 1892, was Liberal senator alongside Prime Minister Alexander MacKenzie (whose family had long been acquainted with the McIlwraiths) as well as Sir John A. Macdonald and a succession of other Conservative prime ministers. Mary's son Tom speculated in his memoir that, for her, "[c]oming to Hamilton must have been an undertaking" and "the boisterous, hilarious, mirthful McIlwraiths" a change from the "narrow Methodist teetotal family" from which she came ("Genealogy"). As his father's successor in the coal dealership, her husband was quite prosperous when they married, and the couple travelled to England for their honeymoon. Soon enough, however, their fortunes began to slide, largely because business at the wharf was rapidly being replaced by railway transport, and one source of Mary's chronic unhappiness was the family's failure to maintain an impressive social standing in Hamilton. The couple reluctantly gave up their first home to move into Cairnbrae in order to look after Mr. McIlwraith after Jean had left for New York. All three of their children grew up in the old family home on the wharf until 1912, when they moved to 179 Duke Street, "our best house," as Tom wistfully called it in later years. His father was finally edged out of business in 1919, and he accepted "a very small job in [a] larger insurance company" for the remainder of his working life ("Genealogy").

An exceptionally gifted child, Tom was enrolled at the independent High-field School for Boys (now Hillfield Strathallan College) in 1908. Highfield was founded in 1901 with support from two future lieutenant governors, Sir John Strathearn Hendrie and Sir John Morison Gibson, and a former governor general and his chatelaine, Lord and Lady Aberdeen. Viceregal support continued, and Lord and Lady Grey attended Sports Day in 1907, " 'len[ding] additional éclat to the occasion'" (qtd. in Wansbrough et al. 12). John H. Collinson, the first headmaster, was a Yorkshireman who had come to Canada in 1892 to teach higher mathematics at Upper Canada College, where he made friends with another ardent imperialist, Stephen Leacock. The school's senior day fee was a substantial $75 per annum, and some of Hamilton's wealthiest and most influential families, many of them headed by businessmen and politicians, enrolled their sons, including the Crerars, Hendries, Woods, Ferries, Nord-heimers, Zimmermans, and Childs. By the time he entered, Tom's parents were not well-to-do, but the school made allowances because of their son's many prizes and awards. Nellie Holt, who often generously supported her nephew, helped out. Through Jean and Kennedy, the McIlwraiths' network extended to Upper Canada College, and these connections may also have been of assistance in having Tom placed at Highfield.

The school was designed as a preparatory institution for students planning to enter the Royal Military College of Canada, and as many as half of the boys were known to transfer to Kingston upon graduation. Students were immersed in the military tradition through the "[t]he school cadet corps[,] ... an affiliate of the Royal Hamilton Light Infantry" (Gossage 181), and there was a strong emphasis on athletics, including rifle, revolver, and sword practice. Indeed, Highfield operated by the exhortation, repeated by Lord Dufferin with little var-iation throughout his tenure as governor general of Canada between 1872 and 1878, "You are the owners of half a continent, of a land of unbounded prom-ise and unprecedented greatness. Love it, honour it; work for it; fight for it; die for it" (qtd. in Wansbrough et al. 9).[7] The school produced outstanding mili-tary men like General Officer Commander-in-Chief Henry Duncan Graham Crerar, RAF pilot Captain William Otway Boger, and RCAF Air Vice-Marshall H.M. Carscallen. When the First World War broke out, former Highfield

---

7 The exact origin of this quotation remains to be determined. However, Dufferin expressed similar sentiments in other speeches: "You are no longer colonists or provincials. You are the defenders and guardians of half a continent, – of a land of unbounded promise and pre-destinated renown. That thought alone should make men and soldiers of you all. Life would scarcely be worth living, unless it gave us something for the sake of which it was worth while to die ... never should a Canadian forget, no matter what his station in life, what his origin or special environments, that in this broad Dominion he has that which it is worth while both to live for and to die for" ("Lord Dufferin in Canada").

students rushed to join up for combat, including all but 5 of the 23 men then enrolled at the Royal Military College. Out of 270 Old Boys in uniform, 184 were officers and 48 imperial officers, and 45 received decorations (Wansbrough et al. 28). As figures compiled by a former headmaster of Bishop's College by the end of 1915 illustrate, "Young Canada" at other renowned boys' schools displayed a similar eagerness to ensure "the maintenance of the British Empire unimpaired" (E. Kingston 9), including the students at Upper Canada College, St. Andrew's College, Bishop's College School, Trinity College, Ridley College, King's College School, St. Alban's School, Lower Canada College, and Rothesay Collegiate School. Old Boys from these schools were united by common purpose and a spirit of competition. During Canadian Officer Training Corps (COTC) training in Toronto, McIlwraith attended a football game at which "[m]ost of our fellows were from the prep schools of Ontario, a big bunch being Ridley chaps" (CWM, T.F. McIlwraith to Dorothy McIlwraith, 29 November 1917).

As many as thirty-five former Highfield students lost their lives in the Great War in theatres stretching from France to Palestine, and some families – such as the Dobbies and Tinlings – lost more than one son. Tom kept careful tab on the military achievements of all former students in action and noted the deaths of so many with pride and sorrow. "Your letter was the first I had heard of [G.M.] Matheson's death," he wrote to his father. "There is one of the finest men Highfield ever turned out gone under in the war" (CWM, T.F. McIlwraith to his father, 25 September 1918). Here, he is referring to Lieutenant Gordon MacMichael Matheson, captain óf Highfield's hockey and football teams between 1905 and 1910 and a graduate of Trinity University, who used his "many and rich gifts ... with native modesty and a noble heart" before he was killed in combat (Wansbrough et al. 26). Two years before war was declared, Tom borrowed D.H. Parry's *Britain's Roll of Glory, or The Victoria Cross, its Heroes and their Valour: From Personal Accounts, Official Records, and Regimental Tradition* (1898) from the library. He misspelled the title as *Britain's Role of Glory* in his notebook, a telling error because Highfield taught its students to view themselves as passionately committed to fulfilling that "role." As his Aunt Jean's life story and written works have illustrated, Highfield's principles were mirrored in the imperialism embraced by the McIlwraith family, and as a young child Tom was photographed in a miniature Boer War uniform and helmet.

Academically, Tom excelled from the start, and his report cards at Highfield were invariably glowing. As a ten-year-old, he achieved a perfect grade for reading and received prizes in Latin and arithmetic. His assessments in subsequent years ranged from "[a] most promising boy" and "[a]n unusual boy" to "one of a brilliant group of boys who should do remarkably well"; one teacher even wrote, "I never saw such a report as this in all my experience." When he

Young T.F. McIlwraith in Boer War uniform, ca. 1908. TFMP.

matriculated in 1914, he was complimented on his "remarkable Exam. proving better than nearly all matric. boys" (TFMP, report cards). The history of
Highfield refers to 1916 as "the year of Tom McIlwraith and Richard Saunders":
while Saunders won the Bristol Cup the second year in a row, Tom received
both the Governor General's and the Lieutenant General's Medals, along with
the Tinling Gold Medal for character. He had won the Lieutenant General's
Medal the previous year as well (Wansbrough et al. 21).[8] He did not, however,
excel in sports, and his short stature (he was just under five foot five) was to
earn him the nickname "Tiny" in the army. Although he insisted in his memoir
that "fellow students [at Highfield] were not ... athletically snobbish" ("Genealogy"), the company of muscular giants, including a football team featuring
"two or three of abnormal bulk" (Wanbrough et al. 10), may have had something
to do with his fierce determination to be accepted into the military despite his
size and weight. When he finally did succeed in becoming a recruit, he "won
the first prize [he] ever bagged in an athletic event, being half of the winning
wheelbarrow" in "the usual silly games" played on deck of the *Missanabie*, the
troopship taking him to Britain (CWM, T.F. McIlwraith to family, 20 December
1917–2 January 1918).

Tom's education at Highfield continued at home. As with Jean's generation,
his earliest reading included the children's page in magazines, and at thirteen he
won a book prize for solving a puzzle in *Harper's Bazaar* ("Our Puzzle Mill").
As a student at Cambridge he fondly remembered the family sitting together
and reading to each other, sometimes the same books he later studied in anthropology (TFMF, T.F. McIlwraith to family, 22 February 1920). Above all, he
read voraciously on his own, and – like his great-uncle Andrew – he organized
and evaluated his copious reading, including *Britain's Roll of Glory*, by keeping
lists of "non-fiction" books checked out from the library, thirteen for 1913 and
sixteen for 1914. He annotated each with "good," "very good," or "bad" (TFMP,
childhood notebook). Prominent are books about animals (particularly birds),
anthropological works, books about the mission of the British Empire, and travel
books, especially travelogues with an imperial theme. The titles reflect the "masculine" subjects of hunting, sports, anthropology, agriculture, and administrative prowess that characterize colonial writing. A stack of books on Africa, one
of Tom's favourite subjects, included D.C.E. Comyn's *Services and Sport in the
Sudan* (1911), Edgar Allan Forbes's *In the Land of the White Helmet* (1910), Percy
C. Madeira's *Hunting in British East Africa* (1909), C.H. Stigand's *To Abyssinia*

---

8 The Tinling Gold Medal is named after Charles B. Tinling, son of Charles W. Tinling, vice
president and general manager of the National Drug and Chemical Company Montreal.
Charles B. was killed in action. A second son, Captain George E. Tinling, was also killed. See
notice, Toronto *Evening Telegram*, 12 October 1917, n.p.

Through an Unknown Land (1910), Alfred J. Swann's *Fighting the Slave Hunters in Central Africa* (1910), and Karl Weule's *Native Life in West Africa* (1909). As a whole, the list is a remarkably accurate reflection of McIlwraith's ideas about the British Empire while in the army and as a student at Cambridge, but the titles also set a standard by which to gauge subsequent changes in his thinking.

While this annotated booklist is proof of an ambitious and well-organized boy who had been brought up to account to himself, his family, and his teachers how he spent his time, there is also evidence of spontaneity and a seemingly limitless energy that remained a characteristic for years to come. A letter written at the age of eight to his father conveys an enthusiasm for exploration so breathless that it does not have the time to stop for punctuation. At the same time there is a sense of verbal irony – evidenced, for example, in his use of "comfortable" instead of "uncomfortable" when he encounters nettles – that is unusual for such a young child and perhaps reflective of the wit that characterized his family's communication with each other:

> Yesterday we went for a walk Dorothy Mary and I. Mary wanted to get some ferns and Mable showed us a shortcut to Mr Moors the house on the road to Pinks Lake you come to it just a little way after you go around the bend well we got off the path and – got lost well we wandered on for about a mile till we came to a nettle swamp we walked about half a mile through the nettles which was very comfortable for my bare legs then we struck a blazed trail followed it on and on three or four miles till we lost it there was a path in two directions one way we heard a dog barking but we took ... the other, we went a little way and came back when we were passing I saw a blaze and then we saw more and the path went on we didn't know where the trail went to well we went on and lost it and ... never found it again by this time we had know [sic] idea which way home was one thought one way and one another.
> (TFMP, T.F. McIlwraith to his father, 2 September 1907)

Sprinkled with his favourite adjectives "dilly" and "spiffy, " letters written to his mother two years later show him immersed in stamp collecting and reading Alfred W. Drayson's *The White Chief of the Caffres* (1887), along with G.A. Henty's *With Wolfe in Canada* (1887) and *The Young Midshipman* (ca. 1900). At the same time, Tom approves of "the whipcream cake for dinner," "a boxing tournament which is *the* thing the boxers will have a great pow-wow," and some "gymnastical stunts" performed with his seventeen-year-old sister Dorothy on the bed, which were vigorous enough to "sen[d] out a slat and some other things." He dutifully reports on a tooth "that came out, so there are mostly new ones now," as well as on his regular attendance at church and a visit from the bishop of Ottawa, who "heard us sing (two songs only which was enough for him I guess)," after which event Highfield's Headmaster Collinson gave the whole school the rest of the day off. In addition to his love for high jinx, Tom demonstrates a talent inherited from his grandfather for describing with delicate precision the natural world around him: "Some more Song Sparrows have come besides the ones that stayed around all winter and the other day I saw a winter wren and lots of crows. The sillias [sic] are just beginning to show green but theres no sign of the snowdrops" (TFMP, T.F. McIlwraith to his mother, 28 March and 14 March 1909).

University and War

In the few surviving letters from Tom's first, and as it turned out only, year at McGill, his enthusiasm for empire rose to a feverish pitch as war was declared, and it stayed there as the conflict progressed into its first few years. At both McGill and the University of Toronto, students were pressured to join up despite complaints from parents that President Sir Robert Falconer had no business setting himself up as "Recruiting Officer in General" when it was more appropriate to leave this decision "to the boys and their parents" (Friedland 254). As many as five hundred students signed up for the COTC within hours of Falconer's first appeal in October 1914, and by December, eighteen hundred students had become cadets. The program initially involved "basic military and leadership skills while [students were] still enrolled in their regular academic programs," but it was eventually extended to include the affiliated Overseas Training Company. The latter allowed individuals not teaching or studying at the university to train in "technical courses" such as "engineering, ballistics, and mathematics" (Calhoun 15). The COTC's rifle range was located in the Hart House Theatre, where cadets practised on sets depicting "a ruined Belgian village" created by Lawren Harris, later of Group of Seven renown (Friedland 254).

From McGill, Tom wrote little about his academic lectures except to say that he was doing well, "one of the best ... the professor said," and he was informed a couple of months before he left for Britain that he had passed his year at 84 per cent. Often, he argued about conscription with his fellow students, including "a most violent argument ... with the president of the literary and debating society ... He is a senior, and also a dub and not at the front" (TFMP, T.F. McIlwraith to his mother, 13 November 1916). They made enough noise to be reprimanded, but this did not stop him from getting into a "dispute with ... a third year man and blooming nationalist" (TFMP, T.F. McIlwraith to his mother, 13 November 1916), an intolerable attitude given Tom's own imperialist sympathies. The pro-war atmosphere was further heated up by guests like the actor Sir Herbert Beerbohm Tree, who came to Montreal to perform in Shakespeare's *Henry VIII* and visited McGill to "talk ... of how much they were all doing in England, this to a room full of slackers" (TFMP, T.F. McIlwraith to his mother, n.d., November 1916). Fifteen when war was declared, McIlwraith enlisted in the Princess Patricia's Canadian Light Infantry but his parents would not allow him to go to the front until he was eighteen, and enrolment at McGill served first and foremost the purpose of keeping him "busy" ("Genealogy"). Above all, Tom alternately pleaded with his mother to give her consent for him to enlist, assured her that he would respect her decisions whatever they turned out to be, and then reprimanded her with the breathtaking logic of a seventeen-year-old for "letting the fact that you do not want me to be killed, influence you in the question of whether I am to go or not" (TFMP, T.F. McIlwraith to his mother, n.d., November 1916). These letters display extreme variations in tone, and they "sound" at times as if his voice were breaking a second time. There was clearly great turmoil at home, and he was torn between respecting his parents' wishes (including their opposition to his enrolment at Kingston) and following his own inclinations: "Poor little mummy, I suppose you are very much worried these days ... I know just how worried you are, darling, and I am only sorry that I could not get you and father to say something when I was home, I tried as hard as I could, but I know you both successfully persuaded yourself [sic] that the war would be over before I was old enough, and would not realize that my time to go had almost come" (TFMP, T.F. McIlwraith to his mother, n.d., November 1916). He tried emotional blackmail by reminding her that she would "be able to look any mother in the world in the face" by allowing him to enlist (TFMP, T.F. McIlwraith to his mother, 13 November 1916), before abruptly switching to an everyday register in the announcement that his cold was better.[9] When she obtained the advice of his old headmaster, John Collinson, and of a family friend, Frank Hills, the superintendent of the Stephenson's Children's Home in Hamilton, he dismissed them as "old fogies" whom he considered "patriotic and all that, but ... not military men" (TFMP, T.F. McIlwraith to his mother, n.d., November 1916). There is some irony in this comment, considering Highfield's role in fuelling T.F.'s imperialist fervour in the first place. He shed his disdain for these "old fogies" soon enough and was grateful to Collinson and Hills's family for their continued support throughout his military service and into his academic career. By the end of the war, Collinson had returned to Britain, and Highfield's survival was uncertain after a major fire in 1918.

Tom's close friend at Highfield was Philip Child, and Will Child, too, tried to hold his son back from the front, first by transferring him from Highfield to Ridley College in the apparent hope of getting him away from Highfield's sabre-rattling, then by taking him on an extended trip to Alaska (Calhoun 12–13). To no avail: by 1916, Philip had joined the COTC at the University of Toronto and tried to persuade Tom to enrol with him at the Royal Military College in

---

9 On the relationship between mothers and sons in war, see Roper, *The Secret Battle*.

Kingston (TFMP, T.F. McIlwraith, letter to his mother, n.d., November 1916). Because he was a year older than Tom, his decisions influenced McIlwraith's own. This, in addition to joining the University of Toronto's COTC, included application to the British imperial forces because they promised prompt military action overseas and because doing so kept Tom away from the Canadian "slackers" who suddenly filled the army after conscription ("Genealogy"). Philip was tall and, as a footballer, had the requisite weight. As a result, he had no difficulty enlisting, completed his officer training in late 1917, reached France in early 1918, and was wounded a few months later, though Tom was informed it was "only ... a scratch." Child's novel *God's Sparrows* (1937), for which he won the Governor General's Award, suggests that though the physical wounds may have been superficial, the trauma of trench warfare haunted him for years after. When McIlwraith encountered a number of problems preventing him from enlisting, the refrain "He's lucky to be in it; wish I were" appeared in his letters at every stage of his own training (CWM, T.F. McIlwraith to Dorothy McIlwraith, 20 May 1918).

When McIlwraith finally did get to Britain, the two friends instantly met up in London for meals, shows, and sightseeing. Philip, already an officer and so forbidden, strictly speaking, to walk around with his friend, was not overly bothered by army regulations, and the two investigated "various winding and smelly streets" near the Wapping docks and observed how the "sights" had been transformed by the war: both the crypt in St. Paul's and the basement of a large hotel served as shelters, and during blackout, it was not easy to get around in fog or after dark (CWM, T.F. McIlwraith to family, 2 January 1918). They met up often while they were in Europe, and after the war some of their studies overlapped as well. In 1921, as Philip Child prepared to follow McIlwraith to Cambridge, Mary Stevens wrote to her son: "Isn't it strange how you and Philip are so mixed up in your lives? He was the first to meet you in London when you went overseas, and now you will be there to greet him" (TFMP, Mary Stevens to T.F. McIlwraith, 10 August 1921). She could not have known that their lives were to become even more "mixed up" when her son married Beulah. There was some rivalry in the friendship, possibly fuelled by Mary Stevens's ambitions for her son. Writing from McGill, Tom found it necessary to point out to his mother that Philip had made three spelling errors in the short letter asking his friend to enrol at Kingston with him (TFMP, T.F. McIlwraith to his mother, n.d., November 1916), and after her son's graduation with a first from Cambridge, his proud mother thought Will Child's "desire that Philip should achieve even a little of your success" rather "pathetic" (TFMP, Mary Stevens to T.F. McIlwraith, 10 August 1921). The competitiveness did not seriously affect the friendship: when Child closed his parents' house on Hess Street in the 1940s, he found a letter describing a holiday he and Tom spent together in Bordighera, Italy in late 1921 and forwarded it to McIlwraith to remind him of these early years (TFMP, Philip Child to T.F. McIlwraith, 22 July 1945).

When he first presented himself at the army recruitment centre for medical inspection after his eighteenth birthday in April 1917, McIlwraith was roughly two pounds shy of the required body weight, and he was rejected. In his 1964 memoir he admitted drastic measures to succeed on the second attempt. Tom – "complexion: sallow, eyes: brown, hair: brown"[10] – not only gorged on as much fattening food as he could lay his hands on, but also "took the reverse of a laxative" and stuffed his cheeks with lead shot to break the weight threshold at slightly more than 110 pounds ("Genealogy"). On his second attempt on 20 June 1917, he was declared "fit for the Canadian Over-Seas Expeditionary Force" ("Attestation Paper") and so was ready to join "[t]he biggest war for thousands of years, in fact ever, and it not only comes off in my lifetime but chooses the exact time when I could get in it" (CWM, T.F. McIlwraith to Dorothy McIlwraith, 14 December 1917). His letters home from COTC training at Burwash Hall capture the city's wartime excitement, as one famous motivational speaker after another paraded through town. Among them were the Scottish entertainer Sir Harry Lauder, whose own son had been killed in action, the naval-affairs expert Arthur Pollen, and Theodore Roosevelt, who was "escorted ... by air mechanics with fur caps who wrote [sic] on motorcycles" (CWM, T.F. McIlwraith to Dorothy McIlwraith, 29 November 1917). Tom's unit marched through Toronto to advertise the Victory Loan, fired up by bands playing "Land of Hope and Glory" and "Rule Britannia" (CWM, T.F. McIlwraith to Dorothy McIlwraith, 29 November 1917). The crowds enjoyed "Over There" too, but because of the Americans' delayed entry into the war, Tom was angry every time he had to listen to "that rotten Yankee song" (CWM, T.F. McIlwraith to Dorothy McIlwraith, 29 November 1917). When he was travelling with the troops to St. John, New Brunswick to ship out for Europe, his world was finally in order, especially as his parents had been stoic in their farewells: "You and father [are] the bravest people I think I ever saw" (CWM, T.F. McIlwraith to family, 14 December 1917). On his last weekend with his parents in Hamilton, Tom felt peaceful enough to observe "a very fine specimen of cecropia cocoon on the pussy willow tree in our back yard" (TFMP, T.F. McIlwraith to Dorothy McIlwraith, 10 November 1917).

Wartime Correspondence

On the train travelling towards the *Missanabie*, McIlwraith immediately began writing letters and postcards to his family, and because there was little else to

---

10 "Thomas Forsyth McIlwraith," Attestation Paper, University of Toronto Training, Canadian Over-Seas Expeditionary Force, Soldiers of the First War, LAC, http://www.bac-lac.gc.ca/eng /discover/military-heritage/first-world-war/personnel-records/Pages/item.aspx?IdNumber =155743 (accessed 27 July 2017).

do, he had the leisure to turn the first few letters into a blow-by-blow report of his observations. The journey became a condensed lesson in Canadian history, including his first vote in a federal election, first-hand experience of French Canadians' hostile response to conscription, and the fallout from the devastating explosion in Halifax in early December 1917 when a French cargo ship laden with wartime explosives collided with a Norwegian vessel.

As the clocks were changed to Atlantic time and the Intercolonial Railway train came close enough to the St. Lawrence to reveal "rough ice packs drifting around everywhere" (CWM, T.F. McIlwraith to family, 16 December 1917), word came that McIlwraith and his fellow soldiers were able to vote en route under the Military Voting Act, a privilege so exciting that he described the process in three different letters: "[a] warrant officer was sent aboard as a deputy returning officer at Montreal. We swore that we had not before voted in this election and marked our ballots which were then put into a heavy locked bag" (CWM, T.F. McIlwraith to family, 16 December 1917). He regretted that neither his mother nor his sister Marjorie was able to take advantage of the special dispensation for female relatives of soldiers to be allowed to vote because "a soldier must be out of Canada to qualify them and the time for being enumerated stops tomorrow" (CWM, T.F. McIlwraith to Dorothy McIlwraith, 29 November 1917). He was keen for his family to send him a Hamilton paper or the Toronto *Globe* so he could read up on the results for Ontario now that he had cast his first-ever vote for Conservative Thomas Joseph Stewart in Hamilton West, and he was eager to know whether the soldiers' vote had made any difference.

In November 1917, he had attended Sir Robert Borden's "big mass meeting ... for Union government" at Massey Hall (and two years later shook hands with him in Cambridge when the Canadian prime minister received an LLD). McIlwraith joined the crowd in yelling "traitors" when Borden referred to Quebec's lack of support for Union (CWM, T.F. McIlwraith to Dorothy McIlwraith, 18 November 1917). Conscription was supported by Borden's camp but opposed by French Canadians, and McIlwraith's train was booed in Montmagny. He treated the hostile reception with contempt: "If the artillery men were ever let loose there sure would be a grand clean-up as our men are a rough crowd," and "Laurier would get mighty little encouragement from the votes cast by our men" (CWM, T.F. McIlwraith to family, 16 December 1917). There were "a few, very few, posters in French for the Victory Loan." The peacetime stereotype of quaint North American Frenchmen filling in for their European equivalents when Anglophone tourists were unable to get to the real thing is here transformed into the advance guard of the enemy, represented by a "greasy Frenchman" or a "fat and voluble" one (CWM, T.F. McIlwraith to family, 16 December 1917). Some exceptions did exist, such as "a Frenchman [at Rivière-du-Loup who] came out to the street and played God Save the King on an old out-of-tune mouth organ" (CWM, T.F. McIlwraith to family, 20 December

1917–2 January 1918). McIlwraith mailed postcards with bulletins about the intense voting observed at various railway stops. In the town of Rogersville, in New Brunswick, he and his companions tried, unsuccessfully, to get "solid Laurier" folk "to come over and be convinced to vote for Borden" (CWM, T.F. McIlwraith to his mother, 17 December 1917). Moncton was "doing nothing but vote" (CWM, T.F. McIlwraith to Dorothy McIlwraith, 17 December 1917). In St. John, he finally had word that "Union is in, cheers for Borden" (CWM, T.F. McIlwraith to Dorothy McIlwraith, 18 December 1917). In Rivière-du-Loup, they spied "a large motor truck with Halifax relief on it" (CWM, T.F. McIlwraith to family, 16 December 1917). Because of the Halifax explosion, the train had to detour to St. John, New Brunswick for passengers to board their ship. Although censorship forbade him to give the name of the port to his family, his wartime diary indicates that the ship did pass through Halifax on its way out, but that the soldiers were unable to see any of the devastation because of dense fog.

Detailed descriptions of these and other events occur in an extensive and carefully managed correspondence begun by McIlwraith and his family even before he left Canadian soil. A small saga involving astonishingly efficient communication by letter, postcard, and telegraph developed over a package that Aunt Nellie sent "out to the boat by the pilot" on the day he was expected to leave "Montreal by boat." When there was a delay, she retrieved the parcel by sending a telegram to Halifax, making him briefly nervous that he had "let ... out military secrets" by indicating their port of departure. To conclude the episode, one of the first letters to reach him in Britain was a message from Nellie forwarded from Burwash Hall to assure him that the errant parcel had been safely retrieved and to wish him Godspeed (CWM, T.F. McIlwraith to Dorothy McIlwraith, 4 December 1917; T.F. McIlwraith to family, 17 January 1918). For mutual orientation, the McIlwraiths dated and numbered letters and packages, and they conscientiously acknowledged receipt. This system proved helpful because it repeatedly allowed them to account for mail that had gone down with a torpedoed ship, such as the *Andania* (CWM, T.F. McIlwraith to Dorothy McIlwraith, 27 January 1918), and the prospect of losing mail almost instantly raised its head when a fire, fortunately hosed down before too much damage was done, broke out on the *Missanabie* and "bags and bags of mail [were] pulled out" to save them (CWM, T.F. McIlwraith to family, 20 December 1917–2 January 1918). As well, the McIlwraiths' tracking system brought some narrative order to the family's communication because letters arrived in either a trickle or in floods and were often wildly out of sequence. As Tom put it, the mails were often "doing ... gymnastics" or "funny stunts" (CWM, T.F. McIlwraith to Dorothy McIlwraith, 28 April and 20 May 1918). Too much mail was preferable to too little, and he was delighted when a procession of nurses deposited five parcels from home on his bed when he was convalescing from influenza in Cambridge, or when as many as thirty letters accumulated as he was marching across Belgium towards Cologne.

Tom and his immediate circle of correspondents would, of course, not have been McIlwraiths if their wartime connections had confined themselves to family. Names related to their Hamilton circle – Hardy, Hills, Collinson, Heming, Beasley, and Cruikshank, to name only a few – show up often as he receives greetings, letters, and packages from them. McIlwraith begins his networking on board the *Missanabie*, where he "got talking with one of the V.A.D.'s" and found she was a "Miss Joseph ... from Quebec who had met Dorothy there. Another Quebec V.A.D., a Miss Gibson, ... said she knew [McIlwraith's cousin] Willis quite well" (CWM, T.F. McIlwraith to family, 20 December 1917–2 January 1918). Also on board were friends of Philip Child, one of whom trained for "the kite balloon section of the navy" at the Caldale Airship Station in the Orkneys and later visited McIlwraith in Cambridge (CWM, T.F. McIlwraith to family, 23 March 1918). Once he was in Great Britain, McIlwraith received an introduction to the dean of Peterborough Cathedral from Mr. Aldous, Jean's collaborator on *Ptarmigan*, and Tom paid a visit to the dean when he was staying in Sheffield with the in-laws of his army friend Walter Burd. In Ayr, on his first extended trip to Scotland, Tom had an excellent lunch with Jean's friends, the Ritchies and Steeles, and was regaled with stories about his parents' younger days. A Miss Jameson wrote from Paris (where she was probably a V.A.D. with the Red Cross) and invited him to drop in. And so on.

In addition to his family keeping careful track of their correspondence with Tom, his own letters were backed up by a diary. Such diaries were, strictly speaking, forbidden by military regulations but nevertheless kept by numerous soldiers.[11] Tom used his journal entries to ensure there was a substitute for any information lost in the mail and also to record items that he did not consider suitable for letters to his family, such as lectures on venereal disease, a bout of dysentery on arrival in France, episodes of serious drinking when he was stationed in Germany, and his feelings of abject misery when he had to leave his KOSB friends behind. His longer letters were themselves a kind of journal as he often kept up a running commentary over several days, writing in as many as ten "spasms" (CWM, T.F. McIlwraith to Dorothy McIlwraith, 29 November 1917). Sometimes, he lost his thread among the mass of new impressions and repeated information contained in an earlier part of the letter because he was too tired to read it over before mailing it. At other times, the chronology became scrambled when events in real time, such as an air

---

11   Carol Reid (collections manager, CWM Archives) explains in an email to Eva-Marie Kröller, 23 December 2014: "While soldiers were ordered not to keep diaries (or take photographs) nonetheless they did and in great numbers. I think we have about 200 from the First World War in our collection."

raid, interrupted the description of events in the past, including a sightseeing tour of Westminster Abbey: "Right here I had to stop for a reason I will tell you about, and I will let the Abbey stop too for the present" (CWM, T.F. McIlwraith to Dorothy McIlwraith, 27 January 1918). While he requested that his own letters be preserved for future reference, he kept his luggage light by destroying most incoming mail in a periodic "grand clean-up" after ensuring that "any points in them that seem to want answering" had been attended to, sometimes in a rather shapeless list (CWM, T.F. McIlwraith to Dorothy McIlwraith, 29 November 1917). Except for a couple of his sister's letters that he decided to keep because they contained descriptions of victory celebrations in New York, Dorothy's detailed reports on New York in wartime, his parents' accounts of daily life in Hamilton while he was away, or any other news from relatives and acquaintances are lost. As a result, a few of McIlwraith's responses now lack some of the necessary context but his own very detailed letters mostly make up for these gaps.

All of his correspondents became adept at paying close attention to customs and censorship regulations, the advantages of registering a letter, and the need to write McIlwraith's name and rank the correct way: "My address is Cadet T.F. McIlwraith, 'E' company, 2nd Officer Cadet Battalion, Peterhouse, Cambridge. Special Request to Dorothy – please do not address any more envelopes to Tom McI. Thomas if you like, but not Tom" (CWM, T.F. McIlwraith to his mother, 8 February 1918). He pleaded, "If I get my commission for goodness sake address letters to 2nd lieut, not lieut." (CWM, T.F. McIlwraith to family, 15 February 1918). His letters home alternated between mail sent to his parents in Hamilton, to be forwarded to his sister Dorothy in New York, where she was working as an editor, and letters sent to Dorothy, to be forwarded to Hamilton. Correspondence with his sister required up-to-date knowledge of the increasingly complicated regulations for mail to and from the United States, and in the last few months of the war she had to reroute her many packages to him through Canada because, for reasons they do not specify, it was no longer possible to send them directly. Although he feared shortly after arrival in Britain that "there won't be a thing to say when I get properly settled down and you will be disappointed at getting small letters" (CWM, T.F. McIlwraith to family, 17 January 1918), his missives were rarely under ten pages and at their most extreme clocked in at over fifty. One of his bulkier letters roused the wrath of a censor who had to wade through it, and McIlwraith related the episode to his folks in the third person as concerning "[o]ne of the chaps in our company," but gave enough detail to clarify that the story was in fact about him. Probably because it was missing a military address, which, he thought, would have automatically protected the letter from interference, this "chap" had a letter to his sister in New York returned to him with "a printed slip that 'an unnecessarily long letter is a waste of man-power in the censor's office; please re-write this letter so that it can be read quickly and forwarded' " (CWM, T.F. McIlwraith to family, 23 March 1918).

This particular act of censorship may have saved manpower, but it did not save paper, itself an increasingly rare commodity. Label-stickers were introduced to economize on envelopes, and wrapping paper sometimes repeatedly crossed the Atlantic in parcels going back and forth. Recycling paper was not a difficult thing to learn for a McIlwraith because even in peacetime it was a well-established family custom to use every scrap of it. Tom also helped himself to supplies whenever possible until his "letter case [was] bulged away out with odds and ends of sheets of paper" (CWM, T.F. McIlwraith to family, 17 January 1918). His friend Walter Burd wondered if "notepaper annexing [was] a malady in the McIlwraith family" after Tom's father raided the insurance office in which he was now working for paper and sent it to his son (CWM, T.F. McIlwraith to family, 21 July 1918). Stationery from Mr. McIlwraith's various business offices shows up well into his son's studies at Cambridge, and at times it becomes a kind of sketchy family history in its own right. Thus, in March 1921, Tom was using up "a number of foolscap size Delaware and Hudson Coal Co. forms," dated "189-" and showing "signs of both fire and water, perhaps signs of the blaze in the old office at the wharf" (CWM, T.F. McIlwraith to family, 21 March 1921). His mother and sister often included notepads, special " 'overseas' paper" (CWM, T.F. McIlwraith to Dorothy McIlwraith, 29 November 1917), and refills for his diary in their packages to ensure that he did not have to deal with too many cases of "paper famine," which otherwise had him scribble on the back of notes from lectures on military strategy (CWM, T.F. McIlwraith to family, 23 March 1918). One of several advantages of joining the Cambridge Union Society, a privilege extended to cadets for a nominal fee, was that it provided both a peaceful place to write and the notepaper to do it on. The union notepaper joined an eclectic collection that included everything from "Y.M.C.A. On Active Service," "The Royal, St. John N.B.," and "The Canadian Pacific Ocean Services" to "The Gordon Highlanders," "The Plume of Feathers Hotel," and "21 Montague Road, Richmond." The loss of his fountain pen on his way into France was a disaster, both for McIlwraith and for the present-day researcher who has to decipher fading pencil until Tom has found a replacement pen. He liked to illustrate his letters with photographs after his mother had given him "a very nice little pocket folding camera" (CWM, T.F, McIlwraith to Dorothy McIlwraith, 29 November 1917), and supplies of film and technical equipment not easily available in Britain or Germany, such as Vest Pocket Autographic Kodak films or a viewfinder, were forwarded from Canada.

The "epistolary pact" (Lyons 57) between Tom and his family stipulated that his letters were to be shared with the immediate family only, and not with other relatives or acquaintances unless carefully edited. The extended family whose support was welcome in some ways created complications in others, and McIlwraith's mother repeatedly found herself in the unhappy position of having to decide between her son's directives and her obligations to the family at large. He asked her to censor sections written with her interest in everyday detail in mind, such as the names, appearances, and personalities of his closest army friends, but it must have been quite a job for his family to edit his multi-page epistles for more general consumption while sticking to his instructions for what was and was not suitable to pass on: "If necessary omit a page, even if it doesn't make sense and patch up spelling if it can be done without show-ing" (CWM, T.F. McIlwraith to family, 8 March 1918). His mother repeatedly did not even try to fish out appropriate sections and, despite earlier assurances to her son that she would not do so, passed on whole letters to family in the Eastern Townships whom Tom did not consider part of the inner circle. As well, he suspected her – wrongly, as it turned out – of informing the Hamilton *Herald* of his adventures as assistant education officer in Germany, resulting in an article that created unwanted publicity and spread erroneous information. Having nervously consulted with Dorothy shortly after his arrival in Britain whether she thought "the family like[d] such long letters" (CWM, T.F. McIl-wraith to Dorothy McIlwraith, 27 January 1918), Tom was so furious at what he perceived as a breach of trust and a sabotage of his military career that he threatened to write only brief and generic letters in future, or to even stop writ-ing altogether:

> It spoils the pleasure of writing home – makes it a drudgery in fact – to think that as soon as I am out of Canada mother breaks a distinct promise she made to me and passes around letters when knowing my views on the subject. (CWM, T.F. McIlwraith to family, 16 April 1918)

As writing letters was as essential to his own well-being as receiving them was to his family's, he did not succeed long in producing letters of "rational size," but the rift was serious enough for his father to intervene and obtain his son's promise that the letters would continue. During a second altercation, this time in a letter that elsewhere tenderly enquired about her always fragile health, T.F. punished his mother by "confin[ing] himself to the most trivial matters" and "omit[ting] quite a number of things which might have interested you" (CWM, T.F. McIlwraith to family, 3 May 1919). His mother's alleged breach of trust seemed heinous enough to have him compare it with the Germans break-ing their word when they invaded Belgium. The Germans' treachery remained a powerful point of reference for him in later years. From fieldwork in Bella Coola, he wrote to his teacher A.C. Haddon that "[t]he whole life of the people has been broken down by our 'civilization,' and we have treated them in a man-ner that has many points of resemblance with the Germans in Belgium" (*HBCI*, T.F. McIlwraith to A.C. Haddon, 29 August 1922, 68). Fortunately, his mother did not accidentally forward the letter containing his pithy comment on Kennedy McIlwraith's wife May to the wrong people: "My I loathe that woman" (CWM, T.F. McIlwraith to Dorothy McIlwraith, 11 October 1917).

Writing about letters between sons and mothers in the Second World War, Jenny Hartley refers to such correspondence as a crucial component in writers' maintaining and, if necessary, reassembling a sense of "continuous character and identity" that was being jeopardized by the chaos of war. "The calming and reassuring tableau of composition draws attention to the writer as self-creator, and reminds us that the word 'composition' has more than one meaning" (Hartley 192–3). On the *Missanabie*, the image of McIlwraith looking through "the window of the lounge room in front of which [he is] writing" at the convoy of troopships travelling across the Atlantic (CWM, T.F. McIlwraith to family, 20 December 1917–2 January 1918) was meant to be such a reassuring scene, one he knew his mother needed to regain some peace of mind after their recent parting, even if a convoy of troopships may not have been her idea of a peaceful scene. Hartley's term of a silent "tableau" also fits the family's habit of keeping worries to themselves. Misunderstandings were sometimes the result. Thus, McIlwraith confided in Dorothy that their mother mistook his sudden failure to rant about "all the bums who haven't reported, or … the swarms who are claiming exemption" as a newfound readiness not to be so "hard judging people." The real reason was his recent success in enlisting and the fact that he could no longer be mistaken for a "slacker" (CWM, T.F. McIlwraith to Dorothy McIlwraith, 10 November 1917). In turn, the siblings were alert to their mother's "fidgeting" or becoming "blue and flustered" as signals that a situation was becoming too much for her. When she unexpectedly calmed down and she "thought it was religion," Tom expressed his hope that "it sticks with her" (CWM, T.F. McIlwraith to Dorothy McIlwraith, 10 November 1917; TFMF, T.F. McIlwraith to family, 4 January 1920).

Although his sense of imperial mission remained unshaken, T.F. looked for ways to ease his family's anxiety. One method was to use homely comparisons to bring martial rhetoric down to earth. He dwelled on the miseries of seasickness endured by everyone on board, and he sent along the prescription for bromo seltzer he was issued to make him feel better. He suggested that the lookout seemed "exactly like your big, oblong clothes boiler with a lid suspended over it" and he thought the "two engines" that pulled their train from Glasgow to London "looked like peanut roasters" (CWM, T.F. McIlwraith to family, 20 December 1917). He reached for more outlandish comparisons when the *Missanabie* inched up the river Clyde towards Glasgow and he recorded, awestruck, on the military activity on both sides of the river, including "a huge aeroplane factory with a flock of tanks spread out in a field alongside." The tanks had the air of "a bunch of fat slugs at a sewing meeting" (CWM, T.F. McIlwraith to family, 2 January 1918). "Tanks" was one of the divisions he had considered joining, and there clearly had been a hot debate at home as to whether tanks or infantry was the more dangerous posting. McIlwraith picked up on the discussion in one of his first letters after arriving in Glasgow, justifying his decision to join the infantry and alternating between soothing his mother's fears and displaying his bravado. One can only imagine the response at the other end when he writes, "As regards danger[,] mother, I do not think there is much to choose. In every attack tanks go forward and some do not come back. The same is true of the attacking infantry" (CWM, T.F. McIlwraith to his mother, 2 January 1918). Comparing the tanks to "fat slugs at a sewing meeting" was an awkward effort to reconcile the conflicting notions of what thrilled him but appalled his mother.

Dorothy McIlwraith

Such tensions never plagued his relationship with his sister Dorothy (nicknamed "Dorfa" or "Dorf" because of T.F.'s inability, as a young child, to pronounce her name), with whom he was exceptionally close when he was a young man. She graduated from McGill University in 1914, where she had honed her literary and organizational skills by writing poetry, serving on the editorial board of the yearbook, and acting as president of the reading club. Because no suitable jobs were forthcoming at home, she found work in New York publishing thanks to Jean's intervention, beginning with a temporary summer job in 1913 at Doubleday, Page ("Genealogy"). In subsequent years, Dorothy worked for the *American Magazine* and the *Independent* before she moved on to the Rockefeller Foundation, Doubleday, Doran Publishers, and *Short Stories*. Between 1940 and 1954, she became the well-paid editor of the science-fiction magazine *Weird Tales*, where she published Ray Bradbury, Margaret St. Clair, Hannes Bok, Anthony Boucher, Joseph Payne Brennan, and others. This career is outside the scope of the present study but deserves separate study.[12] The Battle of Loos in 1915 demoralized her deeply, and she describes her initial motivation to move to the States as the decision of someone who did not "care ... what happened to [her]." In an unpublished memoir, "CONCERNING US CANADIANS," she wrote that with the disastrous defeat at Loos, "[t]he life [she] had dreamed of living had vanished over night."[13] She does not specify what kind of life that would have been.

---

12 See "Meet the Editor." Scholarly work on Dorothy McIlwraith, and women in science fiction generally, is as yet sparse, but see Yaszek and Sharp 306–13.

13 Yaszek and Sharp have McIlwraith in New York by Christmas 1917, but she arrived sooner, and her letters indicate that she was well settled in the city by October 1917. See also Hanley.

She appears to have rallied, however, and began to write articles about the Canadian war effort for US magazines. The features included "The Canadian Red Cross Carries On" for the *Red Cross Magazine*, "Canada's Half Million" for the *Independent*, and, for the *New Country Life*, a piece of reportage on the wartime contributions of fruit growers in the Niagara Peninsula. The latter bears the wonderfully two-pronged title of "Sending Tommy His Marmalade" but omits to mention that the author has a brother by that name overseas. Because of the Americans' reluctance to enter the war, her attitude towards the States remained conflicted and, as a proud British imperialist, she never became a US citizen. In "CONCERNING US CANADIANS," she expressed her reservations but used greater restraint in expressing her views about Americans than she did in writing to her brother. Despite their numerous family connections in Detroit and elsewhere in the States, brother and sister were very critical of Americans in their correspondence. Dorothy was particularly angered by the Armistice celebrations in New York: "In front of the library where there is a huge map showing the western front, some men were writing U.S. all over Germany and blotting out the battle line," she writes, and in another letter she sums up her impression that "everyone I saw was a perfect idiot. Fed up is the word for me and the U.S.A." (TFMP, Dorothy McIlwraith to T.F. McIlwraith, 8 and 6 November 1918). She was not impressed by the spectacle of "two continuous processions" of people with horns, rattles, and "a flag tied round their hat" travelling up and down Fifth Avenue, with coffins containing effigies of the Kaiser being wheeled through the streets and a blizzard of ticker tape descending from the office windows.

Tom visited Dorothy in New York shortly before going overseas, thanking her afterwards for "one gorgeous time": "you bet I like playing around with mine Dorfa" (CWM, T.F. McIlwraith to Dorothy McIlwraith, 10 November 1917). He praised her as "a sport and just the sort of sister any fellow would like to have" (CWM, T.F. McIlwraith to family, 14 December 1917). Dorothy was his confidante, extra parent, best friend, his "gem," and "cute lady" (CWM, T.F. McIlwraith to Dorothy McIlwraith, 25 April 1918; 9 October 1917). When his "Best Beloved of Dorfas" suffered through a period of bad health while he was a student at Cambridge, he felt "drefful sorry" for her (TFMF, T.F. McIlwraith to Dorothy McIlwraith, 12 August 1920). She understood his loving but difficult relationship with their high-strung mother and helped him navigate it. Although much of his correspondence was relayed from Hamilton to New York and vice versa, Tom frequently wrote letters to her that were obviously not to be shared with the rest of the family because they discussed tensions at home. Variations of "you know what I mean" dot this correspondence. With Dorothy's sympathetic assistance, Tom dealt with his guilt about leaving home. He closely observed their mother's restless anxiety as his departure approached when she "had listened to some idiot who said I would not be able to let her know when I was going and had got it into her head that I had gone when I did not write for a few days" (CWM, T.F. McIlwraith to Dorothy McIlwraith, 29 November 1917). When he reached Britain, he fired off a brief note as soon as he was permitted to confirm arrival, warning that his first detailed letter would likely take some time to get to Hamilton (CWM, T.F. McIlwraith to his mother, 31 December 1917). He complained when Dorothy was not immediately forthcoming with details, such as telling him "how mother is feeling, whether it was altogether too much for her, and a batch of things of that kind which you know that I want to know about." He was relieved that the roses he had ordered for Christmas had safely arrived: "Were they a dozen roses as I ordered, and were they nice ones? Also, what else did mother get for Christmas?" (CWM, T.F. McIlwraith to Dorothy McIlwraith, 27 January 1918). The support was not one-sided either. Dorothy's own departure for New York and her insistence on making an independent life for herself did not meet with her mother's full approval. Despite her obvious pride in her daughter's professional success, Mary wanted her to return to Hamilton and settle down nearby with a family of her own. Dorothy happily reported on her achievements, such as earning $25 for "Sending Tommy His Marmalade," and confided her dreams for the future in her brother, her wish for a house on Long Island "and a flivver and a dog." He therefore made a point of describing any dogs he came across (CWM, T.F. McIlwraith to Dorothy McIlwraith, 14 December 1917), and because she also appears to have been fond of children, especially mischievous little boys, he faithfully reported on any sightings of these too.

Brother and sister were less concerned about their self-sufficient father's ability to cope with his son's absence. Tom often had to encourage him to write more about himself and his doings, assured him that all of his day-to-day news was interesting, and immediately gave in when his father took his mother's side after she had angered her son by showing letters to unauthorized parties. Except for thanks in the family letters for her excellent baking and a separate letter for her birthday written in a much stiffer style than the comfortable slang of his correspondence with Dorothy, their sister Marjorie featured little in the letters, even as he dutifully acknowledged any news about her activities. Although Marjorie was the oldest, neither he nor Dorothy was willing to concede the same privileges of freedom to her they claimed for themselves. When a gardening course took Marjorie to Guelph for three weeks, her brother was in high dudgeon, and he commended the family for "not letting Marjorie take that other course; on any account either she or Dorothy should be at home" (CWM, T.F. McIlwraith to Dorothy McIlwraith, 28 April 1918). After the war, he repeated similar exhortations any time Marjorie tried to create an independent life for herself and impressed upon her (who was, it must be remembered, eleven years his senior) that "none of us children should forget that we must do as [mother] wants" (TFMF, T.F. McIlwraith to Marjorie McIlwraith, 11 January

1920). The parents were well aware that their children were not created equal. In one of her congratulatory letters to Tom, this one to Cambridge when he had earned his BA, his mother cites from the Book of Joshua to characterize Marjorie, who became a missionary in later life. Compared to her glamorous siblings, she was a "sawyer of wood and drawer of water." Mary added: "I hope she will have a reward in Heaven" (TFMP, Mary Stevens to T.F. McIlwraith, 10 August 1921).

Dorothy was interested in absolutely everything about her brother's experience of the war. They shared affection for each other and love for the empire, and one suspects that by enlisting, Tom had chosen a man's version of "the life she had dreamed of living" herself and that the second-best solution was to live the experience through him. She treats him so much as an equal that it is easy to forget that there was an eight-year difference in age. Occasionally she tried to be the older sister when she has something to say about his spelling, questioning "serjeant" (correct in some military contexts) for "sergeant" (CWM, T.F. McIlwraith to family, 8 March 1918), but she appears to have given up on the reprimands because his persistent mangling of "demobilization" as "demobolization" or "Bosche" for "Boche" remain unchallenged. At times, he humours her by anticipating her editorial reproach and annotating the complaint himself in a bracket, as in "(oh you split infinitive)" (CWM, T.F. McIlwraith to Dorothy McIlwraith, 6 April 1918). More importantly, she pressed him for clarification if he did not volunteer it, such as the tartan of his uniform: the KOSB wore the blue-and-green Lesley tartan, he obliged, while the pipers were in the colours of Royal Stuart, "which is very red and gorgeous" (CWM, T.F. McIlwraith to family, 21 May 1919). Their intimacy is one reason why Tom's rather juvenile experiments in coded correspondence – "[w]atch for a bent-in (and then flattened-out) lower left hand corner" (CWM, T.F. McIlwraith to Dorothy McIlwraith, 29 November 1917) – make excellent sense: despite the length of his letters, there were many aspects of their personal lives that required only the briefest of allusions. Before the war was over, an undated letter containing a more elaborate coding system was hand-delivered either to Dorothy or his parents by a friend, one of the few civilians to brave an Atlantic crossing. The letter assumes that the code would assist its recipients in communicating with T.F. should he be taken prisoner of war, but it is of a piece with the siblings' insistence on seeing the war as a Boy's Own adventure. As soon as the Armistice had been declared, she proposed to visit him in Britain, but this plan had to wait until he was installed as a student at Cambridge.[14]

Once he had issued an urgent plea for packages of candy, much of Dorothy's salary went to keeping her "dear boy" in "sweet stuff." Many of the forty-odd

---

14 For wartime brother-sister relationships, see Woollacott, "Sisters and Brothers in Arms."

parcels McIlwraith received between January 1918 and August 1919 came from her, and his companions at Peterhouse College made a habit of toasting "Mac's sister in New York" when they helped her brother to devour the contents – except when "a tube of mints" was revealed to be "made in Austria, and therefore scorned by several of [his] friends" (CWM, T.F. McIlwraith to Dorothy McIlwraith, 6 April and 11 June 1918). He gave specifications of the kind of sweets he liked, such as "several tons of those biscuits shaped like this [rectangle sketched], two layers with soft filling between – cream sandwiches I think they are called," though the "six hot chocolate fudges in a row" he craved were a thing of the distant future and "the making of ice cream or iced custard of any kind" was forbidden in England from early 1918 onwards (CWM, T.F. McIlwraith to Dorothy McIlwraith, 27 January 1918). His sister sent "très fine" Loft's chocolates, including "six whopping soft coconut performances," cans of peaches, salted peanuts, and chocolate cakes, and also sardines, cigarettes, and toothpaste. Any remaining gaps in the packages were filled with lumps of sugar. She took the trouble to wrap each item separately, apparently a tradition from his childhood birthdays when presents were wrapped in many layers and hidden around the house for him to find (CWM, T.F. McIlwraith to Dorothy McIlwraith, 9 April 1918). He even requested that she not tell him the contents of the parcels in her letters so as not to spoil the surprise.

Wartime Reading and Entertainment

The abrupt switches between momentous historical event and everyday domestic worries that characterize McIlwraith's letters are typical of the "paratactic" style that everyday correspondence shares with the diary, but the resulting gaps are often overcome with the help of his copious reading (see Lyons 60, 53). His thorough knowledge of travel writing, historical fiction, and poetry from the British imperial tradition provided him with a repertoire that could be adapted to his wartime adventures. During training at Burwash Hall, he read historical novels, Sir Walter Scott's *Quentin Durward* and William Thackeray's *Henry Esmond*, both featuring Scottish soldiers engaged in historical international conflict. He browsed through the patriotic verse of Alfred Noyes, possibly because Noyes's collaborator Sir Beerbohm Tree had referred to it during his presentation at McGill. Towards the end of his life, McIlwraith recalled how he and Dorothy made a habit of reciting poetry together "by the mile" while doing the dishes ("Genealogy"), and he remembers in his wartime letters that she read him Thomas Macaulay's "The Battle of Lake Regillus" from the *Lays of Ancient Rome* (1842). During fieldwork in Bella Coola in 1923, he was called upon to "coach the youngsters on the town-site [for] a Christmas tree entertainment," and recalling "Dorothy's huge poetry book," he facetiously taught them Lewis Carroll's "The Mad Gardener's Song" and Eugene Fields's "Jest 'Fore Christmas"

(*HBCI*, T.F. McIlwraith to father, 10 December 1923, 107). The siblings were steeped in the English poetry collected in Arthur Quiller-Couch's famous *Oxford Book of English Verse*. "One notice that caught my eye as we were going through [Jesus College] was that Professor Sir A. Quiller-Couch would lecture at a certain hour," McIlwraith reported as he arrived in Cambridge for officer training. "I did not know that he hung out at Cambridge" (CWM, T.F. McIlwraith to family, 15 February 1918). Quiller-Couch had been appointed to the King Edward VII Professorship of English Literature two years before the outbreak of war and was elected fellow of Jesus College.

Above all, brother and sister shared a passion for Rudyard Kipling, whom their Aunt Jean appears to have met through her work at Doubleday, Page, his American publisher. Tom and Dorothy cite or refer to Kipling at least a dozen times in their letters; they had even created a private "Kipling game" (TFMF, T.F. McIlwraith to Dorothy McIlwraith, 8 December 1920), the rules of which they unfortunately do not pass on. To Tom and Dorothy, Kipling's verse supplied a blueprint for everything from heroic sentiment to unfamiliar trees, and monkey puzzle trees in English gardens had McIlwraith ask Dorothy whether she remembered "Kipling's yarn" in the story "The Puzzler" (1906) (CWM, T.F. McIlwraith to Dorothy, 27 January 1918). During a weekend away from COTC training spent with his family in Hamilton, his mother persuaded him to attend a service at St. Paul's Presbyterian Church with her. He found the sermon average, but was impressed when the "beefy old Methodist" preacher, "a Dr. Chown,"[15] quoted from Kipling's poem "The Return" (1903) to illustrate "the dangers to which our troops [are] exposed in England" (CWM, T.F. McIlwraith to Dorothy McIlwraith, 23 October 1917). Tom remembered Kipling's "The English Flag" (1891) as the *Missanabie* crossed the Atlantic, and "the whistling of two other boats from the fog on either side" reminded him of the tolling of "the frighted ship bells" described in this poem (CWM, T.F. McIlwraith to family, 20 December 1917–2 January 1918).

He knew the verse so well that, during his officer training in Cambridge, he could be pressed at short notice into reciting "The English Flag" at an Empire Day celebration. He was "cheered by the troops" for his "strong-lunged" recitation of "Gunga Din" (1890) at a concert on board the *Royal George* during his journey back to Canada ("Genealogy"). On that occasion, he paired Kipling's poem with J. Milton Hayes's "The Green Eye of the Little Yellow God" (1911), while at other times Robert Service's "The Cremation of Sam McGee" (1907) made for a popular duo with either Kipling or Hayes. Books and magazines with stories by Kipling went back and forth in the mail between Tom and Dorothy. On a visit to Scotland he perused the memorial tablet to the Indian Rebellion in St. Giles, Edinburgh, and found "Lest we forget" from "The Recessional,"

---

15 See "Samuel Dwight Chown."

the first time he saw Kipling quoted in such a place although it was surely not the last (CWM, T.F. McIlwraith to Dorothy McIlwraith, 28 April 1918). The McIlwraiths' enthusiasm for Kipling was shared so extensively by wartime readers that Ian Hay was able to parody the writer's popularity in *The First Hundred Thousand*. Here, all of the forty volumes of Kipling in the Service edition weigh down the luggage of a fictitious recruit who has to learn the hard way to pack his Wolseley valise more efficiently. When his sister forwarded *The Years Between*, a collection of melancholy verse published in 1919, when Kipling was grieving the death of his only son John at Loos, McIlwraith found the verse too cryptic for his taste, greatly preferring the straightforward language of earlier poems like "The Grave of the Hundred Dead" and its " '*drip-drip-drip*' from the baskets" containing the bloody heads of the slaughtered of Papengmay (1888).

McIlwraith's reservations when it came to "Kip's" most recent work did not, however, permanently sour his enjoyment. A couple of years later, when he was a student at Cambridge, he went on a walking tour with his army friend Leslie Houstoun in Dunbartonshire, and the two spent an evening in a fisherman's cottage on Loch Long "playing 2 handed bridge and talking Kipling like mad" (CWM, T.F. McIlwraith to Dorothy McIlwraith, n.d. [April 1920?]). That vacation, first planned for August 1919 after demobilization, had been postponed when plans to visit the loch were thwarted by the rush to organize his registration at Cambridge. In between a frenzied program of meeting professors, tutor, and master at St. John's College, filling in complicated application forms, picking up urgent mail at the post office, and wiring the Pirbright Military Training Centre for extension of his military leave, he still made time to visit the library to learn a few new Kipling poems by heart "for use on Loch Long" in case the tour could be squeezed in after all (WD, 9 August 1919). He railed against the cost of the three-volume Inclusive Edition of Kipling's verse published by Doubleday in 1919, but was overjoyed to receive the books for Christmas from Dorothy, with whom he continued to trade titles of poems. He sent her an exegesis of Kipling's "The Bee-Boy's Song" from *Puck of Pook's Hill* (1906) along anthropological lines, and though he thought little of women in academia – or women generally at the time – Mary Kingsley's account of her *Travels in West Africa* (1897) commended itself to him because she quoted Kipling frequently (CWM, T.F. McIlwraith to Dorothy McIlwraith, 30 September and 21 September 1920). McIlwraith's love of Kipling continued unabated in later years and was sometimes put to unexpected use. Even his *The Bella Coola Indians* (1948) contains a quotation from Kipling. There, the line "men in a world of men" from "England's Answer" (1893),[16] a poem composed to mark the opening of the Imperial Institute, is radically reinterpreted to refer not to the "Sons of the Blood" but to

---

16 Rudyard Kipling, *The Cambridge Edition of the Poems of Rudyard Kipling*, Volume I: *Collected Poems I*, 329.

"the faults and follies as well as the elements of strength and wisdom" that make "the Bella Coola ... essentially similar to ourselves" (*BCI* 2: 530).

In describing for his family the scene of his departure from St. John, McIlwraith puts his copious reading of patriotic literature, sea stories, and maritime scholarship to effective and occasionally operatic use. As a boy, he had feasted on C. Reginald's Enock's *The Secret of the Pacific: A Discussion of the Early Civilisations of America, the Toltecs, Aztecs, Mayas, Incas, and Their Predecessors, and of the Possibilities of Asiatic Influence Thereon* (1912), E. Hamilton Currey's *Sea Wolves of the Mediterranean: The Grand Period of the Moslem Corsairs* (1910), H.J. Snow's *In Forbidden Seas: Recollections of Sea-Otter Hunting in the Kurils* (1910), and Frank T. Bullen's *Denizens of the Deep* (1904), and he now drew on these books to shape his observations. With the *Missanabie's* departure, familial and geographical ties were severed, perhaps permanently, for a dangerous crossing. McIlwraith's farewell scene has additional layers that gradually unfold as his adventure takes its course. Above all, he is a recruit from the Dominion of Canada with a mission to defend the empire. As the grandson of immigrants, he is also "returning" to sites that are both new and familiar. Finally, he is a tourist who looks forward to seeing the best of Britain, despite wartime restrictions. Will Child, acknowledging that McIlwraith was a first-time visitor to the Old Country, ordered a Baedeker delivered to Burwash Hall to help him organize his sight-seeing.

McIlwraith's description of his departure underscores the troops' collective determination to conquer the enemy, and thus straighten out the political and ethical balance temporarily skewed by the war. The scene is dynamic and exuberant, but not disorderly. On the contrary: the enemy better watch out with soldiers this agile and this ready to come at him from all sides: "Looking down from our deck on to the one where the troops were gathered was a sight to be remembered," he wrote. "They were all on deck, standing in groups and cheering, a sight a fellow won't be apt to forget. There are men of all types and character yet each was looking happy and cheering, each of them setting out on the big thing in the world. One chap climbed the rope ladder and got into the look-out ... The fellow found two pieces of stick in it and proceeded to beat time with them. All the soldiers were singing, rag-time chiefly, though Rule Britannia and Land of Hope and Glory also appeared" (CWM, T.F. McIlwraith to family, 20 December 1917–2 January 1918).

Because of the wartime context, the crossing both extends the departure scene and anticipates the battlefield on the other side as the convoy responds in well-choreographed manoeuvres to escalating threat. On a calm day that "[made] grand hunting for [German] submarines," he wrote: "The convoy gathered closer, and soon the whole eight of us were in sight. It sure looked fine to see the eight ships steaming along over a perfectly calm ocean with only a few hundred yards between each. Each one was zigzagging too, in strange looking courses but each in a definite way, and each acting when signal flags were raised on the convoying auxiliary cruiser" (CWM, T.F. McIlwraith to family, 20 December 1917–2 January 1918). His anthropomorphic description of this "procession," in which participants gallantly watch out for each other, echoes similar ones in contemporary juvenile writing about the exploits of the British navy, such as John S. Margerison's *Midshipman Rex Carew, V.C.* (191?). In this book that Dorothy had recommended to him, the names of the ships are clustered to evoke military might, sacred mission, and global sweep, as "the fleets [get] under way – *Hyena* towing *Wolf*, *Princess Alice* and *Burma* steaming to port of them, and *Invincible* to starboard as escorts, while still farther out the two light cruisers led their somewhat depleted destroyer divisions as the outer guard. It would have gone hard with any Hun who had tried to interfere with that procession" (135).

Although he browsed through the *Rubâ'iyât* of Omar Khayyám, his response to Kipling's *The Years Between* indicates McIlwraith's dislike of any form of entertainment that he considered too rarefied. He tried opera in Toronto by attending *Lucia di Lammermoor*, but decided that "[i]t looked pretty queer to ... see a bunch of Dagoes trotting around in tartans" (CWM, T.F. McIlwraith to Dorothy McIlwraith, 29 November 1917). In London, he dutifully went to a performance of *Twelfth Night* because he "had read the play at school" but was disappointed with the "very small stage" as well as the costumes, which were "nothing remarkable" (CWM, T.F. McIlwraith to his mother, 14 February 1919). On the *Royal George* back to Canada in 1919 he complained that the concert presented on board was "rather too high-brow" to be enjoyable (WD, 21 August 1919). Instead, along with other members of the British and Dominion troops, he experienced the "unifying effects [of popular culture], its capacity to bond front and home front" (Winter, "Popular Culture" 331). Like many of his fellow soldiers, he preferred light entertainment, lavishly staged, and he had an appetite for detective drama, musical revue, and light opera, the latter inherited from his father, who had seen *The Mikado* on his honeymoon in London and sang tunes from it around the McIlwraiths' home for years ("Genealogy"). Shortly after arrival in London, Tom obtained tickets for the "show that everybody had to see" (J. White 221), Oscar Asche and Frederic Norton's musical comedy *Chu Chin Chow*. This was followed by Bayard Veiller's mystery *The Thirteenth Chair* and a series of comedies and other plays: Max Marcin and Roy Atwell's *Here Comes the Bride*, Walter W. Ellis's *A Little Bit of Fluff*, Dorothy Brandon's *Wild Heather*, Sir Charles Henry Hawtrey's *The Private Secretary* (this one, surprisingly, was adapted from a German original), Walter Hackett's *The Freedom of the Seas*, Austen Hurgon and George Arthurs's *Yes Uncle*, Charles Guernon and Max Marcin's *The Eyes of Youth*. A favourite, Herman Darewski and Edouard Mathe's revue *As You Were Y'Know*, was "a really screaming farce" (CWM, T.F. McIlwraith to his mother, 14 February 1919). Among the few serious plays he enjoyed was Arnold Bennett's *The Title*, as well as anything by J.M. Barrie, but once he was settled in Cambridge, he saw John Martin Harvey as Hamlet and Maurice Moskowitz as Shylock (CWM, T.F. McIlwraith to family, 31 December 1919). Perhaps to capitalize on the success of *Chu Chin Chow*, there were several shows with "oriental" themes, such as Frances Barclay and Lyon M. Lion's crime drama *The Chinese Puzzle* and Isidore Witmark and William Duncan's operetta *Shanghai* at Drury Lane.[17] The oriental theme did not worry him, but he was taken aback when the usual stereotypes were not being implemented. Thus he found *The Chinese Puzzle* to have "a most peculiar ending in that the Chinaman turns out the hero" (CWM, T.F. McIlwraith to his mother, 19 October 1918).[18]

Like the Family Album in the previous generation, Tom's letters offer ample evidence that, despite growing competition from the gramophone, he and his contemporaries were used to providing their own entertainment by singing, playing musical instruments, and reciting poetry on the many occasions when no professional performances were available. One of his army friends, a lawyer, was able "to recite poetry from Service to Browning by the yard, or even prose" (CWM, T.F. McIlwraith to family, 23 March 1918). On the *Missanabie*, he listened to folk songs, ragtime, and wartime marches – some of them very recently composed – as everyone

> [s]pend[s] the evening [by] standing at the end of the promenade deck and listening to the men singing down below ... There is a draft from the 78th battery at Calgary on board who, they say, have been at the game all summer and they sure can sing well together, all knowing the same tunes. There are some pretty good voices among them and it sounds fine in the moonlight. They have great variety and everything of the last fifty years is dished up, "Annie Laurie" "Way Down Yonder in the Corn Field," "Old Black Joe," "My Home in Indiana," and right up through Harry Lauder and all the ragtime of the last ten years to "Home Again," "Over There," "Joan of Arc," and "Pack All Your Troubles" (CWM, T.F. McIlwraith to family, 20 December 1917–2 January 1918).[19]

As the influence of Darewski's "When We've Wound Up the Watch on the Rhine" illustrates, such entertainment was not merely welcome escape: at times it also provided a satirical tool to process stressful situations. By using popular

---

17   On theatre with an oriental theme in the First World War, see Everett; Singleton.

18   For an overview of performances during the period, see Wearing.

19   "Home Again," 1917, music and lyrics by Will J. White; "Over There," 1917, music and lyrics by George M. Cohan; "Joan of Arc They Are Calling You," 1917, music by Jack Wells, lyrics by Al Bryan and Willie Weston, from the musical production *This Way Out*; "Pack Up Your Troubles in Your Old Kit-Bag," 1916, music by Felix Powell, lyrics by George Henry Powell, from the show *Her Soldier Boy*. See "War Songs," Archives and Research Collection, McMaster University, https://library.mcmaster.ca/archives/w/war.songs.1.htm (accessed 16 August 2019).

songs as flashpoints of resistance, imperial troops were able to express their criticism of their American allies, who they thought had taken their time to wake up to their obligations. As we shall see later in this chapter, "Over There" became such a filter, and it is unusual for McIlwraith not to annotate the American songs performed by the Calgarians with his usual caustic remarks. As an important purveyor of simplified ideas, popular entertainment strengthened solidarity within the empire and shone a light on new ties beyond it.

Knowing her brother's literary taste, Dorothy was on the lookout for books that would keep him entertained without insulting his patriotic sentiment. Few recruits obtained such expert advice on the most recent publications and received so many up-to-date magazines, including *Captain*, the *Saturday Evening Post*, *Maclean's*, *Life*, and "that little editorial magazine from you with the nice thing about British militarism in it" (CWM, T.F. McIlwraith to Dorothy McIlwraith, 10 November 1917). His copious reading of magazines primed him to note the name "Blackwood" on one of the tombstones in an Edinburgh cemetery when he first visited there and to acknowledge the editor's military family: "perhaps that is why he always seemed to bag good military stories for the magazine" (CWM, T.F. McIlwraith to Dorothy McIlwraith, 28 April 1918). Some of his mates were envious of McIlwraith's ready supply. When Dorothy sent him Ian Hay's humorous collection of sketches, *The First Hundred Thousand* (1915), about the author's experiences as a second lieutenant with the Argyll and Sutherland Highlanders, which "incidentally [Tom] liked very much," a fellow soldier "pounced on it and asked where he could get it," because Hay was his cousin (CWM, T.F. McIlwraith to Dorothy McIlwraith, 10 November 1917). Along with copious supplies of butterscotch and peanuts, Dorothy sent detective stories such as Thomas W. Hanshew's *Cleek, the Master Detective* (1910) and Clinton H. Stagg's *The Silver Sandals* (1916). The siblings were even mulling over "a story in disguise of a youth of 19 who was at the front for two years" (CWM, T.F. McIlwraith to Dorothy McIlwraith, 28 April 1918), though Tom was not overly keen on the idea and preferred that she find someone else for the job.

Importantly, books that dwelled on the absurdities of army life without being disrespectful of it gave him models of how to capture his own experience for the benefit of his worried family. "Life is better than good. It is amusing," Alan Bott wrote in *An Airman's Outings* (223), and McIlwraith could not have agreed more. He strove to turn as many of his adventures as possible into a "très funny" joke for his loved ones to enjoy. He learned from the books he read just how to do this because they were shrewdly packaged education for soldiers and their folks at home in how to handle the "very unusual and upsetting" circumstances of war (Hay 41).[20] For example, in sketches about the flood of letters,

---

20   On literature as First World War propaganda, see Buitenhuis; on Hay, see Urquhart.

postcards, and packages that filled "eight or ten mailbags a day" for one battalion alone (284), the meaning of military mail and censorship was explained
to civilians and recruits alike.[21] Bott and Hay include vivid descriptions of the
rituals of receiving mail, "the most important moment of the day" (Bott 223),
and of responding to it. McIlwraith's own letters frequently arrived in Hamilton
with the "opened by censor" marking, and once he had become an officer, he
acted as censor himself. In Bott's and Hay's accounts, the military censor is a
godlike creature who gains privileged insight into the men's lives and ensures
that, whenever possible, his charges benefit from "the blessings of literature"
bestowed on them by the regular receipt of letters (Hay 224). Readers learn the
importance of sending newspapers as a way of giving soldiers the larger picture of the war, along with keeping them intellectually stimulated. While some
recruits in the trenches were reduced to "cut[ting magazines] into sections to
make them go round, while even the wrapping paper ... [was] smoothed out
and read as 'literature' " ("More Books"), the McIlwraiths mailed newspapers
and magazines in such numbers that T.F. had to beg them to send clippings
only. In keeping with Hay's dual purpose to instruct and entertain, the tone of
The First Hundred Thousand offers the author's trademark mixture of flippancy
and sentimentality. Thus, the censor curses as "verbose and susceptible" the
youthful Private Cosh, whose "undemonstrative, not to say wooden exterior
evidently conceals a heart as inflammable as flannelette" and who is capable
of "conducting ... no less than four parallel love affairs" by mail. By contrast, a
letter from a husband to his wife displaying "a wealth of homely sentiment and
honest affection which holds up its head without shame" is "sealed and signed
without further scrutiny" (Hay 294–5). By comparison, McIlwraith's letters are
less formulated for unified effect than the ones cited by Hay, and, especially in
his mail to his mother, he often swings between tenderness, playfulness, and
severe reproach, at times extremely so.

The episodic structure of Bott's and Hay's books, both first published serially
in *Blackwood's Magazine*, acknowledges the recruits' fragmented experience,
the loss of control over their lives, and the submersion in the military collective
of any individual identity they previously occupied. Though ostensibly "merely
a record of some ... personal adventures" (Hay, Note, n.p.), as Hay describes
his narrative, these books incrementally organize themselves into recognizable genres with a definite purpose to them. In *The First Hundred Thousand*,
a battalion's training in seemingly pointless (and abundantly satirized) skills
such as military etiquette, tidiness, and punctuality reveals itself to be the methodical apprenticeship "ab ovo" of an "awkward, shy, self-conscious mob" into

---

21 The meaning of wartime correspondence has been discussed by a number of scholars, including
    M. Hanna.

men with "character," "grit," and "discipline" (Hay 6). As a result, they are "going to be an everlasting credit to the cause which roused [their] manhood and the land which gave [them] birth" when they display conspicuous gallantry at Loos (183). In return for such uplifting language, the popularity of Hay's books earned him the commission "to write an introduction to [the National War Memorial in Edinburgh] in 1931" (Strachan 63).

Because Hay writes about "the Jock," his reflections provide a kind of manual for the Scotsman McIlwraith on a variety of subjects ranging from the grand to the trivial. Hay highlighted the loyalty among clansmen, their independence of mind, and their refusal to be overly impressed by authority. Thus, with a "full-throated" rendition of "Loch Lomond," the Seventh (Service) Battalion of the Bruce and Wallace Highlanders swing past "[a]n English battalion" who observe them "curiously." Both battalions are in this war together, but for the Scots "courage, and the joy of battle, and the knowledge of victory" come "with all a Scotsman's ... reserve and contempt for social airs and graces," his disdain of "the effete and tyrannical upper classes," and his ability "to know all [of Scotland's] sons by heart" (Hay 6, 14). Folks with such a sturdy sense of self-worth are not upset by the endless polishing of uniform buttons and boots because they understand the educational purpose of it all. They also know how to deal with friendly people who do not belong to the tribe, and McIlwraith's descriptions of meeting up with Belgian and French natives emulate Hay's sketches of a wily population whose members expertly decode orders of "vinblank one, vinrooge two, bogeys six, Dom one," as well as "a bottle of brute" (302). "Madame appeared from somewhere," McIlwraith wrote from Flemish-speaking Belgium, "and with a beaming smile said: 'Offizier, trink kaffee.' Naturally I said 'Ja,' and down I sat and was fed coffee in a round cup without handles and a sunflower shaped bottom" (CWM, T.F. McIlwraith to family, 17 November 1918). Along with advice on etiquette, he obtained some helpful slang from Hay's book, such as "na pooh," an expression he liberally used throughout his correspondence with his sister. Apparently derived from "il n'y a plus," the expression acquired a variety of meanings: " 'All over!' ... 'Not likely!' or 'Nothing doing!' By a further development it has come to mean 'done for,' 'finished,' and in extreme cases, 'dead.' " In the latter sense, the word could even be conjugated, as in "na-poohed by a rifle-grenade" (Hay 302). Tom applies the term in its whole range from the trivial (his camera is "na pooh" until his folks send him more film) to the tragic (wondering how many fellows "will be na pooh" in a year) (CWM, T.F. McIlwraith to family, 5 and 13 May 1918). Once he has crossed into Germany, however, he instructs Dorothy that "na pooh" is passé and has been "kapooted" by "kapoot" (CWM, T.F. McIlwraith to family, 3 May 1919).

The comedy of Hay and Bott is complemented by McIlwraith's vision of an idealized rural Britain as "[t]his is the country we have read about"

(CWM, T.F. McIlwraith to family, 17 January 1918). Characterized by the "going-to-stayness" of the scenery and by houses that were "big, square, substantial looking affairs" (CWM, T.F. McIlwraith to family, 2 January 1918), these scenes seemed unchanged from the time of "William the Conqueror," he ventured, although "aeroplanes and observation balloons passed overhead occasionally, and notices about sugar cards are on the notice-board (an old fence)" (CWM, T.F. McIlwraith to Dorothy McIlwraith, 27 January 1918). He responded enthusiastically to the village of Grantchester and to Rupert Brooke's poem "The Old Vicarage, Grantchester" (1912) when he and Walter Burd arrived to have tea at the Orchard. They came well prepared because Burd had "read up [on Brooke's poems]" in the morning (CWM, T.F. McIlwraith to family, 23 March 1918). Although he was only just learning about the Georgian poets, McIlwraith identified the peaceful countryside with the best Britain had to offer. From an outing to the tiny village of Haslingfield in Cambridgeshire he unleashed a string of adjectives describing an idealized setting: "The farmhouse was an old, white, low-gabled house with steeply-pitched and neatly-thatched roof ... the kind of place one would imagine the yeomen of England to come from." The Philemon and Baucis inhabiting this idyll were "jovial, healthy, and kindly," and refused to take money from the Canadian soldier for a drink of milk and a handful of eggs because they, too, had sons at the front. Completing the picture, he described the presence of "blue corn-flowers ... while the yard looked as if it had been scrubbed" (CWM, T.F. McIlwraith to family, 16 June 1918). The pastoralism of these descriptions is all of a piece with military mission because the killing takes place to ensure the scene is preserved. His comment, on first arriving in Britain, that "the whole country looked like the landscape pictures they issue to teach the troops musketry" underscores that circulating visual imagery, along with literary and musical propaganda, helped to cement the imperial program (CWM, T.F. McIlwraith to family, 2 January 1918).

These bucolic scenes are lifted out of cliché by Tom's typically attentive observations of plant and animal life. By the time he undertook a canoeing trip on the Cam to Whittlesford, Cambridgeshire with his friends, the initially foreign-sounding birdsong had become "a pretty neat sounding medley" that he was able to decipher for his sister, who was equally versed in reading the natural world. On the "spot between a brush pile and a mound of earth" where he had settled down to sleep, he was awakened in the early morning by the jubilant dawn chorus:

I never in my life heard anything like the birds, even Pelee falling far into the background. There were finches and robins singing in the brushwood a few feet from my ear, and thrushes and blackbirds in nearly every tree. There were sky-larks in regular choruses up above, and cuckoos in action most of the time. I had thought

T.F. McIlwraith in his King's Own Scottish Borderers uniform, ca. 1918. TFMP.

of the English cuckoo as rather a rare bird, but in this place we heard them all the time, and saw them quite often... Goodness only knows what other birds were singing, but whatever they were, they were there in full strength. (CWM, T.F. McIlwraith to Dorothy McIlwraith, 20 May 1918)

On a later outing, he and his friends "[find] a grebe's nest," which he assesses with a practised eye for details, once again providing a helpful comparison for the folks in Hamilton: "As at home it was built of reeds and rushes, and was floating on the water among growing reeds and anchored and interwoven to them, a very neat business. There were three chicks, apparently only hatched a few minutes, and one egg. The young were covered with brownish fluff, and were even too young to be in the water, as I guess they would have been a few hours later" (CWM, T.F. McIlwraith to family, 16 June 1918). Knowing of his interest in birds, his family forwarded clippings of Peter McArthur's nature column in the *Globe*, and he was "really very interested" in a discussion citing his grandfather's *The Birds of Ontario* (CWM, T.F. McIlwraith to family, 23 March 1918; see McArthur). Throughout his later busy life as an academic and administrator at the University of Toronto, he kept a detailed bird diary that concluded only a few weeks before his death in 1964 ("Five notebooks").

"The Greatest Race on Earth"

In his letter of 17 August 1918, McIlwraith informed his family that he was "now cleared for action with a pip" and, having passed his exams, was a second lieutenant in the British army. His new tunic made him feel "horribly self-conscious" and his Glengarry bonnet fell into the dust at least once, but he did enjoy receiving his "first salute." The week before, the newly minted officers of E Company were fêted with a dinner at Peterhouse College and McIlwraith sent the program to his family. In his reply to the toast to the empire, Lieutenant Colonel I.H. Macdonnell, DSO, had everyone sit up and take notice when he told the assembled company, "sort of [spitting] out the words as if he meant them": "We are the English. We have always been top dogs in the world and we always shall be. We have deserved to be top dogs, and it's up to you men to keep the English flag at the top. You will be going out to France soon. I wish you all the best of luck, and I wish I were going with you" (CWM, T.F. McIlwraith to family, 17 August 1918). Later in the week, the colonel once again voiced his conviction that maintaining racial superiority was a chief mission of the war: "The highest kind of esprit de corps ... is pride of race. We belong to the greatest race on earth, the English" (CWM, T.F. McIlwraith to family, 17 August 1918). Although both the Scots and the Dominion soldiers might have complained about the emphasis on the "English," the colonel – a Scotsman himself – was telling the men nothing that McIlwraith had not already been taught at

Highfield, at McGill, and in COTC training. This hierarchical thinking una-voidably affected his views of both army and civilians. After the Armistice a few months later, he commented on the troops' enthusiastic welcome in Belgium, writing that, "[n]aturally one has to be very polite with these people, represent-atives of the British race etc." This was language quite different from the cozy scene that had the Belgian woman serving him coffee in a cup with flowers painted on it, and he became quickly bored by the "pathetic ... way they gather around and almost make a demi-god of you" (CWM, T.F. McIlwraith to family, 17 November 1918).

The toast to the empire was offered by McIlwraith's special friend, Officer Cadet Walter Burd, who had probably been selected for this honour in recog-nition of his seniority and his Distinguished Conduct Medal. During training in Cambridge, McIlwraith associated with a group of Canadians billeted at Pe-terhouse College who were bankers, lawyers, and clerks in civilian life: Harty Wilson Morden, Isaac Foster Fitch, Ralph Bodmore Boles, Denzil Robert Au-gustus Walker, and Burd. They met every Saturday for "eats" from packages sent by their families, and spent their leisure visiting the sights in town and in the surrounding fen country. While the other men, especially Morden the banker, came in for mockery in McIlwraith's letters home for their love of the aristoc-racy and various other alleged shortcomings, he became attached to Burd, "a very quiet, nicely spoken and very polite, sensible fellow ... with brains" (CWM, T.F. McIlwraith to family, 20 December 1917–2 January 1918). A decorated war hero determined to avenge his brother's death in battle, Burd was a theological student who became the Anglican bishop of Saskatchewan after the war ("The Right Reverend Walter Burd, D.C.M., D.D."). When McIlwraith first met him at Burwash, Burd's air of calm reliability was underscored by the presence of his Airedale dog, the company mascot, and by the fact that "two brothers [of the dog were] at the front already as Red Cross dogs in the French army" (CWM, T.F. McIlwraith to Dorothy, 10 November 1917). Burd married a young woman from Sheffield while he was at Cambridge, and his in-laws warmly received McIlwraith in their home in South Yorkshire, as well as taking him on ram-bles through the Derbyshire countryside. In turn, Burd visited Tom's family in Hamilton when he was back in Canada, and in early 1922, when McIlwraith was on his way to Bella Coola, he, Burd, and Boles met up in Toronto for an evening of reminiscences. They were somewhat impeded by the presence of Tom's sister Majorie, Burd's wife, and a new baby that "did nothing but yowl." The friendship continued into McIlwraith's marriage with Beulah Knox (CWM, T.F. McIlwraith, letter to family, 28 February 1922; see also "Genealogy").

Twelve years older than Tom, Burd still endeared himself for his willingness to participate in pranks such as using the bayonet to hack up ancient oak chairs for fuel at Peterhouse College and pushing students who were punting on the Cam into the river. McIlwraith felt comfortable with Burd and the others not only because they were Canadians and good fun, but also because they fit the definition of "the British race" with which he had been inoculated. These distinctions were taken for granted when he talked about his friends: "One thing the army does for you is to teach you how to make friends, and how to stick together," McIlwraith wrote to his family. "Take the six of us here for instance. In the ordinary course of civilian life we would never have met, or if we had would certainly never have been friends. As it is we have stuck together and found out how much more there is in a chap than sticks out on the surface. I am beginning to realize that there are more decent people in the world than I expected, and that when you come down to brass tacks most fellows show up all right" (CWM, T.F. McIlwraith to family, 13 May 1918). Another close companion was his KOSB mate Leslie Houstoun, whom McIlwraith befriended in Germany where both were members of the British army of occupation. Houstoun, son of a mercantile cashier and student of Latin, French, and mathematics at the University of Glasgow when he joined up,[22] remained a steady presence throughout McIlwraith's studies at Cambridge, for vacations in Scotland, time together in London, and at a KOSB reunion. On demobilization, McIlwraith found the separation extremely difficult because Houstoun was "the whitest man I ever knew" (WD, 7 September 1919). The phrase is likely borrowed from the music-hall song "The Whitest Man I Know" (1914) by R. Fenton Gower and J. Milton Hayes. The original line runs, "The greatest friend I'd ever had, the whitest man on earth," but while the jingoism of the song is meant to be ironical (Osborne 243),[23] there is no irony whatsoever in McIlwraith's use of the expression. In his wartime diary, to call a man "white" was the highest compliment he could pay a mate, including the padre who was given a rousing farewell because he had been "damn white to us all through" (WD, 13 July 1919). The alternative was to be "pure swine," as in "Leney is pure swine, and Charley damned white" (WD, 17 July 1919).

McIlwraith was generally impressed with the Dominion troops. Among the Australians, New Zealanders, and South Africans, he favoured the Australians, "nearly all of them husky fellows towering over the English lads" (CWM, T.F. McIlwraith to family, 15 February 1918). He admired them for their courage, irreverence, and dashing slouch hats, and their reluctance to submit to discipline reminded him of the Scots as Ian Hay had painted them. The Australians' evasion of some of the more tedious military routines commended them as clever, such as their replacing the "regular button with the lion and unicorn

---

22 R8/5/37/2; Uh.90, R4/1/12, UGA.

23 In Andrew Magnus Fleming's *Captain Kiddle* (1889), a character explains the phrase "one of the whitest men that ever lived" as meaning "white-livered" (142), that is to say, "cowardly" and therefore the opposite of McIlwraith's usage.

on it" with "bronzed ones with a map of Australia" that were easier to polish (CWM, T.F. McIlwraith to Dorothy McIlwraith, 2 March 1918). In drawing distinctions between the different colonial troops, McIlwraith was probably influenced by standard characterizations circulating in contemporary accounts. These images were all the more persistent because the self-perception of the Australians and the Canadians as good-looking and healthy " 'crack' troops" whose valour was confirmed at Gallipoli and Vimy, could be seen as compensation for the Dominions' "minimal say in operational matters" (Holland 129). McIlwraith reported as often as possible on the Australians' refusal to be cowed by "old army chaps," one of whom was "completely amazed when ... an Australian enquire[d] from the ranks in an interested voice, 'got Mondayitis major?' " in response to the sergeant major's yawns (CWM, T.F. McIlwraith to family, 13 May 1918). Nor, as a member of an "energetic, headstrong people," was one of them afraid to call out, "say Bill, do you know there's a war on?" when drill seemed to get overly fussy (CWM, T.F. McIlwraith to family, 6 August and 30 June 1918).

Because the valour of the Māori at Gallipoli and on the western front was well established (see Cowan), McIlwraith's admiration for the Australasian troops extended to New Zealand's Indigenous people, whom he described as "looking brown and fit in their uniforms" (CWM, T.F. McIlwraith to family, 15 February 1918). Like Eileen Plunket and her family, however, he was reserved about any individuals who did not fit "the pride of race" as proclaimed by his colonel. This attitude began to make itself known at the COTC camp in Toronto where he encountered the first such outsiders. Among the men brought in to train the French-speaking recruits, he noted "a chap named [Job] Boulian who was an engineer from Cleveland who worked for years in northern Ontario and looks like an Indian and in fact is a mixture of Indian, French and British descent" (CWM, T.F. McIlwraith to Dorothy McIlwraith, 4 December 1917).[24] He makes a similar observation at Hare Hall Camp in Essex a month later when he comments that if their "Lewis gun instructor" from Rangoon "has not native blood in him I am a Dutchman" (CWM, T.F. McIlwraith to family, 17 January 1918). As McIlwraith's train journey from Toronto to St. John to board the *Missanabie* has already illustrated, his description of French Canadians is tinged with prejudice, and his censorious views are aggravated by their resistance to conscription. Members of ethnic groups suspected of being "slackers" were doubly shunned, both for their origins and their alleged cowardice. One such group was the Irish, and when his troopship docked in Glasgow, McIlwraith was "hit ... by a hard boiled egg," that he briefly suspected of having been thrown "by a Scotchman who supposed us to be Irishmen coming

24 The literature on First Nations in the First World War is growing; see, among others, Talbot.

over to work at munitions instead of fighting" (CWM, T.F. McIlwraith to his mother, 2 January 1918). Even when they did enlist, the Irish remained suspect. On the *Missanabie*, Burd was "annexed by the joke of the transport, a dirty Irish man who is killing himself with cocaine and who in 15 minutes had given him his own and his relatives' life histories, his views on Home Rule and had wound up by asking for a quarter" (CWM, T.F. McIlwraith to family, 20 December 1917–2 January 1918).

For similar reasons, there is an eruption of antisemitism in McIlwraith's letter describing his arrival in London. Londoners suspected East-End Jewry, many foreign-born, of "communal opposition to military service" and of obtaining economic advantage from the war rather than doing their duty at the front (J. White 84–9). When he objected to being marched through London with a group of "fellows ... from Whitechapel and other choice east end haunts" (CWM, T.F. McIlwraith to family, 17 January 1918), his response was probably sharpened by perusal of antisemitic coverage in the Canadian press. In his perception, military bravery did exempt Jewish men from prejudice, and when he was recovering from influenza at the hospital in Cambridge, he briefly shared a ward with "a Jew from Victoria, Australia, and a first class chap" as well as an outstanding athlete (CWM, T.F. McIlwraith to family, 16 June 1918). The name of the patient was Phillips, and a later section in this chapter will discuss another Jewish family named Phillips that was well known to the McIlwraiths and whose sons served in the Dominion army of South Africa.

McIlwraith inhabited a world in which skin colour was measured by a chromatic scale developed by the anthropologist Felix von Luschan, whose critics complained that "a few more dark shades would have been useful for Africa, a blue-black in particular" (N.W. Thomas 160).[25] In this world it was all right to consume a candy named "nigger-toes" (CWM, T.F. McIlwraith to Dorothy McIlwraith, 21 July 1918), wear hats in a fashionable shade of "nigger-brown" ("Oh, Those Tricornes!"), own a dog named "Nigger" (Gutsche 67), and to talk about working "like a nigger" (used in several of McIlwraith's letters). Therefore it also seemed all right to refer to some of the few students remaining at Cambridge as "African negroes, ... China-men, and all intermediate types" (CWM, T.F. McIlwraith to family, 13 May 1918) and to laugh with Dorothy at the sighting of a KOSB "nigger" in New York (CWM, T.F. McIlwraith to family,

---

25 Von Luschan was opposed to systemic racism, but his theories are nevertheless difficult to disentangle from it. At the Universal Races Congress in 1911, he angered delegates by claiming that "racial antagonism" served a purpose: "Whatever was good about humanity came from ambition, from the struggle for life." He was challenged by the astronomer Wilhelm Foerster, who insisted "that the great majority of the people of Germany did not agree with the glorification of war" but "approved and praised ... the humanitarian and peaceful spirit of that Congress" ("Universal Races Congress").

3 May 1919). Along with other Black ex-servicemen, that soldier was facing a "Red Summer" of race riots and social unrest (Gallagher and Lippard 1045). A particular target was "dark-haired Hindoos with grey trousers inclined to be floppy, and low shoes" (CWM, T.F. McIlwraith to his mother, 8 February 1918). Also referred to as "big greasy Indian students" (CWM, T.F. McIlwraith to family, 17 August 1918), these students were at Cambridge to study for the Indian Civil Service. McIlwraith and his gang, including the otherwise clear-headed Walter Burd, were delighted when they managed to inconvenience or play a joke on some of them. Like the "French native troops, muscular looking chaps with a cheerful grin and wearing turbans" he saw in France, the Indian students seemed all skin, teeth, and strange costume (CWM, T.F. McIlwraith to family, 22 October 1918). Some of these attitudes may have been imbibed from his reading of Kipling.[26] A few years earlier, in addressing the Conference on Nationalities and Subject Races in 1910, Gilbert Murray, Regius Professor of Greek at Oxford, thought Kipling was to blame for provoking his readers into "a blind and savage contempt for the Bengali" (G. Murray 321). Whatever the immediate cause of their contempt, the attitude was not one invented by the soldiers but was already well established at Cambridge by the time they got there. The Indians' perspective was described by the social reformer Samuel Satthianadan in his memoir *Four Years in an English University* (1890) and has been documented in Shompa Lahiri's study of Indians in Britain. The routine stereotypes for students from India had them as either "niggers" or "princes." Reminiscing about the Armistice, a Newnham student remembered rather flippantly the death of one of "a number of dark-skinned gentlemen whom we designated the 'Indian Princes.' " The women's "dearest and most popular 'Prince,' an obese gentleman with a round smiling pudding-face, [was] snuffed out like a candle in the terrible Spanish flu epidemic at the end of the war, sorely lamented by all" (D.C. Booth 120).

This statement is all the more ironical coming from a female student because women were routinely lumped in with coloured students as not fitting in at Cambridge. At the beginning of the war, the economist John Maynard Keynes complained to a student in the trenches that he was reduced to lecture to "blacks and women."[27] One of the objections raised against "blacks and women" was the reputation of both groups as "swotters" from whom the ordinary undergraduate was advised to keep his distance. Describing a typical pre-war scene, an "Old Don," who was firmly opposed to women's admission to Cambridge, wrote in the *Evening Standard* in 1920 that "[b]efore a lecture you would see a

---

26 Kipling's views about "Orientals" and the empire are famously complex. See, for example, D. Scott.

27 Letter to Frederick McMahon "Freddy" Hardman, 25 October 1914, qtd. in Skidelsky 294.

close clot of girls round the door of the hall waiting for it to open; behind them a gang of Indians – for they were hard swotters too. Then, a long way off, you saw the ordinary undergraduates who didn't want to have anything to do with either crowd."[28] This "Old Don" lamented the ease with which, after the war, undergraduates began to ignore these segregations – at least in some contexts.

When McIlwraith landed in France and boarded the train to the front, he found that it was occupied by "most of the allies fighting on the western front ..., everybody from Chink coolies up" (CWM, T.F. McIlwraith to family, 22 October 1918). The "coolies" – that is, members of the Chinese Labour Corps (CLC) hired by both the French and the British – "loaded cargoes, dug trenches, filled sandbags, repaired tanks and artillery; ... laid railway lines, repaired roads, built ports and aerodromes; ... removed animal carcasses and ammunition from the battlefield, collected the bodies of the dead and built the graves to bury them" (M. O'Neill, *Forgotten Chinese Labourers* 1–2). Dressed in "odds and ends of uniforms, stuff which once belonged to men of all the armies," the CLC attracted McIlwraith's attention because, of the 94,400 labourers the British recruited by spring 1918 (O'Neill 18), more than 3,500 were shipped from Vancouver to Halifax, where they embarked for Europe. They were transported in a sealed train across Canada to prevent any of the passengers from attempting to stay in the country because head tax laws had been enforced since 1885 to restrict Chinese immigration. Efforts were made to censor news or photographs of this transport, but American papers nevertheless reported on the operation (O'Neill 31). In France, McIlwraith took a blurry photo of the workers from his train and suspected them of being "busily engaged in doing nothing but watch the train go by" (CWM, T.F. McIlwraith to family, 22 October 1918).

The Americans

McIlwraith minded very much when his accent was mistaken as American. As mentioned earlier, he and Dorothy were critical of the Americans and considered them little better than the "slackers" among his fellow Canadians. Brother and sister were angered when the Americans were cheered on parade in Toronto, though he surmised that this was because they were a novelty: "One thing that peeved me was the way the Yankee soldiers were cheered while our own men went through silent crowds. I think our cavalry and artillery got a bit more cheering than the infantry, [but] I know that we got practically none at all" (CWM, T.F. McIlwraith to Dorothy McIlwraith, 18 November 1917). He was angered when "notices of welcome" in Belgium cited Woodrow Wilson and Lloyd George together, "in that order" (CWM, T.F. McIlwraith to family, 2

---

28 "Old Don," *Evening Standard*, 7 October 1920, qtd. in McWilliams-Tullberg 168.

December 1918). Conversely, he was gratified when a Cambridge audience responded by making "not a sound" when a Pathé newsreel was shown displaying the US flag (CWM, T.F. McIlwraith to family, 8 March 1918), or when members of the audience dismissed public lectures by professors from Chicago as "a series of apologies for the Yanks not having come in sooner" (CWM, T.F. McIlwraith to Dorothy McIlwraith, 20 May 1918). As with "Die Wacht am Rhein" and its reinterpretation in "When We've Wound Up the Watch on the Rhine," it was a song that took the brunt of his resentment. He never could resist quoting parodies of "Over There" (written immediately after the States' entry into the war) that punctured its triumphalist self-confidence. At COTC training in Toronto, "various rude people proceeded to sing (?) that rotten Yankee song 'Over There' with variations, the chief of which was 'They won't be over till it's over over there' " (CWM, T.F. McIlwraith to Dorothy McIlwraith, 29 November 1917). A similar sentiment was expressed in Cambridge by "a kilted boy" from the Argyle and Sutherland Highlanders who "when somebody started 'Over There' ... said, 'weel, it seems to me it is aboot time they stopped coming over and actually came' " (CWM, T.F. McIlwraith to Dorothy McIlwraith, 2 March 1918). He admitted that "Over There" did "sound ... better coming across the water" when his convoy, including a transport carrying American troops, moved out of Halifax Harbour, but he still found it tolerable only because their ship was flying the British flag (CWM, T.F. McIlwraith to family, 20 December 1917–2 January 1918). Having made his feelings known, he raised no objections when the singing Calgarians on the *Missanabie* included "Over There" in their repertoire.

The "Hun"

On the train travelling into France, McIlwraith saw his first "Huns," these in the form of "German prisoners at work" (CWM, T.F. McIlwraith to family, 22 October 1918). During the nine months he spent with the British army of occupation in Wald (Solingen), he was able to study the Hun from up close, and although the British occupation has generally been judged to be more lenient than its French and Belgian counterparts (Limburger 115), he was gratified by the numerous regulations that kept the Germans in their place. By order of the British commander, Sir Herbert Plumer, the clocks were turned back by one hour to bring them in line with standard time in Britain and France (CWM, T.F. McIlwraith to family, 3 April 1919).[29] In addition, Germans had to observe numerous directives that restricted their freedom of movement and activity.

---

29 Limburger 98; see also Nanni. Nanni discusses the policing of time in colonial imperialism but his observations apply to the wartime takeover of one empire by another as well.

These prohibitions included curfew from 9:00 p.m. to 5:00 a.m., and for all citizens over the age of twelve a mandatory pass in English and German was issued, stamped by the occupation authorities. In some districts, inventories had to be posted on each building listing all occupants by name, citizenship, sex, age, and profession. The press and postal system were strictly censored, and assemblies of any kind had to be registered with day, time of day, place, and topic. Once the permission had been obtained, gatherings were supervised by the British troops. Only the British national anthem was permitted, and all German nationalist hymns were strictly forbidden – especially, one assumes, "Die Wacht am Rhein." Initially, all men were required to salute the British flag and doff their hats when they passed British officers. Individuals who did not obey had their hats removed and trampled into the ground, or they were pelted with rocks. Guards were posted at the border crossings from the occupied to the neutral zones and vice versa, and border traffic was strictly controlled.

The regulation that all men remove their hats when they encountered a British officer was cumbersome to one party and resented by the other, and was soon changed to requiring a salute by uniformed men (including "policemen, firemen, conductors, watchmen," as McIlwraith explained to his family), whereas civilians had to remove their hats only when spoken to by an officer. Tom made a point to "acknowledge their salute as curtly as I can" (CWM, T.F. McIlwraith to family, 3 April 1919), but he and a companion chased all over town to take "snaps" of some of the resulting encounters, and unlike the local population, they were free to take as many photographs as they wanted. "Whenever we saw a big Bosche with a sword," he wrote to his family, "we turned and chased him, then sauntering into position as casually as possible. Sometimes the Bosche was wily and moved away, sometimes we missed fire, however the one snap was quite a success. It was a scream chasing madly around in pursuit of a Hun large enough to look important and the bearer of a sword" (CWM, T.F. McIlwraith to family, 15 June 1919). Likewise, he took as many photos as possible of civilians having to produce identification, pointing out that "[t]he real fun is at the neutral zone where everybody is stopped and searched ... People who try to enter or leave without proper authority also get it hard in the neck" (CWM, T.F. McIlwraith to family, 3 April 1919).[30] The status of the occupation troops was underlined by the ruling that they did not have to wait their turn in shops or pay for fares on trains and trams. In some districts troops confiscated bread, milk, butter, and eggs for their own use, sometimes in large quantities. For a population already suffering from food shortages, this was a particular hardship.

---

30 For everyday aspects of the occupation, see Limburger; Jeffery. These accounts differ in some details, such as the specifications for the curfew, perhaps because regulations changed over time.

Hotels, schools, and private homes were requisitioned to accommodate troops. Just in Cologne, living space for fifty-five thousand troops had to be found. Individual rooms were requisitioned, and sometimes whole apartments and buildings. Occupants were required to remove themselves as promptly as possible but were not allowed to take any furniture with them. In Wald, McIlwraith and his friends settled in the mansions of local industrialists, first, it seems, in a villa owned by the umbrella-maker Kortenbach & Rauh, whose factory had been repurposed for military production during the war,[31] and second in the home of Hugo Lauterjung, maker of knives and razors. Indeed, knives and razors were such normal objects in Wald that one family presented each of the soldiers billeted with them with a knife for Christmas. The opulence of the Kortenbach mansion, separated by a lawn from the main street and equipped with every modern convenience, impressed McIlwraith deeply and he wrote a detailed description of it, sketching out scenes in which he and his crew reminded "Mr. and Mrs. Hun" of the new conditions of occupancy in their home. When the couple complained about rowdy behaviour, the men responded with reminders of Belgium and the sinking of the Lusitania (CWM, T.F. McIlwraith to his mother, 14 February 1919). "They are frankly keen on being on friendly terms with us," he concluded. He temporarily forgot that his reluctant hosts did have the option of complaining to the Occupation Bureau when he added, "as is natural since we would otherwise be disposed to wreck [this] place" (CWM, T.F. McIlwraith to family, 27 January 1919). The owners did, in fact, eventually file a report, but by then a fair amount of damage had already been done.

The soldiers' main contact was "Mrs. Hun," a "very capable housewife" who spoke fluent English and French. As a first point of contention, she objected to the army cook in her kitchen who used her "dish towels to dry plates, wash his hands, or wipe his sweaty face" (CWM, T.F. McIlwraith to family, 27 January 1919). Similar problems erupted in Cologne after the Treaty of Versailles had been signed when soldiers' wives and children were allowed to join them and invaded the kitchens of German citizens with no concern for their "pristine cleanliness" (D. Williamson, "Cologne and the British" 701). In Wald, this particular problem was resolved when a separate officers' mess was established, but as elsewhere in occupied territory there was "an ... upsurge of boisterous undergraduate behaviour" in response to the relief that came with the Armistice (700). In Cologne, two inebriated soldiers crowned statues of Wilhelm I and his empress with chamber pots, and a bust of Wilhelm II in the Kakushöhle, a grotto near Mechernich, was used for target practice. McIlwraith's version of this kind of rowdiness was to pin a cartoon torn out of *Life* magazine on

---

31 Several photographs taken by McIlwraith, along with his detailed description of the house and its location, suggest that this was the August Kortenbach villa. See Kirchhoff 351–9.

the wall of the Kortenbachs' sitting room when he "found that the Huns had gone on the sack rampage and were generally a bit rambunctious." The developing situation sounds considerably more tense in the clipped language of McIlwraith's diary than in his letters and, rather than serving as an aide-mémoire as it did earlier, the diary now often functions as an complement to correspondence that is increasingly diminished by a lack of news appropriate to pass on to his family. He and his friends "declared war" on the Huns, ignoring the angry objections of the owners who did not want a depiction of the Kaiser addressing an army of skeletons displayed in their home. Several days of domestic warfare ensued during which both parties repeatedly swapped the picture back and forth between a prominent place over the mantelpiece in the living room, "with a notice not to take away," and the soldiers' bedrooms. With satisfaction, McIlwraith noted the Germans' efforts to defuse the tension as they make "unsuccessful efforts to taffy us with teaching German and wine." These attempts "got absolutely no change, in fact [they] were only shown another cartoon and got into an argument about war." It was only when the soldiers became tired of the game, but particularly when the maid refused to enter their rooms to tidy up, that a truce was declared. Also left out of the letters were wild parties during which ornaments were smashed and "Houstoun led a bayonet charge at a Japanese screen" (WD, 2, 3, 4, and 10 January 1919), along with noisy pillow fights and piano playing until the small hours of the morning. Presumably there was also full-throttle music from the "very fine large gramophone with plenty of records" he had described earlier. It was displayed in the music room with "mandolins and things spread around the walls. Of course we use the piano and things whenever we feel like it" (CWM, T.F. McIlwraith to family, 27 January 1919). He was particularly careful not to mention to his family how often he and his friends became "very tight" during these parties, including a time when he feared that he was vomiting up blood only to remember – to his relief – that he had earlier eaten a dish of strawberries.

At his second billet, he and a friend went out of their way to inconvenience a large group of "Bolshevically inclined Bosche" who wanted to collect chairs and tables for a meeting but were prevented from doing so until the soldiers had completed their tennis match (CWM, T.F. McIlwraith to family, 15 June 1919).[32] This particular episode occurred on Whitsun, and as he had done at Christmas, McIlwraith reported on local customs. He was not always sure about their meaning, as indicated by his bafflement at a *Wandervogel* group

---

32 McIlwraith may be exaggerating here to entertain his family because expressions of Bolshevism were strictly controlled under the British occupation, and he does point this out elsewhere in his letters.

Philip Child in his Royal Garrison Artillery uniform, ca. 1917–18. Hamilton Public Library.

and their songs:[33] "A great habit here seems to be for people to go around in their shirt sleeves with fiddles tied around their necks with pink ribbon and swarms of other young toughs following and singing in chorus. Strangely enough one of the favourites at present is the 'Marsaillais' [sic], or rather a Bosche version of the same tune" (CWM, T.F. McIlwraith to family, 15 June 1919).[34] The bafflement was sometimes mutual, and the curiosity of the local children unrestrained: "the children followed our band. The kilts had a great attraction for them and none of their parents apparently made the slightest effort to check them. It was precisely the way the youngsters in Belgium did" (CWM, T.F. McIlwraith to family, 27 January 1919). In Cologne especially, one cannot help but suspect that the children enjoyed the Scots' "bunte Röckchen" ("little colourful skirts"; my translation) and bagpipes as a substitute for the region's normally exuberant carnival celebrations, summarily cancelled in 1919 ("Erster Weltkrieg"). Their parents were not so thrilled with the pipes: Leslie Houstoun, a skilled piper, annoyed the Germans in his billet with his playing.

The Hills-Phillips Collection

Managing McIlwraith's postal connections with his family from his various locations in Great Britain and on the Continent would have been infinitely more difficult without the assistance of what he calls the "Hills-Phillips Collection" or "Hills-Phillips Combination" (CWM, T.F. McIlwraith to his mother, 14 February 1919). Shortly after arrival in London, Tom travelled to the village of Petersham, near Richmond, to visit Hilda Phillips and her mother, Mrs. Hills, old friends from Hamilton. He came laden with parcels from their relatives and his own family, and the recipients were "pleased with the various stuff, sugar included, though the cakes were pretty sadly stale" (CWM, T.F. McIlwraith to family, 2 January 1918). In turn, parcels from his sister and the Hamilton church ladies were waiting for him in Hilda's house. Mother and daughter "were awfully decent, couldn't have been kinder in fact" (CWM, T.F. McIlwraith to family, 2 January 1918). For much of his time in Britain, Hilda agreed to receive and pass on his mail. She stored any of his belongings that were not needed in camp or that, like his camera, he was not always allowed to use. Her mother took charge of mending his socks when he was getting ready to leave for France, and when neither Hilda nor Mrs. Hills was at home, the maid served him lunch

---

33 On the *Wandervogel* movement, see J. Williams.
34 "Frisch auf zur Weise von Marseille," or "Reveille," by Ferdinand Freiligrath was written for the first anniversary of the 1848 revolution. As a result, the Marseillaise became conflated with the revolutionary songs of that generation. This connection was revived in the workers' movement, but became problematic in the wake of the French occupation of Germany and the Treaty of Versailles. See Brophy 83; also Widmaier et al.

and pressed his clothes. Except when they had other visitors or there was a new baby, McIlwraith stayed with Hilda when he was on furlough, and their hospitality extended to Philip Child whenever he and Tom happened to be in London at the same time. The Phillipses became used to the spectacle of McIlwraith rushing madly into and out of their house. On his last visit before travelling to Southampton for his transport home, he raced "[o]ut to Richmond where [I] found Hilda and Harold and had tea[;] huge rush. About half-an-hour to pack which meant throwing out surplus stuff, did it all right and got my gear away in a taxi, violent rush train to Waterloo and plenty of time for 19.30 to Southampton West" (WD, 14 September 1919). On the other side of the Atlantic a couple of years later, Mrs. Hills was the usual "brick" after his return from Cambridge when his parents were staying with Dorothy in New York. Before fieldwork in Bella Coola, he interrupted his journey in Hamilton. Mrs. Hills "washed up a huge pile of clothes" for him, helped sort his luggage, "with my stuff all over the floor of the dining room," sent "one suit to be cleaned, fearing that its dust and dirt might collect moths," and directed him to "scrap ... a few socks" (TFMF, T.F. McIlwraith to family, 3 and 4 March 1922).

Like the stories of Eileen Plunket and Doris Blackwood in Beulah Knox's life, the Hills-Phillips connection illustrates aspects of imperial networking that were not part of the McIlwraiths' usual milieu but to which they gained access as the result of carefully nurtured friendship. Outlining this connection takes this chapter deeper into the psychological complications and economic injustices of the empire than McIlwraith's encounters with the Dominion troops are able to convey on their own. Conversely, his wartime letters allow reconstruction of the story of Hilda Phillips that, despite her marriage into a prominent South African family, has not been told. Born at Bethnal Green in London in 1892, Hilda Wildman Hills was the daughter of Frank Hills and his wife Evelina, both natives of England ("Valued Citizen"). In 1913, Hilda married Harold Phillips, son of the South African randlord Sir Lionel Phillips and his wife Florence. The McIlwraiths and Hilda's family were close friends, and Dorothy served as bridesmaid at Hilda's wedding in Wentworth, for which she endured an outfit "in pale eau de Nil voile over silk of the same shade, girdle and sash of silk, [a] large leghorn hat ... in poke style with streamers of green," the whole accessorized with a "shower bouquet of pink roses and lilies of the valley" ("A Wedding of Wide-Spread Interest" n.p.). Unlike Beulah's connection with the Dufferin granddaughters, the McIlwraiths' friendship with Evelina Hills and Hilda Phillips lasted a lifetime. Hilda and her mother were still in Richmond when T.F. returned in November 1919 to study at Cambridge. When he travelled to Britain in 1934 to attend the International Congress of Anthropology and Ethnology in London, he made a trip to Hampshire to spend the day with Mrs. Hills, who appears to have moved frequently back and forth between Canada and Britain to keep up with the widely dispersed members of her family.

Harold Phillips's parents were born into relatively modest circumstances. Lionel Phillips came from a lower-middle-class Jewish merchant family in London's East End while Florence Ortlepp was the daughter of a South African land surveyor. However, the couple amassed a fortune in the diamond business, acquiring large estates in South Africa and Britain. Lady Florence became an influential patron of garden architecture and the arts, and the popular Edwardian painter Giovanni Boldini captured the couple's flamboyance in individual portraits.[35] The Hills must have thought that their daughter had struck gold when the Phillipses' older son proposed to her. The Hamilton *Spectator* certainly thought so: the feature on the wedding in its society pages pointed out that Sir Lionel's story was the stuff of novels: "the father of the bridegroom ... is mentioned by Sir Gilbert Parker in his recent book *The Judgement House*" ("A Wedding of Wide-Spread Interest" n.p.). A year earlier, Lionel Phillips had been made a baronet (and not several years earlier, as the *Spectator* claimed). The reporter might have added that John Buchan had recently dedicated his novel *Prester John* (1910) to Sir Lionel, with whom he had become friends when Buchan was private secretary to Alfred Milner, high commissioner for southern Africa, and member of his famous "kindergarten" of young colonial civil servants. Hamiltonians' curiosity was not as fully satisfied as they would have liked because Sir Lionel and Lady Florence were unable to come to Canada, and Mr. and Mrs. Hills were prevented from travelling to England, where the wedding was originally to have taken place.

Harold met his bride when he was pursuing a bachelor of agricultural science at the Ontario Agricultural College (OAC) in Guelph between 1908 and 1912, in preparation for managing his father's farmlands in northern Transvaal. Nearby, Hilda was attending a home economics program at the Macdonald Institute, where she had been admitted with a letter of reference from Tom's mother.[36] A creation of educator Adelaide Hoodless and the tobacco industrialist Sir William Macdonald,[37] the institute was intended to provide young rural women with a useful education, but it also attracted middle-class women who were suspected of using the proximity of the OAC to find a suitable husband. These marriages occurred so frequently that by the early 1910s, the Macdonald program was known as the " 'diamond ring' course" (Snell 54). When he wrote to his parents about Hilda, Harold underlined that "the very best sort of girls seem to come" (LPP, Harold Phillips to Sir Lionel Phillips, 22 July 1912), and by this he did not mean

---

35 Boldini's portrait of Lady Phillips (1902) serves as the cover of Trumble and Ranger's *Edwardian Opulence*.

36 See Hilda Hills's record at the Macdonald Institute, Archival and Special Collections, UGL, entrance records and transcripts, 1903–41 (RE MAC A0003).

37 See Terry Crowley, "Hunter, Adelaide Sophia (Hoodless);" S.B. Frost, "Macdonald, Sir William Christopher."

women from small farms. Once Harold had proposed to Hilda, she broke off her studies at Macdonald, but in reporting on the wedding, the *S.A. Ladies' Pictorial* thought that "her knowledge of domestic science and scientific farming [would] be quite an acquisition in South Africa, where practical demonstrations of 'Back to the Land' are of untold value" ("Wedding Announcements" 26).

Through her marriage, Hilda moved into a circle that featured some of the most prominent names of the Edwardian era. Sir Lionel's business associates included Alfred Beit, Julius Wernher, Hermann Ludwig Eckstein, and Cecil Rhodes. Although never shy to display their wealth, the Phillipses' discriminating taste distinguished them from other randlords who were "eager to accrue markers of taste and status that they then displayed in London townhouses and English country homes" (M. O'Neill, "Colonial Nationalism" 245). At their estates in South Africa and in Britain, Florence Phillips worked with the architect Edward Lutyens and the landscaping artist Gertrude Jekyll, as well as collectors and curators Robert Ross and Hugh Lane. Lane, director of the Dublin Art Gallery, assisted Lady Florence in establishing the foundations of the Johannesburg Art Gallery (see Carman). Lionel and Florence Phillips imported international art but also sponsored local arts and crafts, and they were both "ardent nature conservationists" (J. Foster, *Washed with the Sun* 42). Botanist Rudolf Marloth's six-volume *The Flora of South Africa* (1913–32) was published at Florence Phillips's instigation, and she and her husband worked towards the establishment of the National Botanical Gardens at Kirstenbosch.

After a visit to Niagara Falls and Tylney Hall, the Phillipses' mansion in Hampshire, Hilda and Harold spent much of their honeymoon driving through England buying "pedigree cattle" for Lionel Phillips' farms (Gutsche 305). When the couple arrived in South Africa, Johannesburg society was enchanted with the "young Canadian [in] her crisp white muslins with blue sashes to match her eyes" (308), and Sir Lionel presented the newly-weds with the "Westfalia portion" of his Woodbush estate in a lush area of northern Transvaal. This was a "soft, rich, and fascinating garden-land" rhapsodized by John Buchan as the South African Hesperides (Buchan, *The African Colony* 114, 117),[38] with "virgin forests and waterfalls" and orchards where "apples thrive[d] on the upper levels, and bananas, pineapples, citrus, mangoes, paw-paws, [grew] beneath" (Phillips 83, 84). Despite this Edenic environment, it became clear within days that Hilda had come to a dangerous place. In December 1913, the same month in which the couple arrived in Johannesburg, Sir Lionel was shot and seriously wounded by an unhappy former employee whom the international papers variously reported to be either a Russian or a Boer named Nissun or Missum.[39] This was not the

---

38 Also see J. Foster, "John Buchan's *Hesperides*" 119–43.

39 According to Maryna Fraser, "Sir Lionel Phillips," the assassin was "J.L. Misnun, a former hawker, at one of the mines."

first time Sir Lionel's life had been in jeopardy, and when he did eventually die, at the age of eighty, his obituaries cited as a special accomplishment the number of times he had defied imminent death by accident, execution, and assassination.[40] To begin with, he survived a three-hundred-foot drop in his youth as he was descending into a diamond shaft. For his role in the Jameson Raid in 1895–6 against the Kruger regime, often considered a prelude to the Boer War, he was sentenced to death with other leaders of the revolt, but the sentence was commuted to eight years in British exile, from which he returned in due course. The Hamilton *Spectator* cited the raid in its coverage of his son's wedding.

It also became clear soon after their arrival in South Africa that the couple was not ideally suited to each other. Harold's letters to his father from Guelph had registered plenty of danger signals in behaviour that was familiar to his parents but not yet to his bride and her own parents. Having Harold train as a cattle and citrus farmer at Guelph was only the most recent of his parents' efforts to get him settled, and in order to have their son accepted into the school, they had mobilized the support of a powerful ally – namely, Lord Grey, Canada's governor general, a man with strong ties to South Africa and "a consummate networker" (Magee and Thompson 206). Harold dutifully reported home on his academic work, complaining about courses that he found useless for his purposes as a future cattle farmer such as beekeeping, raising chicks in an incubator, and analysing soil. Not that he was all that thrilled with any other aspects of his studies: his true enthusiasm was for sports, dancing, and flirting. A romance still in progress overseas as he settled into Guelph had become "the other affair" (LPP, Harold Phillips to Lionel Phillips, 22 July 1912) by the time he began courting Hilda. This "other affair" may or may not have involved the young woman with whom he entered into "an impetuous engagement in Johannesburg" that was dissolved not long after it had been entered (Gutsche 271). He concludes the letter in which he asks for his parents' permission to marry Hilda with the announcement that "[p]robably one of the leading + most popular girls in Toronto society today was here and a very good friend of mine. In fact she still is + I often see her" (LPP, Harold Phillips to Sir Lionel Phillips, 22 July 1912). His parents knew him as a "charming [and] goodlooking" fellow, but also one who was lazy, "moody and difficult," and fond of drink (Gutsche 188, 176, 140). His mother periodically extracted him from sloth and got him organized, and as her rages were known to move grown men to tears, he had reason to be afraid of her. In a post scriptum to the letter asking his father for permission to marry Hilda, he disingenuously adds: "I only suggested not telling Mother perhaps at present, Father, because she is not very strong, and if

---

40   "Death of Sir Lionel Phillips: 80-year-old survivor of Jameson Raid: His 'Charmed Life,' " unidentified newspaper clipping inserted in the University of Victoria's copy of L. Phillips, *Some Reminiscences*.

she did not understand, it might worry her" (LPP, Harold Phillips to Sir Lionel Phillips, 22 July 1912). He even raised the prospect that his intended career in farming could well become another failure when he gave his reasons for wanting to marry Hilda: she struck him as "the kind of girl who would, no matter what happened, be a real wife and friend to me" (LPP, Harold Phillips to Sir Lionel Phillips, 22 July 1912). Despite any misgivings he may have had, Harold's father agreed to mediate between son and mother, advised Harold on effective courting techniques, and sent money for the purchase of a diamond ring at Ryrie Jewellers in Toronto.

Harold had been given every educational and professional opportunity that money could buy. He was educated at Eton, but his tutors' blunt assessments set the tone for the difficulties in the remainder of his life: unlike his well-behaved younger brother, he was criticized for his "naturally volatile disposition," for "being a nuisance," "too selfwilled and impatient," and "ostentatiously inattentive," and for rarely managing to be "quiet, except in warm weather at 2.45 p.m. and then his fixed gaze and unmoved limbs are susceptible of another explanation than wrapt attention." The best praise his tutor could muster was that Harold "has got a good place in a weakish division." The consensus appeared to be that he was an individual who "thinks too much of himself and his personal ease and comfort," and when he left Eton, his house master worried whether he was equipped to "resist shady companions, or all the various traps which are laid about for young men" (LPP, Harold Phillips, Reports, Eton College). No wonder that Sir Lionel supplied the table of Edward Compton Austen-Leigh, Harold's master at Eton and the Phillipses' personal friend, with pheasants and partridges from Tylney to compensate for their son's behaviour (Gutsche 166). On graduation, Harold announced his intention to attend Magdalen College, Oxford, followed by "Toronto College," presumably meaning the Ontario Agricultural College in Guelph, where he enrolled later in the decade.[41] His brother Francis did well at Balliol and generally does not seem to have put a foot wrong in his life, but Harold did not thrive at Oxford. He did spend a year at Magdalen but, "aiming for a degree in Pass Moderations," failed his "preliminary exams in Classics."[42] In response to Harold's most recent plan – that is, to join the

---

41 Penny Hatfield, college archivist, Eton College, email to Eva-Marie Kröller, 14 August 2013.

42 Robin Darwall-Smith, archivist, Magdalen College, email to Eva-Marie Kröller, 14 August 2013. The information on Harold Phillips at Magdalen draws on the "President's Notebooks" by Herbert Warren, president of Magdalen, 1885–1928, Magdalen College Archives PR/2/15, which also quote the Tutorial Board meeting, 20 December 1905, 335–6. His admission form at the Ontario Agricultural College (OAC) and other biographical sources summarily claim that he attended Oxford for two years, but they do not indicate completion of a degree (see OAC Bureau of Records, graduates, ca. 1890–1944, RE1 OAC A0811). Jan Brett, archivist, UGL ASC, and Anna Sander, archivist of Balliol College, along with their colleagues at Eton and Magdalen College, helped me sort out the complicated history of Harold's college education.

army – Magdalen permitted him to repeat his exams and his father fixed him up with a "first-class tutor" (Gutsche 188), but this was apparently in vain: there is no record that he completed an academic program of any kind at Oxford. He may have failed again, or he (or, rather, his parents) may have given up on Oxford, where he "was going to the devil headlong," as his father confided in his business associate, Sir Julius Wernher (Fraser and Jeeves 197).

Despite Florence and Lionel Phillips's efforts, Harold and Hilda's marriage was soon in difficulty. Judging by his letters to his father, Harold was attracted to Hilda because she was a pretty, guileless, and carefully chaperoned twenty-year-old who excelled at playing the piano. It also helped that another suitor proposed marriage to her at the same time but was unable to compete with Harold's glamour. Unlike the solid education of the McIlwraith girls, Hilda's had been fitful: she attended the Alexandra School for French and Music in 1910 and the Technical School for Drawing and Designing in 1911 and broke off a degree in English at the University of Toronto after one year.[43] Despite her brief training at the Macdonald Institute, there is little to indicate that she was prepared for life in the isolation of the Broederstroom Farm without her own family nearby to support her. Mrs. Hills had relatives in New Zealand, and Hilda and her parents may have concluded that, by moving to South Africa, she was merely settling in an area of the empire that, although remote, was still part of a sort of global home. When he proposed to her, she told Harold that she "would not mind the loneliness of the farm, for the first few years especially when we would have to be up there almost all the time" (LPP, Harold Phillips to Sir Lionel Phillips, 22 July 1912), but neither Harold nor Hilda had a good understanding of what was ahead of them. She sounded desperately lonely when she wrote to a neighbour, Emma Eastwood, asking for "lunch at the tennis court" after Harold had been called to his father's bedside following the assassination attempt: "I don't know if you will think it heartless or not but ... I simply couldn't spend my first Christmas away from home all day by myself – I'm such a baby." Her PS adds: "I'm so lonely" (LPP, Hilda Phillips to Emma Eastwood, n.d. [December 1913?]). She played tennis with other protégés of Emma Eastwood, such as Kenneth McGaffin from the Forest Station and Barney McMagh, the manager of Koningskroon Farm, halfway between Haenertsburg and Broederstroom. As she was six months pregnant by December when she wrote this unhappy note to Mrs. Eastwood, it is unlikely that she played much tennis before the birth of her baby in March 1914 (G. Thompson 109).

Eastwood, the wife of the government forestry officer for the Woodbush Forestry Station near Haenertsburg, was a "neighbour" only in relative terms: there

---

43 Hilda Wildman Hills, Entrance Record, Macdonald Institute, Archival and Special Collections, UGL.

was a distance of well over two hundred miles between Haenertsburg and the Broederstroom Farm. A sociable and cultured woman, Mrs. Eastwood took Hilda under her wing, probably sympathizing with her because she, too, had suffered "a dreadful shock to be landed in the wilds of the Northern Transvaal" (G. Thompson 31) after attending the Riebeeck College for Girls in Uitenhage, and working as a governess in Johannesburg for the family of Robert George Fricker, mining engineer and manager of Consolidated Gold Fields of S.A. Ltd. Hilda came to depend on Eastwood's caring presence. On leaving for Britain after the outbreak of war, she hoped that Emma Eastwood would not forget her, and she sent along a gift of riding gloves (LPP, Hilda Phillips to Emma Eastwood, n.d.).[44] Along with her daughter Awdry, a skilled amateur botanist better known under her nickname Googoo and married name Thompson,[45] Mrs. Eastwood observed the rapid deterioration of the Phillipses' marriage. She knew that Harold had been given the farm to "get him away from the wild and dissipating life of Johannesburg," but she also realized that he would find ways to ensure his entertainment once playing the "gentleman-farmer" was not enough to keep him occupied. In describing Harold's disastrous management of the farm, some observers also appear to blame Hilda, suggesting that, "town-bred" as she was, she joined him in giving "many parties, wild and otherwise" (Klapwijk 18) and preferred as he did "the high life of the Johannesburg set" ("Artefacts"). From what we know about her until her departure for South Africa, these sources either get the reasons for Hilda's unhappiness wrong or we must assume that, under her husband's influence, she changed rapidly from her demure self that had Harold think she was "a little young for her age" when they first met (LPP, Harold Phillips to Lionel Phillips, 22 July 1912). In the early 1920s, Lionel Phillips built a mansion for the couple in Balfour to give them an urban escape, but Crestlands did not resolve their marital difficulties, especially as his father soon had to bail Harold out of major debt (LPP, Harold Phillips, letters to Sir Lionel Phillips, 17 and 18 March 1924). To entertain himself and his guests, Harold built a racetrack at the farm,[46] and Thompson remembers that he "organised a hunt in his own bush, with Africans as drivers." The hunt "was more of a slaughter than a hunt" and made onlookers ashamed to witness the carnage (G. Thompson 108). The shoot was arranged for the benefit of Australian-born Sir Kenneth Beatty, then public prosecutor for the Transvaal who was appointed a few years later chief justice first of Bermuda and later of the Bahamas. He was only one of numerous close acquaintances of the Phillips

---

44 The letter, written from Villa Arcadia in Johannesburg, is undated, but suggests a "momentous" departure.
45 The nickname "Googoo" is derived from the Sepedi *Koko*, meaning grandmother. On Thompson's botanical work, see Figueiredo and Smith.
46 Maryna Fraser, email to Eva-Marie Kröller, 28 September 2013.

family who spent their working lives "careering" throughout the empire (see Lambert and Lester).

Except for the repeated reference to messages sent from one distant farm to another "by a boy," Harold and Hilda's letters never indicate how extensively they relied on Black workers. Thompson's memoir, which describes this type of relay as managed "by 'piccanin,' " gives a more differentiated picture: of her own deferential visits to the Rain Queen Modjadji, of Indigenous woodcutters in the Woodbush, "the piccanin Mogedigedi" who looked after Awdry when she was a child, and "a girl named Julia" who "slept in my room at the foot of my bed on a small mattress" because Julia's parents would not allow her "to wander." Thompson also discusses the frequent cohabitation among whites and blacks and the injunction that prevented the offspring from even legal unions from inheriting property (G. Thompson 36, 57). Despite her independence that had her set out on "a long walk, all on my own, along the Limpopo to Pafuri" when she was fifty (189), Thompson's views were ruled by the racial categories of her time, and in this regard some of her narrative resembles the ambivalence of Doris Lessing's story "The Old Chief Mshlanga" (1951). By contrast, there is no ambivalence whatsoever in the writings of Hilda's father-in-law. Echoing Sir Thomas McIlwraith's views of Native and Chinese labour in Queensland and his criticism of "Exeter-Hall philanthropy," Lionel Phillips's *Transvaal Problems: Some Notes on Current Politics* (1905) and *Some Reminiscences* (1906) denounce the "humanitarian imperialism" of the Aborigines' Protection Society (Heartfield) as advancing the views of "many ill-informed people of benign intent." The society's ideas were forceful enough to impress the Colonial Office, but Phillips advised his readers that "but for [the white man's] advent, South Africa would have become a veritable wilderness ... The Kaffir, left to himself, would have ever remained the unprogressive savage" (*Reminiscences*, xxxvii, xxxviii–xxxix, xl). When he advocated the import of Chinese workers into South Africa as more reliable than the "kaffirs," Phillips acquired the nickname of "Li Phi." He expected the Chinese to be uncomplaining and humble workers, but they resisted the harsh conditions in the Witwatersrand gold mines (see Ngai). Since there were eventually more than sixty-three thousand Chinese recruits, at times amounting to as much as "35 percent of the work force" (Northrup 59), any organized protest from this group was bound to register.

Ironically, the war temporarily propped up Hilda and Harold's marriage. Life near the front appears to have suited Harold's reckless and athletic nature better than farming, and he was awarded the Military MBE for service in Africa and in France. After serving with the Witwatersrand Rifles, of which his father was honorary colonel, Harold joined the Royal Artillery in England and was at the front in France when McIlwraith arrived in 1918 (L. Phillips 228). During the war, Sir Lionel moved his whole family to London, where he became chairman of the Central Mining and Investment Corporation, and "was appointed a member of the Imperial Munitions Committee, which was concerned with the development of Britain's mineral resources" (M. Fraser, "Sir Lionel Phillips"). Tylney Hall served as an army hospital until Major Herbert Cayzer of the Union Castle Line purchased it at the end of the war. In Richmond (just east of Walton-on-Thames, where Eileen Plunket's father presided over the hospital for New Zealand soldiers), the Phillipses established the Springbok Hospital for South African troops, the Springbok Club for soldiers, and a club for nurses. In *The History of the South African Forces in France* (1920), John Buchan describes the hospital, including its founders' efforts to create a home-like atmosphere by naming "[t]he principal corridors and rooms ... after well-known streets and places in South Africa, all the principal towns in the Union being represented" (328). To entertain the troops, Lady Phillips commandeered a "stuffed ostrich on wheels" for the Christmas festivities (Gutsche 346). The hospital was known for the quality of its facilities and care, including rehabilitation of the wounded, and Sir Lionel stopped by every day after work "to have a friendly chat with the men who were not too ill and to cheer them up as best [he] might" (L. Phillips 230). Meanwhile, his family stayed nearby in Petersham at Rutland Lodge.

At the outbreak of war, Hilda put her home economics training to good use when she "organized sewing parties at the Villa Arcadia," the family's Johannesburg home (Gutsche 326). She found an even better place for herself at Rutland Lodge, where Tom McIlwraith visited her shortly after he arrived in Britain. Because Harold was away at the front and Mrs. Hills had bravely crossed the Atlantic to be with her daughter and grandchildren, Hilda had reason to be happier than she had been at the Broederstroom Farm. Tom found Hilda "changed" from the last time he had seen her in Hamilton. He did not elaborate, but to judge from photos, her appearance had become more matronly in the five years since her wedding. She had settled well into her "job," McIlwraith told his mother, and he approved of the patriotism that had her plough up her lawn to plant potatoes. Several rooms, including the cavernous dining room, were closed to save on fuel, and the house was freezing. Nevertheless Hilda fed her guest well on pheasant eaten in front of the gas grate and "an excellent breed of green fig South African [jam]" brought along from the farm (CWM, T.F. McIlwraith to family, 2 January 1918).

Despite some austerity measures, the Phillipses lived in style. The lodge, a seventeenth-century mansion originally built for the lord mayor of London, had been leased in 1915 by John Stuart Wortley, husband of Harold's sister Edith Minnie ("Petersham Remembers"). Wortley was killed in action in 1918, necessitating the Phillipses' departure from Rutland Lodge and several moves to different addresses in the Richmond area over the next couple of years. One of these relocations had not been conveyed to McIlwraith, and he had to search for the Phillipses and his kit when he returned from Germany (WD, 27 July 1919). By far the largest of these various dwellings, the lodge had a staff of eight, including a nursemaid each for young Lionel and his baby sister, soon to be joined by a third child, also a girl. Like Beulah when she was confronted with a crowd of European aristocrats at the *Pensionat* in Dresden, Tom refused to be impressed, described the lodge as "certainly like a barn," and related his adventures at Hilda's in a series of comical sketches. These included encounters with a baby that spent "most of its time grinning," a maid who tried to unpack his bag and "arrange [his] clothes," and a canopy bed in a room "about a million feet wide and long" with "a monstrous sofa with white velvet cushions and cover" on which his dirty collar was displayed when Mrs. Hills arrived to say goodnight (CWM, T.F. McIlwraith to family, 2 January 1918). He seems to have had some preconceived notion of what Hilda's in-laws were like, probably from Hilda's letters home to her mother. He met Sir Lionel over lunch, and agreed with his daughter-in-law, who got along well with him, that he was "not a bad sort at all, cheerful old duffer in fact." By contrast, Lady Phillips's tantrums appear to have been reported to Hamilton, and when she was unable to attend, he heaved a sigh of relief: "[t]hank goodness ... and the rest of the party wasn't at all deadly." Either because no negative reports about Hilda's husband had been forwarded to Hamilton or because Tom was pleasantly surprised, McIlwraith is restrained in his comments about Harold, who suddenly appeared for a two-week leave from the front and "seems quite decent and was very fat" (CWM, T.F. McIlwraith to Dorothy, 27 January 1918). Tom also reports meeting Harold's brother Frank, then serving in Salonica, and Lady Phillips's cousin, Dora Poultney, who was working with the wounded at Tylney. Given Tom's juvenile sense of humour, it was probably a good thing that he did not know that the Phillipses' children referred to Mrs. Poultney and her daughters as "the Poultry" (Gutsche 234). Still, there was enough to keep him amused. When the Phillipses' car would not start, despite a cumbersome compressed-gas bag that made it look as if it was transporting a large duvet on the roof, he was delighted. The fact that the occupants had to take the bus to the Springbok Club seemed even more hilarious.

His tone became instantly respectful when Mrs. Hills took him and Phil Child, who had come along to Petersham for a visit, sightseeing in London. The Baedeker that Will Child had given McIlwraith as a farewell present was not needed because Mrs. Hills expertly "piloted" him in interesting directions and was "a good one to go with as she points out lots of little things that I would never have noticed in the world." A vigorous two-day program, some of it without Philip, took them from Petersham's village church to Westminster Abbey, the Houses of Parliament, St. Paul's, the Inns of Court, and the Tower. Everywhere, Tom made a point of noting connections with Canada, such as "a tablet in memory of Franklin with an Arctic scene carved on it" and "a rather fine carved assortment of boats and cliffs in memory of Wolfe" with "a whole batch of flags of Canadian battalions ... resting against it." These flags

Hilda Wildman Phillips with her son Lionel, ca. 1917. Richard N. Speaight, photographer, London. Clive Hunt, personal collection.

were among several reminders of the current war: tombs in the abbey were "sandbagged against air-raids," he observed. They paid a visit to the East End, where Mrs. Hills's husband had directed a children's home before emigrating to Canada. Lunch at Lyon's and dinner at the Trocadero on Shaftesbury Avenue rounded off the day before they lined up for the musical comedy *The Boy* with W.H. Berry as Mr. Meebles. He made a note to see *Billeted* next (CWM, T.F. McIlwraith to Dorothy McIlwraith, 27 January 1918). Mrs. Hills organized a similarly lavish program for him when he prepared to cross the Channel to France in October of that year. At other times, his stays were more relaxed.

He retrieved Mrs. Hills's Pekinese dog from the police station when it had run away yet again, wandered across Petersham Meadows with her and young Lionel, admired the rhododendron at Kew Gardens, or joined in a river cruise to Hampton Court. Surprisingly, given his interest in exploration narratives, he does not mention visiting Captain George Vancouver's grave in St. Peter's churchyard in Petersham, just a few steps away from Rutland Lodge.

The Phillipses returned to South Africa in early 1920, and McIlwraith – by then a student at Cambridge – surmised that their son would now finally have a father to look after him and teach him some discipline. Mrs. Hills, whose husband appears to have come for a brief visit to Britain as soon as the war was over, returned to Canada shortly after. Six years later, Harold died suddenly of pancreatic bleeding, apparently – as an autopsy concluded – the delayed result of a war injury. His mother's biographer writes that he "was at the time on good terms with his wife," who – unusual for Hilda – was in the Transvaal while Harold was at Crestlands (Gutsche 378). Hilda, who travelled to Canada for a visit soon after her husband's death, was remarried in the mid-1930s to John Dewar Lammie of South Africa. Her son Lionel inherited the baronetcy, and he and his sisters Pamela and Elizabeth came into their grandparents' wealth. Lionel was killed in action in the Second World War.

The Sewards

The story of a second family, the Sewards, complements that of the Hills-Phillips clan, extending this narrative into the imperial networks of academia and helping to set the stage for the next phase in Tom's life, his studies at Cambridge. On Empire Day 1918, a reluctant Thomas McIlwraith was cajoled along with fifteen other colonial cadets to participate in the celebrations at what he disrespectfully referred to as a "giddy club" meeting in "a barn down in the slums of Cambridge." His willingness to recite Kipling's "The English Flag" to a crowd of "about 200 women ... and absolutely countless children" introduced him to a remarkable couple and resulted in one of the most useful contacts he established in Cambridge (CWM, T.F. McIlwraith to family, 29 May 1918). In April 1918, he had reported to Dorothy that "[t]here has been a funny old boy chasing around with us last week. He is 'The Master' of Downing College, otherwise a grey-haired and venerable old don. The old boy has joined the volunteers and is attached to us to learn warfare." Tom found that the gentleman looked "like a stray duck in a thunderstorm" and that he was so unmilitary as not to be sure how to respond to a salute: "[He] acknowledged it very carefully, almost a bow." The master, usually gracious with the cadets billeted at Downing and Peterhouse Colleges, was, however, "quite peeved" when several soldiers climbed through the window of his college. "Big joke," Tom commented dismissively (CWM, T.F. McIlwraith to Dorothy McIlwraith, 6 April 1918). In a letter to family a month later, he reiterated the story in slightly more courteous language and appreciatively added that the master had begun to include the Canadians billeted at Peterhouse College in his Sunday-night gatherings for cadets at the Master's Lodge, where they were fed refreshments a little too frugal for their large appetites but where they enjoyed themselves nevertheless: "There were about a dozen cadets in all and we sat around the fire and talked for a bit. Then one of the chaps played on the piano and we generally amused ourselves. He produced a game sort of like glorified hunt the slipper, not bad sport" (CWM, T.F. McIlwraith to family, 5 May 1918).

Aged fifty-five in 1918, the "funny old boy" was A.C. Seward, professor of botany at Cambridge between 1906 and 1936, the year of his retirement and also the year in which he was knighted. In addition to serving as master of Downing College between 1915 and 1936, he was vice chancellor of the University of Cambridge from 1924 to 1926, author of a long list of influential books, and recipient of numerous professional honours. His publications included, among many others, the four volumes of his *Fossil Plants: For Students of Botany and Geology* (1898–1919), the four *Catalogues of the Mesozoic Plants in the Department of Geology of the British Museum* (1894–1915), an edition of Darwin's letters with Darwin's son Francis (1903), a centenary volume commemorating Darwin's birth and the fiftieth anniversary of the publication of *The Origin of Species* (1910), and *Plant Life Through the Ages: A Botanical and Geological Retrospect* (1931). He was general editor of the *Cambridge Botanical Handbooks* and the *Cambridge Manuals of Science and Literature*. Despite an abundance of scholarly obligations, Seward joined the Volunteer Training Corps at the beginning of the war as a "distinguished ... recruit," the role in which Tom first encountered him.[47] Seward's military activities were obviously limited, but he was a supportive presence during cadet drill and he facilitated relaxed camaraderie in his home. After some initial mockery, the cadets learned to appreciate his friendliness. Seward and his wife Marion were not only gracious hosts to Tom and his military friends, however, but also opened up an invaluable support system for him.

Marion Seward was of course present at the Downing Lodge at-homes, perhaps along with some or all of their four daughters – Phyllis, Dorothy, Carola, and Margery – but she had a program all of her own that was so daunting that it was blamed for her sudden death from heart disease only a few years after the war's end. In addition to numerous other charitable activities, Seward helped to initiate an undertaking that became synonymous with her name: the Tipperary Club in Cambridge, one of several such organizations across Britain. Its

---

47 Clipping, *Cambridge and University Journal*, 15 December 1915, n.p. Downing College Archives, DCHR/1/2/SEW.

work attracted high-level attention when Queen Mary and the Princess Royal came to call ("Court Circular"), as well as Admiral of the Fleet John Jellicoe and other dignitaries (*Marion Seward* 4). M.R. James, provost of King's College, medievalist, and author of famous ghost stories, spoke at the unveiling of the honour roll in 1916 for club members' fallen relatives. He quoted from *Macbeth* and reminded everyone that "[t]o us Christians the sum of our thought about the dead is that they are alive, that they are the same persons that they were on this earth, and that we have a prospect of meeting them again" (M.R. James 4). Taking its inspiration from a similar initiative during the Boer War, the club was open to "Soldiers' and Sailors' Wives" and their children in order to give low-income families "a rallying point and central meeting ground, to their mutual advantage." The club offered domestic training, babysitting, sewing and mending lessons, a library with magazines and books, and social evenings with music and dance to which "the girls were allowed to bring men friends, either soldiers or civilians" ("Fitzroy House Opened"). The underlying purpose of the club was education in practical patriotism, and to remind everyone of what they were there for, it hosted a thunderous speech by Mrs. Hudson-Lyall, "of the Ministry of Food," reminding women of "Their Power for Good": "She wanted every woman and girl to be ashamed of herself if she was not in the great army of war savers ... She would like to see all the food hoarders taken to prison, or even somewhere worse" ("Women's War Weapons"). More enjoyable than this philippic were picnics featuring three-legged and needle-threading races in the grounds of Downing Hall, at which the older club members proved that "the sporting instinct even in women of advanced age and many sorrows is difficult to crush." Winners received prizes from Mrs. Seward ("Tipperary Club"). She was so popular with the club's working-class women that at her funeral "they gathered in close ranks ... and with bowed heads formed her body-guard while the beloved friend was borne between their lines." At the next meeting of the club – which, at Marion Seward's instigation, had become the New Tipperary Club after the war – a college bedmaker proposed to "make that Club 'her living monument'" (*Marion Seward* 3). It is not clear, however, for how long the club did continue past the war and without Seward's leadership.

For Empire Day 1917, Marion Seward offered a series of "water colour sketches of Australian scenery" ("Empire Day Celebrations") for display at the club. She had brought these back from the Sewards' adventurous trip to the 1914 Conference of the British Association for the Advancement of Science (BAAS) in Sydney. Delegates were informed about the outbreak of war by "marconigram ... which fell like a bomb amongst us" (SD, 2 August 1914) while they were travelling on the *Euripides* and other ships to Australia. Some conference attendants – such as the anthropologist Bronislaw Malinowski, the physicist Peter Pringsheim, and the geographer Fritz Graebner – were declared enemy aliens on arrival and interned, while others like the anthropologist Felix von

Luschan and his wife managed a quick escape by an American-owned ship and returned to Europe via the United States.[48] By the time the scholars returned to Britain, the SMS *Emden* was prowling through the Indian Ocean and, by 20 September, had sunk "six British ships off Penang," including the SS *Indus*, which was destined for use as an Indian Expeditionary Force transport (SD, 20 September 1914). As a result, the return journey was completely dominated by the imperatives of war. Marion Seward was nevertheless undeterred from completing her diary and embellished it with a collection of small watercolours that she presented to her husband on the birthday he celebrated near Sri Lanka (he forgot hers, and hastily purchased a late present in Kandy). The Empire Day display at the Tipperary Club was a selection from this portfolio. In addition to a show of "pictures, products and photographs of Australia, New Zealand, South Africa, and Canada," several "Colonial cadets" had been drafted to speak on subjects related to their country of origin, and they were rewarded with rapt attention from "the hearers, who listened to their overseas kinsmen with close attention and evident appreciation" ("Empire Day Celebrations").

The watercolours of Australian scenery that Seward exhibited at the club and the two sketches of Cambridge she gave Tom as a memento when he left for France in 1918 were not an amateur's work. She was a botanical artist who regularly illustrated her husband's scholarly books and, when her wartime work issued "more urgent calls" (Seward, *Fossil Plants* vii) than those represented by her husband's publications, their daughter Phyllis, who studied painting at the Slade School of Fine Art with Henry Tonks (Sampson, *The Anatomist* 2), filled in for her.[49] Marion Seward furthermore belonged to a group of landscape painters who recorded the crumbling coastline of Suffolk. She may have derived part of her inspiration for this work from her background as the daughter of Robert Brewis, a Hartlepool shipowner. At "Old Farm," the cottage occupied by the Sewards in Walberswick since 1880, she was tutored by Alfred Rich,[50] and she and her family befriended numerous artists who frequented the village, including Francis and Jessie Newbery from the Glasgow School of Art. On the walls of Downing Lodge, McIlwraith might have seen a collection of contemporary paintings, including work by D.S. MacColl, C.J. Holmes, Roger Fry, and Rich. The outbreak of war and the Defence of the Realm Act severely curtailed plein-air painting, especially in coastal areas. Charles Rennie Mackintosh, architect of the Glasgow School of Art and a visitor to the village in 1914, was briefly arrested on suspicion of espionage and was subsequently "followed by

---

48 See Scheckter and Balfour. On von Luschan and his "escape" from Australia, see J.D. Smith.
49 Tonks, who was also a surgeon, produced drawings of First World War facial injuries to assist in the reconstructive work of plastic surgeon Harold Gillies.
50 "Alfred William Rich"; see also Mcinnes and Stubbings.

detectives everywhere he went" (Fox 47). Because of these restrictions, along with Marion Seward's work for the club, it is unlikely that the Sewards spent much time in Walberswick between 1914 and 1918, and they appear to have terminated their lease for "Old Farm" by 1919. In Australia, she narrowly escaped arrest herself when a sentry found her sketching outside a fort in Townsville, Queensland, in the company of the geologist Margaret Crosfield. On the voyage out she obtained "the Captain's permission to go on the forbidden part of the deck near his cabin [to draw] the bows of the boat with sea and sky beyond," and was gratified that he allowed her to sketch out in the open even on a Sunday: "one never knows how easily a Scotchman may be shocked," she explained her concern. By contrast, she was prevented from sketching much from the bows or anywhere else on the return journey when the *Montoro* and, from Kuala Lumpur onwards, the *Kashima Maru* had to observe restrictions imposed by "martial law" (SD, 9 and 12 July and 7 September 1914).

As Marion Seward's travel diary makes abundantly clear, she and her husband kept comfortable company with the large circle of scholars travelling to and from the BAAS congress with them, and identifying themselves as conference delegates repeatedly produced privileges for the group that were otherwise extensively restricted once war had been declared. When their ship was detained in Townsville, for example, the captain advised them to "wire the Federal Premier, Sir Joseph Cook, to complain" (SD, 8 September 1914), and sentries on Thursday Island were satisfied when they declared themselves members of "the Brit. Ass. party" (SD, 12 September 1914). To name only a few members of this high-powered gathering, their fellow passengers included the anthropologist W.H.R. Rivers (who was accompanied by John Layard), the physicist Sir Ernest Rutherford, the geologist Sir Thomas Holland, the mathematician and physicist Thomas Henry Havelock, the botanist and past governor of Fiji Sir Everard im Thurn,[51] the resident commissioner of the British Solomon Islands Protectorate Charles Morris Woodford, the anthropologist Henry Balfour, the physiologist Sir Edward Albert Sharpey-Schafer, and the chemist N.V. Sidgwick. Marion Seward became particularly fond of the anthropologist Major A.J.N. Tremearne, who, she imagined, "would find it easy to govern men, at one time he had 12,000 under him" when he served in the Boer War (SD, 11 July 1914). Tremearne, a native of Melbourne, joined the army immediately on return to Britain and was killed soon after at the Battle of Loos. Despite the general tension, there was occasional comic relief when, on the return voyage, the eccentric George Forbes, an electrical engineer, began a feud against the howling babies on the ship who, he thought, were not being disciplined by their languorous ayahs. Incidentally, nobody seems to have been concerned that these

---

51 On Everard im Thurn, see Dalziell.

ayahs would find it virtually impossible to get back to their country of origin during the war when it was difficult enough to organize their return even in times of peace (see Visram). Forbes reminded Marion Seward of "a war horse" when he announced that "despite his age and deafness" he hoped to join up and that "he actually enjoy[ed] the sight of bloodshed and battle, and that it [was] the only thing living for," a sentiment he did not expect her to "realize" because she "was a woman" (SD, 14 October 1914). The usual entertainments of tennis, quoits, pillow fights, Coon Can, tableaux vivants, and "Book Dinners" with passengers dressed up as their favourite literary characters seemed frivolous once war had been declared, and instead members of this potent group of experts volunteered their services teaching German to each other, or they watched Japanese passengers in second class perform martial arts. On the voyage out, they had attended lectures by some of the many scholars on board. A few of them were happy to have a captive audience, such as Sir Everard im Thurn, "a delightful old boy but a tedious speaker" (SD, 28 July 1914), who could not get his lantern slides to work. By the time the *Euripides* reached Australia, even the BAAS lectures were censored, and to everyone's regret Sir Joseph Ernest Petavel had to remove everything from his talk on aeroplanes that had to do with the war. On the return voyage, the Sewards sat in on lectures to the troops on board. They "watch[ed] the soldiers drill, and B. had a very interesting talk with one of the officers" (SD, 5 October 1914).[52] This appears to be where A.C. Seward began his own habit, later observed by T.F. McIlwraith, of expressing his solidarity with the soldiers by attending drill in the morning when there were otherwise few military things that he was equipped to do.

In addition to this circle of scholars, the Sewards connected with a large nexus of colleagues and former students wherever the couple went ashore. This routine began with their first landfall in Cape Town, where the BAAS had met in 1905. Here they were welcomed by Henry Harold Welch Pearson, Harry Bolus Professor of Botany at the South African College. Inspired by A.C. Seward's lectures to study botany, Pearson issued a plea at the 1905 BAAS meeting for the creation of a botanical garden, and – as mentioned above in the section on the Hills-Phillips family – Sir Lionel Phillips became a political ally in the foundation of Kirstenbosch National Botanical Garden. The Sewards were motored to the garden on arrival, admired the beauty of the scenery, and returned to the ship "laden with flowers," including "delicious violets" (SD, 20 July 1914). Also awaiting the Sewards' arrival was the Astronomer Royal Sydney Samuel Hough, who had been a fellow at St. John's College, Cambridge between 1895 and 1901. Depending on their professional and marital status, these men and their wives provided accommodation, invitations, introductions, and

---

52 Marion Seward refers to her husband as "B.," possibly short for "Bert" or "Bertie."

transport. In Sydney, the Sewards were hosted by "Dr. Radford, Warden of St. Paul's College" and "a contemporary of B's at St. John's Cambridge" (SD, 19 August 1914).[53] In Singapore, they were received by "Mr. Faulkner, an old pupil of Caius College"; in Penang, they saw "Mr. Stone of Sidney Sussex [who] is in the P&O office here," as well as "Mr. South (an Emmanuel man and a pupil of B's)"; in Kuala Lumpur, they met up with "Mr. Lewton-Brain ... an old pupil of B. and head of the Agricultural Department here" (SD, 27, 30, 29, and 28 September 1914). In Colombo, they dined with A.C. Seward's former student Father Maurice James Le Goc, who had arrived in Sri Lanka earlier that year. A botanist, astronomer, and member of the Oblates order, Le Goc had spent six years at Cambridge, where he became a particular favourite of Carola Seward. Former fellow students and pupils offered their services as interpreters when the Sewards wanted to purchase local specialties such as ostrich feathers at the Cape and "a fine piece of old Indian embroidery" as well as "finely coloured silk sarongs" in Kuala Lumpur (SD, 29 and 27 September 1914). Maintaining liaison with Cambridge men, no matter how long ago they had been A.C. Seward's students, was a matter of course for him and for them, and it was from this rich store of connections that McIlwraith was able to benefit when the Sewards took him under their wing. Of course, the outbreak of war diminished the number of friendships the Sewards had previously enjoyed, and if they had been concerned about the fate of Professors Graebner and Pringsheim when the possibility of war first raised its head, this sympathy was replaced by animosity shortly after. Everyone was relieved when these colleagues were prevented from travelling back to Britain: "it would have been a great strain having them, also they are both officers in the German army and it would have been straining even the magnanimity of science to take them back to kill our soldiers" (SD, 6 September 1914).

The Sewards were both amused and annoyed by an acquaintance in Melbourne who responded to each new name mentioned in conversation with "she or he is my wife's first cousin." Soon after these "cousins" were said to include Florence Nightingale, the Sewards tore themselves away from him in the middle of a sentence beginning with "she's my wife's ..." (SD, 14 August 1914). However, Marion Seward had her own densely woven web of cousins, or cousins of friends, spread across the empire. One of the passengers on the *Euripides* is "cousin of a friend of ours, a Mr. Shelford who stayed with us a few days but who is now dead. This Mr. Shelford's brother is Captain of the 'Orvieto' on the Orient Line" (SD, 30 July 1914). In Adelaide, she had "a long talk to a Mr Backhouse, who is one of the Darlington family of that name and we discussed all the old Darlington families" (SD, 11 August 1914). Shortly after,

---

53 On the Reverend Lewis Bostock Radford, later bishop of Goulburn, see K.J. Cable.

she received a telephone call from "Senator McColl (the son of my mother's old friend)," along with an invitation to lunch at which the senator unfortunately displayed "a very dirty collar" (SD, 13 August 1917). In Brisbane, she "took a tram out to Norman Park to see Mrs Snowdon (sister to my friend Agatha Barlow)" (SD, 1 September 1914). Margery Seward attended Bedales School in Hampshire, and this school, too, became a means of introduction when a member of the Harbour Commissioners in Sydney received Phyllis with "You were at Bedales were you not, my son was there." After straightening out the confusion between two Seward daughters, "we had a long talk about Bedalians generally" (SD, 25 August 1914). Family connections between Great Britain and the Sewards' various ports of call crop up constantly, and they repeatedly serve as a kind of passport confirming an individual's social cachet. Thus, Marion Seward, who bridles at being referred to as an "overseas member," chatted with "a Miss Wright, sister to the Archbishop of Sydney, who is taking the Archbishop's daughter back with her, we shall probably meet in Sydney" (SD, 7 August and 12 July 1914).[54] She also met "[a] Miss White ... she is a friend of the D H Scotts and her brother is Bishop of Carpentaria" (SD, 8 August 1914),[55] and she called on the bishop on Thursday Island during the return voyage. During sightseeing by trolley in Brisbane, Marion Seward met "a Doctor from Katoomba" who aptly summarized the paradoxical ties within the imperial family for her: "He came out there 22 years ago as locum tenens, and there he still is, he says he has a very good practice without having to work too hard and he married an Australian girl, as he thought that an English girl would always be wanting to go back to the Old Country. He took his wife to England on a visit, and in spite of being an Australian, she is longing to go home again!" (SD, 29 August 1914).

In contrast to individuals commended by their professional or familial connections, there was exclusion based on racism, colonial snobbery, and prejudice of long standing, and Seward was not always free of these attitudes either. She does not appear to have participated in a BAAS excursion to Coranderrk, where Aboriginals performed "boomerang throwing [and singing]" and Professor von Luschan measured their skulls (I. Clark 87). She also rolled her eyes when Arnold Lupton, professor of engineering and member of Parliament, repeatedly committed gaffes with his Australian hosts, and in one town put "his head out of the window and shout[ed] to the Mayor, who came to the station, 'Three cheers for ... what's the name of this place?' " (SD, 29 August 1914). However, at one of the many dinners organized for delegates, she thought that "Bishop Wilson, a delightful character, who had lived 18 years in the Solomon

---

54 See S. Judd, "Wright, John Charles."
55 See Teale.

Islands" was "just the right type to deal with natives" (SD, 10 August 1914).[56] In Sri Lanka, she commented that "[t]he Singalese or Sinhalese as they are now called, are a much taller and better developed race than the Malays or Javanese, and some are quite handsome!" (SD, 9 October 1914). Seward was also relieved that the captain of the *Kashima Maru* was "a very genial and talkative little man, and good type of Japanese," and she was enchanted by the "high caste Japanese travelling by this boat, the little ladies are very picturesque in their native costumes" (SD, 4 October 1914). She reached another impasse, this one sounding much like Eileen Plunket's view of French troops, when their ship reached Marseilles: "Before breakfast the [British] soldiers were inspected and went on to the quay where they formed in marching order and went for a six mile march. They looked very smart and seem a fine lot of men, very different from the French soldiers who whatever they may be in the field look very slack and sloppy in the town even when they are marching" (SD, 28 October 1914).

The Sewards' interest in McIlwraith's welfare did not stop with invitations to tea while he was a cadet or with the gift of two of Seward's sketches and a handy Wayfarers Library copy of Mark Twain's *The Innocents Abroad & Jumping Frog* for Christmas 1918. Passing through Britain on his way home to Canada in August 1919 and using a delay in embarkment to research his options for future university education, McIlwraith was taken in hand by the couple, who welcomed him with open arms. On a visit to Downing Lodge, McIlwraith and the professor stayed up chatting until the early hours, and the guest had to spend the night "in a pair of pyjamas belonging to a super-respectable professor of botany." He was invited to dinner in hall and into the senior combination room after, and the cigars and drinks in male company following dinner made him "a bit homesick for our mess anteroom" (CWM, T.F. McIlwraith to family, 3 August 1919). The doddery professors at high table did not make up for his army companions, especially "a bearded old imbecile on my right who was deaf and about 100 years old," but as a result of the dons' interest in his wartime experiences, the college environment instantly felt like a companionable fit: "Various professors came and talked to me, but, as they all seemed more or less keen on comparatively true stories of life in Germany, all went well" (CWM, T.F. McIlwraith to family, 3 August 1919). Seward himself "was wonderful," advised him that "[he] should take anthropology if [he] was to deal with peoples" ("Genealogy"), and introduced him to two of the leading men in the field at Cambridge, A.C. Haddon and W.H.R. Rivers. Both immediately supported McIlwraith's application and eventually became his teachers. The Sewards' friendship continued into his studies between 1919 and 1921, and McIlwraith

---

56   See "Wilson, Cecil."

often dropped in on them. They introduced him to celebrities like the geologist James Mann Wordie, who had participated in Shackleton's second Antarctic expedition, and at one of their at-homes he obtained a much-sought-after invitation to join the university's Natural Science Club.

In their generosity, the Sewards practised the principle of the university as family (see Irish, "Fractured Families") to a fault. The couple's keen social conscience towards townsfolk, soldiers, and young scholars had them run Downing College as if it were a kind of large vicarage. In this, they did not limit themselves to natives of Britain but included young soldiers from around the empire. They were eager to prove their gratitude for the "reinforcements from India, Canada and Australia" (SD, 28 August 1914) that had them hope on their return journey from Australia that Britain would not be permanently outnumbered by the Germans. Indeed, by the time they reached Suez, they saw "camel corps with Indian soldiers" patrolling the canal (SD, 21 October 1914). The Sewards were attentive to McIlwraith when he was billeted at a college emptied of students, and they looked out for him after he had departed for the front, when he returned after demobilization, and when he became a student at Cambridge.

When Marion Seward died in 1924, her husband eulogized her as one whose "religion was service" (*Marion Seward* 12). Tom McIlwraith benefited from that religion, and he appears to have befriended the next generation of Sewards as well. Specifically, he remained in touch with Phyllis Seward and her husband Michael Sampson, son of the eccentric scholar of Romani culture, John Sampson. Michael, a war hero decorated with the Military Cross and future scientist with ICI (Imperial Chemical Industries), was McIlwraith's contemporary and friend at St. John's College, where they formed "a mutual aid society in regard to such details as sugar and tea" (TFMF, T.F. McIlwraith to family, 8 August 1921). In addition to Sampson's military distinction, which was bound to impress T.F., there were a number of other connections between the two. Indeed, Sampson "relished the wildlife, particularly the birds," when he grew up in South Wales (*The Gypsy Scholar* 103). He also had family in Canada: two of his paternal uncles lived in Gananoque, not far from Hamilton, and Michael's brother Amyas trained in Toronto and Texas with the Royal Flying Corps (126). After he went missing in action in France, Amyas's name was included on the war memorial in Gananoque. When he visited London in 1934 for a conference and on business for the ROM, McIlwraith met up repeatedly with "the Sampsons" and "their youngsters, three nice kiddies, but very strenuous" (TFMP, T.F. McIlwraith to Beulah McIlwraith, 16 August 1934). Thirty years later, his memoir praised Michael Sampson along with Leslie Houstoun – both of whom had died in the 1950s – as the only two people he had known in his lifetime who might have taken Bella Coola "in their strides" ("Genealogy").

One of the "very strenuous" children was Anthony Terrell Seward Sampson, editor of the South African *Drum Magazine* between 1951 and 1955, a journalist active in the anti-apartheid movement, friend of Nelson Mandela, and author of Mandela's authorized biography. Sampson wrote the acclaimed *The Anatomy of Britain* (1962), and in other books he documented the networks – some sinister – of international banking, the oil and arms industries, and the European Common Market. Certain aspects of Anthony Sampson's career duplicate McIlwraith's intellectual switch, following Cambridge and beginning with fieldwork in Bella Coola, from endorsement to criticism of imperial ideas. These developments will be related in the next chapter and the conclusion.

Chapter Seven

T.F. McIlwraith at Cambridge

Demobilization, a Scots Identity, and Enrolment at Cambridge

Arriving in Cambridge after a hectic few days in Glasgow with his KOSB mate Leslie Houstoun, followed by a quick trip to the military camp in Pirbright to have his leave extended, Tom McIlwraith completed formalities towards enrolment at the university and lined up lodging. He

> [s]tarted filling in application forms at once, in spite of tired and a headache and worked till 2.45, everything needing to be very exact. Was called for early breakfast, what a [dub?] to get up, and started out to look for digs at 08.00. Hired a bicycle it soon played out and had to be repaired. Used a search for address of [army friend] Irwin as a start and chased around like mad, getting two half promises. Went to [Walter] Burd's old digs and used same excuse, but with quite good results as found place where room likely available. Ran them to earth successfully and got definite promise, praise be. Went at once to [Tutor E.A.] Benians, he told me to book them, but was busy and said he would see me at 17.30. Called ... on [W.H.R.] Rivers ..., got list of several books from him and broached idea of Canada,[1] he not objecting, my chances looking up. Went to appointments people and talked to them, rather youthful person in charge, who told me no board was needed, the real power being the Master of the college. They also said that Canada would be sound, and promised to let me know, things still looking up. Also heard that a recommendation from Rivers would help grant along, needing another trip to him, even after borrowing large book from him. Back to lodgings and definitely booked them, also held another set for Benians. Swore to statement of income before a commissioner for oaths. Rivers not in, so nothing to do and had tea, first

---

1 The reference to Canada alludes to McIlwraith's plan to pay a short visit to his family before the beginning of the Michaelmas term.

meal since breakfast. Saw Benians at 17.30, very amiable owing to extra diggings, thought Canada all clear, and no need to see Master, gave me papers and so forth, guess all clear. Wired to Pirbright to send my papers to Victoria. Back to chase Rivers and found him changing for dinner, no time to write anything for my papers but he promised to see the Master, which comes to even better provided he doesn't forget. Back to "University Arms" and wrote Master, sending whole affair, no time to re-read it and post, in fact I only made 20.35 train by a taxi. No room in Liverpool St. Hotel so chased across to Victoria and had to go to Queen Mary's Hostel, right up near Sloane Square, then they chased me to the Annexe as not leaving for France to-morrow. (WD, 13 September 1919)

Between 8 and 15 August, McIlwraith pursued a program that has the reader of his diary gasping at its relentless pace. The immediacy of his entries is particularly noteworthy because, once on board the *Royal George* on his way back to Canada, he confesses that he has had to catch up with four weeks' worth of writing. Unless his memory was truly photographic, this may have been done with a brief prompt for each day that allowed him to fill in the details when he had the time to do so. Contrary to the comedy in his letters home and despite his gratitude to Professor Seward, the diary describes his encounter with the ancient professors at high table in Downing College with abject misery at the prospect of leaving his KOSB mates behind for this decrepit "mob" (WD, 31 July 1919). Versions of "utterly fed-up, hungry, and cross," "hopelessly fed up with life," feeling "hellish unsettled," and "[i]n a bad state of blues" litter his notes. Fortunately, his flying visit to Scotland "bucked [him] up endlessly," as did several bottles of Scotch emptied with "Blue-Eyes" Leslie Houstoun: "verily great are whisky and L." (WD, 4 August 1919). One attraction of study in Edinburgh or Glasgow would have been to stay close to Houstoun, whose demobilization several weeks before his own had left McIlwraith feeling lonely and lost. On his brief visit to Scotland he did consult with university advisers but in the end decided for Cambridge, probably because of the instant support he received there for his plans.

This chapter describes McIlwraith's transition from the military to studies at Cambridge and his search first for a post in the Colonial Service and then an appointment to a major university within the empire. These early stages in his academic career progressed alongside developments in his personal life, with a shift from the camaraderie with his army friends to filial relationships with his professors.

Despite his decision to go to Cambridge, McIlwraith swore to Houstoun that he would "never be an Englishman" (WD, 7 August 1919). Although he does not record these particular discussions with his mates, membership in his KOSB unit had obviously pushed him towards a strong acknowledgment of his Scottish roots. The heavy loss of life among soldiers from Scotland, along with general unrest caused by a declining economy, had him and his friends develop an animosity towards the English that is not apparent in the romanticized descriptions he sent home shortly after arriving in Britain in early 1918.[2] Several trips north before and during his studies at Cambridge strengthened an emotional attachment in which his military experience, professional aspirations, and his family's origins became strongly linked. In March 1920, a walking tour on Loch Long in Dunbartonshire with Houstoun had him admire the "clouds ... coming up the valleys" and "burns racing down the hillsides" (TFMF, T.F. McIlwraith to family, 29 March 1920).[3] Amazed, they noted the dozens of learned books on astronomy, theology, and "goodness knows what" filling the shelves of the fisherman's cottage in which they were staying, and spent the evenings conversing with the owner who was "verra glad to hae a wee bit crack wi' ye on bees and astronomy" (TFMF, T.F. McIlwraith to family, 3 and 4 April 1920). When Dorothy came to visit later that summer, brother and sister toured Scotland together, and McIlwraith confessed afterwards that "[i]f any question ever turns up here with regard to Scotland and England I always catch myself thinking of it from the Scots rather than the English point of view in spite of the fact that I have been in England nearly two years and in Scotland less than that many months." The siblings toured Culloden, and he evoked for his parents the melancholy scene of "the gray moor, made still grayer under the sky that was never bright" where it was easy to imagine "the skirl of the pipers and the wild charge of the Highlanders" (TFMF, T.F. McIlwraith to family, 17 August 1920). Like the new Scottish war memorials that preserved the names of "all those who had fallen defending the nation against its enemies, aligning its First World War dead with the warriors of the past, not just Robert the Bruce but also Alexander III and William Wallace," McIlwraith drew a parallel between Culloden and First World War battlefields – especially, one suspects, with Loos, where the Scots had suffered heavy losses and won five Victoria Crosses (Strachan 55–6). The recent war transformed the historic markers commemorating the deaths of Jacobite chiefs and clansmen into a graveyard that had "the weird Burns memorial at the Brig o'Doon" in the McIlwraiths' native Ayr appear a mere frivolity by comparison (TFMF, T.F. McIlwraith to family, 17 August 1920). On these occasions, the English seemed a long-time enemy made newly objectionable by their apparent failure to acknowledge Scotland's role in the war as much as

---

2 The actual figure for Scotland's war dead has been the subject of some debate. Strachan questions the accuracy of 26.4 per cent Scottish war dead, more than twice the percentage for the remainder of Britain, as used in Winter, *The Great War and the British People*; Ferguson, *The Pity of War*; and Devine, *The Scottish Nation*.

3 I consulted the letters from Cambridge when they were in family possession. Most of them were deposited in TFMF in 2019.

it deserved. McIlwraith was gratified when a reason could be found to conflate the Hanoverian monarchs with the German enemy. When Jean sang "The Wee Wee German Lairdie" to him during her visit in Cambridge, he tacked the Jacobite song ridiculing George I on the wall of his room at St. John's College once Dorothy had sent him the typed-up lyrics, even if it was all "to the amusement of [his] Sassenach friends" (TFMF, T.F. McIlwraith to family, 24 January 1922).

The strongest expression of just how pronounced McIlwraith's identity as a Scotsman had become occurred shortly after his graduation from Cambridge when he attended his first BAAS congress. McIlwraith motored to Edinburgh in the company of a fellow student in chemistry, "a super-worthy and respectable individual [who] had lost a leg in the war" (TFMF, T.F. McIlwraith to family, 31 August 1921). Their vehicle, a three-wheeler not unlike "an overgrown perambulator" (TFMF, T.F. McIlwraith to family, 31 August 1921), broke down frequently as they travelled north, providing them with more leisure to contemplate the countryside than they had bargained for. McIlwraith's descriptions of the pair's progress towards Edinburgh are interspersed with professional news, enclosing a copy of Sapir's letter offering him fieldwork in Bella Coola, detailed accounts of conference presentations, scientific activities (including skull-measuring), and discussions with scholars who promised to be useful in future. With Jean, who had attended his graduation and travelled north ahead of him, there was sightseeing in Jedburgh and in Walter Scott's house in Abbotsford, and from a distance they saw the "new home" of Field Marshall Sir Douglas Haig, "a most beautiful spot" (TFMF, T.F. McIlwraith to family, 15 September 1921). Normally, McIlwraith was inclined to dismiss his aunt as an eccentric old lady, but he could not help but be impressed by her knowledge of Scottish genealogy, literature, and music and by her virtuoso mobilization of their family's local connections. When he took time off from his conference in Edinburgh to travel to Greenock to say goodbye to Jean and cousin Helen Service, he expected to "wave them off at the dock from among the common herd." Instead, he was swept off his feet and packed into a lighter by "Mr. Steele of Ayr" (presumably one of the Steeles and Ritchies T.F. had visited at Jean's instigation during the war), who had rushed to the port for a last-minute meeting with Jean, "telephoned to the steamship people for permission to go aboard, and stretched this doubtful claim so as to include me." The group talked among piles of luggage in Jean's cabin until it was time to return by tender, and "as we pushed off the anchor began to be raised" (TFMF, T.F. McIlwraith to family, 20 September 1921). She continued to pass on information about the McIlwraiths' roots, and towards the end of his time at Cambridge, she forwarded "a letter from the author of a book on Skye who claims we are descendants of an ancient Skye family" (TFMP, T.F. McIlwraith to family, 24 January 1922). At the BAAS conference, he had also talked to the Reverend Roderick MacLeod, president of the Gaelic Society, who pointed out that the origin of the McIlwraith name

was "unquestionably Gaelic" and that the family was "rather out of [its] area in
Ayrshire" (TFMF, T.F. McIlwraith to family, 26 September 1921).

Like his aunt, McIlwraith appears to have had a remarkable ability to im-
itate accents and, back in Hamilton, his family found that he sounded like a
Glaswegian. In the army, learning to appreciate the diversity of their speech
helped him to bond with Scots from various backgrounds. On demobilization,
he was given a "send-off [from] a C.S.M. [command sergeant major] who was
rather a pal of mine. I believe his civvy occupation is poaching, and I fancy he
would be an expert. He came up to my room when he heard I was going, sat
down peaceably, and with a broad Dumfries accent came out with 'You're going
awa', you're going awa', you wee divvle, I love ye' " (TFMF, T.F. McIlwraith to
family, 3 August 1919). On one of his trips to Scotland, it became apparent to
McIlwraith that "[m]ost of my friends were Lowlanders and it was quite interesting to me to hear the Inverness accent. I had met it before but had always
simply put it down to individualism" (TFMF, McIlwraith to family, 17 August
1920). Although he appreciated the charm of "a broad Dumfries accent," it was
not McIlwraith's intention to look and sound endearing when, on his chase
for lodgings in overcrowded Cambridge, he flourished his own new Glasgow
accent along with his KOSB uniform and swagger stick to impress on future
landlords that it was their patriotic duty to help him out. He flared at the suggestion that a veteran could be held back in civilian life by a technicality like
housing: "This ... was too much for a K.O.S.B. officer." The thought angered him
so much that even a full forty-five years later he recalled this episode ("Genealogy"). His Scots accent was, however, no match for the influence of Cambridge.
By the time he returned to Canada in 1922, he imitated the pronunciation of
his teachers, none of them Scots. This, in turn, was soon enough dropped for a
Canadian accent that, according to his family, he maintained for the remainder
of his life. Without their knowledge, he may of course have slipped back into his
Scots and English accents in conversation with old friends.

Despite the emergence of a Scottish identity while he served in the KOSB,
demobilization shook McIlwraith's sense of personal balance so strongly that
the resulting turmoil, as recorded in his diary, became an unsuitable subject
for the letter that he wrote to his family describing the same few weeks. At
twenty-five pages, it is only half as long as the letter describing his march into
Germany with the British army of occupation, but its length and detail are nevertheless remarkable because it was written three weeks before he expected to
catch the boat back to Canada, delayed by the Liverpool police strike that in the
end obliged him to embark from Southampton. The cable alerting his parents
to his arrival in Halifax would, he speculated, probably reach them well before
this letter. Yet for him, writing was clearly an important way (and one not easily replaced by talking) to justify his thinking, explain his intentions, and put
up a sensible front. He was to repeat an abbreviated version of this exercise in

the subsequent months every time promising career prospects emerged variously in New Guinea, South Africa, Uganda, and finally Canada. McIlwraith's description of demobilization and his efforts to decide what he was going to do with himself helped him to shape his plans into a workable prospect. While the concurrent diary entries suggest nervous uncertainty, his letter alternates between a well-organized accountancy sheet and shrewdly calibrated emotional expression. Thus, he firmly pushed aside the prospect of homesickness should he decide to take up a colonial post in the far reaches of the empire, though, given how much he had already enjoyed himself away from Canada, this admission may have been more for his family's reassurance than diagnosis of a real problem. More surprisingly, he accused himself repeatedly of having "a horrible inclination to let things slide" (TFMF, T.F. McIlwraith to family, 3 August 1919). There is certainly no evidence of this alleged tendency in this letter, nor for that matter in any of his other correspondence, and perhaps this odd self-accusation is his way of justifying the briskness with which he lays out his plans. Thanks to a visit from an education advisory officer in Germany earlier in the year, he had already learned that his service record provided him with an Imperial Settlement Scholarship, and he had received "No[, it should be] Oxford or Cambridge" in response to his own preference for Glasgow or Edinburgh ("Genealogy"). These choices and the money that came with his military service represented educational opportunities that his family's limited financial resources alone would not have made possible. To reassure his parents that his thoughts about the future – whatever his final decisions – were well considered, he gave them a comprehensive report on his financial situation, including any savings from army pay and cash brought over from Canada when he shipped out. The same sense of responsibility prevailed later in the fall when "it seemed rather a pity to turn ... down" his veterans grant because Helen Holt had topped it with a generous gift of money to pay his expenses, but "it would not [have been] square to take" more than his fair share (TFMF, T.F. McIlwraith to family, 26 October 1919). When he graduated with a first in anthropology two years later, she repeated the gesture "in ... a substantial way, for she [was] most awfully pleased and proud" (TFMP, Mary Stevens to T.F. McIlwraith, 10 August 1921).

The pragmatism of McIlwraith's explanations is enlivened with the occasional outburst of army language that has him declare one situation after the other "a regular scream" and that "would have [his family] laugh for a week" (TFMF, T.F. McIlwraith to family, 3 August 1919). Generally, his military experience spilled into this new phase of his life, and this letter and subsequent ones are replete with references to fellow soldiers who seemed to show up everywhere and in unexpected places well into his studies at Cambridge. Shortly after his arrival, he met a young man named Scott, "a KOSB officer" and now "a freshman at Christ's" (TFMF, T.F. McIlwraith to family, 26 October 1919), and as late as 1921, he ran into a Canadian with whom he had shared his cabin on the *Royal George* on his short visit home.

A particularly elaborate encounter just before his return to Canada involved "a toughish-looking individual in civvies" who turned out to be "a l/cpl [lance corporal] in the Gordons at Colchester" in rank and a "rather homesick Yankee from Bridgeport" in personal life (TFMP, T.F. McIlwraith to family, 3 August 1919). The American, apparently hoping for help in finalizing his own demobilization, chased McIlwraith's bus because he mistakenly believed that T.F. would be able to use his influence in getting him home faster. Despite his amusement at these delusions about a second lieutenant's clout with the military authorities, McIlwraith himself relentlessly began to pursue the connections he had gained through his military service. Though T.F.'s conversation with Professor Seward turned out to be decisive in making up his mind to study anthropology, it was only one of a series of interviews with a variety of officials. There was all the more opportunity to do this when he arrived from Germany because the Hills-Phillipses were "all at the sea-side," leaving him – as he put it in a favourite analogy – to "tear ... around London like a lost duck in a thunderstorm," with only the musical "The Maid of the Mountains" to distract him (TFMP, T.F. McIlwraith to family, 3 August 1919). To obtain the necessary information and advice, he looked up influential people in their offices, presented himself uninvited in their homes, and criticized their lack of hospitality if they fell short of his expectations. William Graham,[4] the brother of his KOSB mate T.N. Graham, was member of Parliament for Central Edinburgh, and McIlwraith had obtained a letter of introduction to him, which he "unearth[ed]" along with "snaps and addresses from all corners of [his] kit" (TFMP, T.F. McIlwraith to family, 3 August 1919). If the meeting was not a success, it was not for lack of trying. Graham was a busy Labour politician with duties on numerous committees, such as the Royal Commission on Income Tax and the Speaker's Conference on Devolution, but when McIlwraith failed to locate him at the Houses of Parliament despite a four-hour wait and did not receive an immediate response to a letter, he obtained Graham's home address from a policeman and "tracked him down to his digs away in the wilds of North London." McIlwraith stayed "until [he] had pumped him dry" and had been promised information on university studies at Edinburgh (TFMP, T.F. McIlwraith to family, 3 August 1919). Graham's note saying that he preferred to communicate in writing rather than in person had been delayed in the mail, but it is doubtful that receiving it in time would have deterred his visitor, who commented critically after the meeting that "[Graham] was decent enough, but not superabundantly so, considering what a good friend of mine his brother

---

4 See P. Williamson, "Graham, William."

is" (TFMP, T.F. McIlwraith to family, 3 August 1919). After all, only ten days earlier McIlwraith had steered T.N. Graham home to his billet in Germany after a whisky-sodden night at the officers' mess (WD, 20 July 1919). In contrast to his brother, William Graham had been turned down for military service for medical reasons, and it is possible that McIlwraith's sceptical response to the MP is shaped by the censorious attitude that he continued to adopt when he suspected a "slacker."

In reporting to his family the outcome of his discussions with various officials, McIlwraith blends his personal plans with the rhetoric of empire, imbibed at Highfield School and in the army and from his copious reading of imperial literature. Returning to McGill remained an option but not a particularly attractive one as he felt that in the United Kingdom, "the opportunities of big things are greater ... and I would feel more than keen to give a hand in the getting ahead" in "this empire of ours," which he did not "for a moment" expect to falter (TFMP, T.F. McIlwraith to family, 3 August 1919). Systematically, he perused the available choices, dismissing "an Arts course" as a degree probably "useless" in attempting to find a paying profession, science as too competitive and different from what he had done before, and forestry as "overcrowded" (TFMP, T.F. McIlwraith to family, 3 August 1919). Instead, he was attracted to an education that would improve his prospect of research work "with one of the museums" or prepare him for a post as "a junior commissioner or official in Africa, India, Malay States, Southern Pacific, I am not over-particular where!" In his consultation with the Appointments Department at the Ministry of Labour, he declared that he wanted "[t]o take up research or exploration work in the Outer Empire" (TFMP, T.F. McIlwraith to family, 3 August 1919) and was promptly shown a list of both British and French posts ranging from "a police inspector in British Guiana to an assistant resident in the Gilbert Islands, not forgetting ... a job in a rubber company on the Gold Coast ... [or] a secretary's post at Teneriffe" (TFMP, T.F. McIlwraith to family, 3 August 1919). His contempt for "an Arts course" as "a useless degree" may have created some discussion with Dorothy, who had been a literary light at McGill and – as discussed in the previous chapter – was making a career for herself in New York publishing. However, McIlwraith's dismissal of the arts as the basis for his future profession echoes the debate, in Cambridge and elsewhere, about the apparently waning influence of the classics-centred humanities, compared to disciplines that emphasized "bread-winning" or "Empire-building."[5] For these goals, empirically oriented areas of study seemed more obviously suited than the arts. Perhaps the career counselling he received from the education advisory officer in Germany had further primed McIlwraith to adopt this kind of thinking.

---

5   Sir George Kekewich, "Classics and the University Curriculum," *Cambridge Magazine*, vol. 1, 25 May 1912, 369, qtd. in Wang 114.

Cambridge After the War

When McIlwraith returned to Cambridge after a brief interlude in Canada, he was part of a large influx of undergraduates, "literally swarms of them," and the city was so crowded that it was "difficult to get [one's] laundry done" (TFMF, T.F. McIlwraith to family, 12 October and 9 November 1919). Numbers leapt from their lowest at 233 in 1916 to 3,844 by May 1919 – that is, several hundred more than the 3,181 enrolled in 1914. By the Michaelmas term, when McIlwraith began his studies, there were 4,200 undergraduates.[6] Students included "190 United States servicemen on a short course" as well as "400 naval officers whose education at Dartmouth had been interrupted by the demand of them as midshipmen on active service" (Howarth 25; see also Irish, *The University at War*, 62). These officers were going to be of particular interest to McIlwraith because he did his first university lecturing, an introduction to anthropology, to a group of fifty of them in the fall of 1921.[7] From the start, the officers attracted public attention. Citing an announcement in the "daily papers," Kipling celebrated them in his poem "The Scholars" (1919), and exhorted the Proctor to "[t]enderly ... let them down, if they do not walk as they should: / For, by God, if they owe you half a crown, you owe 'em your four years' food!"[8] Not walking "as they should," however, was the least of their disciplinary problems. Instead, the officers helped to create a volatile mood in Cambridge during "the strange year following the peace" (Glover, *Cambridge Retrospect* 113). Together with other demobilized soldiers they resisted the university discipline, were hostile to pacifists, exchanged provocations with the Bolsheviks, and – when they were not roaring around town on their motorbikes with them – battled the full admission of women to the university as unfair competition to ex-servicemen. A first signal of what lay ahead came when the offices of the pacifist *Cambridge Magazine*, edited by the philosopher C.K. Ogden, were destroyed on Armistice Day (Cope 127). A year later, on 12 November 1919, the proctor noted that "RN [Royal Navy] Commanders" came to him "with tale of 200 Bolsheviks [who] vowed to strip Navy of its uniforms, of naval organiz[ing] to protect itself + retaliate; + they have gated all navy at 8 tonight!" The day after, there was "an alarm as to story of naval students meaning to rag a Socialist soc[iety] mtg in ev[ening], so off + saw Captain Fullerton, who will prohibit the mtg. Commander [illegible] then called with

---

6 *Cambridge Review*, 30 October 1913, 56, and 31 October 1913, 56, qtd. in Levsen 189.

7 See "Lectures delivered at Cambridge University: Lectures to Naval Officers, Michaelmas Term, 1921," TFMF, UTA, B 1979-0011/007 (16). Unfortunately, the file does not contain any details about his students.

8 Rudyard Kipling, "The Scholars" (1919), *The Cambridge Edition of the Poems of Rudyard Kipling*, Volume II: *Collected Poems II*, 1388.

report of 3 u.g. [= undergraduate] bands going round town, singing anti-naval songs!" (TRG, 12 and 13 November 1919). Captain Roskill, in his discussion of "the navy at Cambridge," cites "the hoisting of the White Ensign on the lantern of Trinity College hall" as "the best remembered" (Roskill 192), but this prank was mild compared to some of the others.

One of the worst rags erupted around the visit of Norman Angell, co-founder of the Union of Democratic Control and future winner of the Nobel Peace Prize (1933), but dismissed as a "worm" by the Debating Society of St. John's College.[9] During the demonstrations against Angell, the proctor had a "flour bag thrown at [him]," and there was almost a casualty when "[a] naval officer fell from outside window and was badly hurt" (Wood 125).[10] Undergraduates were barely prevented from throwing Angell into the river along with dunking the policemen who had come to his rescue, and the house of the chairman who had introduced Angell's speech was pelted with rocks and mud.[11] The incident created deep divisions within the city of Cambridge. Labour protested against the "resumption of the Town and Gown bitterness" when undergraduates stormed the railway station on Angell's arrival and "danced and capered on top of trains." Railway workers threatened to lay down their jobs should there be a repetition of this behaviour ("Labour and 'Rags' "). Parliament became interested in the incident, and the parliamentary secretary to the Admiralty was asked in exasperation "whether his department have any control over naval officer undergraduates at Cambridge" ("The Norman Angell 'Rag' "). These were widely publicized events, but the proctor also inserted clippings in his diaries documenting problems that were not so extensively disseminated, including an "outbreak of cerebro-spinal fever" that killed five of the naval officers. Another sombre note was added to the post-war exuberance by a rash of suicides among university lecturers and their wives, some of whom were driven to despair by their sons' deaths in action (TRG, inserts, diaries for 1919 and 1921).[12]

McIlwraith, who was instantly immersed in his studies, did not participate in rags (or at any rate did not write home about doing so) although he probably

---

9   The Records of St. John's College, Clubs and Societies, Debating Society, SJCS/15/4/3 (1902–1921), 13 March 1920. However, as recorded in the minutes, the debate, on the motion "That the break up of civilization is imminent," was so nonsensical that it is not clear how much weight should be given to this comment: "Norman Angell was a worm, beer is the only thing worth having, Norman didn't like beer, ergo Norman wasn't worth having."

10 Wood cites from Glover's diary for 1920. This volume is currently missing from the T.R. Glover papers, St. John's College Library.

11 Cambridge *Daily News*, 24 February 1920, 25 April 1920, and 26 April 1920, qtd. in Levsen 305. Ceadel suggests that the reasons behind the rag were more complex than opposition to Angell's pacifism.

12 The undated clipping about "cerebro-spinal fever" appeared in the *Daily News*.

shared the hostility towards Angell and other pacifists. He did describe celebratory events such as the conferral, in May 1920, of honorary degrees on Admiral of the Fleet Sir John Jellicoe and Field Marshall Earl Douglas Haig. McIlwraith reported that "hordes of [undergraduates] proceeded to 'chair' both Haig and Jellicoe" with "Haig balancing precariously on the shoulders of about 10 undergrads with a red gown over his khaki and a velvet and floppy hat hanging with difficulty to one ear" until the crowd reached Emmanuel College and the two men "were allowed to escape to eat." This rowdy event was preceded by an equally lively evening at the Union, with "huge cheering and stamping," after Haig "warned us that the [L]eague of Nations was not yet ready to stop the next war, in other words don't get too much out of army ways" (TFMF, T.F. McIlwraith to family, 25 May 1920). Other high-ranking military and politicians continued to parade through the Union, among them Winston Churchill, then secretary of state for air and war, Vice Admiral Alfred Francis Blakeney Carpenter, Major Raymond Priestley, and Lieutenant Colonel Francis Younghusband (TFMF, T.F. McIlwraith to family, 29 February 1920; T.F. McIlwraith to Jean McIlwraith, 2 March 1920). Despite their warnings, these distinguished visitors underscored that Britain and her allies had the global situation in hand, but McIlwraith's letters to his family do refer to political and social turmoil. During a visit in London in fall 1920 with Leslie Houstoun, in town for a civil-service examination following graduation with an MA from Glasgow, McIlwraith found it difficult to get a train back to Cambridge because of an impending strike called by the Scottish coal miners. He does not criticize the miners, but he and his family confirmed that the reservations held by the previous McIlwraith generation about the Irish had not dissipated. Following the Easter Rising of 1916, the situation was volatile, and McIlwraith and Houstoun were further held up by the funeral of the lord mayor of Cork, with "Metropolitan police marching along and guarding Sinn Fein people" (TFMF, T.F. McIlwraith to family, 29 October 1920). Terence MacSwiney had died in Brixton Prison after a hunger strike lasting for more than two months. Earlier that year, the Irish Patriotic Strike, organized partly in support of MacSwiney, tied up New York's docks for weeks. McIlwraith's parents, on an extended visit with Dorothy, disapprovingly wrote to him about these events and also Eamon de Valera's visit earlier that year, "seeking support for Sinn Fein and an Independent Irish Republic" and "rais[ing] $ 10 million for his cause" among "New York's Irish population" (McNickle 351). In the summer of 1920, McIlwraith was appalled to learn of the assassination of Lieutenant Colonel Gerald Bryce Ferguson Smyth by the IRA, and he immediately pledged a contribution to his memorial. His response confirms that he was not in sympathy with the Irish cause: he felt "sick" about de Valera's enthusiastic reception in the United States (TFMF, T.F. McIlwraith to family, 8 February 1920) and thought that Smyth's assassins were "a miserable lot of Irish mongrels" (TFMF, T.F. McIlwraith to family, 4 August 1920).

After he had left Cambridge, his teacher Sir William Ridgeway – himself a fiercely Anglo-Irish Protestant – kept him informed about events in Ireland, specifically the destruction of country houses owned by Anglo-Irish Protestant aristocrats or by Catholics "who became members of the Senate" and were therefore seen as supporters of the Irish Free State (TFMF, William Ridgeway to T.F. McIlwraith, [23?] March 1923).

Ridgeway also intervened extensively in another debate that fuelled the incendiary atmosphere at the university. Because of the crowd of ex-servicemen, post-war Cambridge was even more insistently male than it had been before 1914, a situation that intensified the debate over admitting women as regular members of the university who would be in competition with returning soldiers. Opposition to accepting women fully into academia was strong, and male students developed a habit of "stamp[ing] their feet in time with [a woman's] steps as she went to her place and ... mark[ing] her sitting down with a tremendous 'bang.' " This custom had an irate reader in *The Times* wonder if it were "a pathological exhibition of sex hatred of young men leading a monastic life, or merely bounderish bad manners?" ("The Newnham Incident"),[13] but in her reminiscences of Newnham College, the social anthropologist Audrey Richards writes about the custom of "stamping" that occurred "[a]fter the war, when the University was crowded with returning soldiers, [and] women were of course resented" (A.I. Richards 133). In her comparison of student life in Cambridge and Tübingen between 1900 and 1929, Sonja Levsen connects the increase in such rowdy behaviour to the presence of recently demobilized military who felt the university's disciplinary regulations did not apply to them and were outdated in any case (see Levsen 220).

Female students were forcefully reminded to stay in their place when male undergraduates celebrated the defeat of women's admission as regular members to the University of Cambridge in 1921 by vandalizing the bronze gates of Newnham, a memorial to its first principal, Anne Clough ("Women at Cambridge"). When a male student was sent down as a result, the *Old Cambridge* protested that "[t]he acrimonious critics of Cambridge would do well to remember that Englishmen won the war because they had more devil in them than our late enemies."[14] Richards's "women were *of course* resented" (emphasis added) is poignant, but female students were not easily cowed and treated Professor Arthur Quiller-Couch to "a little rhythmic clapping" of their own when he insisted on addressing a room full of women as "[g]entlemen" (Cusack 100). Women's resilience was further demonstrated in their refusal to shrink into the background during lectures and laboratory demonstrations, for which

---

13 See also McWilliams-Tullberg 195.
14 *Old Cambridge*, 29 October 1921, 1, qtd. in Levsen 304n141.

they were promptly criticized as "so pushing, so regardless of other people, and altogether too aggressive," and they were instructed by the "Mother of an undergraduate" to develop "more gracious manners and pleasing ways" ("The Newnham Incident"). Outside of the lecture hall, ex-servicemen did not object to the presence of women nor were female students opposed to the advantages of suddenly having hundreds of young men in town "who got fond of dancing in the Army."[15] The naval officers in particular were popular, as partners in *thés dansants* and ice skating and for teaching the women to ride motorbikes "on the road to Ely (then an undiscovered country because beyond the range of [female students'] bicycle rides)" (D.C. Booth 125). Nevertheless, compared to the ease with which students like Tom McIlwraith roamed the city and its surroundings or wandered into their teachers' rooms as they were changing their shirts for dinner, women students' freedom of movement continued to be restricted by complicated rules of decorum. Even when they observed all of these, there were pitfalls. Thus, on a visit to the house of Sir William Ridgeway in Fen Ditton, one Newnham student was mistakenly guided to the group of ladies attending his wife's tea party instead of upstairs to his study where the students were being entertained (Halliday 141). A maid eventually ushered this young woman to the correct location, but there was no help for those who wilfully flouted etiquette. One "fourth-year student, noted for her brilliant auburn hair and exotic appearance," was "sent down ... for riding pillion down Sidgwick Avenue on a young man's motor-bicycle" (D.C. Booth 126).

Some of McIlwraith's teachers did their best to keep the university an enclave for men. Ridgeway, the most militant opponent to women's admission among them, startled McIlwraith on a visit to his professor's home by " pounding the table and remarking that he was proud of the fact that he had been chairman of the last meeting to oppose woman suffrage in Cambridge" (TFMF, T.F. McIlwraith to family, 1 February 1920). Ridgeway waged a relentless war on as many fronts as possible against the presence of female students. He wrote to *The Times* in 1920 that "[t]he higher education of men is far more important for the community than that of women," that male students would be distracted by "too much philandering," and that – having taken "up valuable space in laboratory and the time of university teachers" – most women would get married in any case and thereby lose all interest in education and career (Ridgeway, "Women at Cambridge"). The "philandering" worried him especially, and he complained to his colleague T.R. Glover that "the dance clubs are getting so many + ill controlled + engagements follow" (TRG, diary, 17 February 1921). Laced with "scientific" evidence, his views were so extreme that his colleague A.C. Haddon could not help but remember even in Ridgeway's obituary that

---

15   "Old Don," *Evening Standard*, 7 October 1920, qtd. in McWilliams-Tullberg 168.

"he strained the forbearance of many friends, even occasionally to the break-
ing point" ("Sir William Ridgeway," 275). Seward, who led the "*placet*" faction
for the admission of women, challenged Ridgeway with a letter of his own to
The Times ("Women at Cambridge"). Not that Seward, despite his formidable wife and four accomplished daughters, was always reliably on the side of
women either, especially when they became too ostentatiously ambitious. He
was popular with women scientists at Cambridge, and on arrival in Albany,
Australia, in 1914 was immediately swept up by the geologist Margaret Crosfield and the botanists Edith Saunders and Margaret Benson to have him look
at "some flower they knew of" (SD, 4 August 1914). However, as if to anticipate the "Mother of an undergraduate" in *The Times* who complained about
pushy female students, he complained to his wife about a scene at Buitenzorg
Botanic Gardens in Java where Dr. Benson was "most insatiable, and ... fairly
swamped the poor Director with her anxiety to get to know about things, and
others had not much chance of getting an innings" (SD, 23 September 1914).
More seriously, Seward considered a "botanical gynocracy [unacceptable]"[16]
and closed ranks with his male colleagues from the Royal Society to prevent the
botanist Agnes Arber from obtaining the presidency in Section K at the 1921
BAAS meeting in Edinburgh. For his part, W.H.R. Rivers served on the Royal
Commission on Oxford and Cambridge, and its report (1922), despite making
some concessions to female students, insisted that "Cambridge remain mainly
and predominantly a 'men's University' by limiting the number of women graduates to 500." Furthermore, women were to be kept out of senior university administration and denied the offices of "chancellor, vice-chancellor or proctor"
(Wang 123). The two dissenting commissioners were Blanche Athena Clough,
the principal of Newnham College, and William Graham, the MP whom McIlwraith had chased down in London after demobilization.

Ridgeway saw no contradiction between his hostility to women at Cambridge and his devotion to his wife and daughter. Management of Ridgeway's
own career would have been impossible without the assistance of Lucy and
their daughter, named Lucy as well and married to the economist John Archibald Venn. Ridgeway was so devastated by his wife's death that he passed away
a mere two months later. "Hardly less interested than he was in his work" (Conway), she "was his prop for very many years as his eyesight increasingly failed"
(Haddon, "Sir William Ridgeway" 276), and Ridgeway confided in Glover that
"they had been friends since he was sixteen" (Glover, *Cambridge Retrospect* 79).
Nevertheless, neither Lucy Ridgeway nor Lucy Venn was present, nor any other

---

16   Frederick Orpen Bower collection, GB248 DC2/14/13, Albert Seward to I.B. Balfour, qtd. in
     a letter by I. Bayley Balfour to F.O. Bower, 18 January 1921, UGA. For a discussion of the epi-
     sode, see Boney. On Arber, see Schmid.

woman for that matter, at the presentation of a Festschrift to mark Ridgeway's sixtieth birthday in 1913, apparently the first time an Irishman had been so honoured.[17] It took another twelve years, until 1925, for "the first occasion [to arrive] on which ladies dined in Hall" (Quiggin and Fegan 100). The event was A.C. Haddon's seventieth birthday dinner at Christ's.

McIlwraith benefited from the hospitality of Lucy Ridgeway, Fanny Haddon, and Marion Seward, but encouraged by the reactionary views that surrounded him and by the influence of his recent military life, he, too, was hostile to the prospect of admitting women as full members of the university or even allowing them to be overly visible and so obstruct the male company he had learned to enjoy. At one of the last concerts with his military friends in Wald, two participants recited poems by Kipling that characterized women as a disruptive bother. McIlwraith volunteered "The Betrothed" (1888), with its punchline that "a woman is only a woman, but a good Cigar is a Smoke,"[18] while a friend presented "The Ladies" (1891),[19] in which a soldier lists the romances during his itinerant life followed by the refrain "An' I learned about women from 'er!" (WD, 16 July 1919). When the battalion's padre confided in Tom "about being a blighter in love," his friend thought it was "a damn scream" (WD, 10 July 1919). McIlwraith was not happy when only four men showed up at a KOSB reunion in Glasgow because marriage kept several of his mates from attending (TFMF, T.F. McIlwraith to family, 26 September 1921), and his nose was particularly out of joint when manly conversation was interrupted by noisy babies such as Walter Burd's firstborn (TFMF, T.F. McIlwraith to family, 28 February 1922). On board the Metagama taking him back to Britain in early fall 1919, he sounded like the cranky George Forbes on Marion Seward's return voyage from Australia when he described the deck as resembling a "nursery ... most of them yowling," with "women, as thick as wheat" in attendance (TFMF, T.F. McIlwraith to family, 3 October 1919), and he approved of a Christmas dinner with the Hills-Phillipses because there were "a few nondescript females on the horizon but nothing like a mob" (TFMF, T.F. McIlwraith to family, 31 December 1919). He was irked when a tennis partner insisted on bringing his wife, and her game, although it "was good for a female," reminded him that he did "not appreciate mixed tennis" (TFMF, T.F. McIlwraith to family, 17 August 1920). In Haddon's lectures, a degree of formality prevailed "because a pile of other people come to them, females and so on," and T.F. and his fellow students had to

---

17 Niall ó Closâin, "An Obscure Centenary," History at Galway (blog), 30 May 2013, https://
    historyatgalway.wordpress.com/2013/05/30/an-obscure-centenary/ (accessed 8 August 2015).
18 "The Betrothed" (1888), The Cambridge Edition of the Poems of Rudyard Kipling, Volume I:
    Collected Poems I, 108.
19 "The Ladies" (1891), The Cambridge Edition of the Poems of Rudyard Kipling, Volume I:
    Collected Poems I, 439.

refrain from lounging in easy chairs and smoking their pipes (TFMF, T.F. McIlwraith to family, 2 November 1919). Astonishingly, it appears that McIlwraith
tried to stir up a discussion about the admission of women to Cambridge in the
Sewards' house, but there were strong views in this household full of educated
women, and to keep the peace "they suggested that [the subject] be dropped"
(TFMF, T.F. McIlwraith to family, 17 December 1920). As might be expected,
Dorothy did not keep quiet either, and she "wax[ed] sarcastic" at her brother's
show of misogyny. He was, however, "entirely unconvinced" because, as he informed her, she did not have "the full details of the argument here" (TFMF, T.F.
McIlwraith to family, 9 March 1921). This is one of several exchanges between
brother and sister to remind us of the pity that, with few exceptions, he made a
habit of tearing up his mail from home. Even in later years, when his views of
women had become distinctly more positive, Dorothy would have had reason
to pull him up short when, in a letter to Haddon, he referred to female students
as "undergraduettes" although, in the same letter, he praised one of his own
students as "a rather clever girl" (HCUL, T.F. McIlwraith to A.C. Haddon, 2
February 1926). Fittingly, the term "undergraduette" originated in 1919, the
first year of McIlwraith's studies at Cambridge (see Romaine 143–4). Brother
and sister do seem to have agreed on Lady Astor, however, whom they "heard"
on their visit to the House of Commons and believed to have "hinder[ed]" the
chances of any other woman who might want to have a shot at [entering Parlia-
ment]" (TFMF, T.F. McIlwraith to family, 25 August 1920).

It is a surprise, then, to see a female writer among his readings for anthropology: the ethnographer Mary Kingsley commends herself to him because "she
certainly knows how to write an interesting story" and, as mentioned earlier,
because she quotes "copiously" from Kipling (TFMF, T.F. McIlwraith to family,
2 September 1920). However, he criticizes her tendency to bury her information in "a mass of personal anecdotes about ants and snakes." In this, he sounds
not unlike A.R. Radcliffe-Brown, also a student of Rivers and Haddon, who
is famously rumoured to have referred to the Australian anthropologist Daisy
Bates as possessing a mind "somewhat similar to the contents of a well-stored
sewing basket, after half a dozen kittens had been playing there undisturbed for
a few days."[20] In later years, McIlwraith proved his support of female candidates
when, in 1946, Marius Barbeau requested a list of possible applicants towards
an opening at the National Museum in Ottawa, but he was also aware of the
continued institutional prejudice against hiring women. McIlwraith put the
anthropologist A.G. Bailey at the top of his choices, but his strongest support
was with number two on his list. Aware of the possible objections, he qualified
his recommendation with the addition, "[i]f a woman could be considered,"

20 Grant Watson, *But To What Purpose: The Autobiography of a Contemporary* (1946), qtd. in
    Langham 267.

before enthusiastically proposing Isabel Brown Crook, who "did a considerable amount of anthropology with me as part of her master's requirement in the Department of Psychology"[21] and subsequently studied at the London School of Economics with Raymond Firth. Barbeau also favoured Crook, but she chose China instead, and one feels that she made a lucky escape when he responds that "[s]he could help me with my studies on the origins of the northwestern Indians and their prehistory in Asia"[22] rather than confirming his support for her own research interests.

Terrot Reaveley Glover

In contrast to his practice during the war, McIlwraith does not appear to have kept a separate diary while at Cambridge. The presence of another diarist in this chapter, the classicist T.R. Glover, must, however, be acknowledged. A man not easily overlooked on the King's Parade or in Heffers bookshop because of "his vast frame, his dark complexion, and large gold spectacles" (Laski), Glover cannot be given full attention here, but some background is nevertheless in order to give a sense of the colourful perspective he brings to this narrative. He was one of Cambridge's great chroniclers whose diaries span sixty years between 1883 and 1943; he is author of the memoir *Cambridge Retrospect* (1943), and his career knits together strands of university life across the empire and the United States even more intimately than the prodigious academic connections maintained by McIlwraith's teachers. Glover had a link to T.F.'s family, established when he spent the years 1896 to 1901 teaching Latin at Queen's University in Kingston – among them the "noughty-noughts" of the class of 1900 (Glover and Calvin, 149) – before he returned to Cambridge for the remainder of an academic career that was illustrious despite his failure to obtain a chair. He knew of T.F.'s grandfather, "[a] great old bird-man from Western Ontario" (Glover and Calvin, 39), and his many Canadian friendships included a close bond with members of the Saunders family, linked to the McIlwraiths by marriage. At the Saunders home in Kingston, Glover met May Saunders and her future husband Kennedy McIlwraith, and he became friends with May's sister Lois, first librarian of Queen's University in Kingston, as well as a poet and translator.[23] Although both men were affiliated with St. John's College, neither Glover's diaries nor McIlwraith's letters record a personal meeting between the two. There may be simple reasons for this omission: Glover's diary for 1920 is currently missing, and there are gaps in McIlwraith's letters home between 1919 and 1922, especially during the weeks surrounding his final examination

---

21 T.F. McIlwraith to Marius Barbeau, 18 June 1946, TFMF, UTA, B1979- 0011/01(12).
22 Marius Barbeau to T.F. McIlwraith, 25 June 1946, TFMF, UTA, B1979-0011/01 (12)
23 On Lois Saunders, see McNeill.

in 1921. And yet by implication Glover features from the start in T.F.'s reports from Cambridge. He was the proctor who monitored the clashes between naval officers, pacifists, and Bolsheviks in town, and he was the public orator who eulogized Jellicoe and Haig when they received honorary degrees in May 1920. For the fallen members, choristers, and servants of St. John's College, Glover composed "For men who heard their country's call," a hymn performed at the memorial service that opened the Michaelmas term of 1919 ("The Memorial Service"). As cox of the college rowing team, Tom became familiar with another of Glover's creations, the Lady Margaret Boat Song (see "The Lady Margaret Boat Song"). Glover's comments on Cambridge for the years of McIlwraith's residency are threaded throughout this chapter, but a brief digression focusing on Glover's five years in Canada will give a sense of this particular episode in the professor's biography.[24]

Despite periodic eruptions – usually on Sundays when he was prevented from doing any work – of "[d]eadly sick of Canada all day," "[w]hat will be the end of this awful exile?," or "very sad and weary to get free + back to England from our captivity here" (TRG, 26 January 1897; 23 February 1900; 18 December 1898), Glover became so attached to the place and its people that, whenever possible, he included trips to Kingston during the twenty-odd times he crossed the Atlantic to North America on return visits because "those years at Queen's University set the New World for him in the background of a perpetual sunlight." (The latter quotation is from Laski's tribute to Glover, "On Not Having Known T.R. Glover" [1943], which locates Queen's in California and has Glover admire "the generous vitality of American youth." Surprisingly, Laski himself had spent two years at McGill during The First World War.) In between visits, Glover kept in touch by letter, and one of his Canadian friends received so many of them (at least 384) that his tribute to Glover in the Queen's Quarterly was aptly entitled "Letters from 'T.R.'"[25] The recipient of this correspondence was one of his students at Queen's, D.D. Calvin, member of a prominent lumber and shipbuilding family, as well as an architect and historian of Queen's University. Glover was interviewed in London for his position by Principal George Monro Grant and Chancellor Sandford Fleming, but as a trustee of Queen's, Calvin's father, Hiram, also "had a ... share in bringing [Glover] to the University" (Calvin 394), not least because Glover was a fellow Baptist whose father, Richard Glover of Tyndale Chapel, Bristol, was a famous preacher. Calvin and Glover subsequently co-authored A Corner of Empire: The Old Ontario Strand (1937), in which they viewed Kingston as a "corner" – that is, a strategic meeting point – of

---

24 On Glover, with an emphasis on his years at Queen's, see also Kilpatrick.

25 The St. John's College Library catalogue entry for TRG's letters to D.D. Calvin clarifies that there may be even more letters because "[s]ome items were missing at the time of cataloguing."

the British, French, and American Empires until the fight between these powers "to control the place" (Preface, n.p.) was decided in favour of the British. The book splendidly evokes the skill and drama of timber rafting, but it also indicts the destructions caused by empire building, such as the environmental damage provoked by deforestation. In doing so, the book makes for instructive reading alongside similar observations in *The Birds of Ontario*.

As an important institution located in this "corner," Queen's University features prominently, and in the book Glover transformed the zesty notes populating his diary into diplomatic language, such as the quip about Principal Grant who was "less objectionable than usual" when "his wife was present" (TRG, 9 October 1897). Glover, who was a Scotsman, appreciated the presence of other Scots at the university and became friends with the philosopher John Watson and the classicist John Macnaughton. A regular guest at his home was E.W. MacBride, professor of biology at McGill, who came from St. John's College like Glover and, also like him, eventually returned to the United Kingdom, in his case to Imperial College London. Likewise, Glover was "much interested in the appointment of W.B. Anderson, who was Professor of Latin at Queen's from 1906–1913, as a Fellow of St. John's College in 1936." Anderson, too, was a Scot (Calvin, "Letters" 397), and Glover enjoyed meeting the economist James Mavor from the University of Toronto, "a sandy loose hung Scot of some power" (TRG, 24 September 1899).[26] After his return to Cambridge and during numerous visits to North America in subsequent years, Glover kept up with former students from Queen's: " 'Bricks' Nimmo at Detroit in 1935, J.A. Richardson and D.H. Laird in Winnipeg in 1930, 'Billy' Baker at the Cavendish Laboratories" (Calvin "Letters," 397).[27] Several diary entries refer to visits with or from the economist and civil servant Oscar Skelton and his wife, "both pupils of mine" (TRG, 3 September 1919). His close connections with Canada impelled Cambridge University Press to propose that Glover write a history of the country. Nothing came of the plan but he made up for it by "bagging" anything Heffers had for sale on a Canadian subject. In the years after his return to Britain, he declined offers of chairs at Queen's, McMaster, and the University of Toronto, not to mention the repeated offer of a chair at Yale. The connection to Canada was strengthened in the next generation when his

---

26 Compiled from TRG, diary of 1897, 9 October 1897; diary of 1899, 24 September 1899; diary of 1900, 18 April 1900.

27 "Bricks" Nimmo was Harry M. Nimmo, who became editor of the *Detroit Saturday Night* (see "Harry M. Nimmo"). James A. Richardson entered his family's grain-exporting firm in Winnipeg and became a leader in the aviation industry. The Winnipeg International Airport is named after him (see "Richardson, James Armstrong"). David Henry Laird was a prominent lawyer in Winnipeg (see "David Henry Laird"). "Billy" Baker was William Coombs Baker, who became Robert Waddell Professor of Experimental Physics at Queen's (see "William C. Baker").

student Christopher Charles Love was appointed at Bishop's, and when, after earning a doctorate at Harvard, his own son Richard Gilchrist Glover became one of Canada's first military historians (see R. Glover). Canada remained so uppermost in T.R. Glover's mind that his students kept score on the number of times he mentioned it in his lectures (Linehan 459n5). As public orator, he eulogized Mackenzie King with a lyrical evocation of "Canada, coloniarum omnium Britannicarum primaria" when the Canadian prime minister received an honorary degree in 1926 (qtd. in Wood 133). A few years later, he paid homage to Gugliemo Marconi for his work on long-distance wireless transmission, and the *New York Times* reported on his impressive speech that once again featured a reference to Canada: "The Public Orator ... had a splendid sentence about the 'camporum infinitorum Canadensium,' where in the widely scattered little homes, once in the midst of waste and solitude, to-day out of the sky comes a human voice singing, or speaking, or preaching the gospel." In this way, as the *Times* further paraphrased Glover's Latin original: "the happiness of men is increased, and life itself is made more humane" ("Marconi's Degree").[28] Ironically, the year 1933 was also a landmark in the fascists' use of radio broadcasts for political propaganda. These did anything but increase the happiness of men or make life more humane.

Glover's biography by the theologian Herbert George Wood duly acknowledges its subject's scholarly achievements, his accomplishments as proctor and public orator, and his spiritual life as "a God-intoxicated man." Harold Laski borrows this memorable description from the German Romantic poet Novalis who, in turn, had applied it to Spinoza. By contrast, accounts of Glover's daily life are limited to various anecdotes about his young children as recorded in his diaries or reported by members of the family. Either Wood was self-conscious about the tradition of "lives of great men" as published by a renowned university press, or Glover's wife intervened to protect the family's privacy, especially her own: she was not a self-effacing individual, but she barely appears in the narrative and, unlike all of the Glovers' children and various relatives, she is not listed in the index (which she helped to compile) under either her maiden or her married name. Peter Linehan, in his history of St. John's College, dwells on Glover's splenetic responses to his colleagues, but he, too, seems to consider the don's domestic life, including "the artless antics of his young children," largely irrelevant (Linehan 458). Yet, as several of the preceding chapters have demonstrated, there is much to be learned by looking at the details of family life, and studies of empire now routinely include investigations of the "everyday" (see, for example, Ishiguro). Glover's five years in Canada began with a year-long separation from his "lover" Alice Few, an educated and self-confident woman with

---

28   For a discussion of Glover's speeches as public orator, see Getty.

plans to attend Girton before she became engaged to Glover in Berlin, where she was studying music and he was working in the archives. Their year apart was followed by life as a young couple in an unfamiliar environment, where they were often bewildered by their new domestic duties and, in his case, disrupted by depressions that afflicted him throughout his life. Social obligations in Kingston descended on them with a vengeance. When the newlyweds arrived from Britain in the fall of 1897, the Glovers' at-homes attracted 25, 34, and 49 callers, respectively, on three subsequent days. They were obliged to respond with an exhausting round of 51 return visits. At least, Alice's presence cancelled out the need for their frantic letter-writing the previous year when, having arrived at the end of September, he was already up to his nineteenth letter to his fiancée by early November. Efficient communication between the Glover and Few families was of the utmost importance for professional and personal reasons and, like Jean McIlwraith, Glover faithfully noted the postal improvements: "Penny postage between England, Canada + Cape to come in" he jots down in July 1898. In December he buys the "new British Empire stamps – curious device," and in January 1899 he reports "People jubilant over 2 cent inland postage as well as Ocean penny." He was grateful for the speed of communication by cable, and he sent one "in code" to Alice when he was house hunting for their life together.

He spent mornings at Queen's teaching Latin, stamping out two plagiarists' "joint production," and dealing with "chattering" students, and on Sundays he might be taken aback by the distribution of "Woman suffrage pamphlets" at church. There were social obligations in the evenings, and on weekends he met with members of the Saturday Club, which he had helped to found, for intellectual debate. In between, however, Glover gamely looked after domestic jobs by going "[o]ut to plant tomatoes, kill Colorado beetles + inspect robin's nest with five blue eggs." Ontario's punishing winters had him do battle with frozen pipes and confront "Taylor the plumber [who] smiled and smiled and left us nowhere." A never-ending series of unsatisfactory servants paraded through the house. Two of the Glovers' six children were born in Canada, and their father accompanied his pregnant wife to Eaton's and Laidlaw's, where he watched her make "a terrible lot of feminine purchases." The birth of his first child had him feeling like a helpless bystander at the "strangest scene I was ever at," and he was relieved that his mother-in-law had undertaken the long journey to Canada to supervise the situation. He unsentimentally referred to baby Mary as "a little troublesome + howly," watched her "eating cornstarch + drinking milk like an Antediluvian," and recorded with alarm when she "added No to her vocabulary," which "Alice thinks ... charming, I ominous." Reports followed on Mary's first word (in this book-mad household, it was, appropriately, "boo" for "book") and her "first needlework, sewing the woolen hair on to the rag doll," with the result judged "fearful + wonderful but done." He fretted for hours when he thought he had scolded her too hard. These entries sit next to accounts of updates, first

anxious, then triumphant, about the outcome of the Boer War, while the purchase of furniture or a bicycle competes for space with young Winston Churchill's lecture in Toronto on "his adventures in Natal." Before Alice's arrival, Glover
was gratified to be told that "Miss [illegible] one of my seniors thinks me like
St. Paul" (it does not occur to him that perhaps his leg is being pulled), and as a
devoted husband he still paid attention to "fine frocks with low necks + plentiful shapely shoulders that seem the vogue now." The researcher going through
Glover's diaries must be prepared not only to leap back and forth with him between the momentous and the quotidian in the ten lines set aside for each day,
but also to find locks of hair, samples of fabric for dresses and drapes, specifications for a frock coat, and a baby tooth wrapped in a paper cone.

Like Glover's large correspondence, his reading constituted a network in its
own right. Any number of books – both classics and the current bestsellers –
were read alone or aloud to his wife: Francis Parkman and John George Bourinot
on Canada, anything by Walter Scott, J.M. Barrie, Robert Louis Stevenson, and
Rudyard Kipling, works by Neil Munro, Susan Ferrier, Sir Arthur Conan Doyle,
Anthony Hope, Charles Kingsley, Kinglake's *Eothen*, Ford Madox Brown's diary, the Grossmiths' *Diary of a Nobody*, Charlotte Brontë, Jane Austen, and
Mark Twain. Alice practised her German by reading Wilhelm Hauff's *Das
Wirtshaus im Spessart*, and Glover read Alphonse Daudet in translation. Latin
was as natural to him as English, and in working through a scholarly tome, he
thought it a "relief to have a German writing in readily intelligible Latin instead
of his own barbarous tongue." When the couple made a return visit to Britain
during the summer of 1899, he prepared for the voyage by buying "75 c worth
of cheap books." The books almost did not make it on to the boat because he
immediately started on Olive Schreiner's *Story of an African Farm* on the train,
"a hysterical ... book with a very inadequate interpretation of life." He was not
impressed by G.W. Steevens's *With Kitchener in Khartoum* either, "written in
journalistic + rather cheap way." Back in Cambridge, Heffers occasionally tried
to save Glover from himself by lending him books, such as Walter H. Page's *Life
and Letters*, but Glover appears to have kept up his voracious book-buying and
reading throughout his life, and in December of 1919 he sheepishly realized
that he had purchased "339 volumes this year so far," though he felt he deserved
credit for selling or swapping some of them. Repeating the outrageous number, he pretended shock at the fact that James Cappon, professor of English
at Queen's, was hoarding "179 (179) bks out of library" at home.[29] His own

---

29 Compiled from TRG, 2 November 1896; 8 December 1896; 14 December 1896; 26 March
    1897; 21 April 1898; 6 May 1898; 26 May 1898; 18 July 1898; 9 December 1898; 14 December
    1898; 1 January 1899; 2 January 1899; 12 February 1899; 18 April 1899; 2 May 1899; 30 Oc-
    tober 1899; 28 December 1899; 19 January 1900; 21 February 1900; 18 April 1900; 2 January
    1901, 25 February 1901; 20 December 1919.

Drawing of Magdalene Street, Cambridge, ca. 1918, by Marion Seward. TFMP.

preference appears to have been to buy them, and Laski acknowledged that "he knew how to comb a bookshop as few people know that art, and ... he understood that a good bookseller is, next to a great writer, the noblest work of God." The trail of books that followed Glover wherever he went developed a kind of life of its own. D.D. and Eleanor Calvin estimated that over the years "they amassed some 150 books presented or left behind by T.R.G." On one occasion, he brought twenty-nine books with him to North America, left eight behind, and bought or received nine new ones (Wood 188).

There was good reason for McIlwraith's teacher W.H.R. Rivers to describe Glover to Harold Laski as "a fine combination of Dr. Johnson and Charles Lamb" (qtd. in Laski). Laski, whose world view was completely different from Glover's, "suspect[ed] ... that he would have rejected angrily most of my ideas" and, somewhat unusual for an obituary, spent several paragraphs chastising Glover for derivative scholarship, but he nevertheless celebrated him as a man who "lit a bright lamp on that road to the childhood of the world" and in doing so was "adorably insatiable in his enthusiasm and his curiosity" (Laski).[30] Glover's fascination with daily human existence, not to mention the frequent absurdity of university life, carries over into his observations about men like Rivers and Ridgeway that are cited elsewhere in this chapter. *The Eagle*, the house magazine of St. John's College, captures his delight in combining his own scholarly expertise, that of his colleagues, and his life as a family man when it cites a memorable letter he wrote to *The Times* in 1932. Based on his knowledge of "Aelian's *Natural History*," Glover defended the parental instincts of the crocodile in response to a critical article on its lack of emotion: "I am not a crocodile myself," he solemnly intones to prove that he is "wholly disinterested," but, apparently referring to the "mask with a crocodile head" (Herle, "Life-Histories" 80) deposited by A.C. Haddon in the Cambridge Museum of Archaeology and Anthropology, "one of my colleagues is a crocodile – he was admitted to the tribe long ago in Torres Straits."[31] According to Aelian, the newborn crocodile is accepted as a bona fide reptile when it "at once snaps at something" thus filling its parent with relief that it is "a chip off the old block." This, Glover concluded, demonstrated "a real sense of moral responsibility" in the animal, and he requested that *The Times* "rectify [the] injustice" (M.P.C., "Terrot Reaveley Glover" 194) by printing a retraction.

Students of Anthropology

At the beginning of term McIlwraith was deeply moved by the memorial service for the 153 fallen members of St. John's College for which Glover had written a hymn. T.F. admitted to his parents that he was overcome when he heard a barrel organ play "Till the Boys Come Home," although he ascribed this surge of emotion to "Celtic sentimentality." He often longed "for the days of the battalion" and proclaimed that "a finer lot of real gentlemen would be hard to find," but after all was said and done, life in Cambridge was "quite correct" (TFMF, T.F. McIlwraith to family, 11 January 1920; 26 October 1919; 31 December 1919). One reason to feel at home was surely that his new milieu was after all not dominated by the geriatric dons who had frightened him at Downing College and knew about the trenches only by rumour. Considering his contempt

---

30 "Childhood of the World" is the title of Edward Clodd's bestselling introduction, intended for children, to Darwin's theory of evolution (1872), but it may be safely assumed that Glover and Clodd did not agree on the nature of this "childhood."

31 Probably a reference to Haddon since Rivers had died in 1922. The turtle-shell mask was deposited in the MAA after Haddon's first visit to Torres Strait in 1888, but the 1898 expedition also brought back objects with crocodile motifs, including "Arrows Carved to Represent a Crocodile," *Reports of the Cambridge Anthropological Expedition to Torres Straits*, vol. 4, plate xxi, n.p.

for "slackers," his respect for the scholarly excellence of his teachers and fellow students was enhanced by their military record and the casual demeanour they had retained from their days in the army. "None of us give[s] a damn for the traditions and so forth of the university, so all is quite happy," he told Philip (TFMF, T.F. McIlwraith to Philip Child, 12 November 1919).

Anthropology was a relatively new discipline at Cambridge in 1919, and the Board of Anthropology Studies had been established only fifteen years earlier. Approval of the Tripos followed in 1915, but establishment of the new program was delayed by the war, and there are no class lists until 1921 (see Rouse, "Haddon and Anthropology"). The small group of six students in McIlwraith's year was composed of "a mongrel crew of two Australians, 1 Irishman, 1 Englishman, 1 Yankee and myself." Now styled "Mac" rather than "Tiny," McIlwraith was the youngest in his cohort, most of whom had taken previous degrees, and he found the achievements that some of them brought to the program intimidating: "The more I see of the work to be done the more do I think that I had infernal cheek to put my nose into the business at all. People admit that it is a very hard subject and I believe them" (TFMF, T.F. McIlwraith to family, 11 January 1920). There was no textbook, and along with extensive background reading, copious notes had to be taken in courses focused on "(1) Totems, (2) Disposal of dead, (3) Kinship terms, (4) Polyandry, (5) Divination, (6) Trepanning, (7) Twins," as well as "Lectures in ethnology and comparative anatomy," and demonstrations with Haddon where "we play around with skulls and dope of that kind" (TFMF, T.F. McIlwraith to family, 26 October 1919). Lectures familiarized students with their teachers' expertise, much of it gained in pioneering fieldwork. The group learned of newly formulated practices and theories, such as Rivers's genealogical method, refined during the Torres Strait Expedition and often acknowledged as pivotal in the history of anthropology (see Stocking, *After Tylor* 111–13). Less acclaimed even then was Rivers's theory of diffusionism, developed alongside Elliott Smith and W.J. Perry, which caused some of his associates to wonder whether he had taken leave of "his scientific caution and good sense" (Slobodin 73). This theory had Rivers lecture to his students about "Egyptian influence" on Pacific custom, an assumption that McIlwraith mistakenly anticipated "would become orthodox in time" while it was still a "heresy" in 1920 (TFMF, T.F. McIlwraith to family, 13 April 1920). T.F., too, was to encounter some strong resistance to the theory when he presented a paper related to the subject at the BAAS conference in Edinburgh.

A year later, when he was seeking employment in the Anthropological Division of the Geological Survey of Canada, McIlwraith summarized the highlights of his training in a letter to Edward Sapir, as concentrating on physical anthropology, arts and crafts, stone implements, races of man, religion, and his "special subject," social institutions, the latter studied primarily under

T.F. McIlwraith, in front, at the Museum of Archaeology and Anthropology, Cambridge, ca. 1921. Behind him: L.W.G. Malcolm (far left), A.C. Haddon (centre), and J.D. Newsom (right of Haddon); the other two men are not identified. TFMP.

Rivers's guidance.[32] In his letter of reference to Playfair McMurrich at the University of Toronto a few months later, Haddon explained that he and Rivers operated on the "principle ... that we consider it advisable for a student to master some definite area."[33] The understanding of "area" is geographical to begin with, and Haddon explains that, because of their participation in the Torres Strait Expedition of 1898, "[Rivers and I] might have chosen Melanesia ... but we thought it better for students to get up another area, as incidentally they would learn a good deal about Melanesia and New Guinea in the ordinary course of instruction." In McIlwraith's case, this other area was Africa (HCUL, A.C. Haddon to Playfair McMurrich, 25 January 1922).

---

32   T.F. McIlwraith to Edward Sapir, 9 August 1921, CMH, Edward Sapir papers (I-A-236M), Correspondence, Folder: McIlwraith, T.F. (1921–1923), Box 628, folder 23.

33   Mastering "some definite area" is a variation on the "intensive study of limited areas." This widely cited "watchword" apparently first appears in a letter from Haddon to the Finnish anthropologist Edward Westermarck, where it is applied to the training of students and its contribution to the professionalization of anthropology. See Haddon to Westermarck, 20 July 1908, qtd. in Lagerspetz 16.

Just as they had attracted his attention during officer training some two years earlier, the Australians among this cohort were particularly memorable. E.W.P. Chinnery, who had joined the Australian Flying Corps in the war, was appointed government anthropologist of the Mandated Territory of New Guinea in 1924. In New Guinea, he remained an important contact for Haddon when it came to sending young scholars for fieldwork to the area (see Stocking "Gatekeeper to the Field"), and Haddon may have conferred with him when there were plans to find a post for McIlwraith in the Pacific. As early as 1920, Chinnery assisted McIlwraith in strengthening his professional connections by proposing him for membership in the RAI.[34] The second Australian, Malcolm, was the future conservator of the Wellcome Historical Medical Museum and, from 1937 onwards, curator of the Horniman Museum. Because Haddon had given him the run of his library during the Christmas vacation, McIlwraith had ample opportunity to chat with L.W.G. Malcolm, who was the Haddons' permanent houseguest for the duration of his studies at Cambridge. Using a typewriter obtained from Malcolm, who had himself requisitioned it during military deployment in German Cameroon, McIlwraith treated his family to the Australian's adventurous biography:

> Malcolm is one of the people taking anthropology here and perhaps the best at the job. He is of a type that I had never met before, one [of those] lucky people who seems able to succeed at anything. He is an Australian who went to an Australian university on a Scholarship and took a degree in mining engineering, and in some way got a scholarship in anatomy to a Swiss university while he was studying anthropology at Melbourne. When war broke out he was sitting for his [PhD] in Switzerland and naturally came back at once and spent the next few years in potting Bosche in the Cameroons ... As a final leg in the war he was a King's messenger between Paris and the War Office at the time of the peace conference. Naturally as a result of Melbourne and a Bosche professor in Switzerland he knows a heap more anthropology than the rest of us. (TFMF, T.F. McIlwraith to family, 11 January 1920)

Malcolm also disabused McIlwraith of the expectation, gained during his encounters with imperial troops in officer training, that Australians were by definition wary of the empire: "The thing that amuses me is that he is one of the most rabid Imperialists that I have ever met: a regular Jingo in fact, which differs from so many Australians" (TFMF, T.F. McIlwraith to family, 11 January 1920). One undisclosed reason for Malcolm's jingoism may have been a wish to compensate for his father's German background. Malcolm's original name was "Büchner," to which he added his mother's maiden name "Malcolm" when he

---

34   "Thomas F. McIlwraith," Past Fellows, the RAI Collection, RAI, London.

enlisted in 1915. His first names "Ludwig William Gunter" were transformed to "Louis William Gordon" but usually abbreviated to L.W.G. By the time he arrived at Cambridge, his name had become L.W.G. Malcolm (Clark, Ian D. 81–84). McIlwraith and Malcolm stayed in touch: Malcolm visited McIlwraith in Toronto in late 1926 or early 1927, and asked for his assistance in obtaining a totem pole for the Wellcome Museum. When McIlwraith pointed out that the government of British Columbia was reluctant to export poles, Malcolm brought in Dr. J.N.E. Brown, "who was in the Yukon years ago" and "a very intimate friend of Malcolm's," as go-between.[35] It is not clear from McIlwraith's subsequent exchange with Marius Barbeau whether a pole was obtained; what is clear is the extent of Malcolm's connections and the speed with which they could be mobilized. Brown's wife, incidentally, was the journalist Faith Fenton, who interviewed Jean McIlwraith in 1895.

Even the lone American in the group passed muster because John D. Newsom had served in the British army, and McIlwraith therefore stifled his usual criticism and declared him "a most worthy soul" and "one of the soundest Yanks I have ever met" whose "accent [was] his chief crime" (TFMF, T.F. McIlwraith to family, 19 December 1919; 1 February 1920). Born in Shanghai of American parents and raised in France, the "Yank," too, had an intriguing background, and McIlwraith cites him repeatedly because this fellow student helped him "read" the enigmatic W.H.R. Rivers, who arranged for Newsom to do fieldwork in Melanesia. However, following a series of difficulties, Newsom did not make a career of anthropology, and his failure in Melanesia appears to have affected McIlwraith's own chances of obtaining a position there.[36] Instead Newsom used his experience living and working in Africa to write pulp fiction about the Foreign Legion, "that crack-brained, polyglot crew," and other subjects. He became Michigan director and then national director of the Federal Writers' Project, followed by military service in the Second World War and an appointment as associate editor with Harcourt, Brace publishers after the war (see "J.D. Newsom"). Any support he may have expressed for the British and French Empires during his days at Cambridge had been modified by the time he reached the mid-thirties, when he worried about the justification of "a colonial empire ... in this day of hypertrophied nationalism" and the "pleasant-faced, good-natured young men [who] were being trained to murder one another for the greater

---

35 T.F. McIlwraith to Marius Barbeau, 27 June 1927, TFMF, UTA, B1979-0011/001 (11).

36 See Langham 301: "J.D. Newsom – , a student of Rivers ... [,] was granted money from the Percy Sladen Trust Fund to make a field trip to New Caledonia. Newsom's ethnographic adventures, and with them the hope of a career in academic anthropology, came to a miserable end following illness in the field, shortage of funds and the discovery that the indigenous culture he had been sent to investigate was largely inoperative due to the influence of missionaries."

glory of their respective Fatherland." His only blind spot in this remarkably prophetic response to pre–Second World War Europe was his belief that the United States represented an alternative, "a new form of civilization, cut loose at last from the shackles of the old and musty continent of Europe" ("The Men").

Although he was impressed with several of them, McIlwraith did not form as strong a bond with his fellow students in anthropology as he did with the KOSB officers, and he cites only a few of his contemporaries at Cambridge by name. The group was small to begin with, and both Chinnery and Newsom left Cambridge early in McIlwraith's program. As well, despite the strong reluctance among former soldiers to submit to the disciplinary traditions of Cambridge, this new set of students was conscientious about their studies (see Levsen 208; see also Lahiri 72). This did not mean that McIlwraith suddenly preferred his own company. Especially after he finally obtained rooms at St. John's College, T.F. became his usual gregarious self, and reminders of his pleasant life during cadet training at Peterhouse College enhanced his sense of well-being. It was convenient to have a "bedder" clean his room, lay his breakfast table, do the dishes, and bring in a hip bath that "look[ed] like nothing on earth except an overgrown flat flower-pot" for him to splash in. When he had company for lunch, he ordered food up to his rooms, "and up it came, très handy" (TFMF, T.F. McIlwraith to family, 10 July 1921). He was, as usual, popular, and "joshed" by "a good circle of friends ... for [his] singing voice and [his] vile tobacco" ("Genealogy"). When he was laid up with an injured knee, he "was never alone" from morning to midnight as he lounged in his new dressing gown on the sofa (TFMF, T.F. McIlwraith to family, 24 January 1922). Some of these friends may have joined the delegation that took him to the train station when he left Cambridge. There he gave everybody a final demonstration of his off-key singing by bursting into "No token of love, adieu, farewell, but harken I hear the sound of a bell," causing onlookers to assume that he "was being sent down and these were drunken cronies" ("Genealogy").[37]

Professors of Anthropology

McIlwraith's connections with his teachers were strong from the start. Like his fellow students, McIlwraith's professors commended themselves to him as much for their wartime efforts as for their scholarship, even if some of them were too old and frail for active service. The most impressive military work was that of W.H.R. Rivers. As related in the discussion of Marion Seward's diary in the previous chapter, he experienced the outbreak of war together with colleagues from Cambridge on his way to the 1914 BAAS meeting in Sydney.

---

37 A free adaptation of lines from *The Beggar's Opera* (1728).

He stayed on for fieldwork in Melanesia but was back in Britain by 1915, where he put his training in neurology and psychiatry to use assisting in the recovery of wounded soldiers. His experimental treatment of psychological disorders resulting from combat gained wide exposure in lectures such as "The Repression of War Experience" (1917), subsequently printed in the medical journal *The Lancet* (see Rivers, "Repression") and perhaps one of the documents behind Virginia Woolf's conception of the shell-shocked Septimus Smith in her novel *Mrs. Dalloway* (1925). Rivers worked at Moss Side Military Hospital in Maghull and with the Royal Air Force, where he conducted "research on the mental aspects of military aviation" (Head 977). Most famously, he treated traumatized soldiers at Craiglockhart War Hospital near Edinburgh, where Siegfried Sassoon and Wilfred Owen were grateful patients. One patient repeatedly visited the library of St. John's College as late as 1963 to "stand, at the salute" before Rivers's portrait and thank him "for all he did for him."[38] The encounter between Rivers and Sassoon, as well as the connections between Rivers's research in Melanesia and his treatment of traumatized soldiers, inspired a chapter in Elaine Showalter's *The Female Malady* (1987)[39] and was fictionalized in Pat Barker's *Regeneration* trilogy (1991–5),[40] and McIlwraith, too, was aware of Rivers's wartime work. When he had an opportunity to go through his teacher's books while he was away lecturing in the States, McIlwraith located a privately printed copy of Sassoon's *Picture-Show*, containing "To a Very Wise Man," a poem dedicated to Rivers. He immediately asked his family to purchase the book for him just as soon as it became available in New York (TFMF, T.F. McIlwraith to family, 28 April 1920). Although he had "heard parts and spasms of it at intervals," he did find Rivers's theories about "psychology and the war business ... much too deep and complicated for [him]" (TFMF, T.F. McIlwraith to family, 13 April 1920).

As McIlwraith's diary for the frantic few days before his return to Canada in 1919 illustrates, Rivers, who had recently been appointed praelector in natural sciences, immediately leapt to his aid when McIlwraith tried to organize his registration at the university for the fall. Rivers's "magnetism and charm" (Showalter, "Male Hysteria" 183) were the stuff of legend around Cambridge, despite his shyness and stuttering. In addition to meeting renowned researchers like Henry Head, Elliot Smith, and Paul Radin, visitors to Rivers's soirées might encounter celebrities like H.G. Wells, Harold Laski, Arnold Bennett, Siegfried Sassoon, Robert Graves, and, before the war, Bertrand Russell (see Bartlett,

---

38 N.C. Buck, Note in the St. John's College Archive, 1963, 1, qtd. in Whittle 22.

39 See also Showalter, "Rivers and Sassoon."

40 For the connections, evoked in Barker's novel, between Rivers's work on shell shock and his ethnographic studies during the Percy Sladen Trust expedition, see Hviding and Berg, especially "Introduction," 15–16, and Appendix 2, 293.

"W.H.R. Rivers"). Like Jean McIlwraith, Tom read H.G. Wells, and both his short stories and the enormously successful *The Outline of History*[41] show up in McIlwraith's letters; "vilely contracted, but it seems sound" was his judgment on the *Outline* (TFMF, T.F. McIlwraith to family 14 December 1919). He was keen to meet the author in person, and in February 1920, while Rivers was away in the United States, Wells was occupying his rooms, and McIlwraith and a fellow student ventured "up to see if we could get into conversation with him[,] a case of pure curiosity I am afraid, coupled with a degree of cheek in that neither of us knew him in the slightest." However, "H.G. was just sitting down to breakfast with a number of friends so that the time was to say the least unstrategic" (TFMF, T.F. McIlwraith to family, 8 February 1920).

McIlwraith praised the all-male company, the comfortable easy chairs set out in Rivers's college rooms, the permission to smoke, the casual tutorial style, and their teacher's tolerance for serendipitous discussion: "He talks for about twenty minutes and then we start heaving in questions and the original subject gets quite forgotten" (TFMF, T.F. McIlwraith to family, 26 October 1919). Especially in his early months at Cambridge, however, McIlwraith found Rivers to be "a queer man and a hard man to work for," and Rivers's stutter made him seem even more remote because it prevented him from lecturing without notes. His teacher's impenetrable manner made McIlwraith uncomfortable, and he "would never [have thought] of talking to him the way [he did] with Haddon or even with Ridgeway" (TFMF, T.F. McIlwraith to family, 28 April 1920). Other observers drew a line between Rivers's pre- and post-war personae, with the "ways of life and thought, ... hopes and fears" of the former largely unknown to "many people," while the latter "was here there and everywhere, the heart and spirit of all manner of schemes, writing and working in a feverish hurry" (Bartlett, "Cambridge, England" 104). His plans, shortly before his sudden death in 1922, included running for political office with the Labour Party. To McIlwraith, he remained the unknown Rivers although he realized that he was always able to rely on his teacher's professional support. In trying to describe the effect to his family, McIlwraith – who was then certainly a self-confident and quick-witted fellow – was driven to remember his own discomfort as "a kid" when he "always used to feel awkward when speaking with strangers, as if I wanted to stutter all the time, and that is exactly the way [that] Rivers still makes me feel" (TFMF, T.F. McIlwraith to family, 28 April 1920).

J.D. Newsom confirmed the impression by quoting Arnold Bennett: Rivers made even this close friend and well-known writer feel "like a school boy"

---

41 McIlwraith cites the title as *History of the World*, but given the date of his letter and the details he gives about its publication in fortnightly instalments, of which he has read two by 14 December 1919, he seems to be referring to *The Outline of History* rather than *A Short History of the World*.

(TFMF, T.F. McIlwraith to family, 28 April 1920). In an affectionate recollection he wrote for the *New Statesman* after Rivers's death, Bennett speculated
that one root of Rivers's aloofness lay in the anthropological perspective that
had him view "[a]ll civilized society [as] a sort of South Sea Island" (rpt. in
Bennett 6), but there was enough of a mystery surrounding him that it even
affected accounts of his appearance, as Rivers's biographer was puzzled to
observe (Slobodin 82). While Bennett thought him "a man of insignificant
aspect, small ... [a] quiet voice, capable of silences without self-consciousness"
(Bennett 1), Rivers's student Frederic Bartlett remembered his teacher as
"rather tall, trim, quick and light in his movements, in navy blue. You got
a swift impression of straight, broad shoulders and a jutting chin" (Bartlett,
"Cambridge, England" 104). McIlwraith, while he does not describe Rivers's
physical appearance in such detail, comments on his penetrating glance.
When he met Edward Sapir, his employer at the Geological Survey of Canada,
McIlwraith had a similar response. He found Sapir "a most brilliant individual" (HCUL, T.F. McIlwraith to A.C. Haddon, 3 May 1922), and "a person far
above the mental average of ethnologists in America" who "left [him] gasping
in almost the way Rivers does" (TFMF, T.F. McIlwraith to family, 28 February
1922), but "more of a machine than Rivers" (HCUL, T.F. McIlwraith to A.C.
Haddon, 7 May 1923). Glover, a man not easily intimidated, thought Rivers at times "a bit doctrinaire + dogmatic" and was taken aback to be told
"that when it comes to religion I (TR) don't use my intell[igence]." Nevertheless, Glover was fond of Rivers and, when the latter announced his political
plans, he worried that "he is physically + mentally (not intellectually) unfit
for H[ouse] of C[ommons] life." Rivers returned the affection: when Glover
walked away from this particular conversation, "[h]e called from window:
'... think as well as you can of Bill!' "[42]

Concerned about Rivers's celibate life, Bennett organized a dance on his
yacht, only to be rewarded the next morning with "pricelessly Marquesan"
commentary on the "social phenomenon" (Bennett 7), which had the young
men rowing their dates to the yacht as if it were part of a South Sea ritual.
More perceptive observers have related Rivers's reserve towards women to his
homosexuality, repressed by shyness and inhibited by a strong sense of social
decorum (Shephard 38). In his letters, McIlwraith never speculates about the
reasons for Rivers's manner. Indeed, in contrast to his praise for Rivers's relaxed
tutorials, he depicts their own relationship as that of an almost comically traditional teacher-student duo. For a book review, Rivers required McIlwraith's expertise on Africa, and following a Sunday's worth of library research, the latter

---

42   TRG, diary of 1919, 17 November 1919; diary of 1921, 8 June 1921; diary of 1922, 3 February
     1922.

hauled a suitcase of "14 books, the smallest of which was 350 pages" into Rivers's office for a report. He was grilled on the subject "[f]or three solid hours" and worried that his instructor might "slay" him when McIlwraith later located a mistake in his conclusions that required Rivers to rewrite parts of the review (TFMF, T.F. McIlwraith to family, 28 April 1920).

Despite his student's worries, Rivers was consistently supportive, kept influential colleagues like Ridgeway "primed up with [him]" (TFMF, T.F. McIlwraith to family, 1 February 1920), looked over his first conference paper for the BAAS meeting in Edinburgh, and asked him after graduation "to make arrangements to stay on the next term and they could find me plenty to do" (TFMF, T.F. McIlwraith to family, 7 October 1921). Rivers also stood by as an additional referee when Haddon recommended McIlwraith to Playfair McMurrich for a position at the University of Toronto (HCUL, A.C. Haddon to Playfair McMurrich, 25 January 1922). Rivers's sudden death shocked everyone, and McIlwraith, too, was "broken up" by the news (HBCI, T.F. McIlwraith to A.C. Haddon, 29 August 1922, 66). The Haddons acknowledged Rivers's importance to McIlwraith when Fanny Haddon wrote in some detail to describe the circumstances of his death (TFMP, Fanny Haddon to T.F. McIlwraith, 10 June 1922). T.F. regretted being "so far away [that] he could not even have the satisfaction" of helping to arrange Rivers's papers (HBCI, T.F. McIlwraith to A.C. Haddon, 29 August 1922, 66), and as a special favour, he asked Haddon to forward a copy of his obituary for Rivers in Nature (Haddon, "Dr. W.H.R. Rivers"). William Ridgeway did not easily express tender sentiment, but he confessed that he, like everyone else in Cambridge, "miss[ed] Rivers terribly" (TFMF, William Ridgeway to T.F. McIlwraith, [23?] March 1923).

It is more difficult for an outsider to anthropology to obtain a sense of A.C. Haddon's intellectual legacy, and he even colluded in assuming second place to his colleague: his obituaries insistently mention that "he used to say that his claim to fame was that he had induced W.H.R. Rivers to accompany him" on the Second Torres Strait Expedition (see Quiggin and Fegan 98). What is a literary scholar to make of the extravagantly negative judgments that historians of anthropology have been known to pass on their colleagues and rival programs? Fredrik Barth, for example, described "[a]nthropology at Cambridge ... as a disaster," and he referred to Haddon's influence as "inept and unfortunate" (Barth 26). Similarly dismissive, Edmund Leach blamed Haddon's modest social background for his alleged dilettantism as a researcher and university politician (see Leach). In these accounts, the accomplishments of both Haddon and Rivers pale in comparison with their brilliant student Bronislaw Malinowski and his circle at the London School of Economics. Malinowski himself did not hesitate to tilt the comparison to his own advantage by ranking himself with the modernist Joseph Conrad and Rivers with Rider Haggard, popular author of adventure novels.[43] Indeed, Malinowski appears to serve often as a measuring stick to establish excellence, and McIlwraith, too, has been judged by his example (Barker, "T.F. McIlwraith and Anthropology" 253).

Like Rivers, Haddon – who was fifty-nine in 1914 – was in Australia at the outbreak of war. He had travelled there to receive an honorary degree from the University of Perth and to attend the meeting of the BAAS. For most of the war, he stayed on for fieldwork in New Guinea, but his biographer Alison Hingston Quiggin is careful to chronicle his wartime activities as well. Haddon joined YMCA headquarters near Ypres in France between April and July 1917 until poor health forced him to return home. His colleague Miles Crawford Burkitt, also one of McIlwraith's teachers, kept him company. Like numerous other Cambridge professors, Haddon volunteered to lecture at the front, giving presentations on "New Guinea Cannibals" to as many as 150 men at a time, but he also helped with mundane jobs such as working in the canteen, where, as he reported with the casual racism that always comes as a surprise in the later stages of his career, the sound of "gun-firing stimulate[d him] like the drum-beating of savages." As a "counter-jumper," he juggled "English, French and Belgic money of all denominations, all in a terrible rush" (qtd. in Quiggin 139, 140),[44] and he reported on his experiences near the front in the YMCA's publication *The Red Triangle*.[45] Among his first students when academic business at Cambridge resumed was Louis Mountbatten, one of the naval officers catching up with their education at the university and enjoying a lecture series in ethnology presented by Haddon and L.G.W. Malcolm (see Roskill 188). Over tea at Haddon's home, McIlwraith met the future (and last) viceroy of India, assassinated by the IRA in 1979. He "was telling us how utterly weary" the Prince of Wales had been on his recent tour through Canada. A tour of Australia, with Mountbatten as aide-de-camp, was up next. T.F. found him "an interesting man," but was far from star-struck and found the complaints he conveyed about the Canadian tour "rather a joke" (TFMF, T.F. McIlwraith to family, 25 January 1920). At the Cambridge Union, he thought Mountbatten "distinctly feeble" in debate with Winston Churchill who, despite a lisp, "ha[d] a wonderful power of putting his words together" (TFMF, T.F. McIlwraith to family, 29 February 1920). This debate occurred some twenty years after T.R. Glover heard Churchill lecture in Toronto, speaking about his South African adventures. T.F. was

---

43 The quotation has not been fully confirmed: "The apocryphal remark, attributed by Raymond Firth to Brenda Seligman's recollection of what Malinowski said to her, has nonetheless passed into legend" (see M. Young 236).

44 See also Rouse, "Haddon and Anthropology" 176. For Rivers' wartime work and that of other anthropologists who had participated in the 1898 Torres Strait Expedition, see Shephard 149.

45 Haddon, "Three Days," Museum of Archaeology and Anthropology, Cambridge, AA1/1/41, Box 328.

equally unimpressed with the presence, at Trinity College, of the Princes Henry and Albert, though his folks thought his proximity to royalty very exciting.

Haddon, McIlwraith's most important mentor, was appointed reader at Cambridge as late as 1909 when he was in his fifties, following many professional disappointments that had to be bridged by holding simultaneous posts in Dublin and Cambridge. Energetic networking by Ridgeway, Sir James Frazer, and Fanny Haddon (who ensured that powerful individuals at the university remembered him while he was away in the Pacific) was necessary to get Haddon established at Cambridge (see Rouse, "Haddon and Anthropology" and "Expedition and Institution"). As a consequence of these delays he was only a few years away from retirement in 1926 when McIlwraith arrived in 1919, but that did not diminish his professional influence or the "tremendous energy" that had him "tearing around like a youngster" (TFMF, T.F. McIlwraith to family, 21 March 1920; 15 November 1919). Even towards the end of Haddon's life, a visitor, expecting a frail old man, acknowledged that "there [was] something about him like fire" (Quiggin and Fegan 97). "A gentle and empathetic person by nature" (Stocking, *After Tylor* 99), one who was remembered for his "broad humanity and kindliness" (Seligman 850), Haddon was an outgoing man, a powerful physical presence, and a popular lecturer despite a speech impediment. His appearance was characterized by a mop of unruly hair and very large hands and feet, and his manner displayed an abhorrence of pretence of any kind. He had "a keen sense of humour" that – despite "a somewhat unexpected streak of Puritanism" – could even be "frivolous" (Seligman 850). In his letters home, McIlwraith mercilessly lampooned the eccentrics among his professors, such as Burkitt, who had slipped into outlandish mannerisms during fieldwork in France and made a habit of addressing prehistoric specimens with "My pet devil, isn't he attractive[?]" (TFMF, McIlwraith to family, 26 October 1919). By contrast, McIlwraith never caricatured Haddon's oddities, and the two seem to have instantly developed a strong bond of respect and affection that continued well after McIlwraith had left Cambridge. Haddon included him in a select list of students who had obtained appointments,[46] and McIlwraith was slated as a contributor to a Festschrift planned, but not published, for Haddon's eightieth birthday.[47] Perhaps Haddon's humble origins were one reason for their affinity. As well, his apparently inexhaustible intellectual curiosity and appetite for hard work matched his student's, and because Haddon's "research plans were always expansive," he found it easy to support such plans in his students too (Rouse, "Haddon and Anthropology" 50). Haddon's early journals are often reminiscent

---

46 Haddon, *A Brief History*, pamphlet, Museum of Archaeology and Ethnology [sic], 21 June 1923, MAA, AA1/1/41, Box 328.

47 Letter from Alisa Nicol Smith to Miss Fegan, 6 November 1934, MAA, AA1/1/41, Box 328.

of McIlwraith's exuberant childhood letters, though the Canadian seemed more content (or else his fastidious mother had convinced him to be) to enjoy what he saw in nature rather than dissect it and bottle it up in formaldehyde. Thus, Haddon's diary has him "spread open the slugs, sea cucumber etc." in his room, or it reports that he "Rebottled [his] cobra. did tree frog etc. etc. cut [his] finger in the middle of it all and did not know it. washed it well, when found no evil consequences. before breakfast dissected a small banded fish" (qtd. in Quiggin 11–12). As underscored by these excerpts, the origins of Haddon's career were in zoology, but his participation in two expeditions to the Torres Strait, especially the Cambridge Torres Strait Expedition of 1898–9, definitively shifted his scholarly interests towards anthropology. His publications featured sweeping surveys such as *The Study of Man* (1898), *History of Anthropology*, co-authored with A. Hingston Quiggin (1910), and *The Races of Man and Their Distribution* (1909). He was one of the editors of the six-volume *Reports of the Cambridge Anthropological Expedition to Torres Straits* (1901–35) and author of a popular volume on the same subject, *Head-Hunters: Black, White and Brown* (1901), that he rushed through the press a mere two years after the return of the expedition. He published specialized investigations into the "Life-Histories of Designs" in *Evolution in Art* (1895), and wrote about *The Decorative Art of British New Guinea* (1894), *Iban or Sea Dayak Fabrics and Their Patterns* (1936), as well as the design of canoes in the three-volume *Canoes of Oceania*, with James Hornell (1936–8).

McIlwraith repeatedly acknowledges Haddon's ease with people from all backgrounds that, among others, had him launch into an animated discussion with Jean McIlwraith on the head brasses for horses she had begun to collect. In contrast to the attention he pays to Rivers's connections with Siegfried Sassoon, H.G. Wells, Arnold Bennett, and others, however, McIlwraith does not discuss Haddon's own affiliation with two remarkable groups of intellectuals whose interests went well beyond the study of anthropology or zoology, but they are worth pointing out because their influential ideas, particularly those of Nevinson and Clodd, show up elsewhere in this book. As a reviewer for the *Daily Chronicle*, Haddon became acquainted with the editor of the literary page, H.W. Nevinson, a progressive journalist and supporter of women's suffrage, whose career is vividly narrated in his autobiography, *Fire of Life* (1935).[48] Like Miklouho-Maclay, Nevinson worked with Ernst Haeckel in Jena, and together with his formidable wife Margaret, he was affiliated with Toynbee Hall in London's East End, the original university-affiliated Settlement House from which Mary Kingsbury Simkhovitch's Greenwich House and others derived their inspiration. The large group of writers, essayists, critics, scholars, and travellers

---

48   An abridgement of three original volumes (1923–8).

who contributed to, or were highlighted in, the *Chronicle* included George Bernard Shaw, Lionel Johnson, William Archer, W.B. Yeats, Hubert Bland, Edward Fitzgerald, Andrew Lang, J. Cotter Morison, Eliza Lynn Linton, Sir Henry Thompson, Sir William Huggins, Sir Laurence Gomme, Sir John Rhys, Paul du Chaillu, Edward Whymper, Alfred Comyn Lyall, Sir E. Ray Lankester, and others. This group overlapped with another, equally important to Haddon's intellectual life: the Strafford House parties organized by Edward Clodd in Aldeburgh, in which Haddon participated, attracted important contemporary figures such as Thomas Hardy, Grant Allen, George Gissing, and Mary Kingsley. Clodd was a banker, but, like Thomas McIlwraith and Will Child, he managed a dual career and made important contributions to the study of anthropology in works such as *The Childhood of the World*. Although Haddon did introduce him to the folklore scholar Edwin Sidney Hartland, who belonged to Clodd's circle, Haddon (whose origins were in a devoutly Baptist family) was probably well aware that McIlwraith did not share the agnosticism and socialist convictions that propelled these groups.

The scholarly range of Rivers and Haddon was matched by William Ridgeway, Disney Professor of Archaeology and Reader in Classics when McIlwraith met him and professor of Greek at Cork University and lecturer in natural religion at Aberdeen before then. His scholarship extended from the *Origins of Metallic Currency and Weight Standards* (1892) and *The Early Age of Greece* (1902) to *The Origin and Influence of the Thoroughbred Horse* (1905) and *The Dramas and Dramatic Dances of Non-European Races* (1915). No wonder that McIlwraith instantly found him "undoubtedly extraordinarily clever, and it seem[ed] to sprout out without the slightest effort" (TFMF, T.F. McIlwraith to family, 26 October 1919). As the details of William Ridgeway's hostility to the admission of women to Cambridge have already illustrated, the man was sui generis, and obituaries and recollections of him luxuriate in anecdotes about his towering intellect and his odd behaviour. His poor eyesight prevented even volunteer work in the war, but Ridgeway still proclaimed his patriotism by refusing to admit known members of the Union of Democratic Control into his lectures (Irish, *The University at War* 71). His opposition to pacifists was at times compounded by his opposition to women in academia, as demonstrated when, in a thinly veiled attack on the classicist Jane Ellen Harrison, he accused Newnham College of serving as "a notorious centre for Pro-German agitation."[49] In typically extreme fashion, he opposed T.R. Glover's election to university orator on the grounds that as a Baptist and critic of war (though not a declared pacifist), he "would not be in sympathy with many of the best

---

49   William Ridgeway, "Letter," *Cambridge Review*, 14 February 1917, 224, qtd. in Shelley, 178n79.

recipients of Honorary degrees, such as the great soldiers and sailors who have kept the roofs over our heads."[50]

And yet Glover, who was too old to sign up at the outbreak of war but would have become subject to conscription in 1916, had not been idle. At the suggestion of the Reverend Kenneth J. Saunders,[51] he spent a month in the fall of 1915 observing the work of YMCA welfare officers at the Military Hospital for Venereal Diseases in Le Havre in order to give him "experience of Y.M.C.A. work under some of the most difficult conditions" (Wood 97). He then sailed for a year in India as part of a contingent that included other well-known Nonconformists such as the Reverend James Hope Moulton from Manchester, as well as a group of clergymen and divinity students. Their purpose was to jump into the breach for members of India's YMCA National Council who were deployed in France, Greece, and other theatres of war. The intention behind the expedition to India was missionary and bluntly imperialist, and among the tasks undertaken by this group was to organize sightseeing for troops and so teach them "the material and social advantages of British rule in the Great Dependency" ("The Work of the Y.M.C.A." 200). Scholars like Glover had little contact with soldiers, but lectured "on religious and other subjects, with reference to the war and its lessons, for the benefit of the highly educated Hindus and Mahomedans" (200). Unlike Saunders and Moulton, who studied Buddhism and Zoroastrianism, respectively, Glover could not bring himself to appreciate the local religions to which his travels exposed him, and any effect from the encounter remained one-sided. On his return, he assembled his lectures in what became one of his most popular books, *The Jesus of History* (1917), but he also assisted in "training [YMCA] candidates for service at home and abroad" at the Mildmay Institute in London (Wood 115).[52]

None of this impressed Ridgeway as an acceptable equivalent of military service, but he did relent after Glover's election to university orator and congratulated him on his success (Wood 129).For his part, Glover did not bear a grudge, but instead invited Ridgeway to be his guest at a College Feast evening in 1921. He was "good company," telling "stories of his ancestors settling in Ireland, of Sinn Fein + Black + Tan outrages" (TRG, 8 November 1921). Twenty-two years later, in *Cambridge Retrospect*, Glover – for whom an individual's

---

50 Ridgeway to Glover, 1 January 1920, qtd. in Linehan 448. Contrary to Linehan, Wood claims that Glover was sympathetic to pacifism rather than a pacifist (95).

51 Born in South Africa and a specialist on Buddhism, Saunders was educated at Emmanuel College, Cambridge. He taught at Trinity College, Kandy, Sri Lanka, and during the First World War was "director of studies of men in war service" at Mildmay Training College in London. After the war, he was appointed professor of history of religion at the Pacific School of Religion. See "Fellows," John Simon Guggenheim Memorial Foundation, https://www.gf.org/fellows/all-fellows/kenneth-james-saunders/ (accessed 29 June 2017).

52 On the Victorian roots of the Mildmay institutions, see "Mildmay and its Institutions."

human interest generally seemed to make up for most shortcomings – paid him an affectionate tribute as "a great splendid, unchastened, belligerent Irishman" (76).

Ridgeway's near-blindness had him look "persistently ... away from whomever he was speaking to" (TFMF, T.F. McIlwraith to his mother, 19 October 1919). Students flew forward to prevent him from walking through windows mistaken for doors, waiters leapt backward when they attempted to serve him soup "on his blind side" (Brooke 238), and colleagues steered him down the winding stairs from an upper-story boardroom "like Antigone and Oedipus" (Glover, *Cambridge Retrospect* 77). Despite his frailty, Ridgeway was feared around the university for his "temper of the soldier, who delights in the clash of arms and smoke of battle" ("Obituary for William Ridgeway" 4), and he was known for his "ability to provoke the mildest and most tranquil people" (Glover, *Cambridge Retrospect* 76). His intransigence made permanent enemies of several of his opponents on the Senate, where in addition to his fight against the equality of female students, he battled the abolition of the compulsory Greek requirement, the advancement of the sciences, the acceptance of government funding by the university, and the granting of study leaves. Indeed, he not only "trampled on many of the frontiers between archaeology and anthropology with a polemical fierceness which took the breath away," but was also capable of making "any cause ludicrous by his advocacy" (Brooke 237, 247–8).

McIlwraith was afraid of Ridgeway (and, as it turned out at his first BAAS conference in Edinburgh, had reason to be) and from the start identified him as "weird with longish hair, projecting eyebrows," as well as a "queer old fish" and "a mad man in all ways at once" (TFMF, T.F. McIlwraith to his mother 19 October 1919; to his family 26 October 1919; 9 August 1920), but he benefited from Ridgeway's support at Cambridge, which continued after his return to Canada. When his former student's application for a post at University College London was not successful, Ridgeway commented with characteristic abandon on both the applicant who *was* appointed and his supporter: "Elliott Smith ha[s] gotthat insti[t]uted for Perry, his follower, not tosay jackal" (TFMF, William Ridgeway to T.F. McIlwraith, 23 March 1923). (As is apparent in this quotation, much of the text of Ridgeway's letters was run into a single paragraph because the writer's poor eyesight made the spacebar difficult to navigate; the recipient's first job was to separate the words by pencil marks.)

Because Ridgeway admired the missionary John Roscoe, McIlwraith was treated to "a violent 'Hear, Hear,' after nearly all my sentences" when he gave a demonstration of the Roscoe collection to the Anthropological Club at the Museum of Archaeology and Anthropology in Cambridge (MAA) (TFMF, T.F. McIlwraith to family, 9 March 1921). However, even as a protégé, he repeatedly "got it in the neck" (TFMF, T.F. McIlwraith to family, 9 August 1920). On one such occasion, T.F. incautiously asked how "one of the finest brasses in the country" located in an old church "had escaped from Cromwell," and like Glover he related Ridgeway's response as if it were a dramatic performance complete with mime and sound effects. While Glover exclaimed "I wish I could reproduce, in letters, the 'Hay! hay! Or 'heh! heh!' ... which came when he had pulled off an argument that seemed good" (Glover, *Cambridge Retrospect* 78), McIlwraith has Ridgeway "[shoot] his head out at me till I thought his neck would crack" and intersperse his disapproval with exclamations of "hgh": "Cromwell, what do you mean, (hgh), Cromwell (hgh) never destroyed any memorial to the dead in his life (hgh), he pulled down some of the blasphemous idols (hgh) that so deface the continental churches (hgh), those tawdry, disgusting things (hgh), it is all down in the diary (hgh) of the man who was [in] charge (hgh)" (TFMF, T.F. McIlwraith to family, 9 August 1920).

One of Rivers's most important acts of professional kindness towards McIlwraith was to steer him as well as he could through Ridgeway's wrath at the BAAS meeting in Edinburgh in 1921, where McIlwraith presented a paper on "Egyptian Influence on African Death-Rites." The situation, which had T.F.'s presentation delayed by Sir Everard im Thurn, the talkative "old boy" whom the Sewards had met on their eventful trip to Australia, developed into a presenter's nightmare from the start:

> The only person I was afraid of was Sir Wm. Ridgeway, who was in the front seat. I knew he was strongly opposed to any idea of Egyptian influence anywhere, and tried to taffy him along a bit, a pure waste of time ... The chairman ... announced there was no time for discussion, at which there was a loud grunt from Ridgeway, "What a pity." I had begun to think that if that was the way he felt about it, it was lucky for me that there was no time for discussion. I might as well have saved myself the trouble of any such thought, because Ridgeway is a law unto himself. He had no sooner come out with his regrets about time, than he hopped up and began to slay. The chairman should have ruled him out of order, but Lord Abercromby is a nice gentle old man who could be bossed by anyone, let alone by a fire-eater of the type of Ridgeway. The annoying part was that I knew there would be no chance or time for any of my supporters, or myself, to answer the old man. I must have trod on more of his pet theories than I knew of, because he became quite excited and vengeful. First of all he chewed me to pieces as it were, and then sort of annihilated the pieces one by one. He objects on principal [sic] to any theory of transmission of culture and is opposed to independent evolution and this was the first chance he had had in some time of attacking a theory of this ... I was rather annoyed at this, but Rivers seemed to think it was wiser [to keep quiet] otherwise I would have had Ridgeway really sore instead of being pleased with himself. I shall have a most interesting discussion with him as I am quite prepared to stand to my guns and fight back (TFMF, T.F. McIlwraith to family, 21 September 1921).

The fracas in fact worked out to McIlwraith's advantage because the RAI secretary invited him to repeat the paper in London;[53] Harold Peake urged him to produce a similarly controversial presentation for the next BAAS meeting, and he was interviewed by *The Scotsman*. Either because it was true or because he felt that McIlwraith was owed some reassurance, Haddon later claimed that Ridgeway was feeling apologetic about his attack. At Rivers's request, McIlwraith sent him the revised paper in March 1922 so that it could be submitted for publication, but Rivers died not long after, and Elliot Smith, his literary executor, returned it to McIlwraith.[54] It appears to have remained unpublished (*HBCI*, T.F. McIlwraith to W.H.R. Rivers, [21?] March 1922, 33).

By their patriotism and unconventional manner, Haddon, Rivers, and Ridgeway assured McIlwraith that he had not landed in mildewed civilian company as he feared when he left the KOSB. However, the university's antiquated traditions continued to irk him even if he never became as aggressive in his opposition as some of the naval officers. Shortly after his arrival in Cambridge, he expressed a fierce resentment against "customs that must have come from the arc [sic]" in a letter replete with "damn" and "damnable" to Philip Child, who was then enrolled at McGill. "Most of the undergrads are demobbed officers, quite decent on the whole," McIlwraith continued, even if they were "obviously not in the same class as the ones in your own battalion. Ça va sans dire" (TFMF, T.F. McIlwraith to Philip Child, 12 November 1919). His irritation, submerged over the coming months, erupted once more in his long description of graduation ceremonies in 1921. Exhaustion from his exam preparations may have played a role, and perhaps he was still rattled by an anxious moment just before graduation when Haddon had to step in to assure the Senate that he "was a suitable candidate" as it was suddenly found that his "two years at McGill were really one plus war service" ("Genealogy"). Whatever the immediate reason, he was angered that the graduation rituals, now so quaint as to be bizarre, had survived the war. Perhaps typing his account on the back of a crossed-out academic paper was an additional expression of his disdain. It helped to be briefly transported back into a military community when his sentiments were shared by "the undergrads queuing up for the thing, [in] remarks expressed in the choicest of army language." He repeatedly lambasted "the stupidity of going forward under the introduction of a man who does not know you," and was unable to suppress his anger at marching along, to no apparent purpose, "in fours and looking like a flock of black and white sheep being led off to the slaughterhouse, except that I never saw sheep that looked as disgusted and annoyed as we did." He was particularly incensed by a custom that required four supplicants for

---

53   The minutes suggest that there was a lively discussion with Rivers in the chair. See "Proceedings of the Royal Anthropological Institute, 1921."
54   See Harold Averill, Finding Aid for TFMF, UTA, 19 April 1979, B1979-0011/ 009 (03-06).

T.R. Glover as praelector, with four undergraduates, June 1905. Item inserted in Glover's diary for 1905. By permission of the Master and Fellows of St John's College, Cambridge.

the BA degree to grasp a finger each of the praelector, the medievalist C.W. Previté-Orton, as they were presented to the vice chancellor:

Finally ... the four of us stood immediately in front of the V.C. who sat on a chair raised on a platform. Previté-Orton stuck out his right hand along in front of us and we each clutched a finger[;] he then raised his square politely at the V.C. and [said] something in Latin. I suppose it was to introduce the four of us who were under his wing, or rather clutching his finger, as four who had completed the instruction and were worthy to take their degree. Needless to say it was a farce and I am sure the man did not know a quarter of the men he introduced ... [O]ne man wished to grab a finger with his left hand. A horrified whisper came from

Previté-Orton, though why one cannot be equally well introduced by a man whom you do not know in a language that you do not know when holding his little finger in the left as in the right hand is a mystery which is beyond my power to fathom.

A profusion of Latin included the pronouncement that "may have been a curse, but was probably a statement that [the vice chancellor] hereby made me a B.A.," and as a last straw – though he was relieved to have his name for once pronounced correctly – he found himself described as "Canadiensis," with the apology added that this was probably "bad Latin." McIlwraith's clarification that there were "various warblers having Canadiensis in their labels" suggests that he suspected condescension towards a colonial, but the only way he knew to protest against proceedings that he considered childish and undignified was to be childish himself. He was delighted that a group of undergraduates created a disturbance by throwing pennies from the galleries onto the assembly below and that others, in their hoods and tabs, "play[ed] marbles on the steps of the Senate House." His own "protest" was "to play bowls" in evening dress as he waited to sign "for [his] scholarship" (TFMF, T.F. McIlwraith to family, 27 June 1921).

The Museum of Archaeology and Anthropology

McIlwraith's later career was influenced by his work at the MAA, which eventually had him switch his plans from a career in the Colonial Service to one in academia and, once he was hired by the University of Toronto, prepared him for his cross-appointment to the ROM. Moreover, the community of scholars and staff working at the MAA became the kind of close-knit group in which McIlwraith typically prospered, and on his return to Canada, he immediately mailed a box of apples from the Niagara Peninsula as a return gift for the many teas he had enjoyed with the staff at the museum. On a visit to Cambridge more than ten years later, he "arrived just in time for tea ... and talked to everyone, feeling very much at home again," and was delighted to spot "a temporary diagram which I put up as a makeshift in 1921" (TFMP, T.F. McIlwraith to Beulah McIlwraith, 8 August 1934). He assisted Haddon, named curator while Anatole von Hügel was away on a medical leave (see Haddon and Maudslay), in the onerous job of creating a well-organized and accessible teaching facility from the previous "very much run-down and ill-sorted place" over which L.W.G. Malcolm had been temporarily presiding and from where he provided T.F. with the informal loan of books (TFMF, T.F. McIlwraith to family, 2 September 1920). It was crucial to complete the reorganization while the Baron was away and therefore unable to prevent boxes and books from leaving the hoard amassed in his office. With the collusion of Rivers, Haddon had von Hügel's "priceless Fiji collection" (Pickles 3) and other specimens unpacked and arranged, and McIlwraith was given a key that allowed him to work evenings and weekends in the museum. In keeping with his interest in Africa, his work concentrated on the Ugandan objects from the Roscoe collection. Perhaps he also had a hand in sorting items that had belonged to Marion Seward's friend and Haddon's student, Major Tremearne, who had left his collection of Ugandan artefacts to the MAA. In his letter of reference for McIlwraith to the University of Toronto, Haddon praised the results: "a card catalogue of the specimens" and "an attractive and instructive" display. Haddon, whose son Ernest was a civil servant in Uganda and a lecturer in Bantu languages at Makerere College, concluded that McIlwraith's "knowledge of African ethnology [was] really remarkable" (HCUL, A.C. Haddon to Playfair McMurrich, 25 January 1922). In July 1921, it was all hands on deck as von Hügel was expected to return shortly, and McIlwraith's job was to do "combs and hairpins" from "a batch of Nigerian objects" that, despite the "dust and dirt," reminded him of "fine brass paper-cutters" (TFMF, T.F. McIlwraith to family, 10 and 17 July 1921). Recently introduced to theories of diffusionism, he was also "tremendously interested in seeing several of the 'typical' Celtic patterns on these African combs" (TFMF, T.F. McIlwraith to family, 17 July 1921).

Next door, the books were being organized by Ethel Sophia Fegan, who had read classics at Girton and remained an important contact after McIlwraith had left Cambridge. She forwarded Haddon's letters from his trip to the Second Pan-Pacific Conference in Australia containing news of academic prospects in South Africa he hoped to open up for his former student. McIlwraith thanked her with a note written in the woods of Bella Coola and smeared with jam from his lunch, expressing his hope to see her on his way to Cape Town should the position materialize (*HBCI*, T.F. McIlwraith to Ethel Fegan, 13 October 1923, 85–6). Fegan's accomplishment as a librarian was as formidable as the organization, by others, of the display of objects in the museum. Some eight thousand volumes that were scattered through various rooms had to be consolidated into one library that could be easily accessed by faculty and students. Bookcases from her late husband's library were obtained "at bargain prices" from Mrs. Quiggin, a numismatologist and archaeologist with whom McIlwraith took a course in "[b]asketry."[55] Chairs and tables were found in second-hand shops. There were recollections of the recent war when a door was improvised from "an old wire mattress found in the Museum, a relic of the Belgian refugees." Because it proceeded without official authorization, all of the "work was carried through in great secrecy," and at its next meeting Haddon confronted the Library Committee with the fait accompli, after forcing "them to admit that they had done nothing" (Pickles 3).

---

55 "Lecture Notes Taken at Cambridge University," Harold Averill, Finding Aid for TFMF, 19 April 1979, UTA, B1979-0011/ 006 (53). The lecture is erroneously listed as one in "masketry."

W.H.R. Rivers. Elliott & Fry Photographers, London, no date available but probably close to 1922. By permission of the Master and Fellows of St John's College, Cambridge.

The Imperial Job Market

Soon after he began his studies at Cambridge, McIlwraith's fellow student Ernest Chinnery and his teachers began to introduce him to individuals whom they considered useful in obtaining a position as colonial civil servant or researcher in the "Empire of Scholars" (Pietsch). Prominent among the connections that needed to be established were the "élite of scholar-official mandarins" affiliated with the Colonial Office and the Royal Colonial Institute, but also missionaries and entrepreneurs with an interest in anthropology (Hyam 259). Cambridge seems to have swarmed with such people, and for some time after he had left the university, McIlwraith referred to individuals to whom he had been introduced. From Yale in 1924, he asked Haddon for details about Sir Arthur Francis Grimble, colonial administrator in the Gilbert and Ellice Islands on furlough in the United Kingdom after the war, because the latter's anecdote about "a black demon who insisted on the ghosts doing Cat's Cradles before they reached their land of bliss" was useful to his current research on the disposal of the dead (HCUL, T.F. McIlwraith to A.C. Haddon, 14 December 1924). Before he left for New Guinea, Chinnery had written a letter introducing McIlwraith to Sir Harry Wilson, British colonial secretary, and McIlwraith demonstrated his own initiative by having a well-connected fellow student accompany him to the meeting: "It seemed to work and the old boy was very decent," McIlwraith told his family, and he was confident that Sir Harry was on side to support him in future applications (TFMF, T.F. McIlwraith to family, 21 April 1920). Ridgeway wanted him to talk to the recently retired British colonial administrator Charles William Hobley, "one of the very big men in the Colonial Service in East Africa,"[56] but the invitation to tea in Fen Ditton did not reach McIlwraith in time, and the opportunity to meet with Hobley was lost for the time being. However, Hobley assured Ridgeway that he would be ready to help on the strength of Ridgeway's own support of McIlwraith (TFMF, T.F. McIlwraith to family, 9 August 1920).

Rivers presented him to Sir Ralph Furse from the Colonial Office[57] and Rivers insisted that his student be found a position in the interior of German East Africa (TFMF, T.F. McIlwraith to family, 17 August 1920). McIlwraith probably did not know that, in addition to relying on the testimonial of trusted teachers at select public schools and universities, the method of assessing candidates for the Colonial Service during a lengthy interview was based on a type of unofficial anthropometry for white men, with uncomfortable parallels to the assessment endured by Ernst Kromayer when it came to establishing his Aryan credentials in 1937. One applicant created a favourable impression because of his "good open face with a good deal of grit in it," not to mention his achievements as "a very good athlete."[58] Handshakes especially served as a code of identifying the worthy. The "limp fingers" of one applicant worried Furse until on saying goodbye he found"[h]is palm was as hard as nails." The applicant promptly made a success of his difficult posting in Palestine (Furse 230–1). Recruiting officers were advised to pay closer attention "to character, personality, physique and habits" than to academic achievement (141), and a fourth-class honours degree was by no means a deterrent to employment. Colonial officers had to be "of the right stamp" because they were expected to deal with "native chiefs and headmen," who would become instantly alert to weakness of

---

56 On Hobley, see Northcote.

57 On Furse, see Kirk-Greene, "Furse, Sir Ralph Dolignon."

58 Interviewer's notes, qtd. in Heussler 23.

character because "[l]ike children" they had "exceptional powers of intuitive observation" (142). Indeed, British district officers worth their salt viewed the natives as "attractive children," while their lesser French and Belgian counterparts saw them "as barbaric nuisances" (Heussler 122). To their credit, both Furse and Haddon did have their doubts about imperial methods and stereotypes: Haddon felt that Britain had disgraced itself in its dependencies with "The Red-Paint of British Aggression" (see Stocking and Haddon), and in his memoir Furse wondered if the practices of "British imperialism" had at times not been been "rather obtuse" (286).

McIlwraith was introduced to Furse two years before the latter made two extended trips to Canada. The recruiting officer thought of the Dominions as rather parochial until these visits taught him otherwise (see Kirk-Greene, "White Man's Burden"), and he agreed with Charles E. Saunders, agronomist at the University of Toronto, that because of its role in the Great War, Canada had "gained immensely in confidence and national self-respect" (Furse 115–16). Furse met with university presidents and politicians across the country in order to organize the Dominion Selection Scheme, which was later extended to Australia, New Zealand, and South Africa. McIlwraith had attended neither Eton nor Harrow, and he was no athlete, but his teachers must have been certain that his perseverance, friendliness, team spirit, and handshake would carry the day, and that his outstanding academic record would not speak against him. Perhaps their endorsement helped to alert Furse to the potential of candidates from the Dominions for the Colonial Service. The suggestion that he "would be almost sure of getting it" recurs frequently in McIlwraith's accounts of openings in the service, emphasizing just how aggressively his teachers promoted his prospects, often in the face of stiff competition from Oxford. There was a string of disappointments, but it never seemed to take long for the next position to materialize. When McIlwraith and his teachers began to concentrate on an appointment in Canada, he used similarly confident language in reporting to Haddon about his negotiations: in a meeting with Robert Falconer, president of the University of Toronto, he was "assured ... that I was the one person seriously considered, in fact their choice" (HCUL, T.F. McIlwraith to A.C. Haddon, 27 September 1924).

One of the first placements under discussion was a lectureship in Cape Town, and possible appointments in South Africa persistently recur throughout McIlwraith's early career, usually with Haddon as mediator. In fall 1920, Haddon had learned from "somebody who was connected with the University of Cape Town" that "they are planning to have classes in anthropology," for which both a professor and a lecturer were needed. The professorship went to Alfred Radcliffe-Brown, a pupil of Haddon and Rivers, and Haddon informed "this person ... that they had a man in Cambridge who would be well qualified for [the lectureship] if he would take it," always provided the money could be

found to fund the position. Haddon and Rivers pledged their support to McIlwraith, and Haddon even intended to put in a personal word with Prime Minister Jan Smuts. As an honorary fellow of Christ's College, Smuts was "inclined
to be friendly" to Cambridge, and although candidates from Oxford posed "the
greatest danger" because "the Cape Town people ... might want to put in an Oxford man to even up with [Alfred Radcliffe-]Brown from Cambridge," Haddon
argued that it would be judicious to appoint two men from Cambridge because
their training at the same university assured consistency in scholarly method
(TFMF, T.F. McIlwraith to family, 24 September 1920). As with his professional
plans following demobilization, McIlwraith details all the advantages and disadvantages of this appointment for his family, including the expected salary. In
language that is remarkably more civil than similar discussions in his wartime
letters, he also begs them not to let anything slip to the "Hills-Phillips Collection" so as to avoid gossip circulating through the mails between Canada, South
Africa, and Great Britain, where both the Hills and the Phillips families had numerous relatives, before the job could be finalized. This is one of several times
when his academic network overlaps with his family's personal connections: he
also mentions that Highfield's headmaster, John Collinson, is acquainted with
Robert Ranulph Marett. Marett oversaw the Oxford equivalent of the nexus
that, at Cambridge, was controlled by Haddon and Rivers (TFMF, T.F. McIlwraith to family, 17 August 1920).

Nothing more is heard of the prospect in Cape Town in 1920, but three years
later, Haddon revived the idea with former students Radcliffe-Brown, Winifred Hoernlé, and A.J.H. Goodwin when he stopped over at Cape Town on
his way to the Second Pan-Pacific Science Congress in Melbourne and Sydney.
All pledged "to do all they can to help you & and they can do a great deal."[59]
Radcliffe-Brown contacted McIlwraith after this meeting and proposed "an appointment as ethnologist to the Transvaal Museum in Pretoria," underlining
that the position had not yet been advertised.[60] As related earlier, Haddon himself followed up with McIlwraith through Ethel Fegan at the MAA. McIlwraith,
whose permanent employment with the Geological Survey of Canada or the
University of Toronto remained at that point uncertain, was tempted (HCUL,
T.F. McIlwraith to A.C. Haddon, 13 October 1923), but there is no further correspondence about this post. When Radcliffe-Brown moved to Sydney in 1925,
McIlwraith was in discussion as the successor to his professorship in Cape
Town. The two even had a chance to talk things over in person when both attended the Second Conference of the Institute of Pacific Relations in Honolulu
two years later. McIlwraith demurred for a variety of reasons, however, one of
which was his growing conviction that Canada was "a better country" (HCUL,

59   A.C. Haddon to T.F. McIlwraith, 23 July 1923, TFMF, UTA, B1979-0011/002 (01).
60   Alfred Radcliffe-Brown to T.F. McIlwraith, 25 July 1923, TFMF, UTA, B1979-0011/002 (01).

T.F. McIlwraith to A.C. Haddon, 8 February 1926). As late as 1934, McIlwraith wrote to his four-year-old daughter "Marykins" to "tell mummy that [he was] not applying for a job in South Africa" (TFMP, T.F. McIlwraith to Mary Agnes McIlwraith, 20 August 1934). The circumstances of that particular position are not clear, but McIlwraith's decision not to pursue it may have something to do with his growing opposition to South Africa's racial policies. From the same trip, McIlwraith reported to his wife on his "first contact with a sufferer from the Nazis" in London, a Jewish collector of Chinese artefacts who had fled from Hamburg and from whom he intended to purchase items for the ROM (TFMP, T.F. McIlwraith to Beulah McIlwraith, 8 August 1934).

Another African connection came through John Roscoe, whose collection of artefacts McIlwraith helped to sort at the MAA and whom he met at the 1921 BAAS meeting in Edinburgh if not before. In 1920, Roscoe had returned from the Mackie Expedition to some acclaim, and "Winston Churchill, then the colonial secretary, ... consult[ed] [him] about African affairs" (D. Richards 160). Roscoe had left on the expedition in 1919, handicapped by the scarcity of qualified men who were only just beginning to return from the trenches. Initiated by Sir James Frazer and funded by the whisky distiller Sir Peter Mackie, the expedition was intended to obtain "details of the social anthropology which would be of value to science and to the Government, especially in regard to customs affecting land tenure, inheritance, marriage and birth." According to Roscoe, the Colonial Office concluded that "the natives would benefit" and unnecessary conflict could be avoided if "Administrative Officers and Missionaries" familiarized themselves with these traditions (Roscoe 217). The year after his return from the expedition, Roscoe published his anthropological memoir *Twenty-Five Years in East Africa*, intended as an information manual for imperial workers in Africa.

When it became known that Roscoe's research had helped to resolve land disputes in Uganda, the Colonial Office concluded that a systematic study of Indigenous "land tenure" by a government-appointed ethnographer would serve its administrative purposes even better. Supported by Sir Richard Temple and other senior colonial administrators at the BAAS meeting a year before the war (J.A.H., "Anthropology") the idea of bringing university-trained anthropologists and ethnographers into the work of the Colonial Office to give its activities scientific "backbone" was now being revived, and once again, McIlwraith seemed first in line for the job: "Roscoe ... thought that the government would accept anyone on his ... recommendation, which would apparently mean myself if I want it" (TFMP, T.F. McIlwraith to family, 13 February 1921). The appointment did not come through, but the notion that anthropology was useful training for colonial administrators and missionaries stayed with McIlwraith, and shortly after his appointment at Toronto he began to teach anthropology "to missionaries home on furlough and probationers" at the Canadian School of Missions (HCUL, T.F. McIlwraith to A.C. Haddon, 2 February 1926).

Discussion of his employment prospects introduced McIlwraith to the difficult question of funding for anthropological posts and expeditions, and to the tireless lobbying that anthropologists like Frazer, Haddon, and Rivers had to keep up to obtain the money for their research and find placements for their students. Before securing funds from Mackie, Frazer had unsuccessfully approached the Carnegie Trust, the Royal Society, and the Colonial Office (Michaud 65). Realizing that Mackie was pleased with the result of the expedition, Rivers "hop[ed] to 'tap' Sir Peter Mackie for some money for research work in the Pacific." McIlwraith elaborated that "Dr. Rivers had seen Roscoe in London on Friday ... Roscoe will be in Cambridge next term, and both Dr. Rivers and Dr. Haddon will go into the pros and cons of the business with him then. As Dr. Rivers said last night it would be research work with a salary attached. It would also be just the training required for an academic post of some kind if such were available later on." Once again, McIlwraith was told that "[i]f any money did appear this way ... I would be almost sure of getting it" (TFMF, T.F. McIlwraith to family, 13 February 1921).

Plans to obtain a post for McIlwraith continued into the summer of 1921, but there is no further talk of possible financial support from Mackie, and "the decided difficulty of whether the funds will allow it" becomes a refrain (TFMF, T.F. McIlwraith to family, 18 February 1921). An additional complication was an apparent reluctance at Cambridge to accept American money, and with it outside influence on British scholarship, in the context of "[i]nter-allied projects in the 1920s" (Irish, *The University at War* 178–83). Without providing details of what he was to do there, McIlwraith writes about a US-funded "job in the Pacific" that came with a salary of "about $1500 a year – with all expenses paid." However, it was not "the part of the Pacific in which Cambridge [was] most interested, Melanesia." On its own, Cambridge would cover his "expenses, no salary, but I think it would be up to me to go, and into the bargain I would simply be tumbling over myself to do it." He was aware "that the people here would prefer to keep me in touch with Cambridge rather than be turned over to the Yanks. Naturally I have not been told this last directly but I believe it is the way the cat really jumps" (TFMF, T.F. McIlwraith to family, 14 March 1921). A month later, he had to report that the posting in the Pacific had fallen through because the previous occupant – probably J.D. Newsom – had "chucked up and Dr. Rivers who got the money for him from these various societies will probably have to repay it from his own pocket" (TFMF, T.F. McIlwraith to family, 17 April 1921).

Immediately, another "proposition" emerged in New Guinea, where the services of a government ethnologist were required. This post did not materialize either, to the great puzzlement and irritation of McIlwraith's teachers, who "had thought [he] was almost safe for the job and as a result none of them had worried to hunt elsewhere for a job on my behalf" (TFMF, T.F. McIlwraith to family, 27 June 1921). Although this appointment would have been "the type of job that appeal[ed] tremendously to [him]," there is now a new element in McIlwraith's response when he describes the posting as an interim to his final goal, a position with the "Canadian Ethnologic Service." This is the first time that McIlwraith mentions "one Dr. Sapir," friend of Paul Radin, an American anthropologist from the University of California who was visiting Cambridge in 1921 and with whom McIlwraith was "on good terms" (TFMF, T.F. McIlwraith to family, 17 April 1921). The ensuing correspondence illustrates the indispensable role of patronage in this web of academia and government agencies, so densely woven as to evoke the imperial networks feeding into, and preventing, Sir Thomas's attempted annexation of New Guinea. Citing Radin, McIlwraith's first letter to Sapir was sent in June, with a summary of his qualifications and enquiry about possible employment.[61] Radin himself wrote a month later, describing the T.F. as "a remarkable find if you could secure him," referring to him as "Rivers' favourite pupil," and suggesting that "he would be worth a grant for field-work."[62] When Sapir responded that there was no vacancy for regular employment but that fieldwork might be available, McIlwraith followed up with details about his training and expertise.[63] Just before McIlwraith's departure for the BAAS meeting in Edinburgh, where his first conference paper was savaged by Ridgeway, he received a letter proposing study of the Bella Coola under the auspices of the Anthropology Division of the Geological Survey of Canada,[64] and he copied the whole letter triumphantly to his family (TFMF, T.F. McIlwraith to family, 8 September 1921). Having suggested that it was a good idea to "grab" McIlwraith, Radin prodded Sapir again in November to make McIlwraith a formal offer, explaining that he had begun to train McIlwraith in "phonetics! And N.W. coast grammar!"[65] Sapir responded immediately and enclosed a note from Deputy Minister Charles Camsell agreeing "to employ Mr. McIlwraith as a field assistant."[66] On 25 January 1922 a telegram

61 T.F. McIlwraith to Edward Sapir, 24 June 1921, CMH, Archives, Ethnology Documents, Edward Sapir (I-A-236M), Folder: McIlwraith, T.F. (1921–1923), Box 628, f. 23.

62 Paul Radin to Edward Sapir, 9 July 1921, CMH, Archives, Ethnology Documents, Edward Sapir (I-A-236M), Folder: Radin, Paul (1919–1925), Box 632, f. 3.

63 T.F. McIlwraith to Edward Sapir, 9 August 1921, CMH, Archives, Ethnology Documents, Edward Sapir (I-A-236M), Folder: McIlwraith, T.F. (1921–1923), Box 628, f. 23.

64 Edward Sapir to T.F. McIlwraith, 19 August 1921, CMH, Archives, Ethnology Documents, Edward Sapir (I-A-236M), Folder: McIlwraith, T.F. (1921–1923), Box 628, f. 23.

65 Paul Radin to Edward Sapir, 16 November 1921, CMH, Archives, Ethnology Documents, Edward Sapir (I-A-236M), Folder: Radin, Paul (1919–1925), Box 632, f. 3.

66 William McInnes to Edward Sapir, 30 November 1921, CMH, Archives, Ethnology Documents, Edward Sapir (I-A-236M), Folder: McIlwraith, T.F. (1921–1923), Box 626, f. 23; Edward Sapir to Paul Radin, 30 November 1921, Ethnology Documents, Edward Sapir (I-A-236M), Folder: Radin, Paul, Box 632, f. 3.

reading "Appointment Authorized Report Ottawa" asked McIlwraith to return to Canada immediately. Because his student was laid up with an injury, Haddon ran up three flights of stairs to his room at St. John's College to let him know ("Genealogy"), and by 8 February McIlwraith was on his way back to North America.

But there was more. Shortly before his departure, he found Haddon "established in front of [the] fire" in his room, with a letter from Playfair McMurrich at the University of Toronto, "an old friend of his, saying that they were planning to found Anthropology at Toronto, could Dr. Haddon suggest a suitable person to take charge of it?" (TFMF, T.F. McIlwraith to family, 24 January 1922). When he met up with them in New York in February, McIlwraith told his family who, fired up by his success at Cambridge, hoped that he would obtain a position there, that they were "wrong in advising [him] to turn ... down" the opportunity to work at the University of Toronto: "it is bad to stay too long in any one place, and it is now high time for me to leave Cambridge" (TFMF, T.F. McIlwraith to family, 4 March 1922). Haddon was a formidable ally, and although Radin's efforts on McIlwraith's behalf were impressive, they dwindle in comparison to the campaign staged by T.F.'s mentor. For the next few years, he tenaciously went after McMurrich on the repeated occasions when this plan seemed to sputter. His four-page recommendation, sent the day after he had appeared in McIlwraith's room, outlined his student's academic preparation, expertise in museum displays, and teaching experience from the course for the naval officers that Haddon had passed on to him, and he concluded with an appraisal of the upcoming fieldwork in Bella Coola. Haddon underscored McIlwraith's personal qualifications "as a cheerful soul, easy to work with, and enthusiastic in all that he undertakes" (HCUL, A.C. Haddon to Playfair McMurrich, 25 January 1922). Because, as usual, the funds were slow to be approved, the run-up to the appointment in Toronto turned into a complicated performance, with Haddon as skilful coach. By June 1922, McIlwraith feared that "the Toronto job had fallen through" and that he was once again looking for a position following Bella Coola. He repeatedly asked Sapir about further employment, but also – though probably with reluctance – reviewed the possibilities of "return[ing] to Cambridge" or applying for a post with the "African Colonial Service" since an academic appointment appeared to be elusive. He dismissed Reed College, in Portland, Oregon, as too insignificant when he was approached by W.D. Wallis, a faculty member there who had studied under Marett in Oxford (HBCI, T.F. McIlwraith to A.C. Haddon, 7 June 1922, 50). Possibly alerted by the offer from Reed College to look out for vacancies in the United States as well, Haddon put in a word with Berthold Laufer at the Field Museum of Natural History in Chicago. McIlwraith was grateful but was influenced by Rivers's critical comments about the museum's methods (HBCI, T.F. McIlwraith to A.C. Haddon, 29 August 1922, 67).

In November, Haddon wrote another urgent letter to McMurrich: "McIlwraith is such a good man that it would be a thousand pities if his services could not be retained for Canada." To ensure that McMurrich knew there was competition for "a good man" such as this, Haddon added that he was holding back other prospects for his student until he had heard back from McMurrich (HCUL, A.C. Haddon to Playfair McMurrich, [10 or 16 November?] 1922). The response from Toronto was inconclusive (HCUL, Playfair McMurrich to A.C. Haddon, 11 January 1923), but Haddon was undeterred. He undoubtedly had an urgent word with McMurrich when both attended the Second Pan-Pacific Science Congress in Australia in August of that year. At the same time he alerted McIlwraith to possible additional openings in South Africa and Australia "because from what I have heard about Toronto there does not seem much chance in that direction,"[67] and he urged him to check out the advertisements of academic posts in *Science*, the publication of AAAS, the American Association for the Advancement of Science (*HBCI*, T.F. McIlwraith to Haddon, 16 March 1924, 143). Haddon's decisive opportunity came with the 1924 BAAS meeting in Toronto. Supported by testimony from other influential delegates such as Harold Peake from the West Berkshire Museum and Sir John Myres from Oxford, whom Haddon quite possibly urged to weigh in with recommendations, he tackled McMurrich after McIlwraith had presented a well-received paper on "Certain Aspects of the Potlatch among the Bella Coola" (see *HBCI*, 161–9). Haddon "said almost too much, as if [he] were a reporter singing [McIlwraith's praises]" (HCUL, T.F. McIlwraith to A.C. Haddon, 27 September 1924). Indeed, McMurrich appears to have been rather overwhelmed and suspected that others were too. He persuaded Haddon to refrain from meeting with President Falconer or even "write to him – as he was well primed."[68]

As usual, McIlwraith did not rely on his teachers to do all the work for him, but accessed the networking opportunities at large academic gatherings, nurturing the links carefully once they had been established. Peake knew of him because, in Edinburgh in 1921, McIlwraith had done his best to "pump ... [Peake] for information," encouraged by Haddon and Rivers's endorsement of Peake as a "first class" scholar and T.F.'s own realization that he was "a good businessman" (TFMF, T.F. McIlwraith to family, 20 September 1921). After the conference in Toronto, McIlwraith instantly reciprocated by asking William A. Newcombe at the Royal British Columbia Museum in Victoria to host a party of anthropologists who were travelling to the West Coast after the BAAS meeting, especially Peake and Henry Balfour from Oxford, and "give them the advantage of your knowledge." As this particular letter makes clear, the importunate energy with which McIlwraith pursued his contacts in London and

---

67 A.C. Haddon to T.F. McIlwraith, 22 July 1923, TFMF, UTA, B1979-0011-002 (01).
68 A.C. Haddon to T.F. McIlwraith, 15 August 1924, TFMF, UTA, B1979-0011-002 (01).

Cambridge on demobilization had acquired professional polish: "I know that this is an imposition, and I would not write except that I feel you would enjoy meeting English anthropologists, and they would certainly be fortunate to have you act as guide in Victoria."[69] As is repeatedly the case in his letters after Cambridge, he pitches the British system against its American counterpart in his thank-you note to Newcombe and views himself as "liaison officer between the New Yorkers and the Englishmen."[70] While he is conciliatory, his wartime hostility towards the Americans does emerge in this context as well, especially when it becomes paired with his dislike of Germans. From a research position he briefly occupied with Clark Wissler at Yale between 1924 and 1925, once again obtained through Haddon's intervention, he recommended an American anthropologist to Haddon. The young man, unlike other Americans they both knew, was "a gentleman" and would not fare well with Franz Boas at Columbia University "since [he] is essentially a man and not an intellectual machine"[71] (HCUL, T.F. McIlwraith to A.C. Haddon, 15 February 1925). Although both his military and professional life had already taught him a thing or two about discretion, McIlwraith was not shy in his criticism of colleagues. In steering Peake towards Newcombe in Victoria rather than towards the "official guide" who was standing by in Vancouver to receive the visiting anthropologists, he hoped that they would thereby avoid the "long-windedness" of "H.I.S." The "official guide" was Harlan Ingersoll Smith from the Geological Survey of Canada, with whom McIlwraith was otherwise on good terms.[72]

The correspondence between Haddon and McIlwraith was often split into official and confidential parts in order to handle their long-distance communications with the necessary diplomacy, thus practising on a smaller academic scale the busy "traffic [of] unofficial correspondence" that helped to maintain a multilayered system of information among colonial officials (see Laidlaw 94–126). Haddon's approach was to "deal" professional correspondence as if he were setting up a well-played game of cards, and he shared his communications and their results with other players as he considered strategic. He did not hesitate to let T.F. know just how strongly he supported him. When McIlwraith required an open "testimonial" because he feared that a mailed

69   T.F. McIlwraith to William A. Newcombe, 15 August 1924, BC Archives, MS-1077, Newcombe family papers, Box 4, Folder 94, Reel A01748.

70   T.F. McIlwraith to William A. Newcombe, 29 September 1924, BC Archives, MS-1077, Newcombe family papers, Box 4, Folder 94, Reel A01748.

71   The question of whether McIlwraith's own scholarship was inflected by British or American influences has been raised in an exchange between Darnell, "Canadian Departments of Anthropology," and Barker, "Reply to Regna Darnell."

72   T.F. McIlwraith to William A. Newcombe, 29 September 1924, BC Archives, MS-1077, Newcombe family papers, Box 4, Folder 94, Reel A01748.

request would not always be fast enough to reach Haddon, who frequently travelled overseas, Haddon immediately produced one to use at McIlwraith's own discretion (HCUL, T.F. McIlwraith to A.C. Haddon, 27 September and 7 November 1924). Every bit of information could be valuable in building up his tactic, and the back of a notice announcing a General Meeting of the Royal Irish Academy was as good a place as any to copy down Newcombe's complimentary note that McIlwraith was "one of the brightest workers I have met & I expect great things of him" (HCUL, A.C. Haddon papers, 7 April 1924). For his part, McIlwraith – well trained by the polyphonic correspondence with his family during the war – designated letters to Haddon as suitable for sharing with Rivers but probably not "sufficiently diplomatic to circulate further," though he politely added that his teacher would be "the best judge" (HCUL, T.F. McIlwraith to A.C. Haddon, 5 March 1922). Likewise, he urged Haddon to use his attendance at the BAAS conference in Toronto to visit Ottawa, so that "someone from England" might inspire the staff of the Victoria Memorial Museum to cast off the tyranny of "red-tape ... before a nail could be driven or a specimen moved" and to replace it with efficient do-it-yourself, adding that "needless to say this is NOT official" (HCUL, T.F. McIlwraith to A.C. Haddon, 15 November 1922). At times the information was so confidential that it needed to be separated physically from the rest of the communication. In a note hand-written from his home address, McIlwraith reported on his successful negotiations with Toronto's university officials (HCUL, T.F. McIlwraith to A.C. Haddon, 8 February 1926). By contrast, a letter describing the shrewd measures McIlwraith had already initiated to gain approbation for the new field of anthropology at Toronto was dictated to an assistant and typed on letterhead from the ROM. Among his activities, he listed consultation with colleagues in psychology, history, political economy, and social service, formalizing undergraduate and graduate programs, establishing connections with the Canadian School of Missions, and sorting the museum collections into more effective displays by ordering cases and stands from the ROM's carpenter. Getting his lectures listed independently in the university calendar under anthropology rather than another departmental heading was a coup that "virtually [made] anthropology a department" (HCUL, T.F. McIlwraith to A.C. Haddon, 2 February 1926).

Although he had the foresight to separate some of his more momentous news into public and confidential portions, McIlwraith did have a few things to learn about prudence because he not only openly criticized Harlan Ingersoll Smith in the letter to Newcombe cited earlier but was also blunt in correspondence dictated to his assistant. One of these letters contained criticism of one colleague's scholarship on the Jesuit *Relations* as "exceedingly bad" and referred to another professor, the eminent (but to McIlwraith's mind aptly named) historian "Professor Wrong," as "not as conversant with anthropology as I would

like" (HCUL, T.F. McIlwraith to A.C. Haddon, 2 February 1926).[73] His deference to Haddon notwithstanding, McIlwraith's sharp tongue in sizing up his
fellow man at times matches his Aunt Jean's at her most outspoken moments,
such as when he wrote about Charles T. Currelly, the ROM's curator: "He struck
me (I speak frankly) as a curio hunter who has got his museum full of stuff
about which he knows very little, and who is chiefly concerned with getting
stuff which will be of interest to Members of Parliament and wealthy visitors"
(HCUL, T.F. McIlwraith to A.C. Haddon, 5 March 1922).

Despite all of his precautions in sharing the right information with the right
person, he had also inherited some of Jean's and his grandfather's talent for getting himself into embarrassing situations. Particularly delicate were occasions
when McIlwraith sent Haddon objects he had collected in his fieldwork, in-
tending them for display in the Cambridge MAA rather than the Victoria Memorial Museum in Ottawa. He learned his lesson the hard way when he failed
to include an explanatory letter in a package of items he had received as personal gifts in Bella Coola, and Haddon mistook it as coming from McIlwraith's
employers in Ottawa and thanked them for it (HCUL, T.F. McIlwraith to A.C.
Haddon, 15 November 1922). The ensuing muddle replays the embarrassment
his grandfather experienced when correspondence with John Macoun went
astray in the labyrinths of the Geological Survey of Canada. The second time
McIlwraith sent artefacts to Cambridge, he mailed the package to Haddon's
home address, requesting that he forward the contents to the MAA, all to avoid
"unpleasantness if anyone [at the Victoria Memorial Museum] knew" (HCUL,
T.F. McIlwraith to A.C. Haddon, 14 May 1923).

As is apparent from his support for T.F., Haddon's professional connections
with colleagues and former students had been growing for several decades by
the time McIlwraith became his student, and his contacts included every chair
in anthropology in the British Empire and the United States (Rouse, "Ethnology" 14). Haddon's continually updated store of information about academic
posts worldwide was part of a larger effort to obtain "intelligence" by collecting,
via correspondence and wherever possible by personal contact, "all published
and hitherto unpublished information, of an authoritative character, respecting
the developed or the undeveloped resources, industries and commerce of all
our dependencies" (Stocking and Haddon 5). As a brief he prepared in 1891
towards the creation of an Imperial Bureau of Ethnology indicates, Haddon
was guided by the conviction that such knowledge, together with the careful
selection of scholars and administrators to wield it, would work against col-
onizers' contempt for Indigenous populations, "which is the fertile mother of
injustice, cruelty, & legalised murder" (8). The energy Haddon brought to the

---

73 On George McKinnon Wrong, see J.B. Brebner, rev. Philip Buckner.

task of placing students such as McIlwraith has him resemble a diplomatic en-
voy rather than a desk-bound academic, and he was keenly aware of rivals in
this game such as Marett, who had taught the New Zealander Diamond Jenness
and the Canadian Marius Barbeau, McIlwraith's colleagues from 1922 to 1924.
To strengthen and expand his connections, Haddon rarely missed an opportunity to attend international conferences and expositions. Among the many
conferences he attended in the pre-war years, he travelled to the 1884 BAAS
meeting in Montreal, the 1904 Alaska-Yukon-Pacific Exposition in Seattle, the
1905 BAAS meeting in South Africa, the 1906 Congress of Americanists in
Quebec City, and the 1914 BAAS meeting in Sydney, Australia, not to mention
important conferences closer to home such as the 1911 Universal Races Congress in London. Whenever possible, he combined attendance at conferences
with trips to academic institutions. The 1884 BAAS meeting was followed by
visits to "Boston and Harvard, Yale, New York, Philadelphia, Baltimore and
Washington," where "he aimed at 'seeing all the museums and laboratories.' "
He felt that "even a cursory visit to a place and a short acquaintance with people
gives one's reading & correspondence ... a definition & vitality which would be
otherwise unobtainable."[74] Although he cites the ideas of BAAS president Max
Müller as his source, Haddon's understanding that an Imperial Bureau of Ethnology would gain from the example of the Bureau of American Ethnology was
probably shaped by a personal visit in Washington in 1884 (Stocking and Haddon 10). As his support of McIlwraith amply illustrates, Haddon was ruthless in
pursuing his students' interests, and he found informal conversations, such as
those "on the precipice-poised Dufferin Terrace" at the Congress of Americanists, more useful than scholarly sessions, declaring many of the latter "of limited interest" (Haddon, "The Congress of Americanists" 596). At this particular
congress, he seemed almost glad that many American delegates were prevented
by military conflict with Cuba from attending because cancellation of sessions
freed up more time for personal conversation. The result of his intervention
in 1924 was, as we have seen, definite progress towards an appointment for
McIlwraith at Toronto, and McIlwraith thanked Haddon for undertaking "a
long trip for such a short stay and you can be sure that I, who understood just
why you came, fully appreciate what you did for me" (HCUL, T.F. McIlwraith
to A.C. Haddon, 27 September 1924).[75]

Once his student had gained a foothold at the University of Toronto following a brief appointment at Yale, Haddon gave him the strategic advice to apply
for the Cape Town professorship, recently vacated by Radcliffe-Brown, implying that he use this prospect as leverage for a permanent position at Toronto.

---

74 A.C. Haddon to Patrick Geddes, 6 July 1884, qtd. in Rouse, "Haddon and Anthropology" 45.
75 On the importance of travel to academic networking at Cambridge, see Jöns, "Academic
    Travel from Cambridge" and "Cambridge, Academic Expertise, and the British Empire."

McIlwraith sounded out McMurrich, Charles Currelly, and President Falconer, with the result that he was made an assistant professor (HCUL, T.F. McIlwraith to A.C. Haddon, 8 February 1926). As soon as McIlwraith was settled at Toronto, these manoeuvres ceased for the time being, but quite possibly Haddon was the one who advised him to enter into negotiations for the position, mentioned earlier, at the University of Cape Town in 1934. By coincidence or not, the University of Toronto's Department of Anthropology was formally created two years later in 1936, and "McIlwraith was appointed professor and head" (*HBCI*, Introduction, 7).

The Academic Family

Although Haddon's attentiveness stands out, several of McIlwraith's teachers became substitute parents as well as academic mentors. Perhaps to delight his mother with the way he felt he was being singled out, Tom assured his family that it was "not a customary thing" for professors to be so attentive to their undergraduate students (TFMF, T.F. McIlwraith to family, 16 September 1920). In this, he was mistaken: it was a well-established tradition for teachers at Cambridge to develop close parental relationships with students and junior colleagues. The classicist W.E. Heitland alerted T.R. Glover's father to his son's fragile health shortly after Glover junior had become a fellow at St. John's College, assuring Glover senior that "I value him so highly that I watch him narrowly" (qtd. in Wood 28). As well, "he sat up with [his very sick tutorial pupil] Dicky Benthall three consecutive nights" (Glover, *Cambridge Retrospect* 38). Other students, too, boasted to their mothers that they received a great deal of attention, and Glover wrote to his parent that he was "getting very thick with the Master himself [the Hebraist Charles Taylor at St. John's College]," and he had "had four notes from him in 48 hours." Reciprocity was expected, however, and the master put his protégé to work correcting proofs (Wood 27).

Ridgeway, whose interest in McIlwraith may have been increased because he had a nephew farming in Canada, frequently invited T.F. to Fen Ditton for meals and to his college rooms for tea. It became so much of a habit for the young man to drop in on Sundays that the Ridgeways missed the routine after McIlwraith had left Cambridge. Letters were a poor substitute for Tom's good-natured patience in listening to Ridgeway's rants, but Ridgeway responded by return post when he wanted to get his thoughts about the political turmoil in Ireland off his chest. The couple lived in Flendyshe House, an imposing seventeenth-century mansion "with ... high outside walls," an "old-fashioned garden," "oak beams in the ceiling," and a gigantic fireplace. The grandeur was no match for the chaos in the study, with the "typewriter balanced precariously on a huge pile of papers on a table," and documents and books spread out several inches deep on the floor. Flendyshe House was "a library, a museum, a work-shop" (Myres and Haddon 174), and McIlwraith was shown some of the choice specimens in Ridgeway's collection. A cabinet of ethnographic treasures revealed, among coins, weapons, and various ornaments, "the skull of an Irish priest who had been hanged as one of the ring leaders of the rebellion [of] 1798" (TFMF, T.F. McIlwraith to family, 13 April 1920).

Once again, Haddon stood out as he repeatedly assumed the role of a fond parent dropping everything to admire what the youngster had found. When McIlwraith moved to the village of Comberton during the summer months to save money on rent and, while there, convinced himself that he had found an archaeological site, Haddon pedalled out on his bicycle to investigate the situation: "I piloted him down the front pasture to look at my circle in the ground, he said it would be nothing but that by all means I should dig it out," which McIlwraith proceeded to do "to the infinite amusement of the people here and as many of the youthful generation of Comberton as can line the fence" (TFMF, T.F. McIlwraith to family, 16 and 24 September 1920). Unlike Glover, McIlwraith was not set to work correcting proofs in return for his teacher's attention, but he was called upon to keep Fanny Haddon company when her husband was away for the evening (not an easy task as she was quite deaf), or he was summoned by postcard to prune the hedges and trees in the Haddons' garden on the Cranmer Road: "I was told that a job was waiting for me, and was turned loose on two trees of crab apples that needed picking ... I usually run into a job of some kind there, everything from digging dandelions to preparing patent bug-killer" (TFMF, T.F. McIlwraith to family, 16 September 1920). After his return to Canada, Fanny Haddon deplored that they no longer had a "kind Mac. coming to chop wood," that they "missed [him] very much," and "frequently talk[ed] of [him]" (TFMF, Fanny Haddon to T.F. McIlwraith, 10 June 1922). The Haddons' hospitality was so lavish that, at least in the beginning of his acquaintance with them, it made him uncomfortable. He tried to resist, only to head back the next day "for lunch ... as a sort of peace offering" (TFMF, T.F. McIlwraith to family, 19 December 1919). When the Haddons were absent, the maid stood by to give him a substantial tea after he had done the gardening.

Haddon kept a close eye on McIlwraith's health, and to prevent overwork in the months leading up to his Tripos invited him to join him and his wife on an excursion to Dorset. The solicitor and ethnographer E.S. Hartland, a member of Edward Clodd's circle, was also of the party. The Haddons intended to cover the cost of this trip but, when McIlwraith "objected violently," agreed to a compromise that had him pay for any days exceeding the week during which he was their guest (TFMF, T.F. McIlwraith to family, 22 February 1921). The letter he wrote home after this vacation demonstrates that Haddon's plan had worked: refreshed, T.F. delivered an exuberant account about all he had seen and done.

Their destination was Tollard Royal, near Stonehenge in Dorset, a village with "1 inn, 1 church, 1 smithy, and 1 P.O." There McIlwraith was fed by an excellent cook, slept to his heart's content, and accompanied Haddon on expeditions in the neighbourhood, "a place literally studded with prehistoric sites, dating chiefly to Neolithic and Bronze Ages" (TFMF, T.F. McIlwraith to family, 25 March 1921). Professor and student enjoyed each other's company, and although leisure was foremost on the agenda, professional networking was not forgotten. The previous year, Haddon had arranged for McIlwraith to spend a short vacation with Charles and Brenda Seligman in Oxford to enlarge his circle beyond Cambridge. From Tollard Royal, McIlwraith wrote to Seligman about "the queer beast," an object from the Solomon Islands they had seen at Pitt Rivers Museum in Farnham Royal. A sketch produced by Haddon was enclosed. The ensuing correspondence vividly illustrates the chain reaction of such contacts as Seligman several years later approached Captain Pitt Rivers about a photograph of the object for use in a forthcoming "joint paper" with Camilla Wedgwood.[76]

McIlwraith's professors were also attentive to his family and friends. In anticipation of Philip's admission to Christ's College in August 1921, the Childs spent the fall of 1920 in Cambridge, where Will Child attended lectures in anthropology and McIlwraith introduced him to Miles Burkitt (TFMF, T.F. McIlwraith to family, 18 October 1920). When Dorothy and Jean arrived for visits, they met his mentors and their families as a matter of course. Mrs. Seward organized a picnic for Jean and cousin Helen Service, and the Haddons laid on tea for them in their garden (TFMF, T.F. McIlwraith to family, 28 July 1921). Despite her frequent comments on the ravages caused by Cromwell's troops, Dorothy did not suffer from Ridgeway's wrath, as her brother enviously observed, perhaps because the old man thought that as the weaker sex women were owed gallantry even if they did not deserve admission to the university. McIlwraith's frequent references to invitations to tea had his mother offer to crochet a "tea cosey" in "delicate or dainty shades" to give to Mrs. Haddon (TFMP, Mary Stevens to T.F. McIlwraith, 1 September 1921). Ever concerned that her children put their best foot forward, Mary Stevens complained a little about the wrinkled socks he displayed in one of the photos he had forwarded, having scolded him earlier for mixing up "shall" and "will" in his letters (TFMP, Mary Stevens to T.F. McIlwraith, 27 July and 1 September 1921). The acquaintance continued on the other side of the Atlantic: McIlwraith's parents attended public lectures by Rivers and Haddon in New York and went up to chat with them afterwards. In a letter written after McIlwraith had returned to Canada, Fanny Haddon asks him to thank his mother for her letter from New York (TFMF, Fanny Haddon

---

76 T.F. McIlwraith to Charles Gabriel Seligman, 27 and 31 March 1921, Charles Gabriel Seligman, 20 January 1927, Seligman, Charles Gabriel, Manuscript Collection (MS 364), RAI, London.

to T.F. McIlwraith, 10 June 1922). There was even the occasional item of interest to his teachers in McIlwraith's mail from home. Thus, Haddon was pleased to be given a copy of the December 1920 issue of *World's Work* because it featured an article on the Black leader Moses Garvey (TFMF, T.F. McIlwraith to family, 8 February 1921).

Haddon's parental role came powerfully to the fore after the death of Mary Stevens in 1923 and T.F.'s sudden engagement to Beulah Knox the year after. In a letter written several months after his mother's death, McIlwraith veers between delight at Haddon's impending visit to Toronto, apologies for "no longer [having] any home" in which to receive him, an account of his efforts to keep up with the five-hundred-thousand-word report on his Bella Coola fieldwork, and the daily "selling, storing, giving away, and burning [of] the accumulated articles of fifty years" that came with closing his parents' home on Duke Street in Hamilton after his father had joined his sister Jean in her recently purchased house in Burlington (HCUL, T.F. McIlwraith to A.C. Haddon, 14 May 1924). McIlwraith was close enough to Fanny Haddon to confide the "nightmare" of his mother's decline in a personal letter free of the professional discussion with which he attempts to balance, not always successfully, this private news in writing to Haddon (HCUL, T.F. McIlwraith to Fanny Haddon, 9 December 1923).

When he had happier events to report, he supplemented an official letter to Haddon with a separate sheet. He announced his engagement to Beulah Knox in this way, an event confirming that he had abandoned the wariness he displayed towards women following his military service. Through the Childs, he had met his future wife several times before, but they became close at the Childs' cottage in August 1924, perhaps spurred on by unhappiness following both of their mothers' recent deaths. It would be good to have Beulah's letters to Carlos and Neilson describing the event from her perspective, but in their absence there are snapshots of T.F., Beulah, and Philip Child as matchmaker, all glowing with happy relief. Haddon had met Beulah, not yet engaged to T.F., in Hamilton when he attended the BAAS conference in Toronto. McIlwraith took his mentor to Burlington to meet his father, but the Childs also appear to have hosted Haddon at their house on Hess Street. McIlwraith justified his choice in a wife to Haddon as one might to a parent. He professed his belief "that a man should marry," sketched her family background as "an American, though her father came from Scotland" and "of old England stock on her mother's side," and commended her for being "of the type who could fit in anywhere, and takes a very great interest in my work" (HCUL, T.F. McIlwraith to A.C. Haddon, 7 November 1924). She was willing to accompany him to a university post no matter how far away from North America. In this, his justification for offering marriage to Beulah resembles Harold Phillips's wish to have a loyal companion in the Transvaal, although here any similarity between the two men ends abruptly. The Haddons were as quick with congratulations on the announcement of the engagement as they had been with their condolences on his mother's death, and Haddon approved of his choice especially because Beulah promised to " 'fit in' – which is a most desirable qualification in a wife – as I know full well."[77] Soon enough, McIlwraith's new wife had opportunities to demonstrate that she "fit in," by accompanying her husband first to the Second Conference of the Institute of Pacific Relations in Honolulu in 1927 and then the following year on a trip to Britain, where McIlwraith spent two busy months working with Haddon and lecturing about his work in Bella Coola. After Honolulu, Beulah even published a paper on "Some Aspects of Race Contacts in the South Pacific," and John Barker has acknowledged her assistance as "an able and enthusiastic co-researcher at the early stages" of his work on McIlwraith's career and publications (Barker, "T.F. McIlwraith and Anthropology" 252). She easily "fit in" socially as well: the couple made the rounds among McIlwraith's colleagues in Cambridge and Oxford, including the Seligmans. There were particularly friendly times with the Haddons who, among other get-togethers, met them in London for a day at the zoo (HCUL, T.F. McIlwraith to A.C. Haddon, 15 August 1928). The easy rapport between teacher and former student continued in their follow-up correspondence. To Haddon's pretended envy,[78] one of McIlwraith's talks attracted the attention of *Punch*: "We don't see anything extraordinary in Professor G.F. [sic] McIlwraith's description of the supernatural influence which occasionally impels him, as a member of a secret society of Indians in British Columbia, to rush about biting people. Professors are often like that."[79]

McIlwraith even confided in Haddon that there was a previous attraction to Iris Peers Scott, a young schoolteacher in Bella Coola, and he talked about "the considerable worry" the episode had caused him (HCUL, T.F. McIlwraith to A.C. Haddon, 7 November 1924). "[N]eedless to say," Haddon wrote after his visit to Hamilton, "it was a great delight to me to see you again and to have your confidences." He signed the letter with "Best of luck my dear boy."[80] By contrast, McIlwraith's extant letters to his family depict the schoolteacher as never more than "a kid from Victoria, who is rather lost in Bella Coola" (*HBCI*, T.F. McIlwraith to father, 11 November 1923, 93) or praise her, as if she were one of his army friends or his sister, as "one of the best sports I have ever met" (*HBCI*, T.F. McIlwraith to father, 19 December 1923, 109). She was enjoyable company with whom to attend dances and "play ... crib till all hours of the morning," followed by searching the kitchen for food "at 2.00 a.m." (*HBCI*, T.F. McIlwraith to father, 1 January 1924, 116). Against the background of his confession to Haddon, however, a walk home from a bridge party on a moonlit

77 A.C. Haddon to T.F. McIlwraith, 20 November 1924, TFMF, UTA, B1979-0011/002 (01).

78 A.C. Haddon to T.F. McIlwraith, 20 September 1928, TFMF, UTA, B1979-0011/002(01).

79 "Charivaria," *Punch*, issue 4581, 19 September 1928, 309.

80 A.C. Haddon to T.F. McIlwraith, 15 August 1924, TFMF, UTA, B1979-0011/002(01).

night, "with the glaciers covered with new snow, ... the dark waters rushing underneath, and the inky black trees on the lower slopes," sounds like the perfect backdrop for romance, despite his effort to redirect the reader's attention to "a sea of mud through which I had to pilot the school teacher" (*HBCI*, T.F. McIlwraith to father, 27 November 1923, 98). With this context in mind, his announcement in early January 1924 that Miss Scott had "left for good last boat" sounds forlorn rather than a mere statement of fact (*HBCI*, T.F. McIlwraith to father, 1 January 1924, 116). Because the episode continued to "worry" him well into the summer, when he confided in Haddon, it may be assumed that possible efforts to pursue the relationship came to nothing. He had been unhappy enough to tell Haddon, in the same letter in which he announced his engagement to Beulah, that he "was thankful to the B.A.A.S. for giving me a new interest in my work and finally clearing my mind, which I had all along realized was desirable" (HCUL, T.F. McIlwraith to A.C. Haddon, 7 November 1924). A mere month later, he sent a triumphant cable to Beulah in Ohio, indicating that – with Haddon's dedicated assistance towards finding him academic employment – the path was now clear to marriage: "Toronto has arrived. You know what that means."[81]

By way of conclusion, the following chapter steps back by a couple of years for an account of McIlwraith's fieldwork in Bella Coola, his mother's death, and the reception of his published scholarship by his peers and, more importantly, by the Nuxalk who hosted his research.

---

81 T.F. McIlwraith to Beulah Knox, 16 December 1924, TFMF, UTA, B1979-0011/001 (8).

Bella Coola and After

Death of Mary Stevens

As McIlwraith would soon realize, it was not so much the difficulty of securing a permanent post that caused his certainties to unravel but his mother's death from cancer. T.F., who arrived in Bella Coola on 9 March 1922 and stayed until August, was unable to return to the West Coast for the second phase of his research until September 1923 because of Mary Stevens's illness during the summer and her death the previous month. As a result, his fieldwork was not concluded until March 1924.

In June 1921, the arrival of a telegram from Cambridge with the message "Passed First" had spurred his parents into a practised relay of spreading the news among family and friends, and the collaboration his mother describes is all the more affecting because Mr. McIlwraith would soon be forced to take on the role of chief correspondent previously occupied by his wife:

> Father was as excited as I (but he did not shed tears) and carried the telegram downtown where he went to send a return cable. I am sure he showed the telegram to many, & of course we called up particular friends to let them rejoice with us. Father & Mr. Child exchanged mutual congratulations over their sons' success ... Father telegraphed Aunt Nellie and wrote Dorothy as we knew that with the office closed she would not receive a message until Monday morning. I wrote Marjorie at once also ... Auntie Jean will write fully I am sure. (TFMP, Mary Stevens to T.F. McIlwraith, 12 June 1921)

Despite the animation he displays in this scene, letter-writing was an awkward business for Mr. McIlwraith, and as is apparent in his son's wartime correspondence, he could be persuaded to add a comment or two to his wife's letters only at their children's repeated insistence that they enjoyed his news "about the little things, work in the garden and so on" (CWM, T.F. McIlwraith to family, 5

May 1918). When his father had to replace his wife, Tom appreciated the effort to produce "long newsy letters" to send to Bella Coola all the more because he realized "how much [his father] dislike[d]" writing them.[1] From Cambridge, Tom had written to his mother, who was already ailing at the time: "You must look after yourself little mother because if anything should happen to you it would be just the end of all things" (TFMF, T.F. McIlwraith to his mother, 15 February 1920). When she died, it did feel like the end of all things. The great gap left by Mary Stevens's death had her husband and son "so thankful to have each other and Dorothy" that they moved as quickly as they could to shore up the bond among them (T.F. McIlwraith to father, 18 October 1923).

It was all the more important to nurture these relationships because they had begun to shift quite disastrously even during Mary Stevens's illness. Mr. McIlwraith, whose reticence his son described as "obviously apparently indifferent" with "never a word about anything I feel to do or anything" when T.F. went off to war (CWM, T.F. McIlwraith to Dorothy McIlwraith, 10 November 1917), was unable to cope with the emotional strain of his wife's suffering and abdicated the role of head of the household to Tom and Dorothy. T.F. explained to Fanny Haddon that it was for the son to accompany his mother to a specialist in New York and for him to "[break] the news ... to father" that her cancer was incurable. In a detailed account of this "nightmare" to Haddon's wife, he characterized his "father and ... sister" as "wonderfully brave, and [able to stand] the strain better than I thought possible" (HCUL, T.F. McIlwraith to Fanny Haddon, 9 December 1923). Yet some details were too private to share even with Fanny Haddon, and in his memoir McIlwraith describes family tensions that must have been severe enough to stay with him until the end of his life: "Dorothy was able to take [a] long leave from her job and I was able to defer going back to Bella Coola ... Father seemed to have lost touch; Dorothy and I were the ones who spent hours at the hospital, phoning father when mother seemed well enough to see anyone" ("Genealogy"). To make matters worse, Mr. McIlwraith was plunged into a "feud" with Marjorie, who, as indicated earlier, had always occupied a difficult place in the family. The reasons for their quarrel are not explained but may be connected to her refusal "to come [home], much to everyone's irritation," for her share of the vigil by her mother's bedside, and bad feelings may have been exacerbated by her failure to take her father's financial advice and, as a result, her losing all of her money. Tom struggled to keep some members of the family together and others apart because it was for him to ensure that "father and Marjorie did not meet" ("Genealogy"). The son's

---

1 T.F. McIlwraith to his father, 18 October 1923. The letter, also cited below, is partly reproduced in *HBCI*, 86–7. My thanks to John Barker for providing me with a copy of the complete letter and also with copies of the letters dated 6 January 1924, 26 February 1924, and 18 October 1923 cited below.

role had become parental, and McIlwraith's own letters from Bella Coola during the second season of his fieldwork were written in the knowledge that his badly shaken father needed steadfast support to carry on.

Repairing the Family

McIlwraith wrote faithfully to his father every week, and the regular flow of mail was interrupted only when he missed the mail boat. If his letters to his family after demobilization and from Cambridge seek to master uncertainty by systematically setting out his plans, his correspondence from Bella Coola deals with his troubles more obliquely, by keeping largely silent about the crises themselves, let alone talking about his own sadness. The most he admits to is not having any "pep" (*HBCI*, T.F. McIlwraith to father, 29 January 1924, 132). Commiseration with his father over having to leave the family home and moving in with his sister is hinted at rather than articulated: "Of course I knew that Aunt Jean would be doing everything possible for you, and it makes me feel a lot better to know that you are fairly comfortable but – well I know dad, dear."[2] He does not give vent to his own grief when his father begins to talk about selling the family home, admitting that he has "been deliberately trying not to think about it" and asking merely that his father wait "till I get back before doing anything, don't you agree?"[3] The subject of Mary Stevens's death is almost completely avoided, except for a note on New Year's Eve when he writes: "whatever may come it can be nothing as terrible as the last year. But there is nothing to be said about that" (*HBCI*, T.F. McIlwraith to father, 1 January 1924, 114). He tries to cheer his father up with congratulations on having the new "Murray St. School" named after him and on his successful re-election to the Board of Education.[4] To strengthen the weakened connections among the immediate family, he continues the tradition of reporting any familiar names or faces from Hamilton and the Eastern Townships he comes across. He describes a photo of his mother's brother Sidney and his wife Hattie that he discovers hanging on the wall in a Bella Coola home (*HBCI*, T.F. McIlwraith to father, 18 October 1923, 81), and relates a conversation with "the school-teacher next door, a most respectable fish who was born in Guelph and knows the name Goldie" (*HBCI*, T.F. McIlwraith to father, 6 February 1924, 134). There is also a reference to Aunt Jean's collaborator, the composer J.E.P. Aldous, and the complicated tale of a musician from Ocean Falls, in town to teach the local band. He turns out to be a Cockney with an adventurous international life who at one time conducted the Bowmanville band "when it played in Hamilton" (*HBCI*, T.F. McIlwraith to father, 6 February 1924, 134).

---

2 T.F. McIlwraith to father, 6 January 1924. The letter is partly reproduced in *HBCI*, 116–20.
3 T.F. McIlwraith to father, 26 February 1924. The letter is partly reproduced in *HBCI*, 137.
4 T.F. McIlwraith to father, 18 October 1923. The letter is partly reproduced in *HBCI*, 86–7.

T.F.'s most consoling letters direct his father's attention to the outdoors in descriptions that are anchored in childhood recollections: paper chases at Highfield or picnics on Twelve Mile Creek. Thus, he composes a long account of "going after bear at Kwatna" with two Norwegians and an American hunter. He begins with a lavish version of one of his set pieces, the frantic organization of a sudden departure, in this case involving "a hunter's license" obtained at short notice from the local police as well as the "borrowed plumage" of guns, blankets, and other equipment (*HBCI*, T.F. McIlwraith to father, 6 October 1923, 78). Various comical adventures, all evoked with suspenseful drama, occupy the narrative, as well as reminiscences of his "army days" (85) when the whisky flowed as freely as it does on this occasion. At the heart of the letter are several hours spent in surveying the river from "the river bank, a place where a huge tree had fallen down so that its roots rose to a height of about 20 ft. from the water, and from which I had a good view both up and down" (82). To a literary mind, it is difficult not to see the deracinated tree as the disruption Mary Stevens's death had brought to her son's life, and his contemplative perch on it as a moment of healing. The plan was to shoot a bear, but when none showed up, McIlwraith – who shortly after arriving for his first season at Bella Coola had requested that his parents send him a pocket guide to western birds – slipped into his family's ornithological habits. Earlier, on his way to his prospect point, he had been treated to "what I had never met before, a ruffed grouse with its ruff all preened up parading before a couple of hens" (80). From his seat, he observes eagles, ravens, ducks, and geese either "established near at hand" or drifting by on the river. Their rhythmic movement, "entirely ignorant of my presence," creates moments of restorative peace:

> After a time three mallards drifted downstream within 20 feet of where I was sitting. Three seemed to be a popular number and soon three mergansers did the same, feeding as they went ... A little later and the geese, Canada, went by, first three, then eight, and finally ten. All fine plump birds, some swimming lazily downstream, and occasionally diving for food, others waddling along the bank and getting something from among the stones ... It began to get dark and a mist rose from the water. (83)

Because the McIlwraiths were so reluctant to express their feelings, even items requested and forwarded became an act of pulling the family closer. Objects were enhanced by their emotional significance. When he was away from them, his family always sent anything McIlwraith needed or asked for, and his father continued the tradition after his wife's death. His son sometimes made a request that he thought would keep his father enjoyably busy, knowing him to have "the time of his life, building things with odds and ends of material" (CWM, T.F. McIlwraith to Dorothy McIlwraith, 27 January 1918). Writing from Cambridge, T.F. had suggested a custom-made filing cabinet for the slips on which he recorded his research, and his father built one and sent the bulky package to Britain, along with blank slips cut to specifications. Gifts mailed to Bella Coola after the "terrible" summer contained ample supplies of Gold Flake cigarettes; candy and slippers for Christmas; Christmas cards to distribute among his friends in Bella Coola; and copies of *The Times* (presumably the Hamilton *Times*) and *World's Work*. Once his father had moved to Burlington, there was also a steady supply of socks knitted or repaired by Aunt Jean. When Tom was "negotiating for some Indian bracelets" and he had to "produce the equivalent in metal" to purchase them, Mr. McIlwraith was asked to obtain "a $20.00 gold piece – or two tens – or four fives" (*HBCI*, T.F. McIlwraith to father, 27 November 1923, 99). One of the bracelets went to Dorothy, who also kept a small totem pole on her desk in New York that she either purchased herself when she visited her brother in the summer of 1922 or received as a gift from him.

New Networks and Learning to Understand Them

Describing the beauty of the Pacific Northwest helped to tether McIlwraith to previous periods of contentment in his life. So did recollections of the army and Cambridge, but these reference points became quickly transformed by his new environment. If his trench coat, which was coming apart at the seams, hardly ever dried out in the torrential rains and his army boots had to be patched up by "a decent individual with a last and nails" (*HBCI*, T.F. McIlwraith to family, 28 April 1822), then both his experience of the war and his scholarly training were challenged by his interviews with the Nuxalk. Shortly after his arrival in Bella Coola, one of his hosts suggested that the "angels at Mons" believed to have assisted the British army were "due to siut power" (*HBCI*, T.F. McIlwraith to W.H.R. Rivers, [21?] March 1921, 34).[5] When McIlwraith investigated the concept of land ownership, some wanted to know "how it had been possible ... for the allies ... to annex territory from Germany" because it was "unthinkable" to the Nuxalk to seize land (*BCI* 1: 132–3). The responses, as rendered in *The Bella Coola Indians*, are filtered through McIlwraith's academically impersonal language, but their assertive tone nevertheless anticipates the Resolutions Adopted by the Indian Members at the North American Indian Today conference in Toronto in 1939. Organized by McIlwraith and C.T. Loram from Yale, the meeting began three days after a new war with Germany had been declared:

> [W]e Indians appreciate having been invited to take part in the Conference and by way of returning the compliment we wish to assure the Conference that you, our white brothers, will be invited to participate in any conference that we Indians may

---

5 See Clarke. The "Bella Coola-English Vocabulary" in *BCI*, vol. 2, 611, provides a detailed entry for "siut," with the meaning of "[a]ny supernatural being" at the top.

call in the future for the purpose of finding solutions to the white man's dilemma
in a social and economic order that has, during the past decade, gone on the rocks.
(Loram and McIlwraith 349)

In his review of the conference proceedings, the anthropologist A.G. Bailey –
who had written his thesis on the conflict between European and Eastern Algonkian cultures under the supervision of McIlwraith and Harold Innis (see
Bailey, *Conflict*) – reads this statement as "invoking an ancient trait of reciprocal courtesy" (review of *The North American Indian*). It is also possible to read
it as an expression of irony, all the more blistering because it is so polite. In
laying out his qualifications to Sapir in his first letters to him from Cambridge,
McIlwraith had assured him that he "would like nothing better than ... to do
field work among the dying races."[6] In the course of his research in Bella Coola,
he quickly learned that the Nuxalk and their culture were very much alive.

Decisive for McIlwraith's evolving understanding of anthropology were
the challenges he encountered as soon as he tried to apply Rivers's genealogical method to his research. Rivers had warned investigators of the "danger of
falling into error if one merely attempts to obtain the equivalents of our own
terms," but his recommendations towards avoiding this problem by "ask[ing
his] informant the terms which he would apply to the different members of his
pedigree" (Rivers, "The Genealogical Method" 3) did not adequately prepare
McIlwraith for the complications. He complained that his collaborators had
forgotten pedigrees and kinship terms, and he was confused by the "multiplicity
of names" owned by each individual (*HBCI*, T.F. McIlwraith to A.C. Haddon,
14 March 1922, 32). As Barker warns, the forgetfulness may in reality have been
a reluctance to share information about their families with someone the Nuxalk did not know (*HBCI*, Introduction, 25). McIlwraith did observe that "the
people know with what families they are connected" (*HBCI*, T.F. McIlwraith to
A.C. Haddon, 14 March 1922, 32) and that villages were "virtually endogamous
through the desire of the people to prevent their 'story' from going to strangers"
(*HBCI*, T.F. McIlwraith to Edward Sapir, 2 April 1922, 39). In the early stages
of his research, the vagueness of their responses was evidence to McIlwraith
that the people had lost touch with their cultural roots (*HBCI*, Introduction,
20), but when information was finally forthcoming, he realized he had come to
a community that knew to protect its names, stories, and ceremonies not only
from outsiders but also, where necessary, from each other. Rivalries over ownership erupted when he attempted to cross-check his information with several
individuals. He lived through a particularly uncomfortable day when he was

---

6 T.F. McIlwraith to Edward Sapir, 9 August 1921, CMH, Archives, Ethnology Documents,
   Edward Sapir (I-A-236M), Correspondence, Folder: "McIlwraith, T.F. (1921–1923)," Box 628,
   Folder 23.

wrongly suspected of having reported to the Indian agent that one of the men he had interviewed "was no chief" as he had claimed, and "that [this man] was stirring up trouble against the government ... Some of them suspected me as the one who had been prying into ancient history, and I have been busy vindicating myself and trying to turn their suspicions elsewhere" (*HBCI*, T.F. McIlwraith to family, 12 May 1922, 47). At times, his presence appears to have stirred up hostilities of long standing and occasionally it may have made them worse. Repeatedly, he found himself in situations that were meant to be sociable such as a dance but that "featured four cliques, including several that would not speak to one another" (*HBCI*, T.F. McIlwraith to father, 20 November 1923, 97).

In their edition of McIlwraith's letters from Bella Coola, Barker and Cole underscore that fieldwork "at once engenders personal transformation and provides insight into alien cultural ways" (Introduction, 3). McIlwraith never spells out parallels between situations he observed in Bella Coola and any that prevailed in his own family, but by the time he observed the "cliques ... that would not speak to one another," he had endured family discord of his own. The deaths in quick succession of Rivers, his mother, and his Nuxalk friend Captain Schooner, "a fine old man, a true gentleman" (HCUL, T.F. McIlwraith to A.C. Haddon, 13 October 1923), repeatedly forced him to realign his own genealogies around the gaping holes they left. McIlwraith's romance with Iris Peers Scott and his role, performed with hectic zest, of go-between for his friends Andy Christensen and Dorothy Clayton as they prepared for their wedding against resistance from their families, may be seen as part of these efforts. The friendships that developed through his interviews with the Nuxalk gave him additional stability. It was consoling that "they all kept asking for me" (*HBCI*, T.F. McIlwraith to father, 26 September 1923, 76) when he was away and that they were "really sorry to see me go" when he left for good (*HBCI*, T.F. McIlwraith to A.C. Haddon, 16 March 1924, 145). The ceremonies he observed in Bella Coola soon after his arrival offered haunting and elaborate models of how grief could be expressed in the grand style, and he reached for a comparison with playing of "pipes over a grave" to convey the dignity of the scene (*HBCI*, T.F. McIlwraith to family, 30 June 1922, 56). In the same letter that tells his family about Rivers's death, he describes burial ceremonies for Jessie King, "the chief's wife," who was "a daughter of old Schooner, one of the men I am always working with." The detached observational style he had been taught in his studies, and that has him write even in a personal letter that "The songs were of the early history of the people, whence they came and whither the dead would return," is undermined by the shock of mortality when he listens to the "cry sings" featuring a "choir of six old men, who beat a time on the floor and led the singing, while the women sang." He admits that "[i]t was the most mournful creepy thing I ever heard." (*HBCI*, T.F. McIlwraith to family, 30 June 1922, 55). The section entitled "Death" in *The Bella Coola Indians* draws on his experience of Jessie King's funeral, and his full account was possible only because the participants agreed to help him recapitulate their contributions to it. In a note he clarifies: "It was impossible to record these speeches verbatim at the time of their delivery. The writer was able to make notes, which were amplified by each speaker later telling him what he had said" (*BCI*, 1: 449n19).

Most impressively, as a result of his adoption by Captain Schooner, McIlwraith was appointed "prompter" in the winter ceremonials during his second research season and so gained an entirely new understanding of his duty to "family." Participation in the dances absorbed so much of his energy that there was little left for his regular interviews, he complained, but since he now had "an official name and position in the community, ... it would be disastrous should I stay away" (*HBCI*, T.F. McIlwraith to Harlan I. Smith, 7 January 1924, 121–2). To lose the regard of the community would indeed have been disastrous, both to their respect for him and to his self-esteem. A month before he left Bella Coola for good, he wrote to his father:

> I have been given rather a funny job. Each dancer has his song which is made by the choir only a few hours before his dance, and which is bellowed forth line by line while the people sing. These songs are repeated night after night and it is a brute for the man whose duty it is to remember these to do so, often thirty or forty songs. In the old days there would have been three or four of these men sitting by the announcer to whisper to him what he should call forth: now there is only one man who combines in himself the duties of announcer and remembrancer. This individual got the happy inspiration of having me write down the words and be ready to whisper them to him whenever he poked me in the ribs. So I am an established member of the choir, and when I walk in the evening go straight up to the head of the hall and greet the choir with, "Hello, fellow-singers." Some of the Indians of course do not like it a bit, but the combined announcer-remembrancer made a speech to them saying how much I was helping him, and they could do nothing. There is really no doubt but that the dances are going off in better shape through my help, but it makes me chuckle inwardly when I find myself bellowing out, "No, watch your step, there are six lines to the assikotl," or whatever the particular thing may be (*HBCI*, T.F. McIlwraith to father, 1 January 1924, 115).

Barker and Cole suspect that with his tendency, shown especially in the descriptions of the winter ceremonials, to style himself "the White man ... who is elevated by the Natives to be their leader," McIlwraith "was not able to escape the underlying assumptions of his own class and culture" (*HBCI*, Introduction, 23). It is true that the description above is contradictory. It demonstrates both the respect and the resistance he encountered among the Nuxalk, and it also contains more than a hint of white man's arrogance. Compared to the attitudes expressed in his previous correspondence, however, especially the sense of imperial entitlement conveyed by his wartime letters, McIlwraith's views did change quite substantially in Bella Coola. If the quotation above displays an assumption of superiority ("there is really no doubt but that the dances are going off in better shape through my help"), it is also possible that, for the benefit of his correspondents, he was playing a role that he had already begun to outgrow. The self-irony in his earlier letters, often conveyed in small dramas in which he makes a fool of himself for the entertainment of his family, makes it doubtful that he felt "embarrassment ... towards his very public participation in Nuxalk ceremonial," as claimed by a reviewer of the field letters (Thom 117).What is new in these letters is his willingness to be conspicuous and still remain respectful towards the people who are the cause of the awkward feeling. "His field descriptions are among the most humane I have read," Douglas Cole commented well before his and Barker's edition of the letters was finally published.[7] In his landmark study *Captured Heritage*, Cole underscored McIlwraith's reluctance to collect Native artefacts (279) that had him write to the curator of the Museum of Archaeology and Anthropology in Cambridge: "I have been able to obtain very few specimens [of Native artefacts], partly, it is true, through my unwillingness to take away many of the few that remain; practically no new ceremonial objects are being made, and any losses curtail the already too much curtailed sacred life to that extent" (*HBCI*, T.F. McIlwraith to Louis C.G. Clarke, 16 January 1924, 129).

Finding the appropriate language to express the transformation of his thinking or to apply the insight to a variety of contexts presented a difficulty of its own, and there were few contemporary models by which McIlwraith was able to orient himself. Inconsistencies in his language usage are the result. By 1927, he avoided the word "savage" that still populated his notes for the lectures he gave to the naval officers in Cambridge, and he now preferred "native."[8] By contrast, prejudicial terms applied to Blacks and the Chinese linger in the letters from Bella Coola (*HBCI*, Introduction, 27). Similarly, in letters written from the United Kingdom in 1934 he tells his young daughter that she need not become a "pickaninny" now that he is turning down a post in South Africa but that Uncle Carlos, who is moving to Shanghai, is becoming a "Chinaman." At the same time, the antisemitic sentiment in some of his wartime writing is replaced by dismay at the Jewish refugees in London who must dispose of valued possessions in order to survive (TFMP, T.F. McIlwraith to Mary Agnes McIlwraith, 20 August 1934; T.F. McIlwraith to Beulah McIlwraith, 8 August 1934).

---

7 Douglas Cole to Allan Smith, 20 May 1986, F-35-1-1-38, Correspondence, 2/2 1986, DCF, SFU Archives.

8 T.F. McIlwraith, "Some Missionary Problems From an Anthropological Viewpoint," Second Conference, Institute of Pacific Relations, Honolulu, 1927, Data Paper, Mimeo, TFMF, UTA, B1979-011, Series XIII, Box 10, Folder 16.

A few years later, as mentioned earlier, he joined Haddon in vocal opposition to the Nazis' racial politics.

By the summer of 1922, McIlwraith had begun to doubt the racist stereotypes that had been part of his scholarly training. Shortly after his arrival in Bella Coola, he used one of the standard tropes of Colonial Office reports when he writes, "[l]uckily the Indian is like a child in his willingness to swallow taffy and be pacified" (*HBCI*, T.F. McIlwraith to family, 26 March 1922, 37), but he began to question this and other clichés a few months later: "[w]hatever the traditional, unemotional Indians may be, these are the reverse" (*HBCI*, T.F. McIlwraith to family, 24 June 1922, 54). He gained an understanding of white men's culpability with the "conviction that our treatment of the Indians is a disgrace to Canada … It is nothing less than a crime that conditions are not improved" (T.F. McIlwraith to William A. Newcombe, 22 August 1922).[9] By late 1923, he had become convinced that "[i]n hospitality and kindness the Bella Coolas could teach many white people valuable lessons" (HCUL, T.F. McIlwraith to Fanny Haddon, 9 December 1923). The same letter that talks about Rivers's death and Jessie King's funeral takes a critical look at the culture that has so far defined McIlwraith and expresses "a profound disgust for our so-called civilization which is so intolerant that it tries to stop such rites" (*HBCI*, T.F. McIlwraith to family, 30 June 1922, 56). His perspective on religious practices among the Nuxalk became more complex. When the observance of the Sabbath stopped several of his informants from talking to him on a Sunday (*HBCI*, T.F. McIlwraith to Edward Sapir, 2 April 1922, 39), he was annoyed but had to accept it. Though he "miss[ed] most of his teeth … and [was] practically deaf" (Barker, Introduction, *BCI* 1: xv), his ideal source of information was the man who was to adopt him, Captain "Schooner … an old fellow about 80, a devout pagan, scorning the missionaries and regretting the changes and loss to the culture of the Bella Coola" (*HBCI*, T. F. McIlwraith to family, 17 June 1922, 52). Yet McIlwraith also became captivated by Joshua Moody's interpretation of Christian theology, his reading of "theophany," the parallel he drew between a murder in his community and the burning of Ridley and Latimer (*HBCI*, T.F. McIlwraith to family, 26 March 1922, 37), and his cool analysis of the various Christian faiths in action: "The Methodists say that the English Church is bad, the English Church that the Presbyterians are bad, they all say that the Catholics are bad, and the Jews likewise say all are bad, henceforth I shall have nothing to do with any of them but shall stick to the Bible alone" (*HBCI*, T.F. McIlwraith to father, 20 November 1923, 96).[10] Moody's appropriation of some

---

9   T.F. McIlwraith to William A. Newcombe, 22 August 1922, BC Archives, MS-1077, Newcombe family papers, Box 4, Folder 94, Reel A01748.

10 The episode parallels another related by the missionary Arthur Brigg about the Xhosa, qtd. in Nanni 174.

T.F. McIlwraith with Bella Coola Nuxalk in ceremonial regalia, Bella Coola River Valley, British Columbia, 1922. Barker and Cole identify the individuals in the photo, from left to right, as T.F. McIlwraith, Willie Mack and son, (possibly) Clayton Mack, Joshua Mack, Mary Mack, and Eliza Moody on the Bella Coola reserve, 25 June 1922 (72). Harlan I. Smith, photographer, Canadian Museum of History, 56872.

of the theological concepts is not so much erased as highlighted by his mispronunciations ("chèobany," "litley and lattimer"). For one thing, these alternative pronunciations force a discussion between him and his interviewer about the meaning of words and ideas. Their exchange would otherwise not have been half so thorough.

Teaching Missionaries, Instructing the Public

He enjoyed his and his wife's company when he first arrived, but McIlwraith soon began to dislike the local missionary, the Reverend Samuel Spencer Peat. Peat was a recently arrived Englishman whose reluctance to learn Chinook suggested to T.F. that he was "out of place" in Bella Coola (*HBCI*, T.F. McIlwraith to family, 26 March 1922, 36). At Cambridge McIlwraith had been taught that anthropology, in imparting an understanding of other cultures to Colonial Office personnel and missionaries, could serve as a valuable diplomatic tool in interviewing, governing, and converting Native people (Haddon, "A Plea for a Bureau of Ethnology" 574). Bella Coola taught him to rethink the question of the relationship between missionaries and anthropology in ways that affected his future university teaching. In a voluntary commitment that continued until 1962, he began to lecture at the Canadian School of Missions (CSM) shortly after his appointment at the University of Toronto. Important contacts emerged from his work at the CSM, such as his friendship with Jim and Mary Endicott, missionaries in China. Robert A. Wright has criticized McIlwraith's work for the CSM, but there is little in McIlwraith's field letters to prove an "unsympathetic attitude toward those whose societies had been ravaged by foreign contact" or to substantiate a failure to "communicate ... an appreciation for the integrity of other cultures to his students" (163).[11] Nor does the archival evidence confirm Wright's claim that McIlwraith worked in "isolation from the cultural intercourse" of his profession (163). On the contrary, primed by the habits of his own family, he continued the professional and intellectual networking to which Cambridge had introduced him. Wright relies on Barker's article about McIlwraith's career at the University of Toronto, published four years before Wright's book, which concludes that the anthropologist "failed to make his own intellectual mark amongst his peers or to shape the work of his students" (Barker, "T.F. McIlwraith and Anthropology" 254). Neither the 1992 edition of *The Bella Coola Indians* nor *At Home with the Bella Coola Indians*, in both of which Barker offers appreciative assessments of McIlwraith's achievements, had appeared in 1991, when Wright's book was published. Judging by McIlwraith's insistent criticism of the missionary in Bella Coola, an equally likely reading is that he saw his CSM course as an opportunity to prevent the insensitivity he saw embodied in individuals like the Reverend Peat (*HBCI*, T.F. McIlwraith to A.C. Haddon, 29 August 1922, 69). In 1927, his paper on "Some Missionary Problems from an Anthropological Viewpoint," delivered at the Second Conference of the Institute of Pacific Relations in Honolulu, outlined the reasons why "[t]he missionary must study the culture of the people among whom he is working." McIlwraith held missionaries responsible for effective communication with Native people because the latter will shun "one

---

11   Wright cites Barker, "T.F. McIlwraith and Anthropology," but misrepresents what is being said
     there. Barker writes that "The best passages of McIlwraith's *The Bella Coola Indians* (1948)
     show an exceptional sensitivity for and alertness to the intricate interconnections among
     cultural elements. Presumably he communicated some of his appreciation for the integrity of
     other cultures to his students" (260).

who assumes a supercilious attitude of disinterested superiority," and he listed
the disastrous consequences of failing to create a situation of "mutual respect."[12]

The realization that Native people's points of view had to be considered of
equal importance to the researcher's carried over into McIlwraith's teaching.
McIlwraith used this approach in his supervisions, such as A.G. Bailey's doctoral
research on the contact between Europeans and Algonquians (Trigger 5–6) and
Isabel Brown Crook's MA work. It is, however, also evident in his involvement
in various public projects, including art and pageantry, and in his teaching of
the public at large. In making his expertise available to a non-academic audience, McIlwraith followed the example of Haddon, who emphasized "public
lectures and community education work for the London County Council and
the Horniman Museum" as part of his mandate (Herle and Rouse, Introduction, 22). McIlwraith's professional correspondence contains numerous exchanges that are tangential to his discipline, and his responses are mostly brief
and polite. His response became lengthy and his tone stern, however, when he
suspected disrespect towards Indigenous people. In 1938, the journalist and
author Mabel Burkholder, at work on a popular history of Hamilton, requested
information on the region's Native population. In answer to her question "Were
the Neutrals very low in the scale of intelligence?," McIlwraith wrote angrily:

> The Neutrals were not "low in the scale of intelligence." As a matter of fact, it is
> definitely known to-day that there is no such thing as varying scales of intelligence
> throughout the world. All varieties of man are Homo sapiens with nothing to sug-
> gest any differences in intelligence between them.[13]

He hotly objected to Burkholder's use of "cruel," "savage," "grunting," "squaw,"
and to her emphasis on the practice of scalping. Not surprisingly, no further
letters from her are included in his files. When the post-war revival of the
Brébeuf pageant at Martyrs' Shrine in Midland, Ontario was being discussed
in 1946, some of the planning committee's ideas worried him enough to write
to the chairman, Sir Ellsworth Flavelle, asking him to consider the consequences of portraying "the Iroquois as fiends of brutality." An Iroquois who
had "reached the rank of brigadier" in the Second World War had "recall[ed
to him] how badly he felt at school to read about the brutality of his ancestors," and McIlwraith warned that Native people in general would be equally

---

12   T.F. McIlwraith, "Some Missionary Problems from an Anthropological Viewpoint," Data
     Paper, Mimeo, TFMF, UTA, B1979-011, Series XIII, Box 10, folder 16.
13   Mabel Burkholder to T.F. McIlwraith, 4 March, 1938; T.F. McIlwraith to Mabel Burkholder,
     10 March 1938, TFMF, UTA, B1979-0011/001 (13). For information on Burkholder, see
     Canada's Early Women Writers, Simon Fraser University: http://digital.lib.sfu.ca/ceww-869
     /burkholder-mabel-grace.

offended. He underscored his support for Indigenous veterans when, the next year, he testified before the Special Joint Committee of the Senate and the House of Commons as its members were working toward amendments to the Indian Act (see Special Joint Committee). Besides, he added in his letter to Flavelle, seventeenth-century Europe under the Inquisition "was likewise a cruel region."[14] Although McIlwraith appears to have forgotten the prejudice he himself witnessed and shared in the Great War, all of this evidence contradicts Wright's conclusion that McIlwraith's "appraisal of the cultural dislocation that invariably accompanied the transplantation of religions was clinical and insensitive" (163).

Censorship and Publication

In his preface to *The Bella Coola Indians*, McIlwraith explains that publication of the book was delayed because there were "questions ... about its size and the suitability of detailed studies of social anthropology in a government publication." He also cites a lack of funds during economically troubled times for two such large volumes and insists that he did not want to carve up his research into "short articles" (*BCI* 1: xxxix). Because it was the most clearly formulated reason for the delay, reviewers of the 1948 edition responded most strongly to his reluctance to divide up the work, and they read it as proof of his professional integrity.[15] None of them seems to have considered a delay of twenty years particularly odd, probably because the Depression and the Second World War had seriously interfered with scholarly publishing in general and other books had also been put on hold.[16] Reviewers agreed that this was an "important" and "valuable," and even a "luxurious" and "monumental,"[17] publication that had been well worth waiting for. The work attracted attention beyond anthropology, and the *American Journal of Psychiatry* attested that "these 2 volumes can be read to advantage ... by workers in any field interested in human development and functioning" (Steer 879).

As a prominent academic with numerous public duties, McIlwraith appears to have thought it wise to exercise diplomacy to the point of vagueness in his preface, and it was not until the republication of *The Bella Coola Indians* in 1992 and John Barker's account of its publication history in his introduction that the details behind the delay of the book became more generally known. Barnett Richling's even more expansive discussion of the circumstances followed in 2005, as an example "of institutional constraints on the research and writing of Canada's first generation of professional anthropologists" (57). The delay was certainly

---

14 T.F. McIlwraith to Sir Ellsworth Flavelle, 9 January 1947, TFMF, UTA, B1979-0011/001 (17).
15 See, for example, the reviews by Barnett; Bott; Garfield.
16 Several chapters in *History of the Book in Canada*, vol. 3, address the problems in Canadian publishing during the Great Depression.
17 See reviews by Barnett; Bott; Garfield; Gunther.

not due to any procrastination on McIlwraith's part. After his return from Bella Coola, he rented a room in Hamilton so as to be able to divide his time between clearing out his family's home on Duke Street and "working as hard as may be at my report" (HCUL, T.F. McIlwraith to A.C. Haddon, 14 May 1924). Once he had moved to Yale, he wrote for up to "eleven hours a day," producing between "15000 or 20000 words a week" and completing the manuscript for the first volume by mid-February 1925 (HCUL, T.F. McIlwraith to A.C. Haddon, 1 and 15 February 1925). If he had still been in Cambridge while this marathon was in progress, Haddon and his wife would have been sure to prescribe another vacation. He began work as assistant professor at the University of Toronto later that year and, as he reported to Haddon, immediately became very busy with administration, university politics, and consulting with other departments that he expected to be supportive of anthropology, all in addition to museum work, teaching, supervisions, and his lectures at the CSM (HCUL, T.F. McIlwraith to A.C. Haddon, 2 February 1926). By February 1927, however, Sapir's successor, Diamond Jenness, thanked him for recently submitting the manuscript and congratulated him on "a splendid piece of ethnological work."

Nevertheless, Jenness cautioned immediately "that obscene or unpleasant matter must be ruled out absolutely"[18] because a government publication containing such material would be sure to be vetoed before it even reached the printer. It was not he who was "squeamish," he assured McIlwraith repeatedly, but the politicians who had to answer to their constituents, including "the most innocent" among them (TFMF, Diamond Jenness to T.F. McIlwraith, 3 February 1927). The implied precedent that had him issue these warnings was William Mechling's *Malecite Tales* (1914), specifically the story of "The Talking Vagina," which had slipped through the departmental censors, scandalized parliamentarians, and put them on unwelcome alert for anything issued in print by the Anthropological Division (Richling 59). Failure to render his work appropriately "innocuous" might result in censure not only of McIlwraith's report, Jenness was told after a "severe castigation" from his superiors, but "all anthropological publications might thereafter be banned." The norm for acceptable subject matter and language was variously said to be provided by "the most sensitive old maid," "a twelve-year-old school-girl," and "a child" (TFMF, Diamond Jenness to T.F. McIlwraith, 30 January 1929). Two examples of objectionable material cited by the printer that McIlwraith and Jenness had missed were some six pages on childbirth and repeated references to chamber pots and urine (TFMF, Diamond Jenness to T.F. McIlwraith, 27 February 1929). Looking back on the episode, McIlwraith later estimated that there were "no more than

---

18 Diamond Jenness to T.F. McIlwraith, 3 February 1927, TFMF, UTA, B1979-0011/002 (02). All subsequent quotations from the correspondence between Jenness and McIlwraith are from this file.

15 pages of Rabelaisian material" all told ("Genealogy"), but they were enough to delay publication until 1948.

This particular crisis, which had Jenness and McIlwraith exchange numerous letters, several very long, between January and early March 1929, occurred after they had already worked on revisions for two years. Some offensive passages were eliminated altogether and others were translated into Latin with the assistance of the classicist Gilbert Norwood at University College, "who enjoyed himself" doing the work, as McIlwraith reported in retrospect ("Genealogy"). The energy with which Jenness and McIlwraith, both very busy professionals, tackled the job was impressive, but solutions that had been approved by one government official were rejected by others higher up after the work had already been done. The strenuous efforts these two men undertook to extract logic where no logic could be expected in return were so futile that they are distressing to witness even now. As communication between the two became increasingly difficult, each fell back on analogy in order to make his specific difficulties understood. McIlwraith, up to his eyebrows in teaching, used the example of marking "a thousand examination papers" and having nothing to show for it (TFMF, T.F. McIlwraith to Diamond Jenness, 22 February 1929), while Jenness – who had been a gunner with the Canadian field artillery in the First World War – repeatedly pleaded that McIlwraith "think of a government department not as a scientific institution, but like the army, only controlled by parliament and the cabinet" (TFMF, Diamond Jenness to T.F. McIlwraith, 27 February 1929). To Jenness's mind, both the army and the Victoria Memorial Museum featured a chain of command in which each link was able to annihilate decisions taken below it, without any necessity to justify its actions (TFMF, Diamond Jenness to T.F. McIlwraith, 4 March 1929).

If their exasperation had allowed McIlwraith and Jenness to stand back from the situation, they might have appreciated the linguistic interest of having each of the several parties in this conflict speak a completely different idiom despite using the same language. Thus, McIlwraith, who keeps asking for precise guidelines and definitions, writes: "what assurance have I that, having done this work, it will not be lost for two more years, and then returned for alteration in some other respect?" and "I feel strongly that [your department] should not require an author to prepare his material in one form – as I did at her behest – with publication as a 'bait,' and then ask him to put it in another form" (TFMF, T.F. McIlwraith to Diamond Jenness, 26 January 1929). McIlwraith does not appear to have consulted with Haddon on the matter, perhaps because he was embarrassed by the delays of his scholarly work and the bigotry of Canadian government officials, but his teacher, too, had had his brush with censorship and might have been able to advise him. In Haddon's case, the problem had been a paper by the trader Edward Beardmore on the customs of Mowat, New Guinea that the *Journal of the Anthropological Institute of Great Britain and*

Ireland refused to print because passages in it were considered obscene. Frederick William Rudler, president of the RAI, told Haddon to summarize Beardmore's account in acceptable language and avoid a "full description," adding that in his own role as juryman, "people have been brought up before us for publishing statements less offensive than certain parts of Beardmore's paper."[19]

Initially, Jenness and McIlwraith propped each other up in their ordeal, and Jenness reiterated even after enduring "severe castigation" by his superiors that the "report [was] the finest work ever offered us, or that we are likely to get for a long time." He insisted that it was essential for "the museum's reputation [to have] it published as soon as possible" (TFMF, Diamond Jenness to T.F. McIlwraith, 30 January 1929). As time went on, however, there was escalating friction between them. Jenness began to remind McIlwraith that he had spent hours on his manuscript "in preference to others which might seem to have a higher claim" (TFMF, Diamond Jenness to T.F. McIlwraith, 27 February 1929). He may have been goaded by McIlwraith's approving references to Edward Sapir, Jenness's predecessor, and to Sapir's manner of running his department. Jenness's instincts would have been right: in McIlwraith's view, he did not measure up to Sapir. Some thirty-five years later, McIlwraith assessed Jenness as "unsure of himself" whereas Sapir is cited as having called the delay in publication "an international disgrace" ("Genealogy"). In addition, Jenness was incensed by what he took to be suggestions of professional impropriety. That interpretation was hotly disputed by McIlwraith, but his angry phrasing was in fact easy to misunderstand. What was he to do, McIlwraith enquired, with an announcement in the *Journal of American Folk-Lore* that *The Bella Coola Indians* was "in the press"? And did Jenness think it "quite ethical" to refer to McIlwraith's research in his own publications when "your department has rejected it in a curt, if dilatory manner"? (TFMF, T. F. McIlwraith to Diamond Jenness, 26 January 1929).[20] In an extended exchange in which they struggled to remain courteous, each clarified not quite successfully what he had meant to say. Jenness tracked down the origin of the erroneous "in the press" as stemming from correspondence between his department and Franz Boas and offered to ask for a correction. No such correction had appeared in the journal by the early 1930s.

Various alternative venues for publication were discussed. McIlwraith wondered if "the American Ethnological Society and other learned societies" would consider publishing a monograph, but felt that the initiative had to come from

---

19 A.C. Haddon Papers, CUL, Frederick William Rudler to A.C. Haddon, 28 March 1890, Env. 21, qtd. in Rouse, "Ethnology, Ethnobiography, and Institution," 66n10. Also see Beardmore. The paper is prefaced by the annotation that "Professor A.C. Haddon gave a verbal abstract of the following paper."

20 The notice reads: "McIlwraith, T.F. Bella Coola mythology (400 stories) 500 Ms pp. to appear in: Bella Coola Indians of British Columbia. In press National Museum of Canada" (Lesser 22).

Jenness because, "as the author of a rejected mss.," he could hardly do so himself. In response, he was informed that "Dr. Collins," the director of the Geological Survey of Canada, "could see no reason why it should be published elsewhere" (TFMF, Diamond Jenness to T.F. McIlwraith, 4 March 1929). In turn, Jenness suggested "the Royal Society or the Research Council," only to be told by Charles Camsell, the deputy minister of mines, that "they also were government institutions and could not run the risk" (TFMF, Diamond Jenness to T.F. McIlwraith, 27 February 1929). When McIlwraith broached the subject of a grant from the Victoria Memorial Museum towards publication elsewhere since "your department is willing to spend a certain amount of money on the publication of a mutilated mss." (TFMF, T.F. McIlwraith to Diamond Jenness, 22 February 1929), this idea – as could be anticipated – was rejected out of hand. Jenness suggested preparing one or two articles for the *American Anthropologist* from the discarded sections but realized that "it would be impossible to lift out more ... without re-writing considerable portions of the remaining" (TFMF, Diamond Jenness to T.F. McIlwraith, 4 March 1929). A large section of the manuscript did make it to the printer by early 1930, with galley proofs expected later in the year. But "none arrived" because Jenness's department could not afford the cost (Richling 63), and any subsequent plans to revive the work were routed by the Depression ("Genealogy"). Sapir wrote in 1934 that he "often hear[d] references to your Bella Coola work and the general feeling is that it should be out. Have you any news on it?" McIlwraith responded:

> Conditions in Ottawa seem to be even worse than formerly and I am afraid that publication of any reports is out of the question. My own manuscript has been waiting for years although it needs drastic revision now in view of the effort by lay editors. As a matter of fact, Boas has had part of it for a long time, and if I can ever get time to go at it again I hope to make the matter up with him.[21]

In addition to using up great amounts of his time with no result, the experience with *The Bella Coola Indians* appears to have paralyzed McIlwraith's motivation towards undertaking further scholarship of comparable ambition. For a man of his normally boundless energy, this was a serious outcome.

There was repeated talk of filing the manuscript "for the use of students and not [have it] published at all" (TFMF, Diamond Jenness to T.F. McIlwraith, 27 February 1929). Whether or not the manuscript was in fact made available to students is not clear, but it was stored by a succession of administrators at the Victoria Memorial Museum (TFMF, Diamond Jenness to T.F. McIlwraith, 10 December 1941). By 1933, the "1737 pages plus 41 pages of notes and excerpts,

---

21 Edward Sapir to T.F. McIlwraith, 21 May 1934; T.F. McIlwraith to Edward Sapir, 16 July 1934, TFMF, UTA, B1972-0030/008 (15).

44 photographs and 31 drawings" were in such tatters that G.C. Monture, acting editor-in-chief of the Editorial Division, Department of Mines, advised to have parts of it retyped "[i]f it is proposed that this Ms. be stored for any length of time." Even worse, he found that it was "impossible to restore the original version" of individual chapters because "the so-called 'discards' " had by then been lost.[22] One wonders if Gilbert Monture, a mining engineer with a distinguished career ahead of him, as well as a "Mohawk from the Six Nations Reserve in Hagersville, Ontario" and "a descendant of Joseph Brant," took a personal interest in keeping the manuscript intact ("Big Feather"). There is, however, no documented follow-up to his request. The next available communication about *The Bella Coola Indians* with the museum, now renamed the National Museum of Canada, occurred eight years later in 1941, when McIlwraith asked for permission yet again to publish the work elsewhere, this time with the assistance of the Canadian Social Science Research Council ("Genealogy"). Jenness appears to have forgotten the details of their acrimonious exchange in the late twenties, recalling that "you long ago received permission to publish it outside, if facilities were available" (TFMF, Diamond Jenness to T.F. McIlwraith, 10 December 1941). If such permission was indeed issued "long ago," there is no trace of it in McIlwraith's files. Further delayed by the war, the book finally appeared with the University of Toronto Press in 1948, following laborious efforts to restore the missing passages, in some cases by retranslating the Latin versions into English. Given the McIlwraiths' thrifty habits, it is easy to believe that there were "portions ... scribbled on old cigarette boxes,"[23] as his assistant told Barker. When the work was typeset, the phonetic symbols "fell off and had to be rechecked and reset" after a worker accidentally walked over the original. Along with the printers, McIlwraith "went nearly out of [his] mind" over this never-ending series of mishaps ("Genealogy"). It was probably no comfort to him that other research out of the Anthropological Division of the National Museum was held up too, including Harlan Smith's *Materia Medica of the Bella Coola and Neighbouring Tribes of British Columbia* and Leonard Bloomfield's *Sacred Stories of the Sweet Grass Cree*. In any case, the former did appear in 1927 and the latter in 1930 because, unlike McIlwraith's manuscript, they did not present "seemingly intractable difficulties" in subject matter and size (Richling 60).

The belated publication of *The Bella Coola Indians* did result in a number of inconsistencies. McIlwraith explains in his preface that, except for minor editorial changes, the manuscript "is presented as it was written in 1924–26." He defends his decision with the explanation that "[t]o the student of social institutions, the significant fact is that a certain group of *homo sapiens* has

---

22 G.C. Monture to W.H. Collins, 20 December 1933, TFMF, UTA, B1979-0011/002 (2).

23 John Barker citing McIlwraith's assistant Margaret Thomson Tushingham, Introduction, *BCI*, vol. 1, xxvii.

practised certain customs, whether in 1922 or 1948 is immaterial." His training at Cambridge, he explained, emphasized the intensive and clearly delineated study of "aboriginal customs [that] were passing away," and because the culture was endangered, "data collected between 1922 and 1924 are more valuable than those acquired today" (xl). As a result of this decision, however, parts of the preface and especially the concluding chapter, "The Man Himself," are anomalies because they do not adequately reflect McIlwraith's professional development in the intervening years or even the direction it had already begun to take during his fieldwork in Bella Coola. The explanation that the dates are "immaterial" seems to have more to do with his exasperation at having to deal with a "manuscript, which was dusty, stale" to him ("Genealogy") than with a well-considered methodology. With its dated application of anthropometry, "The Man Himself" reads like a throwback to the 1921 BAAS conference and to an anthropological perspective of the 1920s generally, but it is not contextualized as a historical reflection. A few of McIlwraith's reviewers promptly responded to the work in equally outdated language. One comments that "[t]he Indians were very helpful towards a man who was sympathetic to their situation and wanted to record fast-disappearing customs" (Gschaedler 133). Another who agreed with the notion that McIlwraith was "reconstructing a dying culture," was alert to the gap between "verbal statements" and "observations of actual behaviour" (Bott, "Review of *The Bella Coola Indians*" 143), but she does not include current behaviour in her understanding of "actual behaviour." That "current behaviour" is of no interest is implied in yet another reviewer's confirmation that McIlwraith was able to obtain "a better ethnography in 1922 to 1924 when he was in the field than could be obtained today" (Gunther 333).

Any impression of McIlwraith's work as outdated was, however, challenged by the field letters collected in *At Home With the Bella Coola Indians*, and one reviewer suggests that the two works are so closely connected that the field letters may be considered a third volume of *The Bella Coola Indians* (Nusqumata). Indeed, the 1992 edition of *The Bella Coola Indians* appears to have expedited the publication of *At Home with the Bella Coola Indians*, a volume that, for a number of reasons, was also delayed by over twenty years.[24] In this case, the delay may even have been fortunate because the final version included a richer selection of letters, and the scholarly reception benefited from the post-structuralist

---

24 For some of the background, see Douglas Cole, letter to Michael Ames, 30 January 1983, "The Bella Coola Field Letters of T.F. McIlwraith, 1922, 1923, 1924" (typescript), BIBRRS-AAM-2468, Audrey and Harry Hawthorn Library and Archives, MOA, UBC; also DCF, SFU Archives, especially Randy Bouchard to Douglas Cole, 8 May 1985, F-35-1-1-36, Correspondence 2/2 1985; Douglas Cole to Allan Smith, 20 May 1986, F-35-1-1-38, Correspondence, 2/2 1986; John Barker to Douglas Cole, 5 September 1986, F-35-1-1-37, Correspondence 1/2 1986.

commentary initiated by Barker's introduction to the 1992 reprint of *The Bella Coola Indians*. As discussed below, this reading was forcefully confirmed by Julie Cruikshank's review of *The Bella Coola Indians*. One review speaks of the letters as "open[ing] a door to a historical critique of *The Bella Coola Indians* – not to denounce the work as flawed but to reclaim it as an essential part of a living and continuously evolving Nuxalk culture."[25]

Spurred by Barker's essay, in typescript, on McIlwraith's career at the University of Toronto and by a complimentary comment about McIlwraith's work in Bella Coola he had located in the Newcombe files,[26] Douglas Cole first approached members of the family about obtaining copies of the field letters in 1979. By 1983, a number of letters had been edited, but when publication was delayed, Cole deposited copies of the typescript with Michael Ames at the UBC Museum of Anthropology, Peter McNair at the Royal BC Museum, and George MacDonald at the Canadian Museum of Civilization for reference. A set also went to the ethnographer Randy Bouchard, whose interests overlapped with some of McIlwraith's fieldwork.[27] Barker expressed an interest in reviving the project in 1986, but was delayed by other research until 1999 (two years after Cole's death), when he submitted a substantially augmented manuscript to UBC Press.[28] When the field letters finally did appear, in 2003, there had already been the positive reception, among scholars and the Nuxalk alike, of the reprint of *The Bella Coola Indians* by the University of Toronto Press.

Indigenous Ownership

His work with the Nuxalk gave McIlwraith material for his research, and it helped him regain his equilibrium at a turbulent time of his life. In ways that exceed his own intentions, he returned the favour by helping to "encourage ... the spiritual renewal of our proud nation" (*BCI*, vii), as Hereditary Chief Lawrence Pootlass writes in the foreword to *The Bella Coola Indians*. Pootlass provided a similar endorsement for *At Home with the Bella Coola Indians*. By their reception of both of these books, the Nuxalk proved wrong those reviewers who worried about the

---

25 SirReadaLot.org, 27 August 2004, HBCI, UBC Press Fonds, UBC Archives.

26 The comment was addressed to Haddon, and – as discussed in the previous chapter – a copy of it is also located in Haddon's papers at CUL. Cole identifies the source as "Dr. Newcombe to A.C. Haddon, 7 April 1924, Newcombe Collection, Msc. Ethno. 58, Provincial Archives in Victoria." For the exchange with Mary Brian and T.F. McIlwraith (b. 1941), see F-35-1-1-24, Correspondence 1/2 1978-1980, DCF, SFU Archives.

27 Randy Bouchard to Douglas Cole, 8 May 1985, F-35-1-1-36, Correspondence 2/2 1985, DCF, SFU Archives.

28 Memorandum, meeting of editorial assistant with John Barker, UBC Press Fonds, University of British Columbia archive. For documents related to the publication of *HBCI*, see box 80, file 11, and box 83, files 90 and 91.

response of the people of Bella Coola. A leading scholar of BC Indigenous people who assessed the edition of the field letters for UBC Press was concerned that there might be "a backlash from the community" because the Nuxalk would be offended by "the extensive reporting of feuding and drunkenness, complete with personal names." The reader suggested that the editors' introduction distance itself more emphatically from McIlwraith's views and language and that the title of the work be changed from the proposed "Certainly an Interesting Life: T.F. McIlwraith in Bella Coola, 1922–24" to another quotation from the letters, "Pretending to Be Duly Impressed: Letters from the Field – T.F. McIlwraith in Bella Coola, 1922–24." "This is not about McIlwraith's life," the assessor explained, but about "the field experience of a young Canadian anthropologist" (Reader's Report A, University of British Columbia Press Fonds, UBCA). The introduction to the published book does not subscribe to this distinction when it insists that fieldwork affects researchers as much as it does the individuals they study and when it subtitles one of its sections "T.F. McIlwraith's Life and Work." Although not all of the discussion is recorded in the UBC Press files, the question of the title appears to have been worrisome enough to switch to a third option, *At Home with the Bella Coola Indians*. This is also the title of an article, included among the appendices to the field letters, that McIlwraith contributed to the Toronto *Star* in 1924 ahead of the BAAS meeting in Toronto.[29] Using this title underscored the place of the Bella Coola letters in a specific historical moment and the language that came with it.

In his scholarly work, McIlwraith did invariably adopt the dispassionate tone of objectivity he had been taught at Cambridge. One reviewer of *The Bella Coola Indians* concluded that McIlwraith was limited by the "intellectual grid" he had been taught and that he "dismiss[ed]" its implications as far as he could even be said to be aware of them (R. Cook, 92, 91).[30] By contrast, other commentators were quick to point out the various methods by which he questioned the authority of that grid, the problematic last chapter notwithstanding. Even the original 1948 edition had reviewers take notice that, by repeatedly arranging the sequence of his narrative to suit the logic of the culture he described rather than the logic of the scholarship applied to it, McIlwraith had variously undermined "a monograph form which was so rigid as to devitalize the most enthralling account" (M. Smith 561). McIlwraith insists that he cannot "begin with the social organization of the people," but must discuss religion first "since [the] religious beliefs [among the Bella Coola] colour every aspect of their life" (*BCI* 1: 116). He frequently uses the words "fluid" or "fluidity," referring both to the Bella Coola River, which "frequently changes its course" (8), and to communal traditions

29 See also Barker, " 'At Home with the Bella Coola Indians,' Introduced and Annotated by John Barker."

30 Cook somewhat compromises the accuracy of his review by referring to Joshua Moody as "John Moodie."

that can, if necessary, be adapted to circumstances, "since the Bella Coola is never such a slave to legal privileges that he fails to be guided by common sense" (136). McIlwraith makes the latter assertion in the body of the text, but more frequently it is his footnotes that signal deviations from the "common anthropological practice," as he explains when he introduces a discussion of "Origin Myths" not in the appendix, as would be the norm, but in an earlier position where it seems to "interrupt ... the sequence." He nevertheless perseveres with the apparent irregularity because it reflects "the essential interactions of this type of myth upon [the] whole life" of the Nuxalk (292). In the notes, McIlwraith alerts readers to his use of one tense over another, to the problems of translating certain concepts, to the blurred distinctions between history and myth, to questions that were interesting to him but not to the people with whom he conversed, to the effect of circumstances on accurate note-taking. Much of this may sound like a list of technicalities, but in her review of the 1992 edition, Julie Cruikshank makes a substantial claim for the notes as the place where McIlwraith initiated, among others, a dialogue with Franz Boas, "sometimes confirming, sometimes challenging the latter's observations" (Cruikshank 139). One such challenge underscores McIlwraith's growing conviction that "the high pitch of accuracy and detail" that was central to Boas's approach (HCUL, T.F. McIlwraith to A.C. Haddon, 7 May 1923) would get him nowhere in a context where "[e]ach man, convinced of the authenticity of his own family account is quite willing to believe that the one belonging to someone else is equally correct" (*BCI* 1: 294).[31] As so often in McIlwraith's approach, Haddon's influence is apparent not only in the method of research, "which paid close attention to details provided by individual informants" (Herle, "Life-Histories" 86), but also in the manner in which the method is applied. Cautiously subverting the conventions of academic writing in *The Bella Coola Indians* is one approach, and – although these were not originally written for a large readership – the vividly personal accounts in the field letters are another. Deliberately or not, the letters especially parallel Haddon's interest in "popular genres, autobiographical and meditative, as a means to develop reflexive accounts of fieldwork" (Herle and Rouse, Introduction, 21).

The same sense of autonomy that McIlwraith encountered among the Nuxalk when he interviewed them prevails in their reception of *The Bella Coola Indians* in 1948 and 1992. McIlwraith, who in his preface and the notes named the individuals who had assisted him in his work (Joshua Moody, Captain Schooner, Jim Pollard, Willie Mack, Mr. and Mrs. Tallio Charlie, and Mr. and Mrs. Lame Charlie), forwarded the two volumes to Jim Pollard, and he heard from the painter Mildred Valley Thornton that Pollard's granddaughter "read [from] them to him regularly."[32] Once again, McIlwraith's work mirrors that of

---

31 On Boas's concept of "accuracy," see Zumwalt 71.
32 Mildred Valley Thornton to T.F. McIlwraith, 15 May 1950, TFMF, UTA B1979-0011/01 (08).

his mentor. Haddon sent copies of the *Reports of the Cambridge Anthropological Expedition to Torres Straits* (1901–35) and of *Head-Hunters: Black, White and Brown* (1901), his popular account of the expedition, to his Indigenous hosts who had provided verbal accounts and drawings. They were named and "often quoted verbatim," an acknowledgment "of special filial importance to the descendants" (Herle and Rouse, Introduction, 18–19). McIlwraith, who remained vividly interested in Bella Coola and its people,[33] may have sent his book to others in Bella Coola who were still alive in 1948, even if he never returned there. But the Nuxalk did not wait for books to be sent to them: "at least thirty copies [were] purchased [by] Nuxalk families," and "one set [has been] kept under lock and key at the Nuxalk Band offices" (Barker, Introduction, *BCI*, xxxiv–xxxv). The book became "an important instrument of reclamation" (Nusqumata 120) because, in addition to the narrative itself, the rich documentation in "photographs, ... diagrams, genealogies, place names, maps, songs and narratives provide reference material for programs initiated by the Nuxalk Cultural Centre and for Nuxalk collaborations with the Canadian Museum of Civilization [now Canadian Museum of History]" (Cruikshank 123–4). On a more modest scale, *At Home with the Bella Coola Indians* had a similar effect. One First Nations reviewer was "very interested to learn about [her] ancestral past" from the letters, obtain new details about her grandfather, and discover that she was connected to the Christensen family. She also draws attention to the existence of alternative versions of myths when she declares herself curious to see what "families and individuals" had been interviewed, and which " 'smayustas' (origin stories and cultural property) were represented as common Nuxalk culture" (Nusqumata 121). In enquiring about the names of "families and individuals," this reviewer, too, does not confirm the fears of the UBC Press reader who worried that naming unruly individuals would provoke "a negative reaction from the Nuxalk community about this portrayal of their community by an outsider" (Reader's Report A). Instead, the reviewer concentrates on the additional cultural information that might be gained from having even more names available.

The most important dialogue in *The Bella Coola Indians*, according to Cruikshank and other reviewers, is provided by the oral narratives on which McIlwraith's account is based. If at first sight the exchange between anthropologist

---

33 In 1949, McIlwraith received a letter from Fritz Knechtel, owner of a furniture store in Hanover, Ontario, written in response to *BCI*. Knechtel talks about a number of Bella Coola masks and whistles that had been sent to Ontario by a man who was stationed in Bella Coola during the Second World War (Fritz Knechtel to T.F. McIlwraith 15 July 1949, TFMF, UTA, B1979 0011/001 [08]). McIlwraith responds with interest and opens his letter with "The world is sometimes much smaller than it seems, to judge from the number of people I have met who have had some connection or other with Bella Coola, a place so small that I would have expected no one to have heard of it" (T.F. McIlwraith to Fritz Knechtel, 19 July 1949, TFMF, UTA, B1979 0011/001 [08]).

and Nuxalk seems to be professionally and emotionally weighted in McIlwraith's favour, much of the response to *The Bella Coola Indians* says otherwise and indicates that a balance was achieved. In a process in which, as Cruikshank has it, "[m]anuscripts have a life of their own, quite independent of authors" (124), Indigenous assertiveness and post-structuralist theory worked in tandem to produce a revisionist reading of McIlwraith's research when the reprint of *The Bella Coola Indians* was published in 1992 and the field letters appeared in 2003. The relationship between McIlwraith and the people he interviewed gained legitimacy because the Nuxalk "were paid for their time" (D. Kingston 166). One reviewer insists that the volumes were "coauthored by Nuxalk people, although this is not acknowledged on the title page," and he points out that the book set out to do one thing (namely, to document a dying culture) but accomplished another: the Nuxalk "were looking forward rather than backward" (Marles 387).

Understanding McIlwraith's book as a collaborative work in no small measure shaped its assessment as an "important instrument of reclamation" (Nusqumata 120). There was isolated resistance to Barker's "postmodern" reading of McIlwraith's research as collaborative, with the implication that this was a modish approach not supported by evidence (Rubel and Rosman 772). It would be interesting to know these particular commentators' response to an Indigenous reviewer like Nusqumata for whom co-authorship is an indisputable fact. Another sceptical reviewer, who did not think McIlwraith was "a pioneering anthropologist," still admitted to being impressed with the "warmth of feeling" in Pootlass's endorsement and reluctantly conceded that "given reasonably adequate fieldwork ... how the anthropologist views his role and his relationship with those with whom he works may not be as important as how the people studied choose to use the product" (Lane 142). The most typical response, however, was accolade: the author was "a pioneer" (D. Kingston 165) and *The Bella Coola Indians* a "definitive ethnography" (Marles 387), a "seminal ... ethnography" (Thom 116), and "one of the major ethnographies of the Northwest Coast" (Lane 141). The word "classic" recurs insistently (Newell 581), and Ramsay Cook compares the significance of the work to Harold Innis's *The Fur Trade in Canada* (87). If McIlwraith's overall "intellectual legacy" has elsewhere been called "somewhat qualified" (Buchanan 99), there is no evidence of such qualification in these assessments, nor in the documented response of the Nuxalk to McIlwraith's achievement.

The story of the "imperial" McIlwraiths concludes in a place similar to the one where it began. Queensland and British Columbia were both considered places, to borrow Adele Perry's phrase, "on the edge of Empire." They were seen to exist on a frontier as yet untamed by metropolitan civilization, but precisely because of this lack of polish, these "edges" were also locations where the presumption of imperial thought was exposed to observers willing to pay attention and learn. This moment never came swiftly enough for Indigenous people to be spared exploitation, indoctrination, and brutality, but their descendants have retooled the empire's decaying "girdle round about the earth" to assert their own history. The annexation of New Guinea initiated by Sir Thomas McIlwraith and the anthropological work conducted by T.F. McIlwraith among the Nuxalk under the auspices of the Geological Survey of Canada were intended as confirmation of imperial power around the Pacific, but the life stories of Pacific Islanders and the Nuxalk that can be extrapolated from the Parliamentary Papers and from McIlwraith's field letters have instead become important means to reconstruct "everything as it used to be" (Haddon qtd. in Philp 58), not as an act of nostalgia but as one in support of a living culture.[34]

"[E]verything as it used to be" is a quotation from Haddon's journals of the 1898 Torres Strait expedition that, with the participation of Pacific Islanders, have been published by Anita Herle from the MAA in Cambridge and Jude Philp from the Macleay Museum at the University of Sydney. As Herle explains, "[t]he project involved extended consultation with the families and communities where Haddon worked, with field trips to [the Torres Strait] in 2016 and 2018 to discuss the journals as well as hosting numerous Islanders in Cambridge."[35] In addition, the genealogies established by Rivers have supported "land-claim cases," and "[i]nformation from the *Reports* was used as evidence in the landmark *Mabo* case on Mer (1992) which overturned the 200-year-old doctrine of *terra nullius* in Australian law" (Herle and Rouse, Introduction, 15, 18–19; see also Herle, Philp, Introduction). The result was the Native Title Act of 1993. This interrelation between the "Atlantic world in the Antipodes" (see Fullagar) on the one hand and the Pacific network on the other is also apparent in the work of "Indigenous Conversations about Biography," a special issue of *Biography* (2016) co-edited by Alice Te Punga Somerville (Māori), Daniel Heath Justice (Cherokee), and Noelani Arista (Hawai'ian) following a conference at the University of Hawai'i that "focus[ed] on the things Indigenous people want to talk about when it comes to biography" (Somerville and Justice 239). The presentation of the papers incorporates seemingly simple reversals such as placing the introduction at the end of the collection, scrambling the alphabetical order, and alternating presentations with responses. The contributions discuss, and practise themselves, life writing both traditional and creative, often reinterpreting the work as "life-speaking" and moving backwards, forwards, and sideways in time. The result is an important revision of the genre, both from an anthropological and literary perspective, and one that parallels and exceeds McIlwraith's own experiments with the scholarly monograph as a form of collective life writing.

In 1991, just prior to the publication of the second edition of *The Bella Coola Indians*, McIlwraith's children were invited, along with Barker, to attend the

---

34 For a parallel process, see Solomonian on Harlan I. Smith's fieldwork photographs.
35 Anita Herle, email to Eva-Marie Kröller, 20 October 2019.

Hereditary Chief Lawrence Pootlass (Nuximlayc), with the two volumes of the original
1948 edition of *The Bella Coola Indians* at the memorial potlatch, October 1991.
Connie Brian, photographer. Mary Brian (McIlwraith) estate.

Pootlass-Brown Memorial Potlatch, "an occasion in which the Nuxalk people
honoured [their] father's memory and his work among them nearly seventy years
earlier." Chief Lawrence Pootlass (Nuximlayc), an important figure in the revival
of contemporary Nuxalk culture (see NoiseCat), assured his guests that "these
books are worth more than gold to us," and McIlwraith's Nuxalk name "Weena"
was passed on to his son.[36] At the invitation of T.F's children, Pootlass and his wife
attended the book launch in Toronto. In a suitable coda, T.F's grandson, Thomas
(Tad) McIlwraith, has cited the potlatch as motivating him in his decision to become an anthropologist himself, with an emphasis on Indigenous rights to land.

---

36 Thomas F. McIlwraith, "Words from Weena II," 4.

McIlwraith Genealogies[*]

A. The Australian McIlwraiths

(a) John McIlwraith (1808–1885) + Janet Howat (1809–1886), lived in Ayr, Ayrshire, Scotland
- John (1828–1902) + Mary Whannell (1832–1915)
- Euphemia (1831–1902) + John Mackay (1821–1882)
- Margaret Baird (1833–1923) + William McIlwraith (1833–1914); see **B. The Ontario McIlwraiths** below
- (Sir) Thomas (1835–1900). See **A(b1)** and **A(b2)** below
- Elizabeth (1837–1924) + John Taylor
- Janet (1839–1847)
- Agnes (1842–1934) + James McLachlan
- Andrew (1844–1932) + Mabel Campbell; second marriage to Holte Leichenberger
- Anne (1846–1935) + Charles Reid; second marriage to Joseph Gray
- Hamilton (1848–1900) + Lavinda Wood
- Janet Margaret (1851–1935) + Matthew Gilmour
- Mary Jane (1853–1937) + Allan Stevenson

(b1) Sir Thomas McIlwraith (1835–1900) + Margaret Whannell (1835–1877) (first marriage)
- Thomas (1863–1864)
- Jessie Maggie (1864–1942) + Fanshawe Gostling
- Mary Campbell (1866–1952) + Montagu Stanley
- Blanche Margaret (1872–1943) + Forrester Alexander

---

[*] The information in these genealogies has been compiled from a variety of sources, including Beanland, Twaddel, Holman and Kristofferson, and information from Professor Thomas F. McIlwraith (b. 1941) and Duane McIlwraith.

(b2) Sir Thomas McIlwraith (1835–1900) + Harriet Mosman (second marriage)
- Leila Harriet (1880–1944) + James McGowan

B. The Ontario McIlwraiths

(a) Thomas McIlwraith (1785–1856) + Jean Adair Forsyth (1787–1875), lived in Ayrshire, Scotland
- Helen (1810–1893), later Mrs. Hunter
- Jean Smith (1812–1862)
- Margaret (1814–1889), later Mrs. Logan
- Thomas (1816–1817), died in infancy
- John (1820–1875)
- Mary Wilson (1822–1841)
- Thomas (1824–1903) + Mary Park; author of *Birds of Ontario*
- Christina (1828–death date unrecorded), later Mrs. Brewster
- Andrew (1830–1891) + Mary Goldie (1834–1911)
- William (1833–1914) + Margaret Baird McIlwraith (1833–1923); see **A. The Australian McIlwraiths** above

(b) Thomas McIlwraith (1824–1903) + Mary Park (1825–1901), emigrated to Hamilton, Ontario in 1853
- Thomas Forsyth (1855–1932) + Mary Stevens; see **B(c)** and **C. Mary Stevens's Family** below
- Mary Duncan (1857–1907) + Robert John Service
  - ○ Marion Reid
  - ○ Helen Forsyth
  - ○ Willis James
- Jean (or Jane) Newton (1858–1938); author and editor
- Helen Adair ("Nellie") (1860–1950) + John Henderson Holt
- Hugh Park (1861–1916)
- Marion Reid (1863–1864)
- John Goldie (1865–1923) + Mattie Chittenden
- Kennedy Crawford (1868–1941) + Mary ("May") Saunders

(c) Thomas Forsyth McIlwraith (1855–1932) + Mary Stevens (1858–1923), of Hamilton, Ontario; see **C. Mary Stevens's Family** below
- Marjorie Spafford (1888–1977)
- Dorothy Stevens (1891–1976)
- Thomas Forsyth (1899–1964) + Beulah Gillet Knox; see **D. Beulah Gillet Knox's Family** below

(d) Thomas Forsyth McIlwraith (1899–1964) + Beulah Knox (1895–1978)
- Mary Agnes (1930–2006) + Michael Brian
- Margaret (Peggy) Knox (b. 1933) + Murray Matheson
- Thomas Forsyth (b. 1941) + Duane Catherine Bell

C. Mary Stevens's Family

Gardner Green Stevens (1813–1892) + Relief Jane Spafford (1816–1882), of Stanstead, Quebec
- Gardner (b. 1850) + Nellie G. Foster
- Sidney (1852–1933) + Harriet Flanders
- Clara J. (1855–1923)
- Mary (1858–1923) + Thomas F. McIlwraith; see **B(c)** above
- Edward A. (b. 1861 or 1866; no further details at hand)

D. Beulah Gillet Knox's Family

Carlos Oscar Child (1827–1904) + Mary Gillet (1831–1908), of Painesville, Ohio
- Albert Gillet ("Letty") (1855–1871)
- Agnes Julia (1860–1923) + Wilm Knox
  - Carlos Child (1892–1976)
  - Beulah Gillet (1895–1978); see **B(c)** above
  - Margaret Neilson (1898–1964)
- William Addison (1862–1935) + Elizabeth Helen ("Nellie") Harvey
  - Helen Mary (1893–1912)
  - Philip Albert Gillet (1898–1978) + Gertrude Helen Potts

Bibliography

Manuscripts and Manuscript Collections

Rudolph Martin **Anderson** and Mae Bell Allstrand Fonds, LAC.

Douglas **Cole**, "The Bella Coola Field Letters," typescript, Audrey and Harry Hawthorn Library and Archives, MOA, UBC.

Douglas **Cole** Fonds, Simon Fraser University Archives.

Downing College, Cambridge, Archives.

Dufferin and Ava Papers, PRONI.

Fannie Hardy **Eckstorm** Papers, Raymond H. Fogler Library, Special Collections, University of Maine, Orono. MS 158, Series 1, Subseries 1, Folder 65, Box 1.

James Henry **Fleming** Fonds, ROM.

Terrot Reaveley **Glover** Fonds, St. John's College Library.

Joseph **Grinnell** Papers, Bancroft Library, UCB.

Services: **Hackett-Lowther** Unit (EN1/3/SER/007), Imperial War Museum.

Alfred Cort **Haddon** Papers, CUL.

Burton J. **Hendrick** papers, HLHU.

Houghton Mifflin Company Records, HLHU.

C.W. **Jefferys** Fonds, Archives of Ontario.

Macdonald Institute, Archival and Special Collections, UGL, entrance records and transcripts, 1903–1941.

The Diary of Lieutenant Colonel Charles Mackesy of the New Zealand Mounted Rifles Brigade, 1919, https://ndhadeliver.natlib.govt.nz/webarchive/wayback /20131021063400/http://www.nzmr.org/diary4.htm. Accessed 3 June 2020.

McDunnough-McInnes Correspondence, Botany Division, Geological Survey, LAC.

G.W. **McCallum**, "Catalogue of Indian and Other Relics" (1887), QUA.

Andrew McIlwraith. Diaries, TFMP.

Dorothy McIlwraith, "CONCERNING US CANADIANS: By One of Minor Importance," unpublished, undated memoir, TFMP.

Jean N. McIlwraith
- "Casual Kate's Letters," JNMP.
- "The Days of the Year, or the Masque of the Months" (also entitled, "Pageant of the Seasons"), unpublished play, JNMP.
- "Dialogue," untitled, undated manuscript, JNMP.
- "Dominick Street," ca. 1905, unpublished novel, JNMP.
- Editorial Correspondence, JNMP.
- "Essay on George Meredith, *Diana of the Crossways,*" assignment for Queen Margaret College, University of Glasgow, JNMP.
- "A Few Unimportant Jottings about Mr. W.H. Page" (cited as "Jottings"), JNMP.
- "New York Impressions," 1902–3, unpublished diary, JNMP.
- "Smiling Water," undated, unpublished novel, JNMP.
- "The Temple of Fame: A Spectacular Play," unpublished play, JNMP.

John McIlwraith (1828–1902) and Company Deposit, AU NBAC 35, press copies of letters sent by John McIlwraith.

Kennedy McIlwraith (1902–1941), "What I Know About Birds and How I Came to Know It (1882–1890)," manuscript, TFRBL.

Mary Stevens McIlwraith, letters to T.F. McIlwraith, 1919–1921, TFMP.

Thomas McIlwraith (1824–1903)
- "Catalogue of Birds Mounted under Glass," a list of 448 specimens compiled in 1891, Ornithology Department, ROM.
- Thomas G. McIlwraith Fonds, Local History and Archives, HPL.
- business postcards and postcards related to ornithology, TMF, HPL. An annotated list, assigning a number to each postcard and providing other commentary, was prepared by T.F. McIlwraith (b. 1941). Consulted when the documents were in private hands.
- *The Birds of Ontario* (1894 edition), annotated typescript.
- Thomas McIlwraith Fonds, LAC.

Thomas Forsyth McIlwraith (1899–1964)
- Fonds of 2nd Lt. Thomas Forsyth McIlwraith, 20110123–001, George Metcalf Archival Collection, CWM; original letters; includes annotated typescript prepared by T.F. McIlwraith (b. 1941) and Duane McIlwraith. Consulted when the documents were in private hands.
- childhood notebook, TFMP.
- five notebooks of daily bird observations, 1929–1964, Thomas Forsyth McIlwraith Fonds, SC 184, ROM.
- report cards, TFMP.
- wartime diary, TFMP.
- letters from Cambridge, 1919–1922, TFMF. Consulted when papers were in private hands.
- Thomas F. McIlwraith Papers, UTA.
- Thomas Forsyth McIlwraith Fonds, SC 184, ROM.

Sir Thomas McIlwraith (1835–1900)/Palmer Papers, JOL.

McLennan Family Fonds, Box 4, file 3, RBSC, UBC.

William **McLennan** Fonds, Rare Books and Special Collections, McGill University.

Archives, Museum of Comparative Zoology, Ernst **Mayr** Library, Harvard University.

Walter Hines **Page** Papers, HLHU.

Sir Lionel **Phillips**, Private Papers, Rand Mines Archive, Historical Papers Research Archive, University of the Witwatersrand, Johannesburg, SA.

Queen Margaret College, Archives, UG.

Ethnology Documents, Edward **Sapir** (I-A-236M), Correspondence, Folder: "McIlwraith, T. F. (1921–1923)," Archives, CMH.

Scrapbook Collection, Nova Scotia Archives, MG 9, volume 10.

Marion **Seward**, 29 August 1914, "Sketchbook and Diary, July to November 1914: Sketches and Notes on a Voyage to Australia to the Meeting of the British Association for the Advancement of Science Held There in 1914," private family papers, Dorothy Meade estate.

Smithsonian Institution, United States National Museum, Division of Birds.

Frederick **Sykes**, Presidents Historical Collection. Linda Lear Center for Special Collections and Archives, Connecticut College.

Una **Troubridge** diaries, Lovat Dickson collection, MG30 D237, volume 1, LAC.

University of Waterloo Library, Elizabeth Smith Shortt Fonds, WA-10, File 280.

University of British Columbia Press Fonds, UBCA.

A.P. **Watt** Records, 1888–1982, #11036, Rare Book Literary and Historical Papers, the Wilson Library, University of North Carolina at Chapel Hill, US.

Publications by the McIlwraiths (Selected)

NB: Publications by Jean N. McIlwraith appear under Forsyth, McIlwraith, and Newton. She sometimes used her middle initial N. and sometimes omitted it.

Duncan, Mary. "A Day in the Highlands of Scotland." *Our Young Folks*, vol. 9, no. 11, 1873, p. 690.

Forsyth, Jean. "Bracing Outings on the Great Lakes." *Country Life in America*, vol. 9, Dec. 1905, pp. 175–80.

– "A City of Fountains." *The World To-day*, vol. 18, June 1910, pp. 186–96.

– "George Meredith on Women." *The Globe*, 18 Apr. 1895, p. B13.

– *The Making of Mary*. Fisher Unwin, 1895.

– "A Singing-Student in London." *Harper's Magazine*, vol. 88, no. 525, 1894, pp. 385–91.

– "The Earthquake Region." *Harper's Bazaar*, vol. 23, no. 38, 1890, p. 730.

Loram, C.T., and Thomas F. McIlwraith, eds. *The North American Indian Today*. U of Toronto P, 1943.

McIlwraith, Beulah Knox. "Some Aspects of Race Contacts in the South Pacific." *Social Welfare*, vol. 12, no. 7, 1930, pp. 150–1.

McIlwraith, Dorothy. "Canada's Half Million." *The Independent*, 26 Feb. 1917, p. 354.

– "The Canadian Red Cross Carries On." *Red Cross Magazine*, vol. 12, no. 7, 1917, pp. 265–9.

– "Sending Tommy His Marmalade." *New Country Life*, vol. 34, no. 4, 1918, p. 64.

McIlwraith, Jean N. *A Book About Longfellow*. Nelson, 1900.

– *A Book About Shakespeare Written for Young People*. Nelson, 1898.

– "A Dialogue in Hades: Omar Khayyám and Walt Whitman." *Atlantic Monthly*, vol. 89, 1902, pp. 808–12.

– "Emerson's Choice of Representative Men." Canadiana Online, *Canadian Magazine*, vol. 1, no. 8, 1893, pp. 689–91.

– "The Assimilation of Christina." Canadiana Online, *Canadian Magazine*, vol. 41, no. 6, 1913, pp. 607–14. Also published as "Wah-sah-yah-ben-oqua," *Cornhill Magazine*, new series, vol. 128, no. 168, 1910, pp. 820–31, and as "On Georgian Bay" in *Hampton's Magazine*, vol. 24, 1910, pp. 867–72. The latter is not identical with the story "On Georgian Bay" published in *Cornhill Magazine* (see below).

– "A Bright Girlhood: Autobiographical Sketch by Miss McIlwraith." *Mail and Empire*, 29 June 1901, n.p.

– *Canada*. The Children's Study. T. Fisher Unwin, 1899.

– *The Curious Career of Roderick Campbell*. Houghton Mifflin, 1901.

– *A Diana of Quebec*. Bell & Cockburn, 1912.

– "Hardy, Thomas." *The New International Encyclopedia*, vol. 9, ed. Daniel Coit Gilman, Harry Thurston Peck, and Frank Moore Colby. Dodd, Mead, 1903.

– "Household Budgets Abroad: Canada." *Cornhill Magazine*, vol. 17, 1903, pp. 806–21.

– "How to Be Happy Though Single." *Harper's Bazaar*, May 1902, pp. 454–5.

– *Kinsmen at War*. Graphic Publishers, 1927.

– *The Little Admiral*. Hodder and Stoughton, 1923.

– "Motor Rides Around Quebec." *Canadian Magazine*, vol. 61, no. 2, 1923, pp. 128–37.

– "On Georgian Bay." *Cornhill Magazine*, vol. 9, no. 50, 1900, pp. 179–95.

– "A Primitive Coaster." *A Book of Winter Sports: An Attempt to Catch the Spirit of the Keen Joys of the Winter Season*, edited by J.C. Dier, Macmillan, 1912, p. 258.

– "Ptarmigan, or, A Canadian Carnival." *Canada's Lost Plays*, vol. 1: *The Nineteenth Century*, edited by Anton Wagner and Richard Plants, CTR Publications, 1978, pp. 194–223.

– "Reenacting 300 Years of Quebec History." *World's Work*, vol. 16, 1908, pp. 10371–3.

– "Robbing the Clydesdales." Canadiana Online, *Canadian Magazine*, vol. 62, no. 6, 1924, pp. 373–81.

– *Sir Frederick Haldimand*. Makers of Canada. Morang, 1904.

– "Wintersports Old and New: The Joyous Possibilities of Sleighing, Snow-Shoeing, Skeeing, Curling, Bobbing, Tobogganing – What Canada Can Teach Us in Open-Air Holiday-Making." *Country Life in America*, vol. 9, 1905–6, pp. 175–80.

McIlwraith, Kennedy Crawford, "Prothonotary Warbler in Ontario." *The Auk*, vol. 5, no. 3, 1888, pp. 322–3.

McIlwraith, T.F. *The Bella Coola Indians*. 1948. U of Toronto P, 1992. 2 vols.

– "Race and Race Concepts." Presidential Lecture, *Proceedings of the Royal Canadian Institute*, series IIIa, vol. VIII, 1943, 18–26.

McIlwraith, Thomas. *The Birds of Ontario, Being a Concise Account of Every Species of Bird Known to Have Been Found in Ontario, With a Description of their Nests and Eggs, And Instructions for Collecting Birds and Preparing and Preserving Skins, Also Directions How to Form a Collection of Eggs*. 1886. Rev. ed., W. Briggs, 1894.

– "The English Sparrow." *Twentieth Annual Report of the Fruit Growers' Association of Ontario, 1888*. Warwick and Sons, 1889, pp. 83–7.

– "List of Birds Observed in the Vicinity of Hamilton, C.W. Arranged after the System of Audubon." *Canadian Journal*, new series, vol. 5, 1860, pp. 387–96.

– "List of Birds Observed Near Hamilton, C.W." Essex Institute, *Proceedings* (Salem, MA), vol. 5, 1866, pp. 79–96.

– "Notices of Birds Observed Near Hamilton, C.W." *Canadian Journal*, new series, vol. 6, 1861, pp. 6–18, 129–38.

– "The Starling." *Canadian Horticulturalist*, vol. 14, 1891, pp. 134–5.

McIlwraith, Thomas F. (b. 1941), and Thomas F. McIlwraith (b. 1969). "Who is Methuselah: Author Footnotes with Thomas F. McIlwraith," *UTP Blog*, 22 Nov. 2012, https://utorontopress.com/ca/blog/2012/11/22/who-is-methuselah-author-footnotes-with-thomas-f-mcilwraith/. Accessed 21 Dec. 2018.

McIlwraith, Thomas F. "Words from Weena." Letter to the Editor. *The Beaver*, Apr.–May 2005, p. 3.

McLennan, William, and Jean N. McIlwraith. *The Span o' Life: A Tale of Louisbourg and Quebec*. Harper, 1899.

Newton, Jeannie. "Burned to the Water's Edge." *Our Young Folks*, vol. 9, no. 12, 1873, pp. 755–6.

– "Under the Sea." *Kind Words, for Boys and Girls*, 1 Aug. 1874, pp. 243–4.

– "What We Did at the Beach." *Our Young Folks*, vol. 9, no. 8, 1873, pp. 497–8.

Selected Biographical and Critical Publications about the McIlwraiths and Extended Family

"Active Mind Is Stilled; Noted Citizen Passes" (Obituary of W.A. Child). Hamilton *Spectator*, 16 Oct. 1935, pp. 7, 10.

"The Birds of Western Canada." *Journal of the Board of Arts and Manufactures for Upper Canada*, vol. 7, 1867, pp. 142–3.

Baigent, Elizabeth. "McIlwraith, Sir Thomas (1835–1900)." *Oxford Dictionary of National Biography*, https://doi.org/10.1093/ref:odnb/17540. Accessed 25 July 2019.

Bailey, A.G. Review of *The North American Indian Today*, ed. C.T. Loram and T.F.
McIlwraith. *Canadian Journal of Economics and Political Science*, vol. 10, no. 1, 1944,
pp. 110–12.

Barker, John. " 'At Home with the Bella Coola Indians,' Introduced and Annotated by
John Barker." *BC Studies*, no. 75, 1987, pp. 43–60.

– "T.F. McIlwraith and Anthropology at the University of Toronto, 1925–63."
Canadian Review of Sociology and Anthropology, vol. 24, no. 2, 1987, pp. 252–68.

Barker, John, and Douglas Cole, eds. *At Home with the Bella Coola Indians: T.F.
McIlwraith's Field Letters, 1922–4*. UBC Press, 2003.

Barnett, H.G. Review of *The Bella Coola Indians. American Anthropologist*, vol. 51,
1949, pp. 632–5.

Beanland, Denver. *The Queensland Caesar: Sir Thomas McIlwraith*. Boolarong Press,
2013.

"Books and Authors" (Review of *The Span o' Life*). Canadiana Online, *Canadian
Magazine*, vol. 13, no. 1, 1899, pp. 91–2.

Bott, Elizabeth. Review of *The Bella Coola Indians. Man*, vol. 50, Oct. 1950, p. 143.

Calhoun, James R. Introduction. Philip Child, *God's Sparrows*. 1937. Dundurn, 2017,
pp. 7–31.

Campbell, Sandra, and Lorraine McMullen, eds. *New Women: Short Stories by
Canadian Women, 1900–1920*. U of Ottawa P, 1991.

"Charivaria." *Punch*, vol. 175, no. 4,582, 19 Sept. 1928, p. 309.

Child, W.A. "Iron Trade Built By Determined Men." Hamilton *Spectator*, 15 July 1926, n.p.

– "Notes on Ethnology: A Lecture Delivered Before the Hamilton Scientific
Association, 2 December 1910." *Journal and Proceedings of the Hamilton Association
for Sessions of 1911–1912* (handwritten correction: 1910–1911). Heath and Lockhart,
1911, pp. 50–70.

– *Notes on Ethnology: A Lecture Delivered Before the Hamilton Scientific Association on
4 December 1914*. Scientific Association, 1914.

"Chit Chat" (on "The Temple of Fame"). *The Globe*, 27 Feb. 1900, p. 8.

Cook, Ramsay. Review of *The Bella Coola Indians. BC Studies*, no. 102, 1994,
pp. 87–91.

Coues, Elliott. "Recent Literature: The New Canadian Ornithology" (Review of *The
Birds of Ontario*). *The Auk*, vol. 4, 1887, pp. 245–6.

Cruikshank, Julie. "Ethnography as Dialogue: Review of *The Bella Coola Indians*."
Canadian Literature, no. 140, spring 1994, pp. 122–4.

Dean, Misao. "Jean Newton McIlwraith." *Canadian Writers, 1890–1920*, edited
by William H. New, Gale, 1990. *Dictionary of Literary Biography*, vol. 92. Gale
Literature Resource Centre. Accessed 27 July 2019.

Dickson, James A.R. "Mr. Andrew McIlwraith." *"Ebenezer": A History of the Central
Presbyterian Church, Galt, Ontario; with Brief Sketches of Some of Its Members who
Have Passed on to the Other Side*. W. Briggs, 1904, pp. 306–8.

Dignan, Don. "Sir Thomas McIlwraith (1835–1900)." *Australian Dictionary of Biography*. Vol. 5, Melbourne UP, 1974, http://adb.anu.edu.au/biography /mcilwraith-sir-thomas-4099. Accessed 25 July 2019.

– "Sir Thomas McIlwraith: His Public Career and Political Thought: A Short Essay." Honours thesis, University of Queensland, 1951.

Fenton, Faith. "A Talk with Jean Forsyth: Faith Fenton Interviews the Popular Authoress." *The Globe*, 5 Oct. 1895, p. 16. Rpt. from *Canadian Home Journal*.

"Fiction" (Review of *The Making of Mary*). *The Speaker*, vol. 12, 21 Sept., 1895, p. 322.

Fisher, A.K. "In Memoriam: Thomas McIlwraith." *The Auk*, vol. 21, no. 1, 1904, pp. 1–7.

"Flashlights on Nature: Life of Thomas McIlwraith is Worthy of Study." Hamilton *Spectator*, 5 Oct. 1946, p. 12.

Forkner, John LaRue. "John G. McIlwraith." *History of Madison County, Indiana: A Narrative Account of its Historical Progress, Its People, and Its Principal Interests*, vol. 2, Lewis, 1914, pp. 777–8.

Garfield, Viola E. Review of *The Bella Coola Indians*. *The Pacific Northwest Quarterly*, vol. 41, no. 4, 1950, pp. 358–9.

Gschaedler, André. Review of *The Bella Coola Indians*. *Boletín Bibliográfico de Antropología Americana* (Mexico), vol. 13, no. 2, 1950, p. 133.

Gunther, Erna. Review of *The Bella Coola Indians*. *The Journal of American Folklore*, vol. 64, no. 253, 1951, p. 33.

"Hamilton Woman Secures Prize" (about Jean N. McIlwraith, *The Little Admiral*). Hamilton *Spectator*, 1 Mar, 1923, n.p.

Hammond, M.O. "Life and Letters" (about Jean N. McIlwraith, *A Diana of Quebec*). *The Globe*, 5 Oct. 1912, p. 18.

Henley, J. Brian. "Thomas G. [sic] McIlwraith." *Hamiltonians: 100 Fascinating Lives*, edited by Margaret Houghton, Lorimer, 2000, p. 108.

Hincks, W. "Catalogue of Birds Known to Inhabit Western Canada." *Journal of the Board of Arts and Manufactures for Upper Canada*, vol. 7, 1867, pp. 9–12.

Holman, Andrew C., and Robert R. Kristofferson, eds. *More of a Man: Diaries of a Scottish Craftsman in Mid-Nineteenth-Century North America*. U of Toronto P, 2013.

Hone, J. Ann. "McIlwraith, John (1828–1903)." *Australian Dictionary of Biography*. Vol. 5, Melbourne UP, 1974, http://adb.anu.edu.au/biography/mcilwraith-john-4098. Accessed 25 July 2019.

"H.P. McIlwraith Called By Death." New Castle *News*, 3 Jan. 1916, n.p.

"H.P. M'Ilwraith Dies Suddenly." New Castle *Herald*, 3 Jan. 1916. n.p.

Huyck, Wendy Ratkowski. "Adapting Through Compromise: Jean Newton McIlwraith and Her Major Novels." MA thesis, University of Guelph, 1988.

– "McIlwraith, Jean Newton." *Dictionary of Hamilton Biography*. Vol. 3, Dictionary of Hamilton Biography, 1992, pp. 136–7.

"Interim Copyrights" (on "The Temple of Fame"). *Canada Gazette*, vol. 26, no. 22, 1892, p. 1002.

Irmscher, Christoph. " 'So That Nothing May Be Lost': Thomas McIlwraith's *The Birds of Ontario.*" *Other Selves: Animals in the Canadian Imagination*, edited by Janice Fiamengo, U of Ottawa P, 2007, pp. 145–69.

"Jean McIlwraith." *World Biographies*, vol. 32, no. 5, 1 May 1901, p. 76.

J.L.G., "Browsings among Books: *The Birds of Ontario.*" *Canadian Baptist*, n.d. (but after 1894), p. 586, clipping, TFMP.

"John G M'Ilwraith Dies at Miami, Fla." Anderson *Herald*, 27 Feb. 1923, p. 1.

"John Goldie, Gardener and Botanist" (Obituary). *Botanical Gazette*, vol. 11, no. 10, 1886, pp. 272–4.

Kingston, Deanna. Review of *At Home with the Bella Coola Indians*. *Oregon Historical Quarterly*, vol. 105, no. 1, 2004, pp. 165–6.

"Knox, William." *The Book of Clevelanders: A Biographical Dictionary of Living Men of the City of Cleveland*. Burrows, 1914, n.p., https://accessgenealogy.com/illinois/biographical-sketch-of-william-knox.htm. Accessed 15 Aug. 2019.

Kröller, Eva-Marie. "McIlwraith, Jean Newton." *Dictionary of Canadian Biography*, vol. 16 (1931–1940), forthcoming.

Lane, Robert B. Review of *The Bella Coola Indians*. *American Indian Quarterly*, vol. 18, no. 1, 1994, pp. 141–3.

"Leads the Reader a Dance" (Review of *The Making of Mary*). New York *Times*, 10 Aug. 1895, p. 3.

Lemoine, James Macpherson. "Thomas McIlwraith, the Canadian Ornithologist." *Canadiana Online*, *Canadian Magazine*, vol. 3, no. 1, May 1894, pp. 91–4.

"*The Making of Mary* (Review)." *Saturday Review*, vol. 80, no. 2073, 20 July 1895, p. 88.

MacMurchy, Marjory. "Canadian Celebrities XXIV: Miss Jean McIlwraith." *Canadiana Online*, *Canadian Magazine*, vol. 17, no. 2, 1901, pp. 131–4.

– "Retrospect of a Year's Books: Review of a Steadily Increasing Output by Canadian Writers in Fiction, Politics, Biography and Poetry" (includes review of *A Diana of Quebec*). *Canadian Courier*, vol. 13, no. 1, 30 Nov. 1912, p. 7.

Marles, Robin J. Review of *At Home with the Bella Coola Indians*. *Canadian Journal of Native Studies*, vol. 16, no. 2, 1996, p. 387.

McIlwraith, Jean Newton. *Woman's Who's Who of America: A Biographical Dictionary of Contemporary Women of the United States and Canada*. Edited by John William Leonard. American Commonwealth Company, 1914, p. 521.

McIlwraith, Thomas F. "An Evening with Thomas McIlwraith." *The Cardinal*, no. 193, Nov. 2003, pp. 24–5.

– "McIlwraith, Thomas." *Dictionary of Canadian Biography*, vol. 13 (1901–1910), http://www.biographi.ca/en/bio/mcilwraith_thomas_13E.html. Accessed 26 July 2019.

"McIlwraith, Thomas Forsyth." *Dictionary of Hamilton Biography*. Vol. 3, Dictionary of Hamilton Biography, 1981, p. 136.

McIlwraith, Thomas F., and Duane McIlwraith. "508, 389, 179, et al: McIlwraith and Child Houses in Hamilton, 1853–1945," typescript, Dec. 2013, TFMP.

"Meet the Editor: Dorothy McIlwraith, Editor, *Short Stories* and *Weird Tales*." *Writers' Journal*, Nov. 1942, p. 4.

Middleton, Diana, and David Walker. "Thomas McIlwraith: Hamilton Coal Merchant and Forwarder, 1871–1893." University of Waterloo, unpublished paper, 20 pp., TFMP.

Morgan, Henry James, ed. "McIlwraith, Miss Jane [sic] Newton." *The Canadian Men and Women of the Time: A Handbook of Biography*, W. Briggs, 1898, pp. 740–1.

– "McIlwraith, Miss Jean Newton." *The Canadian Men and Women of the Time*, 2nd ed. W. Briggs, 1912, pp. 769–70.

"Mort de M.J.H. Holt." *L'Action catholique* (Quebec), 27 July 1915, n.p.

"Mrs. Helen Holt Dies in 90th Year" (Obituary). Quebec *Chronicle-Telegraph*, 26 Oct. 1950, p. 3.

"Négociant très connu qui disparaît" (Obituary John Holt). *L'Action catholique* (Quebec), 27 July 1915, n.p.

Newell, Diane. Review of *At Home with the Bella Coola Indians*. *Canadian Historical Review*, vol. 85, no. 3, 2004, pp. 579–81.

"New Fur House Opens: Holt Renfrew & Company's Store a Dreamland." Montreal *Gazette*, 3 Nov. 1910, n.p.

"New Novels" (Review of *The Making of Mary*). *The Academy*, vol. 48, no. 1214, 24 Aug. 1895, p. 143.

"Notes on Novels" (Review of *The Span o' Life*). *The Academy*, vol. 56, no. 1411, 6 May 1899, p. 508.

"Novels" (Review of *The Span o' Life*). *Saturday Review*, vol. 87, no. 2273, 20 May 1899, p. 631.

Nusqumata (Jacinda Mack). Review of *At Home with the Bella Coola Indians*. *BC Studies*, vol. 141, 2004, pp. 120–1.

"Old Resident Gone" (Obituary, Thomas McIlwraith). Hamilton *Spectator*, 2 Feb. 1903, n.p.

"Our Most Enterprising Colony: An Interview with the Ex-Prime Minister [sic] of Queensland," *Pall Mall Budget*, Part I: 15 Aug. 1884, p. 20; Part II: 22 Aug. 1884, pp. 21–2.

Pringle, Gertrude. "Jean McIlwraith, Canadian Authoress." *Saturday Night*, vol. 41, 30 Jan. 1926, pp. 21, 28.

Review of *At Home with the Bella Coola Indians*, ed. John Barker and Douglas Cole, *SirReadalot.org*, no. 64, Sept. 2004, n.p. http://www.sirreadalot.org/reviews/0065 .htm. Accessed 3 June 2020.

Review of *The Span o' Life*. *The Bookman* (London, UK), vol. 16, no. 93, June 1899, p. 83.

Richling, Barnett. "Scaenae ex matrimonio infelici (Scenes from an Unhappy Marriage)." *Museum Anthropology*, vol. 28, no. 1, 2005, pp. 57–65.

Rubel, Paula, and Abraham Rosman. Review of *The Bella Coola Indians*. *Man*, vol. 29, no. 3, 1994, pp. 771–2.

Saunders, William E. "In Memoriam – Thomas McIlwraith." *Bulletin of the Michigan Ornithological Club*, vol., 4, no. 1, 1903, pp. 1–5.

– Review of *The Birds of Ontario*. *The Auk*, vol. 4, no. 3, 1887, pp. 246–9.

"A Short Guide to New Books" (Review of *The Curious Career of Roderick Campbell*). *World's Work*, vol. 2, no. 2, June 1901, p. 891.

"Sir T. M'Ilwraith, Return to Australia, Account of His Travels, Lady M'Ilwraith's Illness, Hospitality in Canada, The Canadian Route to England, Prospects of Trade, The Pacific Cable, Land-Grant Railways, Secret of Cheap Railway Freights, A New Railway Policy, Solution of the Railway Problem (By Electric Telegraph)." Trove, Brisbane *Courier*, 4 June 1894, p. 5.

Smith, Marian W. Review of *The Bella Coola Indians*. *Canadian Journal of Economics and Political Science*, vol. 15, no. 4, 1949, pp. 560–2.

"South African War." *Carleton Place Local History* (blog), https://carletonplacelocalhistory.wordpress.com/tag/bates-innes-woollen-mill/. Accessed 5 July 2017.

Steer, H.O. Review of *The Bella Coola Indians*. *American Journal of Psychiatry*, vol. 106, no. 11, 1950, p. 879.

"The Temple of Fame." ProQuest, *The Globe*, 26 Oct. 1892, p. 6.

"The Temple of Fame." ProQuest, *The Globe*, 13 Feb. 1897, p. 21.

"The Temple of Fame." ProQuest, *The Globe*, 5 Oct. 1901, p. 9.

"The Temple of Fame: A Brilliant Dramatic Entertainment at Woodstock." ProQuest, *The Globe*, 27 June 1892, p. 5.

Thom, Brian, Review of *At Home with the Bella Coola Indians*. *Anthropologica*, vol. 46, no. 1, 2004, pp. 116–7.

"Thomas G. [sic] McIlwraith." *Dictionary of Hamilton Biography*. Vol. 1, Dictionary of Hamilton Biography, 1981, p. 132.

"Thomas McIlwraith" (Obituary). *The Auk*, vol. 20, 1903, p. 242.

"Thomas McIlwraith" (Obituary). *Emu*, 3, 1903, p. 79.

Tubbs, Frank H. "Shakespeare's Pupils" (about "A Singing-Student in London"). *The Vocalist: A Progressive Magazine Devoted to Science and Art in Music*, vol. 12, 1896, pp. 301–3.

Twaddel, Patricia Ellen. *Back to My Roots and Beyond: An Authenticated History of the Descendancy of the McIlwraith's [sic] of Ayr, Commencing with Thomas of Newton, the Founder of Our Dynasty, Covering the Years from 1740 to the 1980's*. Broadbeach, QLD: McIlwraith Family, 1999.

"U.S. Negro 100 Per Cent Aryan Says Anthropology Professor [T.F. McIlwraith]." *Globe and Mail*, 2 Sept. 1944, p. 5.

Waterson, Duncan. *An Ayrshire Family: The McIlwraiths of Auchenflower, Ayr and Australia*. Ayrshire Archaeological and Natural History Science, 1978.

– "McIlwraith, Andrew (1844–1932)." *Australian Dictionary of Biography*. Vol. 10, Melbourne UP, 1986, http://adb.anu.edu.au/biography/mcilwraith-andrew-7370. Accessed 25 July 2019.

– *Personality, Profit and Politics: Thomas McIlwraith in Queensland, 1866–1894*. U of Queensland P, 1978.

- "Thomas McIlwraith: A Colonial Entrepreneur." *Queensland Political Portraits, 1859–1952*, edited by D.J. Murphy and R.B. Joyce, U of Queensland P, 1978, pp. 119–42.

"What They Read" (Review of *The Curious Career of Roderick Campbell*). *Vogue*, vol. 17, no. 16, 19 Apr. 1901, p. 284.

Wilbor, Elsie M. "What Private Griefs They Have" (about "A Singing-Student in London"). *Werner's Magazine*, vols. 15–16, Mar. 1894, pp. 104–5.

Wilson, Anne Elizabeth. "Beloved Friend" (Obituary of Jean N. McIlwraith). *Saturday Night*, vol. 54, no. 7, 14 Dec. 1938, p. 28.

Government Papers and Law Reports

Deutscher Reichstag. *Weissbuch: Deutsche Interessen in der Südsee*, 1. Session 6. Legislaturperiode. Heymanns, 1885.

Great Britain, Parliament, House of Commons. *Correspondence Respecting Natives of Western Pacific and Labour Traffic*. Parliamentary Papers, C3641. Eyre and Spottiswoode, 1883.

- *Correspondence Respecting New Guinea and Other Islands, and The Convention in Sydney of Representatives of the Australasian Colonies*. Parliamentary Papers, C3863. Eyre and Spottiswoode, 1884.

- *Further Correspondence Respecting New Guinea*. Parliamentary Papers, C3617. Eyre and Spottiswoode, 1883.

- *Further Correspondence Respecting New Guinea*. Parliamentary Papers, C3691. Eyre and Spottiswoode, 1883.

Journals and Printed Papers of the Federal Council of Australasia, January 25 to February 6, 1886. William Thomas Strutt, 1886.

"The Labour Trade." *Report of the Royal Commission to Enquire into Kidnapping of Labourers in New Guinea and Adjacent Islands*. Trove, Brisbane *Courier*, 4 May 1885, pp. 2–3.

The Law Reports: Appeal Cases Before the House of Lords and the Judicial Committee of the Privy Council, Also Peerage Cases, 1882–1883. Vol. 8, Clowes, 1883.

"Post and Telegraph Act 1901" (C1901A00012). Federal Register of Legislation, Australia, https://www.legislation.gov.au/Details/C1901A00012. Accessed 1 August 2019.

Special Joint Committee of the Senate and the House of Commons, Appointed to Continue and Complete Examination and Consideration of the Indian Act. *Minutes of Proceedings and Evidence No. 29. Tuesday, June 3, 1947. Witness: T. F. McIlwraith, M.A., F.R.S.C., Professor of Anthropology, University of Toronto*. Edmond Cloutier, 1947.

General

Adam, Thomas. *Germany and the Americas: Culture, Politics, and History*. ABC Clio, 2005. 3 vols.

Adams, Francis. *The Australians: A Social Sketch*. 1893. Cambridge UP, 2011.

Adams, J.F.A. "Is Botany a Suitable Study for Young Men?" *Science*, vol. 9, no. 209, 1887, pp. 116–7.

Adickes, Sandra. *To Be Young Was Very Heaven: Women in New York Before the First World War*. St. Martin's Griffin, 1997.

Adler, Jacob. "The Oceanic Steamship Company: A Link in Claus Spreckels' Hawaiian Sugar Empire." *Pacific Historical Review*, vol. 29, no. 3, 1960, pp. 257–69.

Adler, Jeremy. "On Steely Wings: Wordsworth, Klopstock and the Poetry of Skating." *TLS*, 4 Dec. 2018, pp. 15–16.

"Advertisements: Grand Garden Fete in Aid of Veterans' Home." Papers Past, *Evening Post* (Wellington), 15 Oct. 1924, p. 6.

De Aguirre, Gertrude G. "A Woman from Altruria." *The Arena*, vol. 27, no. 90, May 1897, pp. 929–34.

Ainley, Marianne Gosztonyi. "Foreword: Thomas McIlwraith (1824–1903) and the Birds of Ontario." *Ornithology in Ontario*, edited by M.K. McNicholl and J.L. Cranmer-Byng, Special Publications No. 1, Ontario Field Ornithologists, Hawk Owl Publishing, 1994, pp. viii–xiii.

– "From Natural History to Avian Biology: Canadian Ornithology 1860–1950." PhD diss., McGill University, 1985.

"Alfred William Rich." *Suffolk Artists*, https://suffolkartists.co.uk/index.cgi. Accessed 26 July 2019.

Amyot, Chantal, and John Willis. *Country Post: Rural Postal Service in Canada, 1880–1945*. Canadian Museum of Civilization, 2003.

Anderson, Duncan. *Lays of Canada, And Other Poems*. Lovell, 1890.

Askey, Jennifer Drake. " 'Von dir hätte ich nur lernen können': The Nineteenth-Century 'Luisenkult' and Literature for Young Women." *Colloquia Germanica*, vol. 39, nos. 3–4, 2006, pp. 317–37.

Ashton, Susanna. *Collaborators in Literary America, 1870–1920*. Palgrave Macmillan, 2003.

Auerbach, Jeffrey A. *Imperial Boredom: Monotony and the British Empire*. Oxford UP, 2018.

Bailey, A.G. *The Conflict of European and Eastern Algonkian Culture, 1504–1700: A Study in Canadian Civilization*. 1937. U of Toronto P, 1969.

Baker, Conrad. "Conesus Steamship Captain was a 'Lincoln Avenger' for Killing John Wilkes Booth." https://geneseesun.com/conesus-steamship-captain-was-a-lincoln -avenger-for-killing-john-wilkes-booth/. Accessed 8 Sept. 2020.

Baker, Deborah. *The Last Englishmen: Love, War and the End of Empire*. Graywolf, 2018.

Balfour, Henry. Diaries of Henry Balfour (1863–1939), Anthropologist and Museum Curator, Australia 1914, BAAS, 3 notebooks, Pitt Rivers Museum, Oxford. https:// www.prm.ox.ac.uk/australia-1914-baas-british-association-advancement-science -meeting-sydney-etc. Accessed 30 Nov. 2017.

Ballantyne, Tony. *Orientalism and Race: Aryanism in the British Empire*. Palgrave, 2002.

Ballantyne, Tony, and Antoinette Burton. *Empires and the Reach of the Global, 1870–1945*. Belknap. 2014.

– eds. *Moving Subjects: Gender, Mobility and Intimacy in an Age of Global Empire*. U of Illinois P, 2009.

Banholzer, Kuno. "Emil Deckert" (Obituary). *Frankfurter Universitäts-Zeitung*, vol. 3, no. 20, Nov. 1916, pp. 23–6.

Banivanua-Mar, Tracey. "Shadowing Imperial Networks: Indigenous Mobility and Australian Pacific Past." *Australian Historical Studies*, vol. 46, no. 3, 2015, pp. 340–55.

– *Violence and Colonial Dialogue: The Australian-Pacific Indentured Labor Trade*. U of Hawai'i P, 2007.

Banivanua-Mar, Tracey, and Nadia Rhook. Introduction, *Counter Networks of Empire: Reading Unexpected People in Unexpected Places*, edited by Nadia Rhook, special issue of *Journal of Colonialism and Colonial History*, vol. 19, no. 2, 2018, n.p.

Bannet, Eve Tavor. *Empire of Letters: Letter Manuals and Transatlantic Correspondence, 1680–1820*. Cambridge UP, 2005.

Barker, John. "Reply to Regna Darnell, 'Toward a History of Canadian Departments of Anthropology.'" *Anthropologica*, vol. 42, no. 1, 2000, pp. 95–7.

Barrie, J.M. *Margaret Ogilvy*. 1896. Hodder and Stoughton, 1924.

Barrow, Mark V. "The Specimen Dealer: Entrepreneurial Natural History in America's Gilded Age." *Journal of the History of Biology*, vol. 33, no. 3, 2000, pp. 493–534.

Barth, Fredrik. "Britain and the Commonwealth." *One Discipline, Four Ways: British, German, French, and American Anthropology*. U of Chicago P, 2005, pp. 3–57.

Bartlett, F.C. "Cambridge, England: 1887–1937." Golden Jubilee Volume, *American Journal of Psychology*, vol. 50, nos. 1–4, 1937, pp. 97–110.

– "W.H.R. Rivers." *The Eagle* (St. John's College Cambridge), vol. 62, no. 269, 1968, pp. 156–60.

Beardmore, Edward. "The Natives of Mowat, Daudai, New Guinea." *Journal of the Anthropological Institute of Great Britain and Ireland*, vol. 19, 1890, pp. 459–66.

Begg, Alexander. *History of British Columbia from its Earliest Discovery to the Present Time*. W. Briggs, 1894.

Belgum, Kirsten. "Popularizing the World: Karl Andree's 'Globus.'" *Colloquia Germanica*, vol. 46, no. 3, 2013, pp. 245–65.

Belich, James. *Replenishing the Earth: The Settler Revolution and the Rise of the Anglo-World, 1783–1939*. Oxford UP, 2009.

Bell, Joshua. "'For Scientific Purposes a Stand Camera is Essential': Salvaging Photographic Histories in Papua." *Photography, Anthropology and History: Expanding the Frame*, edited by Elizabeth Edwards and Christopher Morton, Ashgate, 2009, pp. 143–70.

Bellow, Saul. "Chicago: The City That Was, The City That Is." *There Is Simply Too Much to Think About: Collected Nonfiction*, edited by Benjamin Taylor, Viking, 2015, pp. 374–9.

Benoît, Jean. "Renfrew, George Richard." *Dictionary of Canadian Biography*, vol. 12
    (1891–1900), http://www.biographi.ca/en/bio/renfrew_george_richard_12E.html.
    Accessed 26 July 2019.

Bennett, Arnold. "W.H.R. Rivers: Some Recollections." *Things That Have Interested Me:
    Second Series*. Chatto and Windus, 1923, pp. 1–7.

Bergantz, Alexis. " 'The Scum of France': Australian Anxieties towards French
    Convicts in the Nineteenth Century." *Australian Historical Studies*, vol. 49, no. 2,
    2018, pp. 150–66.

Bernays, Charles Arrowsmith. *Queensland Politics During Sixty (1859–1919) Years*.
    Government Printer, 1919.

"Big Feather: Dr. Gilbert Monture." Veterans Affairs Canada, https://www.veterans.
    gc.ca/eng/remembrance/those-who-served/indigenous-veterans/native-soldiers/
    feather. Accessed 26 July 2019.

Binnema, Ted. *Enlightened Zeal: The Hudson's Bay Company and Scientific Networks,
    1670–1870*. U of Toronto P, 2014.

Blainey, Geoffrey. *Black Kettle and Full Moon: Daily Life in a Vanished Australia*.
    Penguin, 2003.

– *The Tyranny of Distance: How Distance Shaped Australia's History*. 1966. Pan
    Macmillan, 2010.

Birk, Hanne, and Birgit Neumann. "The Tree and the Family: Metaphors as Discursive
    Supports of British Imperial Culture in Froude's *Oceana*." *AAA* [*Arbeiten aus
    Anglistik und Amerikanistik*], vol. 31, no. 1, 2006, pp. 63–79.

Böhmert, Viktor. "Die Staatsangehörigkeit und Gebürtigkeit der sächsischen
    Bevölkerung nach den fünf Volkszählungen von 1871–1890." *Zeitschrift des k.
    Sächsischen Statistischen Bureaus*, vol. 38, 1892, pp. 219–33.

Boney, A.D. "The Botanical 'Establishment' Closes Ranks: Fifteen Days in January
    1921." *The Linnean*, vol. 11, no. 3, 1995, pp. 26–37.

"Books as Main Motif in House-Furnishing Scheme." Trove, Sydney *Morning Herald*,
    12 Mar. 1936, p. 24.

Booth, D.C. "Armistice Day Siege." *A Newnham Anthology*, edited by A. Phillips,
    Cambridge UP, 1979, pp. 119–26.

"Booth, William Stone." *The National Cyclopaedia of American Biography*. Vol. 20,
    James T. White, 1929, pp. 261–2.

Bott, Alan. *An Airman's Outings*. Blackwood, 1917.

Bottoms, Timothy. *Conspiracy of Silence: Queensland's Frontier Killing Times*. Allen and
    Unwin, 2013.

Bouchier, Nancy B., and Ken Cruikshank. *The People and the Bay: A Social and
    Environmental History of Hamilton Harbour*. UBC Press, 2016.

Bowman, Joyce. "Reconstructing the Past Using the British Parliamentary Papers: The
    Anglo-Zulu War of 1879." *History in Africa*, vol. 31, 2004, pp. 117–32.

Boyle, Michael. "Major General Sir Henry Hugh Tudor (1871–1965)." *Canadian
    Journal of Irish Studies*, vol. 34, no. 2, 2008, p. 65.

Bracq, Jean Charlemagne. *The Evolution of French Canada*. Macmillan, 1924.

Brebner, J.B., revised by Philip Buckner. "Wrong, George Mackinnon (1860–1948)." *Oxford Dictionary of National Biography*, https://doi.org/10.1093/ref:odnb/37043. Accessed 26 July 2019.

Breckinridge, Mary. *Wide Neighbourhoods: A Story of the Frontier Nursing Service.* UP of Kentucky, 1981.

Brewster, William. "The Present Status of the Wild Pigeon (*Ectopistes Migratorius*) as a Bird of the United States, with Some Notes on its Habits." *The Auk*, vol. 6, no. 4, 1889, pp. 285–91.

Brodie, Nick. *Kin: A Real People's History of Our Nation.* Hardie Grant, 2015.

Brogiato, Heinz Peter. "Deckert, Friedrich Karl Emil." *Sächsische Biografie*, edited by Institut für Sächsische Geschichte und Volkskunde, http://www.isgv.de/saebi/. Accessed 26 July 2019.

Brooke, Christopher. *A History of Gonville and Caius College.* Boydell, 1985.

Brooks, Marjorie. "Allan Brooks – A Biography." *The Condor*, vol. 40, no. 1, 1938, pp. 12–17.

Broomhead, Frank. *The Zaehnsdorfs, 1842–1947: Craft Bookbinders.* Private Libraries Association, 1986.

Brophy, James. *Popular Culture and the Public Sphere in the Rhineland, 1800–1850.* Cambridge UP, 2007.

Brown, Judith M., and Wm. Roger Louis, eds. *The Oxford History of the British Empire*, Vol. 4: *The Twentieth Century.* Oxford UP, 1999.

"Browne, Michael Wilson." *Dictionary of Hamilton Biography.* Vol. 1, Dictionary of Hamilton Biography, 1981.

Browne, Spencer R. *A Journalist's Memories.* Read Press, 1927.

Brunken, Otto, et al., eds. *Handbuch zur Kinder- und Jugendliteratur: Von 1850 bis 1900.* Springer, 2008

Buchan, John. *The African Colony: Studies in the Reconstruction.* Blackwood, 1903.

– *The History of the South African Forces in France.* Nelson, 1920.

Buchanan, Colin. "Canadian Anthropology and Ideas of Aboriginal Emendation." *Historicizing Canadian Anthropology*, edited by Regna Darnell and Julia Harrison, UBC Press, 2006, pp. 93–106.

Buitenhuis, Peter. *The Great War of Words: British, American, and Canadian Propaganda and Fiction, 1913–1933.* UBC Press, 1987.

Burroughs, John. "The Nature Library and What It Means to the Reader." Introduction to Neltje Blanchan, *Bird Neighbors: An Introductory Acquaintance with One Hundred and Fifty Birds Commonly Found in the Gardens, Meadows and Woods About Our Homes.* 1897. Doubleday, 1918, pp. ix–xv.

Cabajsky, Andrea, and Brett Joseph Grubisic, eds. *National Plots: Historical Fiction and Changing Ideas of Canada.* Wilfrid Laurier UP, 2010.

Cable, K.J. "Radford, Lewis Bostock (1869–1937)." *Australian Dictionary of Biography.* Vol. 11, Melbourne UP, 1988, http://adb.anu.edu.au/biography/radford-lewis-bostock-8147. Accessed 19 Nov. 2017.

Caine, Barbara. *From Bloomsbury to Bombay: A Biography of the Strachey Family.* Oxford UP, 2005.

Calvin, D.D. "Letters from 'T.R.' " *Queen's Quarterly*, vol. 50, no. 4, 1943, pp. 394–401.

Cameron, Elspeth, with Gail Kreutzer. *A Tale of Two Divas: The Curious Adventures of Jean Forsyth and Edith J. Miller in Canada's Edwardian West*. J. Gordon Shillingford, 2016.

Campbell, Marjorie Freeman. *A Mountain and a City: The Story of Hamilton*. McClelland and Stewart, 1966.

Carman, Jillian. *Uplifting the Colonial Philistine: Florence Phillips and the Making of the Johannesburg Art Gallery*. Witwatersrand UP, 2006.

Carter, Kathryn D. "A Contingency of Words: Diaries in English by Women in Canada, 1830–1915." PhD diss., University of Alberta, 1997.

– *The Small Details of Life: Twenty Diaries by Women in Canada, 1830–1996*. U of Toronto P, 2002.

Casey, Gilbert. "The Q.N. Bankrupt Party, and Their Leader, M'Ilwraith." *The Worker* (Brisbane), 21 Oct. 1893, p. 3.

Catalogue of Books in the Legislative Library of the Province of Ontario, on November 1, 1912. L. K. Cameron, 1913.

A Catalogue of Books Recommended by the Church Library Association, for Sunday School and Church Libraries. Cambridge, MA: s.n., 1909.

Catalogue of the Library of the Illinois State Penitentiary, Joliet, Illinois. Joliet Republication Printing, 1902.

"Miss Cathlin Cicely du Sautoy." *British Journal of Nursing*, vol. 49, 28 Dec. 1912, p. 516.

"Cathlin Cicely du Sautoy." *British Journal of Nursing*, vol. 69, 18 Nov. 1922, p. 324.

Caves, Roger W. *Encyclopedia of the City*. Routledge, 2004.

Ceadel, Martin. *Living the Great Illusion: Sir Norman Angell, 1872–1967*. Oxford UP, 2009.

Cella, Laurie. *The Personal and the Political in American Working-Class Literature, 1850–1939: Defining the Radical Romance*. Lexington Books, 2019.

Chamberlain, Montague. *A Catalogue of Canadian Birds, with Notes on the Distribution of the Species*. McMillan, 1887.

Châtenay, Victor. "Des bagnards au Gotha, mon journal de 14–18, "*Mémoires de Victor Chatenay, sapeur-mineur au 1er génie 22e battalion, 28e compagnie puis chauffeur au 9e escadron du train des équipages militaires*. Imprimerie de l'Anjou, 1968, http://www.chtimiste.com/carnets/Chatenay%20Victor/Chatenay%20Victor.htm. Accessed 27 July 2019.

"Children from Cuba Held on Ellis Island." New York *Times*, 2 Nov. 1902, p. 7.

"Chronik vom Tage," *Vossische Zeitung*, 7 May 1933, n.p.

Clark, Ian D. "*A Peep at the Blacks*": *A History of Tourism at Coranderrk Aboriginal Station, 1863–1924*. Walter de Gruyter, 2015.

Clarke, David. *The Angel of Mons: Phantom Soldiers and Ghostly Guardians*. Wiley, 2005.

A Classified Catalogue of 3500 Volumes Suitable for a Public Library. McClurg, 1901.

Cleall, Esme, et al., eds. *Imperial Relations: Histories of Family in the British Empire*, special issue of *Journal of Colonialism and Colonial History*, vol. 14, no. 1, 2013.

Cohen, Deborah. *Household Gods: The British and their Possessions*. Yale UP, 2006.

Cole, Douglas. *Captured Heritage: The Scramble for Northwest Coast Artifacts*. 1985. UBC Press, 1995.

Cole, Rose Owen. *Lessons in Cookery: Hand-book of the National Training School for Cookery (South Kensington, London) to which is added, The Principles of Diet in Health and Disease*, by Thomas K. Chambers. 1877. M.D. Appleton, 1878.

Coleman, Daniel. *White Civility: The Literary Project of English Canada*. U of Toronto P, 2014.

The Collection of Mr. Henry Lanier of New York City, with Additions: Early American Furniture. Anderson Galleries, 1923.

Colley, Linda. *Britons: Forging the Nation, 1707-1837*. Yale UP, 1992.

Collier's New Practical Guide to Dresden, 14th ed. Tittmann, 1910.

Conway, R.S., rev. A.M. Snodgrass. "Ridgeway, Sir William (1858-1926)." *Oxford Dictionary of National Biography*, https://www.oxforddnb.com/view/10.1093/ref:odnb/9780198614128.001.0001/odnb-9780198614128-e-1004504. Accessed 27 July 2019.

Cook, Della Collins. "Neglected Ancestors: Robert Wilson Shufeldt, MD (1850-1934)." *The Global History of Paleopathology: Pioneers and Prospects*, edited by Jane Buikstra and Charlotte Roberts, Oxford UP, 2012, pp. 192-6.

Cook, Tim. "From Destruction to Construction: The Khaki University of Canada, 1917-1919." *Journal of Canadian Studies*, vol. 37, no. 1, 2002, pp. 109-43.

Cooper, John A. "A Literary Rendezvous of Quebec." Canadiana Online, *Canadian Magazine*, vol. 7, no. 6, Oct. 1896, pp. 511-14.

Cooper, John Milton. *Walter Hines Page: The Southerner as American, 1855-1918*. U of North Carolina P, 1977.

Cope, K.B. MacP., " 'Poisonous Place.' " *A Newnham Anthology*, edited by A. Phillips, Cambridge UP, 1979, pp. 126-31.

Corfield, William. *Reminiscences of Queensland, 1862-1899*. A.H. Frater, 1921.

"Court Circular." *The Times* (London), 10 Oct. 1918, n.p.

Cowan, James. *The Maoris in the Great War*. Whitcombe & Tombs, 1926.

Crowley, T.A. "Johnstone, James, known as the Chevalier de Johnstone." *Dictionary of Canadian Biography*, vol. 4 (1771-1800), www.biographi.ca/en/bio/johnstone _james_4E.html. Accessed 27 July 2019.

Crowley, Terry. "Hunter, Adelaide Sophia (Hoodless)." *Dictionary of Canadian Biography*, vol. 13 (1901-1910), http://www.biographi.ca/en/bio/hunter_adelaide _sophia_13E.html. Accessed 27 July 2017.

"Cummings, James." *Dictionary of Hamilton Biography*. Vol. 1, Dictionary of Hamilton Biography, 1981, p. 5.

Cunniff, M.G. "The New York Subway." *World's Work*, vol. 8, no. 6, 1904, pp. 5346-64.

Cunniff, M. G., and Arthur Goodrich. "The Rebuilding of New York." *World's Work*, vol. 3, no. 2, 1901, pp. 1485-511.

Cusack, O.J.M. "Paley's Ghost." *A Newnham Anthology*, edited by A. Phillips, Cambridge UP, 1979, pp. 100-1.

Daley, Paul. " 'Wholesale Massacre': Carl Feilberg Exposed the Ugly Truth of the Australian Frontier." *Guardian*, 20 Sept. 2018, https://www.theguardian.com /australia-news/postcolonial-blog/2018/sep/21/wholesale-massacre-carl-feilberg -exposed-the-ugly-truth-of-the-australian-frontier. Accessed 17 July 2019.

Dalziell, Rosamund. "Everard im Thurn in Guiana and the Western Pacific." *Writing, Travel and Empire: In the Margins of Anthropology*, edited by Peter Hulme and Russell McDougall. Tauris, 2007, pp. 97–118.

"Dan R. Hanna Dies Suddenly in Bed." ProQuest, New York *Times*, 4 Nov. 1921, p. 17.

Darnell, Regna. "Toward a History of Canadian Departments of Anthropology." *Anthropologica*, vol. 40, no. 2, 1998, pp. 153–68.

Davey, Ian E. "Educational Reform and the Working Class: School Attendance in Hamilton, Ontario, 1851–1891." PhD diss., University of Toronto, 1975.

"David Henry Laird (1875–1952)." Manitoba Historical Society, *Memorable Manitobans*, http://www.mhs.mb.ca/docs/people/laird_dh.shtml. Accessed 17 Aug. 2019.

"The Dawdle and Circumlocution Offices." Trove, *Pall Mall Gazette*, n.d, rpt. in Brisbane *Courier*, 9 Feb. 1885, p. 3.

Deacon, Desley, et al., eds. *Transnational Lives: Biographies of Global Modernity, 1700– Present*. Palgrave Macmillan, 2010.

"Death of Lord Plunket: Passing of a Popular Ex-Governor." Papers Past, *Press* (Christchurch, NZ), vol. 56, no. 16741, 26 Jan. 1920, p. 6.

Deckert, Emil. *Das Britische Weltreich: ein politisch- und wirtschaftlichgeographisches Charakterbild*. Keller, 1916.

– *Die Kolonialreiche und Kolonisationsgebiete der Gegenwart: Kolonialpolitische und kolonialgeographische Skizzen*. 1884. Baldamus, 1888.

– *Über die geographischen Grundvoraussetzungen der Hauptbahnen des Weltverkehrs*. Frohberg, 1883.

Dembski, Peter E. Paul, ed. *Travels and Identities: Elizabeth and Adam Shortt in Europe, 1911*. Wilfrid Laurier UP, 2016.

Devine, T.M. *The Scottish Nation 1700–2000*. Penguin, 1999.

– *To the Ends of the Earth: Scotland's Global Diaspora, 1750–2010*. Penguin, 2011.

Devine, T.M., and John M. Mackenzie. "Scots in the Imperial Economy." *Scotland and the British Empire*, edited by T.M. Devine and John M. Mackenzie. Oxford UP, 2011, pp. 227–54.

Dexter, Mary. *In the Soldier's Service: War Experiences of Mary Dexter, England – Belgium – France 1914–1918, edited by her mother*. Houghton Mifflin, 1918.

Dickens, Charles Jr. *Dickens' Dictionary of London*. Macmillan, 1882.

Dietmar, Carl. "Erster Weltkrieg: Befehl der Engländer: In Köln gehen die Uhren anderst." *Kölner Stadt-Anzeiger*, 24 Sept. 2014, n.p.

Dilke, Charles Wentworth. *Problems of Greater Britain*. Macmillan, 1890. 2 vols.

"A 'Disloyal' Chief Justice." Trove, Moreton *Mail*, 1 Mar. 1889, p. 9.

Distad, Merrill. "The Postcard – A Brief History." *Peel's Prairie Provinces*, Peel Library, University of Alberta, http://peel.library.ualberta.ca/postcardhistory.html. Accessed 28 July 2019.

Doan, Laura. "Primum Mobile: Women and Auto/mobility in the Era of the Great War." *Women: A Cultural Review*, vol. 17, no. 1, 2006, pp. 26–41.

Dodge, Mary Mapes. "Jack-in-the-Pulpit." *St. Nicholas*, vol. 1, no. 1, Nov. 1873, p. 46.

Doubleday, F.N. *The Memoirs of a Publisher*. Doubleday, 1972.

Doust, Janet L. "Two English Immigrant Families in Australia in the 19th Century." *History of the Family*, vol. 13, no. 1, 2008, pp. 2–25.

Downie, Jill. *A Passionate Pen: The Life and Times of Faith Fenton*. HarperCollins, 1996.

Drazin, Charles. *Mapping the Past: A Search for Five Brothers at the Edge of Empire*. Heinemann, 2016.

Driver, Elizabeth. *Culinary Landmarks: A Bibliography of Canadian Cookbooks, 1825–1949*. U of Toronto P, 2008.

Duchesne, Raymond. "Science et société coloniale: les naturalistes du Canada français et leurs correspondants scientifiques (1860–1900)." *HSTC [History of Canadian Science, Technology and Medicine] Bulletin*, vol. 5, no. 2, May 1981, pp. 99–139.

Dufour, Pierre, and Jean Hamelin. "Sales Laterrière, Pierre de. " *Dictionary of Canadian Biography*, vol. 5 (1801–1820), http://www.biographi.ca/en/bio/sales_laterriere_pierre_de_5E.html. Accessed 28 July 2019.

Duffy, Dennis. "Child, Philip." *Canadian Writers, 1920–1959*: First Series, edited by William H. New, Gale, 1988. *Dictionary of Literary Biography*, vol. 68. Gale Literature Resource Centre. Accessed 7 Aug. 2019.

Dülffer, Jost, et al. *Vermiedene Kriege: Deeskalation von Konflikten der Grossmächte zwischen Krimkrieg und Erstem Weltkrieg, 1865–1914*. Oldenbourg, 1997.

Dunne, Pete. *On Birdwatching: A Beginner's Guide to Finding, Identifying and Enjoying Birds*. Stackpole Books, 2015.

Dyrenfurth, Nick. "The Fat Man in History," *The Monthly*, June 2012, https://www.themonthly.com.au/issue/2012/june/1342072733/nick-dyrenfurth/fat-man-history. Accessed 28 July 2019.

– " 'Truth and Time Against the World's Wrongs': Montagu Scott, Jim Case and the Lost World of Brisbane *Worker* Cartoonists." *Labour History*, no. 99, Nov. 2010, pp. 115–48.

"Eckstorm, Fannie Pearson Hardy (Mrs. Jacob A. Eckstorm)." *The National Cyclopaedia of American Biography*. Vol. 36, James T. White, 1950, p. 199.

Eidelberg, Martin, Nina Gray, and Margaret K. Hofer. *A New Light: Clara Driscoll and the Tiffany Girls*. New York Historical Society and Giles, 2007.

"Elevation in Rank of Fair Women Who Have Married Heirs to Great Names Will Further Americanize British Peerage." Chronicling America: Historic American Newspapers, *San Francisco Call*, vol. 94, no. 126, 4 Oct. 1903, p. 1.

Elliot, Robert. *Robert Elliot's Poems*, edited by John Dearness and Frank Lawson. Lawson & Jones, 1904.

"Empire Day Celebrations." Gale Primary Sources, Cambridge *Independent Press*, 25 May 1917, p. 5.

"An Engagement, Wedding, and Viceregal Visit." Trove, *The Register* (Adelaide), 4 Mar. 1926, p. 3.

"Englishwomen with the French Army: Miss Toupie Lowther's Unit." *Times Digital Archive, 1785–1985, The Times* (London), 5 Aug. 1919, p. 13.

E.Q.V. "Canadian Celebrities: William McLennan." Canadiana Online, *Canadian Magazine*, vol. 13, no. 3, 1899, pp. 251–3.

Errington, Elizabeth Jane. *Emigrant Worlds and Transatlantic Communities: Migration to Upper Canada in the First Half of the Nineteenth Century*. McGill-Queen's UP, 2007.

Evans, Raymond. "The Country Has Another Past: Queensland and the History Wars." *Passionate Histories: Myth, Memory and Aboriginal Australia*, edited by Frances Peters-Little et al. ANU Press, 2010, pp. 9–38.

– "Done and Dusted." *Griffith Review*, special issue: *Hidden Queensland*, ed. 21, 2008, https://griffithreview.com/articles/done-and-dusted/. Accessed 28 July 2019.

Everett, William A. "Chu Chin Chow and Orientalist Musical Theatre in Britain during the First World War." *Music and Orientalism in the British Empire, 1780s-1940s: Portrayal of the East*, edited by Martin Clayton and Bennett Zon, Ashgate, 2007, pp. 277–96.

Exporters' Encyclopedia, 10th ed. Dun and Bradstreet, 1914.

Fairclough, Henry Rushton. *Warming Both Hands: The Autobiography of Henry Rushton Fairclough, including His Experiences Under the American Red Cross in Switzerland and Montenegro*. Stanford UP, 1941.

"Fancy Dress Ball at Government House." Trove, Brisbane *Courier*, 29 May 1875, p. 5.

"Fancy Dress Ball at Te Koraha." Papers Past, *The Star* (Christchurch), no. 19841, 9 Jan. 1920, n.p.

Farge, Arlette. *The Allure of the Archive*. Translated by Thomas Scott-Railton. Yale UP, 2013.

– *Le Goût de l'archive*. Editions du Seuil, 1989.

Farrell, Ella G. *Among the Blue Laurentians, Queenly Montreal, Quaint Quebec, Peerless Ste. Anne de Beaupré*. P.J. Kenedy, 1912.

Farrell, J.G. *The Siege of Krishnapur*. Phoenix, 1973.

Ferguson, Niall. *The Pity of War: Explaining World War I*. Penguin, 1998.

– *The Square and the Tower: Networks and Power, from the Freemasons to Facebook*. Penguin, 2017.

Fiamengo, Janice. "Rediscovering Our Foremothers Again: The Racial Ideas of Canada's Early Feminists, 1885–1945." Academic Search Premier, *Essays on Canadian Writing*, no. 75, Winter 2002, pp. 85–117.

Figueiredo, Estrela, and Gideon Smith. "Who's In a Name: Eponymy of the Name Aloe Thompsoniae Groenew, with Notes on Naming Species after People." *Bradleya*, vol. 29, no. 201, pp. 121–4.

Fisher, Laura R. "Writing Immigrant Aid: The Settlement House and the Problem of Representation." *MELUS*, vol. 37, no. 2, 2012, pp. 83–107.

Fitzpatrick, Sheila. "On the Trail of Miklouho-Maclay: A Russian Encounter in the Antipodes." *The Atlantic World in the Antipodes: Effects and Transformations since the Eighteenth Century*, edited by Kate Fullagar. Cambridge Scholars Publishing, 2012, pp. 166–84.

"Fitzroy House Opened: Cambridge Club for Soldiers' and Sailors' Wives." Gale Primary Sources, Cambridge *Independent Press*, 26 Feb. 1915, p. 7.

Fleming, Andrew Magnus. *Captain Kiddle*. John Alden, 1889.

Fleming, C.A. *How to Write a Business Letter: A Manual for Use in Colleges, Schools, and for Private Learners*. Northern Business College Steam Press, 1890.

Flynn, Barry. *Political Football: The Life and Death of Belfast Celtic*. History Press, 2009.

"For Women." Papers Past, *Press* (Christchurch and Canterbury, NZ), vol. 77, no. 23424, 3 Sept. 1941, n.p.

"For Women: Current Notes." Papers Past, *Press* (Christchurch and Canterbury, NZ), vol. 79, no. 23996, 10 July 1943, n.p.

Foster, Jeremy. "John Buchan's *Hesperides*: The Aesthetics of Improvement on the Highveld." *Washed with the Sun: Landscape and the Making of White South Africa*, edited by Jeremy Foster. U of Pittsburgh P, 2008, pp. 119–43.

Foster, Jeremy, ed. *Washed with the Sun: Landscape and the Making of White South Africa*. U of Pittsburgh P, 2008.

Foster, John. *Ayrshire*. Cambridge UP, 1910.

Foster, Stephen. *A Private Empire*. Pier 9, 2010.

"Four Scenes of Life in Five Years' Time under the Glorious McIlwraith Government." Trove, Mackay *Mercury*, 5 May 1888, p. 2.

Fox, James. *British Art and the First World War, 1914–1924*. Cambridge UP, 2015.

Francis, Mark. "Gordon, Arthur Charles Hamilton, First Baron Stanmore (1829–1912)." *Oxford Dictionary of National Biography*, https://doi.org/10.1093/ref:odnb/33459. Accessed 8 Aug. 2019.

Fraser, Maryna. "Phillips, Sir Lionel, First Baronet (1855–1936)." *Oxford Dictionary of National Biography*, https://doi.org/10.1093/ref:odnb/39343. Accessed 28 July 2019.

Fraser, Maryna, and Alan Jeeves, eds. *All that Glittered: Selected Correspondence of Lionel Phillips, 1890–1924*. Oxford UP, 1977.

Friedland, Martin. *The University of Toronto: A History*. U of Toronto P, 2002.

Frost, Lucy, ed. *No Place for a Nervous Lady: Voices from the Australian Bush*. McPhee Gribble/Penguin, 1984.

Frost, Stanley Brice. "Macdonald, Sir William Christopher." *Dictionary of Canadian Biography*, vol. 14 (1911–1920), http://www.biographi.ca/en/bio/macdonald_william_christopher_14E.html. Accessed 27 July 2017.

Fullagar, Kate, ed. *The Atlantic World in the Antipodes: Effects and Transformations since the Eighteenth Century*. Cambridge Scholars Publishing, 2012.

Furse, Ralph Dolignon. *Aucuparius: Recollections of a Recruiting Officer*. Oxford UP, 1962.

Fussell, Paul. *Abroad: British Literary Travelling Between the Wars*. Oxford UP, 1980.

Gailey, Andrew. *The Lost Imperialist: Lord Dufferin, Memory and Mythmaking in an Age of Celebrity*. John Murray, 2015.

Gallagher, Charles A., and Cameron D. Lippard, eds. *Race and Racism in the United States: An Encyclopedia of the American Mosaic*. ABC-CLIO, LLC, 2014.

Gammond, Peter. "Ayer, Nat D." *Oxford Companion to Popular Music*. Oxford UP, 1991, p. 28.

– "Darewski, H.E." *Oxford Companion to Popular Music*. Oxford UP, 1991, pp. 147–8.

– "Guilbert, Yvette." *Oxford Companion to Popular Music*. Oxford UP, 1991, pp. 245–6.

– "Tango." *Oxford Companion to Popular Music*. Oxford UP, 1991. pp. 564–5.

Garrett, A.S. "Robert Elliott Was Known as Poet-Naturalist – Native of London Township Became Famed as Writer and Student – Forced from School Through Ill Health – Devoted Himself to Favorite Work During Life at Old Family Homestead." London *Free Press*, 29 Aug. 1936, p. 15. Clipping reproduced in Judd, *Memorabilia of Robert Elliott*, p. 18.

Gendreau, Bianca. "Putting Pen to Paper," *Special Delivery: Canada's Postal Heritage*, edited by Francine Brousseau. Canadian Museum of Civilization/Goose Lane Editions, 2000, pp. 23–33.

Gerber, David A. *Authors of Their Lives: The Personal Correspondence of British Immigrants to North America in the Nineteenth Century*. New York UP, 2006.

Germer, Ernst. "Miklucho-Maklai und die koloniale Annexion Neuguineas durch das kaiserliche Deutschland 1884." *Beiträge zur Völkerforschung: Hans Damm zum 65. Geburtstag*, edited by Dietrich Drost and Wolfgang König, vol. 1, Akademie-Verlag, 1961, pp. 153–70; illustrations in vol. 2, pp. 51–4.

"A German on Our Colonies." Trove, *Morning Bulletin* (Rockhampton, QLD), suppl., 30 May 1884, p. 1.

"A German View of the British Empire." Trove, *Western Star and* Roma *Advertiser*, 31 May 1884, p. 3.

Gerson, Carole. *Canadian Women in Print, 1750–1918*. Wilfrid Laurier UP, 2010.

Gerson, Carole, and Jacques Michaud, eds. *History of the Book in Canada*, Vol. 3: *1918–1980*. U of Toronto P, 2007.

Getty, Cassandra. *Arthur Heming: Chronicler of the North*. Museum London, 2013.

Getty, R.J. "The Orator Emeritus" (About T.R. Glover). *The Eagle* (St. John's College Cambridge), vol. 51, no. 224, 1939, pp. 211–36.

Gibbney, H.J. "Musgrave, Sir Anthony (1828–1888). *Australian Dictionary of Biography*. Vol., 5, Melbourne UP, 1974, http://adb.anu.edu.au/biography/musgrave -sir-anthony-4283. Accessed 28 July 2019.

Gibson, Sarah Katherine. " 'In Quist of a Better Hame': A Transatlantic Lowland Scottish Network in Lower Canada, 1800–1850." *A Global Clan: Scottish Migrant Networks and Identities since the Eighteenth Century*, edited by Angela McCarthy, Tauris, 2006, pp. 127–49.

Gillis, Robert Peter. "George Bryson." *Dictionary of Canadian Biography*, vol. 12 (1891–1900), http://biographi.ca/en/bio/bryson_george_12E.html. Accessed 28 July 2019.

Glazer, Penina Migdal. "Neilson, William Allan (28 March 1869–13 February 1946)." *American National Biography*, vol. 16, edited by John A. Garraty and Mark C. Carnes, Oxford UP, 1999, pp. 273–4.

Glover, Richard. "War and Civilian Historians." *Canadian Military History*, vol. 23, no. 2, 2015, pp. 165–85.

Glover, T.R. *Cambridge Retrospect*. Cambridge UP, 1943.

Glover, T.R., and D.D. Calvin, *A Corner of Empire: The Old Ontario Strand*. Cambridge UP, 1937.

Golden, Catherine. *Posting It: The Victorian Revolution in Letter Writing*. U of Florida P, 2009.

Goldstein, Daniel. " 'Yours for Science': The Smithsonian Institution's Correspondents and the Shape of Scientific Community in Nineteenth-Century America." *Isis*, vol. 85, no. 4, 1994, pp. 573–99.

Goody, Jack. *The Logic of Writing and the Organization of Society*. Cambridge UP, 1986.

Goodyear Kirkman, Grace. *Genealogy of the Goodyear Family*. Cubery, 1899.

Gopal, Priyamvada. *Insurgent Empire: Anticolonial Resistance and British Dissent*. Verso, 2019.

Gossage, Carolyn. *A Question of Privilege: Canada's Independent Schools*. Peter Martin, 1977.

Government of Canada. "History of Canadian Passports," 2014, http://www.cic.gc.ca /english/games/teachers-corner/history-passports.asp. Accessed 13 July 2017.

Gräbel, Carsten. *Die Erforschung der Kolonien: Expeditionen und koloniale Wissenskultur deutscher Geographen, 1884–1919*. Transcript, 2015.

Granovetter, Mark S. "The Strength of Weak Ties." *American Journal of Sociology*, vol. 78, no. 6, May 1973, pp. 1360–80.

Grattan, C. Hartley. "The Walter Hines Page Legend." *American Mercury*, vol. 6, 1925, pp. 39–51.

Green, Judy, and Jeanne LaDuke. *Pioneering Women in American Mathematics: The Pre-1940 PhDs*. *History of Mathematics*, vol. 34, American Mathematical Society, 2008.

Greenwalt. Emmett A. *The Point Loma Community in California, 1897–1942: A Theosophical Experiment*. U of California P, 1955.

Greer, Kirsten. "Placing Colonial Ornithology: Imperial Ambiguities in Upper Canada, 1791–1841." *Scientia Canadensis*, vol. 31, nos. 1–2, 2008, pp. 85–112.

Greer, Kirsten, and Laura Cameron. "Swee-ee-et Cán-a-da, Cán-a-da, Cán-a-da: Sensuous Landscapes of Birdwatching in the Eastern Provinces, 1900–1939." *Material History Review/Revue d'histoire de la culture matérielle*, vol. 62, 2005, pp. 35–48.

Greer, Kirsten, and Jeanne Kay Guelke. " 'Intrepid Naturalists and Polite Observers': Gender and Recreational Birdwatching in Southern Ontario, 1791–1886." *Journal of Sport History*, vol. 30, no. 3, 2003, pp. 323–46.

Grove, George, and John Alexander Fuller-Maitland. *Dictionary of Music and Musicians, 1450–1889*. Theodore Presser, 1895. 4 vols.

Gutsche, Thelma. *No Ordinary Woman: The Life and Times of Florence Phillips*. Howard Timmins, 1966.

Haddon, A.C. *A Brief History of the Study of Anthropology at Cambridge.* Museum of Archaeology and Ethnology (now the Museum of Archaeology and Anthropology), 1923.

- "The Congress of Americanists at Quebec." *Nature,* vol. 74, 1906, pp. 595–6.
- "A Plea for a Bureau of Ethnology in the British Empire." *Nature,* vol. 56, 1897, pp. 574–5.
- "Three Days in the Thick of It: With the Y.M.C.A. in an Advanced Position on the Western Front." *Red Triangle* (YMCA), 20 July 1917, pp. 652–4.
- "Sir William Ridgeway" (Obituary). *Nature,* vol. 118, no. 2964, 21 Aug. 1926, pp. 275–6.
- "Dr. W.H.R. Rivers, F.R.S." (Obituary). *Nature,* vol. 109, 17 June 1922, pp. 786–7.

Haddon, A.C., and Alfred P. Maudslay. "Baron Anatole von Hügel" (Obituary). *Man,* vol. 28, 1928, pp. 169–71.

Haeckel, Ernst. *Englands Blutschuld am Weltkriege.* Kayser, 1914.

Hagen, Carrie. *We Is Got Him: The Kidnapping that Changed America.* Overlook Books, 2012.

"Halifax County: Dartmouth Agricultural Society, 1 July 1887." *Journal and Proceedings of the House of Assembly of the Province of Nova Scotia,* Session 1888. Queen's Printer, 1888, pp. lx–lxiii.

Halliday, D.L. "Years of Renaissance." *A Newnham Anthology,* edited by A. Phillips, Cambridge UP, 1979, pp. 136–43.

Hamel, Nathalie. "Coordonner l'artisanat et le tourisme, ou comment mettre en valeur le visage pittoresque du Québec (1915–1960)." *Social History/Histoire sociale,* vol. 34, no. 67, 2001, pp. 97–114.

Hamer. Emily. *Britannia's Glory: A History of Twentieth-Century Lesbians.* Cassell, 1996.

Hamilton, Michelle. *Collections and Objections: Aboriginal Material Culture in Southern Ontario, 1791–1914.* McGill-Queen's UP, 2010.

Hamilton & Gore Mechanics' Institute, *Act of Incorporation and Catalogue of Library, as Revised 1867.* Lawson, 1867.

Hanley, Terence E. "Tellers of Weird Tales: Dorothy McIlwraith, Part I." https://tellersofweirdtales.blogspot.com/2012/04/dorothy-mcilwraith-1891-1976.html. Accessed 3 June 2020.

"Hanna, Daniel Rhodes," *Encyclopedia of Cleveland History,* https://case.edu/ech/articles/h/hanna-daniel-rhodes. Accessed 29 July 2019.

Hanna, Martha. "War Letters: Communication Between Front and Home Front." *1914–1918 Online: International Encyclopedia of the First World War,* edited by Ute Daniel et al., Freie Universität Berlin, 2014, doi:10.15463/ie1418.10362. Accessed 9 July 2019.

Hardach-Pinke, Irene. "Weibliche Bildung und weiblicher Beruf: Gouvernanten im 18. und 19. Jahrhundert." *Geschichte und Gesellschaft,* vol. 18, no. 4, 1992, pp. 507–25.

Harding, Bruce. *Ngaio Marsh: A Companion to the Mystery Fiction.* McFarland, 2019.

Hare, Jan, and Jean Barman. *Good Intentions Gone Awry: Emma Crosby and the Methodist Mission on the Northwest Coast.* UBC Press, 2006.

Harkin, Natalie. "The Poetics of (Re) Mapping Archives: Memory in the Blood." *Journal of the Association for the Study of Australian Literature*, vol. 14, no. 3, pp. 1–14.

Harper, Marjory. *Adventurers and Exiles: The Great Scottish Exodus.* Profile Books, 2003.

Harris, Harry. "Robert Ridgway, With a Bibliography of His Published Writings and Fifty Illustrations." *The Condor*, vol. 30, no.1, 1928, pp. 4–118.

Harris, Katherine D. *Forget Me Not: The Rise of the British Literary Annual, 1823–1835.* Ohio UP, 2015.

"Harry M. Nimmo; A Founder and Editor of Detroit Saturday Night Dies." ProQuest, New York *Times*, 1 May 1937, p. 19.

Hartley, Jenny. " 'Letters are everything these days': Mothers and Letters in WWI." *Epistolary Selves: Letters and Letter-Writers, 1600–1945*, edited by Rebecca Earle, Ashgate, 1999, pp. 183–95.

Hay, Ian. *The First Hundred Thousand, Being the Unofficial Chronicle of a Unit of "K. (1)."* W. Blackwood, 1915.

Head, Henry. "W.H.R. Rivers, M.D., D.Sc., F.R.S.: An Appreciation." *British Medical Journal*, 17 June 1922, pp. 977–8.

Heartfield, James. *The Aborigines' Protection Society: Humanitarian Imperialism in Australia, New Zealand, Fiji, Canada, South Africa, and the Congo, 1837–1909.* Hurst, 2011.

Hebden, John. *Sermon preached in the Church of the Ascension, Hamilton, Ontario, on the 3rd of July, 1870, the Sunday following the lamentable yacht accident, by which the three children, Amy Florence, Constance Ada, and Irene Augusta Margaret Donalda, daughters of Thos. Swinyard, Esq., lost their lives.* Hamilton *Spectator*, 1870.

Hendrick, Burton J., ed. *The Life and Letters of Walter H. Page.* Doubleday, Page, 1922–5. 3 vols.

"Hendrie, William." *Canadian Horse Racing Hall of Fame*, https://www .canadianhorseracinghalloffame.com/1976/01/11/william-hendrie/. Accessed 11 Aug. 2019.

Henkin, David M. *The Postal Age: The Emergence of Modern Communications in Nineteenth-Century America.* U of Chicago P, 2006.

"Henry Philemon Attwater" (Obituary). *The Auk*, vol. 49, no. 1, 1932, p. 144.

Herle, Anita. "Creating the Anthropological Field in the Pacific." *The Atlantic World in the Antipodes: Effects and Transformations since the Eighteenth Century*, edited by Kate Fullagar, Cambridge Scholars Publishing, 2012, pp. 185–218.

– "The Life-Histories of Objects: Collections of the Cambridge Anthropological Expedition to the Torres Strait." *Cambridge and the Torres Strait: Centenary Essays on the 1898 Anthropological Expedition*, edited by Anita Herle and Sandra Rouse, Cambridge UP, 1998, pp. 77–105.

Herle, Anita, and Jude Philp, eds. *Recording Kastom: Alfred Haddon's Journals from his Expeditions to the Torres Strait and New Guinea, 1888 and 1898.* Sydney UP, 2020.

Herle, Anita, and Sandra Rouse, eds. *Cambridge and the Torres Strait: Centenary Essays on the 1898 Expedition.* Cambridge UP, 1998.

Heussler, Robert. *Yesterday's Rulers: The Making of the British Colonial Service.* Syracuse UP, 1963.

Higgitt, Rebekah, and Charles W.J. Withers, "Science and Sociability: Women as Audience in the British Association for the Advancement of Science, 1831–1901." *Isis*, vol. 99, no. 1, 2008, pp. 1–27.

Hill, Rowland. *Post Office Reform: Its Importance and Practicability*, 3rd ed. Vol. 1, C. Knight, 1837.

"Hillfield Strathallan College celebrates 100 years." Hamilton *Spectator*, 8 Sept. 2001, p. A8.

Hind, Andrew. "Summer Theatre at the Gravenhurst Opera House," *Muskoka Life Magazine*, 16 June 2017, https://www.muskokaregion.com/community -story/7363050-canadian-summer-theatre-at-the-gravenhurst-opera-house/. Accessed 29 July 2019.

Historische Addressbücher, Sächsische Landesbibliothek – Staats- und Universitätsbibliothek Dresden (SLUB), https://adressbuecher.sachsendigital.de /tour/ergebnisse/adressbuch/Book/list/dresden/1913/. Accessed 29 July 2019.

Hoffman, Frances, and Ryan Taylor. *Much to be Done: Private Life in Ontario from Victorian Diaries.* Natural Heritage/Natural History, 1996.

Holland, Robert. "The British Empire and the Great War, 1913–1918." *The Oxford History of the British Empire*, Vol. 4: *The Twentieth Century*, edited by Judith M. Brown and Wm. Roger Louis, Oxford UP, 1999, pp. 114–37.

"House Harold Phillips Crestlands, Balfour Mpumalanga." *Artefacts.co.za*, http://www .artefacts.co.za/main/Buildings/bldgframes.php?bldgid=5448. Accessed 29 July 2017.

Houston, Susan E., and Alison Prentice. *Schooling and Scholars in Nineteenth-Century Ontario.* U of Toronto P, 1988.

Howard, June. *Publishing the Family.* Duke UP, 2001.

Howarth, T.E.B. *Cambridge Between Two Wars.* Collins, 1978.

Hunter, Douglas. *Beardmore: The Viking Hoax That Re-Wrote History.* McGill-Queen's UP, 2018.

Hviding, Edward, and Cato Berg, eds. *The Ethnographic Experiment: A.M. Hocart and W.H.R. Rivers in Island Melanesia, 1908.* Berghahn, 2014.

Hyam, Ronald. "Bureaucracy and 'Trusteeship' in the Colonial Empire." *The Oxford History of the British Empire*, Vol. 4: *The Twentieth Century*, edited by Judith M. Brown and Wm. Roger Louis, Oxford UP, 1999, pp. 254–79.

Hyland, Christopher James. "Merciless Marches and Martial Law: Canada's Commitment to the Occupation of the Rhineland." MA thesis, University of New Brunswick, 2008.

"Inglis, David." *Dictionary of Hamilton Biography*. Vol. 1, Dictionary of Hamilton Biography, 1981, pp. 107–8.

Inglis, Ken. "Mateship." *The Oxford Companion to Australian History*, edited by Graeme Davison et al., Oxford UP, 2013.

"Interesting Engagement." Papers Past, *Evening Post* (Wellington), vol. 112, no. 107, 2 Nov. 1931, p. 10.

"An Interview with Mr. William Shakespeare." *Musical Herald and Tonic Sol-Fa Reporter*, 1 Mar. 1891, pp. 67–9.

Irish, Tomás. "Fractured Families: Educated Elites in Britain and France and the Challenge of the Great War." *Historical Journal*, vol. 57, no. 2, 2014, pp. 509–30.

– *The University at War, 1914–1925: Britain, France and the United States*. Palgrave Macmillan, 2015.

Ishiguro, Laura. *Nothing to Write Home About: British Family Correspondence and the Settler Colonial Everyday in British Columbia*. UBC Press, 2019.

Jacob, Jane M. *Edge of Empire: Postcolonialism and the City*. Routledge, 1996.

James, Edward T., Janet Wilson, and Paul S. Boyer, eds. *Notable American Women, 1607–1950: A Biographical Dictionary*. Belknap, 1971. 3 vols.

James, M.R. *Address at the Unveiling of the Roll of Honour of the Cambridge Tipperary Club on July 12, 1916 by the Provost of King's College*. Cambridge UP, 1916.

"J.D. Newsom, Headed U.S. Writers Group" (Obituary). Proquest, New York *Times*, 27 Apr. 1954, p. 29.

Jeffery, Keith. " 'Hut ab', 'Promenade with Kamerade for Schokolade', and the Flying Dutchman: British Soldiers in the Rhineland, 1918–1929." *Diplomacy and Statecraft*, vol. 16, no. 3, 2005, pp. 455–73.

Jenkyns, Richard. *Westminster Abbey: A Thousand Years of National Pageantry*. 2004. Profile Books, 2011.

Jerome, Jerome K. *Three Men on the Bummel*. 1900. Oxford UP, 1998.

"Jessie Campbell of Tullichewan." *The University of Glasgow Story*, https://www.universitystory.gla.ac.uk/biography/?id=WH1110&type=P. Accessed 27 Aug. 2019.

J.H.A. "Anthropology at the British Association." *Nature*, vol. 92, no. 2301, 4 Dec. 1913, pp. 412–13.

Johann, Klaus. *Grenze und Halt: Der Einzelne im "Haus der Regeln": Zur deutschsprachigen Internatsliteratur*. Winter, 2003.

"John Proctor" (Obituary). Hamilton *Spectator* 18 Aug. 1908, n.p.

Johnston, A.J.B. "McLennan, John Stewart." *Dictionary of Canadian Biography*, vol. 16 (1931–1940), http://www.biographi.ca/en/bio/mclennan_john_stewart_16E.html. Accessed 29 July 2019.

Johnston, C.M. *The Head of the Lake: A History of Wentworth County*. Wentworth County Council, 1958.

Jones, Dorothy. "Sheridan, Richard Bingham (1822–1897)." *Australian Dictionary of Biography*. Vol. 6, Melbourne UP, 1976, http://adb.anu.edu.au/biography/sheridan-richard-bingham-4573. Accessed 29 July 2019.

Jöns, Heike. "Academic Travel from Cambridge and the Formation of Centers of Knowledge, 1885–1954." *Geographies of Science*, edited by Peter Meusburger, et al., Springer, 2010, pp. 95–117.

– "The University of Cambridge, Academic Expertise, and the British Empire, 1885–1962." *Mobilities of Knowledge*, edited by Heike Jöns et al., Springer, 2017, pp. 185–210.

Jordan, Elizabeth Garver. *Three Rousing Cheers*. D. Appleton Century, 1938.

Joyce, R.B. "MacGregor, Sir William (1846–1919)." *Australian Dictionary of Biography*. Vol. 5, Melbourne UP, 1974, http://adb.anu.edu.au/biography/macgregor-sir -william-4097. Accessed 29 July 2019.

Judd, Stephen E. "Wright, John Charles (1861–1933)," *Australian Dictionary of Biography*. Vol. 12, Melbourne UP, 1990, http://adb.anu.edu.au/biography/wright -john-charles-9202. Accessed 19 Nov. 2017.

Judd, W.W. *Memorabilia of Robert Elliott (1858–1902) Poet and Naturalist of Plover Mills, Middlesex County, Ontario*. Phelps, 2001.

Karr, Clarence. "Dunsmuir, James." *Dictionary of Canadian Biography*, vol. 14 (1911–1920), http://www.biographi.ca/en/bio/dunsmuir_james_14E.html. Accessed 29 July 2019.

Katz, Michael. *The People of Hamilton, Canada West: Family and Class in a Mid-Nineteenth-Century City*. Harvard UP, 1975.

Keefer, Thomas. *Philosophy of Railroads: Published by Order of the Directors of the St. Lawrence and Ottawa Grand Junction Railway Company, 1849*, 4th ed. Lovell, 1853.

Kendrick, Brent L. ed. *The Infant Sphinx: Collected Letters of Mary E. Wilkins Freeman*. Scarecrow, 1985.

Kennedy, Hubert. *Anarchist of Love: The Secret Life of John Henry Mackay*. 1983. Revised and expanded, Peremptory Publications, 2002.

"Kerr, Bobby." *Canada's Sports Hall of Fame*, https://www.sportshall.ca/hall-of-famers /hall-of-famers-search.html?proID=87&catID=all&lang=EN. Accessed 3 June 2020.

Kiefer, Nancy. "Huldah S. McMullen." *Dictionary of Canadian Biography*, vol. 13 (1901–1910), http://www.biographi.ca/en/bio/mcmullen_huldah_s_13E.html. Accessed 30 July 2019.

Kilpatrick, Ross S. "Terrot Reaveley Glover at Queen's University, 1896–1901." *Échos du monde classique: Classical Views*, vol. 42, no. 3, new series, vol. 17, no. 3, 1998, pp. 489–507.

Kingston, Edward J. "Young Canada and the War." *Living Age*, vol. 290, no. 3756, 1 July 1916, pp. 3–9.

Kipling, Rudyard. *The Cambridge Edition of the Poems of Rudyard Kipling*. Edited by Thomas Pinney, Cambridge UP, 2013. 3 vols.

Kirchhoff, Axel. *Der Architekt Heinrich Plange (1857-1942): Ein Baumeister des Unternehmertums in der bergischen Region*. PhD Diss, Bergische Universität Wuppertal, 2004.

Kirk-Greene, A.H.M. "Furse, Sir Ralph Dolignon (1887–1973)." *Oxford Dictionary of National Biography*, https://doi.org/10.1093/ref:odnb/31129. Accessed 28 July 2019.

Kirk-Greene, Anthony H. M. " 'Taking Canada into Partnership in 'The White Man's Burden': The British Colonial Service and the Dominion Selection Scheme." *Canadian Journal of African Studies*, vol. 15, no. 1, 1981, pp. 33–46.

Kirkpatrick, Robert J. *From the Penny Dreadful to the Ha'Penny Dreadfuller: A Bibliographic History of the Boys' Periodical in Britain, 1762–1950*. British Library and Oak Knoll Press, 2013.

Klapwijk, Menno. *Westfalia Estate Before 1929: The Biography of Heinrich Schulte Altenroxel and Conrad Plange on Their Farms in Magoebaskloof*. [N.p., 1980?].

Knaplund, Paul. *Gladstone's Foreign Policy*. 1935. Frank Cass, 1970.

Kotin, David B. "Graphic Publishers and the Bibliographer: An Introduction and Checklist." *Papers of the Bibliographical Society of Canada*, vol. 18, no. 1, 1979, pp. 47–54.

Krohn, William B. *Manly Hardy (1832–1910): The Life and Writing of a Maine Fur-Buyer, Hunter, and Naturalist*. Maine Folklife Center, 2005.

Kröller, Eva-Marie. "Jacobites in Canadian Literature." *Canadian Literature*, no. 94, autumn 1982, pp. 169–72.

"Kromayer, Ernst." *Catalogus professorum halensis*, http://www.catalogus-professorum-halensis.de/kromayerernst.html. Accessed 4 July 2017.

Kuttainen, Victoria. "Dear Miss Cowie: The Construction of Canadian Authorship, 1920s and 1930s." *English Studies in Canada*, vol. 39, no. 4, 2013, pp. 145–71.

"Labour and 'Rags.' " Gale Primary Sources, Cambridge *Independent Press*, 5 Mar. 1920, p. 10.

Lack, Clem. "Bernays, Charles Arrowsmith (1862–1940)." *Australian Dictionary of Biography*. Vol., 3, Melbourne UP, 1969, http://adb.anu.edu.au/biography/bernays-charles-arrowsmith-3317. Accessed 30 July 2019.

"The Lady Margaret Boat Song." *The Eagle* (St. John's College Cambridge), vol. 93, 2011, pp. 70–1.

"Lady Munro Ferguson: Woman of Many Activities. Her Attractive Personality." Trove, Bathurst *Times*, 31 Mar. 1914, p. 4.

Lagerspetz, Olli. "Introduction." *Evolution, Human Behaviour and Morality: The Legacy of Westermarck*, edited by Olli Lagerspetz et al., Routledge, 2016, pp. 1–11.

Lahiri, Shompa. *Indians in Britain: Anglo-Indian Encounters, Race and Identity, 1880–1930*. Frank Cass, 2000.

Laidlaw, Zoe. *Colonial Connections, 1815–45: Patronage, the Information Revolution and Colonial Government*. Manchester UP, 2005.

Lake, Marilyn. "The Politics of Respectability: Identifying the Masculinist Context." *Historical Studies*, vol. 22, no. 86, 1986, pp. 116–31.

Lake, Marilyn, and Henry Reynolds. *Drawing the Global Colour Line: White Men's Countries and the International Challenge of Racial Equality*. Cambridge UP, 2008.

Lambert, David, and Alan Lester, eds. *Colonial Lives across the British Empire: Imperial Careering in the Long Nineteenth Century*. Cambridge UP, 2006.

Lange, Kerstin. "The Argentine Tango: A Transatlantic Dance on the European Stage." *Popular Musical Theatre in London and Berlin, 1890–1939*, edited by Len Platt et al., Cambridge UP, 2014, pp. 153–69.

Langham, Ian. *The Building of British Social Anthropology: W.H.R. Rivers and His Cambridge Disciples in the Development of Kinship Studies, 1898–1931*. Reidel, 1981.

Lanman, Susan Warren. " 'For Profit and Pleasure': Peter Henderson and the Commercialization of Horticulture in Nineteenth-Century America." *Industrializing Organisms: Introducing Evolutionary History*, edited by Susan Schrepfer and Philip Scranton, Routledge, 2004, pp. 19–42.

Laski, Harold. "On Not Having Known T.R. Glover." *New Statesman and Nation*, vol. 26, no. 666, 1943, p. 351.

"Latest Intelligence: The New Guinea Question." Times Digital Archive, 1785–1985, *The Times* (London), 7 Feb. 1885, p. 5.

Laurel School: Academic Catalogue 1912–1913. Horace Carr, 1913.

Leach, Edmund R. "Glimpses of the Unmentionable in the History of British Social Anthropology." *Annual Review of Anthropology*, vol. 13, 1984, pp. 1–23.

LeJeune, Philippe. "The 'Journal de jeune fille' in Nineteenth-Century France." *On Diary*, edited by Jeremy D. Popkin and Julie Rak, U of Hawai'i P, 2009, pp. 129–44.

Lemoine, James Macpherson. Introduction to Chevalier de Johnstone, "A Dialogue in Hades: A Parallel of Military Errors, of which the French and English were Guilty During the Campaign of 1759, in Canada." *Manuscripts Relating to the Early History of Canada, Recently Published Under the Auspices of the Literary and Historical Society of Quebec*, 2nd series, Middleton & Dawson, 1868, n.p.

– *Maple Leaves: A Budget of Legendary, Historical Critical, and Sporting Intelligence*. Hunter, Rose, 1864.

Lepore, Jill. "Historians Who Love Too Much: Reflections on Microhistory and Biography." *Journal of American History*, vol. 88, no.1, 2001, pp. 129–44.

Lesser, Alexander. "Bibliography of American Folklore 1915–1928." *American Journal of Folk-Lore*, vol. 41, no. 159, 1928, pp. 1–60.

"A Letter from London: Society, the Drama, and Art." Trove, *The Register* (Adelaide), 27 Jan. 1925, p. 9.

Levine, Allan. "McLennan, Hugh." *Dictionary of Canadian Biography*, vol. 12 (1891–1900), http://www.biographi.ca/en/bio/mclennan_hugh_12F.html. Accessed 30 July 2019.

Levsen, Sonja. *Elite, Männlichkeit und Krieg: Tübinger und Cambridger Studenten 1900–1929*. Vandenhoeck & Ruprecht, 2006.

Lewis, Daniel. *The Feathery Tribe: Robert Ridgway and the Modern Study of Birds*. Yale UP, 2012.

Lewis, Jane. "Gender and Welfare in the Late Nineteenth and Early Twentieth Centuries." *Gender, Health, and Welfare*, edited by Anne Digby and John Stewart. Routledge, 1996, pp. 208–28.

Limburger, Iris. "Die Rheinlandbesetzung nach dem Ersten Weltkrieg: Leben unter alliierter Besatzungsherrschaft in Köln und in der Eifel, 1918–1926," *Geschichte in Köln: Zeitschrift für Stadt- und Regionalgeschichte*, vol. 57, 2010, pp. 93–118.

Linehan, Peter. "The Twentieth Century." *St. John's College Cambridge: A History*, edited by Peter Linehan. Boydell, 2011, pp. 397–639.

A List of Books for Junior College Libraries, compiled by Foster E. Mohrhardt for the Carnegie Corporation of New York by the Advisory Group on Junior College Libraries. American Library Association, 1936.

Little, Jack I. " 'Like a Fragment of the Old World': The Historical Regression of Quebec City in Travel Narratives and Tourist Guidebooks, 1776–1913." *Urban History Review/Revue d'histoire urbaine*, vol. 40, no. 2, 2012, pp. 15–27.

Locke, Stefan. "Ein Sioux in Sachsen." *Frankfurter Allgemeine Zeitung*, 19 June 2012, https://www.faz.net/aktuell/gesellschaft/dokumentarfilmerin-bettina-renner-ein -sioux-in-sachsen-11791887.html. Accessed 30 July 2019.

"Lord Dufferin in Canada." *The Spectator* (London), 15 June 1878, p. 7. http://archive .spectator.co.uk/article/15th-june-1878/7/lord-dufferin-in-canada. Accessed 28 July 2019.

"Loss of the Mail Steamer Rangoon Off Galle Harbour: Letter to the Editor." Trove, South Australian *Register*, 28 Nov. 1871, p. 5.

"The Loss of the Rangoon." Papers Past, Grey River *Argus* (From the *Ceylon Observer*, 4 Nov.), 16 Dec. 1871, n.p.

"The Loss of the Rangoon." Papers Past, Otago *Daily Times*, 9 Dec. 1871, p. 6.

"Loss of the Rangoon." Trove, Portland *Guardian and* Normanby *General Advertiser* (Victoria), 30 Nov. 1871, p. 2.

"Lotus Buds start for California Home." Proquest, New York *Times*, 8 Dec. 1902, p. 3.

Lovell's Montreal Directory for 1881–82. Lovell, 1881.

Lutkehaus, Nancy. " 'She was *very* Cambridge': Camilla Wedgwood and the History of Women in British Social Anthropology." *American Ethnologist*, vol. 13, no. 4, 1986, pp. 776–98.

Lutz, Catherine. "Empire Is in the Details." *American Ethnologist*, vol. 33, no. 4, 2006, pp. 593–611.

Lux, David S., and Harold J. Cook. "Closed Circles or Open Networks? Communicating at a Distance during the Scientific Revolution." *History of Science*, vol. 36, no. 2, 1998, pp. 179–211.

Lyons, Martyn. *The Writing Culture of Ordinary People in Europe, c. 1860–1920*. Cambridge UP, 2013.

MacDougall, Pauleena M. *Fannie Hardy Eckstorm and Her Quest for Local Knowledge, 1865–1946*. Lexington, 2013.

Mackay, George H. "Fire-lighting." *The Auk*, vol. 8, no. 4, 1891, pp. 340–3.

– "Observations on the Knot (*Tringa Canutus*)." *The Auk*, vol. 10, no. 1, 1893, pp. 25–35.

MacLachlan, R.W. *Fleury Mesplet, the First Printer at Montreal*, Proceedings and Transactions of the Royal Society of Canada, 2nd series, 1906–7, vol. 12, section II. J. Hope and Sons, 1906.

MacMurchy, Archibald. *Handbook of Canadian Literature*. W. Briggs, 1906.

MacNab, Sophia. *The Diary of Sophia MacNab: Written at Dundurn Castle, Hamilton, 1846 Age 13*. Edited by Charles Ambrose Carter. W.L. Griffin, 1968.

Magee, Gary B., and Andrew S. Thompson, *Empire and Globalisation: Networks of People, Goods and Capital in the British World, c. 1850-1914*. Cambridge UP, 2010.

"Mails for England via Panama." Trove, Sydney *Morning Herald*, 12 June 1866, p. 4.

"Major Vernon Harcourt de Butts Powell." *Little Shelford History*, http://www.littleshelfordhistory.co.uk/little-shelford-people/major-vernon-harcourt-de-butts-powell. Accessed 17 Jan. 2020.

"Marconi's Degree." ProQuest, New York *Times*, 27 Aug. 1933, p. E4.

Margerison, John S. *Midshipman Rex Carew, V.C.* Nelson [191?].

Marion Seward: Born 24 September 1861, Died 13 November 1924. Commemorative Volume. Cambridge UP, 1925.

Marquis, T.G. "Spanish John vs. Mr. William McLennan." *The Bookman* (New York), vol. 7, no. 1, Mar. 1898, pp. 40-3.

Mason, Otis Tufton. *Primitive Travel and Transportation, from the Report of the U.S. National Museum 1894*. Government Printing Office, 1896.

Maull, Otto. "Emil Deckert" (Obituary). *Geographische Zeitschrift*, vol. 23, no. 2, 1917, pp. 57-62.

McArthur, Peter. "The Bird Row." Proquest, *The Globe*, 16 Feb. 1918, p. 7.

McCarthy, Angela. "Ethnic Networks and Identities among Inter-war Scottish Migrants in North America." *A Global Clan*, pp. 203-26.

– ed. *A Global Clan: Scottish Migrant Networks and Identities since the Eighteenth Century*. Tauris, 2006.

McConnel, Katherine. " 'Our Wayward and Backward Sister Colony': Queensland and the Australian Federation Movement, 1859-1901." PhD diss., University of Queensland, 2006.

– *The People's Stories: Queensland and Federation*, Memoirs of the Queensland Museum, Cultural Heritage Series, vol. 2, part 2, The State of Queensland. Queensland Museum, 2002.

McDonald, Lorna. *Rockhampton: A History of City and District*. U of Queensland P, 1981.

McFarland, Gerald W. *Inside Greenwich Village: A New York City Neighborhood, 1898–1918*. U of Massachusetts P, 2001.

Mcinnes, Robin, and Hope Stubbings. *Art as a Tool in Support of the Understanding of Coastal Change in East Anglia*. Crown Estate, 2010.

McLaren, Sheryl Ann Stotts. "Becoming Indispensable: A Biography of Elizabeth Smith Shortt (1859-1949)." PhD diss., York University, 2002.

McLean, Gavin. *The Governors: New Zealand's Governors and Governors-General*. Otago UP, 2006.

McLennan, William. Response to "Spanish John vs. Mr. William McLennan." *The Bookman* (New York), vol. 7, no. 2, April 1898, p. 138.

McNeill, W.E. "Lois Saunders" (Obituary). *Queen's Review*, Aug. 1942, pp. 167-70.

McNickle, Chris. "When New York Was Irish, And After." *The New York Irish*, edited by Ronald H. Bayor and Timothy J. Meagher. Johns Hopkins UP, 1997, pp. 337-56.

McQuesten, Mary Baker. *The Life Writings of Mary Baker McQuesten*. Edited by Mary J. Anderson. Wilfrid Laurier UP, 2004.

McWilliams-Tullberg, Rita. *Women at Cambridge*. Victor Gollancz, 1975.

Megarrity, Lyndon. " 'White Queensland': The Queensland Government's Ideological Position on the Use of Pacific Island Labourers in the Sugar Sector 1880–1901." *Australian Journal of Politics and History*, vol. 52, no. 1, 2006, pp. 1–12.

"Melbourne News." Trove, *The Critic* (Adelaide), 10 Sept. 1919, p. 32.

"The Memorial Service for the Members of the College and of The Choir School and for College Servants who Died on Active Service, 1914–1919." *The Eagle* (St. John's College Cambridge), Dec. 1919, pp. 12–21.

"The Men Who Make The Argosy: J.D. Newsom." *The Argosy*, vol. 253, no. 4, 16 Feb. 1935, p. 140.

Meskimmon, Marsha. "Visual Arts and Life Writing." *Encyclopedia of Life Writing: Autobiographical and Biographical Forms*, vol. 1, edited by Margaretta Jolly and Fitzroy Dearborn, 2001, pp. 916–18.

Michaud, Maud. "The Missionary and the Anthropologist: The Intellectual Friendship and Scientific Collaboration of the Reverend John Roscoe (CMS) and James G. Frazer, 1896–1932." *Studies in World Christianity*, vol. 22, no. 1, 2016, pp. 57–74.

"Mildmay and its Institutions." *The Quiver*, vol. 18, no. 877, Jan. 1883, pp. 303–7.

Miller, Carman. "Hutton, Sir Edward Thomas Henry." *Dictionary of Canadian Biography*, vol. 15 (1921–1930), http://www.biographi.ca/en/bio/hutton_edward _thomas_henry_15E.html. Accessed 31 July 2019.

Miller's Canadian Farmer's Almanac for the Year of the Lord 1870. Robert Miller, 1869. https://ia601602.us.archive.org/29/items/millerscanadianf00mont /millerscanadianf00mont.pdf. Accessed 24 Sept. 2014.

Mitchell, Sally. *The New Girl: Girls' Culture in England, 1880–1915*. Columbia UP, 1995.

Moffat, J. Alston. "Platysamia Columbia." *Canadian Entomologist*, vol. 26, no. 10, 1894, pp. 281–3.

Monkman, Leslie G. "William McLennan." *Dictionary of Canadian Biography*, vol. 13 (1901–1910), http://www.biographi.ca/en/bio/mclennan_william_13E.html. Accessed 31 July 2019.

Moore, Clive. "Oral Testimony and the Pacific Labour Trade to Queensland: Myth and Reality." *Oral History Association of Australia Journal*, vol. 1, 1978–9, pp. 28–42.

Moore, John. "Zoology of the Pacific Railroad Surveys." *American Zoologist*, vol. 26, 1986, pp. 331–41.

"More Books and Magazines Wanted." *Red Triangle* (YMCA), 20 July 1917, p. 658.

Morrison, Arthur. "Family Budgets: 1. A Workman's Budget." *Cornhill Magazine*, vol. 10, 1901, pp. 446–56.

Morrison, Madelaine. "Domestic Harmonies: Musical Activities in Southwestern Ontario, 1880–1920," PhD diss., Carleton University, 2013.

Moruzi, Kristine. *Constructing Girlhood through the Periodical Press, 1850–1915*. Ashgate, 2012.

Mount, Nick. *When Canadian Literature Moved to New York.* U of Toronto P, 2005.

M.P.C. "Terrot Reaveley Glover" (Obituary). *The Eagle* (St. John's College Cambridge), vol. 52, nos. 227 and 228, 1943, pp. 191–7.

"Mr. and Mrs. George Case." Papers Past, Thames *Star*, vol. 7, no. 1985, 15 May 1875, n.p.

Mullen, Richard, and James Munson. *"The Smell of the Continent": The British Discover Europe, 1814–1914.* Macmillan, 2009.

Müller, Simone. *Wiring the World: The Social and Cultural Creation of Telegraph Networks.* Columbia UP, 2016.

Mullins, Steve. "Queensland's Quest for Torres Strait: The Delusion of Inevitability." *Journal of Pacific History,* vol. 27, no. 2, 1992, pp. 165–80.

Munro, J. Forbes. *Maritime Enterprise and Empire: Sir William Mackinnon and his Business Network, 1823–1893.* Boydell, 2003.

Murphy, Miriam B. " 'If Only I Shall Have the Right Stuff': Utah Women in World War I." *Utah Historical Quarterly,* vol. 58, no. 4, 1990, pp. 334–50.

– "World War One Heroine Maud Fitch lived in Eureka, Utah." *History Blazer,* Apr. 1995, n.p., http://digitallibrary.utah.gov/awweb/awarchive?type=file&item=30778. Accessed 31 July 2019.

Murray, Gilbert. "Discussion: Empire and Subject Races." *Sociological Review,* vol. 3, no. 3, 1910, pp. 227–32.

Murray, Heather. *Come, Bright Improvement! The Literary Societies of Nineteenth-Century Ontario.* U of Toronto P, 2002.

Murray-Smith, S. "Adams, Francis William Lauderdale (1862–1893)." *Australian Dictionary of Biography.* Vol. 3, Melbourne UP, 1969, http://adb.anu.edu.au /biography/adams-francis-william-2865. Accessed 31 July 2019.

Myers, Christine D. "The Glasgow Association for the Higher Education of Women, 1878 to 1883." *The Historian,* vol. 63, no. 2, 2007, pp. 357–71.

Myres, John L., and A.C. Haddon. "Sir William Ridgeway, August 6, 1853–August 12, 1926." *Man,* vol. 26, Oct. 1926, pp. 173–6.

Nanni, Giordano. *The Colonisation of Time: Ritual, Routine and Resistance in the British Empire.* Manchester UP, 2012.

National Council of Women of Canada. *Women of Canada: Their Life and Work.* Compiled at the Request of the Hon. Sydney Fisher, Minister of Agriculture, for Distribution at the International Exhibition, Paris, 1900, and Pan-American Exposition, Buffalo, 1901.

"The National Training School for Cookery at Kensington." Proquest, New York *Times,* 27 Dec. 1874, p. 4.

The Naturalists' Directory of the United States and Canada. S.E. Cassino, 1895.

Neatby, Nicole. "Meeting of Minds: American Travel Writers and Government Tourist Publicity in Quebec, 1920–1955." *Social History/Histoire sociale,* vol. 36, no. 72, 2003, pp. 465–95.

Nevinson, Henry W. *Fire of Life.* Harcourt & Brace, 1935.

– *A Modern Slavery.* Harper, 1906.

New, William H. *Dreams of Speech and Violence: The Art of the Short Story in Canada and New Zealand.* U of Toronto P, 1987.

"The Newnham Incident." Letter to the editor by an "M.A., and Mother of an undergraduate." Times Digital Archive, 1785–1985, *The Times* (London), 25 Oct. 1921, p. 10.

Nielson, Carmen J. *Private Women and the Public Good: Charity and State Formation in Hamilton, Ontario, 1846–93.* UBC Press, 2014.

Ngai, Mae M. "Trouble on the Rand: The Chinese Question in South Africa and the Apogee of White Settlerism." *International Labour and Working-Class History,* vol. 91, 2017, pp. 59–78.

"Nineteenth Annual Exhibition of the Agricultural Association of Upper Canada." *Journal of the Board of Arts and Manufactures for U.C.,* vol. 4, Nov. 1864, pp. 326–34.

Noël, Françoise. *Family Life and Sociability in Upper and Lower Canada, 1780–1870: A View from Diaries and Family Correspondence.* McGill-Queen's UP, 2003.

NoiseCat, Julian Brave. "The Resurgence of the Nuxalk." *Canadian Geographic,* 12 Oct. 2018, https://www.canadiangeographic.ca/article/resurgence-nuxalk. Accessed 19 Oct. 2019.

Nolan, Melanie. *Kin: A Collective Biography of a Working-Class New Zealand Family.* Canterbury UP, 2005.

"The Norman Angell 'Rag.' " Gale Primary Sources, Cambridge *Independent Press,* 19 Mar. 1920, p. 7.

Northcote, Sir Geoffrey. "C.W. Hobley, C.M.G.: An Appreciation." *Journal of East Africa Natural History Society,* vol. 19, no. 5, 1948, p. 256.

Northrup, David. *Indentured Labour in the Age of Imperialism, 1834–1922.* Cambridge UP, 1995.

"Nursing Guild Bazaar." Papers Past, *Evening Post* (Wellington), 30 Aug. 1904, p. 5.

"Obituary for William Ridgeway." *Classical Bulletin,* vol. 3, no. 1, 1926, p. 4.

"Oh, Those Tricornes! London's World of Fashion." Trove, *The Straits Times* (Singapore), 21 Nov. 1931, p. 14.

O'Neill, Mark. *The Chinese Labour Corps: The Forgotten Chinese Labourers of the First World War.* Penguin, 2016.

O'Neill, Morna. "Colonial Nationalism and Closer Union: Hugh Lane in South Africa." *Transculturation in British Art, 1770–1930,* edited by Julie Codell. Ashgate, 2012, pp. 243–59.

O'Neill, T.P. *British Parliamentary Papers: A Monograph on Blue Books.* Irish UP, 1968.

"On the Rhine: Something More Than Geography." Times Digital Archive, 1785–1985, *The Times* (London), 13 Nov. 1918, p. 11.

Oppenheimer, Melanie. " 'The Best P.M. for the Empire in War'? Lady Helen Munro Ferguson and the Australian Red Cross Society, 1914–1920." *Australian Historical Studies,* vol. 33, no. 119, 2002, pp. 108–34.

– "The 'imperial girl': Lady Helen Munro, the Imperial Woman and Her Imperial Childhood." *Journal of Australian Studies,* vol. 34, no. 4, 2010, pp. 513–25.

"Ormiston, William." *Dictionary of Hamilton Biography*. Vol. 1, Dictionary of Hamilton Biography, 1981, p. 161.

Osbaldeston, Mark. *Unbuilt Toronto 2: More of the City that Might Have Been*. Dundurn, 2011.

Osborne, J. *Larkin, Ideology and Critical Violence: A Case of Wrongful Conviction*. Palgrave Macmillan, 2008.

Otis, Fessenden Nott. *Isthmus of Panama, History of the Panama Railroad and of the Pacific Mail Steamship Company*. Harper, 1867.

"Our Letter Box." *Our Young Folks*, vol. 9, no. 5, May 1873, pp. 315–20.

"Our Puzzle Mill." *Harper's Bazaar*, vol. 46, no. 7, July 1912, p. 366.

Pache, Walter. "Kipling in Kanada: Aspekte des literarischen Imperialismus." *AAA* [*Arbeiten aus Anglistik und Amerikanistik*], vol. 12, no. 1, 1987, pp. 41–55.

Page, Walter Hines. *A Publisher's Confession*. Doubleday, Page, 1905.

"The Panama Steam Route to Australia, and the Pacific Trade. " *The Merchant's Magazine, Statist and Commercial Review*, vol. 2, Jan. 1853, pp. 664–72.

Parker, Gilbert. *Round the Compass in Australia*. Hutchinson & Company, 1892.

Parrinder, Patrick. "The Time Traveller Goes Backwards" (about H.G. Wells's *The Outline of History*). *TLS*, 25 Oct. 2018, pp. 17–18.

"Particulars of the Loss of the Rangoon." Trove, Ovens and Murray *Advertiser*, 28 Nov. 1871, p. 2.

Patrick, Rhianna. "The Cambridge Expedition to the Torres Strait (1898)," curator's notes on "Yamaz Sibarud," a traditional song performed by "Maino of Yam." *Australian Screen, National Film and Sound Archive*, https://aso.gov.au/titles /music/1898-torres-strait-recordings/notes/. Accessed 1 Aug. 2019.

Penloup, Marie-Claire. *La Tentation du littéraire: essai sur le rapport à l'écriture littéraire du scripteur "ordinaire."* Didier, 2000.

Perron, Jean-Marie. "Léon Provancher." *Dictionary of Canadian Biography*, vol. 12 (1891–1900), http://www.biographi.ca/en/bio/provancher_leon_12E.html. Accessed 1 Aug. 2019.

Perry, Adele. *Colonial Relations: The Douglas-Connolly Family and the Nineteenth-Century Imperial World*. Cambridge UP, 2015.

– *On the Edge of Empire: Gender, Race, and the Making of British Columbia, 1849–1871*. U of Toronto P, 2001.

Peterman, Michael, and Jane Friskney. " 'Booming' the Canuck Book: Edward Caswell and the Promotion of Canadian Writing." *Journal of Canadian Studies*, vol. 30, no. 3, 1995, pp. 60–90.

Peters-Little, Frances, et al., eds. *Passionate Histories: Myth, Memory and Aboriginal Australia*. ANU Press, 2010.

"Petersham Remembers." https://petershamremembers.wordpress.com/2014/03/29 /john-stuart-wortley-1880-1918/. Accessed 29 July 2017.

Pettit, Clare. "The Origin of the Thesis: Why Charles Darwin's Approach to Science Should Not Be Misunderstood." *TLS*, 15 Dec. 2017, p. 4.

Philadelphia Centennial Exhibition of 1876–1875: Official Record, Containing Introduction, Catalogues, Official Awards of the Commissioners, Reports and Recommendations of the Experts, and Essays and Statistics on the Social and Economic Resources of the Colony of Victoria. McCarron, Bird & Co., 1875.

Phillips, Ann, ed. *A Newnham Anthology.* Cambridge UP, 1979.

Phillips, Lionel. *Some Reminiscences.* Hutchinson, 1924.

Phillips, Michelle H. " 'Along the Paragraphic Wires': Child-Adult Mediation in *St. Nicholas Magazine.*" *Children's Literature,* vol. 37, 2009, pp. 84–113.

Philp, Jude. " 'Everything as it used to be': Recreating Torres Strait Islander History in 1898." *Cambridge Journal of Anthropology,* vol. 21, no. 1, 1999, pp. 58–78.

Pickles, J.D. "The Haddon Library, Cambridge." *Library History,* vol. 8, no. 1, 1988, pp. 1–9.

Pietsch, Tamson. *Empire of Scholars: Universities, Networks and the British Academic World, 1850–1939.* Manchester UP, 2013.

Piper, Alana. "All the Waters of Lethe: An Experience of Female Alcoholism in Federation Queensland." *Queensland Review,* vol. 18, no. 1, 2011, pp. 85–97.

"Plagiarism Extraordinary (about William McLennan, *Spanish John*)." *Publishers' Weekly,* vol. 53, no. 1365, Mar. 1898, p. 586.

"Political Froth. By An Abstainer." Trove, *The Queenslander,* 9 Sept. 1882, p. 328.

Powell, Graeme. "A Diarist in the Cabinet: Lord Derby and the Australian Colonies, 1882–85." *Australian Journal of Politics and History,* vol. 51, no. 4, 2005, pp. 481–95.

Prendergast, Patricia A. "Chalmers, James (1841–1901)." *Australian Dictionary of Biography.* Vol. 3, Melbourne UP, 1969, http://adb.anu.edu.au/biography/chalmers -james-3187. Accessed 1 Aug. 2019.

Pringle, Gertrude. *Etiquette in Canada: The Blue Book of Canadian Social Usage.* McClelland and Stewart, 1932.

"Proceedings of the Royal Anthropological Institute, 1921." *Journal of the Royal Anthropological Institute of Britain and Ireland,* vol. 51, Dec. 1921.

Proceedings of the Royal Colonial Institute. Vol. 25: *1893–1894.* Royal Colonial Institute, 1894.

Pryke, K.G. "McCormick, William." *Dictionary of Canadian Biography,* vol. 7 (1836– 1850), http://www.biographi.ca/en/bio/mccormick_william_7E.html. Accessed 1 Aug. 2019.

"Queen Margaret College: Correspondence Classes." *Chambers's Journal,* 30 Aug. 1884, pp. 555–7.

"The Queensland Government and Captain Wright." Grey River *Argus,* 26 Oct. 1888, p. 10.

Quiggin, A. Hingston. *Haddon, the Head Hunter: A Short Sketch of the Life of A.C. Haddon.* Cambridge UP, 1942.

Quiggin A.H., and E.S. Fegan. "Alfred Cort Haddon, 1855–1940." *Man,* vol. 40, 1940, pp. 97–100.

Quinn, Michael S. "Fleming, James Henry." *Dictionary of Canadian Biography,* vol. 16 (1931–1940), http://biographi.ca/en/bio/fleming_james_henry_16F.html. Accessed 1 Aug. 2019.

"Rags or Tags." Trove, *The Daily News* (Perth), 28 Nov. 1931, p. 5.

Rantanen, Terhi. "The Struggle for Control of Domestic News Markets (I)." *The Globalization of News*, edited by Oliver Boyd-Barrett and Terhi Rantanen. Sage, 1998, pp. 35–48.

"Recent Historical Fiction" (about William McLennan, *Spanish John*). *The Dial*, vol. 24, Jan.–June 1898, p. 295.

Redmann, Jennifer. "Doing Her Bit: German and Anglo-American Girls' Literature of the First World War." *Girlhood Studies*, vol. 4, no. 1, 2011, pp. 10–29.

Reeve, William C. *Peter Pringle, Master Decoy Maker*. McGill-Queens UP, 2002.

Regehr, T.D. "Hanna, David Blythe." *Dictionary of Canadian Biography*, vol. 16 (1931–1940), http://www.biographi.ca/en/bio/hanna_david_blythe_16E.html. Accessed 4 Dec. 2014.

Reid, John G. "Adams, Mary Electa." *Dictionary of Canadian Biography*, vol. 12 (1891–1900), http://www.biographi.ca/en/bio/adams_mary_electa_12E.html. Accessed 1 Aug. 2019.

Report of the British Association for the Advancement of Science, 1936. BAAS, 1936.

Reports of the Cambridge Anthropological Expedition to Torres Straits, vol. 4, edited by A.C. Haddon and W.H.R. Rivers, Cambridge UP, 1912.

"Review of *Spanish John*, a novel by William McLennan." *The Academy*, vol. 53, no. 1363, 11 June 1898, p. 626.

Reynolds, Henry. *This Whispering in Our Hearts*. Allen and Unwin, 1998.

Rich, Arnold R. "Men and Books: Dr. William George Maccallum." *Canadian Medical Association Journal*, vol. 51, no. 6, 1944, pp. 570–3.

Richards, A.I. "An Isolated Community." *A Newnham Anthology*, edited by A. Phillips, Cambridge UP, 1979, pp. 131–5.

Richards, David. *Masks of Difference: Cultural Representations in Literature, Anthropology and Art*. Cambridge UP, 1994.

Richards, Eric. "Scottish Voices and Networks in Colonial Australia." *A Global Clan: Scottish Migrant Networks and Identities since the Eighteenth Century*, edited by Angela McCarthy, Tauris, 2006, pp. 151–82.

"Richardson, James Armstrong," *Queen's Encyclopedia*, https://www.queensu.ca /encyclopedia/r/richardson-james-armstrong. Accessed 17 Aug. 2019.

"Rickards' Vaudeville Company." Papers Past, *Evening Post* (Wellington), 15 Oct. 1906, p. 2.

Ridgway, Robert. "Is the Love of Trees and Flowers a Sign of Effeminacy?" Olney *Times* (IL), 28 Mar. 1925, p. 5.

Ridgeway, William. "Women at Cambridge: The Issue for the Senate" (Letter to the Editor). Times Digital Archive, 1785–1985, *The Times* (London), 22 Nov. 1920. p. 8.

"The Right Reverend Walter Burd, D.C.M., D.D.," http://www.eagle.ca/~ben /familyhistory/walter.htm. Accessed 30 Nov. 2017.

Rivers, W.H.R. "The Genealogical Method of Anthropological Inquiry." *Sociological Review*, vol. 3, no. 1, 1910, pp. 1–12.

- "The Repression of War Experience." *The Lancet*, vol. 191, no. 4927, Feb. 1918, pp. 173–7.

Roberts, Sam. "Revisiting the Era of Automatic Dining." New York *Times*, 17 June 2012, https://cityroom.blogs.nytimes.com/2012/06/17/revisiting-the-era-of-automatic-dining/. Accessed 1 Aug. 2019.

Roemer, Hans. "Deckert, Friedrich Paul Emil." *Neue Deutsche Biographie*, vol. 3, 1957, p. 549, https://www.deutsche-biographie.de/pnd116043776.html#ndbcontent. Accessed 1 Aug. 2019.

Roland, Charles G. "Garnier, John Hutchison." *Dictionary of Canadian Biography*, vol. 12 (1891–1900), http://www.biographi.ca/en/bio/garnier_john_hutchison_12E.html. Accessed 1 Aug. 2019.

Romaine, Suzanne. *Communicating Gender*. Lawrence Erlbaum, 1999.

Roper, Michael. *The Secret Battle: Emotional Survival in the Great War*. Manchester UP, 2009.

- "The Unconscious Work of History." *Cultural and Social History*, vol. 11, no. 2, 2014, pp. 169–93.

Roscoe, John. "Preliminary Report of the Mackie Ethnological Expedition to Central Africa." *Proceedings of the Royal Society of London*, series B, vol. 92, no. 645, 1921, pp. 209–19.

Rosenfeld, Jean. " 'A Noble House in the City': Domestic Architecture as Elite Signification in Late 19th Century Hamilton." PhD diss., University of Guelph, 2000.

Roskill, S.W. "The Navy at Cambridge, 1919–23." *The Mariner's Mirror: The Journal of the Society for Nautical Research*, vol. 49, 1963, pp. 178–93.

Rothschild, Emma. *The Inner Life of Empires: An Eighteenth-Century History*. Princeton UP, 2011.

Rouse, Sandra. "Expedition and Institution: A. C. Haddon and Anthropology at Cambridge." *Cambridge and the Torres Strait: Centenary Essays on the 1898 Anthropological Expedition*, edited by Anita Herle and Sandra Rouse. Cambridge UP, 1998, pp. 50–76.

Rouse, Sandra Louise. "Ethnology, Ethnobiography, and Institution: A.C. Haddon and Anthropology at Cambridge 1880–1926." PhD diss., University of Cambridge, 1996.

"A Russian View of the Germans in New Guinea." Trove, Sydney *Morning Herald*, 26 May 1885, p. 4.

Sampson, Anthony. *The Anatomist: The Autobiography of Anthony Sampson*. Politico's, 2008.

- *The Gypsy Scholar: The Quest for a Family Secret*. Murray, 1997.

"Samuel Dwight Chown." *Canadian Encyclopedia*, 12 Dec. 2013, https://www.the canadianencyclopedia.ca/en/article/samuel-dwight-chown. Accessed 16 Aug. 2019.

Satgé, Oscar de. *Pages from the Journal of a Queensland Squatter*. Hurst & Blackett, 1901.

Satthianadan, Samuel. *Four Years in an English University*. Lawrence Asylum Press, 1890.

Saunders, Kay. " 'Troublesome Servants': The Strategies of Resistance Employed by Melanesian Indentured Labourers on Plantations in Colonial Queensland." *Journal of Pacific History*, vol. 14, no. 3, 1979, pp. 168–83.

Scheckter, John. " 'Modern in Every Respect': The 1914 Conference of the British Association for the Advancement of Science." *Journal of the European Association for Studies of Australia*, vol. 5, no. 1, 2014, pp. 4–20.

Scheffler, Harold W., and Rodney Needham. "Radcliffe-Brown and Daisy Bates." *Man*, vol. 10, no. 2, 1975, pp. 310–13.

Schmid, Rudolf. "Agnes Arber Robertson (1879–1960): Fragments of Her Life, Including Her Place in Biology and in Women's Studies." *Annals of Botany*, vol. 88, no. 6, 2001, pp. 1105–28.

Schmitz, Christopher. "James Robert Millar Robertson (1844–1932)." *Australian Dictionary of Biography*. Vol. 11, Melbourne UP, 1988, http://adb.anu.edu.au /biography/robertson-james-robert-millar-8235. Accessed 1 Aug. 2019.

Schreber, D.G.M. *Medical Indoor Gymnastics, or, a System of Hygienic Exercises for Home Use*. Translated by Herbert A. Day, Williams & Norgate, 1899.

Scott, David. "Kipling, the Orient, and Orientals: 'Orientalism' Reoriented?" *Journal of World History*, vol. 22, no. 2, 2011, pp. 299–328.

Scott, William E.D. "Bird Pictures." *Scribner's Magazine*, vol. 21, 1897, pp. 500–3.

Sedgwick, Ellery. "Walter Hines Page." *World's Work*, vol. 37, no. 4, 1919, pp. 375–8.

"Selects Dr. F.H. Sykes: Columbia Professor First President of Connecticut Women's College." *New York Times*, 9 Feb. 1913, p. 3.

Seligman, C.G. "Dr. A.C. Haddon, F.R.S." (Obituary). *Nature*, vol. 145, 1 June 1940, pp. 848–50.

Selles, Johanna M. *Methodists and Women's Education in Ontario, 1836–1925*. McGill-Queen's UP, 1996.

Seton, Ernest Thompson. *Ernest Thompson Seton: Trail of an Artist-Naturalist*. 1940. Windrush, 2015.

75th Anniversary Meeting, 29 April 1932, Hamilton Association for the Advancement of Literature, Science and Arts. Heath and Fairclough, 1932.

Seward, A.C. *Fossil Plants: A Text-Book for Students of Botany and Geology*. Cambridge UP, 1917.

– "Women at Cambridge: The Case for Membership" (Letter to the Editor). Times Digital Archive, 1785–1985, *The Times* (London), 29 Nov. 1920, p. 10.

Shelley, Arlen. " 'For Love of an Idea': Jane Ellen Harrison, Heretic and Humanist." *Women's History Review*, vol. 5, no. 2, 1996, pp. 165–90.

Shephard, Ben. *Headhunters: The Search for a Science of the Mind*. Bodley Head, 2014.

"Sherring, Billy." *Canada's Sports Hall of Fame*, http://www.sportshall.ca/hall-of -famers/hall-of-famers-search.html?proID=165. Accessed 11 Aug. 2019.

Shorter, Edward. *Partnership for Excellence: Medicine at the University of Toronto and Academic Hospitals*. U of Toronto P, 2013.

Showalter, Elaine. "Male Hysteria: W.H.R. Rivers and the Lessons of Shell Shock." *The Female Malady*. Pantheon, 1985, pp. 167–194.

– "Rivers and Sassoon: The Inscription of Male Gender Anxieties." *Behind the Lines: Gender and the Two World Wars*, edited by Margaret R. Higonnet et al., Yale UP, 1987, pp. 61–9.

Simkhovitch, Mary. *Neighbourhood: My Story of Greenwich House*. Norton, 1938.

Singleton, Brian. *Oscar Asche, Orientalism, and British Musical Comedy*. Praeger, 2004.

Skidelsky, Robert. *John Maynard Keynes: A Biography*. Vol. 1: *Hopes Betrayed, 1883–1920*. Penguin, 1983.

Slack, Nancy G. "Nineteenth-Century American Women Botanists: Wives, Widows, and Work." *Uneasy Careers and Intimate Lives: Women in Science, 1789–1979*, edited by Pnina G. Abir-Am and Dorinda Outram, Rutgers UP, 1987, pp. 77–103.

Slobodin, Richard. *W.H.R. Rivers*. Columbia UP, 1978.

Smith, Elizabeth. *"A Woman with a Purpose": The Diaries of Elizabeth Smith, 1872–1884*. Edited by Veronica Strong-Boag, U of Toronto P, 1980.

Smith, John David. "I would like to study some problems of heredity: Felix von Luschan's Trip to America, 1914–1915." *Felix von Luschan (1854–1924): Leben und Wirken eines Universalgelehrten*, edited by Peter Ruggendorfer and Hubert Szemethy. Böhlau, 2009, pp. 141–63.

Smyth, Adam. *Autobiography in Early Modern England*. Cambridge UP, 2010.

– "Social networking, early modern style" (review of June Schlueter, *The Album Amicorum and the London of Shakespeare's Time*, British Library, 2012). *TLS*, 15 June 2012, p. 10.

Snell, James. *Macdonald Institute: Remembering the Past – Embracing the Future*. Dundurn, 2003.

Solomonian, Adam. "Reclaiming the Gaze: Mining Contemporary Nuxalk Perspectives on Harlan I. Smith's Fieldwork Photographs, 1920–1924." MA thesis, University of British Columbia, 2009.

Somerville, Alice Te Punga, Daniel Heath Justice, and Noelani Arista, eds. *Indigenous Conversations About Biography*, special issue of *Biography*, vol. 39, no. 3, 2016.

Spate, O.H.K. "Foreword." E.M. Webster. *The Moon Man: A Biography of Nicolai Miklouho-Maclay*. U of California P, 1987, pp. vii–ix.

Sprache des Körpers – Tanz in Dresden, special issue of *Dresdner Hefte*, vol. 26, no. 95, 2008.

Sprengel. Peter. *Literatur im Kaiserreich: Studien zur Moderne*. Erich Schmidt, 1993.

Stagl, Justin. "Nikolai Nikolajewitsch Miklouho-Maclay oder das Dilemma der vorkolonialen Situation." *Zeitschrift für Ethnologie*, vol. 114, 1989, pp. 195–204.

Stanley, Edward Henry. *The Diaries of Edward Henry Stanley, 15th Early of Derby (1826–93) between 1878 and 1893: A Selection*. Edited by John Vincent, Leopard's Head Press, 2003.

Starke's Pocket Almanac, Advertiser and General Register 1874. Starke, 1874.

Stebner. Eleanor J. "The Settlement House Movement." *Encyclopedia of Women and Religion in North America*, edited by Mary Skinner Keller and Rosemary Radford Ruether. Indiana UP, 2006, pp. 1059–69.

Steel, Frances. "Re-Routing Empire? Steam-Age Circulations and the Making of an Anglo Pacific, c. 1850–1890." *Australian Historical Studies*, vol. 46, no. 3, 2015, pp. 356–73.

Steinhart, Allan L. *The Postal History of the Post Card in Canada, 1871–1911*. Mission Press, 1979.

Stenberg, Freda. "Woman's Share in War: An Interview with Lady Helen Munro-Ferguson." Trove, Beaudesert *Times*, 30 Oct. 1914, p. 3.

Stimson, Sam S. "Howells discovers a new literary light, W.B. Trites: Author of *John Cave* Tells How He Knocked at the Door of Publishers Here and Abroad Without Result, then Became His Own Publisher and Won Fame. " New York *Times*, 16 Feb. 1913, p. 9.

Stirling, A.W. "The Political Outlook in Queensland." *Fortnightly Review*, vol. 44, new series, Dec. 1888, pp. 721–7.

Stocking, George W. Jr. *After Tylor: British Social Anthropology, 1888–1951*. U of Wisconsin P, 1995.

– "Gatekeeper to the Field: E.W.P. Chinnery and the Ethnography of the New Guinea Mandate." *History of Anthropology Newsletter*, vol. 9, no. 2, 1982, pp. 1–12.

– "Maclay, Kubary, Malinowski: Archetypes from the Dreamtime of Anthropology." *Colonial Situations: Essays on the Contextualization of Ethnographic Knowledge*. U of Wisconsin P, 1993, pp. 9–74.

Stocking, George W. Jr., and Alfred Cort Haddon. "The Red-Paint of British Aggression, the Gospel of Ten-Per-Cent, and the Cost of Maintaining our Ascendancy: A.C. Haddon on the Need for an Imperial Bureau of Ethnology, 1891." *History of Anthropology Newsletter*, vol. 20, no. 1, June 1993, pp. 3–15.

Stoler, Ann Laura. *Along the Archival Grain: Epistemic Anxieties and Colonial Common Sense*. Princeton UP, 2008.

Stone, Dorothy. *The National: The Story of a Pioneer College: The National Training College of Domestic Subjects*. Robert Hale, 1976.

Strachan, Hew. "The Scottish Soldier and Scotland, 1914–1918." *A Global Force: War, Identities and Scotland's Diaspora*, edited by David Forsyth and Wendy Ugolini, Edinburgh UP, 2016, pp. 53–70.

Strupp, Karl, and Hans-Jürgen Schlochauer, eds. *Wörterbuch des Völkerrechts*. de Gruyter, 1960–2. 3 vols.

Sullivan, Rodney. "Casey, Gilbert Stephen (1856–1946)." *Australian Dictionary of Biography*. Vol. 7, Melbourne UP, 1979, http://adb.anu.edu.au/biography/casey-gilbert-stephen-5528. Accessed 2 Aug. 2019.

Sutherland, Stuart R.J. "Robert Mathews." *Dictionary of Canadian Biography*, vol. 5 (1801–1820), http://biographi.ca/en/bio/mathews_robert_5E.html. Accessed 7 Mar. 2015.

Swaisland, Charles. "The Aborigines Protection Society, 1837–1909." *Slavery and Abolition: Journal of Slave and Post-Slave Studies*, vol. 21, 2000, pp. 265–80.

Szuberla, Guy. "Peattie's *Precipice* and the 'Settlement House' Novel." *Midamerica: The Yearbook of the Society for the Study of Midwestern Literature*, vol. 20, 1993, pp. 59–75.

Talbot, Robert J. " 'It would be best to leave us alone': First Nations Responses to the Canadian War Effort, 1914–1918." *Journal of Canadian Studies*, vol. 45, no. 1, 2011, pp. 90–120.

Teale, Ruth. "White, Gilbert (1859–1933)." *Australian Dictionary of Biography*. Vol. 12, Melbourne UP, 1990, http://adb.anu.edu.au/biography/white-gilbert-9072. Accessed 19 Nov. 2017.

Temperley, Harold, and Lillian M. Penson, eds. *A Century of Diplomatic Blue Books, 1814–1914*. Cambridge UP, 1938.

Temple, Richard. "The Manipur Blue-Book." *Contemporary Review*, no. 306, June 1891, pp. 917–24.

Ten Days in Quebec. G.R. Renfrew, 1894.

Ther, Philipp. *In der Mitte der Gesellschaft: Operntheater in Zentraleuropa, 1815–1914*. Oldenbourg, 2006.

Thomas, N.W. "Hautfarbentafel, by Professor von Luschan." *Man*, vol. 5, 1905, p. 160.

Thompson, Googoo, with Brigitte Wongtschowski. *Between Woodbush and Wolkberg: Googoo Thompson's Story*. Protea Book House, 2003.

Thompson, Mark L. *Steamboats & Sailors of the Great Lakes*. Wayne State UP, 1991.

Thompson, Roger C. *Australian Imperialism in the Pacific: The Expansionist Era, 1820–1920*. Melbourne UP, 1980.

Thorp, Margaret Farrand. *Neilson of Smith*. Oxford UP, 1956.

"Tipperary Club." Gale Primary Sources, Cambridge *Independent Press*, 23 Aug. 1918, p. 6.

Toepfer, Karl. *Empire of Ecstasy: Nudity and Movement in German Body Culture, 1910–1935*. U of California P, 1997.

Traill, William Henry. "Historical Review of Queensland." *Australasia Illustrated*, edited by Andrew Garran. 1886. Vol. 2, Picturesque Atlas Publishing Company, 1892, pp. 599–770.

Trainor. Luke. *British Imperialism and Australian Nationalism: Manipulation, Conflict and Compromise in the Late Nineteenth Century*. Cambridge UP, 1994.

Trigger, Bruce G. "A.G. Bailey – Ethnohistorian." *Acadiensis*, vol. 18, no. 2, 1989, pp. 3–21.

"Troops Return Home: The Remuera's Draft." Papers Past, New Zealand *Herald*, vol. 56, no. 17301, 27 Oct. 1919, n.p.

Trotter, Reginald George. *Canadian History: A Syllabus and Guide to Reading*. Macmillan, 1926.

Trumble, Angus, and Andrea Wolk Rager, eds. *Edwardian Opulence: British Art at the Dawn of the Twentieth Century*. Yale UP, 2013.

Trumpener, Katie. *Bardic Nationalism: The Romantic Novel and the British Empire.* Princeton UP, 1997.

Turmarkin, Daniel. "Miklouho-Maclay: 19th Century Russian Anthropologist and Humanist." *RAIN [Royal Anthropological Institute of Great Britain and Ireland Newsletter]*, no. 51, 1982, pp. 4–7.

An Unknown Writer. "The Unknown Writer and the Publishers." *World's Work*, vol. 2, no. 5, 1901, pp. 1217–22.

"Universal Races Congress." Times Digital Archive, 1785–1985, *The Times* (London), 27 July 1911, p. 4.

Urquhart, Gordon. "Confrontation and Withdrawal: Loos, Readership and 'The First Hundred Thousand.' " *Scotland and the Great War*, edited by Catriona M. Macdonald and E.W. McFarland, Tuckwell Press, 1999, pp. 125–44.

"Valued Citizen is Summoned by Angel of Death" (Obituary of Frank Hills). Hamilton *Spectator*, 24 Oct. 1927, n.p.

Vibert, Elizabeth. "Writing 'Home': Sibling Intimacy and Mobility in a Scottish Colonial Memoir." *Moving Subjects*, edited by Tony Ballantyne and Antoinette Burton, U of Illinois P, 2009, pp. 67–88.

Visram, Rozina. *Ayahs, Lascars and Princes: Indians in Britain, 1700–1947.* 1986. Routledge, 2016.

Volkmann, Hans. "Johannes Kromayer." *Pommersche Lebensbilder*, vol. 4, edited by Walter Menn, Böhlau, 1966, pp. 422–31.

Wagner, Anton, and Richard Plant, eds. "Introduction: Reclaiming the Past." *Canada's Lost Plays*, vol. 1: *The Nineteenth Century.* CTR Publications, 1978, pp. 4–15.

Waiser, W.A. *The Field Naturalist: John Macoun, the Geological Survey, and Natural Science.* U of Toronto P, 1989.

Wang, Zuoyue. "The First World War, Academic Science, and the 'Two Cultures': Educational Reforms at the University of Cambridge." *Minerva*, vol. 33, no. 2, June 1995, pp. 107–27.

Wansbrough, M.B., et al., *Echoes that Remain: The Amazing Story of the School that Did.* Hillfield-Strathallan College, 2001.

"Was 'Spanish John' Stolen?" *Canadian Magazine*, vol. 10, Nov. 1897–Apr. 1898, pp. 546–7.

Waterston, Elizabeth. "The Lowland Tradition in Canadian Literature." *The Scottish Tradition in Canada*, edited by W. Stanford Reid, McClelland and Stewart, 1976, pp. 203–31.

Wearing, J.P. *The London Stage, 1910–1919: A Calendar of Productions, Performers, and Personnel.* Scarecrow Press, 2013.

Weaver, John C. *Hamilton: An Illustrated History.* James Lorimer, 1982.

Webster, E.M. *The Moon Man: A Biography of Nicolai Miklouho-Maclay.* U of California P, 1987.

"Wedding Announcements." *S.A. Ladies Pictorial*, July 1913, p. 26.

"A Wedding of Wide-Spread Interest ..." Hamilton *Spectator*, 12 June 1913, n.p.

Weiske, H.A. "Johannes von Gruber (Nekrolog)." *Zeitung für das höhere Unterrichtswesen Deutschlands*, vol. 5, no. 50, 14 Dec. 1876, pp. 395–6.

Wendell, Winifred Lee. "The Modern School of Canadian Writers." *The Bookman* (New York), vol. 11, no. 6, 1900, pp. 515–26.

Wertheimer, Douglas. "Gosse, Philip Henry," *Dictionary of Canadian Biography*, vol. 11 (1881–1890), http://www.biographi.ca/en/bio/gosse_philip_henry_11E.html. Accessed 2 Aug. 2019.

Wetmore, Alexander. *Biographical Memoir of Robert Ridgway, 1850–1929*. National Academy of Sciences of the United States of America, 1931.

Weyers, Wolfgang, with A. Bernard Ackerman, ed. *Death of Medicine in Nazi Germany: Dermatology and Dermatopathology under the Swastika*. Lippincott-Raven, 1998.

Wheatly, W.W. "Transporting New York's Millions." *World's Work*, vol. 6, no. 1, 1903, pp. 3423–36.

Wheeler-Bennett, John, rev. Roger T. Stearn. "Fergusson, Sir Charles, of Kilkerran, Seventh Baronet (1865–1951)." *Oxford Dictionary of National Biography*, https://doi.org/10.1093/ref:odnb/33111. Accessed 23 July 2019.

White, Hervey. *Differences*. Small, Maynard, 1899.

White, Jerry. *Zeppelin Nights: London in the First World War*. Bodley Head, 2014.

Whittle, Paul. "W.H.R. Rivers and the Early History of Psychology at Cambridge." *Bartlett, Culture and Cognition*, edited by Akiko Saito, Routledge, 1999, pp. 21–35.

Widmaier, Tobias, et al. *Populäre und traditionelle Lieder: Historisch-kritisches Liederlexikon*. Deutsche Forschungsgemeinschaft Projekt, http://www.liederlexikon.de. Accessed 8 Sept. 2020.

Wilkie, Benjamin. "Family Networks and the Australian Pastoral Industry: A Case Study of the Port Phillip District and Victoria in the Late Nineteenth Century." *Agricultural History*, vol. 91, no. 1, 2017, pp. 78–95.

"William C. Baker." Proquest, New York *Times*, 6 Dec. 1937, p. 27.

Williams, John A. *Turning to Nature in Germany: Hiking, Nudism, and Conservation, 1900–1940*. Stanford UP, 2007.

Williamson, David G. *The British in Germany, 1918–1930: The Reluctant Occupiers*. Berg, 1991.

– "Cologne and the British, 1918–1926." *History Today*, vol. 27, no. 11, 1977, pp. 695–702.

Williamson, Philip. "Graham, William (1887–1932)." *Oxford Dictionary of National Biography*, https://doi.org/10.1093/ref:odnb/33508. Accessed 2 Aug. 2019.

"Wilson, Anne Elizabeth." Canada's Early Women Writers, Simon Fraser University, https://digital.lib.sfu.ca/ceww-669/wilson-anne-elizabeth. Accessed 10 Aug. 2019.

"Wilson, Cecil (1860–1941)," *Solomon Islands Historical Encyclopedia, 1893–1978*. http://www.solomonencyclopaedia.net/biogs/E000752b.htm. Accessed 19 Nov. 2017.

Winearls, Joan. "Allan Brooks, Naturalist and Artist (1869–1946): The Travails of an Early Twentieth Century Wildlife Illustrator in North America." *Scientia Canadensis*, vol. 32, nos. 1–2, 2008, pp. 131–54.

Winks, Robin. *The Blacks in Canada: A History*, 2nd ed. McGill-Queen's UP, 1997.

Winter, Jay. *The Great War and the British People*. Palgrave, 1986.

– "Popular Culture in Wartime Britain." *European Culture in the Great War: The Arts, Entertainment, and Propaganda, 1914–1918*, edited by Aviel Roshwald and Richard Stite, Cambridge UP, 1999, pp. 330–48.

Wisker, John. "Troubles in the Pacific." *Fortnightly Review*, vol. 31, no. 186, 1882, 711–34.

– "The Victim of Civilisation." *Victorian Review* 6, 1 Sept. 1882, 540–51.

"Women at Cambridge." *The Spectator*, 29 Oct. 1921, p. 7, http://archive.spectator. co.uk/article/29th-october-1921/7/women-at-cambridge. Accessed 15 Oct. 2017.

"Women's War Weapons." Gale Primary Sources, Cambridge *Independent Press*, 1 Feb. 1918, p. 4.

Wood, H.G. *Terrot Reaveley Glover: A Biography*. Cambridge UP, 1953.

Woollacott, Angela. *Settler Society in the Australian Colonies: Self-Government and Imperial Culture*. Oxford UP, 2015.

– "Sisters and Brothers in Arms: Family, Class and Gendering in WWI Britain." *Gendering War Talk*, edited by Miriam Cooke and Angela Woollacott, Princeton UP, 1993, pp. 128–47.

"The Work of the Y.M.C.A." *The Times History and Encyclopaedia of the War*. Vol. 9, *The Times* (London), 1916, pp. 178–201.

Wright, Robert. *The Life of Major-General James Wolfe: Founded on Original Documents and Illustrated by His Correspondence*. Chapman and Hall, 1864.

Wright, Robert A. *A World Mission: Canadian Protestantism and the Quest for a New International Order, 1918–1939*. McGill-Queen's UP, 1991.

Yale, Elizabeth. *Sociable Knowledge: Natural History and the Nation in Early Modern Britain*. U of Pennsylvania P, 2016.

Yaszek, Lisa, and Patrick B. Sharp, eds. *Sisters of Tomorrow: The First Women of Science Fiction*. Wesleyan UP, 2016.

Youmans, Eliza A. "Preface to the American edition." Rose Owen Cole, *Lessons in Cookery*, M.D. Appleton, 1878, pp. iii–ix.

Young, Brian. *Patrician Families and the Making of Quebec: The Taschereaus and McCords*. McGill-Queen's UP, 2014.

Young, Michael W. *Malinowski: Odyssey of an Anthropologist, 1884–1920*. Yale UP, 2004.

Zenck, Claudia Maurer, et al., eds. *LexM Lexikon verfolgter Musiker und Musikerinnen der NS-Zeit*. Universität Hamburg, 2007, https://www.lexm.uni-hamburg.de /content/index.xml. Accessed 2 Aug. 2019.

Zumwalt, Rosemary Lévy. *American Folklore Scholarship: A Dialogue of Dissent*. Indiana UP, 1988.

Index